The Indian Constitution

Cornerstone of a Nation

'Long years ago we made a tryst with destiny, and now the time comes when we shall redeem our pledge, not wholly or in full measure, but very substantially. At the stroke of the midnight hour, when the world sleeps, India will awake to life and freedom.' *Jawaharlal Nehru, just before midnight on 14 August 1947, in a speech to the Constituent Assembly.*

The Indian Constitution

Cornerstone of a Nation

Granville Austin

OXFORD
UNIVERSITY PRESS

Oxford University Press is a department of the University of Oxford.
It furthers the University's objective of excellence in research, scholarship,
and education by publishing worldwide in. Oxford is a registered trademark of
Oxford University Press in the UK and in certain other countries

Published in India by
Oxford University Press
YMCA Library Building, 1 Jai Singh Road, New Delhi 110 001, India

First Edition published in 1972
Oxford India Paperbacks 1999
Twenty-fifth impression 2015

ISBN-13: 978-0-19-564959-8
ISBN-10: 0-19-564959-1

Typeset in Adobe Garmond Pro 11/13
by BeSpoke Integrated Solutions, Puducherry, India 605 008
Printed in India by Sapra Brothers, New Delhi 110 092

To

W.S.R., R.H.N., and N.M.A.
for faith, hope, and charity.

Contents

Preface to the Oxford India Paperback Edition, 1999

INDIA'S founding fathers and mothers established in the Constitution both the nation's ideals and the institutions and processes for achieving them. The ideals were national unity and integrity and a democratic and equitable society. The new society was to be achieved through a social-economic revolution pursued with a democratic spirit using constitutional, democratic institutions. I later came to think of unity, social revolution, and democracy as three strands of a seamless web. The founders believed that none of these goals was to be pursued, nor could any be achieved, separately. They were mutually dependent and had to be sought together.

During recent years it has become fashionable among some citizens to disparage the founders and their document. These individuals, disappointed by developments in the country since 1950, have called for changing the Constitution, explaining that it has not 'worked.' Such thinking, in my view, is misguided. Constitutions do not 'work,' they are inert, dependent upon being 'worked' by citizens and elected and appointed leaders.

Looking back over fifty years, I am struck by the extent to which the framers were successful in articulating the nation's goals and in designing the necessary governing structures. The Constitution has served the nation remarkably well. Each and every contingency the framers did not foresee—nor, realistically, could they have been expected to. A combination of idealism and the multitude of issues confronting the country during the framing period apparently obscured their appraisal of several future contingencies. Other contingencies, which they may have foreseen, they did not provide for in the Constitution—aware, I believe, that no founding document can contain solutions to every situation, and that leaders in the future should find, within the Constitution's principles, their own way out of difficulties that might confront them. As Chief Justice John Marshall has said, a Constitution is framed for ages to come, but 'its course cannot always be tranquil.'[1]

The essential element of the framers' foresight was their concept of the seamless web, the interdependence of the nation's three grand goals, and their building into the Constitution the institutions and processes for their pursuit.

National unity and integrity were to be served by the Constitution's highly centralised federalism, characterised, among other elements, by central government distribution of much revenue, national development planning, continuation of the inherited central civil services, state governors who were presidential appointees, the well-known Emergency Provisions, and a wide variety of state-centre coordinating mechanisms. Each of these was to benefit from the Congress Party's mass character and its own central-command federal structure. That this centralisation would become counter-productive over-centralisation, particularly beginning some two decades after the Constitution's inauguration, is another matter. It would be unreasonable to think the framers should have foreseen this. Moreover, during the period from 1946 to 1950 creating a united India to pursue national development was the government's and the framers' highest priority.

The democratic features of the Constitution were as risk-taking as the unity features were cautious. Representative government with adult suffrage, a bill of rights providing for equality under the law and personal liberty, and an independent judiciary were to become the spiritual and institutional bases for a new society—one replacing the traditional hierarchy and its repressions. Other constitutional provisions were designed to spread democracy by protecting and increasing the rights of minorities, by assisting under-privileged groups in society to better their condition, and by ending the blatant oppression of the Scheduled Castes and Tribes. These provisions have brought into, or closer to, the mainstream of society individuals

---

[1] For a history of constitutional developments from 1950–1985 see the author's *Working a Democratic Constitution: The Indian Experience*, Oxford University Press, New Delhi, 1999.

and groups that would otherwise have remained at society's bottom or at its edges.

The Constitution, by its very existence, was a social revolutionary statement. It was to be a modernizing force. Social revolution and democracy were to be the strands of the seamless web most closely related. Democracy, representative government, personal liberty, equality before the law, were revolutionary for the society. Social-economic equitableness as expressed in the Directive Principles of State Policy was equally revolutionary. So were the Constitution's articles allowing abolishing zamindari and altering property relations and those allowing for compensatory discrimination in education and employment for disadvantaged citizens.

The Constitution's many and detailed administrative provisions and their accompanying, if often cumbersome, bureaucracy supported pursuit of these goals. Inherited from the 1935 Government of India Act, the framers included them in the Constitution in preference to building an administration afresh under a Constitution embodying only general principles.

But the founders' foresight was not perfect. There were situations that future governments might confront that they realistically could have been expected to foresee, and that should have been taken into account in the drafting process. Some eventualities they did not provide for, purposely leaving them for their heirs in government. Other developments must have been beyond their imaginations.

Among those in the first category were the situations that brought about the early amendments to the Constitution. It was not foreseen, for example, that there would be a conflict between the fundamental rights provisions for equality before the law and for special treatment for backward classes of citizens. Nor was it expected, although it is fair to say that it should have been, that the word 'compensation' in the property articles would be given its traditional meaning by the courts in zamindari abolition and property-takings cases. (And it is difficult to understand how these longtime Congress Party members did not appreciate—or were they unwilling to admit to themselves?— that the most significant opposition to land reform efforts would not be in the courts, but among their fellow party-men in the states.)

Among the unimagined developments was that President's Rule would come to be abused and that the power to declare a national emergency would be invoked for the personal benefit of a prime minister. Otherwise, the Emergency Provisions might not have been placed in the Constitution—or, if so, perhaps they might have been circumscribed along the lines of the Forty-fourth Amendment. Few among the framers could foresee that implementing the socialism of the Directive Principles would have a dark side, namely corruption, and harm national development by depriving the country of the economic engine of private enterpreneurship—whose excesses, of course, would have to have been curbed. None could have foreseen the vast changes in legislative representation that economic change and adult suffrage would bring about. The framers surely would have deplored the self-serving conduct of many in public life today.

Although the framers provided for adult suffrage expressly to break the mould of traditional society, they did not foresee, so far as one may discern in the historical record, the extent to which the social revolution would at once empower new groups while, in the pattern of traditional society, allowing these groups to oppress others. The most the founders could do was to set a social revolution in motion and hope for the best. They could not prescribe the shape of things to come. Their successors would have to cope.

Among the things that the founding fathers and mothers could have imagined, but did not provide for in the Constitution, were the consequences of a decline in the Congress Party's popularity and legislature representation—especially in Parliament—that would result in its being a partner in a coalition government or out of office replaced by a coalition of other parties. Although from the vantage point of the late Forties, this was remote, it nevertheless was conceivable. If privately they did consider this, it seems probable that they did not think it an abnormal development in a parliamentary system, and did think it one whose political intricacies could not be provided for wisely in advance.

Constitutional conventions were another area where the framers declined to prescribe their successors political conduct, although the Constituent Assembly had direct experience with the contentiousness of conventions. For example, despite the controversy over the President's powers, they did not write into the Constitution the conventions surrounding them. And they did not include an instrument of instructions for governors, although this was contemplated. Evidently believing that the conventions of parliamentary government would be observed, they seem not to have expected the violation of several—leave alone the consequent writing into the Constitution by amendment those concerning presidential powers and the declaration of emergencies.

These are small oversights, if they are oversights at all, when set against the founders' achievements in the Constitution. Under it, national unity has been assured, despite difficulties in Kashmir. Democracy is vibrant, although subject to excesses and shared unequally among citizens. The social-economic revolution has changed the face of the country even if it, too, has far to go. If the dream of the Constitution has not yet wholly been realised, India has become a great nation under it.

Impelled and sustained by a compound of vision, practicality, ambition for the Congress Party, idealism, and faith, the founders laid the cornerstone for the new India. This volume attempts to describe how they did it.

Preface to the Indian Edition

MORE than twenty years have now passed since the adoption of the Indian Constitution. A thorough study of its working—going beyond the few books that have been written about developments under certain parts—would be welcome. Perhaps, on the occasion of this edition, I may offer some brief comments.

The Constitution, it seems to me, has worked very much as the framers intended it should. All their hopes have not been fulfilled; nor was their foresight perfect. Yet a constitution, no matter how well conceived, can only establish institutions on paper. Breathing life into them is up to the succeeding generations. In India, the creation of parliamentary political institutions by the Constitution has itself provided an impetus for their strengthening and growth. The people of India have accepted and worked these institutions. Despite attacks by the radical left and government breakdowns in the states at various times, government in India has operated under the Constitution. Perhaps most important, the institutions of the Constitution have accommodated, to use Professor Morris-Jones' phrase, the 'languages' of Indian politics.

One test of a Constitution is whether it can provide a durable framework for government in the midst of great social and economic change. This, the Indian Constitution has so far done. Furthermore, as we know, the framers had an additional task in mind for the Indian Constitution: that it should be itself a 'modernizing' force. This was to be true on several levels. In the first place, the very institutions of parliamentary government would have, it was believed, a profound effect on the Indian social structure by replacing traditional with 'modem' political techniques and goals. Secondarily, particular parts of the Constitution were to play an especial role in bringing about a social revolution in India. Prominent here were the Fundamental Rights and Directive Principles and the provision for universal, adult suffrage.

The Fundamental Rights have provided a rallying point for the increase of civil liberties of the common man. Yet the Rights, as written, can only work so much change. It may be that government, particularly at the Centre, will have to be a more active advocate of fundamental liberties (for example in villages where the dominant caste or group can effectively deny certain liberties to other groups) for the Rights to attain their fulfilment and true meaning.

The point applies as well to the Directive Principles. The framers' object in including the Principles was to foster the social conditions in which an individual could be free. The governments of India have sometimes seemed to be more interested in assuring the support of their most powerful backers than in pursuing this goal. Yet the goal has not been forgotten and changes in the power bases of politics may awaken governments' enthusiasm for implementing the spirit of the Principles.

The framers' hopes that adult suffrage would create a new dimension in the life of the voter and would avoid the proliferation of political parties have, on balance, been realized. Adult suffrage has been a source and a vehicle for social change, but there is still ample room for the effects of this to be felt on the lower rungs of the political ladder. The influence derived by Parliament from its roots in adult suffrage have given that body a power that has figured vitally in the working and preservation of democracy in India. Parties have proliferated, especially at the state level. But the ebb and flow of party fortunes, even without the major victory of Mrs. Gandhi's Congress in the spring of 1971, has indicated that a kind of equilibrium had been reached and that the number of parties would not importantly increase.

The amending process has been most controversial in the area of Fundamental Rights. And fears have been expressed that a government with a two-thirds majority may amend virtually at will. This ignores, of course, the existence of the entrenched provisions, but it does reflect a genuine fear that was given its most cogent expression in the majority opinion of the Supreme Court in the Golak Nath case. Although 'flexibility' seems to have been one of the framers' aims, governments in the future may have to treat this principle with increasing care.

The tension between the 'centralizers' and the 'federalists' that existed in the Constituent Assembly, not surprisingly, persists today. The Constitution has provided a firm framework for this pull and tug; it has allowed healthy political development. The result has been that India is increasingly federal. 'President's Rule' has proved its worth and this provision has seldom been abused by the Centre. Paradoxically, this non-parliamentary device has helped preserve parliamentary institutions in the states. The use of the parts of the Emergency Provisions since 1962 have little affected the federal structure. But there can be little doubt that the central government grew overly fond of its augmented strength in relation to the parliamentary and legal systems. The end of the emergency came none too soon.

The matter of language remains unsettled. The issues and forces present in the Assembly were prophetic. Unable to resolve the issue, the Assembly left the matter, especially so far as the use of English goes, to Parliament, which remains free to continue the use of English for whatever purposes it choses [Art. 343(3)]. The language issue will move toward solution only with time, providing the Indian people with perhaps the greatest test of their maturity.

Introduction

THE Constituent Assembly, brought into being by the will of the Indian people and, in the last scene of the last act, with the help of the British, drafted a constitution for India in the years from December 1946 to December 1949. In the Assembly Indians were for the first time in a century and a half responsible for their own governance. They were at last free to shape their own destiny, to pursue their long-proclaimed aims and aspirations, and to create the national institutions that would facilitate the fulfilment of these aims. These tasks the members approached with remarkable idealism and a strength of purpose born of the struggle for independence. A constitution, Assembly members realized, could not by itself make a new India, but they intended it to light the way.

The Constitution was to foster the achievement of many goals. Transcendent among them was that of social revolution. Through this revolution would be fulfilled the basic needs of the common man, and, it was hoped, this revolution would bring about fundamental changes in the structure of Indian society—a society with a long and glorious cultural tradition, but greatly in need, Assembly members believed, of a powerful infusion of energy and rationalism. The theme of social revolution runs throughout the proceedings and documents of the Assembly. It provided the basis for the decisions to adopt parliamentary government and direct elections, the Fundamental Rights and the Directive Principles of State Policy, and even many aspects of the Executive, Legislative, and Judicial provisions of the Constitution.

Rivalling the social revolution in importance were the goals of national unity and stability. Desirable as ends in themselves, they were also considered to be necessary prerequisites for a social renascence. Although evident in many parts of the Constitution, unity stood out as the central issue during the framing of the federal and language provisions as well as during the drafting of the Legislative provisions. The need for domestic stability affected the shape of the federal structure in general and particularly caused the inclusion of the Emergency Provisions. Other aims also played their part in shaping the Constitution—aims such as the protection of minority interests, the creation of efficient government and administration, and national security. All these aims were either explicitly or implicitly embodied in the Constitution as were, Assembly members hoped, the institutions that would be the means of achieving them.

The Indian Constitution is, then, a document in which provisions expressing general principles and humanitarian sentiments—vows of purpose, if you will—mingle with those embodying level-headed practicality and administrative detail. And as the idealism that marks the Constitution was predominantly a product of the social content of the Independence Movement, which in turn stemmed from an awareness of the plight of the mass of Indians, so the practical provisions were largely a product of the Assembly members' experience in government and of the exigencies of the times. The members of the Constituent Assembly did not work in a vacuum. Not only did they act as the nation's parliament from August 1947 until January 1950, but many of their number were also the leaders of the Union and provincial governments. Hence domestic conditions—food shortages, communal riots, communist subversion— had a marked effect on the content of the Constitution, and events abroad also carried lessons. The news dispatches carried by New Delhi's major newspaper of the period, *The Hindustan Times,* for the month of September 1948, a few weeks before the members debated the Draft Constitution, show the atmosphere in which the Assembly worked.

The issue of 1 September carried news of the continuing trial of Mahatma Gandhi's murderer, Nathuram Godse. Headlines announced that floods in Kanpur had left twenty thousands homeless, that the Law Ministry of the Union Government had recommended that consideration of the controversial Hindu Code Bill be postponed, and that a large Pakistani attack near Poonch in Kashmir had been beaten off. The issue of 4 September reported that Parliament had discussed the 'inflationary crisis' and that Nehru had assured the House that the rupee was not to be devalued. Sardar Patel praised the Gaekwar of Baroda for inaugurating full responsible government in that Princely State. Events in Kashmir made the headlines on 6 September—and on nearly every day—as did the Russian blockade of Berlin. Troops of the Chinese Red Army were reported advancing on Chiang Kai-shek's positions in Honan. And G. S. Gupta presented his Hindi translation of the Draft Constitution to a press conference, saying that it should be accepted along with the English version to give it legal validity. On 12 September banner headlines and black borders announced the death of Jinnah, the founder of Pakistan. Two days later news of the invasion of the State of Hyderabad by Indian troops covered the front page, and on 18 September came word that the Nizam had surrendered. That same day the dispatches from Palestine reported that Bernadotte had been murdered by the Stern gang. For the last ten days of the month the paper was full of the intentions of provincial food and agriculture ministers to reinstitute food controls, of a plan for cloth rationing in Delhi, and of a communist revolt in East Java. India, no less than the world at large, was in ferment, and amidst such daily events the members of the Constituent Assembly had to lay the foundations of the future India.

Many of the articles of the Constitution, either in wording or in content, have their origins in foreign constitutions. The members of the Assembly were not so chauvinistic as to reject the experience of other nations. Yet although the Assembly borrowed freely, it fashioned from this mass of precedent a document to suit India's needs. Although the Constitution at some point defies nearly all the rules devised by constitutional lawyers for success, it has worked well. The credit for this lies —insofar as it can be assigned—in part with the British, who brought the vision and some of the reality of parliamentary democracy with them to India, in part with fortuitous circumstances, and in largest part with Indians themselves. Indians had for years demanded a constitution establishing parliamentary democracy; when the opportunity came they framed one; and for the past decade and a half they have demonstrated that they have the ability to make it work.

The Constituent Assembly was able to draft a constitution that was both a declaration of social intent and an intricate administrative blueprint because of the extraordinary sense of unity among the members. The members disagreed hardly at all about the ends they sought and only slightly about the means for achieving them, although several issues did produce deep dissension. The atmosphere of the Assembly, generally speaking, was one of trust in the leadership and a sense of compromise among the members. The Assembly's hope, which it frequently achieved, was to reach decisions by consensus. And there can be little doubt that the lengthy and frank discussion of all the provisions of the future constitution by the Assembly, followed by sincere attempts to compromise and to reach consensus, have been the principal reason for the strength of the Constitution.

This book is a political history of the framing of the Constitution, of how past and present, aims and events, ideals and personalities, moved the members of the Constituent Assembly to write the Constitution as they did. It has been called a political history to distinguish it from the many volumes having a more legalistic approach. Several of these have been valuable contributions in their field, but they have not contributed greatly to our knowledge of India in the years since World War II. The author has intended to do this in some measure. It is hoped that the book will provide the general reader with some insight into the political bases and motivations of Indian life and at the same time provide the close student of Indian affairs with the first account, based on manuscript sources, of the working of the Constituent Assembly.

Note

THE reader may find it helpful if certain technical points in connection with the text and the footnotes are explained.

Prior to independence, India was, generally speaking, divided into two political categories: the provinces of 'British India' and the 'Indian States'. These differences have now disappeared, and, with the exception of certain Union Territories, the major political units of India are called 'states'. In the Constituent Assembly, the provinces and often the states-to-be were called provinces. The practice in this work has been to consider the words 'states' and 'provinces' interchangeable, but to endeavour to use 'provinces' when referring to the years before 1950 and 'states' when speaking of the years after the adoption of the Constitution. Throughout, the 'Indian States' have been referred to as the 'States' or the 'Princely States', for the author believes that these feudally governed areas were no more *Indian* than the remainder of the country.

The Government of India in New Delhi is referred to variously as the Centre, the Central Government, the Federal Government, and the Union Government. On independence, in August 1947, this government actually became a Dominion Government and remained so until India became a republic with the adoption of the Constitution on 26 January 1950. Since then the proper term has been the Union Government. To avoid confusion, however, the term Union Government has been used here for the Government of India since independence.

Before India adopted the Constitution, the highest judicial body in the land was the Federal Court, although prior to independence appeals could lie from this Court to the Privy Council in London.

After January 1950 the Federal Court became the Supreme Court. This terminology has been used in the text.

Although today the term 'chief minister' has come into use for the heads of cabinets in the states, the practice in the Assembly was, with few exceptions, to call these men 'prime ministers' and 'premiers' and this precedent has been followed here.

The rendering of Indian first and family names into English produces almost innumerable variations—Mukerjee, Mookerjee, Mookherjee, Mukerji, etc. Not infrequently, an Indian will use one name, although his given name is something else. For the sake of uniformity, and of at least reasonable accuracy, the form and spelling of personal names has been taken from that given in the Constituent Assembly Debates when the member signed the Assembly register. In several places the author has used what he considers the commonly accepted, or the commonly recognized, spelling.

In the footnotes, there will be found frequent references to the Constituent Assembly Debates (*CAD*), the principal source of published material on the Assembly's work. These are arranged so that the volume number, corresponding to the session, is given first. The number, corresponding to the proceedings of each day's sitting, is given second, and the page numbers are given last—e.g. *CAD* II, 3, p. 35 means Volume II, the second session, number 3, the third day, and the page from which the citation was taken. The first edition of the Constituent Assembly Debates was published during the framing period. A second edition was published in 1956 and the proceedings of certain days have been reprinted several times. The page numbering of these editions and reprints, reportedly due to technical difficulties, varies from one to four pages. A reader desiring to investigate a quotation or citation beyond what is to be found in the footnote is urged, therefore, to search several pages to each side of the reference given if the page cited appears to be in error.

At the end of the book will be found a bibliographical note, an index, and three appendixes. The first appendix contains the portions of the Cabinet Mission Plan under which the Assembly came into being; the second lists the most important of the Assembly's committees and their members; the third is mainly biographical and is divided into two parts. Part A consists of brief biographies of the twenty-one individuals who were closest to the centre of Assembly affairs; Part B lists all Assembly members mentioned in the text and provides certain information about them, including the provinces they represented, their political parties, their classifications in the Assembly (Muslim, Sikh, or General—Hindu and all others—or Princely States), their communities (Hindu, Christian, Parsi, etc.), and their probable caste affiliations. The information about caste—in some cases the varna and not the caste is given—is included for general interest not because of its political significance. There is little if any evidence that caste considerations influenced Assembly members in the framing of the Constitution.

Writing a book is seldom a one-man job. The author is more than usually indebted to others for their assistance and takes this opportunity to express his gratitude to some of them. At the top of the list by a goodly distance is the late Francis Carnell, Lecturer in Commonwealth Government at Oxford University, without whose unstinted, patient help and keen insight this book would not have survived even its infancy. Next in Oxford comes Dr. C. C. Davies, former Reader in Indian History, for his constant and warming encouragement. Then thanks to Dr. K. C. Wheare and Professors Max Beloff, and W. H. Morris-Jones—of Durham University—and to Mr. Guy Wint for their help. The author has also benefited from the help of the librarians at the Indian Institute, Oxford, who are always willing to put their time at the researcher's disposal.

In India the list of persons to whom the author is indebted is especially long. Particular thanks are due to the late President Rajendra Prasad and to K. M. Munshi, both of whom were generous with their time and advice and who made their extensive collections of papers available to the author. The enormous value of these documents was enhanced by the kindness of the Indian National Archives (especially V. C. Joshi) in microfilming them so that they could be studied at leisure in Oxford. The late Prime Minister Nehru also helped in gaining access to certain documents. The author wishes to express his gratitude to B. Shiva Rao for his kind help and advice and for the use of documents from B. N. Rau's papers and from his own. This thanks extends to Mr. Rao's research assistants, Messrs. Kashyap, Tiwari, and Ayyangar, who are preparing for publication a most valuable collection of constitutional documents. R. C. S. Sarkar of the Law Ministry, Government of India, has also been helpful in unearthing documents. Kindness is a distinguishing characteristic of Indians, and when gathering material for this book the author profited fully from this trait, especially from persons of note who gave generously of their time for interviews.

Dr. Gopal Krishna read the entire manuscript and commented trenchantly upon it, and others were kind enough to read and advise on particular portions. Dr. Ralph Retzlaff must also be mentioned, for it was he who placed the author on the trail of many of the documents that made the writing of this book possible. Finally, there were those who helped type, edit, and proof-read the manuscript both at Oxford and in India, and who worked both long and well.

New Delhi
November 1964

1

The Constituent Assembly—
Microcosm in Action

This cannot be done by the wisest of lawyers sitting together in conclave;
it cannot be done by small committees trying to balance interests and
calling that constitution-making; it can never be done under the shadow
of an external authority. It can only be done effectively when the political
and psychological conditions are present, and the urge and sanctions come
from the masses.

Jawaharlal Nehru

GANDHI expressed the truth first—that Indians must shape their own
destiny, that only in the hands of Indians could India become herself— when in 1922 he said that Swaraj would not be the gift of the
British Parliament, but must spring from 'the wishes of the people
of India as expressed through their freely chosen representatives'.[1]
Twenty-four years later these words were repeated during the opening session of the Constituent Assembly: they were, some said, the
Assembly's origin; all agreed that they were its justification.

The Indian National Congress made the demand for a constituent
assembly part of its official policy in 1934. Refusing to accept the
1933 White Paper,[2] because it did not express 'the will of the people
of India', the Congress Working Committee stated:

---

[1] To Gandhi, Swaraj meant more than independence from the British. It meant
both national and personal (for all Indians) self-realization; it meant throwing off
foreign ways as well as foreign rule, so that Indians could emerge as masters of
their own souls as well as of their political future.

[2] The *Proposals for Indian Constitutional Reform*, of 1933; Cmd 4268. This was one
of the constitutional bases of the 1935 Act.

The only satisfactory alternative to the White Paper is a constitution drawn up by a Constituent Assembly elected on the basis of adult franchise or as near it as possible, with the power, if necessary, to the important minorities to have their representatives elected exclusively by the electors belonging to such minorities.[3]

Thereafter, in many provincial legislative assemblies and in the central legislative assembly in 1937, at the Congresses at Faizpur, Haripura, and Tripuri, and at the Simla Conference in 1945, the Congress reiterated that India could only accept a constitution drawn from the people and framed 'without any interference by a foreign authority'.[4]

During World War II, the mood of the Indian people became increasingly one of self-assertion, of a readiness to take its destiny into its own hands. By the time of independence, an acute observer wrote, Indians had 'a general awareness of nationality and national dignity. The Indian public felt itself a corporate unit and felt itself adult. Independence had been an ideal, a desideratum to be worked for; now it was an axiom of public life.'[5] In such a mood, even more than previously, Indians would accept only a constitution drafted by themselves.

As a result, in December 1946 a constituent assembly which 'derived from the people . . . all power and authority'[6] was convened. It prospered and ultimately provided Indians with an 'Indian-made' constitution. And its indigenous nature has been the major reason for the Constitution's success. Indians have been less likely to fault the Constitution and more likely to view it with pride, both because they did themselves create it and because, having written it themselves, it was better suited to their needs.[7]

---

[3] P. Chakrabarty and C. Bhattacharya, *Congress in Evolution*, page 30. For the background' role of the Swaraj Party in this declaration, see Tendulkar, *Mahatma*, III, 335 and 338–9 and *CAD* (Constituent Assembly Debates) I, 1, 5.

[4] From a Resolution of the Tripuri Congress; Chakrabarty and Bhattacharya, op. cit., Pan II, p. 35.

[5] Percival Spear, *India*, p. 407.

[6] Objectives Resolution passed by the Assembly; *CAD* I, 5, 59.

[7] This desire for a 'home-made' constitution, instead of one written in the Colonial Office of the imperial power and passed by the British Parliament, is the source of what K. C. Wheare has named the 'principle of constitutional autochthony', or the desire for a constitution sprung from the land itself. See K. C. Wheare, *Constitutional Structure of the Commonwealth*, p. 89.

Before turning to what the Assembly did, it is best to look at the way in which the Assembly came into being and how it worked, and so understand what an unusual body it was. The Constituent Assembly was, in effect, a one-party assembly, in the hands of the mass party, the Indian National Congress. Yet it was representative of India, and its internal decision-making processes were democratic. The leaders of the party, who were also the most important members of the Union Government and of the Assembly, were charismatic in their appeal and thus possessed immense power. In both thought and action, however, they were supported, and sometimes controlled, by the rank and file in the Assembly. This first chapter will be concerned with the origin of the Constituent Assembly itself and the manner in which the members approached the shaping of India's destiny.

The Origins and Creation of the Assembly

By the end of the War, as we have seen, India was ready for a constituent assembly and her leaders were demanding one.[8] Gandhi had changed his sceptical attitude of 1934 and had proclaimed himself more and more 'enamoured' of an assembly.[9] Most important, Britain, in the person of Sir Stafford Cripps, had accepted the idea that an elected body of Indians should frame the Indian constitution.[10]

The greatly increased demand for self-determination was supported by India's war-augmented power—her industry had expanded, many of her men had been trained and armed, and her people had a new, stronger sense of unity—and coincided with a marked decrease in the force Britain could exert in India, occupied as the British were with

---

[8]   There were also a number of books published during the war years calling for an assembly. Exceptions to this trend were Dr. B. R. Ambedkar and Mohammed Ali Jinnah. Ambedkar told the Scheduled Castes Federation, of which he was president, that a constituent assembly was not needed, the 1935 Act would do. Speech to S.C.F., 6 May 1945. *Indian Annual Register* (*IAR*) 1946,1, pp. 321–4. Jinnah's reasons will be examined below.

[9]   In an article in *Harijan*, 12 November 1939, entitled, 'The Only Way'. To Gandhi, and to other leaders, a constituent assembly seemed the best way to approach the communal problem.

[10] The proposals that Cripps put forward on his mission to India in 1942 were not accepted for a variety of reasons, but Cripps for the first time made it clear that Indians would write their own constitution.

Palestine and other problems abroad and war-weariness at home. It was in this atmosphere that the newly elected Labour Government announced in September 1945 that it was contemplating the creation of a constituent body in India and ordered that national elections be held during the winter so that freshly created provincial legislatures would be ready to act as electoral bodies for a constituent assembly.[11] The London government followed this move in January 1946 by sending a Parliamentary Delegation to India, which reported that the tide of independence was running fast, and then by dispatching a Cabinet-level mission the following March.

The Cabinet Mission arrived in New Delhi with the avowed purpose of assisting 'the Viceroy in setting up in India the machinery by which Indians can devise their own constitution', and of mediating between the Congress and the Muslim League in order to find a middle ground upon which the communities of India could be constitutionally united.[12] It was a task that non-Indians should never have attempted; it was almost certainly foredoomed to failure. There had always been conflicts of interest between Muslims and other Indians, particularly the Hindus. During the late nineteen twenties and thirties, disagreement had led to considerable communal tension. Muslim dissatisfaction, hitherto unchannelled, found its leader in Mohammed Ali Jinnah, who turned the infant Muslim League into his vehicle for power by championing Muslim rignts, both real and fictional, and by making an *a priori tenet* of Muslim politics the 60-year-old two-nation theory—the theory that Muslims were culturally as well as religiously a group apart, that they were neither Hindu nor Indian, and that they must seek their fulfilment in a state of their own.[13]

[11] The policy and the general dates of the forthcoming elections were announced by the then Viceroy, Lord Wavell, on Delhi Radio, 19 September 1945. *IAR* 1945, II, 148. The creation of a constituent assembly by indirect elections with provincial assemblies as electoral bodies was a holdover from the Cripps proposals, which were still alive, at least to the British Government, as a basis for negotiation in India.

[12] Lord Pethick-Lawrence, Secretary of State for India and senior member of the Cabinet Mission, in a broadcast over Delhi Radio, 16 May 1946. *IAR* 1946, 1, 152.

[13] In the early thirties, few Muslims looked to the League as their means of political expression. In the 1937 elections the League showed little strength, although 424 of 482 Muslim seats were won by non-Congress Muslims. By 1946, basing its claim on the results of the 1945 elections, however, the League could justly

Distrusting Hindus, the Muslim League opposed the organization to which most Hindus (and many Muslims as well as other Indians) belonged: the much larger Indian National Congress. While the Congress called for a constituent assembly and Indian self-determination, Jinnah's League derided the idea, preferring British presence in India as a deterrent to Congress power, which they said would be synonymous with Hindu domination. Instead of supporting a constituent assembly, the League in 1940 demanded that before independence Muslims must be assured the sanctuary of autonomous areas.[14] In 1945 Jinnah took this a step further: India must have two constituent assemblies, he said, one for Hindustan and one for Pakistan. And the British must remain to see that justice (to the Muslims) was done; independence should come when the constitutions had been completed, when the two nations were established.

The Congress viewpoint was the reverse of the League's. The people of India were Indians; no matter what their religion, they were one nation. The British must leave India—only then could independent Indians come together, settle their differences, and begin to shape their future. India should be one nation under one constitution, the Congress believed, and although the rights of all groups would be protected by the constitution and as much autonomy as possible allowed, government must be sufficiently strong to bring about the social revolution that India must achieve if it was to survive.

These were the views that the three members of the Cabinet Mission hoped to reconcile by a compromise plan.[15] India was to remain one state, but the power of the Central Government would be confined to foreign affairs, communications, and defence. The provinces would be grouped geographically into three regions, one of which would be predominantly Muslim, one predominantly Hindu, and in the third the population of the two communities would be nearly equal. The provincial representatives to the All-India Constituent Assembly, after a preliminary meeting of that body, would meet in three group assemblies to frame constitutions for their

---

say that it spoke for Indian Muslims. This growth of League power did not make the Congress a Hindu organization, which the League claimed was the case.

[14] The famous Lahore Resolution.

[15] For the text of the Cabinet Mission Plan, see M. Gwyer and A. Appadorai, *Speeches and Documents on the Indian Constitution*, pp. 577–84. Only the essence of the Plan is summarized here.

component provinces and, if desired, for their group as well. Among these constitutions, in a manner unspecified by the Cabinet Mission Plan, would be distributed the functions of government other than the three reserved for the centre. When all this was done, the representatives would return from the group constituent assemblies to the All-India Assembly to draft the national constitution.

The Mission made its plan public on 16 May 1946. By the end of June, after infinitely detailed negotiations, both the League and the Congress had accepted it, but both had publicly and privately recorded their reservations. Jinnah accepted the Cabinet Mission Plan 'because the foundation of Pakistan is inherent in compulsory grouping and because it (the League) hopes it will ultimately result in independent Pakistan.'[16] The Congress accepted the Plan subject to its own interpretations of certain provisions being accepted by the British and the League.

This detente lasted through July, long enough to see the Constituent Assembly elected under the terms of one portion of the Cabinet Mission Plan.[17] Rejecting adult suffrage as too cumbersome and slow, the Plan provided that the provincial legislatures elect the Assembly—a decision with which the Congress agreed, forsaking its long-held demand for a constituent assembly created by adult suffrage.[18] The provinces were to be represented in the Assembly in the approximate ratio of one to one million of their population. The members of three communal categories in the legislatures, Muslim, Sikh, and General (Hindus and all other communities), would elect separately, according to their percentage of the province's population, their proportion of the provincial delegation. The Princely States, according to the Mission Plan, were to have ninety-three representatives in the Assembly, but the method of selecting them was left to consultation between the Assembly and the States' rulers.[19]

[16] Muslim League Resolution of 6 June 1946, accepting the Mission Plan; *IAR* 1946,. I, 183-

[17] Paragraph 18; for the text of this paragraph, see Appendix I and Gwyer and Appadorai, op. cit., pp. 581–3.

[18] The Congress did this because the preparations for general elections would have long delayed the creation of the Assembly.

[19] The negotiations between, the CA States Committee and representatives of the Princes resulted in an agreement that provided for at least 50 per cent, of the States' representatives being elected to the Assembly; the rulers could nominate members up to 50 per cent, but it was hoped that the greater proportion would be

The Assembly, although elected, was far from being in session. Jinnah liked the Mission Plan only a little and the Congress's conditional acceptance of it even less. Finding an excellent pretext in some unguarded and tactless remarks Nehru made about 'grouping' and the Congress's intentions in the Assembly,[20] he withdrew his acceptance and instructed League representatives to boycott the Assembly.[21] The League never lifted this boycott; the only League representatives to enter the Assembly did so because they had remained in India after Partition. The Cabinet Mission had failed. It failed because the Congress and the League had almost certainly become too estranged for reconciliation, which in any case was out of the question so long as the British were a third party to whom each side could appeal against the other. Yet if the three members of the Cabinet Mission could not hold together Muslim and non-Muslim India,[22] something that only Indians, if they, could have accomplished, a portion of the Mission's efforts lived on in the Indian Constituent Assembly.

In August 1946 all this was still in the future. India was headed towards independence and the problem was how to bring the Congress and the League together in the Constituent Assembly and obtain their cooperation in forming the Interim Government envisaged in the Cabinet Mission Plan. Throughout the summer and autumn of 1946 the Viceroy, Wavell, had the impossible assignment of reconciling the disparate views and quieting the suspicions that had confronted the Cabinet Mission and that had flared up again in July after the Mission's return to England. Meanwhile, the Congress went ahead with its plans for the Assembly, appointing an Experts Committee to draft fundamental rights and to arrange the early sessions.[23] And the Congress, at the Viceroy's invitation, formed the Interim Government; Nehru was its head, as Vice-President of the

---

elected. *Report of the Committee Appointed to Negotiate with the States Negotiating Committee*, 28 April 1947; Constituent Assembly, *Reports of Committees, First Series*, p. 9.

[20] At a press conference in Bombay on 10 July; *IAR* 1946, II, 145–7.

[21] 29 July 1947.

[22] It is important to remember here that the Indian Muslim community had a population of about 100 millions, of which approximately 65 millions became Pakistanis. The 1951 census figures for both countries show India with 35½ million Muslims and Pakistan with 65 million.

[23] The Experts Committee met in July and August 1946. Nehru was its chairman. For more about this Committee, see below, esp. Chapters II and III.

Viceroy's Executive Council, or *de facto* Prime Minister. The League continued to ignore the Assembly. It refused to join the Interim Government, but later changed its mind and joined with the stated purpose of wrecking it.

Wavell, in the middle, could neither coax nor command from either side the cooperation that would have brought peace and unity to India, and, more particularly, that would have permitted him to convene the Constituent Assembly. It was thought unwise to call the first Assembly session for late September or early October, as the Interim Government at one time wished to do, because it might interfere with a Congress-League *rapprochement*. And it was not until 20 November that Wavell announced that the Assembly would meet on 9 December and that invitations to attend were being sent to those elected.[24]

The Muslim League's boycott of the Assembly was still in force. The Attlee government's last minute efforts to effect an agreement failed, although Nehru, Jinnah, and Baldev Singh (representing the Sikhs) flew to London in early December for a final attempt at unity. When the Assembly began its three-year task on 9 December, the representatives of nearly 100 million Indian Muslims were absent. All the other communities of India were there.[25]

The beginnings of a new India rested on a small portion of what was otherwise a moribund dream: the Constituent Assembly was meeting with the permission of the British Government, and a fourth of the nation was not represented at the Assembly's deliberations. Had such a body any power or authority of its own? Could it speak and act for India? Was it sovereign? Gandhi believed not (because 'it is no use declaring somebody else's creation a sovereign body'), although

---

[24] It had been hoped at one time to convene the Constituent Assembly in August 1946. See B. N. Rau letter to G. E. B. Abell, Wavell's private secretary, 15 June 1946, in B. Shiva Rao, *The Framing of India's Constitution: Select Documents*, I. Then Nehru called for convening the Assembly in mid-September, see G. E. B. Abell to B. N. Bau, 17–18 August 1946, ibid. Late October was then considered. Finally, to allow for further negotiations with the Muslim League, to permit the communal situation to cool, and to allow time for a meeting of the Central Legislative Assembly, the 9 December date was set. See J. Nehru to B. N. Rau, 16 September 1946, ibid., as well as other letters exchanged by them on 7 and 8 September, ibid.

[25] Several Sikh members had, at one stage, also boycotted the Assembly, but in August had expressed their faith in the Congress and their intention to join the Assembly.

he thought that all parties should join the Assembly in an effort to make it work.[26] Maulana Azad, Nehru, and Rajendra Prasad, who had been elected the President of the Assembly at its second sitting, believed that it was sovereign because the Assembly's authority came from the people of India—although they recognized that the Cabinet Mission Plan placed certain limitations on its activities.

The Assembly gave its own answer to these questions, in its Rules, when it arrogated to itself the authority to control its own being: 'The Assembly shall not be dissolved except by a resolution assented to by at least two-thirds of the whole number of members of the Assembly'.[27] The Assembly was the people's. As Nehru said, the British could now dissolve the Assembly only by force. 'We have gone through the valley of the shadow, and we will go through it again for true independence', he said.[28]

Nehru and other Assembly leaders continued to hope throughout December that the League would instruct its members to join the Assembly, and both inside and outside that body the Congress changed or deferred policies to this end. The hope was small and the efforts unrewarded. By the second session of the Assembly in late January 1947, it was all but certain that the League would never come in. Nevertheless, the Assembly restricted itself to the preliminary work of adopting an Objectives Resolution, of electing committees to begin drafting fundamental rights and a federal system, and of opening negotiations with the Princely States.

Partition was in the air at the end of April when the Assembly met for the third time.[29] For this reason it postponed debate on preliminary federal provisions. Throughout May, however, Assembly committees continued to work, as they had during the previous six

---

[26] To Louis Fischer in an interview held about 22 July 1946; see Tendulkar, op. cit, Vol. VII, pp. 189–90.

[27] *Constituent Assembly, Rules of Procedure and Standing Orders*, Rule 7, Chapter III. Nehru had suggested in July 1946 that the Assembly should be dissolved only by its own vote. See Minutes of Experts Committee meeting, 20 July 1946; *Prasad papers*, File 35-C/47.

[28] Nehru at the AICC meeting, 5 January 1947 in Delhi—A. C. Banerjee, *Constitutional Documents*, p. 284—and in the Assembly; *CAD* I, 6, 70.

[29] Nehru had told the All-India States Peoples' Conference at Gwalior on 19 April that 'The Punjab and Bengal will be partitioned.' See *The Hindustan Times*, 20 April 1947.

months, within the framework of the Cabinet Mission Plan.[30] The Constituent Assembly was still marking time.

June 3, 1947: the day of decision. Lord Mountbatten, Viceroy since March, announced that on 15 August England would recognize the existence of two independent states on the sub-continent, India and Pakistan.[31] India and more than half of her Muslims under Jinnah were to go separate ways. The Indian Independence Act passed by the British Parliament came into effect on 15 August 1947, giving legally to the Constituent Assembly the status it had assumed since its inception.[32] The Cabinet Mission Plan became outmoded, and the Constituent Assembly settled down to draft free India's constitution.[33]

India In Microcosm

I. The Assembly, the Congress, and the Country

The Constituent Assembly was a one-party body in an essentially one-party country. The Assembly was the Congress and the Congress was India.[34] There was a third point that completed a tight triangle, the

---

[30] Patel told the Advisory Committee meeting of 21 April 1947 that the Assembly must proceed on the basis of the Cabinet Mission Plan and that the committee must make no decision that 'will prevent them (the Muslim League) from coming in'. Proceedings of the meeting in B. Shiva Rao, *Select Documents*, II.

[31] The date of British withdrawal from India, so long indeterminate, had been set as June 1948 by Prime Minister Attlee in a speech in London on 20 February 1947. Lord Mountbatten convinced the British Government that British withdrawal should come even earlier.

[32] According to the Indian Independence Act the Constituent Assembly became, as the Constituent Assembly (Legislative) the Dominion Parliament. Hence the Assembly sat as a constituent body and as the national legislature, although at different times. The Central Assembly, which had been elected at the same time as the provincial legislatures in 1945, ceased to function as of 15 August. The I.I. Act also provided that the 1935 Act would remain the basis of government in India until the new Constitution was completed. The 1935 Act, among other things, provided for a parliamentary system in India.

[33] The Assembly had met in July and, on the basis of the June 3 Plan, had already begun to frame the Constitution in the light of Partition and the moved-up date of independence.

[34] Of the Muslims remaining in India after Partition, some were Congress members or supporters. Those who were former Muslim Leaguers were divided among

government (meaning the apparatus of elected government both provincial and national), for the Congress was the government too. The Assembly, the Congress, and the government were, like the points of a triangle, separate entities, but, linked by over-lapping membership, they assumed a form infinitely meaningful for India.

One might assume, aware of the character of monolithic political systems in other countries, that a mass-party in India would be rigid and narrow in outlook and that its powerful leadership would silence dissent and confine policy and decision-making to the hands of the select few. In India the reverse was the case. The membership of the Congress in the Constituent Assembly and outside held social, economic, and political views ranging from the reactionary to the revolutionary, and it did not hesitate to voice them. The leaders of the Assembly, who played the same role in the Congress and in the Union Government, were national heroes and had almost unlimited power; yet decision-making in the Assembly was democratic. The Indian Constitution expresses the will of the many rather than the needs of the few.

The Congress's overwhelming majority in the Constituent Assembly resulted from the December 1945 provincial legislature elections and from Partition. Both the Congress and the League campaigned furiously in 1945, knowing that seats in a constituent assembly might be at stake and trying to establish the strongest possible claim to popularity for the negotiations that lay ahead. The election gave the League most of the Muslim seats in all the provinces and all the Muslim seats in some provinces. Of the total of 1,585 seats in the provincial assemblies, the Congress won 925 or 58 per cent., but it captured about 85 per cent, of the non-Muslim seats. Under the scheme of indirect election in the Cabinet Mission Plan,[35] the Constituent Assembly reflected the complexion of the provincial legislatures. Hence in the July 1946 elections to the Assembly,

themselves and had no political organization worthy of the name, for the League was understandably suspect in India, and, with Pakistan a reality, it had lost its motivating force. And it is fair to say that, except on the issue of Muslim rights, few Leaguers would have quarrelled with Congress policies. And after Partition, many sided with the Congress on this issue, also. Admittedly, however, many Indian Muslims still feared Hindu domination, and they now turned to Nehru, Patel, and the Congress leadership for the protection of their interests.

[35] See pp. 8–9 above, and Appendix I.

League members won all but seven of the seats reserved for Muslims. Congress candidates filled 203 of the 212 General places (representing every community except Sikhs and Muslims). Additionally, the Congress parties in the provincial legislatures elected four Muslims and one Sikh, giving the Congress 208 seats of the total of 296 allotted to the provinces under the May 16 Plan. The remaining sixteen places went to five small groups.[36] Thus the Congress had a built-in majority of 69 per cent, in the Assembly, and, after Partition, when the number of Muslim League representatives fell to twenty-eight, the Congress majority jumped to 82 per cent.[37]

To the weight of numbers, the Congress added the prestige of its senior members. In the Assembly were six past or present Congress presidents, fourteen Provincial Congress Committee presidents, and, in 1949, fourteen out of eighteen members of the Congress Working Committee were also active in the Assembly. Among these and other notables were the four chiefs of the party: Jawaharlal Nehru, Vallabhbhai Patel, Maulana Azad, and Rajendra Prasad.

Although the outcome of the Assembly elections in July 1946 had made the Congress master of the Assembly, party policy ensured that Congress members there represented the country. This was a result of the unwritten and unquestioned belief that the Congress should be both socially and ideologically diverse and of a deliberate policy that representatives of various minority communities and viewpoints should be present in the Assembly. The electoral process itself could not have produced a representative body because it was based on the restricted franchise established by the Sixth Schedule of the 1935 Act, which excluded the mass of peasants, the majority of small shopkeepers and traders, and countless others from the rolls through tax, property, and educational qualifications. Only 28.5 per cent, of the adult population of the provinces could vote in the provincial assembly elections of early 1946.[38] But because the Congress and

---

[36] These groups were: Akali Sikhs and the Unionists—both Punjab parties, three seats each; the Communists and the Scheduled Castes Federation (Dr. Ambedkar), one each; and eight Independents.

[37] The representatives of the former Princely States, when finally seated, added some- what to the Congress majority.

[38] Reforms Office telegram 2189G from V. P. Menon to Gilchrist (Secretary of State's office); Reforms Office File 94/4/45-R, *Indian National Archives*

its candidates covered a broad ideological spectrum, those elected
to the assemblies did represent the diverse viewpoints of voters and
non-voters alike.

Congress leaders had long believed that the party should speak for
the country. Nehru wrote in 1939:

> The Congress has within its fold many groups, widely differing in
> their viewpoints and ideologies. This is natural and inevitable if the
> Congress is to be the mirror of the nation.[39]

During the war years the base of the Congress became even broader
as its character more and more resembled that of a national front: as
a national movement the Congress's role was to blend hitherto disparate elements. If this were to continue to be the case in the post-war
period, the party must bring forward capable men representing the
country's new dynamism.

Congress election committees undertook this task in the autumn of
1945, the responsibility mainly falling to the Provincial Congresses,
which selected candidates for the provincial legislatures with very
little interference from the Central Elections Committee created by
the All-India Congress Committee (AICC).[40]

(*INA*). 'Adult population' meant persons aged 20 and over. The author's own
calculations produced a figure of nearly 28 per cent. This figure is an average; proportions of the electorate to the adult population varied from 43.5
per cent, in Sind to 14.8 per cent, in Bihar; ibid. Economically and socially
depressed portions of the population were virtually disenfranchised by the
terms of the 1935 Act. In Madras, for example, according to the author's calculations, approximately 10 per cent, of the Scheduled Caste adult population
was entitled to vote, and in the United Provinces only 2.5 per cent, could
vote—although the ratio for the U.P. generally was 25 per cent. The rolls for
the January to March 1946 provincial assembly elections were based on those
of 1941. They were brought up to date during the autumn of 1945. Persons
not on the 1941 rolls who believed that in 1945 they qualified as voters could
make applications to this effect. For further material, see Reforms Office File
101/45-R- Part I; *INA*.

[39] J. Nehru, *Unity of India*, p. 139.

[40] The Elections Committee of the AICC was concerned with the selection of
candidates for the Central Assembly. Its members were Azad, Patel, Prasad,
Asaf Ali, Pattabhi Sitaramayya, and Shankarrao Deo. Pandit Pant of the United
Provinces, and a Congressman of national stature wrote to Prasad: The 'selec-
tions for the provincial seats have to be made essentially by the Provincial Boards';

One of the primary qualifications for a candidate, it is certain, was a record of active work in the Independence Movement, a qualification that produced a group of determined men of above average ability whose viewpoints, for two reasons, were varied: the Congress, as has been said, had always sought variety, and this qualification did not preclude it, and without central direction in the selection of candidates ideological uniformity was impossible.

When the time came for the election of Constituent Assembly members by the provincial legislatures, the Congress high command adopted much the same policy; i.e., let the provincial machinery select its own members. This preserved the diversity already present in the legislatures and added to it in an important way. As the Constituent Assembly would determine the distribution of powers between the Union Government and the provinces, and would consider the rights of the provinces in general, each Provincial Congress Committee made sure that its delegation, or as many individual members of it as possible, would represent the province's interests at the bargaining table—a precaution that broadened the debate and has helped to make the federal provisions of the Constitution durable.

As a matter of policy, however, the national leadership of the Congress made certain exceptions to this general rule, intervening in the affairs of the Provincial Congresses to assure that persons of exceptional ability found places in the Constituent Assembly and that the minority communities were justly represented. The Cabinet Mission Plan guaranteed seats in the Assembly only for Muslims and Sikhs; it contained no specific provisions for other minorities, and it was the initiative of the Congress high command that brought Parsis, Anglo-Indians, Indian Christians, members of the Scheduled Castes and Tribes, and even women, into the Assembly under the 'General' category. The Constituent Assembly elections were scheduled to take place between 11 and 22 July 1946. Early in the month the Congress Working Committee began to send directions to the various Provincial Congress Committees (PCC) concerning the selection of candidates. The principal communication was sent about 6 July and gave explicit recommendations. The United Provinces PCC, for

---

interference on our part ought to be 'very rare'. Letter dated 15 November 1945; *Prasad papers*, File 14-P/45-6.

example, should list on its slate for the vote of the provincial assembly Nehru, Pandit Pant, Acharya Kripalani, Sir Tej Bahadur Sapru, and H. N. Kunzru.[41] The Bihar PCC should, among others, nominate Mrs. Sarojini Naidu, Rajendra Prasad, and Jayaprakash Narayan. The names for Madras were Pattabhi Sitaramayya, Rajgopalachari, A. K. Ayyar, N. G. Ayyangar, K. Santhanam, and B. Shiva Rao.

The Working Committee's recommendation also stated that the Madras PCC should nominate two Christians; Bihar should nominate one, and so on. Bihar, Orissa, and Assam, should be certain to nominate at least one Adibasi (Backward Tribe member) each, and every province should nominate members of the Scheduled Castes in proportion to the membership of this minority in the particular provincial assembly. The names of several women, among them Mrs. Hansa Mehta and Rajkumari Amrit Kaur, were also recommended to the provinces that should return them.[42] Because the Congress was in the majority in most of the provincial assemblies, it was certain that the legislatures would elect to the Constituent Assembly individuals named by the high command. Except for such names, however, the PCC's had a free hand, and they did not, in most cases, prepare a set slate for the legislature. In Bihar, for example, where Rajendra Prasad, president of the Provincial Congress Committee, headed the selection committee, several candidates named by the committee were not elected by the legislature. In the United Provinces, where Pandit Pant was prime minister, president of the PCC, and head of the selection committee, the PCC nominated 156 persons for election to the Assembly although the province had only 47 General seats.[43]

Some of the names recommended by the Working Committee— such as Nehru, Pant, and Rajgopalachari—were those of Congress luminaries. More than a dozen, however, were not Congressmen, and the Working Committee saw to it that they were elected so that their talents in administration, law, and constitutional law and their

---

[41] See *The Hindustan Times*, 7 July 1946. For a good account of the election activity of the month see this newspaper.

[42] The suggestions regarding specific women candidates was also sent to the provincial prime ministers in an All India Congress Committee circular. See ibid, 4 July 1946. This circular also stated that the candidates selected by the PCC's and their election committees, should be 'suitable for the work to be done by the Constituent Assembly'.

[43] Ibid.

experience in national affairs would be available to the Assembly. Among them were A. K. Ayyar, H. N. Kunzru, N. G. Ayyangar, Dr. Ambedkar,[44] K. Santhanam, M. R. Jayakar, Sachchidananda Sinha, and K. M. Munshi—an estranged Congressman.[45] The well-known statesman and Liberal Party member, Sir Tej Bahadur Sapru, who was also named, as we have seen, declined because of illness, but his influence was nevertheless felt in the Assembly.[46]

As a result of Congress policy, the minority communities were fully represented in the Constituent Assembly, usually by members of their own choosing. The Indian Christians had seven representatives in the Assembly, the Anglo-Indians three (chosen by the national leaders of the community), the Parsis three (chosen in the same manner), and so on. After Partition, when the composition of the Assembly, except for the representation of the Princely States, had become settled, the minorities had 88 of the 235 seats alloted to the provinces, or 37 per cent, of the provincial membership.[47] Additionally, as has been pointed

[44] Dr. Ambedkar was originally elected to the Assembly as the member for the Scheduled Castes Federation, but he lost his seat with the partition of Bengal. The Bombay Congress re-elected him at the request of the Congress high command. See letter from Prasad to B. G. Kher, prime minister of Bombay, 30 June 1947; *Prasad papers*. Later on in the life of the Assembly, the high command occasionally instructed a PCC to find a seat for a Cabinet minister who was not already a member of the Assembly and needed to be to retain his place in the Cabinet.

[45] A version of what happened has been given by B. Shiva Rao, a member of the CA, a prominent journalist with *The Hindu* of Madras, and a man long involved with public affairs in India. Rao informed the author that in June 1946 he presented Gandhi with a list of fifteen prominent Indians, his own name among them, whom he thought should be elected to the Assembly. Gandhi agreed with the idea and with the names and sent it on to Nehru and Patel, who arranged that the persons be named as candidates.

[46] See a letter on this subject from M. R. Jayakar to Sapru dated 10 January 1947. Letter No. J199, *Sapru papers*. For further mention of Sapru, see Chapt. III, especially.

[47] Minority representation was as follows: Nepalis, one (elected from Bengal); Sikhs, five (one more than provided for in the Cabinet Mission Plan); Parsis, three; Christians, seven; Anglo-Indians, three; Backward Tribes, five; Muslims, 31 (three more than provided for in the Mission Plan); and Scheduled Castes, 33. For a summary of the composition of the Assembly during the first session in December 1946, given by Assembly President Prasad in response to the slurs on the Assembly made by Winston Churchill and Viscount Simon in Parliament in London, see *CAD* II, 1, 267. The composition of the Assembly during its entire

out, the ideological spectrum of the Assembly was broadened by the inclusion of non-Congress 'experts' as well as by the diverse nature of the Congress membership itself. In the words of K. Santhanam, 'There was hardly any shade of public opinion not represented in the Assembly.'[48] Although indirectly elected and therefore not responsible to the mass of Indians, the Constituent Assembly was a highly representative body.[49]

This was true even if three political organizations had no official representation in the Constituent Assembly: the Communist Party, the Socialist Party, and the Hindu Mahasabha. The Communists in Bengal had elected an Assembly member, but, like Ambedkar and others, he had lost his seat with Partition; he was not re-elected and attended only the first three sessions. There were in the Assembly, however, Marxists and supporters of the Forward Bloc, a deviationist Communist group.

The Socialists had been the Congress Socialists from the time of their founding in the mid-thirties until they split from the Congress in early 1948 to become a separate party. In the summer of 1946 this group decided not to join the Assembly on the basis of the Cabinet Mission Plan because its senior members believed that the British were again leading India up the garden path. Their decision kept nearly a half dozen able individuals out of the Assembly. A year later, Jayaprakash Narayan, leader of the group, reconsidered his view of the validity and effectiveness of the Assembly and wrote to Nehru that 'in the changed circumstances' Socialist members could join the Assembly if invited.[50] He requested that he should not be included, because he was 'too occupied', and suggested that those who might be invited include Narenda Dev, Mrs. Asaf Ali, Ramanohar Lohia, Purushottam Trikamdas, Kamaladevi, Rao Patwardhan, and Ashoke Mehta. Nehru replied to this overture

---

existence remained much as it was in August 1947, because bye-elections to the Assembly were held on the basis of separate electorates in order to preserve the original balance.

[48] In an interview with the author. This view was also held by many other persons interviewed.

[49] One need hardly say that the Assembly did not represent the lack of sophistication in the masses, who had a growing social consciousness, but little political awareness.

[50] Letter from J. P. Narayan to Nehru, 3 July 1947; *Prasad papers*, Special File.

that 'we shall welcome the persons you have suggested and we shall try to get them in', but he explained that it was difficult to create vacancies because the election of members was largely a matter for the provinces and there was strong competition for seats.[51] The affair ultimately came to naught. The Socialists were divided among themselves about the desirability of joining the Assembly and it proved too difficult for the Congress to create the necessary seats.[52] By May 1948 the non-cooperationist wing of the, by then, Socialist Party had won the day. Not only did the party refuse to consider sending delegates to the Assembly, but a resolution of the National Executive of the party called for the dissolution of the Assembly and its re-election by adult suffrage.[53] The absence of a formal Socialist group meant little, however, for most members of the Assembly thought of themselves as Socialists, and with few exceptions the members believed that the best and perhaps only way to the social and economic goals that India sought was by the road of government initiative and control of industry and commerce.

Equally, the absence of representatives bearing the label of the Hindu Mahasabha, of the Rashtriya Swayamsevak Sangh (RSS), or of other Hindu communal groups, meant little. Their views on the institutional aspects of the constitution differed little from the Congress; their extreme communal views would not have swayed the Assembly. Besides, the Congress had its own Hindu conservatives— like Purushottam Das Tandon. And, indeed, members of the Hindu Mahasabha were present in the Assembly under other sponsorship. In all, three former Mahasabha presidents were members. Two of them became so on Congress tickets: M. R. Jayakar, as we have seen, and Shyama Prasad Mookerjee, actually a vice-president of the Mahasabha when he entered the Assembly after Nehru made him a member of the Cabinet.[54]

---

[51] Nehru to Narayan, 5 July 1947; ibid.

[52] Ashoke Mehta in an interview with the author.

[53] See the Socialist Party pamphlet, *Resolutions of the National Executive at Belgaum,* 24–26 May 1948, p. 5. Set also Narayan letter to Prasad, dated 30 May 1948, expressing the same sentiments; *Prasad papers,* File.13-C/48.

[54] There is an extensive correspondence in the *Prasad papers* between Prasad and B. C. Roy, prime minister of Bengal, concerning Mookerjee's election.
The third Mahasabha member in the CA was N. B. Khare, one-time Congressman who entered the Assembly as member for the former Princely State

At the apex of the triangle of which the Congress and the Constituent Assembly were the base, stood the government. With the presence in the Assembly of members of the Union and the provincial governments, still working as a legacy of the British period, the system of interlocking memberships was complete. In the July 1946 elections the provincial legislatures had chosen their representatives to the Assembly partly from among their own numbers; the Assembly rules, therefore, sanctioned double membership, and in the Assembly in 1948 there were 106 members of provincial legislatures. Among them were six of the nine provincial prime ministers and nearly a dozen other provincial ministers, who were members of local assemblies by virtue of the parliamentary government of the 1935 Act.[55]

The Constituent Assembly was in its second aspect in fact a part of the government, for, as we have seen, the Constituent Assembly (Legislative) was the Indian Parliament. Moreover, nearly fifty of the more than 300 Assembly members who played this dual role participated even more closely in the processes of government through their assignment to the parliamentary committees charged with overseeing the affairs of Union Government ministries. The ministers of the Union Government had to be members of the Constituent Assembly (Legislative) and thus also participated as constitution-makers. Some members of the Union Government, like Nehru, Patel, and Azad, had been elected to the Assembly before they became ministers; others, like S. P. Mookerjee, had to be seated as a result of their appointment to the Cabinet.[56] There were in the Assembly fourteen Union Government ministers, three ministers of state, and one deputy

---

of Alwar. Because of his suspected communalism, he lost his seat in 1948 after Gandhi's assassination.

[55] The Executive Committee of the Congress Party in Parliament in 1948 moved to bar provincial prime ministers from the CA (Legislative) and to force the resignation of provincial ministers from the CA. See Exec. Comm. Res. of February 1948, sent to Prasad by Exec. Comm. Secretary Mohanlal Saksena; *Prasad papers*, Special File. This decision was not put in force, however, and a year later provincial ministers continued to be active in the Assembly.

[56] Ministers of the Government of India were allowed to attend and participate in Constituent Assembly meetings, but not vote in them, while awaiting election to the Assembly. See Minutes of Steering Committee meeting, 23 January 1948; CA File, *Law Ministry Archives*.

minister. Only two persons did not play this dual role: Rajendra Prasad, as President of the Constituent Assembly did not take part in the proceedings of the Constituent Assembly (Legislative) and the reverse was true of G. V. Mavalankar, Speaker of the latter.

Although the Assembly had sprung from the rank and file of the Congress, there was little immediate cause and effect relationship between the national party machinery and Congressmen in the Assembly. Through their participation in government, Constituent Assembly members acquired a sense of professional corporateness that separated them from the Congress Party as a whole. The Congress Working Committee took part in planning the early sessions of the Assembly, and later certain problems of especially grave import—such as the language and linguistic provinces issues—were taken up by the Working Committee. In general, however, Assembly leaders handled Assembly problems. The exclusion of the lower ranks of the party from participation in Constituent Assembly affairs is very evident. The many bulging files of correspondence between the central Congress organization and the Provincial and District Congress Committees, which the author inspected in the Prasad papers, contained not one letter referring to constitutional matters. At the Jaipur Session of the Congress, held in December 1948, after the Draft Constitution had been before the country for nearly a year, no constitutional issue, other than linguistic provinces, was even alluded to.

There were two major reasons for this. The upper and lower echelons of administration of the Congress were both too preoccupied with their own affairs, primarily with rebuilding the party organization preparatory to general elections, to undertake other responsibilities. Secondly, those Congress leaders who had assumed control of the Union Government had rejected party interference in governmental affairs; the government wing of the Congress had early proclaimed its ascendancy within the party—a condition that would continue until the death of Nehru. The *cause celebre* of this shift in the centre of authority was the resignation of Acharya Kripalani from the presidency of the Congress.[57] The government wing of the party continued

[57] The problem of the role of the Working Committee had become embarrassing by the summer of 1947. Nehru prepared a Secret Note for Kripalani and four others—Gandhi, Prasad, Patel, and C. Rajgopalachari—in which he said that the government's need for quick action and sometimes for secrecy precluded

to respond to the currents of opinion in the mass of the party, occasionally to the ideas of the party theoreticians, and to the counsel of the Working Committee, but it was essentially the government wing of the Congress, not the mass party, that wrote the Constitution.

That the same men were responsible for drafting the Constitution and for governing the country, gave the Assembly an immediate awareness of the issues involved in constitution-making. The members' experience with the major problems and day-to-day affairs of government profoundly affected the content of the Constitution and was one of the most unusual aspects of the Assembly. Constitutions in the past had often enough been drafted by representatives of mutually independent territories who desired to create a common, general government; Switzerland, Australia, and the United States were examples. Independent peoples, such as the Russians in 1936, the French in 1873, or the Germans at Weimar, had framed a constitution while sovereignty lay in their own hands. Many colonial territories, such as Nigeria, would produce constitutions while the colonial power controlled the local government. But India was a unique case. India was an emergent, formerly colonial territory, where a sovereign people framed their Constitution in a Constituent Assembly while at the same time working a federal government that pre-existed independence—the federal system of the 1935 Act. Burma and Pakistan, appearances to the contrary, are not the same. In Burma the Constitution was rushed through a Constituent Assembly by a small group with apparently little thought given to its provisions. Nor could Burma, under the 1935 Act, be called a

---

consultation with the W.C. as a customary procedure. It was a question, Nehru wrote, of the 'freedom of the Government to shape policies and act up to them within the larger ambit of the general policy laid down in the Congress Resolutions . . . It is hardly possible for the Working Committee to consider all of them (government problems, which he had listed) in any detail or give directions in regard to all of them.' Note dated 15 July 1947; *Prasad papers*, File 16-P/45-6-7. Kripalani, on the other hand, wanted the W.C. to have equal or superior status to the Cabinet. He complained that the Cabinet leaders 'do not feel that the Government at the Centre is a Congress Government. After August 15 (1947) they seemed to make a distinction between Congress and the National Government.' From a letter to Prasad, dated 21 December 1947, marked Personal and Confidential; ibid. Because this distinction continued to exist, Kripalani resigned as Congress president.

federation.[58] Pakistan up to 1960 had been notably unsuccessful with its Constituent Assemblies and its Constitutions. And in Pakistan the Constituent Assembly found it impossible to govern the country and at the same time draft a Constitution.[59]

2. Leadership and Decision-making

The form and character of the Constituent Assembly leadership was a product of the inter-relation of government, particularly of the Union Government; with the Assembly, and of both, with the Congress Party. Of supreme significance was that the four leaders of the Assembly were the four heroes of the independence movement—Nehru, Patel, Prasad, and Azad—and that they continued to hold sway in the Congress during the framing period as they had in the days before independence. All were members of the party's highest council, the Working Committee, and Nehru and Patel remained its most influential members. Prasad was Congress president in 1948. At the same time Nehru and Patel held the Prime and Deputy Prime Ministerships in the Union Government.[60] Azad was a minister, and Prasad too, until he resigned his portfolio because it conflicted with his duties as President of the Assembly.[61] It was by virtue of their enormous prestige and their power, both in the Congress and in the Government, that these four men controlled the affairs of the Assembly, a control that they effected through their grip on the Congress Assembly Party and the Assembly's committee system.

The Constituent Assembly had eight major committees[62]—Rules, Steering, Advisory, Drafting, Union Subjects, Union Constitution,

---

[58] See Maung Maung, *Burma's Constitution*.

[59] See Keith Callard, *Pakistan*, especially p. 83. Nor has the constitutional experience of Nigeria, Ghana, or Malaya been like that of India, for the constitutions of all three were drafted in conjunction with officials of the British Colonial Office. It must also be remembered that Ghana and Tanganyika, after they became independent, abandoned the constitutions that had been given them by the British.

[60] Patel was also the Home Minister.

[61] Prasad had been Minister of Food and Agriculture, and Azad was the Minister of Education.

[62] The Assembly had a total of more than fifteen committees with a membership greater than eighty individuals. Seven of them, such as the House and Staff Committee, had minor functions. For the members of the more important Committees, see Appendix II.

Provincial Constitution, and States—with a total membership of approximately three dozen.[63] Either Nehru, Patel, or Prasad chaired each of these committees, and in many cases the other two or Azad were also present. With seven other Assembly members, these leaders constituted an inner circle in the Assembly's committees and demonstrated again the interlocking of the three organizations, for with one exception all were also members either of the Congress or of the Union Government. Those in this inner circle are listed opposite along with the number of committees on which they served, and their position in the Congress and in government.

If we add nine more names to this list we will have included a few lesser committee members, all the members of the Drafting Committee, and some secondary Congress personalities.[64]

Name	No. of Committees	Congress Position	Government Position
Prasad	2	Working Comm.	Pres. of C.A.
Azad	4	Working Comm.	Minister
Patel	4	Working Comm.	Deputy Prime Minister
Nehru	3	Working Comm.	Prime Minister
Pant	3	Working Comm.	Prime Minister, U.P.
Sitaramayya	4	Working Comm.	—
Ayyar	5	—	—
Ayyangar, N. G	5	—	Minister
Munshi	6	Member	—
Ambedkar	3	—	Minister
Sinha, Satyanarayan	2	Member	Minister and Chief Whip[65]

[63] The Advisory Committee had sixty-four members, many of whom served only on this one committee and whose importance was minimal. The committee had two subcommittees. Fundamental Rights and Minorities, whose very important work is described in Chapters 3, 4, and 6.

[64] The names: M. A. Ayyangar, Jairamdas Daulatram, Shankarao Deo, Mrs. Durgabai, Acharya Kripalani, T. T. Krishnamachari, H. C. Mookerjee, N. M. Rau, and Mohammed Saadulla. For more information concerning these persons, see Appendix III.

[65] Again to emphasize the overlapping memberships of the organizations at the points of the triangle: fourteen of the eighteen Working Committee members

These twenty individuals comprised the most influential members of the Constituent Assembly. They brought diverse backgrounds, personalities, and qualifications to constitution-making. All were university graduates; four had university training, or its equivalent, outside of India—Nehru, Patel, Ambedkar, and Azad. Twelve were lawyers or had taken law degrees; one was a medical doctor; two had been teachers; three had been high-ranking officials in civil government; one was a businessman. Two were Muslims, one Christian, and the remainder Hindus. Of the Hindus, Ambedkar was a Harijan, and there were nine Brahmins; the other seven were not of high caste. Only half the group had been active in the Independence Movement or had strong ties with the Congress. Of these, nine had for some years been of Working Committee rank. Six had been, or were during the period of the Assembly, Congress presidents. Five of the group of twenty had never been members of the Congress; two, Ambedkar, particularly, and Saadulla, had been its opponents— Saadulla as a member of the Muslim League.

Ambedkar's skirmishes with the Congress and with Gandhi— primarily over Harijan causes—dated back more than twenty years. Nehru had, however, personally invited him to become a member of the Cabinet.[66] Ambedkar, for his part, had joined the Government because he did not believe in opposition for opposition's sake and because '(1) The offer was without any conditions, and (2) one could serve the interests of the Scheduled Castes better from within the government, than from without'.[67] Through his cooperation, Ambedkar thought the Harijans had got 'some safeguards in the Draft Constitution which we might not otherwise have got'.[68] The Harijans need not fear that the Assembly would make laws or frame the Constitution in a manner prejudicial to their

---

Sat in the Assembly, as well as all Cabinet Ministers. Five members of the W.C. were also Cabinet Ministers.

[66] Nehru in a letter to Ambedkar, dated 29 April 1948; *Prasad papers*, File 14-C/48. Letter marked Secret and Personal; see footnote 67.

[67] Ambedkar in a letter to Nehru, 28 April 1948; ibid. Also marked Secret and Personal. This correspondence was occasioned by a speech that Ambedkar made to the Scheduled Castes Federation in Lucknow on 25 April to which Nehru took exception. Nehru first wrote to Ambedkar on 27 April, and in his reply Ambedkar made the statements quoted here.

[68] Ibid.

interests, Ambedkar believed: 'what they had to fear about was bad administration . . . (which) was due to the absence of men belonging to the Scheduled Castes in the administration'. And, Ambedkar charged, 'the administration was unsympathetic to the Scheduled Castes because it was manned wholly by Caste Hindu officers who were partial to the Caste Hindus' and who 'practiced tyranny and oppression' on the Harijans.[69] In Ambedkar's view, the best way to remedy this situation was for Harijans to become members of the various governments in India and thereby to ensure that Harijans also became members of the civil services.

One more individual, B. N. Rau, must be placed among those important in the framing of the Constitution. As Constitutional Adviser, Rau's advice was heard in the Assembly's inner councils, although he was not an Assembly member. A legalist, an eminent advocate and judge, a student of constitutional history, and an able draftsman, one of the more Europeanized intellectuals in the Assembly, Rau looked to Euro-American constitutional precedent perhaps even more than other Assembly members for the devices to be used in India's Constitution. Rau had also gone to London in 1933 as an emissary of the Assam Government to present evidence before the Joint Select Committee. His role in the drafting of the 1935 Act was, however, marginal. But he did have an intimate connection with the implementation of the Act as a member of the Reforms Office of the Government of India during the years 1935–36.[70]

Two men of this inner group and several other Assembly members had taken a reasonably active part in the creation of the 1935 Act from the Round Table Conferences through the activities of the Joint Select Committee. The most notable, both in London and in the Assembly, was Ambedkar. N. M. Rau, V. T. Krishnamachari, K. M. Panikkar, and K. T. Shah had also been present in London and were subsequently active in Assembly affairs. All of these twenty-one individuals were well educated. Azad, Ambedkar, and to a lesser

---

[69] Ibid.
[70] For more information on Rau, see Appendix III. Rau's and Ambedkar's assistant, the Drafting Officer of the Assembly, was an energetic Bengali, S. N. Mukerjee, to whom Ambedkar gave much of the credit for the careful wording of the Constitution.

extent Munshi and Prasad, could be called learned. Nehru brought to the Assembly the mind of a humanist and wide reading in political theory. He was the Assembly's idealist; he and Azad possessed its most speculative minds. Nehru frequently approached problems from a theoretical starting point, but the theories had to meet the test of facts; he was rarely, if ever, doctrinare.[71] Ayyar had unusual ability as a lawyer and N. G. Ayyangar as an administrator. Patel was an iron-fisted statesman, as his successful negotiations with the Princely States testify, but he could also be, as his dealings with minorities show, conciliatory and considerate. Followed by Pant and Munshi, a man who preferred the middle path, Patel was the most pragmatic among the leaders.

Yet all these men approached the drafting of the Constitution in a practical rather than a theoretical way. They knew that the Constitution must help to bring about the reform, the renascence of Indian society, that it must embody the national goals and subserve their achievement, but they were politicians in the sense that they practiced the art of the possible. They were dedicated to the cause, but they did not allow their dedication to blind them to reality; like the American founding fathers, they had put their minds to use in the national cause.

Experience of national issues, whether in the Congress or in government, and an 'Indian' rather than a parochial—a Madrassi or a Bihari— consciousness, also characterized this select group. Its members were not provincial politicians suddenly summoned to New Delhi; many had been national leaders in pre-independence days and now had responsibilities in the new government. To a Constituent Assembly representing an extremely diverse country they brought a spirit of unity, a national awareness. They also had, and this applies particularly to the four leaders, Nehru, Patel, Prasad, and Azad, the practical experience, the personal popularity, the intellectual ability, and the political power to impress upon the Assembly their concept of the type of constitution best able to bring about the new India—a task made much easier by the Assembly's susceptibility to their ideas.

---

[71] This attitude of testing theories of government by their working became increasingly a part of Nehru's behaviour, as one can detect in his speeches and writings. See also Chapter II.

Nehru, Patel, Prasad, and Azad, in fact, constituted an oligarchy within the Assembly.[72] Their honour was unquestioned, their wisdom hardly less so. In their god-like status they may have been feared; certainly they were loved. An Assembly member was not greatly exaggerating the esteem in which his colleagues held these men when he said that the government rested 'in the hands of those who (were) utterly incapable of doing any wrong to the people'.[73] The oligarchy's influence was nearly irresistible, yet the Assembly decided issues democratically after genuine debate, for it was made up of strong-minded men and the leaders themselves were peculiarly responsive.

The Congress Assembly Party was the unofficial, private forum that debated every provision of the Constitution, and in most cases decided its fate before it reached the floor of the House. Everyone elected to the Assembly on the Congress ticket could attend the meetings whether or not he was a member of the party or even close to it. This included the 'experts' brought into the Assembly by the Congress like A. K. Ayyar, N. G. Ayyangar, and Dr. Ambedkar as well as cabinet ministers like John Matthai, who had never been a Congressman, and S. P. Mookerjee, who was still a member of the Hindu Mahasabha. Assembly members representing the Princely States could also participate in Assembly Party meetings if they were members of the All-India States Peoples Conference (the Congress's organization in the States) or if they had been elected, not nominated, from a State to the Assembly. All in all, therefore, no more than 80 of the Assembly's membership of over 300 were not eligible to attend the party meeting.

The Congress Assembly Party functioned differently from the Congress Parliamentary Party, which was the party group in the Constituent Assembly (Legislative), although the two parties shared

[72] They may also have been an oligarchy in relation to all India and to its governmental machinery, but this complicated subject can only be touched upon here when it applies directly to the affairs of the Assembly. Also, the decision-making process in the Assembly differed from that in the Cabinet, for example, and it would be dangerous to extend the description of decision-making contained in the following pages beyond the walls of the Assembly. This danger increases with the passage of time, with the deaths of Patel and Azad, and with other changes.

[73] *CAD* VII, 18, 760–61; Brajeshwar Prasad.

the same membership.[74] The Parliamentary Party operated in the manner one would expect of such a group.[75] It had an Executive Committee consisting of the party leaders, and its meetings were customarily presided over by the Prime Minister or the Deputy Prime Minister. The Assembly Party, on the other hand, had no Executive Committee, its meetings were presided over by the president of the Congress Party, and in its meetings the leaders of the Government had no *official* status beyond their ordinary membership. The purpose of the Assembly Party was not to assure the passage of a political party's legislative programme, but to serve as the confidential forum and decision-making body. Here the sense of national unity and purpose could express itself in a constitution that would meet the needs and desires of the entire nation.

The shadow of the Oligarchy covered the Assembly Party, yet did not dominate it. The discussions held most afternoons in Constitution House on Curzon Road when the Assembly was in session were full and frank, at times heated and acrimonious. On issues such as the public services, due process in relation to property and personal liberty, the federal provisions and language, the diversity of views within the Congress itself was apparent. The non-Congressmen like Ayyar and N. G. Ayyangar spoke their minds freely; Ambedkar's advice—on legal matters and drafting rather than on policy—was frequently sought. At first the long-time Congressmen showed some impatience with these outsiders, but 'if you were tough and kept at it,' said Pandit Kunzru, 'they got used to it; they became tamer'.[76] The matter under discussion might be a clause from the Draft Constitution, an amendment to it, or the report of an Assembly committee. The Cabinet might

[74] There was one exception: the representatives of the Princely States had 'the right' to participate in C.A. (Legislative) proceedings when business was being discussed 'in respect of which the States had acceded to the Dominion', and they were not 'banned' from participating in other business; they rarely did so, however. See *Report of the Committee on the Functions of the Constituent Assembly*, Para 6, C.A., *Reports of Committees, Second Series*, p. 43. Hence States representatives rarely took part in Parliamentary Party meetings.

[75] For the best discussion of the functioning of the Congress Parliamentary Party and its antecedents in the Central Legislative Assembly before independence, see W. H. Morris-Jones, *Parliament in India*.

[76] In an interview with the author.

have originated the provision or commented upon it. Various other committees would have made recommendations. The technical and policy advice of ministries, both solicited and unsolicited, would be available, as well as that of particularly qualified Assembly members—such as the provincial prime ministers and finance ministers on federal questions. Outside organizations like the Calcutta Bar Association might have made recommendations. And, of course, the views of the Oligarchy would be clear, either their unanimity or their disparate views. But no matter how vital the import or delicate the wording of the provision in question, the Assembly Party had to consider it and make the decision. 'Every amendment and every provision suggested . . . was put before the Congress Party and then it was finally debated upon and passed with or without amendment by the Assembly, which alone had the final say in the matter.'[77] The Assembly Party 'alone' could 'give the imprimatur of adoption in this House'.[78]

The Oligarchy was responsive to the multifold currents of opinion in the Assembly, to the intra-party 'Opposition', for a variety of reasons. The members had not only spent much of their lives working for a free, democratic India; they were practising democrats.[79] Patel, for example, had the reputation for being a stern if not an unbending man. His handling of the minorities problem in the Advisory Committee, however, was remarkable for its patient consideration of minority fears. Moreover, the Oligarchy itself could not always present a united front, because of its own internal frictions. On issues where Nehru and Patel, for example, were divided—as on compensation for expropriated property—each

[77] S. N. Mukerjee in a letter to V. P. Menon, dated 19 December 1949; *Law Ministry Archives*.

[78] *CAD* XI, 7, 733, Mohd. Saadulla. Saadulla was a member of the Drafting Committee. A member of the Muslim League, he had entered the CA after Partition. Contrary to non-Congressmen or foes of the Congress who had entered the Assembly on the Congress ticket, he was not a member of the Assembly Party and was bitter about its control of the Assembly. See also Brecher *Nehru: A Political Biography*, p. 423 for Ambedkar's views of Assembly Party control of the Assembly.

[79] Assembly member Mahavir Tyagi disagreed with this. The attitude of the Government, he believed, approached arrogance: 'Any opposition here even in this House is not seen, is not considered or treated with that much of generosity (sic) as in foreign countries opposition parties are treated.' *CAD* IX, 5, 195.

sought support in the ranks of the Assembly Party, and arbitrary decisions were impossible.[80]

The responsiveness of the Oligarchy can be seen either as cold-blooded practicality or as showing high moral sense. It believed that a Constitution adopted with the maximum of agreement would work better and provide a more stable foundation for the new India; approval should therefore be as nearly unanimous as possible.[81] Nehru enjoined the Assembly to try to reach unanimous decisions. Prasad on occasion postponed debate on the Assembly floor so that the solution to a problem could be worked out privately; a vote, he said once, might well result in 'something not wanted by anybody'.[82] Pandit Pant moved that a particular article be passed over because the Assembly 'had not been able to reach unanimity'.[83]

The Oligarchy certainly used its almost irresistible influence to promote consensus. By replying to questions about, and opposition to, various provisions with full explanations, and by relying on persuasion rather than force, the members of the Oligarchy reinforced the effect of their power and prestige, usually winning over their opponents, even high-ranking ones. There were times, however, when the shoe was on the other foot, when, in search of a workable, lasting agreement, the Oligarchy retreated from its position to meet the mood of the Assembly.

When the Oligarchy faced sustained opposition, or its members had split and sought support against each other, the issue usually came to a vote in the party meeting. If the vote gave one side a *large* majority, this was taken to be a party decision, and in the interests of party discipline a Whip was issued.[84] If the vote was close

---

[80] On certain issues, like the formation of linguistic provinces, the Oligarchy was agreed (in this case they were against it), but the Working Committee and the Congress were deeply divided, and no group could impose its will. Hence the decision hung fire until 1953, and was not really faced until 1956.

[81] For a further discussion of consensus, especially in reference to Indian approaches to constitution-making, see the concluding chapter.

[82] *CAD* VIII, 20, 821.

[83] *CAD* VII, 7, 431.

[84] Assembly Party Whips, backed as they almost always were by the will of much more than a simple majority, were a powerful instrument, silencing even such notables as Pandit Pant. See *CAD* IV, 8, 809ff for Pant, who was bound by the decision of the party because 'members should be guided by the collective wisdom of the many'. The Whip did not quiet every member, however; S. L.

and demonstrated that nothing had been settled, that each faction remained adamant, then there was no Whip; either negotiations continued or the question was settled in the Assembly by a free vote. A Whip was rarely issued on matters of great import or matters involving conscience—such as the language or 'due process' controversies; usually the question remained within the Assembly Party meeting until compromise produced agreement by consensus. The Whip was frequently used on smaller matters, almost as a matter of routine, to point out which of several dozen suggested provisions had received the party meeting's blessing.[85]

Democratic decision-making by the members of the Congress Assembly Party and the Oligarchy's refusal to arrogate to itself all wisdom and authority helped to make possible a generally acceptable constitution. Had the Constitution come from the Constituent Assembly sanctioned by a meagre majority, opposed by many, it would have been attacked as unworthy of general support and unrepresentative of India's best interests. But the Assembly adopted the Constitution, despite some of the members' misgivings, by acclamation. It could be presented to the nation as the realization of Nehru's original aim: it had been drafted with the welfare of four hundred million Indians in mind.[86]

Saksena frequently spoke in defiance of it and was, apparently, never punished for the delinquency. The 'independents' on the Congress ticket, like Kunzru, also did not always heed the Whip.

[85] This account of the decision-making process in the Assembly is based on documentary evidence and on interviews with more than a dozen former members of the Assembly and of the Secretariat staff. For further discussion of decision-making in the Assembly, see Chapter 13.

[86] *CAD* I, 5, 60.

2

Which Road to Social Revolution?

The service of India means the service of the millions who suffer. It means the ending of poverty and ignorance and disease and inequality of opportunity. The ambition of the greatest man of our generation has been to wipe every tear from every eye. That may be beyond us, but as long as there are tears and suffering, so long our work will not be over.

Jawaharlal Nehru

Two revolutions, the national and the social, had been running parallel in India since the the end of the First World War.[1] With independence, the national revolution would be completed, but the social revolution must go on. Freedom was not an end in itself, only 'a means to an end', Nehru had said, 'that end being the raising of the people . . . to higher levels and hence the general advancement of humanity'.[2]

The first task of this Assembly (Nehru told the members) is to free India through a new constitution, to feed the starving people, and to clothe the naked masses, and to give every Indian the fullest opportunity to develop himself according to his capacity.[3]

K. Santhanam, a prominent southern member of the Assembly and editor of a major newspaper, described the situation in terms of three revolutions. The political revolution would end, he wrote, with independence. The social revolution meant 'to get (India) out

---

[1] One recalls in this context the fight against Untouchability, the provisions of the 1931 Karachi Resolution, the 1945 Congress Election Manifesto, etc. For a reference to the parallel courses of the two revolutions, see Acharya Narendra Dev, *Socialism and the National Revolution*, p. 4. See Chapter III below.

[2] Nehru, *Unity of India*, p. II; written in 1938.

[3] *CAD* II, 3, 316.

of the medievalism based on birth, religion, custom, and community and, reconstruct her social structure on modern foundations of law, individual merit, and secular education'. The third revolution was an economic one: 'The transition from primitive rural economy to scientific and planned agriculture and industry'.[4] Radhakrishnan (now President of India) believed India must have a 'socio-economic revolution' designed not only to bring about 'the real satisfaction of the fundamental needs of the common man', but to go much deeper and bring about 'a fundamental change in the structure of Indian society'.[5]

On the achievement of this great social change depended India's survival. 'If we cannot solve this problem soon,' Nehru warned the Assembly, 'all our paper constitutions will become useless and purposeless . . . If India goes down, all will go down; if India thrives, all will thrive; and if India lives, all will live . . .'.[6] In the age of modern communications and Communist revolutions, India could not waste time. To retain her identity, Indians believed, their country must be independent and remain non-Communist. 'The choice for India,' wrote Santhanam, '. . . is between rapid evolution and violent revolution . . . because the Indian masses cannot and will not wait for a long time to obtain the satisfaction of their minimum needs.'[7]

The Constituent Assembly's task was to draft a constitution that would serve the ultimate goal of social revolution, of national renascence. But this was a task far more complicated than the simple drafting of fundamental rights or the moral precepts of a preamble. What form of political institutions would foster or at least permit a social revolution? Moreover, any thought of social betterment for the nation would be mere romantic nonsense if the requisite conditions did not exist in the country. If the country were not united, if the

[4] K. Santhanam in Magazine Section, *The Hindustan Times* (of which he was joint editor), New Delhi, 8 September 1946.

[5] *CAD* II, 1, 269–73. Such views were held by many in the Assembly. President Prasad assured the nation that the Assembly's and the government's aim was 'to end poverty and squalor . . . to abolish distinction and exploitation and to ensure decent conditions of living'; *CAD* V, 1, 2. B. Das said 'It is the Dharma of the Government to remove hunger and render social justice to every citizen'; *CAD* V, 11, 367.

[6] *CAD* II, 1, 317–18.

[7] *The Hindustan Times*, Magazine Section, 17 August 1947.

government were not stable, if the government lacked the cooperation or the acquiescence of the people, there could be no economic progress and no government initiative for social change. What political institutions, therefore, would help to accomplish these subsidiary aims and so establish the conditions in which social change could more easily take place? Should the constitution be unitary, federal, or almost completely decentralized? Should the government be one of benevolent despots, of Nehru, Patel, Azad, and Prasad ruling by decree? Or should there be a democratic Executive, Legislature, and Judiciary, and the commonly accepted hierarchy of government administration? But the major choice was more basic: to what political tradition, to the European or the Indian, should the Assembly look for a constitutional pattern. By which of these routes could India best arrive at the goal of social revolution?

The Alternatives

To look to the Euro-American constitutional tradition for its example, would, in all probability, mean continuing in the direction India had taken during the colonial period. Or if Assembly members searched the nation's rich heritage to find indigenous institutions capable of meeting her needs, it would result, most likely, in basing the Constitution on the village and its panchayat and erecting upon them a superstructure of indirect, decentralized government in the 'Gandhian' manner. In either case the constitution must be democratic; there was to be no return to the Indian precedent of a despot with his durbar; nor would the Assembly have Europe's totalitarianisms or the Soviet system.[8] The following pages are concerned with the Assembly's decision and with its reasons for choosing a parliamentary constitution.

Of the alternatives available to the Assembly, the village-based system needs the closer examination. The village—celebrated by certain Englishmen and Indians alike as the true India,[9] representative even in modern times of her ancient modes of life and

---

[8] The Objectives Resolution had laid down that India must be a Republic in which all power and authority were 'derived from the people'; *CAD* I, 5, 59.

[9] Among the Englishmen, see especially Metcalfe and Baden-Powell; among Indians, see the works of K. S. Shelwarkar and K. T. Shah.

thought, and regarded as the one bastion unbreeched by foreign cultural influence—found its most articulate exponent in Mahatma Gandhi. Gandhi did not believe that life in India's villages was ideal; he hoped that it would be reformed, medically, economically, and socially. Yet in the simplicity of village life, in its removal from the falsity of urban, industrial society's values—as he interpreted them— Gandhi envisaged the environment in which man could live morally, where he could tread the path of duty and follow the right mode of conduct, which to Gandhi was the true meaning of 'civilization'.[10] The village, therefore, was Gandhi's unit of social organization. Its panchayat and its cottage industries would provide government and consumer goods; its farms, food. Resting on this village base would be a stateless, classless society where prime ministers and governments would be unnecessary.[11] Gandhi's incompletely formulated views on government became to some extent systematized in two ways: by Gandhi himself in his suggestion for a Congress constitution, and by disciples who desired to commend them to the Constituent Assembly.

Gandhi submitted two plans—one in January 1946 and the other in January 1948[12]—to the committee charged with revising the Congress Constitution. The second plan, presented on the day of his murder and now called his Testament, is the more comprehensive. It would have disbanded the Congress as 'a propaganda vehicle and a parliamentary machine' and turned it into a social service organization based on a nation-wide network of panchayats.[13] Each village panchayat, in Gandhi's plan, would form a unit; two such panchayats would constitute a working party with an elected leader. Fifty leaders would elect a second-grade leader, who would co-ordinate their efforts and who would also be available for national service. Second-grade leaders could elect a national chief to 'regulate and command all the groups'.[14]

---

[10] Gandhi, *Hind Swaraj*, pp. 61–63; and Gandhi's letters to Nehru in October 1945, see *A Bunch of Old Letters*, pp. 505–12.

[11] N. C. Bhattacharya in *Gandhian Concept of State*, B. B. Majumdar, editor, pp. 30–31.

[12] Both the plans appear in English translation in N. V. Rajkumar, *Development of the Congress Constitution*.

[13] The January 1948 plan; ibid., p. 145.

[14] Ibid., pp. 145–6.

The party's constitution committee, under the influence of the Working Committee, did not accept Gandhi's suggestions, believing that the Congress could neither forego its political role nor become so utterly decentralized.[15] The committee's new constitution did for the first time, however, establish 'Primary Congress Panchayats in a village or a group of villages' as the basic organizational unit of the party.[16] To an extent, also, the hierarchy was to be indirectly elected. Panchayat members elected delegates to the annual Congress; within each province these delegates comprised the Provincial Congress Committee, and they elected the AICC. Decentralization was carried only thus far, however, and the Party's central command maintained its unifying control over party affairs: the powerful Working Committee was chosen by the president, who was elected by the delegates and not by a smaller body such as the AICC, and it was difficult for any other group in the party successfully to challenge the president and his Working Committee. There could be no doubt that the Congress had preserved its unified, centrally controlled structure partly for its own reasons: to win elections and thus savour the fruits of office. But party leadership was dedicated more to national survival than to party profit, and it knew that national unity and social progress demanded a tightly organized Congress Party. This policy was made clear in a party circular issued in the summer of 1947. Rebutting the argument that the Congress should be dissolved, the circular stated:

> . . . If India's destiny is to be fulfilled and it is to rake its proper place in the comity of nations, then its unity is essential, and there is no other organization more fitted for this difficult task than the Congress . . . India requires for its gradual and orderly political, social, and economic all round progress, one big political party, large enough to guarantee a stable government, and strong enough organizationally to maintain its hold and influence over the people. Such a party of

---

[15] Members of the Congress Constitution Committee: Sitaramayya, Tandon, Narenda Dev, Diwakar, S. K. Patil, S. M. Ghose, and Jugal Kishore (Convenor). Of these men, all but Narenda Dev were members of the Assembly. The constitution committee presented its draft to the AICC, which accepted it in April 1948; the annual Congress approved the constitution at Jaipur in December.

[16] *Constitution of the Indian National Congress*, 1948, p. 1.

course must have a programme of radical change aiming at social justice and eradication of exploitation in all its forms.[17]

To Assembly members the consequential question clearly was: If the nation needed a centrally controlled mass party, did it not also need a centralized constitution?

Gandhi's adaptation of his utopian ideals to the Congress was taken a good deal further by one of his followers, Shriman Narayan Agarwal, in the knowledge that, short of his ideal, Gandhi would support organized government if it were based on the villages.[18] Agarwal drafted a *Gandhian Constitution for Free India* and, as Gandhi found in it nothing that 'jarred' him or was 'inconsistent with what he would like to stand for',[19] we may, with some caution, look on it as indicative of the Mahatma's ideas.[20]

Agarwal based his work on the well-known Gandhian principle that 'violence logically leads to centralization: the essence of non-violence is decentralization'.[21] Economic and political decentralization would result, Agarwal believed, in self-sufficient, self-governing village communities, the 'models of non-violent organization'.[22] In Agarwal's draft constitution the primary political unit was to be the village panchayat, whose members would be elected by the adults of the village. The panchayat would

[17] AICC, *Congress Bulletin*, No. 5 of 7 November 1947, p. 17.

[18] Prior to this, Gandhi had allegedly helped to draft, or, more likely, influenced the drafting of, the Aundh State Constitution Act No. 1 of 1939—a panchayat-based system with an indirectly elected governmental hierarchy leading upwards to a paternal Prince. The AICC Constituent Assembly Section distributed copies of this document to all CA members in June 1947. Aundh was a small Princely State lying southeastwards of Bombay.

[19] Gandhi in a Foreword to Agarwal's *Gandhian Constitution*. Gandhi also said that he had not checked Agarwal's every word, and that Agarwal had made some alterations at his request.

[20] K. G. Mashruwala, a member of Gandhi's group in Wardha (Agarwal was also from Wardha), prepared and sent to Prasad *Some Particular Suggestions for the Constitution of Free India*. Mashruwala said that the ideas were not 'Gandhian', but that they would help lay the foundations for a 'Gandhian Order'. Among the suggestions was one for representation (direct or indirect) according to income groups: e.g., 44 per cent of seats were to go to persons earning less than 300 rupees annually.

[21] S. N. Agarwal, *Gandhian Constitution for Free India*, p. 38.

[22] Ibid., p. 39.

control chowkidars (watchmen), patwaris (the men who kept the land and tax assessment registries), and police and schools. It would also assess and collect land revenue, supervise cooperative farming, irrigation, and interest rates, as well as khadi and other village industries. Above the village panchayat come a hierarchy of indirectly elected bodies. First came taluka and district panchayats, each comprised of the sarpanchs (panchayat leaders) of the next lower panchayats and having only advisory powers over them. Members from district and municipal panchayats would make up the provincial panchayat, which would elect a president to serve as head of provincial government. Presidents of provincial panchayats would comprise the All-India Panchayat, whose president would be the head of state and of the government, which would be ministerial in character. Among the responsibilities of provincial panchayats would be transport, irrigation, natural resources, and a co-operative bank. The national panchayat would be responsible for such things as defence, currency, customs, the running of key industries of national importance, and the coordination of provincial economic development plans.

Gandhi believed that the achievement of social justice as the common lot must proceed from a character reformation of each individual, from the heart and mind of each Indian outward into society as a whole. The impetus for reform must not come downward from government, and a reformed society would need no government to regulate or control it. Yet Gandhians recognized that to write a constitution, to create a state, was to sacrifice some of this ideal. To keep this sacrifice to the minimum, thereby preserving as much of the ideal as possible, Gandhians like Agarwal compromised by advocating as minimal a 'state' as possible. 'The state that governs best, governs least', they preached; 'keep government to the minimum, and what you must have, decentralize.'[23] A beneficial by-product of this minimal government, said Agarwal in his constitution, would be to increase the individual's responsibility for his own welfare.

And Agarwal, like other Gandhians, hoped that a 'Gandhian' constitution would do away with the need for that great evil of modern societies, political parties. 'The very large measure of local

[23] These concepts are the burden of Chapter V and XIII of *Hind Swaraj*, op. cit.

self-government' in his constitution, he said, would give rise to no 'regular and rigid political parties'.[24] He meant, presumably, that, national political parties would find no place in a society so compartmentalized by decentralization; there would be no all-India issues to provide the cement necessary for their existence. Equally, a 'Gandhian' constitution would return India to a primarily rural society with its base in agriculture, eschewing all but the most essential industrialization. The result of this, Gandhi and his followers believed, would be to 'elevate the moral being' of Indians, whereas to follow the lead of European and American civilization (urban, mechanized, highly political, based on the exploitation of man by man) would be to 'propagate immorality'.[25]

The ideal of a revived village life with benevolent panchayats and decentralized government bringing democracy to the grass-roots level appealed to Assembly members. Yet when considering the political tradition to embody in the constitution they had to ask themselves several questions concerning the Gandhian alternative: (a) Was the nature of man different in rural from in urban society; would man become a moral being in one and not in the other? (b) Was it possible in 1947 to change India back to a primarily agricultural, village nation? (c) Did the state bear the responsibility for the welfare of its citizens; if it did, could it fulfil the responsibility under a decentralized constitution? (d) Did the villagers have—as they must have with a decentralized constitution and indirect government—the initiative to remake their way of life?

The Assembly's alternative to a Gandhian constitution, as we have said, was a constitution in the European and American tradition—a constitutional tradition with, quite evidently, very different principles. Euro-American constitutions provided for directly elected governments. The tendency among them—even in a large federation like the United States—was towards centralization. Although these constitutions might have been *laissez-faire* at the time of their drafting, they had come more and more to assume responsibility for the citizen's welfare, and the scope of modern government had been

[24] Agarwal, op. cit., p. 95. The debate about whether or not political parties would or could or should operate in a panchayat society goes on in India today; see below, pp. 43ff.

[25] *Hind Swaraj*, p. 63. See also pp. 61–62.

steadily widening, not decreasing. And no Euro-American constitution had been framed—as Agarwal's had been—with the aim of creating a single economy country.

Faced with this choice Assembly members had to decide whether traditional or non-traditional institutions would best bring about a social revolution so profound as to alter fundamentally the structure of Indian society. They had to decide what type of constitution would bring India the unity, stability, and economic gains prerequisite for such a change. And, basic to these two decisions, members of the Assembly had to choose a constitution that, while promoting these aims, would be acceptable to those they represented, the 400 millions of India.

The Road Taken

The Assembly's decision to give India a parliamentary, federal constitution was not made in a day. The process took the two and a half years from the first meeting of the Congress Experts Committee on the Constituent Assembly, held in July 1946, to the debate on the Draft Constitution in November 1948—when panchayats were relegated to the Directive Principles and indirect election died a quiet death. The length of time spent making the decision did not mean, however, that there was a genuine contest between the two major alternatives. Although most Assembly members—one might say all—favoured the development of village life, including greatly increased responsibility for village panchayats, few Assembly members could in the last resort bring themselves to support a full-fledged system of indirect, decentralized government. That India would have a centralized parliamentary constitution was nearly certain from the start, and increasingly during the lifetime of the Assembly the compulsion of events made that choice even more certain.

It was the Congress Experts Committee that set India on the road to her present constitution. This committee, with Nehru as its chairman, was set up by the Congress Working Committee to prepare materials for the Assembly—to which six of its eight members had recently been elected.[26] Patel, although not a member,

---

[26] The Working Committee formed the Experts Committee on 8 July 1946. Its members were Nehru, Asaf Ali, Munshi, N. G. Ayyangar, K. T. Shah, K.

attended many committee meetings.[27] These began in mid-July 1946 with four days of sessions and resumed a month later for a like period. The committee members, working within the framework of the Cabinet Mission scheme, made general suggestions about autonomous areas, the powers of provincial governments and the centre, and about such issues as the Princely States and the amending power. They also drafted a resolution, closely resembling the Objectives Resolution, which would appear that December, laying down that power was derived from the people and naming the social objectives of the constitution.[28] Although the Cabinet Mission had presumably believed that India would find its source of inspiration in the 1935 Act, there was still room within its plan for a system of indirect, panchayat government had the Experts Committee wanted to make such a suggestion to the Assembly. The committee ignored the Gandhian approach, however, considering only the institutions of parliamentary government and recommending tentatively that the constitution be a loose federation.[29]

The Constituent Assembly convened on 9 December 1946. With the Muslim League boycotting the session, the Assembly could not take up the sensitive issue of federalism or go into detail concerning the form or type of the constitution. It did, however, debate the Objectives Resolution, which Nehru apparently had drafted, which the Experts Committee had discussed, and which the Working Committee had approved the night before the first session.[30] The

Santhanam (all Assembly members), Humayun Kabir and D. R. Gadgil. See Chanakya, *Indian Constituent Assembly*, Note, p. 27. As Nehru was acknowledged in the Congress as its leading constitutional thinker, the W.C. would have had no trouble picking him as the committee's chairman. Nehru quite possibly suggested the committee's creation and offered to lead it. One should bear in mind that only four of the eight members had long associations with the congress.

[27] V. K. Krishna Menon was less frequently a guest. Also Dr. Appadorai, Mridula Sarabhai, and Raja Hutheesingh. See minutes of, and notes on, Experts Committee meetings in *Prasad papers*, File 35-C/47.

[28] Ibid.

[29] Ibid. D. R. Gadgil, in an interview with the author, confirmed the rejection of the Gandhian view.

[30] Agenda for the Working Committee meeting, 8 December 1948; *Prasad papers*, File 16-P/45-6-7.

Objectives Resolution said that the new constitution would be dedicated to the goal of social revolution, but it did not specify how these aims were to be achieved. Neither panchayat nor indirect government were mentioned and the allusions to decentralization were obviously made in deference to the Cabinet Mission Plan.[31] It was reasonably clear, however, that the Assembly leadership was not contemplating a Gandhian constitution. In the debate on the resolution, there was neither criticism of the omission of panchayat government nor was the subject mentioned. Members spoke of democracy, socialism, and the responsibilities of legislatures, but not of the necessity for an 'Indian' form of government.

During the next seven months, while the Assembly marked time awaiting the outcome of the League-Congress impasse, two Assembly committees discussed the principles on which the constitution should be based and prepared model constitutions, one for the Union, the other for the provinces.[32] A third committee studied the allocation of subjects between the central and the provincial governments. The reports of the Union and Provincial Constitution Committees,[33] both of which had been revised from earlier versions as a result of the announcement of Partition, recommended a direct, parliamentary, and federal constitution. The committees had borrowed freely from the 1935 Act, although they had deviated from it when they believed necessary. The minutes of the committee meetings contain no mention of a Gandhian constitution, or of panchayat or indirect government.[34] The question of decentralization, when discussed, was considered in the context of Euro-American constitutional precedent, in the context of unitary versus federal government or tight versus loose federalism. A Gandhian constitution seems not to have been given a moment's thought.[35]

---

[31] Resolution, para 3; *CAD* I, 5, 59.

[32] According to B. Shiva Rao, in an interview with the author, these committees to consider constitutional principles were set up at the suggestion of Sir Tej Bahadur Sapru

[33] Constituent Assembly, *Reports of Committees, First Series.*

[34] *Prasad papers*, Files 3-C/47, 4-P/47, and records in the Indian National Archives.

[35] Judging from the records of speeches made by UCC and PCC members in the Assembly and from other documents, none of the members of these committees

When these two committee reports were debated in the Assembly during the fourth and fifth sessions in July and August 1947, only a few members noted the absence of panchayats and only one critical voice was authentically Gandhian. Ramnarayan Singh desired 'that the primary units of government be established in villages. The greatest measure of power should vest in village republics,' Singh argued, 'and then in the provinces and then in the centre.'[36]

With the Assembly's seal of approval on parliamentary principles, the drafting of the constitution was handed by the Assembly to its Drafting Committee and to the Constitutional Adviser, B. N. Rau. The Assembly then adjourned for more than a year. Rau produced his draft in a month. From October 1947 until mid-February 1948 the Drafting Committee was busy converting this document into the Draft Constitution—which consisted primarily of the committee's borrowed and modified provisions of the British and American Constitutions and the 1935 Government of India Act. The word panchayat did not once appear in the Draft Constitution.[37]

Within a few months a reaction to this omission set in as Assembly members had time to consider the Draft. President Prasad was the most prominent among the critics. On 10 May 1948 Prasad wrote to B. N. Rau transmitting and explaining an article that he had received suggesting changes in the Draft Constitution. He said that he was aware of the difficulties that alterations to the Draft would pose, but he hoped that something might be done. 'I like the idea,' Prasad wrote, 'of making the Constitution begin with the village and go up to the Centre'; the village 'has been and will ever continue to be our unit in this country'.[38] Prasad believed that the necessary

---

was an advocate of indirect, decentralized government, or of the Gandhian ideal. For the membership of these committees, see Appendix II.

[36] *CAD* V, 4, 92.

[37] Nor did the Drafting Committee (according to the minutes of meetings inspected by the author, *Prasad papers*, Files 1-D/47 and 1(2)-D/47 and *Munshi papers*) discuss in its meetings the alternative principles of a Gandhian and a parliamentary constitution. The Draft Constitution was published 26 February 1948.

[38] Prasad to B. N. Rau, 10 May 1948. The article was written by one K. S. Venkataramani and appeared in the journal *Swatantra* on 24 April 1948. For a clipping of the article and for the covering letter see *Law Ministry Archives*, File CA/21/Cons/48.II. The text of the letter also appears in an incomplete version in *Prasad papers*, File 5-A/48.

articles could be redrafted, whilst leaving the provincial and central government structure more or less as they were. This 'will put the whole thing in the right perspective,' Prasad wrote, and he added, 'I strongly advocate the idea of utilizing the adult franchise only for the village panchayat and making the village panchayats the electoral college for electing representatives to the provinces and the Centre.'[39] Prasad also called Rau's attention to the AICC's adoption the month before of a Congress Constitution with a panchayat base.

Firmly, but kindly, Rau rejected Prasad's suggestion. In his reply Rau said that the Assembly had already decided on direct election of lower houses both at the centre and the provinces and that he was doubtful if the vote could be reversed—a remark that indicated the general popularity of a parliamentary constitution. He also pointed out that it had become customary for lower houses in federations and unions to be directly elected. Rau protested that to write into the Constitution all the details of local government would make it impossibly long and unduly delay its completion; the details of any such plan should be left to 'auxiliary legislation'. But it might be possible, he said, to redraft several articles so that representatives could be 'chosen either by the voters themselves or by persons elected by the voters'.[40]

As the autumn of 1948 approached, when the Assembly would reconvene, other members submitted amendments to the Draft advocating the development of panchayats.[41] These favoured the

---

[39] Ibid. Prasad, concluding his letter, commented on the possibility of instituting qualifications for office-holders along the lines of the Congress Constitution—an idea he recognized as difficult but perhaps worthwhile because it would bring men of 'high calibre' into the legislative system. Prasad later tried to introduce this idea into the Assembly Party meeting, but failed. See an exchange of letters with R. R. Diwakar in the spring of 1949; *Prasad papers*, Random Letters File.

[40] Rau to Prasad, 31 May 1948, written from Simla; *Prasad papers*, File 27-C/48. With the exception of a few unimportant omissions this letter appears in *India's Constitution in the Making* by B. N. Rau, edited by B. Shiva Rao, pp. 331–3. See also Law Ministry Archives per Footnote 38. Although there is no evidence that he did so, Rau probably took the subject up with the Drafting Committee, which, quite evidently, rejected the idea.

[41] See *Notice of Amendments to the Draft Constitution of India*—hereafter called *Amendments Book*—Vol. I, Amendments 868, 870, 924, 925, 989–91. See also Amendment 2986 *Amendment Book* II, for R. K. Sidhwa's scheme for local government.

development of panchayats as a form of local self-government, as schools of democracy, as instruments of village uplift; and they favoured giving the villages some financial resources and a measure of autonomy. None of them, however, attempted to make panchayats the base for an indirect system of government, nor did these amendments support the decentralization of a Gandhian constitution.[42] More importantly, these amendments were to the non-justiciable Directive Principles of State Policy; their intent was hortatory. None would have changed the centralized, parliamentary system established by the Draft; they only made it the duty of the state to encourage the development of panchayats and the reform of village life below the level of the provincial governments.

The debate in the Constituent Assembly in November 1948 on the Draft Constitution confirmed the popularity of panchayats whilst emphasizing that support for them was not a rejection of either parliamentary government or Indian federalism. Members of the Assembly averred that they were an ancient Indian institution and 'in our blood'.[43] Others recalled that Gandhi had always taught that India must be governed by panchayat raj, and that local governing bodies could improve economic conditions in India. S. L. Saksena thought that if 'light and knowledge' were brought to panchayats they would 'become the most potent forces for holding the country together and for its progress towards Ram Rajya'.[44] Panchayats, their supporters stated, were the expression of government from the bottom up; the Draft Constitution was wrong because it was government from the top down. This overcentralization, they said, was undemocratic and might lead to fascism; Gandhi had said that democracy must be broad-based and decentralized. Village panchayats were needed to train the people in government, M. A. Ayyangar believed. 'Democracy is not worth anything,' he said, 'if once in a blue moon individuals are brought together for

---

[42] The strongest of the amendments was that by M. A. Ayyangar and N. G. Ranga. It read: 'The state shall establish self-governing panchayats for every village or a group of villages with adequate powers and funds to give training to rural people in democracy and to pave the way for effective decentralization of political and economic power.' Amendment 924; ibid.

[43] *CAD* VII, 4, 316; Gokulbhai Bhatt.

[44] *CAD* VII, 3, 285.

one common purpose, merely electing X, Y, and Z to this assembly and thereafter disperse.'[45]

These criticisms were at once a realistic appraisal of one method by which the village revival aspect of the social revolution had to be carried out and a romantic chorus of regret that the Draft had made not even a bow toward 'the heart of India', the village. To a lesser degree, these criticisms expressed a dislike for the amount of power given to the central government; they revealed a fear of over-centralization rather than approval of extensive decentralization.

Yet pro-panchayat as these speeches were they did not constitute a rejection of parliamentary government in favour of a Gandhian constitution. None of the critics, for example, attacked the Draft in detail or offered alternative schemes—one member only referred, and then in a general way, to Agarwal's *Gandhian Constitution*. The critics also supported other aspects of the Draft Constitution that were negations of a Gandhian government system: e.g., centralized planning, great-power status for India, expropriation of property, the development of heavy industry, and so on. S. L. Saksena, though a keen believer in panchayats, saw them as the electoral bodies in an American presidential system.[46] S. C. Majumdar thought that 'the main sources of its (India's) strength' would be in 'revitalized' villages; yet he also thought that real progress 'pre-supposed a strong unifying central authority'. The time has now come, he said, 'to curb the bias in favour of the so-called "provincial autonomy" . . . .'.[47]

Belief in the principles of parliamentary democracy, despite support for panchayats, appears most strikingly in the nearly universal approval of adult suffrage—which had come during the years of the independence movement to mean direct elections. That the espousal of adult suffrage meant the acceptance of a parliamentary constitution and the rejection of the village panchayat as a unit in India's *political* system was made clear in a remark by M. A. Ayyangar. Ayyangar told the Assembly that he had his doubts about the success of adult suffrage in India. 'Left to myself, I would have preferred that the village ought to be the unit,' he said, '. . .

---

[45] *CAD* VII, 5, 352.
[46] *CAD* VII, 3, 285.
[47] *CAD* VII, 5, 377–8.

but we have chosen, in keeping with the times, adult suffrage for this country.'[48]

Assembly members who criticized the Draft for not giving panchayats their due place were, then, not putting forward an alternative, a Gandhian, constitutional philosophy. Their demand was not political, but administrative, and administratively, but not politically, their demand could be met. Seen thus on two levels, the problem of panchayats, of village development and renascence, could be solved by providing for a degree of administrative decentralization below the level of the provincial governments, while politically, Indian cooperative federalism operated from the provincial government upwards. India in this way could have both panchayats and a direct, parliamentary constitution in which the villager was connected by the electoral process to the provincial and national governments.[49] Treated both as an administrative and as a political issue, the apparently incompatible goals of centralization and decentralization, of rejuvenated panchayats and direct government, could be accommodated. The Assembly could write into the Directive Principles that it was the state's duty to foster the development of panchayats, yet the Oligarchy and inner circle of Assembly leaders could retain the centralized, direct constitution they believed to be necessary.

Even so it appears that Assembly leaders intended to omit all mention of panchayats from the Constitution and only under strong pressure did the leadership grudgingly agree that an article concerning panchayats should appear in the Directive Principles. On 22 November 1948, K. Santhanam moved the party's official amendment; the Assembly adopted it and thus Article 40 came into the Constitution.[50] After its approval, H. C. Mookerjee, the acting president of the Assembly, somewhat wishfully said, 'I have

---

[48] *CAD* XI, 5, 663. Ayyangar's meaning is clear despite some confusion in the speech. Ayyangar later became Speaker of the Lok Sabha, and he was Deputy Speaker of the CA (Legislative) when he expressed these views. See also p. 46 below for A.K. Ayyar's views on this subject.

[49] Support for an administrative, but not a political, role for panchayats has been given by the foremost advocate of panchayats in India today, S. K. Dey, in his *Panchayat-i-Raj*, particularly pp. 84 and 88–96.

[50] Article 40 reads: 'The State shall take steps to organize village panchayats and endow them with such powers and authority as may be necessary to enable

not found anyone who has opposed the motion put forward by Mr. Santhanam'.[51] So far as the Constitution was concerned, the panchayat issue was settled and India was surely committed to direct, parliamentary government.

The incorporation of Article 40 in the Constitution has proved to have been less a gesture to romantic sentiment than a bow to realistic insight. And the aim of the article has long been generally accepted: if India is to progress, it must do so through reawakened village life. Panchayat development under the Constitution has had three main aims: to foster the involvement of individuals throughout the nation in the processes of democratic government, to gain the villager's participation in national development from the village-level upwards (an aim which would, it was hoped, increase agricultural and village-industrial production and thus promote an improvement in village conditions), and to lessen the burden of state administration through decentralization.[52]

Since 1952 the development of panchayats and village life has been undertaken by the state governments, with the Union Government's Ministry of Community Development acting as the coordinator and the major source of funds and initiative.[53] The plan has been to cover the country with a network of administrative panchayats and thus achieve Panchayat Raj. But Panchayat Raj and community development have had many growing pains, hardly surprising in a huge new programme demanding for its success, cooperation among so many portions of society ranging from sceptical villagers to often untrained community development workers. It was estimated in 1957 that less than 10 per cent of panchayats were functioning 'effectively'.[54] The situation has since improved, however, and in some areas panchayats have more than fulfilled the

---

them to function as units of self government.' For the adoption of Santhanam's motion, see *CAD* VII, 10, 520.

[51] Ibid., 527. Mookerjee was somewhat premature in his satisfaction, for the lack of attention to panchayats would be criticized during the Third Reading.

[52] Henry Maddick, 'Panchayat-i-Raj', in *Journal of Local Administration Overseas*, October 1962, pp. 204–5.

[53] Strictly speaking, local government is the responsibility of the states by virtue of Item 5 of the State List (II) of the Constitution Seventh Schedule.

[54] *The Balwantrai Report*, p. 30; cited in Hugh Tinker, 'Authority and Community in Village India', *Pacific Affairs*, December 1959, p. 361.

hopes placed in them. They have proved, according to one authority, that 'the system is sound and the will to make it work widespread. It should make for a great advance in Indian government and administration'. And, the judgement continues, they should 'be a world-wide example of democratic decentralization'.[55]

The Reasons for the Choice

I. The Congress had never been Gandhian

According to Nehru the Congress had 'never considered' the Gandhian view of society (as exemplified in *Hind Swaraj*), 'much less adopted it'.[56] Great as Gandhi's influence had been, and profound as his achievement was in putting the village and the peasant on the centre of the Indian stage, he had not succeeded in converting either the country or his own party to his view of how Indians should live and how they should govern themselves. Not having accepted Gandhi's premises, the Congress had little reason to build the institutions Gandhi had based upon them.

Although brought into sharper focus by the approach of independence, and made unmistakably clear by the exchange of letters between Gandhi and Nehru in October 1945,[57] this disagreement was not new. During the many years that Gandhi had held fast to the ideas expressed in *Hind Swaraj*?'[58] Congress and other Indian leaders had been couching their demands for independence in terms of parliamentary democracy, and many had participated in the modified forms of representative government that the British had introduced. The Commonwealth of India Bill[59] and the Nehru Report in the

---

[55] Maddick, op. cit., p. 212.

[56] Nor had Gandhi ever before asked the party to adopt his viewpoint 'except for certain relatively minor aspects of it'. Nehru in a letter to Gandhi, dated 9 October 1945; see *A Bunch of Old Letters*, p. 509.

[57] *A Bunch of Old Letters*, pp. 505–12; and Notes 9 and 56 above.

[58] Gandhi to Nehru, 5 October 1945, ibid., p. 505: 'I have said that I still stand by the system of Government envisaged in *Hind Swaraj*. These are not mere words. All the experience gained by me since 1908 when I wrote the booklet has confirmed the truth of my belief.'

[59] *A Bill to Constitute within the British Empire a Commonwealth of India*, 16 Geo. 5— often called the Annie Besant Bill. Drafted by a group of Indians, including B. Shiva Rao, under the direction of Annie Besant, this Bill was introduced in

twenties both proposed a parliamentary system for free India, as did the Sapru Report of 1945. The Congress's repeated demands in the thirties for a constitution written by a constituent assembly created by adult suffrage indicated that the party continued to hold the beliefs embodied in the Nehru Report. Jawaharlal Nehru had also made his views clear throughout the thirties and expressed them even more plainly to B. N. Rau in November 1945, when he said 'I should also like the new constitution to lay the greatest emphasis on State activities, such as planning, industrial development, relief of unemployment, nationalization of key industries, etc.'[60]

The belief in parliamentary government seemed, in fact, to be nearly universal. The draft constitutions published by groups of the Left, Centre, and Right—those of the Marxist, M. N. Roy of the Socialist Party, and of the communal Hindu Mahasabha—were also all parliamentary, centralized constitutions.[61] Of a large number of articles published in the *Indian Journal of Political Science* from 1940 to 1945 concerning India's future constitution, every one used the Euro-American constitutional tradition as its source of both principles and detailed suggestions.

Gandhi knew that his message had failed to get home, although he continued to press his views. Writing in *Harijan* in July 1946 he said that the Constituent Assembly would be in a position to realize his goals, but predicted that it would not do so. He wrote,

> Congressmen themselves are not of one mind even on the contents of independence. I do not know how many swear by non-violence or the charka (the spinning wheel) or, believing in decentralization, regard the village as the nucleus. I know on the contrary that many would have India become a first-class military power and wish for India to have a strong centre and build the whole structure round it.[62]

Parliament by George Lansbury and supported by other Labour members. The government it envisaged was parliamentary in form, although the franchise was very restricted, and there were detailed provisions for panchayat administration below the level of the provincial governments.

[60] An interview with Nehru by Rau at Wavell's request; held 21 November 1945. Rau, *Indian Constitution*, p. xxxiv.

[61] M. N. Roy, *Constitution for Free India*, 1944; Hindu Mahasabha, *Constitution of Hindus than Free State*, 1944; and Socialist Party, *Draft Constitution of Indian Republic*, 1948—after the breakaway from the Congress.

[62] *Harijan*, 28 July 1946.

Considering the unusually lengthy and relatively (speaking in colonial terms) successful experience India had had with representative government, it is not surprising that Indians should have favoured a parliamentary constitution. They had been associated with local self-government since the late nineteenth century, and from the 1909 Government of India Act through those of 1919 and 1935, Indians came to play an increasing role in both the executive and legislative sides of provincial and central government. The numbers who had participated in these fields of government could not have exceeded several thousand, but their influence was considerable. They had learned to work the system well and to like it— despite the difficulties engendered by their lack of final authority. Why, said K. M. Munshi, should the Assembly turn its back on a hundred-year-old tradition of parliamentary government in India?[63] The electorate, however greatly restricted, totalled nearly thirty millions in 1937 under the 1935 Act, and this had risen to forty millions in 1946, thus giving India an impressive number of persons who had had some experience over the period of a generation with the processes of representative government.[64]

Furthermore, many Indians had become intellectually committed to the liberal democratic tradition through their travels and education, even if they had not been fully exposed to it in colonial India. Their commitment must have been strengthened—and a favourable impression of representative government created among many other Indians—by the victory of the democracies over the Nazis and the Fascists. In the years just after 1945, the stock of representative democracy—especially that of Britain and the United States—probably stood higher than at any time before or since.

2. The Socialist Commitment

The Assembly's belief in parliamentary government was also strengthened in large measure by the intellectual or emotional commitment of many members to socialism. Although they ranged from Marxists through Gandhian socialists to conservative capitalists, each with his

---

[63] *CAD* VII, 24, 984–5. See ibid., pp. 985–6 for Ayyar's like views.

[64] For an illuminating account of the meaning and extent of legislative experience in India, see Morris-Jones, op. cit., pp. 43–73 and especially pp. 57ff. See also Nehru, *The Discovery of India*, pp. 369–85.

own definition of 'socialism', nearly everyone in the Assembly was Fabian and Laski-ite enough to believe that 'socialism is everyday politics for social regeneration',[65] and that 'democratic constitutions are . . . inseparably associated with the drive towards economic equality'.[66] The Constituent Assembly in the Objectives Resolution and the debate on it established that the Constitution must be dedicated to some form of socialism and to the social regeneration of India, and none but Communists would have disagreed with the Congress Socialist Party's resolution of 1947 stating that 'there could be no Socialism without democracy'.[67] That such should have been the intellectual atmosphere of the Indian Constituent Assembly is hardly surprising. By the time the Assembly had come into being, these ideas had gained almost world-wide social and political currency. They were, perhaps, even more a part of the Indian scene because of the country's manifest social needs and because of Nehru's influence on Indian social thought.

Nehru had been interested by Fabianism when at Cambridge, and his studies of Marx and his trip to Europe—including Russia— during 1926–27 had greatly influenced him.[68] Mrs. Besant, one of the original Fabians, as well as a theosophist, had been a close friend of the Nehru family. Yet over the years leading to the Constituent Assembly he changed from a Marxist or a Laski-style socialist to an empirical gradualist.[69] This must not be taken to mean that Nehru had forsaken socialist ideals. It means that he strove after his ideals in a less doctrinaire, in a more empirical, fashion. By 1945, the real problems for Nehru were 'problems of individual and social life'; he had no time for the fine points of doctrine.[70] 'Though he is a professed socialist', wrote a close colleague of Nehru in 1946, 'his

---

[65]   M. Beer's description of Fabian Socialism in his *A History of British Socialism*, Part IV, Chapt. XIV, p. 281.

[66]   Laski in the Preface to the Third Edition of H. J. Laski, *A Grammar of Politics*. For further reference to the influence on the Assembly of Laski and the Webbs, see Chapter 3 below.

[67]   Resolution adopted at the Kanpur Conference, 28 February 1947. Praja Socialist Party, PSP, *A Brief Introduction*, p. 99; cited in Saul Rose, *Socialism in Southern Asia*, p. 29. See also A. Narenda Dev, *Socialism*, p. 95.

[68]   Brecher, *Nehru*, p. 48; Nehru, *Discovery of India*, pp. 15ff.

[69]   The phrase is that of Professor W. H. Morris-Jones. See his 'The Exploration of Indian Political Life', *Pacific Affairs*, December 1959, p. 415.

[70]   Nehru, *Discovery*, p. 17.

activities are largely guided by ideals of democracy and economic betterment of the masses.'[71] This practical, secular approach to India's social needs had become—perhaps without their knowing it—the attitude of many Indians. It was certainly true of the rank and file of Assembly members and, to a lesser extent, of the Oligarchy as well. Prasad, Patel, and Azad—who was apparently less conservative than the other two— understood as well as did Nehru that India's survival depended on improving the lot of her people. And although Prasad and Patel had on occasion opposed Nehru on 'socialist' issues,[72] both of them had won fame in the Congress by leading peasant satyagraha for better economic conditions—Prasad at Champaran and Patel at Bardoli.

One may speculate that it was principally Patel's conservative influence that kept the Constitution from having a greater socialist content than it has; perhaps it was in deference to his wishes that Nehru omitted the word 'socialism' from the Objectives Resolution. Patel probably did have a moderating influence on Nehru, but we have very little evidence for it in the documents of the framing period.[73] Nehru was equally aware of India's social and political realities, and it is very doubtful whether he wanted the Constitution to commit India's government—which he would head for an indeterminate period—irrevocably and in detail to any particular course. The difference between Nehru and the other three members of the Oligarchy was one of approach, not of basic belief. Nehru felt an emotional and intellectual obligation to attack India's social problems. Patel, Prasad, and Azad, somewhat more conservative

[71] Narenda Dev, *Socialism*, p. 205. Dev added to this: 'He (Nehru) is not wedded to any particular "ism" nor is he temperamentally fit to be the leader of a group. He believes in some of the fundamental principles of scientific socialism, yet he is not prepared to swear by everything taught by Marx and Lenin. He does not subscribe to any rigid ideology. He considers himself free to examine the claims of every system of ideas which professes to serve the social purposes, and he is always revising his ideas in the light of new experiences gained.' Ibid., p. 206.

[72] Especially in 1936 over the composition of the Working Committee, and hence the Party programme; see Brecher, op. cit., pp. 223–6 and 391. See also the 'compensation' issue in Chapter 4 below.

[73] Although there may be truth in the legend of Patel's political and social conservatism, it often has assumed the form of unfounded generalities, and the sources of his political outlook have never been studied. For some of his views relative to zamandari-abolition, see Chapter 4, esp. pp. 93ff.

than Nehru, were commited only to effective government. Yet the attitudes of all four were rooted in a humanitarian outlook. If the good of the many demanded the sacrifice of the few—as in zamandari-abolition—it would be done.

Therefore, rather than the common image of a realistic Patel holding back a rampant, 'socialist' Nehru, the Constituent Assembly more likely watched Nehru and Patel, in cooperation with other members with practical experience in government, dampening the zeal of the impetuous, very Laski-ite Assembly members who were more interested in state control and immediate, drastic reforms than in democratic processes and efficiency.

What was of greatest importance to most Assembly members, however, was not that socialism be embodied in the Constitution, but that a democratic constitution with a socialist bias be framed so as to allow the nation in the future to become as socialist as its citizens desired or as its needs demanded. Being, in general, imbued with the goals, the humanitarian bases, and some of the techniques of social democratic thought, such was the type of constitution that Constituent Assembly members created.

3. The Immediate Reasons

The rejection of Gandhi's diagnoses of society's ills—and the consequent doubt of his remedy—and the predilection for the institutions of parliamentary government gained over the years, were the basic reasons why the Assembly drafted a direct, centralized constitution. Yet there were impelling immediate reasons as well. In an earlier age, India might have been able to work a Gandhian constitution, but not in the mid-twentieth century, when, Nehru believed, 'any consideration of these questions must keep present facts, forces and the human material we have today in view, otherwise it will be divorced from reality'.[74]

Some of these 'facts' were problems demanding immediate solution by the Union Government. For example, when the Interim Government took office in September 1946, near-famine conditions existed in parts of Madras. Nationally, the rise in food prices, the low grain reserve, and the conflict of interest between the surplus

[74] Nehru letter to Gandhi, 9 October 1945, op. cit.

and scarcity provinces caused the newly installed Indian government grave concern.[75] As for centuries in the past, food scarcity demanded national government control of grain supplies, prices, and distribution.

During the August sessions of the Congress Experts Committee, Jinnah's Direct Action Day touched off the 'Great Calcutta Killing' and communal upheaval throughout North India. During November, Nehru, Prasad and other members of the Interim Government went to Bihar and Bengal in attempts to stop the rioting. Pilgrim trains were attacked within twenty miles of Delhi and fifty persons killed. Other killings took place in New Delhi, less than a mile from where the Constituent Assembly would meet. This tide of murderous passion would ebb and flow for more than a year, finally receding only in the late autumn of 1947. Partition forced on independent India administrative readjustment on a grand scale and presented North India with six million refugees, many of whom filled camps in Old Delhi or set up vegetables stalls in New Delhi within shouting distance of the Constituent Assembly chamber. Tension increased in New Dehli with the arrival of the refugees. Rioting and bloodshed began in late August 1947; Assembly members attending the fifth session had to have special curfew passes to enable them to get to the Assembly.[76] As late as November that year, Muslim Assembly members requested special protection while in New Delhi.[77] This

[75] A description of the situation and action needed is found in a memorandum, 'Important Tasks Facing the Interim Government', dated 19 August 1946, author unknown; *Prasad papers*, File 1-1/46-7. D. R. Gadgil, a member of the Congress Experts Committee on the CA, prepared a Note for the committee commenting particularly on the difficulty that even a centralized government had had during the War with food distribution; note dated 15 August 1946; *Prasad papers*, File 35-C/47. The Interim Government (and that of independent India) faced such other problems as the need to increase agricultural production, to control inflation, to encourage and protect industry, etc. See 'Important Tasks . . . ' memorandum. See also Brecher, *Nehru*, op. cit., pp. 381ff for the well-known affair of the textile price rise in September 1947 after government controls were removed.

[76] For a description of these weeks, see V. P. Menon, *The Transfer of Power in India*, pp. 421–33. A curfew had also interfered with Assembly proceedings at the end of April 1947.

[77] Begum Rasul, Mohd. Saadulla, and others requested protection. Saadulla believed himself unsafe even with 'armed guards who escorted him from the

violence brought home the lesson that local law enforcement and local—even provincial— government could be frail reeds in time of great distress, that the centre must have the power to preserve order and the processes of government.

Apart from the communal troubles, there were two other major threats during the framing period to India's internal security: that posed by the Princely States, and the Communist, Telengana rebellion of 1948. Central Government power met and resolved both—in the first instance with persuasion and veiled counter-threat, and in the second by the use of armed force. The States issue was at its most crucial from the spring of 1947 until early 1948—the months in which the principles of the constitution were decided upon and given concrete shape in the Draft Constitution[78]—and the Telengana rebellion had begun before the debate on panchayats in November 1948.

In determining the degree of the centralization of power in the new constitution, the Constituent Assembly had to consider also India's external security problems. A successor state, India was heir to issues dating from British times—the defence of the North-East Frontier, for example, figured in Assembly debates. The Government's immediate responsibility was brought forcibly home to Assembly members in October 1947 by the Pakistan-inspired invasion of Kashmir. With a village society and a decentralized constitution, would India have been able to protect herself from foreign aggression? Nehru had doubted it,[79] and the Assembly readily agreed with him. Virtually every issue that the Oligarchy and Assembly members faced in their roles as Congressmen, as governors of a newly independent nation, and as constitution-framers, or that they had faced when provincial ministers during the years 1937–1939, bore out Nehru's judgement that 'The scope of the Centre, even though limited, inevitably grows, because it cannot exist otherwise'.[80] And with the power of the Muslim

---

airport and who remain at his house'. Prasad in a letter to Nehru, 6 November 1947; *Prasad papers*, File 1-H/47-8-9

[78] For more on the problems presented by the Princely States, see Chapter 10.

[79] Nehru in his letter to Gandhi, 9 October 1945, op. cit.

[80] In the damnation of 'Grouping' speech, 10 July 1946; *IAR* 1946, II, 147. For the extent of Union Government power in the Indian federal system, see Chapters 8 and 9.

League shifted to Pakistan, the last great barrier to a strong central government was removed.

Events before and during the life of the Assembly had indicated that India needed a centralized constitution to establish the stability and the unity necessary to the social revolution. The Assembly believed that the third prerequisite, economic progress, also could be fulfilled only with the presence of centralized authority, by central planning, and by the development of modern agricultural methods, transport, communications, heavy and light industry, electric power, and technical advancement in general. And necessary to technical, even cultural, advancement was scientific research. 'We should adopt all that the modern world has to give us to fulfil our needs', said an Assembly member.[81] 'How far', Nehru asked, will this sort of progress 'fit in with a purely village society?'[82] And in Sardar Patel's words: '. . . the first requirement of any progressive country is internal and external security. Therefore, I started planning on the integration of the country . . . It is impossible to make progress unless you first restore order in the country.'[83]

4. The Need for Adult Suffrage

Economic progress—making available to the masses better food, clothing, and shelter—was itself, of course, an objective of the social revolution. As a prerequisite it was also a means, for material progress would help to free the mass of Indians from centuries of mental and psychological stagnation and passivity. A centralized constitution might make this, achievement possible, but the process at best would be a long one. And would material gain, national unity, and governmental stability by themselves foster 'a fundamental alteration in the structure of Indian society',[84] the most basic goal of the social revolution? Was there not a gong, a single note, whose reverberations might awaken—or at least stir —sleeping India?

[81] *CAD* XI, 4, 611; Seth Govind Das, a conservative Hindu, not a 'Westernizer'.
[82] Nehru in his letter to Gandhi, 9 October 1945, op. cit.
[83] In a speech to the Congress Planning Conference, 26 May 1950. See AICC, *Our Immediate Programme*, 1950, p. 25.
[84] See p. 27 above.

There was: direct election by adult suffrage.

> The Assembly has adopted the principle of adult franchise (said Alladi Krishnaswami Ayyar) with an abundant faith in the common man and the ultimate success of democratic rule, and in the full belief that the introduction of democratic government on the basis of adult suffrage will bring enlightenment and promote the well-being, the standard of life, the comfort, and the decent living of the common man.[85]

Since the nineteen twenties, the Congress had demanded adult suffrage for the people of India; it had become a *sine qua non* of independence. Few disputed its desirability, and many believed that to confine adult participation in elections to the creation of panchayats would have been politically dangerous.[86] Direct election was to be the pillar of the social revolution, for, as Nehru wrote, 'an Assembly so elected (would) represent the people as a whole and (would) be far more interested in the economic and social problems of the masses than in the petty communal issues which affect small groups'.[87]

Adult suffrage, the 'acceptance of the fullest implication of democracy', was the most striking feature of the Constitution, K. M. Panikkar believed. 'In fact', he said, 'it may well be claimed that the Constitution is a solemn promise to the people of India that the legislature will do everything possible to renovate and rebuild society on new principles.'[88]

Adult suffrage gave a voice, indeed power, to millions who had previously to depend on the whim of others for even a vague representation of their interests. Direct elections brought—or could bring—national life and consciousness to individuals in the village. This new awareness through a new channel of communication made possible new allegiances, national instead of local,

---

[85] *CAD* XI, 9, 835. Ayyar also said that 'the only alternative to adult suffrage was some kind of indirect election based upon village community or local bodies and by constituting them into electoral colleges . . . That was not found feasible'. Ibid.

[86] This view was expressed by former Assembly members in interviews with the author.

[87] Nehru, *Unity of India*, p. 23. Nehru wrote these words in 1938 about a constituent Assembly, but its applicability to the legislature is evident.

[88] K. M. Panikkar, *Hindu Society at Cross Roads*, pp. 63–64. Panikkar was a member of the Assembly, and had before and since that time a distinguished career in public life.

thus creating an alternative to the caste and other purely local loyalties that impeded national unity. And if one local loyalty merely supplanted another, as a result of direct elections, at least village society had a new fluidity. It is very doubtful if indirect elections would have had this effect.

> . . . Adult suffrage has social implications far beyond its political significance (said Panikkar). . . . Many social groups previously unaware of their strength and barely touched by the political changes that had taken place, suddenly realized that they were in a position to wield power.[89]

It is argued that direct elections and the growth of political parties has abetted caste consciousness, thus promoting what the constitution was designed to defeat. That the selection of candidates and election results have often followed caste lines is true, and perhaps this has been detrimental both to social progress and national unity. Yet on the district and provincial level, outside the small circle of the village, caste groups in politics seem to have resembled the occupational and other pressure and electoral groups found elsewhere in developing democratic societies. Indirect election would almost surely entrench caste at the village level, keeping power in the hands of the traditional upper caste or some economically ascendant minority. Indirect elections, too, would be fought on entirely local issues, possibly giving undue influence to local groups such as the Dravida Munetra Kazagham in Madras.[90] It may be doubted that national issues much concern the peasant deep in the countryside even under adult suffrage, although the Congress has tried to make national issues important in elections. But with indirect elections the creation of such

---

[89] Ibid., p. 64. Panikkar also postulates in this exceptionally thoughtful and rewarding book that India can only become a unified nation if the social, non-religious excrescences of Hinduism, such as caste and the joint family, are sloughed off. The Constitution is admirable, he argues, because 'A legislating state armed with the full panoply of power has come into existence proclaiming its right and affirming its duty to set right social injustices by social action'. Ibid., 4–5. This meaning of secularization seems to add a new dimension to the Assembly's ideal of a secular state in India.

[90] The Dravida Munetra Kazagham (or DMK) is a party of Tamil nationalists that demands autonomy, if not independence, for Tamil-speaking areas. In the 1962 elections, the DMK made unexpected gains in the Madras Assembly.

national consciousness would be virtually impossible, for the representatives dealing with national problems would be several steps removed from the general electorate.

Direct election, it was cogently argued in the Constituent Assembly, might also help protect village society, already schismatic, from increased factionalism.[91] At the time the Constitution was being drafted, India had for political parties the Congress, overwhelmingly large, but full of diverse groups and tendencies, the Socialist Party, the Hindu Mahasabha, the Communists, and a variety of small local parties.[92] It was extremely doubtful if they would have withered away—or that new parties would not have sprouted—no matter what type of constitution the Assembly had adopted, for government in the modern age, unless totalitarian, has always produced groups organized for political ends.

Panchayats, therefore, if India had a Gandhian constitution, would perforce become involved in party politics: 'Rival political parties, even if they do not want to exploit the dissensions in the village, will be used, captured, by the factions for their local ends'.[93] This being so, the argument ran, the panchayat should be kept out of politics, being limited to purely administrative functions by the drafting of a direct, parliamentary constitution. Panchayat development should be encouraged (the purpose of Article 40 in the Directive Principles), but panchayats and the electoral system should be kept separate. 'Throwing the village panchayats in the whirlpool of party polities', said N. M. Rau, might well 'be destroying once (and) for all their usefulness as agencies of village administration'.[94]

---

[91] For some interesting evidence in support of this view, see Hugh Tinker, *Authority and Community in Village India*, pp. 360ff. Also Henry Maddick, *Panchayat-i-Raj*, op. cit., October 1962, p. 208.

[92] In the 1951–2 General Elections these parties won the following seats in State Assemblies. Total 3,370 seats: Congress, 2, 293; Socialists, 126; and a variety of other parties, 457.

[93] Ashoka Mehta, *The Opposition in New States*, p. 5. This was a paper read before the International Seminar on Representative Government and Public Liberties in the New States held at Rhodes, Greece, in October 1958. Mehta was speaking of parties generally in new states, not specifically in countries with direct or indirect elections.

[94] *CAD* VII, 5, 386. Jayaprakash Narayan believes that the co-existence of successful village panchayats, even on an administrative level, with a direct electoral system is impossible because the 'atomism' of parliamentary

Party democracy certainly did not appear to Assembly members as a panacea for India's ills, but its only vocal critics in the Assembly were a Gandhian, Ramnarayan Singh, and the Muslims who feared that simple majority rule would eclipse their community. To Indians, parliamentary government seemed the route to the long demanded egalitarian society, presenting 'the masses with dynamite for the destruction of social institutions based on privileges or on hereditary inequality'.[95]

The Constituent Assembly's rejection of a decentralized, indirect constitution was a repudiation of Gandhi's view that 'if India (were) to attain true freedom . . . people (would) have to live in villages, not in towns, in huts, not in palaces'.[96] The Assembly's adoption of a democratic, centralized parliamentary constitution meant the members believed that to achieve the objective of social revolution India must become a modern state. Yet panchayats and the ideal of reformed village life would be central to the programme for the modernization of Indian society. The development of this Indian institution and the creation of a modern state with an industrialized economy were not incompatible; the two were complementary and must be simultaneously pursued.

India would do as she had done for centuries; take what she desired from other cultures and bend it to her needs.

> As of old (Nehru said), India seeks a synthesis of the past and the present, of the old and the new. She sees the new industrial civilization marching irresistibly on; she dislikes it and mistrusts it to some extent, for it is an attack against and an upheaval of so much that is old; yet she has accepted that industrial civilization as an inevitable development. So she seeks to synthesize it with her own

---

society, with its emphasis on the individual and on party competition, disrupts the community 'and the panchayat is unable to function in the wholesome manner that everyone desires'. Narayan, *A Plea for The Reconstruction of Indian Polity*, p. 68. S. K. Dey, disagrees with this view. Dey argues cogently that it is silly to impose artificial unity on villages, especially as 'Opposition provides the very spark of life.' The first thing, believes Dey, is to get the village out of its stagnation and channel the released energies of the people into constructive effort through panchayats. See Dey, *Panchayat-i-Raj*, op.cit., pp. 113ff.

[95] Panikkar, *Hindu Society*, p. 83.

[96] Gandhi letter to Nehru, 5 October 1945. *A Bunch of Old Letters*, p. 506.

fundamental conceptions, to find a harmony between the inner man and his everchanging outer environment.[97]

Through her age-old ability to synthesize cultures, Assembly members believed, India could become modern, yet remain Indian. With her social revolution under way, yet with her identity preserved, India could take her 'rightful and honoured place in the world' and could make her 'full and willing contribution to the promotion of world peace and the welfare of mankind'.[98]

---

[97] Nehru, *Unity of India*, p. 26.
[98] The Objectives Resolution, op. cit., para (8).

3

The Conscience of the Constitution—

The Fundamental Rights and Directive Principles of State Policy—I

. . . It is the business of the State . . . to maintain the conditions without which a free exercise of the human faculties is impossible.

T. H. Green

THE Indian Constitution is first and foremost a social document. The majority of its provisions are either directly aimed at furthering the goals of the social revolution or attempt to foster this revolution by establishing the conditions necessary for its achievement. Yet despite the permeation of the entire constitution by the aim of national renascence, the core of the commitment to the social revolution lies in Parts III and IV, in the Fundamental Rights and in the Directive Principles of State Policy. These are the conscience of the Constitution.

The Fundamental Rights and Directive Principles had their roots deep in the struggle for independence. And they were included in the Constitution in the hope and expectation that one day the tree of true liberty would bloom in India. The Rights and Principles thus connect India's future, present, and past, adding greatly to the significance of their inclusion in the Constitution, and giving strength to the pursuit of the social revolution in India. In the present chapter we will examine the origin and development of the Rights and Principles, the negative and positive obligations of the State towards the social revolution, prior to the formation of the Constituent Assembly and then within the Assembly itself.

The Assembly's handling of 'due process' as it affected liberty and property will claim our especial attention, for here lies the best insight into the members' approach to the issue of liberty and the social revolution, to the classic dilemma of how to preserve individual freedom while promoting the public good.[1]

The Fundamental Rights of the Constitution are, in general, those rights of citizens, or those negative obligations[2] of the State not to encroach on individual liberty, that have become well-known since the late eighteenth century and since the drafting of the Bill of Rights of the American Constitution—for the Indians, no less than other peoples, become heir to this liberal tradition. These rights in the Indian Constitution are divided into seven parts: the Right of Equality, the Right of Freedom, the Right Against Exploitation, the Right to Freedom of Religion, Cultural and Educational Rights, the Right to Property, and the Right to Constitutional Remedies. The Rights lay down that the state is to deny no one equality before the law. All citizens are to have the right to freedom of religion, assembly, association, and movement. No person is to be deprived of his life, liberty, or property, except in accordance with the law. Minorities are allowed to protect and conserve their language, script, and culture. And various means are provided whereby the citizen can move the Supreme Court and other courts for the enforcement of the Fundamental Rights.

Although the Fundamental Rights primarily protect individuals and minority groups from arbitrary, prejudicial, state action, three of the articles have been designed to protect the individual against the action of other private citizens. Article 17 abolishes untouchability; Article 15(2) lays down that no citizen shall suffer any disability in the use of shops, restaurants, wells, roads, and other public places on account of his religion, race, caste, sex, or place of birth; Article 23 prohibits forced labour—which, although it had been practised by the state, was more commonly a case of landowner versus peasant. Thus the state, in addition to obeying the Constitution's negative injunctions not to interfere with certain of the citizen's liberties, must fulfil its positive obligation to protect the citizen's rights from

---

[1] In this chapter the words 'freedom' and 'liberty' are used synonymously.

[2] The 'notion of "negative" freedom of Sir Isaiah Berlin, in *Two Concepts of Liberty*, see p. 7 and pp. 7–16.

encroachment by society. The Fundamental Rights, therefore, were to foster the social revolution by creating a society egalitarian to the extent that all citizens were to be equally free from coercion or restriction by the state, or by society privately; liberty was no longer to be the privilege of the few.

In the Directive Principles, however, one finds an even clearer statement of the social revolution. They aim at making the Indian masses free in the positive sense, free from the passivity engendered by centuries of coercion by society and by nature, free from the abject physical conditions that had prevented them from fulfilling their best selves.[3]

To do this, the state is to apply the precepts contained in the Directive Principles when making laws. These Principles are not justiciable, a court cannot enforce them, but they are to be, nevertheless, 'fundamental in the governance of the country'.[4] The essence of the Directive Principles lies in Article 38, which, echoing the Preamble, reads:

> . . . the State shall strive to promote the welfare of the people by securing and protecting as effectively as it may a social order in which justice, social, economic, and political, shall inform all the institutions of the national life.

To foster this goal the other provisions of the Directive Principles exhort the state to ensure that citizens have an adequate means of livelihood, that the operation of the economic system and the ownership and control of the material resources of the country subserve the common good, that the health of the workers, including children, is not abused, and that special consideration be given to pregnant women. Workers, both agricultural and industrial, are to have a standard of living that allows them to enjoy leisure and social and cultural opportunities. Among the primary duties of the state is the raising of the level of nutrition and the general standard of living of the people. The Principles express the hope that within ten years of the adoption of the Constitution there will be compulsory primary education for children up to the age of fourteen years. The other

---

[3] This is one aspect of 'positive' freedom as described by Berlin, op. cit., p. 16, when he writes, The "positive" sense of the word "liberty" derives from the wish on the part of the individual to be his own master. I wish my life and decisions to depend on myself, not on external forces of whatever kind'.

[4] Article 37.

provisions of the Principles seek equally to secure the renovation of Indian society by improving the techniques of agriculture, husbandry, cottage industry, etc.

By establishing these positive obligations of the state, the members of the Constituent Assembly made it the responsibility of future Indian governments to find a middle way between individual liberty and the public good, between preserving the property and the privilege of the few and bestowing benefits on the many in order to liberate 'the powers of all men equally for contributions to the common good'.[5]

SIXTY YEARS OF GROWTH

Although the Fundamental Rights and Directive Principles appear in the Constitution as distinct entities, it was the Assembly that separated them; the leaders of the Independence Movement had drawn no distinction between the positive and negative obligations of the state. Both types of rights had developed as a common demand, products of the national and social revolutions, of their almost inseparable intertwining, and of the character of Indian politics itself.

The Indian desire for civil rights had its roots deep in the nineteenth century. It was implicit in the formation of the Indian National Congress in 1885: Indians wanted the same rights and privileges that their British masters enjoyed in India, and that Britons had among themselves in England; they wanted an end to the discrimination inherent in a colonial regime. Perhaps the first explicit demand for fundamental rights appeared in *The Constitution of India Bill*, 1895. Article 16 of this Bill laid down a variety of rights including those of free speech, imprisonment only by competent authority, and of free state education.[6] A series of Congress resolutions adopted between 1917 and 1919 repeated the demand for civil rights and equality of status with Englishmen. The resolutions called for equal terms and conditions in bearing arms;[7] for 'a wider application of the system of trial by jury', and

---

[5] T. H. Green, *Liberal Legislation and Freedom of Contract*, see *T. H. Green*, edited by R. L. Nettleship, Vol. III, p. 372.

[6] *The Constitution of India*, 1895, author unknown: Shiva Rao, *Select Documents*, I.

[7] Resolution of 1917; Chakrabarty and Bhattacharya, op. cit., p. 19.

for the right of Indians 'to claim that no less than one-half the jurors should be their own countrymen'.[8] A further resolution stated the 'emphatic opinion' that Parliament should pass a statute guaranteeing 'the Civil Rights of His Majesty's Indian subjects', which would embody provisions establishing equality before the law, a free press, free speech, etc. The statute should moreover lay down that political power belonged to the Indian people in the same manner as to any other people or nation in the British Empire.[9]

This demand for equality of rights and for self-government exemplifies not only the well-known desire for negative freedom, but also that aspect of positive freedom so perceptively described by Sir Isaiah Berlin as 'the desire for the "positive" freedom of collective self-direction'.[10] 'The "positive" sense of liberty comes to light', wrote Berlin, 'if we try to answer the question, not "What am I free to do or be?", but "By whom am I ruled?" or "Who is to say what I am, and what I am not, to be or do?" '[11] The demand for this particular aspect of positive liberty and the demand for negative freedom were to come to their logical fulfilment with the attainment of independence and of its corollary, adult suffrage, and with the inclusion of fundamental rights in the Constitution.

By the mid-twenties, Congress and Indian leaders generally had achieved a new forcefulness and a consciousness of their Indianness and of the needs of the people, thanks largely to the experience of World War I, to the disappointment of the Montagu-Chelmsford reforms, to Woodrow Wilson's support for self-determination and to Gandhi's arrival on the scene. These influences were reflected in the tone and form of demands for civil rights. These no longer aimed at establishing the rights of Indians *vis-à-vis* Englishmen, a goal that was to be achieved through the Independence Movement; the purpose now was to assure liberty among Indians. The experience of colonial status would, however, continue to be reflected in the demand for rights, for, as a great American judge has said, 'such constitutional limitations arise from grievances, real or fancied,

---

[8] Resolution dated 1917; see ibid.

[9] Ibid., p. 26.

[10] Berlin, *Two Concepts*, pp. 47–48, does not refer to two aspects of 'positive' liberty; the distinction is the author's.

[11] Ibid., p. 15; see also pp. 16 and 41–57.

which their makers have suffered, and . . . they withstand the winds of logic by the depth and toughness of their roots in the past'.[12]

The next major development was the drafting of the seven fundamental rights provisions of Mrs. Besant's Commonwealth of India Bill of 1925. These laid down that individual liberty, freedom of conscience, free expression of opinion, free assembly, and equality before the law were to be ensured. There was to be 'no disqualification or disability on the ground only of sex'.[13] According to two other provisions, all persons in the Commonwealth of India were to have the right to free elementary education (a right that was to become enforceable as soon as arrangements for educational facilities could be made), and all persons were to have equal right to the use of 'roads, courts of justice, and all other places of business or resort dedicated to the public'.[14] Thus were presaged several provisions of the Fundamental Rights and one of the Directive Principles.

Within two years of the printing of the Besant Bill came the announcement that the Simon Commission would undertake a study of possible constitutional reforms in India. In response, the Forty-Third Annual Session of the Congress at Madras in 1927 resolved that the Working Committee be empowered to set up a committee 'to draft a Swaraj Constitution for India on the basis of a declaration of rights'.[15] That a declaration of rights had assumed such importance was not surprising: India was a land of communities, of minorities, racial, religious, linguistic, social, and caste.[16] For India to become a state, these minorities had to agree to be governed both at the centre and in the provinces by fellow Indians—members, perhaps, of another-minority—and not by a mediatory third power, the British. On both psychological and political grounds, there- fore, the demand for written rights—since rights would provide tangible safeguards against oppression—proved overwhelming. 'The community, so to say, is a federal process', Laski wrote.[17] And Indians

---

[12] Judge Learned Hand. See Hand, *The Spirit of Liberty*, ed. by Irving Dillard, p. 18.

[13] *Commonwealth of India Bill*, Clause 8(g).

[14] Ibid., Clause 8(d) and (e).

[15] Chakrabarty and Bhattacharya, op. cit., p. 27.

[16] The Hindu community is a majority community, but, generally speaking, it is so fragmented within itself by caste, and linguistic divisions, that it is better to view it as a collection of closely related minorities.

[17] *The Grammar of Politics*, p. 97.

believed that in their 'federation of minorities' a declaration of rights was as necessary as it had been for the Americans when they established the first federal constitution.[18]

The committee called for by the Madras Congress resolution came into being in May 1928. Motilal Nehru, father of Jawaharlal, was its chairman, and its membership represented the views of Muslims, Hindu orthodoxy, non-Brahmins, labour, and Liberals. The committee's report—known as the Nehru Report—contained an explanation of its draft constitution that speaks for itself.

The first concern of Indians, the report declared, was 'to secure the Fundamental Rights that have been denied to them'. In writing a constitution, the report continued,

> It is obvious that our first care should be to have our Fundamental Rights guaranteed in a manner which will not permit their withdrawal under any circumstances . . . Another reason why great importance attaches to a Declaration of Rights is the unfortunate existence of communal differences in the country. Certain safeguards are necessary to create and establish a sense of security among those who look upon each other with distrust and suspicion. We could not better secure the full enjoyment of religious and communal rights to all communities than by including them among the basic principles of the Constitution.[19]

The Fundamental Rights of the Nehru Report[20] were reminiscent of those of the American and post-war European constitutions, and were in several cases taken word for word from the rights listed in the Common wealth of India Bill. Several clauses had, however, a more particularly Indian origin—such as, 'no breach of contract of service or abettment thereof shall be made a criminal offence', which related directly to forced labour. The rights of the Nehru Report were a close precursor of the Fundamental Rights of the Constitution; ten of the nineteen sub-clauses re-appear, materially unchanged, and three of the Nehru Rights are included in the Directive Principles. The first

[18] It will be remembered here that, although most of the thirteen original states already had Bills of Rights in their state constitutions, it was the general demand of the states that a list of rights be included in the federal constitution that caused the addition of the first ten amendments.

[19] All Parties Conference, *Report of a Committee to Determine Principles of the Constitution for India*, the *Nehru Report*, pp. 89–90.

[20] The rights were listed in nineteen sub-clauses of Clause 4; see ibid., pp. 101–3.

sub-clause of the Rights (that all power and authority of government derived from the people) was the *raison d'etre* of the Constituent Assembly as expressed in the Objectives Resolution. The content, although not the form, of other provisions is also to be found in the Constitution; e.g., the sub-clause on language became Part XVII on Language.

In the Nehru Report the desire to afford protection to minorities was especially prominent. For example, the right to freedom of conscience and to the free profession and practice of religion was included explicitly to prevent 'one community domineering over another'.[21] There was also special provision made for the elementary education of members of minorities. Such rights as these were called Minority Rights in the early days of the Assembly, and they appear in the Constitution as Rights Relating to Religion, Cultural and Educational Rights, and also in Part XVII on Language.

In 1931 a new dimension was added to the demand for constitutional rights. Heretofore almost exclusively devoted to the State's negative obligations, the demand now equally emphasized the State's positive obligations to provide its people with the economic and social conditions in which their negative rights would have actual meaning. The Congress Session held at Karachi in March 1931 adopted the Resolution on Fundamental Rights and Economic and Social Change, which was both a declaration of rights and a humanitarian socialist manifesto. The Karachi Resolution, as it came to be called, meant that the social revolution would have a vital share in shaping India's future constitution, and the provisions did in fact become the spiritual, and in some cases the direct, antecedents of the Directive Principles.

The Karachi Resolution stated that 'in order to end the exploitation of the masses, political freedom must include the real economic freedom of the starving millions'.[22] The state was to safeguard 'the interests of industrial workers', ensuring that 'suitable legislation'

---

[21]   Ibid., p. 29.

[22]   Chakrabarty and Bhattacharya, op. cit., p. 28. The text of the Karachi Resolution given by Chakrabarty and Bhattacharya is actually the corrected version adopted by the AICC in Bombay in the autumn of 1931. The difference between the two versions is, however, not great. The text of the original Karachi Resolution is to be found in the Report of the *45th Indian National Congress*, 1931, pp. 139–41.

should secure them a living wage, healthy conditions, limited hours of labour, and protection from 'the economic consequences of old age, sickness, and unemployment'.[23] Women and children were also to be protected in various ways and accorded special benefits. The state was to 'own or control key industries and services, mineral resources, railways, waterways, shipping and other means of public transport'.[24] Another item called for the reform of the systems of land tenure, revenue, and rent.

Several clauses reflected the Gandhian side of the Congress: for example, the demand for greatly reduced military expenditure, the ceiling of five hundred rupees per month for civil servants salaries, no salt duty, prohibition, and the demand for protection against foreign cloth. The provisions concerning the salt tax, prohibition, and protection for domestic textiles had the ring of a tactical programme for the Independence Movement—these subjects had, indeed, been at the centre of the Civil Disobedience campaign of the previous year— and of them only prohibition reached the Constitution.

The negative rights of the Karachi Resolution were derived, in some cases textually, from those of the Nehru Report. Four new provisions, however, were included: the State should confer no titles; franchise should be on the basis of adult suffrage; there should be no capital punishment; and citizens should have the right to freedom of movement throughout India.

Jawaharlal Nehru has been given credit for drafting the Karachi Resolution, although the 'Gandhian' provisions do not sound particularly like him and the list of negative rights could have been prepared by anyone.[25] The humanitarian cast of the provisions concerning the welfare of workers and of the people generally, the placing of the primary responsibility for social reform on the State, and the emphasis on the legislative approach, however, do reflect Nehru's

---

[23] Ibid.

[24] Ibid., p. 29.

[25] Narendra Dev, *Socialism*, p. 203, and Brecher, *Nehru*, p. 175. Brecher also cites a confidential (British) Government of India document to the effect that M. N. Roy may have had some influence on the drafting. Nehru, himself, has said that he drafted the Resolution, incorporating several of Gandhi's suggestions. Ibid., p. 176. Nehru has himself given the general background of the Karachi Resolution, although it is regrettably incomplete; see *Autobiography*, op. cit., pp. 265–7.

ideas and read as if he had written them. Yet there can be little doubt
that these sentiments were generally accepted, for Patel, as Congress
president, was presiding at Karachi during their adoption, and they
have characterized the Congress's approach to the social revolution
from that day to this.

The next major document on rights of the pre-Assembly era was
the *Sapru Report,* published at the end of 1945. The report suggested
a constitutional scheme for India, and although the portions of the
report dealing with fundamental rights contained overtones of the
social revolution, it addressed itself mainly to the problem of placating
minority fears, which were again overshadowing the political scene.
With independence likely in the not too distant future, the minorities
had to face the responsibility of living together and of creating a state.

The fundamental rights of the new constitution, said the Sapru
Report, will be a 'standing warning' to all

> that what the Constitution demands and expects is perfect equality
> between one section of the community and another in the matter
> of political and civic rights, equality of liberty and security in the
> enjoyment of the freedom of religion, worship, and the pursuit of the
> ordinary applications of life.[26]

Not only must the rights protect minorities, the report went on to
say, but they must prescribe 'a standard of conduct for the legislatures, government and the courts'.

Perhaps the most striking thing about the treatment of rights in
the Sapru Report was the distinction made between justiciable and
non-justiciable rights. The distinction was not made, as it would be
in the Constitution, in the context of positive and negative rights, but
in connection with minority rights. Skilful lawyers, said the report,
should find it possible to divide the assurances and guarantees given
to the minorities 'in such a way that the breaches of some may form
the subject of judicial pronouncement, and the breaches of others
may be remedied without resort to courts of law'.[27] A few months

---

[26] Sir Tej Bahadur Sapru and others, *Constitutional Proposals of the Sapru Committee,*
the *Sapru Report,* p. 260. The Sapru Committee styled itself, with justice, a conciliation committee, and for this reason presumably considered economic rights
extraneous to its report.

[27] Ibid, p. 259; see also p. 258.

more than a year later the Constituent Assembly began framing the Fundamental Rights and the Directive Principles of State Policy.

THE ATMOSPHERE OF 1947

The basic question facing the members of the Assembly was the most easily answered. Should a list of rights be included in the Constitution? The answer was, Yes. In every document concerning rights since 1895[28] Indians had rejected the British view of rights enunciated by Dicey and subscribed to by others, including the British Government, that a proclamation of rights in a constitution 'gives of itself but slight security that the right has more than a nominal existence'.[29] Britain had applied this belief in the Indian context when in 1934 the Joint Parliamentary Committee refused the Indian request to include a list of rights in the 1935 Act.[30] Only in 1946 did the British tacitly acknowledge the validity

---

[28] The near universality of the demand for rights can be seen in the *Nehru Report*, the *Proceedings and Reports* of the Round Table Conference, in the *Sapru Report*, particularly in its appendixes, and in the pronouncements of minority groups during the 1920's, 30's, and 40's—for which the *Indian Annual Register* is an excellent source. See also subsequent pages in this chapter.

[29] Dicey, *Law of the Constitution*, p. 207. Other constitutionalists holding the view are Professor Wheare and Sir Ivor Jennings. See Wheare, *Modern Constitutions*, pp. 54–57, and Jennings, *Some Characteristics of the Indian Constitution*, pp. 49–50 and 54. See even Laski, *Grammar of Politics*, p. 104: 'It is the proud spirit of citizens, less than the letter of the law, that is their (rights) most real safeguard.'

[30] *Report of the Joint Parliamentary Committee*, 1934, H.C.5 (1 Part I), pp. 215–16. The committee's given reason for not including written rights was that abstract declarations of rights are useless unless there exists the will to make them effective, and that written rights might put embarrassing restrictions on the legislature. The relevant passages read: 'The Statutory Commission observed with reference to the subject: "We are aware that such provisions have been inserted in many Constitutions, notably in those of the European States formed after the war. Experience, however, has not shown them to be of any great practical value. Abstract declarations are useless, unless there exists the will and means to make them effective." With these observations we entirely agree . . . But there are also strong practical arguments against the proposal, which may be put in the form of a dilemma: for either the declaration of rights is of so abstract a nature that it has no legal effect of any kind or its legal effect will be to impose an embarrassing restriction on the powers of the legislature and to create a grave risk that a large

of the Indian view when the Cabinet Mission Plan suggested that the Assembly constitute an Advisory Committee on fundamental and minority rights to make recommendations concerning constitutional provisions.

Indians rejected the British view of rights for many reasons. Foremost among them was the belief that independence meant liberty, that rights expressed this liberty and must, both in their positive and negative forms, be enshrined in the Constitution. The desire for written rights was reinforced by the suspicion of government engendered by colonial rule—a suspicion that was certainly not diminished by the scoffing attitude of the imperial government toward such rights. The various minority communities also believed that their safety depended upon the inclusion in the constitution of measures protecting their group rights and character. In the eyes of the minorities, too, the Congress was on trial. During the years when independence had been more of a hope than a reality, the Congress had been loud in demanding written rights. With independence and the Congress's assumption of power near, to reject them would have created a vast and crippling suspicion of the Congress leaders' motives. The party leadership, aware of this, was eager to demonstrate its good intentions.

Moreover Britain had often claimed that it had a special obligation to protect the minorities, because Indians could not find justice at the hands of other Indians. Assembly members in general and the Congress leadership in particular intended to refute this. As Sardar Patel told the first meeting of the Advisory Committee:

> It is for us to prove that it is a bogus claim, a false claim, and that nobody can be more interested than us in India, in the protection of our minorities. Our mission is to satisfy every one of them. . . . At least let us prove we can rule ourselves and we have no ambition to rule others.[31]

The decade of the 1940's generally was marked by a resurgence of interest in human rights. The denial of liberties under German and Russian totalitarianism and elsewhere resulted in the Atlantic

---

number of laws may be declared invalid by the Courts because inconsistent with one or other of the rights, so declared.' Ibid., para 366.

[31] Proceedings of the Advisory Committee, 27 February 1947; Shiva Rao, *Select Documents*, II. In Assembly terminology, followed here, 'Proceedings' means a verbatim record and 'Minutes' means abridged proceedings.

Charter, the United Nations Charter, and the activities of the United Nations Human Rights Commission. Assembly members were sensitive to these currents, which supported their own faith in the validity of written rights.

That the Constitution would contain positive rights as well as negative safeguards was nearly as certain as the appearance of the written rights themselves. For as the inclusion of negative rights was primarily a product of the national revolution and of the minorities situation, so the impetus for the inclusion of the state's positive obligations came largely from the social revolution and reflected the social consciousness that had increasingly characterized the twentieth century both in India and abroad.

By 1947 it was a commonly accepted belief that the state bore a major responsibility for the welfare of its citizens. Nehru, the Indian Socialists, and the very winds of social and political thought had brought to India the ideas of Marx, T. H. Green, Laski, the Webbs, and many others.[32] The expression of such ideas had begun before the end of the nineteenth century with the views of Swami Vivekananda, and continued with those of R. C. Dutt, and M. Visvesvaraya, among others.[33]

Members of the Assembly would have accepted without hesitation the views of other humanitarians and socialists that 'political equality . . . is never real unless it is accompanied by virtual economic equality',[34] and that 'true individual freedom cannot exist without economic security and independence. Necessitous men are not free men.'[35] There would have been equal agreement that 'left to itself, or to the operation of casual benevolence, a degraded population perpetuates and increases itself'.[36] Yet in India these sentiments

[32] 'The ghosts of Sidney and Beatrice Webb stalk through the pages of the text' of the Directive Principles, wrote Sir Ivor Jennings in something of an oversimplification. See *Some Characteristics*, p. 31.

[33] See K. R. Karunakaran, Ed., *Modern Indian Political Tradition*, pp. 720ff for quotations from Vivekananda. See also R. C. Dutt, *India in the Victorian Age*, and M. Visvesvaraya, *Reconstructing India*.

[34] Laski, *Grammar*, p. 162.

[35] A quotation attributed to Franklin D. Roosevelt by K. T. Shah in a letter to Prasad dated 15 February 1947. *Prasad papers*, File 4-C/47. Shah was supporting the inclusion of 'economic and social' rights in the Constitution.

[36] Green, op. cit., p. 376.

of political philosophers—true as they were and influential as they had been—were dwarfed and made commonplace by the needs of India's millions.

Sustained by theory though members of the Assembly may have been, they were actuated by the facts of the situation around them. Most members believed that the type of 'socialism' India should have was not theirs to decide (nor is the issue yet settled), but it was clear to them that 'the utility of a state has to be judged from its effect on the common man's welfare',[37] and that the Constitution must establish the state's obligations beyond doubt.[38] This was the purpose of the Directive Principles of State Policy.

The content of the Directive Principles was also to some extent a product of the anti-colonial revolution. As the negative rights expressed a desire for civil liberty in reaction to the political subservience experienced under an imperial regime, so the positive rights represented the casting off of the economic inferiority of colonial status. In the minds of colonial or recently ex-colonial peoples in the mid-twentieth century, colonialism is associated with capitalism, with the domination of indigenous economic life by foreign capitalists, along with native capitalists who have sided with the colonial government in order to safeguard their property and to increase their privileges. Political independence is associated, by newly independent peoples, if not with socialism, at least with the freedom to determine themselves the status of private property within their own country and their country's economic orientation. Such was the case in India. Notwithstanding the number of Indian capitalists who had contributed to the Congress, the popular image was that of British capitalists exploiting a subject people and of Indian monied interests siding with the British for self-protection. Nor was this image unfounded.[39]

---

[37] *CAD* VII, 2, 221; H. V. Kamath.

[38] See also speeches in the Assembly by Sidhwa, *CAD* II, 1, 259; Nehru, *CAD* I, 5, 60; Mme. Pandit, *CAD* II, 1, 261; Ambedkar, *CAD* I, 7, 98; Banerjee, *CAD* III, 5, 509.

[39] That the Indian economy was run largely with the interests of Britain in mind, and that British business interests had a privileged position in India is too well-known to need documentation here. The relationship between Indian monied interests, particularly land-owners, and the colonial regime, which is equally

The Directive Principles were a declaration of economic independence, a declaration that the privilege of the colonial era had ended, that the Indian people (through the democratic institutions of the Constitution) had assumed economic as well as political control of the country, and that Indian capitalists should not inherit the empire of British colonialists.[40]

THE ASSEMBLY DRAFTS THE FUNDAMENTAL RIGHTS

The Cabinet Mission laid down in its 16 May Plan that the Constituent Assembly should have an Advisory Committee whose duty it would be to report to the Assembly on

> the list of Fundamental Rights, the clauses for the protection of minorities and a scheme for the administration of the tribal and excluded areas and to advise whether these Rights should be incorporated in the Provincial, Group, or Union Constitutions.[41]

The Cabinet Mission's recommendations and the intentions of the Congress coincided: the Working Committee of the Congress drew up a resolution establishing the Advisory Committee at its meeting of 8 December 1946,[42] the day before the Constituent Assembly was convened. The resolution was to be moved during the early days of the first session, but was delayed for a month in the hope that the Muslim League might enter the Assembly.[43] It was not until 24 January 1947 that the Assembly voted to create the Advisory Committee. It was originally to have been elected by the Assembly, but instead the Congress leadership arranged that the members be

---

well documented, appears revealingly in the *Report of the Joint Parliamentary Committee*, pp. 217–18.

[40] The 'private sector' of the Indian economy has continued to expand, however; and the 1956 Resolution of the National Development Council acknowledged the important place of private endeavour. The 'socialist pattern of society' that is the aim of the Indian planned economy includes private enterprise provided it serves the needs of the community. 'Private enterprise, free pricing, private management are all devices to further what are truly social ends; they can only be justified in terms of social results.' *Second Five year Plan*, pp. 22–23.

[41] Cabinet Mission Plan, Para, 20, Gwyer and Appadorai, op. cit., p. 283. See also Para. 19(iv), ibid.

[42] Minutes of the meeting, *Prasad papers*, File 16-P/45-6-7.

[43] *CAD* II, 4, 308–9; Pandit Pant.

chosen in off-the-floor conferences held between Assembly leaders and the chief members of each minority group. For this reason the various religious minorities, the Scheduled Castes, and the backward tribes were all proportionally represented on the committee, and, because the minorities had been consulted when the committee was being established, their representatives were of their own choosing.[44] Twelve well-known, influential Congressmen (including two Women) by another Working Committee decision were also made members of the committee representing a 'general' category. Among them were Patel, who became chairman of the Advisory Committee, and Acharya Kripalani, who was to be chairman of the Fundamental Rights Sub-Committee. Five others from this group were also members of the Rights Sub-Committee.[45]

The membership of the Fundamental Rights and other sub-committees was set up, as, had been the whole Advisory Committee, by the leadership of the Congress in consultation with the leaders of the minority groups themselves. Members of the Rights Sub-Committee were: the two ladies, Rajkumari Amrit Kaur and Hansa Mehta, Acharya Kripalani, Minoo Masani, K. T. Shah, A. K. Ayyar, K. M. Munshi, Sardar Harnam Singh, Maulana Azad, B. R. Ambedkar, J. Daulatram, and K. M. Panikkar—who was appointed to the committee to represent the Princely States by President Prasad in March, but who sat with the committee only from 14 April onward. Three of the members already had some familiarity with the formal consideration of rights issues. K. T. Shah and K. M. Munshi had both been members of the Congress Experts Committee, which had drafted a list of rights for the Assembly's guidance.[46] Ambedkar had attended

---

[44] Ibid., p. 324. The Advisory Committee was established by a motion that was amended by general agreement immediately after it was introduced in the House.' For details of the creating of the committee and choosing its members, see ibid., pp. 308–25. Although the Advisory Committee was originally to have seventy-two members, its maximim membership was sixty-four.

[45] There were three sub-committees of the Advisory Committee: that on Fundamental Rights, one on Minorities, and one on Tribal and Excluded Areas—this sub-committee had supporting committees that examined the condition of tribesmen in selected areas.

[46] See footnote 26, Chapter 2. Shah had also attended the Round Table Conference in 1930, as an advisor to the Indian·Princes, where he may have dealt with rights issues. The original draft of the Expert Committee's list of rights had been prepared by K. Santhanam, who had also written the introductory note to the

the Round Table Conference and taken a strong interest in rights issues. At the sub-committee's first meeting, the members chose Kripalani as chairman.

When the Fundamental Rights Sub-Committee met for the first time on 27 February 1947, it had before it draft lists of rights prepared by B. N. Rau,[47] Shah, Munshi, Ambedkar, Harnam Singh, and the Congress Experts Committee, as well as miscellaneous notes and memoranda on various aspects of rights. These lists, sometimes annotated or accompanied by explanatory memoranda, were lengthy and detailed and contained both negative and positive rights taken from foreign constitutions and from the Indian rights documents that we have considered earlier.[48]

Drawing on this mass of precedent, the sub-committee drafted the rights during ten meetings held in March and April 1947. Early in April it passed its tentative conclusions to the Minorities Sub-Committee of the Advisory Committee for suggestions, and on 4 April completed a draft report. After considering the subcommittee's recommendations and reconsidering their own draft report, the

---

compilation of rights clauses from various world constitutions that was prepared by the Sapru Committee. K. Santhanam in an interview with the author; see also *Sapru Report*, para, 364.

[47] Rau's draft rights were in addition to the extensive passages on rights in his *Constitutional Precedents*, op. cit., See *Precedents*, First Series, Parts 8–12 and Third Series, Parts II-V. Pages 10–24 on rights in the Third Series appeared in Rau, *India's Constitution in the Making*, as Chapter 13.

[48] The importance of European and American constitutional precedent to the framing of the Fundamental Rights (and Directive Principles) is already evident and will become increasingly so. One has only to look at Rau's *Constitutional Precedents* to see an example. The affinity between Ireland and India, as we shall see later, bore special fruits. The unpublished *Annexure II* of the Fundamental Rights Sub-Committee's Report to the Advisory Committee even lists the foreign derivation of each rights, clause; e.g., Clause 4 adopted from Weimer 109(1) and second part from U.S.A. Amend. 14, Section 1, etc., etc.

Rau's additional list of rights is not available in its entirety. Shah's list is in File 4-C/47, *Prasad papers*. Munshi's list is in the *Munshi papers* in two forms, a separate list of Draft Rights, dated 15 March 1947, and one included as part of an incomplete draft constitution. Ambedkar's list of rights appear in B. R. Ambedkar, *State and Minorities, What are their rights and how to secure them in free India*, pp. 27ff and Article H. Harnam Singh's list of rights is to be found in *Law Ministry Archives*, File CA/43/Com/47. And the rights drafted by the Congress Experts Committee are in *Prasad papers*, File 16-P/45-6-7.

Rights Sub-Committee members submitted their report on 16 April to the Advisory Committee as a whole. Five days later the Advisory Committee met and made certain changes in it. Patel, as committee chairman, presented the Interim Report of the Advisory Committee on the Subject of Fundamental Rights to the Constituent Assembly on 29 April 1947.[49] The Assembly debated it for the remainder of the Third Session, and considered the rights a second time in November 1948 during the debate on the Draft Constitution. Except for several controversial provisions, the drafting of the rights was completed by mid-December 1948.

When the sub-committee began drafting the rights in March 1947, the members found that although there was some disagreement on techniques, there was little on principles; history had done much of the members' work for them. What disagreement there was centred primarily around the classic predicament of the degree to which personal liberty should be infringed to secure governmental stability and the public peace, of how conditional the statement of a right should be. The members of the sub-committee quickly decided that the Fundamental Rights should be justiciable, that they should be included in the Constitution, and they decided what form these rights should take. The Rights to Freedom were drafted with only brief argument over the wording of the proviso to the Right of Freedom of Association. The provision abolishing Untouchability was adopted with equal swiftness,[50] as were the provisions giving protection against double jeopardy, ex-post facto laws, etc.

That Fundamental Rights, while protecting individual freedom, were not to prevent state intervention in the interests of the social revolution became apparent in the drafting of several rights provisions. It had long been evident, for example, that a clause protecting freedom of conscience and the profession and practice of religion would be in the Constitution. Yet in sub-committee meetings, Amrit Kaur opposed allowing the free 'practice' of religion since

---

[49] *Interim Report of the Advisory Committee on the Subject of Fundamental Rights Reports of Committees, First Series*, pp. 20–34.

[50] Minutes of the Fundamental Rights Sub-Committee meeting, 29 March 1947, File 4-F/47, *Prasad papers*. The limitations on rights in the form of provisos, however, proved on occasion quite controversial as we shall see subsequently.

this could include such 'anti-social' practices as devadasi (temple prostitution), purdah, and sati, and because it might invalidate such secular gains as the Widows Remarriage Act.[51] Ayyar came to her support with a note saying that the Minorities Sub-Committee's use of the word 'practice' was too wide[52] and cited the example of the 1935 Act, when the British Parliament had 'refused to insert any provision that might interfere with social reform'.[53] This protest had its effect: the Advisory Committee altered the sub-committee's provisions and in its own report laid down that the right freely to practice religion should not prevent the state from making laws providing for social welfare and reform, a provision that was carried into the Constitution.[54]

Equality before the law was another right that might have been thought unexceptionable. Yet Ayyar believed that it could hamper reform. It might prevent the passage of laws differentiating between men and women factory workers, thereby denying women special protection. It might also prevent treating children and adults differently in criminal courts. Equality before the law, Ayyar maintained, was a fine principle of English law, but it was self-defeating when written into a constitution. He preferred using the phrase that 'no person should be denied the equal protection of the law'.[55] The Advisory Committee heeded Ayyar's advice, for despite the contrary precedents in the Nehru Report and in the Fundamental Rights Sub-Committee's report, the clause in the Advisory Committee's Interim Report read that no person should be denied equality before the law—and this wording was carried into the Constitution.[56]

The conflict between individual liberty and the state's responsibility was also evident in the provision concerning forced labour. The

[51] In a note dated 20 April 1947. *Prasad papers*, File 1-F/47. See also sub-committee Minutes for 26 March 1947, File 4-F/47, ibid.

[52] Note dated 20 April 1947, *Ayyar papers*.

[53] Quoted from a letter from Ayyar to B. N. Rau, dated 4 April 1947; ibid.

[54] *Interim Report*, Clause 13, Explanation 3, *Reports, First Series*, op. cit., p. 25.

[55] See his notes on this subject to the Fundamental Rights Sub-Committee, dated 10 and 20 April 1947, *Ayyar papers*.

[56] See Article 14 of the Constitution and Clause 9 of the *Interim Report, Reports, First Series*, p. 25.

Nehru Report had a thinly disguised clause aimed at eliminating it.[57] And the Fundamental Rights Sub-Committee found that they were in no disagreement about abolishing forced labour, *begar* (a form of forced labour practised particularly in the United Provinces), and traffic in human beings (primarily directed against prostitution), but they disagreed strongly on the question of involuntary labour in the form of military or social conscription.

The two ladies, Mehta and Kaur, were against conscription and the latter opposed compulsion in any form.[58] K. T. Shah favoured conscription for social service, and apparently had no objection to compulsory military service.[59] Ambedkar, Munshi, and Ayyar did not want to write into the Constitution a clause prohibiting military conscription. Munshi believed that any such prohibition would be very dangerous in time of war, and Alladi Krishnaswami reminded the sub-committee that although India might not choose to have conscription, it was another matter completely to deny oneself, recourse to it. Fundamental rights in India, Ayyar said, rest on the bedrock of Indian national security.[60]

It is not clear who introduced or championed the clause prohibiting conscription, but the sub-committee adopted it at its meeting of 27 March 1947. Opponents of this move called for another vote at the next day's session and the count was five to three against military conscription. At Dr. Ambedkar's request a second vote was taken on conscription for military training only. The vote was five to four against, and it appears that these five votes were cast by Masani, Kripalani, Kaur, Mehta, and Jairamdas Daulatram.[61] The sub-committee's 16 April report did permit 'compulsory service under any general scheme of education'. The Advisory Committee was not satisfied with the wording of this prohibition of conscription, however, and appointed several sub-committees to scrutinize it. A sub-committee, apparently comprised of Pant, Rajgopalachari, Munshi, and Ambedkar redrafted the provision reversing the stand of the sub-committee. The new wording provided that nothing in the forced

---

[57] *Nehru Report*, clause 4(xvi), p. 103; 'No breach of contract of service or abetment thereof shall be made a criminal offence'.

[58] See their undated minute of dissent (April 1947); *Prasad papers*, File 1-F/47.

[59] In a minute of dissent dated 20 April 1947; ibid.

[60] See Ayyar's note dated 17 April 1947; ibid.

[61] Minutes of the meeting of 28 March 1947, ibid.

labour clause should 'prevent the State from imposing compulsory service for public purposes'[62]—essentially the form in which the provision appeared in the Constitution.

The protection of minorities took two forms. First was the inclusion in the Fundamental Rights of the freedom of religion, and other such provisions, plus those special provisions relating to the protection of script and culture, the rights of minorities to maintain their own educational institutions, and so on, that appear in the Cultural and Educational Rights of the Constitution. Protection of this kind had, as we know, long been part of the rights demand, and this continued to be the case in 1947. Minority groups of all kinds—Buddhists, Jains, Christians, Sanatanists, Shia Muslims, Harijans, Kumaonis, linguistic groups, and so on—wrote letters to the Assembly asking that special consideration be given to their problems and their interests protected. Although the Advisory Committee and the sub-committees took note of these sentiments, they found that minority views were well represented among the Assembly's membership. The Rights Sub-Committee sent a questionnaire, drafted by Munshi, in March 1947 to minority community leaders to determine what political, economic; religious, cultural, and other safeguards they believed should be incorporated in the Constitution. In early April, using replies to the questionnaire and Munshi's draft rights as a model, the sub-committee framed a list of minority rights and included the list in its report to the Advisory Committee. On 17,18, and 19 April the Minorities Sub-Committee under the Chairmanship of H. C. Mookerjee considered the minorities provisions of the report and on 19 April sent its own report to the Advisory Committee, having made few changes of substance in the Rights Sub-Committee's recommendations.[63] The Advisory Committee incorporated several changes suggested by the sub-committee and the rights appear in the Constitution in essentially the same form as they appeared in the

---

[62] See Proceedings of the Advisory Committee meeting, 21 April 1947, Rao, *Select Documents*, II, and minutes of the special sub-committee meeting, 22 April 1947; *Munshi papers*. Also *Interim Report*, Clause II, *Reports, First Series*, p. 25. A later sub-committee of seven members headed by S. Varadachariar recommended the retention of the proviso because the wording of the body of the provision would prevent military conscription. *Report of the* Ad Hoc *Committee on Clause II of the Interim Report of the Advisory Committee*; Shiva Rao, *Select Documents*, II.

[63] For a list of the twenty-eight members of the Minorities Sub-Committee, see Appendix II.

Advisory Committee Interim Report.[64] A most important exception to this was the question of language, which it had been thought at first should be included in the Fundamental Rights. The Advisory Committee, however, omitted it from the Interim Report on rights, and the subject ultimately came to be treated in a separate part of the Constitution.[65]

The second type of protection for minority interests was the inclusion in the Constitution, but not within the Fundamental Rights, of provisions providing for adequate minority representation in legislatures and civil services, and other forms of special consideration. These provisions were a good deal more controversial than the issue of safeguards for religious and cultural rights, where there was little important difference of opinion. The matter of reservation, representation, electorates, etc., was close to the heart of the minorities and involved crucial questions of constitutional and social philosophy. The Minorities Sub-Committee took these matters up in July 1947, separately from rights issues, and they will be treated in later chapters.[66]

As has been said earlier, the corollary to the demand for the positive liberty of independence was adult suffrage, or universal franchise. Although some Assembly members had doubts about enfranchising the masses, in general the right to vote was considered fundamental. The Fundamental Rights Sub-Committee unanimously voted that there should be universal suffrage and secret and periodic elections.[67] The Advisory Committee, when considering this provision in the sub-committee's report, agreed with the principle, but recommended that these provisions find another place in the Constitution.[68] The Assembly adopted this suggestion and provided for adult suffrage in Article 326 of Part XV on elections.

Having made the Fundamental Rights justiciable, the sub-committee next included within the Rights the legal methods by which they could be secured. To do this they adopted the English device of prerogative writs, or directions in the form of writs. Munshi,

---

[64] *Reports, First Series*, p. 26.

[65] See Chapter 12.

[66] See especially Chapter 6, on the Legislature.

[67] Minutes of the meeting, 29 March 1947; *Prasad papers*, File 1-F/47.

[68] Advisory Committee, *Interim Report*, in *Reports, First Series*, p. 22. This was decided at the Advisory Committee meeting of 21 April 1947. See proceedings of the meeting in Advisory Committee, Shiva Rao, op. cit.

Ambedkar, and Ayyar strongly and actively favoured the inclusion of the right to constitutional remedies and the other members of the sub-committee agreed with them. Munshi in his draft constitution had included two clauses relating to prerogative writs; one laid down that every citizen had the right to move for a writ of right, and the second named these rights as habeas corpus, mandamus, prohibition, and certiorari.[69] Ayyar, although favouring the principle of writs, preferred supplanting them with directions in the nature of writs, for in England, he said, these directions had proved to be the more convenient device for the protection of rights.[70] The decision to include the prerogative writs in the Constitution was taken by the Rights Sub-Committee at its meeting on 29 March 1947. At this time Ayyar moved that all High Courts and the Supreme Court should have the power to issue writs of habeas corpus. This suggestion ultimately led to the inclusion in the constitution of a provision saying that Parliament could empower any court in India to issue these writs in the same manner as had previously been done by the Supreme Court and certain High Courts.[71]

Although ordinary remedies exist for the protection of rights, the prerogative writs have put teeth in the Fundamental Rights provisions. The writs have become popular for they are commonly believed

[69] Munshi also suggested the inclusion of a Writ of the Constitution; see Part XVIII of draft rights; *Munshi papers*. Munshi explained to sub-committee members that in England the prerogative writs were an extremely powerful device. He believed that they had been brought to India by Judge Impey who, when drafting its charter, gave the Calcutta Supreme Court the powers of the Kings Bench Division in England; Note of 17 March 1947, *Munshi papers*.

[70] In a note dated 17 March 1947, *Prasad papers*, File 1-F/47. Ayyar frequently reiterated that the rights must be enforceable.

[71] Article 32(3). Today, all High Courts and many inferior courts, in addition to the Supreme Court have this power, the High Courts drawing this authority specifically from Article 226 of the Constitution. At the time that the Fundamental Rights Sub-Committee framed these rights, only the High Courts of Madras, Calcutta, and Bombay were empowered to issue such writs.

The decision to allow Parliament to make such laws was taken after the Advisory Committee submitted its Interim Report on 23 April 1947. This report laid down that the Supreme Court could issue the four writs and that this did not prejudice any powers existing in lower courts to issue such writs. *Interim Report*, Clause 22(2). In the final version in the Constitution, a fifth writ, that of *quo warranto*, was added. Sir Tej Bahadur Sapru claimed some credit for the bestowing on the High Courts of this power, saying that he had made the suggestion to a friend in the Assembly, The *Hindustan Times*, 19 August 1947.

to be 'the corner-stone of freedom and liberty'.[72] The impetus that this belief had given towards the achievement of the social revolution has, one expects, been very great.

Sardar Patel, chairman of the Advisory Committee, presented the committee's Interim Report on Rights to the Assembly on 29 April 1947, the second day of the Third Session.[73] If any one thing characterized the Assembly's debate on this report, it was the favour with which it was received. There was heated debate over one or two principles and over many details, but if all the 189 amendments to the rights provisions had been accepted—and few of them were—it would have made little difference to the content of the rights, whose basic principles were not questioned.[74]

LIMITING THE RIGHTS

Although the rights to be included in the Constitution were considered to be fundamental and enforceable by the courts, they could not, Assembly members realized, be absolute. The question was to what extent and in what way the rights should be limited. The rights, it was decided, could best be limited by attaching provisos to the particular right and by providing for the rights to be suspended in certain circumstances. The device of written provisos to rights was one with

---

[72] Alexandrowicz, *Constitutional Developments in India*, p. 38. For a most illuminating description of the use of the writs up to 1955, see ibid., pp. 35–45.

The popularity of the writs would have been increased had N. G. Ranga's quixotically attractive suggestion been adopted. Ranga would have had the Constitution provide that 'those citizens who are so poor as not to be able to move the Supreme Court, should be enabled, under proper safeguards, of course, at the cost of the State to move the Supreme Court in regard to the exercise of any of these Fundamental Rights.' *CAD* III, 2, 389. The paper-work involved made this suggestion administratively impossible, and the cost would have been overwhelming.

[73] In his letter transmitting the report to the President of the Assembly, Patel wrote: 'We attach great importance to the constitution making these rights justiciable. The right of the citizen to be protected in certain matters is a special feature of the American Constitution and the recent democratic constitutions.' *Interim Report, Reports, First Series*, p. 21.

[74] For the texts of these amendments, see *Orders of the Day*, of the Constituent Assembly, Vol. I, Orders for 28 April 1947 through 2 May 1947, *INA*. For the debate on rights, see *CAD* III, 1–5.

which members of the Assembly were acquainted not only from foreign precedent but from Indian rights documents as well. In the Karachi Resolution, for example, the right of free speech was not to contravene law or morality. A. K. Ayyar explained to the Rights Sub-Committee that the U.S. Constitution laid down civil rights in a general fashion and the scope of the rights had been narrowed and expanded by judgements of the Supreme Court. Later constitutions, particularly those drafted after World War I, attempted to expand the rights and to define them more precisely with provisos by 'compendiously seeking to incorporate the effects of the American decisions'. The Assembly, he said, had to choose between the principles and techniques involved in the two systems.[75] The device of limiting the rights by suspending them, as we shall see, grew in favour as the Assembly proceeded with its work.

Additionally the rights had further to be qualified, Assembly, members found, in two directions. About the need to limit individual liberty by allowing state intervention for certain social purposes, there was little argument. The right to equality was not to prevent the state from making special laws protecting women and children.[76] And, as we have seen, the freedom of religion was not to prevent the state from passing social reform legislation.

About the need to circumscribe the basic freedoms of speech, assembly, association, and movement, however, there was no easy agreement. At issue was the always delicate and explosive question of freedom versus state security and, to a lesser extent, of liberty versus licence in individual behaviour. The two strongest advocates in the sub-committee of the limitation of rights were A, K. Ayyar and K. M. Munshi, and with one or two exceptions their fellow members supported them. At its meeting on 25 March 1947, the sub-committee drafted the 'rights to freedom' of the Constitution and voted to qualify each with the proviso that the exercise of these rights be subject to 'public order and morality'.[77] To the freedom of assembly, it attached the restrictive proviso of the Irish Constitution.[78] At this

---

[75] Ayyar, in a note to the Rights Sub-Committee, undated, but circulated to the sub- committee on 5 March 1947; *Law Ministry Archives*, File CA/43/Com/47.

[76] See Clause 4, *Interim Report,. Reports, First Series*, p. 23 and Article 15 of the *Constitution*.

[77] Minutes of the meeting; *Prasad papers*, File 1-F/47.

[78] Ibid. This proviso is Article 40(6) (i) and (ii) of the Irish Constitution and it allows prevention or control of meetings deemed a danger or a nuisance to the general

meeting the members also decided to limit the rights according to categories of persons. Certain rights were to extend to all persons in India; others were to extend only to Indian citizens. Freedom of association, for example, as well as assembly, the right to bear arms, and secrecy of correspondence were confined to citizens. The inviolability of the home and no deprivation of life or liberty without due process of law extended to all persons.[79] Within several days, however, all the rights to freedom were limited to citizens with the exception of the right to life and liberty, which continued to apply to aliens as well—a distinction carried into the Constitution. Several attempts were also made at this time, principally by K. M. Panikkar, the Princely States' representative on the sub-committee, to have the rights divided into two lists: one, embodying general rights, would apply to the Union, while a second list, consisting of relatively less consequential rights, would be enforceable only by the provinces and States. The sub-committee heartily disagreed with this proposition, believing that the rights must be uniformly applied.

A few days later, Munshi suggested that both the provincial governments and the central government be given the power to suspend these rights to freedom in times of emergency. The majority of the sub-committee balked at this, however, rejecting the idea as one which would make the rights illusory, and refused to incorporate the proviso in its draft rights of 3 April.[80] This decision so perturbed Ayyar that he wrote a letter to B. N. Rau, who, in his position as Constitutional Advisor, usually attended the meetings of the Rights Sub-Committee. 'The recent happenings in different parts of India have convinced me more than ever', wrote Ayyar, referring to unrest in Assam and Bengal, and to communal riots in the Punjab and NWFP, 'that all the Fundamental Rights guaranteed under the Constitution must be subject to public order, security, and safety,

---

public or in the vicinity of the Parliament buildings. Ayyar believed this unnecessary because 'public order and morality' applied to all important contingencies.

[79] Ibid. The right to bear arms was eliminated a few weeks later by the Advisory Committee, as was secrecy of correspondence; 'due process' also underwent changes. See below.

[80] Referred to in Ayyar note of 10 April 1947; *Munshi papers*, Advisory Committee File. Munshi had included in his Draft Rights, op. cit., a provision laying down that rights were exercisable subject to the needs of, among other things, national defence.

though such a provision may to some extent neutralize the effect of the rights guaranteed under the Constitution.'[81] Ayyar followed up this letter with a note to members of the sub-committee in which he suggested that if the rights were not made liable to suspension in times of emergency, the words 'security and defence of the state or national security' be added to the already existing proviso.[82]

Ayyar verbally presented his arguments to the sub-committee at its meeting of 14 April and again put the necessity of limiting rights in time of emergency. On this occasion the members took his advice—and Munshi's—and inserted in the introduction to the 'rights-of-freedom' clause a phrase making the rights subject to suspension in times of emergency when the security of the national or a provincial government was threatened.[83]

The full membership of the Advisory Committee met on 21 and 22 April to consider the reports of the two-sub-committees. The situation in Delhi and India was as turbulent and anxious as the mood of the meetings was calm and analytical. Although an important handful of the Princely States would be sending representatives to the third Assembly session, to begin in a week, the States problem was causing Nehru and his colleagues acute worry. The Nawab of Bhopal, chancellor of the Chamber of Princes, was digging in his heels against the tow of history as he tried to sabotage the entry of the States into the Assembly, and Sir C. P. Ramaswamy Aiyar, Dewan of the Princely State of Travancore, was beginning his intransigence. Within several days the Muslim League was due to hand down its final decision on joining the Assembly or quitting India. The Punjab had boiled intermittently for more than a month. Millions of rupees damage had been done, and 'ghastly, mutilated corpses' lay in drains and sewers.[84] Delhi had had more than a week of all-night curfew. Gandhi and Jinnah had published their joint appeal calling on the population to refrain from disorder and violence. Fundamental Rights were to be framed among the carnage of fundamental wrongs.

---

[81] Letter dated 4 April 1947; *Ayyar papers.*
[82] Note of 10 April; see footnote 80.
[83] Minutes of the meeting; *Munshi papers*, Advisory Committee file. Sec also Report of the Sub-Committee on Fundamental Rights, 16 April 1947.
[84] *The Hindustan Times*, 13 March 1947.

These events had their effect on the members of the Advisory Committee, although a much smaller one than might have been expected. The most important result was the removal of due process as a protection of individual liberty, which will be considered in detail subsequently. The committee also deleted from the sub-committee's list the right to bear arms. S. P. Mookerjee supported its retention, but Patel, the chairman and also the Home Minister, opposed this, saying that 'in the present state of our society (this) will be a dangerous thing'.[85] Opposing a suggestion that the matter be left to the units of the federation to decide, Ambedkar, reflecting the anxiety over the Princely States, said that the law must be applied uniformly to prevent one unit from arming its population against another.[86] Ayyar would have added to the proviso of the freedoms clause that the exercise of free speech, etc., must not 'promote class hatred'.[87] Others would have worded it 'class or communal hatred'. Rajgopalachari held this view and later moved such an amendment in the Assembly. The committee members rejected these recommendations for two reasons. In the first place it was claimed that the preaching of communal hatred could be prevented under the existing Penal Code. Second, the members contended, the preaching of class hatred could not be prohibited in the constitution because the courts might use such a provision to prevent speeches, common in a socialist age, calling for the removal of class distinctions and the reform of the social structure of society. The committee, however, added a clause to the proviso making punishable the utterance of seditious, obscene, and libellous matter.

The Advisory Committee also deleted two other rights from the list submitted by the sub-committee. These had nothing to do with the immediate situation and their omission apparently caused no stir at the time. But more than two years later, as we shall see, the rank and file of the Assembly would use these actions to prise from the leadership a liberalization of other rights. The clauses removed at the April meetings were those providing for secrecy of correspondence and for security of person and dwelling from unreasonable searches

---

[85] Proceedings of the meeting, 21 April 1947; Shiva Rao, op. cit., II.
[86] Ibid.
[87] Ibid.

and seizures and from searches without warrant. Panikkar, Ayyar, Pant, Bakshi Tek Chand, B. N. Rau, Rajgopalachari, and Patel led the attack on the clauses. Secrecy of correspondence might aid spies and criminals, they said, and it would impair the working of the Indian Evidence Act of 1892. As to the second provision, it was claimed that the need was met under the Criminal Procedure Code. Moreover, Ayyar argued, 'under Indian conditions of distance and lack of transport in the interior' there might be need for immediate search when a warrant was unobtainable. If the police had to produce a warrant, the whole case might be lost, said Patel; 'what you are suggesting is a dangerous thing'.[88] Such clauses will help no one but lawyers, said a lawyer and a former High Court judge, and, anyway, said another lawyer, India in 1947 is different from the United States in 1790.

In the Assembly a week later, the provisos received a mixed reception. Their supporters explained that they were to prevent the misuse of the rights by subversive groups and were nothing more than the embodiment of precedent as it had been established by case law. The more common view was that the provisos so circumscribed the rights that they no longer had any meaning. As one member put it, the rights had been framed 'from the point of view of a police constable'.[89] The resistance to the provisos so evident on the floor of the House during the first two days of the session came "to a head in the Congress Assembly Party meeting held on the evening of 29 April. That day had been one of 'Panic and Fear in Delhi City'; the streets and bazaars had been desolate, the coffee houses empty; wives had opened their doors slowly and fearfully before admitting their husbands returning from work.[90] Yet in the evening the members of the Assembly Party resolved to omit all the provisos to the rights to freedom, leaving them qualified only by the condition that the

---

[88] Ibid. See also Panikkar's minute of dissent to the Rights Sub-Committee Report, *Prasad papers*, File 1-F/47. For Ayyar's and Rau's views, see Ayyar letter to Patel, 18 April 1947, *Law Ministry Archives*, File CA/43/Com/47, and Ayyar's note on the subject, 17 April 1947, *Prasad papers*, File 1-F/47. Ayyar also opposed including a provision in the rights prohibiting excessive bail and cruel and unusual punishments; in his note cited above.

[89] *CAD* III, 2, 384; Somnath Lahiri. Pandit Kunzru felt the same way, see ibid., p. 380ff.

[90] From reports in *The Hindustan Times*, 30 April 1947.

rights be exercised subject to public order and morality and subject to exception in grave emergency.[91]

The Drafting Committee during its deliberations of late 1947 and 1948 turned its back on the will of the Assembly and revived the provisos in an even more intricate form, making the rights of free speech, assembly, association, movement, etc., subject to public order, morality, health, decency, and public interest. Furthermore, in the case of speech, the utterance must not be seditious, slanderous, or undermine the authority of the state.[92] The mechanism for suspending all the fundamental rights in emergencies had also been expanded. According to the Emergency Provisions in Part XI of the Draft Constitution, executive action could be taken even in contravention of the rights to freedom of Article 13, and the President of the Republic was allowed to suspend the right to constitutional remedies both during the emergency and for an additional period of six months.[93]

These changes, and the arbitrary manner of their making, aroused the ire of the Assembly, and the members strongly attacked the provisos during the debate on the Draft Constitution in the autumn of 1948. In reply Ambedkar gave the classic defence of the provisos. The rights of the American Constitution are not absolute, he said: 'In support of every exception to the Fundamental Rights set out in the Draft Constitution, one can refer to at least one judgement of the U.S. Supreme Court.' The purpose of the provisos, Ambedkar continued, was to prevent endless litigation and the Supreme Court having to rescue Parliament. The provisos permit the state 'directly to impose limitations on the Fundamental Rights. There is really no difference in the result,' he said.[94] But the attack persisted. The

---

[91] Ibid. The Assembly consolidated into one other proviso several conditions made on the rights, particularly those regarding residence and acquisition of property, in the interests of the Adibasis, the Scheduled Tribes. For Jaipal Singh's strong advocacy of these protections for Adibasis, see proceedings of the Advisory Committee, 21 April 1947, op. cit.

[92] Article 13 of the *Draft Constitution*.

[93] Articles 279 and 280 of the *Draft Constitution*. The Drafting Committee (in a footnote, *Draft*, p. 132) explicitly denied this power to provincial governments and governors thereof. As all emergency powers were later taken from provincial governors and vested in the Union (see Chapter 8 below), this action lost its meaning.

[94] *CAD* VII, 1, 40–41. See also *CAD* VII 2, 3, and 4, and especially VII, 17 and 18. Ayyar also held this view. In a letter to the editor of the *Indian Express*

rank and file of the Assembly were not to be diddled again. Thakur Das Bhargava led the final assault, moving an amendment that would put a 'soul' back in Article 13 by inserting the word 'reasonable' before 'restrictions' in the various provisos.[95] The pressure on the floor and in the Assembly Party had been so great that the leadership capitulated. The Oligarchy agreed to sanction the amendment, and when Bhargava moved it, Ambedkar—chairman of the Drafting Committee—accepted it, and the Assembly adopted it.[96] Liberty had scored a triumph over bureaucracy's desire for maximum security. Thus the Constitution placed a major restriction on the scope of legislative competence, for the judges may review the, reasonableness of restrictions placed upon rights and thus have 'mutatis mutandis the same power in relation to Article 19 (of the Constitution, Article 13 of the Draft) which American judges enjoy generally under the due-process-of-law clause'.[97]

For some unexplained reason, the qualifying of the restrictions in the provisos by the word 'reasonable' was not done in the case of freedom of speech. This oversight—if such it was—was remedied a year later when the first amendment to the Constitution laid down that the right to freedom of speech should not prevent, among other things, 'the State from making any law, insofar as such law imposes reasonable restrictions on the exercise of the right by the said sub-clause in the interests of the security of the State, friendly relations with foreign States, public order', etc.[98]

(Madras), dated 28 July J948, he explained that: 'The Draft Constitution, instead of leaving it to the Courts to read the necessary limitations and exceptions (to the rights) seeks to express in a compendious form the limitations and exceptions.' *Ayyar papers.* See also *The Indian Constitution* by B. N. Rau, reprinted from *The Hindu* of 15 August 1948 in Rau, *India's Constitution*, pp. 363–64.

[95] *CAD* VII, 17, 735–40; Thakur Das Bhargava.

[96] The following day the Assembly adopted a reworded version to the proviso to the freedom of speech. In the new form, the word 'sedition' was omitted, although utterances still should not endanger the security of, or tend towards the overthrow of, the state. This change was apparently made largely on Munshi's insistence (see ibid., pp. 730–2) that sedition had too general a meaning.

[97] Alexandrawicz, op. cit., p. 46.

[98] *The Constitution (First Amendment) Act* 1951, para. 3(a). This amendment to the Constitution was not a result of this omission; the amendment stemmed

The Assembly's next task, so far as the Fundamental Rights were concerned, was to consider again limiting the rights by suspending them in times of emergency. The debate on the two relevant articles of the Draft Constitution took place in August 1949 at the time of the major debate on the Emergency Provisions. The first of the two provisions, which laid down that while a Proclamation of Emergency was in force, nothing in the seven-freedoms article should restrict state action, was passed with a minor change, only three voices raised in dissent.[99] To the critics, whose general point was that sufficient limitations on the rights already existed, Ambedkar replied that the Article did not suspend the rights; it only made certain state actions permissible.[100]

The Assembly's reaction to article 280, which would have allowed the right to constitutional remedies (including habeas corpus) to be suspended not only during the period of emergency, but for six months thereafter, was both sharp and effective. The objections had built up to such a point that, within an hour of the debate being opened, Ambedkar asked that the article be held over pending further consideration by the Drafting Committee. When the article was reintroduced sixteen days later, it had been greatly modified in response to the various criticisms. The new version did not allow the blanket suspension of the right to constitutional remedies, but only the suspension of recourse to the courts for the enforcement of any right specifically named in a presidential order issued under a Proclamation of Emergency. Furthermore, such an order should last only during the declared period of emergency, or for a shorter time; it could apply to parts as well as to the whole of the country; and every presidential order made under the article must be laid 'as soon as may be' before Parliament.[101] The new version appears

---

from other causes to do with court interpretations of the freedom of speech clause. For a detailed account of this, see Alexandrowicz, op. cit., pp. 47–49. For an illuminating discussion of the Fundamental Rights and their provisos, see Alexandrowicz, pp. 46–64 and Chapter 3.

[99] Article 279 of the *Draft Constitution*. The change (see Article 358 of the *Constitution*) established that if any law repugnant to the freedoms of Article 19 (Draft 13) were passed during the Emergency, the law should to the extent of this repugnance be void when the Proclamation of Emergency ceased to operate.

[100] *CAD* IX, 5, 180–6, especially 185.

[101] Article 359 of the *Constitution*.

to have had the tacit support of some of its earlier critics,[102] but it remained unpopular with the rank and file despite the assurances of A. K. Ayyar that the President would not act 'in a spirit of vandalism' and the arguments of Ambedkar and others that the whole article had its source, if not its equivalent, in the power of the American Congress to suspend the right of habeas corpus, and in the American President's interim right to take such action.[103] This provision continues to be disliked and feared a-decade-and-a-half later. There is, however, little evidence that under it the Government has worked injustice on the people of India.

THE ASSEMBLY AND THE DIRECTIVE PRINCIPLES

The Directive Principles of State Policy set forth the humanitarian socialist precepts that were, and are, the aims of the Indian social revolution. With these precepts, few if any Assembly members disagreed. Amid the general acclaim for the Principles, which were the offspring of the Objectives Resolution, almost the only critical voices were those of members who believed that the provisions of the Directives should be justiciable if they were to be adequate to their task, and those of a few members who had a quarrel with a particular provision within the Principles. T. T. Krishnamachari found few supporters for his colourful description of the Directive Principles as 'a veritable dustbin of sentiment . . . sufficiently resilient as to permit any individual of this House to ride his hobby horse into it'.[104]

The roots of the Directive Principles may be traced back to the 1931 Karachi Resolution, or farther, and to the two streams of socialist and nationalist sentiment in India that had been flowing ever faster since the late twenties. It is not unreasonable to conjecture also that the placing on the government of a major responsibility for the welfare of the mass of Indians had an even deeper grounding in Indian

[102] For the debate on this provision, see *CAD* IX, 5, 186–96, and *CAD* IX, 14, 523–4. See particularly the speech of H. N. Kunzru (*CAD* IX, 5, 192–93) in relation to the final version.

[103] *CAD* IX, 14, 549. For a discussion of this provision, see Alexandrowicz, op. cit., pp. 29–30.

[104] *CAD* VII, 12, 583. Some two months after giving this speech, Krishnamachari became a member of the Drafting Committee and his criticisms of the Draft's provisions became much less barbed.

history. Under a petty ruler, a Mogul emperor, or the British Raj, responsibility for both initiation and execution of efforts to improve the lot of the people had lain with the government. What the government did not do, or see done, usually was not done. The masses had, generally speaking, looked to the ruler for dispensations both evil and good. Heir to this tradition, Assembly members believed that the impetus for bringing about the social revolution continued to rest with the government.

There were also many contemporary instances of the same process. Assembly members, and especially the select group in the Fundamental Rights Sub-Committee, knew that in the United States it had become constitutional practice for the federal and state governments to play an ever increasing role in the nation's social and economic life. Their knowledge of the constitutions of Europe—particularly those of Germany and East Europe—framed after the First World War could only have shown them that 'the most characteristic feature of the new constitutions was the recognition of the fact that one of the chief functions of the State must be to secure the social well-being of the citizens and the industrial 'prosperity of the nation.'[105]

Equally, the Congress's long-standing affinity with the Irish nationalist[106] movement made the example of constitutional socialism expressed in the Irish Directive Principles of Social Policy especially attractive to a wide range of Assembly members. The ideal of secular socialism in the European style also received strong support, of course, from members of the small, but influential, Congress Socialist Party. The Hindu outlook and the Gandhian experience would ultimately make themselves felt in the Assembly as we shall see, and would affect the content of the Directive Principles, but at no time did the Assembly attempt to base its socialist aims upon, or to draft the Directive Principles in terms of, a religious ethic

---

[105] Agnes Headlam-Morley, *The New Democratic Constitutions of Europe*, p. 264.

[106] The Irish-Congress relationship extended back to the late nineteenth century. Discussing the question of Fundamental Rights, the authors of the Nehru Report spoke of Ireland as 'the only country where the conditions obtaining before the treaty were the nearest approach to those we have in India'. The first concern of the Irish and the Indians, the Nehru Report continued, was 'to secure the Fundamental Rights that have been denied to then'. *Nehru Report*, op. cit, p. 89.

exhumed from an almost mythical past. Nehru and other Assembly members at times referred to the ancient roots of Indian socialism, but these allusions were made more for the sake of form than from historical conviction.[107]

The framing of the Directive Principles in the Rights Sub-Committee proved the wide acceptance of both the device of precepts, and if the effectiveness of the device itself was questioned, of the sentiments they expressed. The most weighty support came from B. N. Rau and Ayyar, and secondly from Ambedkar and K. T. Shah— whose suggestions proved them to be thoroughly liberal in outlook. Of the four, Rau was the most influential. He approached the question of fundamental rights, unlike Sapru, Ayyar, and many other British-trained lawyers, with a certain scepticism. The difficulty of defining negative rights and then of effectively protecting them led him to skirt this 'controversial ground',[108] and instead to prefer 'to set out the positive rights merely as moral precepts, for the authorities concerned and to bar the jurisdiction of the ordinary courts.. '.[109] This belief, in turn, led to Rau's acknowledged emulation in his *Constitutional Precedents* of the Irish example of distinguishing between justiciable and non-justiciable rights, and to his putting the emphasis on precepts rather than on justiciable rights. His *Precedents*, during the actual drafting of the Directive Principles, supplied the members of the sub-committee with at least five of the original twelve provisions and the preamble of the Principles.[110]

In later months Rau publicly defended the Directives: '. . . Many modern constitutions do contain moral precepts of this kind', he wrote in *The Hindu* in August 1948, 'nor can it be denied that

[107] There are many persons in India, however, who do choose to root Indian socialism in a Hindu base. Of several books on the subject, two are: A. R. Desai, *Social Background of Indian Nationalism*, and a recent volume, Sampurnanand, *Indian Socialism*.

[108] Rau, *Constitutional Precedents, Third Series*, p. 22.

[109] Ibid., p. 11. See pp. 10–24. The major portions of this work appears in Rau, *India's Constitution*, op.-cit., Chapter 13.

[110] Compare ibid., pp. 21–22 with the text of the Directive Principles as they were first, presented to the Assembly in August 1947; *Supplementary Report of the Advisory Committee on Fundamental Rights, Reports, Second Series*, pp. 48-49. In his *Precedents, Third Series*, Rau makes the origin of some of these provisions clear; see pp. 21–23.

they may have an educative value.'[111] He would also have lifted the Principles above the level of precepts. It may be occasionally necessary, he believed, for the state to invade private rights in the discharge of one of its fundamental duties—e.g., to raise the nation's standard of health, of living, etc. But the Fundamental Rights being justiciable and the Directive Principles being without legal force, the private right may over-ride the public weal. It is thus a matter for careful consideration, he continued, whether 'the Constitution might not expressly provide that no law made and no action taken by the state in the discharge of its duties under Chapter III of Part III (the Directive Principles) shall be invalid merely by reason of its contravening the provisions of Chapter II (the Fundamental Rights).'[112]

Munshi, Ambedkar, and Shah would have gone even farther than Rau. They would have made the Directive Principles, or an even more rigorous social programme, justiciable. They disliked mere precepts and in the end, supported them in the belief that half a loaf was better than none. Munshi had included in his draft list of rights 'Rights of Workers' and 'Social Rights', which included provisions protecting women and children and guaranteeing the right to work, a decent wage, and a decent standard of living. In his letter transmitting the list to the Assembly secretariat, he noted that India had special social problems because of the gap between socialist thinkers and the feudalism of some areas.[113] Later, Munshi came out strongly in favour of the Principles: 'Even the non-justiciable rights have to be announced', he wrote, 'in order to form the basis of protest against arbitrary legislation. They are a body of doctrines to which public opinion can rally.'[114]

Ambedkar submitted to the Assembly a lengthy (and one must add, fascinatingly detailed) list of fundamental rights that included the rights proper plus provisions regarding minorities, particularly the Scheduled Castes, and a social scheme to come into force in

---

[111] Reprinted in Rau, *India's Constitution*, pp. 364–5.

[112] Rau, *Notes on Certain Clauses* (of his Draft Constitution of 7 October 1947); Shiva Rao, op.cit., II.

[113] Munshi to H. V. R. Iengar, secretary of the Assembly, 15 March 1947; *Law Ministry Archives*, File CA/43/Com/47. The list of rights is that of 15 March 1947, op. cit.

[114] Munshi, *Notes on a Constitution*, undated, but possibly written late in 1947, *Munshi papers*.

ten years. This scheme provided, among other things, that all key industries should be owned and operated by the state, that all land should be nationalized and agriculture become a state industry—with organized plots to be formed by villagers. Insurance should be a state monoply and every adult Indian should be compelled to have life insurance—an idea akin to American Social Security.[115] His social scheme, as well as many other provisions in his programme, was rejected on several occasions in the Assembly on the ground that such provisions should be left to legislation and not be embodied in the Constitution.[116] From this position Ambedkar retreated to the support of the Directive Principles. The party in power, he said, would certainly 'have to answer for them before the electorate at election time'.[117]

K. T. Shah, a graduate of the London School of Economics, one time member of Gray's Inn, and a Bombay advocate since 1914, was perhaps the most doctrinaire socialist in the Constituent Assembly. He supported Ambedkar in the above instance, believing also that there must be a specified time limit within which all the Directive Principles must be made justiciable. Otherwise they would be mere 'pious wishes' and so much window dressing for the social revolution.[118] Shah also made it plain many times in the Assembly that he thought that all natural resources should be the state's property, as well as key industries and other aspects of the economy.

---

[115] Ambedkar, *States and Minorities*, Section II, Clause 4. Ambedkar's views here show a close relationship to those of T. H. Green. Ambedkar believed that his draft provisions did not go beyond the proper scope of fundamental rights because of the connection between 'liberty and the shape and form of the economic structure'. Many persons have to relinquish their fundamental rights to exist, he said. 'In other words, what is called liberty from the control of the State is another name for the dictatorship of the private employer.' See ibid., Explanatory Note, pp. 31–32.

[116] See correspondence with Kripalani,Patel, and the Steering Committee of the Assembly, plus minutes of Steering Committee meeting 28 April, 1947; *Prasad papers*, File 2-S/48.

[117] *CAD* VII, 1, 41–42.

[118] Shah's minute, dated 20 April 1947. *Prasad papers*, File 1-F/47. Also his letter to the sub-committee of 10 April; 1947; Shiva Rao, op. cit, II. For Shah's support of Ambedkar, see his letter to Prasad, 23 April 1947; *Prasad papers*, File 2-S/48. For Shah's scheme for an economic council to be provided for in the Constitution, see Rau, *India's Constitution*, p. 88.

Alladi Krishnaswami Ayyar held more sceptical views on the Directive Principles. In a note to the Rights Sub-Committee he doubted the effectiveness of such precepts in a federal constitution; yet he supported their inclusion in the Constitution.[119] His position appeared to change somewhat as a result of Partition and as the strongly centralized federalism of the Constitution emerged. By November 1948 he could tell Assembly members critical of the lack of socialism in the Draft Constitution that the legislatures of the nation could evolve such an order because it was 'idle to suggest' that any freely elected legislature would ignore the sense of the Directive Principles.[120]

The initial approach of Rights Sub-Committee members, perhaps even more than Rau and others, was to make no distinction between positive obligations and negative liberties. Since both had long been part of the national demand, why should they now be separated? As the members drafted the negative rights, however, it became evident that some were more susceptible to court enforcement than others, and members began talking of a section of non-justiciable rights. The right to free primary education, for example, was first included among the justiciable rights and then taken out again. The right of equality before the law was taken from the Principles and made justiciable.

At the meeting on 30 March 1947, the sub-committee turned its full attention to the positive rights. Using Rau's draft, his collection of precedents,[121] and particularly the example of the Irish Constitution, the members adopted in rapid succession provisions laying down that the state should promote social, economic, and political justice; that the state should try to secure an adequate livelihood for all citizens and should control the nation's economy and material resources in the common interest; that equal pay should be given for equal work; and a variety of like provisions.[122]

[119] Ayyar, note for the Rights Sub-Committee, dated 24 or 25 March 1947; *Ayyar papers.*

[120] *CAD*, VII, 4, 336.

[121] Rau, *Precedents*, Third Series, op. cit, pp. 21–22. The members also drafted provisions based on Munshi's draft fundamental rights and based on articles in Lauterpacht's 'International Bill of Rights of Man'. See minutes of the meeting; *Prasad papers*, File 1-F/47.

[122] The provisions adopted were those later listed as Clauses 2–7 of the *Supplementary Report on Rights, Reports, Second Series*, p. 48. See minutes of the meeting, op. cit.

The members also drafted a clause stipulating that marriage should be based on mutual consent, but this was later dropped.[123]

At the next day's meeting, the sub-committee decided to introduce the Directive Principles of Social Policy, as they were then called, with a preamble explaining that they were for the general guidance of the government and were not cognizable in any court. The break with the Fundamental Rights had been made. The members went on to adopt provisions based on Rau's draft to the effect that the state should raise the level of nutrition and the standard of living of the people, and promote international peace and just dealings between nations.[124] Certain changes and counter-changes were made during the next several weeks, but, in general, the first stage of drafting the Directive Principles was over.

The framing of the provision regarding a uniform civil code provides an interesting aside to the sub-committee's work. In India in 1947, despite the inroads on personal law during the British period, many Indians lived their lives untouched by secular law, whether civil or criminal. The idea of a uniform civil code, therefore, struck at the heart of custom and orthodoxy, Hindu, Muslim, and Sikh. During the days when the Principles were to be justiciable, Minoo Masani moved in a sub-committee meeting that it was the state's responsibility to establish a uniform code, in order to get rid of 'these water-tight compartments', as he called them.[125] The members voted against the recommendation five to four on the ground that it was beyond the sub-committee's competence.[126] Yet two days later the members approved the inclusion of the provision, but only after it had been decided to create a non-justiciable section of the rights where the clause could be put. The reason behind these actions was not, as it might at first appear, the wish to avoid a clash with Hindu orthodoxy, but a sensitivity, particularly on Nehru's part, to the fears of 'the Muslims and the Sikhs. Had the provision been

---

[123] A provision borrowed from the Japanese Constitution (Art. XXIV) of 1946, ibid.

[124] Clauses 9, 10, and 12 of the *Supplementary Report*.

[125] Minutes of the meeting, 28 April 1947; *Prasad papers*, File 1-F/47. See also Masani's minute of dissent to the sub-committee's draft rights, undated; ibid.

[126] Voting for the justiciable code were Masani, Mrs. Mehta, Amrit Kaur, and Ambedkar; against were Kripalani, Daulatram, Shah, Munshi, and Ayyar. Minutes of the meeting, 30 March 1947; ibid.

in the rights, it would have been justiciable and perforce applicable equally to all communities. In the Principles, action could be taken at the will of Parliament in regard to one community—as happened with the Hindu Code Bill a few years later. That the sub-committee refused to make the clause justiciable largely to calm Muslim fears can be seen in a letter written to Patel, as chairman of the Advisory Committee, in late July 1947 by Masani and Amrit Kaur and Mrs. Mehta, who had supported Masani's initiative the previous March. The letter recalled the earlier rejection of their efforts and went on, 'In view of the changes that have taken place since (meaning, certainly, Partition) and the keen desire that is now felt for a more homogenous and closely knit Indian nation' we wish the Advisory Committee again to consider the matter when it meets on 28 July.[127] Their efforts were unsuccessful, however, and the clause remained one of the Directive Principles.

The second stage in the framing of the Principles took place on the Assembly floor in November and December 1948 during the debate on the Draft Constitution. An earlier debate—held in August 1947 on the occasion of Patel's presentation of the Advisory Committee's Supplementary Report—was of little consequence.[128]

The Assembly's reaction to the draft Principles revealed two major currents of opinion: one that the Directives did not go far enough towards establishing a socialist state, and the other that they should have placed greater emphasis on certain institutions and principles central to Indian practice and to Hindu thought, particularly those glorified by Gandhi's teaching. These two reactions became increasingly evident from March 1948 onward as amendments to the Draft Constitution began to come into the Assembly Secretariat; by November 1948 there were scores of amendments to the Principles.[129]

The majority of the amendments would have encouraged the development of village life and economy and the panchayat system of village organization, as we have seen. Some Assembly members sought to make the promotion of cottage industry a government

---

[127] Letter dated 25 July 1947; *Law Ministry Archives*, File CA/24/Com/47-III.

[128] See *CAD* V, 11, 333–75. The wording of the Directive Principles in the Draft Constitution was virtually that of the Supplementary Report.

[129] For the texts of these amendments, see *Amendment Book* I, pp. 87–106.

responsibility and to make it incumbent upon the government to prevent the slaughter of cattle and to improve the methods of animal husbandry and agriculture. A further provision demanded by this same group was prohibition of harmful drugs and intoxicating drinks—a provision founded largely on Gandhian puritanism and directed primarily towards socially and physically depressed industrial workers.

Gandhi had made cottage industries, particularly home spinning, for psychological if not for economic reasons, a central part of the independence movement. Gandhi's economic aims were two: to attack village poverty and to provide an alternative supply of textiles to the hated foreign cloth. In the Assembly there was, as even Ambedkar admitted, 'a considerable amount of feeling'[130] in favour of government encouragement for cottage industries, and this sentiment forced him, as the spokesman of the Drafting Committee, to accept an amendment placing 'the promotion of cottage industries' in the Directive Principles.[131] The motives of the Assembly members supporting the provision may be described as more romantic than clear-eyed, more well-intentioned than practical. And for good or ill, the Cottage industries programme since 1950 has received less support from the federal and state governments than others named in the Principles—less than, for example, the programme to build up panchayats and to improve agriculture.

The provision pertaining to the improvement of agricultural and animal husbandry techniques and the prohibition of cow slaughter was added to the Directive Principles for a mixture of reasons. The need to improve agriculture was obvious, and cattle generally, the cow particularly, held a place of special reverence in Hindu thought. The religious aspect of cow protection had also long-standing political ramifications. Indian Muslims killed cows both for food and as part of religious ceremonies.[132] Hindus, of course, resented this; cow protection societies had existed for at least sixty years prior to the Assembly, and a religious difference had become a major political

---

[130] *CAD* VII, 2, 535.

[131] See Article 43 of the *Constitution*. The amendment that Ambedkar accepted was moved by I. A. R. Chettiyar; see ibid, p. 532.

[132] Hindus slaughtered cattle, too, of course, and in vastly greater numbers than did Muslims—a fact acknowledged in the Assembly by a supporter of the ban on cow-killing, Thakur Das Bhargava. See *CAD* VII, 12, 578–80.

cause espoused by genuine believers and unscrupulous opportunists alike, for reasons both honourable and otherwise. In the days of the British Raj, many Hindu revivalists had promised themselves that with independence cow killing would stop. Those of this persuasion in the Assembly believed that the time for action was ripe and, as a result of agreement in the Congress Assembly Party meeting,[133] the measure passed without opposition. No one would have quarrelled with the need to modernize agriculture, but many may have found the reference to cow-killing distasteful. There is good evidence that Nehru did.[134] Generally speaking, however, Hindu feeling ran high on the subject, and one may surmise that those who opposed the anti-cow-killing cause bent with the wind, believing the issue not sufficiently important to warrant a firm stand against it. As various provisions of the Irish Constitution show that Ireland is a Roman Catholic nation, so Article 48 shows that Hindu sentiment predominated in the Constituent Assembly.

With prohibition it was a different matter. Hindus relying on Gandhi's teaching and Muslims deriving their authority from the Koran could all inveigh against the evils of drink. Moreover, drinking had never been common among the Indian middle classes. The arguments for prohibition were not wholly unreasonable. In many industrial areas (the steel mills of Bihar and Bengal, for example) and especially in Harijan areas, depressed, underfed workers sought solace in liquor to the great detriment of their health. The advocates of prohibition had both social and doctrinal strings to their bow, and they were supported by the Congress's decade-old official dedication to the cause of prohibition.[135] Opposition to this conservative outlook came from the more liberal elements in the Assembly, who cited the United States' disastrous experience, and particularly from members of provincial governments, who knew to what good use the huge income from liquor excise could be put.[136] The Assembly,

---

[133] *CAD* VII, 12, 568.

[134] See Nehru's letter to Prasad 7 August 1947; *Prasad papers*, File, Important Letters from Various Files.

[135] In 1937, when the Congress ministries assumed office, the party high command ordered them to enforce prohibition within three years regardless of the loss of revenue. R. Coupland, *The Indian Problem*, Vol. II, p. 141.

[136] In the fiscal year 1936–7, excise duties on liquor and drugs yielded an average of 17 per cent, of provincial income (26 per cent, in Bombay, 25 per cent,

however, adopted a revised version of the amendment moved by a Muslim and a Hindu.[137] The prohibition of liquor and harmful drugs (e.g. opium) became a fundamental principle of governance, and today the sale of alcoholic drinks is in varying degrees restricted in nearly every state in India.

The second major criticism, as has been said, of the draft Principles when they were introduced in the Assembly was that they did not go far enough in encouraging a socialist society. The several dozen amendments submitted in this vein called for the nationalization of various industries, and phrases such as 'socialist order' and 'socialist economy' were common. One amendment read that 'the profit motive in production (should be) entirely eliminated in due course of time'.[138] Another was aimed at giving 'the workers in the fields and factories effective control of the administrative machinery of the State'.[139] Most of these amendments were voted down in Assembly Party meetings or were withdrawn by their initiators. Those substantive amendments reaching the Assembly floor were not adopted because the majority of members held with the Oligarchy that the Principles should be kept general, leaving 'enough room for people of different ways of thinking' to reach the goal of economic democracy.[140]

---

in Madras, and 13 per cent, in U.P.); the strict enforcement of prohibition in Bombay cost that government nearly 200 lakhs of rupees—about £1,500,000. Ibid. Despite this, B. G. Kher, the prime minister of Bombay, supported prohibition in the Assembly, *CAD* VII, 12, 561ff.

[137] K. S. Karimuddin and M. Tyagi. See *CAD* VII, 9, 500ff, and *CAD* VII, 10 and 12.

[138] Amendment 894, submitted by V, D. Tripathi, *Amendment Book* I, p. 92.

[139] Amendment 866, submitted by A. R. Shastri, ibid., p. 90.

[140] *CAD* VII, 9, 494–5; Ambedkar.

4

Fundamental Rights—II
Social Reform and State Security Versus 'Due Process'

THE classic statement of the right to 'due process' is that of the Fifth Amendment of the American Constitution:' . . . nor shall any person . . . be deprived of life, liberty, or property without due process of law; nor shall private property be taken for public use without just compensation.' Since 1787 every people who have intended to give themselves a written constitution have had to decide what are the citizen's rights to life, liberty, and property, and within the context of their own aims and experience in what way and to what degree these rights are to be limited for the good of society as a whole. India was no exception to this. The Constituent Assembly's treatment of the due process issue is worthy of detailed study for it shows how the members approached the conflict between, on the one hand, the principles of abstract justice and the desire of all good men to be just and fair, and on the other hand, the need to solve the pressing problems of social reform and state security (stability being a pre-requisite to reform) as a means to advance the common good.

Although many Assembly members first approached the due process issue as if it were one simple issue, experience in constitution making soon taught them that it was intimately connected with two very important problems: with the expropriation of property, and compensation for it, and with preventive detention. It took Assembly, members nearly three years to decide how to treat these matters in the Constitution.

When the Fundamental Rights Sub-Committee took up the question of due process, it voted five to two, with two abstentions, to include the clause in its classic form.[1] Two days later the members reinforced their earlier decision, providing that no private property could be acquired for public use unless the law called 'for the payment, according to principles previously determined, of just compensation for the property acquired'.[2] In this form the matter went to the Advisory Committee.

On 21 April the Advisory Committee as a whole met and considered the due process clause. The importance of the meeting lay as much in its effect on the attitudes of members as in the decision reached.[3] Early in the discussion Pandit Pant gave his opinion that due process would be understood only in a procedural sense. But Ayyar quickly disillusioned him, to be subjected to a return fire of questions from Pant. Could a legislature under the clause empower the Executive to detain a person for six months without trial, Pant asked. Could a legislature pass a law acquiring property for public purposes at ten times the rental value when the market value was thirty times the rental? Could a tenant-at-will be ejected from his holding? Alladi answered. In the first place, he said, the aim of due process is to limit legislative power. He recognized that the clause might endanger property, tenancy, and other legislation, and that much depended on the ideas and interpretations of judges. Yet the Fundamental Rights Sub-committee had taken all this into consideration and had still decided to retain the clause.[4] 'Personally, I am for the retention of the clause,' he said. He told Pant that the acquisition of property in his example might not be 'due process' because the compensation was so small, nor was it certain that tenants could be ejected. Rajagopalachari told Pant that detention without trial could not take place under due process.

What you are saying comes to this, then, said Pant: that the future of the country will be determined 'not by the collective wisdom of

[1] Minutes of the meeting, 26 March 1947; *Prasad papers,* File 1-F/47.

[2] Minutes of the meeting, 28 March 1947; ibid.

[3] All citations from this meeting have been taken from the proceedings in Shiva Rao, op. cit., II.

[4] Ayyar had expressed these views verbally to the sub-committee at the meeting of 25 March, and in a note, undated but probably written in mid-April; see *Prasad papers,* File 1-F/47.

the representatives of the people but by the fiats of those elevated to the Judiciary'. We cannot be subject to varying court judgements, to the whims and vagaries of judges. And, he continued, if we can't put mischief makers in jail 'there is no end to these communal disorders.' He declaimed: 'To fetter the discretion of the Legislature would lead to anarchy.'

Ambedkar and Munshi opposed Pant's view. Ambedkar said he could see Pant's point, but he didn't agree that the leader of the oppo-sition in the United Provinces (where Pant was premier) could be jailed for six months without trial. There is no need to give *carte blanche* to the government to detain with a 'facile provision', he said. The Fundamental Rights, including habeas corpus, could be sus-pended in an emergency, said Ambedkar, and this was enough basis for detention. As to property and tenancy legislation, the latter would not be endangered by due process and a special proviso could keep property legislation out of the courts. Munshi replied to Pant that no provision prohibiting detention had been put in the clause so as not to fetter government action. But, he said, due process prevented leg-islative extravagance, and there should be no fear that judges would replace the legislatures.[5]

At this point Panikkar suggested that life and liberty should be separated from property in the rights. The courts should guard our life and liberty, he said, and there should be no detention. But, 'so far as property is concerned, it must be subjected to legislation'.[6] Patel, who had said little previously, interrupted here, arguing that they must deal with property separately. And a few minutes later he made a motion to this effect. The committee adopted this course—with Pant's parting shot that he didn't agree but would keep quiet. The clause in the committee's Interim Report to the Assembly read that

[5] In their respective lists of draft rights, op. cit., Munshi and Ambedkar had both included due process as a protection for life, liberty, and property.

[6] Panikkar had expressed the view to the Rights Sub-Committee that:' . . . the Judiciary should be the guardian, the upholders, and the champion of the rights of the individual, (but) it should not be entrusted with powers restricting the legislative powers of the Union except to the barest extent possible and solely for the purpose of resisting the encroachments of the State on the liberty of the individual.' Minute of dissent to the Rights Sub-Committee Report, dated April (about mid-month) 1947; *Prasad papers,* File 1-F/47. Panikkar was the States' representative on the sub-committee and joined it on 14 April, 1947.

no person could be deprived of life or liberty without due process of law. A few days later the Assembly adopted the provision without debate.[7] Reference to property had been made elsewhere.

The committee's decision had no clear relation to Indian constitutional precedent. Neither the Nehru Report nor the Karachi Resolution had used the wording of due process, although the phrases employed in them could be interpreted to mean something akin to it.[8] The 1935 Government of India Act had made no mention of personal liberty, but did provide that no person could be deprived of his property except by authority of law and that no legislature could authorize the compulsory acquisition of property unless the law provided for the payment of compensation and either fixed the amount of compensation or the principles on which it was to be paid.[9] The rights drafted by the Congress Experts Committee during the summer of 1946 had also omitted reference to due process and personal liberty, saying only that property could not be taken from its owner without 'compensation prescribed by law'.[10]

B. N. Rau's advice to the Assembly and the committees had been to dispense with due process altogether. In his Precedents series he had explained that due process in the Fifth and Fourteenth Amendments to the American Constitution had been conceived as a limitation on legal procedure, but came to apply to substantive questions as well. He warned the Assembly that:

> The Courts, manned by an irremovable Judiciary not so sensitive to public needs in the social or economic sphere as the representatives of a periodically elected legislature, will, in effect, have a veto on legislation exercisable at any time and at the instance of any litigant.[11]

After the Fundamental Rights Sub-Committee had included the due process clause in its report to the Advisory Committee, Rau

---

[7] *CAD* III, 3, 468. For the text of the provision at this stage, see *Interim Report,* Clause 9; *Reports, First Series,* p. 25.

[8] Both the Nehru Report and the Karachi Resolution used the phrase that liberty and property were the individual's 'save in accordance with the law'. It would be argued subsequently in the Assembly that 'save in accordance with the law' permitted judicial review because it meant natural law, whereas review could be blocked by using the phrase 'according to procedure established by law', which meant law as laid down by the legislature. See below, pages 105 and 113.

[9] 1935 *Act,* Section 299, to which frequent references will hereafter be made.

[10] See *Prasad papers,* File 16-P/45-6-7.

[11] Rau, *Precedents,* Third Series, op. cit., pp. 17–18.

reiterated his warning. Forty per cent of the litigation before the U.S. Supreme Court during the past fifty years had centred around due process, he wrote, and due process means only what the courts say it means. To include it in the Constitution might open to litigation tenancy and property laws as well as laws concerning debt, moneylenders, and minimum wages.[12] 'It must be admitted', he continued, 'that the clauses are a safeguard against predatory legislation, but they may also stand in the way of beneficient social legislation.'[13] He concluded that it might be a wise idea to steer a middle course and to adopt the device in the Irish Constitution, which provided that the exercise of certain rights 'be regulated by the principles of social justice'.[14]

In the following sub-section we shall continue to examine the Assembly's treatment of the property issue. And in sub-section 3 we shall consider the Assembly's discussion of due process as it applied to life and liberty.

1. Due Process and Property

By the decision of the Advisory Committee to remove from private property the protection of due process the Legislature had gained in power at the expense of the Judiciary and perhaps of abstract justice. This trend would become even more marked. The day after the Advisory Committee took this action, it moved to restrict further the power of the Courts to review property legislation.

On 22 April the Advisory Committee took up the Rights Sub-Committee's draft clause that property could be acquired for public use only on the payment of just compensation—'just' being the word that clearly left the provision open to judicial interpretation.

---

[12] In their dislike of due process Rau and later Ayyar seemed prone to seek the Support of U.S. Supreme Court decisions of the early part of the century, when wages and hours legislation had been invalidated on the ground that it violated due process, and not to look to the decisions handed down in the thirties and forties modifying or overturning these judgements. Only in cases concerning compensation and property were more recent opinions cited, cases in which the Court had declared compensation for expropriated property inadequate.

[13] Rau, *Explanatory Notes on Clauses,* Annexure II, to the F.R. Sub-Committee report of April 1947; op. cit.

[14] Ibid. Rau referred to Article 43(2) 1 and 2 of the Irish Constitution, 1937.

Opening the meeting, Pant asked if 'public use' meant tenancy legislation. Ayyar replied that it did not. Patel then called for a vote on the clause. He announced that eighteen members favoured its retention, and that it would be kept as worded.[15] Ambedkar, however, was more cautious. What did 'public use' mean, he wondered. Pant then said: Suppose the government acquires zamindari rights and then abolishes them. Or what if the Government takes over Connaught Place (the central shopping and office area of New Delhi) and then redistributes the buildings to the tenants? The first stage is acquisition. Does that come under this clause? To Ayyar's answer of 'Certainly', Pant replied that he opposed the wording if it meant that the government would not be free to determine the compensation it would have to pay. If this clause covers all cases of acquisition, said Rajgopalachari, then the question of the justness of compensation will go to the courts 'with the result that government functioning will be paralyzed'.

Ayyar replied that the wording of the clause was close to that of Section 299 of the 1935 Act, which had never interfered with the acquisition of property. He added: 'After all, "compensation" carries with it the idea of "just compensation". Therefore the words "just compensation" have been used.' Under the wording of Section 299[16] said Ambedkar, programmes like Pant's Zamindari Abolition Bill in the U.P. might still be affected. To which Panikkar suggested that they should take out the 'just' so that it would not be justiciable. Pant replied that if this covered acquisition for social purposes, 'then I submit payment of compensation should not even be compulsory'. Patel concluded the discussion. 'If the word "just" is kept,' he said, 'we came to the conclusion that every case will go to the Federal

---

[15] All citations here are taken from proceedings of the meeting, 22 April 1947; Shiva Rao, op. cit., II.

[16] Section 299 laid down that no one could be deprived of his property 'save by authority of law'. No legislature in the provinces or at New Delhi could authorize the compulsory acquisition of any sort of property unless the law provided 'for the payment of compensation for the property acquired and either fixes the amount of the compensation, or specifies the principles on which, and the manner in which, it is to be determined'. But essential to the property safeguards of the Section was Clause (3), which provided that no law for the taking of property, or rights in land revenue, could be introduced in any legislature without the previous sanction in his discretion of either the Governor-General or the Governor of the province.

Court. Therefore "just" is dropped.'[17] Yet the matter was not so easily solved. Two years would elapse before the Assembly completed drafting the provision.

The Assembly greeted the committee's actions favourably. Only two members opposed the provision on the grounds that it did not provide for 'just' compensation; others sharing this attitude may have decided to hold their peace, however, rather than publicly support such an unpopular cause.[18] The speakers demanded that positive action be taken to protect the tiller of the soil, that 'landlordism' and capitalism must be abolished, and that if compensation were paid to an expropriated zamindar—the debaters concerned themselves wholly with agricultural land—it should be nominal, perhaps enough for a few years maintenance for himself and his family.[19] Zamindars were subjected to such intense criticism partly because they were popularly associated with support for the British Raj, a belief that had some justification in fact,[20] and partly because they had, generally speaking, rarely improved the land and had rack-rented their tenants for generations. In some areas anti-zamindari sentiment also had a communal aspect; in parts of Bihar and the United Provinces, for example, many Hindu peasants had Muslim landlords, a situation easy to exploit politically, particularly at this time.

Sardar Patel closed the debate with a speech that sounded like a requiem for landlords. Patel began by saying that the clause was not directed primarily at zamindars, although land and 'many other things may have to be acquired'.[21] Moreover, compensation would be paid for property taken; there would be no expropriation. But, he continued, zamindars could not protect their interests with speeches in the Assembly for before the Constitution came into effect 'most of the zamindaris will be liquidated'. Legislation was already being framed in many provinces to eliminate zamindaris,

---

[17] Proceedings, op. cit.
[18] The two were: Jaganath Baksh Singh and Syamandan Sahaya; *CAD* III, 5, 506 and 515–16.
[19] For this debate, see *CAD* III, 506–18.
[20] For example, the *Report of the Joint Parliamentary Committee*, pp. 217–18, said that the 1935 Act should give 'specific attention' to land rights of jagirdars and Talukdars (especially those of Oudh) with rights dating from Mogul and Sikh times, and those given by Britain in return for services.
[21] *CAD* III, 5, 518.

'either by paying just compensation or adequate compensation or *whatever the legislatures there think fit*'.[22] Despite Patel's assurances that landlordism was all but finished, and that the provision under discussion had little to do with it anyway, Assembly members continued to think primarily in these terms.

The property provisions in the Draft Constitution appeared briefly before the Assembly in November and December 1948 during the year-long debate on the Draft Constitution. The first of the two provisions considered was the right 'to acquire, hold, and dispose of property'. This article dated from the Advisory Committee's Interim Report, and the Assembly adopted it with little debate. As part of the omnibus 'freedoms' article, this right was liberalized by Bhargava's amendment, becoming subject only to 'reasonable' restrictions either in the public interest or the interests of Scheduled Tribes.[23]

With the right to possess property guaranteed in the Constitution, the Assembly again considered the extent of the state's power to deprive a person of his property in the name of social justice. Article 24 of the Draft Constitution was little different from Section 299 of the 1935 Act and was thus, in essence, like the provision the Assembly had adopted in May 1947. The power of the Governor-General and Governors in relation to property legislation had, not surprisingly, been omitted, and a new clause, added by the Drafting Committee, stipulated that nothing in the article should prevent the state from passing legislation promoting public health or preventing danger to life or to property. This latter clause was to be, as we shall see, the foundation of the state's 'police power' in matters of property.

But when Article 24 came to the floor for debate on 9 December 1948, the Assembly decided to defer its discussion for the time

---

[22] Ibid.; emphasis added. In both Uttar Pradesh and Madhya Pradesh legislatures, resolutions of intent favouring zamindari abolition had been passed as early as 1946. By the latter part of 1948 zamindari abolition Bills, or land tenure legislation had been introduced into, or passed by, the legislatures of Bihar, Madras, and Assam. Bombay passed various land tenure acts in 1949, and other provinces did so before 1952. Had not these states been anti-zamindari, the powerful influence of Bihar and U.P. on the Assembly would have almost certainly had the same effect.

[23] Article 19(5) of the Constitution. See also page 73 above for the passage of the liberalizing amendment. For this debate in the Assembly, see *CAD* VII, 18, 75off.

being, ostensibly to let the Drafting Committee sort out the large number of complicated amendments to it that members had submitted. The real reason was, however, that the members of the Drafting Committee themselves were not agreed on the wording of the article, and the Assembly Party was even more deeply split on the issue. The differences of opinion had grown steadily since 1947 and primarily concerned two questions: What sort of compensation was economically feasible and morally just? And to what degree could the Union Government interfere in provincial actions to expropriate property?

The Union government's policy on the issue was not clear. The Congress Election Manifesto of 1945 had called for state ownership or control of a wide variety of industries and services and for 'the removal of intermediaries between the peasant and the state'. The rights of the intermediaries, said the Manifesto, should be acquired by the payment of 'equitable compensation'.[24] Nehru, Patel, and others were known to be anti-zamindar, and Nehru was known to favour a larger public sector in industry—which could come about, of course, by creating new state industries and did not necessarily mean expropriating existing ones. The Union Cabinet, early in 1948, in a broad resolution on industrial policy, had noted the inherent right of the state to acquire industrial undertakings and had laid down that if property was acquired by the government 'the fundamental rights guaranteed by the Constitution will be observed and compensation will be awarded on a fair and equitable basis.'[25] Furthermore, two ministries had made their professional advice available. The Ministry of Works, Mines, and Power had suggested to the Drafting Committee that the word 'equitable', 'fair', or 'just' be inserted before 'compensation' in Article 24.[26] And the Ministry of Industry and Supplies had recommended that Article 24 specify 'reasonable' compensation.[27] Yet in contrast to these views, the Advisory Committee under Patel's chairmanship had

[24] AICC, *Congress Election Manifesto*, 1945.

[25] *Government of India Resolution on Industrial Policy,* No. 1(3)-44/(13)/48, dated 6 April 1948. For more on this resolution, see Chapter 8.

[26] Memorandum from the Ministry of Works, Mines, and Power, dated 15 October 1948; included in Constituent Assembly, *Comments on the Draft Constitution by Various Ministries,* hereafter called the *Comments Volume.* The minister at this time was S. P. Mookerjee.

[27] Memorandum from the Ministry of Industry and Supplies, dated 5 October 1948; ibid. N. V. Gadgil was minister at the time.

removed due process and the qualifying 'just' as protections to property, and the Drafting Committee, under the chairmanship of the Minister, of Law, Ambedkar, had decided to leave them out of the Draft Constitution. To add to the confusion, there was some doubt, as there would be many months later, about the meaning of words such as 'equitable'—equitable to whom, the property owner or the masses? Also, the Constitutional Adviser, Rau, had given his opinion that it was not necessary to qualify the word compensation with an adjective such as 'just', because 'the noun compensation, standing by itself, carries the idea of an equivalent'.[28]

Popular sentiment continued to lean towards keeping compensation out of the courts, particularly where it concerned zamindars. Although eight Assembly members had submitted amendments to the Draft Constitution calling for reasonable compensation, a more common view was that of Damodar Swarup Seth. His amendment declared: 'It will be determined by the law in which cases and to what extent the owner shall be compensated.'[29] Other amendments were harsher in tone if not in effect. One would have prohibited compensation for 'large estates which were owned by members of former foreign dynasties or which were granted to individuals by foreign usurping authority'—a provision aimed at certain classes of Hindus, Muslims, and British alike.[30] An amendment by Pandit Pant provoked the most controversy. Pant would have left 'the mode and manner of compensation entirely to the discretion of the legislatures concerned'.[31] This raised the issue not only of the reasonableness of compensation but also a federal question: Should the states of the new India have unfettered discretion over all forms of expropriation?

[28] B. N. Rau in a note appended to the suggestion of the Ministry of Industry and Supply; ibid. In support of his view, Rau cited the U.S. case of Monongahela Navigation Co. *v.* United States—U.S. 148 Lawyers Edition 37—and the speech of Syamandan Sahaya in the Assembly— *CAD* III, 5, 515–16.

[29] *Amendment Book* I, op. cit., Amendment 720, p. 76. Seth, who had been a Congress Socialist but who had not split away with many others to form the Socialist Party, apparently moved this amendment for J. P. Narayan, who as we know, had refused to join the Assembly. Narayan had suggested an identical amendment to the Drafting Committee early in 1948. See *Prasad papers,* File of Suggestions for Amendments to the Draft Constitution.

[30] *Amendment Book* I, Amendment 779, p. 82, by R. S. Chaudhry.

[31] *The Hindu,* 10 December 1948. The text of Pant's amendment is not available, but other reports of it support this version.

And if such was to be the case, was there, indeed, any reason to include the right to property among the Fundamental Rights? Word of Pant's amendment reached A. K. Ayyar and so perturbed him that he wrote to Patel. If what he had heard of Pant's amendment was correct, he said, 'it will have the effect of making capital shy and driving it in some measure out of industry.'[32] He suggested that Patel bring the matter up at the Assembly Party meeting scheduled for two days later. It is doubtful if Pant's amendment was directed at industry, although it nevertheless might have had the effect Ayyar feared. Pant was aiming at zamindars, and, particularly, he must have been trying to create a situation in which his own pet anti-zamindari Bill in the United Provinces Legislature could not be tampered with by the Union Government. Although 'big business' was far from popular in the Assembly, generally speaking members reserved their special wrath for zamindars, whether of the landlord or rent-farmer variety.

The federal aspect of the expropriation issue was to some degree already covered by the Draft Constitution. According to the Concurrent Legislative List of the Draft, both the provinces and the centre could legislate in regard to the principles upon which compensation could be paid.[33] The dual control of the principles of compensation was in the interests of 'uniformity', said the Drafting Committee.[34] To increase Union control of such legislation even further, T. T. Krishnamachari proposed an amendment that reverted to Clause 3 of Section 299 of the 1935 Act. On the same day that Ayyar wrote to Patel, Krishnamachari moved that no expropriation Bill—which included certain kinds of tenancy Bills and rent-control Bills—could be introduced or moved in any provincial legislature or in the Union Parliament without the previous sanction of the President.[35]

The Congress Assembly Party was unable to reconcile such widely conflicting views at its meeting of 7 December. The Assembly therefore postponed consideration of Article 24 to allow time for a solution to the problem to be worked out backstage in Assembly committees and in the Assembly Party.

---

[32] Ayyar letter to Patel, 5 December 1948; *Ayyar papers.*
[33] *Draft Constitution,* List III, Item 35, and List I, Item 43, and List II, Item 9.
[34] *Draft Constitution,* Para 14(c), p. 10.
[35] *Orders of the Day,* Amendment 42, List I of 5 December 1948. On 28 November, B. Das had submitted a nearly identical amendment that would have given this power to the Chief Justice; ibid., 28 November 1948, Amendment 74, List I.

Further attempts at solution began seven months later and continued until the Assembly thrashed out an acceptable formula. The debate began again with the basic principles. Assembly members argued the pros and cons of justiciable compensation and about the manner in which compensation should be paid. They argued about the propriety of singling out zamindari property as liable to expropriation under special terms. The 'federal' issue became submerged in the flood of opinions, to reappear briefly only towards the end of the debate. But settlement of the controversy finally turned on a fine point. It turned not on whether compensation as such should be justiciable, but on the right of the courts to examine one aspect of property acquisition laws: the principles on which compensation was to be paid. This was because of the political power and the personal experience of Sardar Patel.

Patel was not the immovable monolith that he is often pictured. He compromised, and indeed under pressure from Nehru and Pant he compromised to some extent on this issue. His power in the Congress, in the Government, and in the Assembly was such, however, that no action could be taken without his consent. This was true of any Article of the Constitution but especially so of Article 24, for it is generally agreed that the compensation issue was one on which Patel had firm views.[36] He had favoured zamindari abolition, as we have seen, on the floor of the Assembly and in the Advisory Committee, where he had been willing to eliminate due process as applied to property and the word 'just' as qualifying compensation in order to keep 'every case' from going to the Supreme Court. He had favoured zamindari abolition for many years. During his presidency, the Kisan (Peasants) Conference at Allahabad in 1935 had passed a resolution calling for 'a system of peasant proprietorship . . . without the intervention of any zamindar or talukdar', but the resolution had said that expropriated zamindars should be paid 'reasonable compensation'.[37] Patel has also been described as 'against any son of violent expropriation, which he always described as *choree* (theft) or *daka* (dacoity)'.[38]

[36] According to a large number of persons interviewed by the author.

[37] H. D. Malaviya, *Land Reforms in India,* pp. 58–59.

[38] V. P. Menon, *The Integration of the Indian States,* p. 489. For a further, although somewhat too simplified, account of Patel's views, see K. L. Panjabi, *The Indomitable Sardar,* pp. 145–7 and 208–10.

Moreover, Patel had had personal experience with land acquisition legislation passed under the authority of Section 299 of the 1935 Act, which, it will be recalled, laid down that legislation acquiring property for public purposes must either specify the compensation or the principles on which it was to be paid. In 1938 Patel was chairman of the Congress Parliamentary Board, and on the board his special responsibility was the affairs of the Bombay region. Part of the control that the Parliamentary Board exercised over the provincial Congress ministries during the 1937–39 period was to scrutinize certain types of proposed legislation before the ministry could present it in the provincial Legislative Assembly; property acquisition Bills fell in this category. So the board, and Patel particularly, had approved a draft Bill entitled The Bombay Forfeited Lands Restoration Act. And Patel had an additional link with the provision because it had particular force in the Bardoli area of Gujarat, where just ten years before he had led a satyagraha against increased land tax, and was rewarded with renown and the honorific 'Sardar'.

The Bombay Forfeited Lands Restoration Act of 1938 provided for the acquisition by the provincial government of certain lands and rights in land in order to return them to their original owners, who had lost them by confiscation for refusing to pay land revenue to the pre-Congress provincial government during the Civil Disobedience Movement. The confiscated lands had been sold at very low prices to other persons, and it was from these persons, who had profited by the nationalism of other Indians, that the Congress government intended to regain the lands. The Act clearly stated that restoration to the original owners was the 'public purpose' for which the lands were being acquired. Compensation under the Act was to be paid on the following principles: the amount of compensation was to be the price paid to the provincial government for the occupancy rights to the land, plus expenditures on improvements, plus the amount of land revenue paid during the occupancy, plus 4 per cent interest on these amounts. From this total could be deducted profits from the land or the value of damage done to the land. But in no case could the compensation be less than the amount paid for the land plus the cost of improvements.[39] Thus

[39]   *The Bombay Forfeited Lands Restoration Act,* 1938, Bombay Act No. XXII of 1938; *Bombay Code,* Vol. II, 1921–49, pp. 2085–8. The author is indebted to K. M. Munshi for the initial suggestion of the importance of this Act to Patel.

the principles of compensation were laid down as demanded by the 1935 Act, and yet, it was evident, compensation calculated according to these principles would amount to considerably less than the market value of the property.

To Patel, therefore, the wording of Section 299 seemed to provide the solution to the Assembly's dilemma. Under it the power of both the legislature and the courts would be limited. The courts would be unable to invalidate land reform and other property acquisition legislation provided reasonable principles had been established, and the legislatures would be unable to expropriate property without payment of compensation. Justice and social reform would both be served. With Patel's position in mind, we can return to the events that led to the adoption of his view.

The re-opening of the debate on Article 24 was on 24 July 1949, during a series of meetings held by the Drafting Committee with the premiers and finance ministers of the provinces and the ministers of the Union Government. At the meeting, Pandit Pant reiterated his belief that the Legislature alone should have the authority to give such compensation 'as it considers to be fair not only in the sense that it is fair in terms of the market value, but considering the circumstances and the paying capacity of the state and the purpose for which the property is being acquired'.[40] Ayyar replied that in that case there might as well be no Fundamental Right. T. T. Krishnamachari expressed the fear that if there were no provision like Article 24, no foreign capital would come to India. Prime Minister Nehru disagreed with this, saying that foreign capital would be dealt with on special terms by agreement.[41] He added that compensation for property should be paid, but that payment must be made largely or only in bonds. To talk of cash payment when

[40] Proceedings of the meeting, 24 July 1949; *Law Ministry Archives.* All citations from this meeting are taken from this source.

[41] Nehru had made a speech on this subject in April 1949 to the Constituent Assembly (Legislative) in which he had said: '. . . if and when foreign enterprises are compulsorily acquired, compensation will be paid on a fair and equitable basis as already announced in the Government's statement of policy (Resolution on Industrial Policy, op. cit.).' *Constituent Assembly of India (Legislative) Debates,* Vol. IV, No. 1, p. 2386 of 6 April 1949. The reference here to equitable compensation was frequently misquoted thereafter as applying to indigenous property, including zamindaris.

there wasn't enough cash was impractical, he said; 'it just means red revolution and nothing else'.

K. M. Munshi thought that if the manner of compensation was kept out of the courts, the payment of it could be spread over '100 years'. He also believed that leaving the quantum of compensation to legislatures was unwise because some of them might lack a sense of fair play. Yet he was willing to 'exclude the zamindari (from the protection of the article) and let the rest remain'. This idea of applying different rules to the expropriation of zamindaris and other forms of property would be strongly advocated in the coming weeks. During the meeting on 24 July, Patel said nothing indicative of his opinions. The Finance Minister, John Matthai, did not attend the meeting. Away in London on official business, he returned only in time for the consideration of sales tax on the following day. The meeting took no firm decision and the issue continued to simmer.

The next month witnessed a continuous campaign specifi-cally against zamindars. B. N. Rau, acting his self-established part as an impartial adviser and draftsman, prepared for Pant a version of Article 24 that, he said, might prevent the courts from blocking land legislation. A new clause laid down that nothing in the article should affect laws made in the discharge of the state's duties under Article 31—an omnibus provision in the Directive Principles that said, among other things, that the ownership and control of material resources should be distributed to subserve the common good and that the operation of the economic system should not result in the concentration of wealth.[42] Several days later Rau submitted another draft that would have made compensation obligatory and payable

---

[42] B. N. Rau letter to G. B. Pant, 24 July 1949; *Law Ministry Archives,* File CA/19(5)/ Cons/49. Although Rau may have often, in the functions of his office, drafted provisions whose import he disliked, he openly favoured the general welfare over private rights, and he may, therefore, have approved of this provision drafted for Pant. This conclusion is supported by the advice given Rau by Eamon De Valera—on whose views Rau placed considerable weight—that De Valera 'would make the right of property guaranteed in the Constitution expressly subject to laws intended for the general welfare'. Rau, *India's Constitution,* p. 310. A like provision had been moved in the Drafting Committee meeting of 20 January 1948, only to be withdrawn the following day. Only B. N. Rau, N. M. Rau, and Ambedkar, plus staff, were present at these meetings. See Minutes of the meet-ings, 20–21 January 1948; *Munshi papers.*

in cash or securities and that stipulated that no law making such provision should be questioned in court on the grounds that the compensation was inadequate or unjust. On the same day he prepared a note reiterating his belief that the word 'compensation' in fact meant 'just compensation'.[43] There were also circulated that day, 2 August, amendments drafted several days previously by Pant, Ayyar, and N. Gopalaswami Ayyangar. Of these only that by Ayyangar bluntly laid down that the compensation established by law would be deemed adequate. An Assembly Party meeting discussed the amendments that morning, but reached no decision. That afternoon Munshi, Ambedkar, and Ayyar circulated an amendment that would have assured the payment of compensation much in the manner of Article 24. Apparently it had a cool reception.

For the party meeting of 4 August the Drafting Committee drafted a new formula providing that compensation must be paid for all property acquired for public purposes, but that a legislature could prescribe different principles for the payment of property acquired for different purposes.[44] The meeting was able to agree only that compensation could be paid in cash or bonds, the argument on other points being indecisive. The Nehru-Pant forces, which held that the Legislature must be supreme, fought against the Matthai-led group, which believed, in Matthai's words, that 'if the credit of the country was to be maintained, there must be specifically adequate compensation'.[45] Apparently a formula was evolved at the meeting calling for compensation to be paid for all property acquired by the state but providing that 'the transference to public ownership or

[43] Undated note, perhaps written about 26 July 1949; ibid. Precisely what Rau meant here is difficult to determine. The word compensation standing by itself might carry the meaning of 'just' or equivalent value to property acquired. But did it mean this in the context of Section 299? Although some authorities believed so, the experience with The Bombay Forfeited Lands Restoration Act indicated the opposite. In fact, no one could be sure what the wording of any provision meant in the eyes of the courts until the provision had been tested by the new Supreme Court. Nevertheless, the conflicting opinions of the definition of compensation played an important, if largely immeasurable, role in the framing process, for Assembly members opposed or favoured certain versions of Article 24 depending on their interpretation of compensation and whether or not they believed compensation should be justiciable.

[44] *Law Ministry Archives,* File CA/19(5)/Cons/49.

[45] *The Hindu,* 6 August 1949, dispatch dated 4 August.

the extinguishment or modification of rights in land intermediate between those of the cultivator and the state, including rights and privileges in respect of land revenue' should be compensated according to terms established by the Legislature, which would then be deemed 'just and adequate'.[46]

The next day saw another heated party meeting as the members debated this formulas and a new draft by the Drafting Committee—again with a special provision aimed at zamindars. One newspaper reported that a cabinet minister (read Matthai) said that he would rather quit the Government than acquiesce in such a dangerous provision.[47] A letter from Patel, read to the meeting by Munshi, called on the members to remember the Congress's promises to pay just compensation and laid the 'present economic deterioration' in the country to the Congress's failure to take a firm stand on the issue. 'No one', Patel was reported to have written, 'should be discriminated against in the eyes of the law and compensation in all cases should be made justiciable.'[48] Again, the meeting produced no agreement.

During the following three weeks various groups, appointed and informal, as well as individuals, drafted and redrafted new provisions. At one point, members of the Assembly Party voted 57 to 52 to make compensation for commercial and industrial property justiciable and to leave zamindars entirely to the mercy of the Legislature.[49] Yet the issue still was not settled. One suspects that this was in part because a majority of five votes was not considered sufficient on such an important matter—the Assembly preferred to decide matters by consensus rather than by a narrow majority—and in larger part because Patel opposed the provision.

---

[46] *The Hindustan Times,* 5 August 1949. See also *The Hindu,* 7 August 1949. The dates on which these events were reported seem to indicate that either one newspaper made a grave error of time or, more likely, that *The Hindustan Times* reported the formula on the day it was evolved and *The Hindu* on the day it was debated. News from North India frequently appeared in *The Hindu* (published in Madras) a day late.

[47] *The Hindu,* 7 August 1949.

[48] *The Hindustan Times,* 6 August 1949. The same account in all relevant points appeared in *The Hindu* of 7 August.

[49] On 9 August. See *The Hindu,* 11 August 1949 and *The Hindustan Times,* 10 August 1949.

As August progressed, the provisions being drafted in back-stage discussions came more and more to resemble Section 299. According to press reports this was a result of conversations between Patel and several Assembly members in Bombay.[50] By the end of the month a generally acceptable formula had been found. It was much like Section 299 and was said to protect zamindari abolition legislation past and pending. The Assembly Party adopted it by a vote of 56–34.[51] A week later the formula, bearing the names of Nehru, Pant, Munshi, Ayyar, and N. G. Ayyangar, was moved in the Assembly as an amendment to the Draft Constitution.[52] The amendment provided that no one could be deprived of his property except by law and the law must name the compensation or the principles on which it was to be paid. A third clause provided that property acquisition Bills must have presidential assent before becoming law. Clause (5) provided for the state's police power relative to property. Clause (4) and (6) laid down that property legislation enacted in a state one year (later changed to eighteen months) before the inauguration of the Constitution and certified by the President within three months of its inauguration, and property legislation pending at the inauguration of the Constitution, later enacted, and then assented to by the President, could not be questioned in court on the grounds of the compensation or principles named in the law.

The provision had in it everything Patel wanted and was at the same time moderately satisfactory to Pant and Nehru. Others, supporters of complete review powers for the courts, like Matthai, and those in favour of unfettered power for legislatures, must have been disappointed by the compromise. So far as Patel was concerned Clause (2), taken directly from Section 299, provided for his middle-of-the road approach to land acquisition. But because legislatures had the authority to prescribe the principles of compensation, the expropriation of zamindars could be undertaken on different principles than the acquisition of commercial or industrial property—an aspect pleasing to many Assembly members. The clause reserving all property legislation

---

[50] *The Hindu*, 20 August 1949.

[51] *The Hindustan Times*, 1 September 1949.

[52] See Amendment 369, List VII, *Orders of the Day*, 8 September 1949; *INA*. See also *The Hindu*, 9 September 1949. The text of the amendment is essentially that of Article 31 of the Constitution.

for presidential assent must also have been included at Patel's demand. For it meant that, so long as he lived, Patel could block any legislation that seemed to him unjust—'the President', of course, meant the Cabinet, and in the Cabinet Patel had veto power. And Nehru, one presumes, was also not averse to the Union Executive's having the opportunity to dampen unseemly zeal in the states. Clauses (4) and (6), it was made explicitly clear in the Assembly, were included to protect land reform legislation pending in the legislatures of Bihar, Madras, and the United Provinces. Representatives of these governments in the Assembly, particularly Pant, had fought hard for their protection. But here too Patel could exercise his veto, for although the compensation in these laws once enacted would not be justiciable, they must have presidential assent before becoming law.

The meaning of the provision was best explained to the Assembly by K. M. Munshi. Munshi had become Patel's spokesman on the issue, as he had on several others, and he was especially well qualified to interpret the origins of the provision because he had been Home Minister in the Bombay government in 1938. As such he had been closely connected with the passage of the Forfeited Lands Restoration Act. The import of the clauses, Munshi told the members, was that Parliament would be the sole judge of two matters: 'the propriety of the principles laid down, so long as they are principles' and that the 'principles may vary as regards different classes of property and different objects for which they are acquired'. If the legislature lays down genuine principles for compensation, 'the court will not substitute their own sense of fairness for that of Parliament', Munshi assured the Assembly; 'they will not judge the adequacy of compensation from the standard of market value; they will not question the judgement of Parliament unless the inadequacy is so gross as to be tantamount to a fraud on the fundamental right to own property.'[53]

---

[53] *CAD* IX, 32,1299–1300. Dr. Ambedkar later gave a version of the controversy during the drafting of Article 24:

'. . . The Congress Party, at the time when Article 31 (read 24) was being framed was so divided within itself that we did not know what to do, what to put and what not to put. There were three sections in the Congress Party. One section was led by Sardar Vallabhbhai Patel, who stood for full compensation. . . . Our Prime Minister was against compensation. Our friend Mr. Pant had conceived his Zamindari Abolition Bill before the Constitution was being actually framed. He wanted a very safe delivery for his baby. So he had his own proposition.

Nehru also informed the Assembly that 'eminent lawyers have told us that on a proper construction of this clause [Clause (2)], normally speaking, the Judiciary should not and does not come in'. He added that 'no Supreme Court and no Judiciary can stand in judgement over the sovereign will of Parliament representing the will of the entire community'. Nehru also made clear the Congress's longstanding programme to abolish zamindari and its promise of equitable compensation. But equity, he said, applies to the community as well as to the individual: 'No individual can override ultimately the rights of the community at large. No community should injure and invade the rights of the individual unless it be for the most urgent and important reasons.'[54]

Patel remained silent. He knew the provision would be adopted and he had already achieved his aims. Ayyar summed up the debate with sentiments appropriate to the occasion. He spoke of the law 'as an instrument of social progress'. The law, he said, 'must reflect the progressive and social techniques of the age'. Dharma and the duty the individual owed to society were the basis of India's social framework, he continued; capitalism as practised in the West was 'alien to the root idea of our civilization. The sole end of property is Yagna and to serve a social purpose', he concluded.[55] The Assembly adopted the new provision, which became Article 31 of the Constitution.

2. Amending the Property Article

Nehru may or may not have believed that Article 31 would stand the test of time, that it was adequate to India's social needs as he saw them. He may have accepted the compromise because he could move Patel no further. In any case the first moves to amend Article 31 began within five months of Patel's death,[56] and there have been several subsequent amendments to the property provision.

There was thus a tripartite struggle and we left the matter to them to decide in any way they liked.' See *Parliamentary Debates, Rajya Sabha, Official Report,* Vol. IX, No. 19, 19 March 1955, Columns 2450–2, cited in D. N. Banerjee, *Our Fundamental Rights, their Nature and Extent,* p. 313.

[54] *CAD* IX, 31, 1192–95.

[55] *CAD* IX, 32, 1274.

[56] For the views of one who believes this to have been treachery to Patel, see Panjabi, op. cit., p. 146.

The First Amendment Act (1951) was aimed primarily at zamindars and rent-farmers, although it also extended the state's police power. The Act added Articles 31A, 31B and the Ninth Schedule to the Constitution. Article 31A allowed the state, despite any inconsistency with Articles 14, 19, or 31,[57] to legislate for the acquisition of estates, the taking over of property by the state for a limited period in the public interest, and the extinction or modification of the rights of directors or stockholders of corporations. The first part of the article, as Dr. Ambedkar, speaking as Law Minister, explained it, was intended

> to permit a State to acquire what are called estates . . . (It) not only removes the operation of the provision relating to compensation, but also removes the article relating to discrimination . . . It does not apply to the acquisition of land. It applies to the acquisition of estates in land, which is a very different thing.[58]

The second part of the article allowed the state to take over for short periods, without actually expropriating them, such property as businesses whose financial or other condition was harmful to the public interest.

Article 31B gave protection to various land reform acts passed by state legislatures by laying down that none of the Acts, which were listed in the new Ninth Schedule, should be declared void because they controverted any other Fundamental Right.[59]

The next amendment to Article 31, the Fourth Amendment Act, was occasioned by two judicial decisions, one of which had interfered with expropriation legislation, the other with the exercise of the state's police power. Instead of attacking the court's judgement, Nehru and

---

[57] Article 14 provided for equality before the law; Article 19 was the 'freedoms' article, including the right to acquire, hold, and dispose of property; Article 31, of course, concerned expropriation and compensation.

[58] *Parliamentary Debates,* 18 May 1951, columns 9024–8, cited in Banerjee, op. cit., P. 393.

[59] The Ninth Schedule listed such acts as the Bihar Land Reforms Act of 1950. Defending the provision, Nehru said that India's basic problem was land, that measures passed in state assemblies must not be held up, and he reiterated that the Congress was firmly committed to zamindari abolition 'with adequate and proper compensation, not too much'. *Parliamentary Debates,* 16 May 1951, columns 8830–37 cited in Banerjee, op. cit., pp. 388–9. For the texts of Constitutional Amendments Acts I-XIV, see *The Constitution of India,* Edition of 1963.

the Cabinet set about amending the Constitution. The responsibility for the economic and social welfare policies of the nation should lie with Parliament, Nehru said, not with the courts. The decisions of the Supreme Court, he said, showed that there was 'an inherent contradiction in the Constitution between the Fundamental Rights and the Directive Principles of State Policy . . . It is up to this Parliament to remove this contradiction and make the Fundamental Rights subserve the Directive Principles of State Policy.'[60]

The Fourth Amendment Act (1955) made two changes in Article 31. By amending Clause (2), it laid down that no law passed under the article should 'be called in question in any court on the ground that the compensation provided by that law is not adequate'.[61] Parliament made this change because 'in Bela Banerjee's case . . . it was unequivocally held that the compensation that will be paid under this clause (Clause 2) should be the full equivalent of the property'.[62]

The second change made by the Fourth Amendment was the addition of Clause 2 A to Article 31. This new clause laid down that if a law did not provide for the actual transfer of ownership of property to the state, it should not be deemed to have been compulsory acquisition even though persons had been deprived of their property.[63] Thus the state would not be liable for compensation. Parliament made this clarification of the extent of the state's police power primarily in response to the Supreme Court's decision in the second Sholapur Mills case. The Union Government had taken over the operation of the Sholapur Spinning and Weaving Company on the ground that it was being grossly mismanaged to the detriment of the public and of its stockholders. The Government took this action under its police powers, apparently believing that it was constitutional according to the provisions of Article 31A. The Supreme Court, however, held that the Government's action deprived the owners and the stockholders of the company of their property and that compensation should be paid them.[64]

---

[60] See *Lok Sabha Debates*, 14 March 1955; cited in Banerjee, op. cit.

[61] *Constitution*, 1963 Edition, Op. cit., pp. 285–7.

[62] Speech by Pandit Pant. See *Parliamentary Debates*, Rajya Sabha, 20 April 1955, cited in Banerjee, op. cit., pp. 327–8. For Bela Banerjee's case, see *Supreme Court Reports* 1954, Vol. V, Part V, pp. 558–65.

[63] Quoted from Banerjee, op. cit, p. 331.

[64] Ibid., p. 382.

Thus in the nine years from 1947 to 1956 had the demands of the social revolution taken the right to property out of the courts and placed it in the hands of the legislatures. Good sense, fairness, and the commonweal might still be served, but so far as property was concerned, due process was dead.[65]

3. Due Process and Individual Liberty

Just as the story of due process and property in the Constituent Assembly was largely concerned with how the land and land rights of the few could be placed at the disposition of the many for the sake of social and economic gain, so the decline and fall of due process as a safeguard for personal liberty placed the citizen's freedom at the disposition of the legislature for the sake of a public peace in which social and economic reforms could be achieved. And as due process was eliminated from the property provisions of the Constitution because of the substantive interpretations that could be placed upon it, so it was not applied to liberty primarily because of the procedural interpretations that flowed from it. Ultimately, the story of due process and liberty in the Constituent Assembly was the story of preventive detention.

Wealth was the responsibility of the few and liberty was the possession of the many; the members of a Constituent Assembly who would enthusiastically expropriate another's property were loathe to endanger their own liberty. Most of the rank and file supported Nehru on expropriation and compensation. Patel, Matthai, and a few others constituted a minority. But many members, led by more than a dozen ranking Congressmen and several Assembly leaders, opposed the sacrifice of due process as a protection of liberty, although Nehru, Patel, and others favoured its elimination. None would have disputed that stable government and peaceful conditions throughout the country were necessary for the achievement of the social revolution. But many thought that individual liberty should not be imperilled even for such ends, and to save what they could they fought the issue into the final days of the Assembly. The harsh provisions of the Constitution, while bestowing great authority on the state, were at the same time,

---

[65] Since 1956 only the Seventeenth Amendment Act, 1964, has concerned property rights. This Act also removes certain state land reform legislation, particularly in regard to ryotwari holdings, from the purview of the courts.

however, framed to give the individual some protection from the vagaries of state detention laws. It must be remembered, too, that while India has preventive detention, it has allowed Communists to govern a state and to sit in Parliament. Yet in the United States, where according to the Constitution there is more individual liberty than in India, the Communist Party is an illegal organization. Had India not once been a colony, the members of her Constituent Assembly might or might not have provided for preventive detention in the Constitution. But the British had practised preventive detention in India for many years—openly since 1818.[66] It would appear that, along with representative government, preventive detention was also a legacy of the empire of which Britain was so proud.

The elimination of due process was initially a result of B. N. Rau's influence, although other personalities and the events of the times played a part as well. The seeds had been sown even before the Assembly adopted the due process clause in May 1947. Rau, in his comments on the report of the Fundamental Rights Sub-Committee, as we have seen, pointed out how a substantive interpretation of due process might interfere with legislation for social purposes. Then, during the Advisory Committee meeting of 21 April 1947, the procedural difficulties that due process could cause were brought to the attention of Pant and Patel. Rajgopalachari and Ayyar told them that under due process the Executive could not detain persons without trial.[67] The Assembly favoured due process, however, and Rau included the provision in his Draft Constitution published in early October 1947, although he qualified 'liberty' with the adjective 'personal'.[68]

Soon after, Rau began his trip to the United States, Canada, Eire, and England to talk with justices, constitutionalists, and statesmen about the framing of the Constitution. In the United States he met Supreme Court Justice Felix Frankfurter, who told him that he considered the power of judicial review implied in the due process clause both undemocratic—because a few judges could veto legislation enacted by the representatives of a nation—and burdensome to the Judiciary;[69]

---

[66] The Bengal State Prisoners Regulation III of 1818.

[67] See page 85 above.

[68] Rau, *Draft Constitution,* Clause 16. This change greatly narrowed the scope and meaning of liberty. See Alexandrowicz, op. cit ., pp. 11–13.

[69] Rau, *India's Constitution,* p. 303. Rau originally reported this to the President of the Assembly, Prasad, in an airmail letter dated 11 November 1947; *Prasad papers,*

Frankfurter had been strongly influenced by the Harvard Law School's great constitutional lawyer, James Bradley Thayer, who also feared that too great a reliance on due process as a protection against legislative oversight or misbehaviour might weaken the democratic process.[70] Thayer's views had impressed Rau even before he met Frankfurter. In his Constitutional Precedents, Rau had pointed out that Thayer and others had 'drawn attention to the dangers of attempting to find in the Supreme Court—instead of in the lessons of experience—a safeguard against the mistakes of the representatives of the people'.[71] Rau's emphasis at this time—and it remained so in the future—was on the substantive meaning of due process, not on the procedural aspect. But the supporters of due process would have preserved it for its procedural safeguards, primarily against arbitrary Executive action.

As a result of his conversations with Frankfurter, Rau proposed an amendment to his Draft Constitution 'designed to secure that when a law is made by the State in the discharge of one of the fundamental duties imposed upon it by the Constitution and happens to conflict with one of the fundamental rights guaranteed to the individual, the former should prevail over the latter; in other words, the general right should prevail over the individual right'.[72] Rau could not get the members of the Drafting Committee to accept this amendment at their meetings in the autumn of 1947, so he tried to obtain the same result by other means and suggested that the due process clause be eliminated in favour of the phrase 'according to the procedure established by law'. It was Rau's enthusiastic espousal of Frankfurter's views that originally caused the Drafting Committee to reconsider the issue.[73]

File 2-N/47. The account of the trip abroad included in *India's Constitution,* edited by Rau's brother, B. Shiva Rao, is essentially the same as that submitted to Prasad by Rau on 24 November 1947. See *Prasad papers,* File 2-N/47. The book, however, does not indicate the material that Rau thought important enough to deserve immediate transmission.

[70] Felix Frankfurter, *Felix Frankfurter Reminisces,* pp. 299–301.

[71] Rau, *Constitutional Precedents,* Third Series, p. 23.

[72] Rau, *India's Constitution,* p. 302; for the text of his suggested amendment, see ibid., p. 313.

[73] The view of H. V. R. Iengar, once head of the Assembly Secretariat, but at this time Home Secretary, expressed in a letter to A. V. Pai, Nehru's private secretary, dated 22 July 1949; *Law Ministry Archives.*

The Drafting Committee took up the matter again during its meetings of January 1948, and at some time after 19 January the members decided to omit due process. It is not clear precisely what happened, but some reconstruction of the event is possible. Of the seven members of the Drafting Committee at the time (Ambedkar, the chairman, Munshi, Ayyar, N. G. Ayyangar, D. P. Khaitan, N. Madhava Rau, and Mohammed Saadulla), four had been supporters of due process—Munshi, Ayyar, Ambedkar, and Saadulla. Ayyangar apparently did not support it; N. M. Rau's views are not known; and Khaitan, a Marwari who was close to Patel, may be presumed to have opposed it. To eliminate due process, one of the four supporters had to change sides. Apparently this was A. K. Ayyar. B. N. Rau had several times met Ayyar since his return and had convinced him of the dangers inherent in substantive interpretations of due process.[74] And, as we shall see, Ayyar later became one of the most outspoken opponents of the clause. It is doubtful if Ambedkar or Saadulla also changed sides; certainly Munshi did not. But Ayyar's vote was sufficient. An added reason for removing due process may have been an increasing conviction that preventive detention provided the best weapon against the communal violence that had racked North India during the past year. This view, if it existed, could only have been strengthened by the cataclysm of Gandhi's assassination a few days later on 30 January. Justifying its decision to supplant due process with the phrase 'according to procedure established by law', the Drafting Committee said merely that the latter was 'more specific'.[75]

Disapproval of the Drafting Committee's action soon became evident in the amendments to the Draft submitted by Assembly members. K. M. Munshi's voice was heard first. Because of his insistence, the Drafting Committee reconsidered the question during its meetings in March 1948, but declined to return due process to Article. 15.[76] Within several months twenty other Assembly members sponsored amendments that would have made the right to personal liberty justiciable. Twelve of them would have reinserted due process, and the remaining eight members would have replaced 'procedure established

---

[74] K. M. Munshi and others in interviews with the author.
[75] *Draft Constitution,* first footnote, p. 8. The committee cited as its precedent Article XXXI of the Japanese Constitution of 1946.
[76] Minutes of the meeting, 23 March 1948; *Munshi papers.*

by law, by 'save in accordance with law'. In the latter phrase 'law' could be interpreted either as the law passed by a legislature or as natural law or natural justice, as 'lex' or 'jus', while the phrase 'procedure established by law' could only be interpreted as law enacted by a legislature. Had 'save in accordance with law' been used the provision would have been justiciable.[77]

Among the supporters of these amendments were Dr. Sitaramayya, president of the Congress 1948–9, T. T. Krishnamachari, later a member of the Drafting Committee, K. Santhanam, M. A, Ayyangar, deputy speaker of the Constituent Assembly (Legislative), Dr. B . V. Keskar, Deputy Minister of External Affairs and a general secretary of the Congress, S. L. Saksena, Thakur Das Bhargava, Hukam Singh, a leader of the Akali Sikhs, and four of the Muslim League members in the Assembly. In later debates, many members who had not submitted amendments spoke in favour of due process, among them Baksi Sir Tek Chand, at one time a judge of the Lahore High Court.

When Article 15 came to the floor of the House for debate on 6 and 13 December 1948, the supporters of due process immediately attacked it. Mahboob Ali Baig made several points that would bear weight in the debate on preventive detention. The Drafting Committee, said Baig, claimed the Japanese Constitution as its precedent for using the phrase 'procedure established by law'. Yet in the Japanese Constitution several fundamental rights endangered by the omission of due process had been separately guaranteed—for instance, the right of a person not to be detained except on adequate cause and unless at once informed of the charges against him, the right to counsel and to an immediate hearing in open court, and the right of a person to be secure against entry, search, etc., except on a warrant.[78]

K. M. Munshi said that a substantive interpretation of due process could not apply to liberty of contract—the basis on which the United States Supreme Court had, at the beginning of the century, declared

---

[77] See the speeches of M. A. Baig *(CAD* VII, 20, 845) and T. D. Bhargava (ibid, 846). For a Supreme Court decision corroborating this view, see p. 113 below. For the texts of the amendments, see *Amendment Book* I, pp. 55—57.

[78] *CAD* VII, 20, 844–5. Baig was referring to Articles XXXII, XXXIV, and XXXV of the Japanese Constitution—drafted in 1946 under American aegis.

some social legislation to be an infringement of due process and hence unconstitutional—but only to liberty of person, because 'personal' had been added to qualify liberty. 'When a law has been passed which entitles the government to take away the personal liberty of an individual,' Munshi said, 'the court will consider whether the law which has been passed is such as is required by the exigencies of the case and therefore, as I said, the balance will be struck between individual liberty and social control.'[79] Other Assembly members agreed: whilst not wishing to impede the passage of social reform legislation they sought to protect the individual's personal liberty against prejudicial action by an arbitrary Executive.[80]

Munshi also referred to the issue that was on everyone's mind—due process versus preventive detention in the light of public security. He said he realized that many Assembly members believed due process a dangerous luxury considering the unsettled conditions of the country. But it would protect the individual against inroads on his fundamental rights, whilst at the same time the dangers to public security were likely to be so great that the courts would uphold the provincial Public Safety Acts (which in most cases provided for preventive detention). Thus both the individual and society would be protected.[81]

Ambedkar, torn between his belief in due process and his official duty to uphold his committee's decision, remained on the fence. He explained the implications of including due process in the Constitution and of omitting it, and then left the House 'to decide in any way it likes'.[82]

A. K. Ayyar upheld the Drafting Committee's position, revealing for the first time on the Assembly floor that he had changed his mind about due process. He now supported its omission on the grounds that its substantive interpretation might impede social legislation—something, one recalls, that he had been willing to risk in April 1947.[83] Yet he did this without any reference to the procedural

[79] Ibid., p. 852.

[80] For example, two of the amendments submitted to Article 15 expressly stipulated that due process should never be used to say that a person had been denied freedom of contract. *Amendment Book* I, amendments 516 and 518, p. 55.

[81] *CAD* VII, 20, 852.

[82] *CAD* VII, 25, 1001.

[83] See proceedings of the Advisory Committee meeting 21 April 1947, op. cit.

importance of due process, the aspect most crucial to the debate of the moment. Moreover, he supported his position not with new arguments but with points he had rejected earlier, never explaining why he had changed his mind.[84] It was one of the sorriest performances ever put on by the Assembly leadership.

The amendments were defeated, and on 13 December 1948 Article 15, without the due process clause, was confirmed as part of the Draft Constitution. It quite possibly took the Whip to assure its adoption, however, for controversy had been widespread; even Ayyar recognized that 'a good number of members in this House' favoured the retention of due process.[85] And public reaction to the omission of due process during 1949 was most unfavourable. 'No part of our Draft Constitution', reported Ambedkar to the Assembly in September 1949,' . . . has been so violently criticized by the public outside as Article 15.'[86] This reaction, this widespread fear of Executive excesses and repression, had its roots in the Indian preventive detention laws—and to some degree in the manner in which several rights questions had been handled in the Assembly. To understand why the issue was reopened in September 1949 it would be well to pause here and examine this situation.

Preventive detention came to India officially with the Bengal State Prisoners Regulation III of 1818, 'the oldest statute dealing with preventive detention' in India,[87] and it was extended in 1819 and 1827 to Madras and Bombay Presidencies. These three regulations were permanent, and the Bengal regulation was extended to other parts of India during the period from 1879 to 1929. Preventive detention was also authorized in other ways. Provincial assemblies passed such Acts. Detention was either authorized, or power was provided to authorize it, by the Defence of India Acts of 1915 and 1939, by the Government of India Act 1919, by the infamous Rowlatt Act, and

---

[84] *CAD* VII, 20, 854. Ayyar had sent a strong note to Nehru emphasizing many of these points just three days before he spoke in the House. Note dated 3 December 1948; *Ayyar papers.* Ayyar's suspicion of due process later developed to an absurd degree. He once told the Assembly that 'if that expression remained there (in the Constitution) it would prevent the State from having any detention laws, any deportation laws, and even any laws relating to labour regulations'. *CAD* IX, 35,1535.

[85] Ibid., p. 853.

[86] *CAD* IX, 35, 1497.

[87] A.Gledhill, *The Republic of India*, p. 173.

by such other measures as the Restriction and Detention Ordinance III of 1944.[88]

Congressmen had for the most part been on the receiving end of detention orders (including all the Oligarchy and most other leaders). During their two years in office from 1937 to 1939 they had done away with some of these laws, but the Congress ministries had also prosecuted for sedition under special powers and emergency acts.[89] And in the years from 1947 to 1950 there was a rash of Public Order and Public Safety Acts throughout the country. No less than twelve provinces adopted such acts. The Bengal regulation of 1818 was itself brought up to date by the Bengal State Prisoners Regulations (Adaptation) Order, promulgated in 1947 by the Governor-General under the Indian Independence Act.[90]

Although there were similarities between the provincial Public Safety Acts, there were also great differences in the amount of protection accorded the person detained. The Acts allowed detention for from fifteen days to six months, with extensions permitted by some provinces. In all provinces, excepting the United Provinces, the statutes required that the detenu be informed of the grounds on which he was being held. In the United Provinces the law of 1949 allowed detention for six months without informing the detenu of the grounds, and only if this period was to be extended had the person to be so informed and the particulars of the case referred to a special tribunal. All these Acts, excepting that of Bombay, granted the detenu the right to make representation against his arrest and detention, but some laws laid down that only such attention need be paid to this representation as the Governor desired. Few of the provincial laws allowed the detenu counsel. The West Bengal Act

---

[88] Mohammed Iqbal, *The Law of Preventive Detention in England, India and Pakistan*, p. 137.

[89] See Coupland, op. cit., Vol. II, Chapter XII. In 1938, for example, an AICC resolution stated that 'the Congress warns the public that civil liberty does not cover acts of incitements to, violence or promulgation of palpable falsehoods.' *IAR* 1938, II, p. 278. This was aimed at communal troubles. In general, however, Congress ministries lived up to the party's condemnation of detention laws, and many such laws were repealed or lapsed during the tenure of the ministries. See Coupland, ibid.

[90] This action was taken under Section 9 of the Indian Independence Act, Iqbal, op. cit., p. 126.

III of 1948 provided that if detention were to exceed three months, the provincial government was bound to place the case before a Calcutta High Court Judge, who could release the individual for insufficient grounds. If the detention was upheld, the person could be detained for six months before the case again went before the High Court Judge.[91]

There is little evidence that these laws allowing preventive detention were loosely or cruelly used. They were aimed not at thought-control, or at intimidating the masses into subservience, but at actual saboteurs who would have endangered the physical security of the nation by attacking railways or public utility installations or at individuals who incited or abetted communal friction or frenzy. Several of the League Muslims in the Assembly spoke against these 'lawless laws', charging that Hindu governments, particularly in the United Provinces, had been much more severe on Muslims than on Hindus in communally disturbed areas—an allegation in which, one expects, there was some truth. But, in general, Assembly members believed that provisions for preventive detention were necessary and few attacked the principle of detention in the debates.[92] What members did fear was that governments, in exercising their powers of preventive detention, would infringe other fundamental rights.

The reasons for this apprehension reached back to the spring of 1947. At that time, it will be remembered, the Advisory Committee had declined to include among the rights the clauses guaranteeing secrecy of correspondence and no arrest without a warrant.[93] The Advisory Committee also passed over the clause in Munshi's draft those rights providing that no person could be detained without being informed of the grounds for his detention or be denied counsel, and that he must be brought before a magistrate within twenty-four hours of his arrest. During the various debates on the Fundamental Rights, members of the Assembly had called for the inclusion of all these rights. Additional pressure in favour of some of them was brought by persons outside the Assembly. The editor of the

---

[91] Ibid., pp. 161–3.

[92] For example, the subject of preventive detention had come up several times relative to its place on the Legislative Lists (see *CAD* IX, 20, 730; *CAD* IX, 23, 866) and its existence was never questioned. See also *CAD* VIII, 3, 73ff.

[93] See above, page 72.

Indian Law Review of Calcutta and other members of the Calcutta Bar, for example, suggested that the 'no searches and seizures' provision should be added to the Rights.[94] Ambedkar even accepted an amendment to this effect on the floor of the House on 3 December 1948, but at some later date it was quietly dropped.

Ayyar and others might claim that it was reasonable to omit such rights in the interests of crime prevention, but without protection the innocent could also suffer, Assembly members realized—and in any case, the principle was the same. The due process clause would have achieved the purposes of such rights provisions; so long as it was in the Draft, all was not lost. But when it was deleted, Assembly members felt the absence of the other rights even more keenly, particularly in view of the wide variety of detention laws existing in the provinces. They had obeyed the Whip in December 1948; they had adopted Article 15 minus the due process clause. But by September 1949 they were determined to redress the balance of liberty and to restore at least some safeguards for individual freedom.

In May 1949 three Assembly members had moved amendments designed to curtail the Executive's power to detain.[95] Of these the most important was Thakur Das Bhargava's, which called for freedom from detention without trial except for alleged participation in dangerous or subversive activities affecting the public peace, the security of the state, or affecting different classes and communities. Detention, according to Bhargava's amendment, could only take place after a declaration had been made by the Executive that an abnormal or dangerous situation existed—and this declaration itself could not be questioned in court. No person could be detained longer than fifteen days without the case being presented before an independent tribunal presided over by a High Court judge or the equivalent. In cases where detention lasting longer than fifteen days

[94] Item 3, *Suggested Amendments to the Constitution; Prasad papers.*

[95] Amendments 52, 53, and 54 of Consolidated List of 5 May 1949; *Orders of the Day,* 5 May 1949. These amendments were submitted by two Muslims, Z. H. Lari and Mohd. Tahir, and by T. D. Bhargava. Lari's and Tahir's amendments provided that there could be no detention without adequate cause, and they provided for a speedy and public trial. That such amendments were moved was another indication that the Assembly's aim was to control, not to prohibit, preventive detention.

was upheld, there were to be quarterly reviews by the special tribunal. No person was to be detained for more than a year.[96]

The pressure brought by the Assembly on its leaders produced results in August and September, those hectic months when final decisions had to be made on other tangled issues such as federalism, compensation for property, and language. On 15 September Ambedkar submitted to the Assembly a new Article 15A, which provided that any arrested person must be brought before a magistrate within twenty-four hours of his arrest, informed of the nature of the accusation, and detained further only on the authority of the magistrate.[97] The arrested person should not be denied counsel. But these provisions were not to apply to persons held under preventive detention laws. An individual so held could not be detained longer than three months unless an Advisory Board consisting of High Court judges, or persons qualified to be judges, supported further detention, and unless laws permitting greater periods of detention were in existence. Parliament could by law prescribe, according to Ambedkar's article:

> The circumstances under which and the class or classes of cases in which a person who is arrested under any law providing for preventive detention may be determined for a period longer than three months and also the maximum period for which any such person may be detained.[98]

Ambedkar's new article was not as solicitous of individual liberty as Bhargava's, or as Ambedkar himself later claimed it to be. It limited the Executive's power to detain, but gave Parliament authority to prescribe detention for long periods. The article did, however, make all detention beyond a three month's period subject to the control of the Advisory Board. During August, when the provision was being framed, the Home Affairs Ministry, the branch of the Executive most immediately concerned, did not take kindly to this interference with its prerogatives and attacked the measure.

---

[96]   Bhargava's amendment was No. 54 as above.

[97]   For the text of Article 15a, see *CAD* IX, 35, 1496–7, and Amendment I, list I, of 12 September 1949, *Orders of the Day*—where it bore T.T. Krishnamachari's name as well as Ambedkar's.

[98]   Ibid.

The substance of Ambedkar's provision had been communicated to H. V. R. Iengar, secretary in the ministry, by S. N. Mukerjee of the Assembly Secretariat, who explained that certain members believed that Article 15 as then passed would not provide adequate safeguards against unwarranted arrest and detention. 'More recently,' Mukerjee wrote, 'there have been further criticisms of a similar nature from certain quarters.' Would Iengar let him know quickly what were the Home Ministry's comments?[99]

The Home Affairs Ministry's reply, in all likelihood approved by Patel, claimed that the terms of Article 15A would hamper its police activities. The letter conveyed the ministry's 'very strong objections' to the powers projected for Advisory Boards. 'It would not be possible', the reply read, 'for the Executive to surrender their judgement to an Advisory Board as a matter of constitutional compulsion.' The ministry wanted the details of detention to be left in the hands of the legislatures, and the most it would concede was that the Union Government would suggest to provincial governments that they abide by Advisory Board decisions.[100]

Introducing Article 15A in the Assembly, despite the Home Ministry's objections, Ambedkar noted that Article 15 had been violently criticized by the Indian public. And 'a large part of the House, including myself, were greatly dissatisfied with the wording of the Article', he said. 'We are therefore now, by introducing Article 15A, making, if I may say so, compensation for what was done then in passing Article 15.' The new article, Ambedkar believed, 'certainly saves a great deal which had been lost by the non-introduction of the words 'due process of law'. . . . Those who are fighting for the protection of individual freedom ought to congratulate themselves that it has been possible to introduce this clause.' Some powers of preventive detention had to be kept, Ambedkar explained, due to the 'present circumstances in the country'.[101]

The Assembly's reaction to Ambedkar's new article was, in general, favourable. Most speakers agreed that the times demanded

99 Letter from S. N. Mukerjee to H. V. R. Iengar, Home Secretary, dated 16 August 1949; *Law Ministry Archives.*

100 Letter from H. V. R. Iengar to S. N. Mukerjee, dated 19–20 August 1949; ibid.

101 *CAD* IX, 35, 1497–8.

some extraordinary measures, but that detention procedures should be strictly controlled. The more substantial amendments would have given detenus the rights reserved by Article 15A for other classes of arrested persons—those of a speedy public hearing before a magistrate, the use of counsel, etc. Pandit Kunzru spoke most cogently, as was so often the case, against the excesses of preventive detention. He supported the right of a detenu to present his case both at the time of his arrest and later before the Advisory Board. He also favoured a maximum limit for detention. To the argument that the representatives of the people in Parliament could do no wrong, Kunzru replied that in the United States there were safeguards against Congressional excesses, and that even the Japanese under a military occupation had rights not provided by Article 15A.[102]

Ambedkar, replying, conceded these points and moved amendments granting detenus the right to know the grounds for their arrest and to make representation against it. He claimed, however, that the detenu's right to make representation to the Advisory Board was 'implicit' in Article 15A and the right of cross-examination and other rights of accused persons were protected by the provisions of the Criminal Procedure Code.[103] After a closure motion had ended the debate, the Assembly negatived all amendments excepting those of Ambedkar to his own article; the amended provision was passed.

But the issue was not yet settled. The Government, prodded by the Home Ministry, intended to have its way. Less than two weeks before the Constitution was completed, on 15 November 1949, T. T. Krishnamachari moved an amendment in the Assembly embodying the views that the Home Ministry had expressed the previous August: there was to be no interference with Executive action in detention cases.

The amendment gave to Parliament the power to prescribe the maximum period of detention, the power to prescribe the categories of cases in which a person could be detained for longer than three months 'without obtaining the opinion of an Advisory Board', and the power to lay down the procedures to be followed by Advisory Boards. Commending the amendment to the House, Krishnamachari said that a number of members had seen it and agreed with its terms.

---

[102] *CAD* IX, 36, 1551–2.
[103] Ibid., pp. 1560–3.

He called it a 'wholesome' amendment and concluded by saying that indefinite detention had been made impossible.[104] He failed to point out, however, that this amendment made it possible for Parliament to make laws providing for detention unscrutinized by Advisory Boards and could so circumscribe Advisory Board procedure as to make it useless as a protection of individual liberty.

None of the Oligarchy spoke on the amendment. But Ambedkar defended it, somehow contriving to say that he believed that it lessened the 'harshness' of Article 15A. He defended detention unsupervised by the courts on the grounds that there might be cases when it would endanger state security if members of the Judicial Board knew the facts regarding the detention of any particular individual. Ambedkar also pointed out that Parliament must specifically define the categories to which such extraordinary detention would apply.[105] His arguments let in but little sun on a gloomy scene. And one wonders if he could himself have believed them.

Patel had won a victory. The authority of the courts in cases of personal liberty had been lessened and the individual had lost another of the remaining vestiges of the protection of due process. This particular aspect of personal freedom had been whittled down until on paper, at least, it was nearly non-existent. And although Assembly members had resisted this, in the end they had pinned their faith upon the mercy of the Legislature and the good character of their leaders.

4. Preventive Detention since 1950

The Provisional Parliament passed the first Preventive Detention Act within a month of the inauguration of the Constitution, in February 1950. In the Act, 'The courts were expressly forbidden from questioning the necessity for any detention order issued by the Government. The subjective satisfaction of the authorities was to be the determining factor in every case.'[106] And, it was subsequently discovered, the

---

[104] For the text of the amendment, and Krishnamachari's defence of it, see *CAD* XI, 2, 531. These provisions became part of Clause (7) of Article 22 of the *Constitution*.

[105] *CAD* XI, 3, 576.

[106] O. H. Bayley, *Preventive Detention in India*, p. x.

courts could not enquire into the truth of facts put forward by the Executive as grounds for detaining an individual.[107] The nation was indeed at the mercy of the Legislature and the Executive.

Commending this first detention Bill to Parliament, Patel explained that it would be used against those 'whose avowed object is to create disruption, dislocation, and tamper with communications, to suborn loyalty and make it impossible for normal government based on law to function'.[108] He cited labour troubles, the Telengana uprising, and pointed to the Communists in justification of such Executive powers. The original Act has been extended eleven times since 1950 and seems now to be a fixture of Indian life. Subsequent versions of the law have been softened, however, and Advisory Boards now have power to release detenus if they think that the Executive has no case for detention.[109]

That the Constituent Assembly had successfully removed due process from the Constitution so that judicial review of preventive detention cases would not be possible was established in the well-known Gopalan's case.[110] The detention of Gopalan was upheld because the Supreme Court 'found it impossible to interpret the term "law" in Article 21 of the Constitution as meaning *jus* as distinct from *lex* and consequently refrained from examining the consistency of procedure laid down in the Preventive Detention Act with the principles of natural justice'.[111]

The authority thus given to the Government in India is a potential danger to liberty. It has been used with restraint, however, and no one has ever proved the charge that the Executive has used it for partisan purposes. Gopalan and other Communist leaders, for example, were finally released and may 'pursue their political activities as long as they do not amount to violence and subversion'[112]—and Kerala has shown

[107] All India Reporter (AIR) 1954, S.C. 179. See ibid.. Appendix I, p. 129.

[108] Ibid., p. 12.

[109] Ibid., p. 25.

[110] 1950 *SCJ*, pp. 174–311.

[111] Alexandrowicz, op. cit., p. 24. This court decision bore out the arguments M. A. Baig bad made in the Assembly; see p. 105 above.

[112] Ibid., p. 34. For an excellent review of the legal aspects of preventive detention, see ibid., Chapter 2. The number of detenus in India in 1950 was 10,962, of whom over 6000 were Communists in Telengana. In 1951 the figure had dropped to 2316 and in 1960 to 153. Bayley, op. cit., pp. 25 and 32.

that the Union Government can be very tolerant indeed. Those who wish India well can only hope that the Union Government will continue, despite the extreme provocation of such events as the border war with China, its past policy of treating the Preventive Detention Act as primarily a psychological deterrent in the fight against subversive activities throughout India, and will not use it to bring about ideological conformity and the downfall of liberty.

The Fundamental Rights and Directive Principles: A Summing Up

It is quite evident that the Fundamental Rights and the Directive Principles were designed by the members of the Assembly to be the chief instruments in bringing about the great reforms of the social revolution. Have they, one may ask, helped to bring Indian society closer to the Constitution's goal of social, economic, and political justice for all?

Briefly, the answer is yes. The purpose of a Bill of written rights is to create or to preserve individual liberty and a democratic way of life based on equality among the members of society—only in theory are rights and liberties separable from democracy. In India it appears that the Fundamental Rights have both created a new equality that had been absent in traditional Indian (largely Hindu) society and have helped to preserve individual liberty. The character of rights issues and the behaviour of human beings what they are, it is the absence of comment about the state of rights in India, rather than its presence, that is significant: it is the denial of rights, not their existence, that makes news. A strong indication, therefore, of the reasonably healthy condition of civil liberties in India is the lack of criticism of their absence—and there is no reason not to attribute this in some measure to the Constitution. The number of rights cases brought before High Courts and the Supreme Court attest to the value of the Rights, and the frequent use of prerogative writs testifies to their popular acceptance as well. The classic arguments against the inclusion of written rights in a Constitution have not been borne out in India. In fact, the reverse may have been the case. Those who argue against written rights cite public opinion as the greater safeguard of rights, but in a politically underdeveloped country like India, which also lacks the rapid communications necessary to the formation and expression of public opinion, it may be that written rights come close to being a necessity.

The Directive Principles have also been sceptically received by some authorities. Dr. Wheare has doubted 'whether there is any gain, on balance, from introducing these paragraphs of generalities into a Constitution'.[113] Yet as we have seen, the Directive Principles have been a guide for the Union Parliament and state legislatures; they have been cited by the courts to support decisions; governmental bodies have been guided by their provisions. The Government of India Fiscal Commission of 1949, for example, recognized that its recommendations should be guided by the Principles. 'It is obvious', the report said, 'that a policy for the economic development of India should conform to the "objectives" laid down in the. . . . Directive Principles of State Policy.'[114]

K. M. Panikkar believes that both the Rights and the Principles have been the source and inspiration of reform legislation, for under their aegis 'the Indian Parliament has been active in the matter of social legislation, whether it be called by the Hindu Code or by another name'.[115] The Fundamental Rights of other constitutions may have served as well as—or even better than—those of the Indian Constitution in protecting the existing rights and liberties of the peoples concerned. It is very doubtful, however, if in any other constitution the expression of positive or negative rights has provided so much impetus towards changing and rebuilding society for the common good.

---

[113] K. C Wheare, *Modern Constitutions*, p. 69. See also Jennings,. *Some Characteristics*, pp.30ff.

[114] *Fiscal Commission Report*, Chapter devoted to Fundamental Objectives of an Economic Policy, p. 9. See also *The First Five Year Plan, a Draft Outline*, p. I, and *Third Five Year Plan*, pp. 1–6 .

[115] Panikkar, *Hindu Society*, p. 52.

5

The Executive–
Strength with Democracy

*The Parliamentary system produces a stronger government, for (a)
members of the Executive and Legislature are overlapping, and (b) the
heads of government control the Legislature.*

K. M. Munshi

THE members of the Constituent Assembly were committed to
framing a democratic constitution for India, and there was little
doubt that this democracy should be expressed in the institutions
of direct, responsible government, and not in the indirect system
envisaged by Gandhi and some of his followers. In the Euro-
American constitutional tradition, to which the Assembly looked
for its examples, there had grown up three major types of Executive:
the American presidential system, the Swiss elected Executive, and
British cabinet government. Which of these should the Assembly
adopt? Or could some workable combination of them be made?

The Assembly had to find the answer in the context of the past—
India's familiarity with cabinet government—and in the needs of the
present and future. The needs were strength and quick effectiveness,
for huge strides in industrial, agricultural, and social development had to be made and an enormous population well and fairly
governed. In the rapidly moving world of the mid-twentieth century,
a new India had to be built almost overnight. How was the leadership for this task to be provided? What type of Executive would be
stable, strong, effective, and quick, yet withal, democratic?

The Assembly chose a slightly modified version of the British
cabinet system. India was to have a President, indirectly elected for
a term of five years, who would be a constitutional head of state in

the manner of the monarch in England. He could be removed by impeachment proceedings brought against him by the Parliament. A Vice-President, also indirectly elected, would serve as head of state in the event of the President's incapacity or death; he would also be the chairman of the upper house of Parliament. As in England, there was to be a council of ministers, headed by the Prime Minister and collectively responsible to Parliament, to aid and advise the head of state. The President was to be the nominal head of the Executive; the Prime Minister the real head. The remaining member of the Executive named in the Constitution was the Attorney-General.

Because the Indian Constitution includes a constitution for the provinces as well as the Union, the Constituent Assembly had to frame a second set of Executive provisions. The result was that Governors appointed by the President would head the provincial Executives, which in all other major respects were to be like that in New Delhi. To avoid needless repetition, this chapter will therefore make only occasional references to provincial Executives. It should be explained, however, that in the early stages of the drafting process it was thought that Governors might be directly elected. Under this scheme, Governors would also have had some powers to exercise in their discretion, and in other ways they would not have been the figureheads they later became. The Assembly finally rejected the idea of elected Governors, believing, no doubt correctly, that there would be friction between them and popular ministries. The discretionary and other special powers once allowed Governors were removed to bring their status into line with that of the President, many of these powers being transferred to the central government. For this reason it is safe to assume that the greater powers given Governors during the earlier stages of the framing process can in part be accounted for by the concept of looser federalism existing at that time, although this was never explicitly stated in the Assembly. A combination of a tighter federal structure and a belief in the desirability of uniform Executive procedures had worked to make the authority of the Governors and the President nearly identical.[1]

---

[1]   The decision to provide for nominated and not for elected Governors was most frequently couched, however, in terms of ensuring the Executive's efficiency. That the change might affect the federal structure by centralizing it further was alluded to only once, by Nehru, who explained that he had come to favour nominated Governors partly because it would keep the centre in touch with the units and would remove a source of possible 'separatist tendencies'; *CAD* VIII, 12, 454–6.

But these were developments of the future. Having decided that it should adopt the British system of cabinet government, the Assembly had to find answers to subsidiary questions as well. India was to be a republic not a monarchy. Therefore, should there be a separate head of state? Or should the Prime Minister also be the head of state? And how was the head of state to be chosen and what should be his powers? India was a land of minorities. Should there be special provision made for minority representation in the Executive? Under the system of parliamentary government practised in England, the relations between the Executive and Parliament and, within the Executive, between the cabinet and the head of state were largely controlled by unwritten conventions, whereas in Ireland many of these same conventions had been written into the Constitution. How was the problem of controlling and limiting Executive powers to be resolved in the Indian context, bearing in mind always the supreme need for strong, efficient, yet democratic government?

What Kind of an Executive?

During the years of the Independence Movement first thoughts about the constitution of free India had centred on fundamental rights, on the form of election, and the composition of legislatures. These issues were of surpassing importance because they closely involved communal interests and the social revolution. The character of the Executive had received much less attention, although it had not been ignored.

No matter how the Governor was to be chosen, there had been strong pressure from the first that he should be a constitutional head of the unit Executive—see especially the unanimity on this subject of the replies of Provincial Constitution Committee members to Rau's questionnaire; *Prasad papers*, File 4-P/47. Although the election of Governors had, until the last, some supporters, most of the Assembly members who had originally held this view came to favour nominated Governors—among them were T. T. Krishnamachari, Mrs. Durgabai, and, the Prime Minister of Bombay, B. G. Kher. Pandit Pant, Prime Minister of U.P., also supported nomination; see Amend. 2015, *Amendment Book* I, op. cit., p. 205. Three provincial legislatures, one provincial government, and a body of newspaper editorial sentiment also favoured nominated Governors. The newspapers, particularly, did so because they feared friction between an elected Governor and a popular ministry. This view was shared by the Drafting Committee—see Draft Constitution, p. vii—and by Kunzru and other Assembly members—see *CAD* VIII, 11 and 12, and especially *CAD* VIII, 11, 830–3.

According to the Nehru Report, the Executive branch was to have a Governor-General, as head of state, with powers like those in other (pre-Statute of Westminster) Dominions, and an Executive Council of ministers chosen and operating as a responsible government. Collective responsibility of the ministers was explicitly provided for.[2]

The Sapru Report had also favoured a constitutional head of state. But it presented two alternative recommendations for the Executive itself, both of which reflected its preoccupation with communal issues—and which were to reappear in the Assembly. The Executive first proposed was of the parliamentary type but included special provisions for minority representation; the alternative proposal was for a council of ministers elected by proportional representation.[3] Two other items in the Sapru Committee's report are worthy of note. The Punjab Hindu Mahasabha's memorial to the Sapru Committee recommended traditional parliamentary government, while the Akali Sikh Board called for an irremovable Executive with special minority provisions, preferably along Swiss lines, claiming that the parliamentary system had been inefficient, corrupt, and had caused the minorities great suffering.[4] In the Constituent Assembly it was the same: the members of sensitive minorities (Muslims particularly) supported the Swiss system or some form of elected ministry, while the members of larger communities favoured traditional cabinet government.

During the early months of the Assembly, various members tentatively drafted Executive provisions—both for the Union and provincial Executives. Several did so on their own initiative, others in response to a questionnaire prepared by B. N. Rau. With few exceptions these envisaged a parliamentary Executive. K. M. Munshi in his Draft Constitution provided for a head of state with powers like those of the British monarch, for joint responsibility of ministers, etc.[5] He preferred the British system to American presidential government, believing it to be stronger because of the overlapping memberships of government and legislature.[6]

[2] *Nehru Report*, Clauses 22–27, pp. 108–9.
[3] *Sapru Report*, pp. vii–xi.
[4] Ibid. For the Hindu Mahasabha, see p. xxix; the Sikhs, p. lxi.
[5] Munshi, *Draft Constitution*, Clauses XX–XXIII. K. Santhanam submitted a draft provincial constitution; *Law Ministry Archives*, File CA/64/Cons/47.
[6] Munshi, in *Notes on a Constitution*, undated, pp. 9–10; *Munshi papers*. For text, see quotation at the head of this chapter.

B. N. Rau's questionnaire on the Executive included queries about the name, method of choosing, and functions of the head of state and of a vice-president—if there was to be one. There were also questions about the nature and type of the Executive as a whole, the method of choosing and the responsibilities of the ministers, as well as the relationship between the head of state and the council of ministers. Among the questions was one asking if there should be any special provisions to help in achieving a stable Executive.[7]

Rau's questionnaire was sent in mid-March 1947 to members of the Central Assembly and provincial legislatures. Only two answers seem to have been received. In early May, the questionnaire was submitted to the fifteen members of the Union Constitution Committee, which the Assembly had voted to establish on 30 April. This time five replies were received, all supporting cabinet government with a constitutional head of state.[8] One suggested that the Prime Minister could either be elected by the Parliament or chosen for the office as the leader of the majority party in the Parliament.[9]

The questionnaires had been sent to the members of the Union Constitution Committee as a result of a decision taken at the committee's first meeting on 5 May. Having elected Nehru chairman, the committee decided that the replies to the questionnaires should be used as the basis for a white paper on the principles of the Union Constitution that B. N. Rau was to prepare for the committee's use. Rau was also to include his own views and recommendations. He duly produced a lengthy 'Memorandum on the Union Constitution'

The members of the Congress Experts Committee, in their meetings during the summer of 1946, had considered the Executive only in a cursory manner, and one may safely assume that this was largely because the leaders of the Assembly took it for granted that the Constitution would have a parliamentary Executive. D. R. Gadgil, a member of the committee, in an interview with the author.

[7] For text of questionnaire, see Rau, *India's Constitution*, pp. 16–41. The questionnaire did not confine itself to the Executive. Questions were included concerning the Legislature, the Judiciary, and amendment. The question concerning special provision for a stable Executive had roots in the Simon Commission and the Round Table Conference. See ibid., p. 24 and Cmd. 3778, p. 221.

[8] These replies came from K. T. Shah, S. P. Mookerjee, and K. M. Panikkar—see *Law Ministry Archives*, File CA/63/Cons/47-III—and from A. K. Ayyar and N. G. Ayyangar in a joint memorandum—see *Prasad papers*, File 3-C/47.

[9] That of S. P. Mookerjee, who also suggested that the government should fall only of a specific no-confidence motion passed by an absolute majority.

and a set of 'Draft Clauses' which, as he had received so little response to his questionnaire, must stand as his own contribution rather than as a summary of the views of others.[10] As one would suspect, he favoured cabinet government. His memorandum also provided for a president with the powers of a constitutional head of state who was to exercise the executive authority of the Union with the aid and advice of a council of ministers.[11] The members of the Union Constitution Committee who had put their views in writing had all included the office of Vice-President. Rau did not do this, but provided for a committee composed of the Chairman of the Senate, the Chief Justice, and the Speaker of the House of Representatives to act for the president in case of his incapacity or death. The Union Constitution Committee rejected this suggestion during their June 1947 meetings.

India was formally set upon the path of parliamentary government during these early June meetings of the Union Constitution Committee. The definitive moment came at a joint meeting with the Provincial Constitution Committee—set up at the same time as the UCC, with Patel as chairman—on 7 June, to determine the basic principles of the Constitution. The decision was that India should have 'the parliamentary system of constitution, the British type of constitution, with which we are familiar'.[12]

Consequent decisions followed. At meetings held during the next few days, the Union Constitution Committee laid down what the major functions of the Executive should be. Using Ayyangar and Ayyar's joint memorandum and Rau's proposal as guides, committee members made the President Commander-in-Chief of the armed forces, gave him the power to refer Bills back to Parliament, and to dissolve the lower house on the advice of his ministers; he was not to have certain discretionary powers allowed him in Rau's memorandum. As to the Prime Minister, the committee at one time believed that it should be explicitly provided in the Constitution that he be the person most likely to command a

[10] See the introductory note to the memorandum by B. Shiva Rao in Rau, *India's Constitution*, p. 62.

[11] For the text of Rau's *Memorandum and Draft Clauses*, dated 30 May 1947, see ibid., pp. 62–140.

[12] Patel's description of the meeting; *CAD* IV, 2, 578. See also minutes of the meeting and minutes of UCC meeting, 6 June 1947, when preliminary decisions were taken; *Prasad papers*, File 3-C/47.

majority in the lower house.[13] This was not done, however, and the Union Constitution Committee report said only that there should be a council of ministers headed by a prime minister to aid and advise the President.

The committee also decided against including a special provision to ensure greater governmental stability. They believed, presumably, that ministries would be assured of a reasonable stay in office by the unthreatened ascendency of the Congress.[14] And they were probably also influenced by the failure of the Irish to solve this problem through the use of constitutional devices, a fact that Rau had noted in his memorandum. The committee's decisions were gathered together by Rau in a second memorandum, dated 21 June 1947, which became the basis of the UCC's final report, drafted during the closing days of June.

Presenting the report to the Assembly, Nehru carefully explained the ministerial character of the Executive, emphasizing that the President had no 'real power', although the Presidency was a position 'of great authority and dignity'.[15] Assembly members put forward various suggestion's for increasing the President's stature and placing him above the grime of the governmental market-place. They recommended, for example, that he either divest himself of, or declare, his financial assets and that he be above party. Nehru replied that he believed the President should disclose his holdings of stock and securities, but that this should be a convention. He also confessed a 'sneaking sympathy with the proposition that the President should be a non-party man', but said that this would be impracticable and that the best that could be hoped for was the President's impartial behaviour in office.[16]

The President's role as a figurehead was to be reflected in his indirect election. If the President was elected by adult franchise 'and yet (we)

---

[13] Minutes of the UCC meetings, 8–9 June 1947; *Prasad papers*, File 3-C/47. For more on Rau's plan for discretionary powers, see pp. 128ff. below.

[14] Minutes of the meeting, 8 June 1947; *Prasad papers*, ibid. K. M. Panikkar believed that this was not necessary because future party alignments would be based on 'economic and political ideologies, rather than on sectional, religious and communal bases . . . and the elections fought on economic and political ideologies will secure a stable majority to any party which may be in power'. Panikkar in his answer to Rau's Questionnaire, op. cit.

[15] *CAD* IV, 6, 734. For the text of the UCC Report, see *Reports of Committees, First Series*, pp. 45–67.

[16] *CAD* IV, 9, 863–7.

did not give him any real powers, it might become slightly anomalous', said Nehru, especially since 'we wanted to emphasize the ministerial character of the Government, that power really resided in the Ministry and in the Legislature and not in the President as such'.[17] The Union Constitution Committee was fully agreed that the President should be a constitutional head, and the idea of his direct election was considered only in passing.[18] On 8 June it decided that the President should be elected by an electoral college consisting of the lower house of the federal parliament and the lower houses in the units—a basic concept that was amplified but never departed from during the framing of the provision. On 9 June Munshi wrote a letter recommending that the President and Governors be elected by an electoral college directly elected for this purpose.[19] On 10 June two sub-committees of the UCC took up the matter and suggested a somewhat different, but still indirect, method of election. A joint meeting of the UCC and PCC on the morning of 11 June by a majority vote called on the UCC to reconsider its decision on Presidential election, but noted that its recommendations were not binding on either of the two committees in separate session. The UCC meeting that same afternoon took the final decision that the President should be indirectly elected. The electoral college was to be the two houses of the federal parliament plus the lower houses of the provincial assemblies—where the vote was to be calculated according to a formula devised by N. G. Ayyangar to give just weight to the provincial population.[20]

---

[17] *CAD* IV, 6, 713. A further reason Nehru gave was to avoid the expenditure of time and money and the dislocation of political life that a second major election—the first being the general elections to Parliament and the state assemblies—would cause. The Vice-President is also indirectly elected by a joint session of both houses of Parliament using proportional representation.

[18] This sentiment has been used by K. M. Munshi in his book *The President Under the Indian Constitution*, to support his contention that the president under the Constitution is not a figurehead but has wide powers. This is an unwarranted assumption not borne out by the documents. See Munshi, *The President*, pp. 19–24. Neither do the documents bear out Munshi's statement that an unspecified joint meeting of the committee at one point decided that the President should be directly elected; see ibid, p. 22.

[19] For the text of Munshi's letter, see *Law Ministry Archives*, File Union Constitution Committee.

[20] For the minutes of the relevant meetings, other UCC and PCC meetings, and the official documents of that week, see *Law Ministry Archives*, Files Union

The reasons behind this brief flurry in favour of direct election are not clear. Its supporters may have believed that a directly elected President would have greater stature, be a greater symbol of national unity— especially if the election placed him above party, though that was by no means a sure outcome of an election.[21] Such were the reasons put forward on the Assembly floor by the few Hindu members who, while continuing to support traditional cabinet government, advocated the direct election of the head of state. The major resistance to an indirectly elected President, and to a ministerial Executive as well, came from Muslim Assembly members, who favoured a directly elected head of state and an indirectly elected ministry for a variety of reasons, but primarily for self-protection.[22] Elected ministries, they reasoned, would be more stable considering the diversity of India's religious and other groups. In India parties and political groups were based on religion and not on political ideology, said A. A. Khan, and in such circumstances the Swiss system of government was superior to the British because it had proved itself effective 'where religious groups and sectional interests exist'.[23] Another Muslim member spoke against majority rule. Mutual differences in India, he said, can best be settled by having 'the representative of every party in the House included in the ministry'.[24] Ministers, according to some suggestions, ought to be elected by the legislatures from among their own number by proportional representation and ought to have a fixed term of office—as in Switzerland; in this view, ministers could at once be elected and responsible to Parliament.

Constitution Committee, and CA/64/Cons/47 and *Prasad papers*, File 3-C/47.

[21] For K. M. Munshi's version of the sentiments behind the movement, see Munshi, *The President*, pp. 22–23.

[22] Dr. Ambedkar apparently favoured an indirectly elected head of state. But he had opposed traditional cabinet government in his pamphlet *States and Minorities, What are Their Rights*, etc. He did not speak against cabinet government in the Assembly, however. In his pamphlet Ambedkar had advocated an Executive whose term of office should be co-extensive with the terms of the Legislature and with a Prime Minister elected by the legislature by single transferable vote. The representatives in the cabinet of majority and minority communities were to be elected by single transferable vote by the members of the minority and the majority communities in the legislature. Cabinet ministers could resign if they were censured but could be removed only by impeachment, ibid., Article II, Section II.

[23] *CAD* IV, 4, 633.

[24] Ibid., p. 642; K. S. Karimuddin. See also *CAD* IV, 8, and 11.

These ideas immediately drew the fire of Munshi and Nehru. Munshi defended the British system on the ground that candidates for elective ministries would make their appeals primarily to particular groups and that this would 'fragment the political life of the country'.[25] Nehru rejected these suggestions flatly. He could think of 'nothing more conducive to creating a feeble ministry and a feeble government than this business of electing them by proportional representation'.[26] On 28 July 1947, eighteen days before India became independent, the Assembly adopted the last of the principles regarding the Union Executive drafted by the Union Constitution Committee.[27]

The Executive provisions were changed little in the draft constitutions prepared by Rau and the Drafting Committee, although the Assembly considered many alterations.[28] But in future debates the well-known arguments reappeared. Those few who continued to advocate the Swiss system or the even smaller number who supported the American presidential form of government, were again told that for stability and strength the British system surpassed all others, particularly in Indian conditions. 'An infant democracy', said A. K. Ayyar, 'cannot afford, under modern conditions, to take the risk of a perpetual cleavage, feud, or conflict or threatened conflict between the Legislature and the Executive.'[29] Munshi asked: 'Why should we go back upon the tradition that has been built for over a hundred years and try a novel experiment framed 150 years ago and found wanting even in America?'[30] Other members called elected ministers communalism via the back door. Experience provided, the most forceful argument in favour of parliamentary government. Those who supported multi-party cabinets, said M. Tyagi, should recall the fiasco of the Interim Government—when a Muslim League

[25] Ibid., p. 651.

[26] *CAD* IV, 11, 915.

[27] The Assembly ten days earlier had adopted the principles of provincial constitutions as drafted by the PCC, which likewise provided for cabinet government.

[28] Certain substantial changes were made in Presidential (Executive) power in relation to the Emergency Powers. As these changed the structure of parliamentary government not at all, but the federal relationship a great deal, they will be considered in Chapter 8 on federalism and the distribution of powers.

[29] *CAD* VII, 24, 985–6.

[30] Ibid., pp. 984–5.

finance minister had held the whip hand in the Congress-League coalition. With the opposition defeated, the Assembly ratified its previous decision: India was to have an Executive founded on the British model.

Although some of the arguments presented in the Assembly were overstated, the grounds for the decision were sound and compelling. It is hard to imagine how the Swiss or American systems could have worked better, and it was perhaps particularly wise to avoid the Swiss example. The members of the Assembly, and particularly leaders like Nehru, were at pains to frame a direct, parliamentary constitution and not an indirect Gandhian one. Their aim, as we suggested in Chapter 2, was to create a new unity by breaking down the old loyalties that had fragmented and compartmentalized Indian life. Presumably Assembly members understood that having a fixed Executive of ministers elected by proportional representation would be a step back from the goal of national consciousness. All the talk of communalism by the back door was not simply anti-communal, or anti-Muslim; it expressed the realization that only in unity could India find strength and stability sufficient to accomplish her short and long-range tasks,[31] the realization that it would be futile to try to reform Indian society if the government itself was not reformed.

The Executive and Minority Interests

By rejecting the idea of ministers elected by proportional representation, the Assembly closed a major route by which minority groups could enter the government. Yet national unity depended also on communal harmony and on the cooperative efforts of all sections of Indian society. Minority fears were genuine. As Ambedkar had said, in a country so communally minded as India it could not be expected that the authorities would give equal treatment to those not of their own community.[32] This might not be true of Nehru, Patel, and other leaders, but it could be true of lesser officials. Assembly members

---

[31] For example, Pant, in his speech moving the establishment of the Advisory Committee, had warned against the 'unwholesome and to some extent degrading habit of thinking always in terms of communities and never in terms of citizens . . . (whereas) the individual citizen . . . is really the backbone of the state'. *CAD* II, 4, 312.

[32] Ambedkar, *States and Minorities*, Explanatory Note, p. 30.

realized that for minorities to feel that their interests were protected, for minorities to participate wholeheartedly in the national effort, they must in some way be assured of representation in the Executive.

B. N. Rau had asked in his questionnaire: 'Should provision be made to secure representation of different Communities on the Executive? If so, how?'[33] One answer came from Ayyangar and Ayyar in their joint Memorandum on the Principles of the Union Constitution. The President, they-wrote, in appointing ministers should have due regard for minority interests and geographical considerations. Of the other answers, several were affirmative, several negative. In his own Memorandum on the Union Constitution, Rau did not refer specifically to minority representation on the Executive; the President was only to be charged generally with safeguarding the legitimate interests of minorities. The members of the Union Constitution Committee, however, voted against minority representation on the Executive.[34]

This decision disappointed and annoyed several minority representatives, who brought the matter before the Minorities Sub-Committee of the Advisory Committee in July. It was not only Muslims and non-Congressmen, although they reopened the issue. Jagjivan Ram, leader of Congress Untouchables and H. J. Khandekar, a party stalwart from the Central Provinces, had recommended that seats be reserved for minorities in cabinets.[35] After lengthy discussions, however, the sub-committee, by the narrow margin of eight votes to seven, rejected a resolution establishing reserved seats for minorities in cabinets. The national interest would be better served, it was decided, by including an Instrument of Instructions in a Schedule to the Constitution, enjoining Governors and the President as far as practicable to appoint members of the important minority communities to the ministries.[36] The Advisory

---

[33] Question 15; see *India's Constitution*, op. cit., p. 25. Rau cited the Swiss precedent and the conventions of the Canadian constitution, as well as noting that there was no such provision whatsoever in the U.S.A.

[34] Minutes of the meeting, 9 June 1947; *Prasad papers*, File 3-C/47.

[35] See Ram and Khandekar answers to the questionnaire on minority rights drafted by Munshi, op. cit.; *Law Ministry Archives*, File CA/37/Com/47.

[36] See Report of the Minorities Sub-Committee to the parent Advisory Committee, dated 28 July 1947; *Law Ministry Archives*.

Committee concurred with the sub-committee's recommendations and suggested in its report on minority rights that an Instrument of Instructions like that issued under the 1935 Act be included in the Constitution. The Instrument appeared in both Rau's Draft and in the Draft Constitution, but was directed only at Governors, despite the Advisory Committee's recommendation that it apply equally to the President.[37]

Several months later the Drafting Committee recommended that this oversight should be rectified. It prepared an amendment to the Draft Constitution that provided for a similar Instrument of Instructions for the President. The President should, among other things, include among his ministers 'so far as practicable, members of important minority communities'.[38] When Muslim members of the Assembly made their final attack on parliamentary government, citing the Swiss system as true democracy because it provided for the representation of all groups instead of the 'tyranny of the majority', Ambedkar pointed out to them that the new Schedule would protect their interests. The following day the Assembly accepted the new article, and it appeared that there would be in the Constitution written provisions assuring minorities of representation on the Executive.[39]

The Drafting Committee's amendment went beyond the President's obligation to minorities, however, and in its other provisions it was the expression of a movement then current in the Assembly to restrict the authority of the Executive by writing into the Constitution limitations that in Britain had been left to convention. When this movement failed, the Instrument was removed from the Constitution and with it went the instruction to the President and the Governors to include the representatives of important minorities in their cabinets. As a result, only six weeks before the completion of the Constitution, minority representation in the Executive was

---

[37] *Draft Constitution*, Schedule IV.

[38] For the text of the Drafting Committee's suggested Schedule, see printed list of amendments List I of August 1948 and minutes of Drafting Committee meetings 18–20 October 1948; B. Shiva Rao, *Select Documents*, III.

[39] *CAD* VII, 30, 1189. The Instrument of Instructions was only implicitly, not actually, adopted at this time. The Assembly actually adopted a new Clause 62(5)a in the main body of the Constitution, which called upon the President to Act in accordance with the Instrument in the Schedule IIIA.

in fact left to convention.[40] The arrangement has worked reasonably well. Complaints by minority groups have not been, generally speaking, because they were under-represented but because their representatives were creatures of the party in power. This, however, is a political development against which there can be no constitutional safeguard.

Limiting Executive Power

The Constituent Assembly had sought to establish a parliamentary Executive for India because it promised strength, cohesive action, and leadership; yet at the same time it feared Executive power. Its suspicions were understandable, for although Indians had participated to some degree in the legislative institutions' of parliamentary democracy, they had for many years been subject to the rule of autocratic Executives. Like colonial Americans, they had learned to have greater faith in legislatures as protectors of their rights; they had, indeed, conceived 'an ineradicable mistrust of the Executive branch of government'.[41] That this distrust was in some measure offset, particularly as regards the Union Government, by the honour and esteem in which leaders like Nehru, Azad, Prasad, and Patel were held, did not alter the fundamentals of the situation.

Assembly members, no less than the men attending the Constitutional Convention in Philadelphia, realized that an effective balance had to be struck between strong government and responsible, democratic government. Words used to describe the mood in Philadelphia in 1787 aptly reflect that of New Delhi in 1947:

> Over the whole convention still hung the dread of future tyranny as well as of immediate anarchy. The delegates were sure that unless anarchy could be avoided, an early despot was certain to appear, as in the classic pattern of republican failure. They believed that anarchy could be at least postponed by the establishment of an adequate central government, but they could only guess what powers would make it neither too weak for security nor too strong for liberty.[42]

[40] For the details of this affair and the demise of this protection for minorities, see p. 139.

[41] Professor Max Beloff in his introduction to *The Federalist*, p. xvi.

[42] Carl Van Doren, *The Great Rehearsal*, p. 62.

The Assembly feared both that the Executive branch as a whole might become too strong, ignore its responsibility to the Legislature and take arbitrary action on its own initiative, and also that the President might not behave as a constitutional head of state. He might usurp the powers given to his office by the Constitution—which were to be exercised only on the advice of his ministers—and personally assume the authority to govern.

The Assembly included a variety of provisions in the Constitution to limit and to control action by the Executive branch as a whole. It was explicitly stated that the council of ministers was collectively responsible to the Legislature. As we have seen, the Executive's power to practice preventive detention depended on the passage of suitable legislation by Parliament or was subject to the review of independent tribunals. In a later chapter on federalism we shall see how the Assembly made the exercise of emergency powers, both by provincial Executives and by the Union Executive, subject to review by the Union Parliament. Similarly, the Assembly moved to curtail the powers of the Union Government in favour of provincial governments, in an attempt to prevent the aggrandizement of power by the Union Executive. Indeed, it was in part due to the feared misuse of Executive power that the Assembly adopted cabinet government instead of the fixed Executive: members believed that with the separation of powers of the Swiss or American systems, the Executive would not be sufficiently subject to legislative control.

The Constitutent Assembly considered one other mechanism for limiting and controlling Executive power: Instruments of Instructions. These were to have been included in the Constitution as Schedules and, although they were apparently aimed at the Governors and the President, they would have curtailed the powers of the cabinets as well. The Instruments would have limited Executive power in two ways: by establishing supervisory councils, independent of councils of ministers, to advise the President and Governors in the exercise of certain of their functions, and by embodying in written form several of the major conventions of parliamentary government. These written conventions were directed exclusively at Governors and the President, indicating that Assembly members feared most that the heads of the Executive might attempt to escape from ministerial control. The President and the Governors must be, beyond doubt or possibility of error, constitutional heads. It is to the Assembly's credit, however, that ultimately the Instruments of Instructions were not included in the Constitution; supervisory councils would almost certainly have split the Executives into competing groups. Written conventions, if not justiciable, would have been superfluous, and if justiciable they would have been a dangerous source of contention.

I. The President, the Council of Ministers, and Supervisory Councils

The first important suggestion that the President should be advised by a body separate from, and in addition to, his cabinet ministers, came from B. N. Rau. In his first memorandum on the Union Constitution, Rau suggested that the Constitution should provide for a Council of State, which would be 'a sort of Privy Council whose advice shall be available to the President whenever he chooses to obtain it in all matters of national importance in which he is required to act in his discretion',[43] This council, in Rau's view, should consist of the Prime Minister and his deputy, the Chief Justice, the Speaker of the House, the Chairman of the Senate, the Attorney-General, plus all former presidents, prime ministers, chief justices, and others appointed by the President. The Council was to have a dual role. It could advise the President on the appointment of judges and in the exercise of other such functions, and in this sense it would act as a brake on the authority of the head of state. Its second duty was to advise the President in the use of his discretionary power. Rau had given the President special

---

[43] See Rau, *India's Constitution*, p. 71. Rau had got the idea for his Council of State from the Irish Constitution, which he described in his *Precedents*, First Series, p. 51. In none of the memoranda or answers to Rau's questionnaire on the principles of the Union, or provincial constitutions, had suggestions of this kind been made. In his Draft Constitution, however, K. M. Munshi had provided for a kind of council of elders to advise the President. Munshi, who believed at this time that the President should be directly elected, provided for a council comprised of ten vice-presidents (who were to be representative of communal groups and the Princely States) and certain cabinet ministers. Only on the advice of this council could the President dissolve Parliament, assent or refuse assent to Bills, and promulgate ordinances. With the concurrence of six members of this council, the President could take action against the will of Parliament. Munshi's scheme would have thus split the Executive into two sections, yet he expected that otherwise the practices of cabinet government would be followed. See Munshi, *Draft Constitution*, Article XX.

responsibilities, like those of the Governor-General under the 1935 Act,[44] for the prevention of grave menace to the Union, for the safeguarding of the financial stability and credit of the Union, and for the protection of the legitimate interests of the minorities, which he was to fulfil in his discretion. Here again the Council of State would have restricted the use of Presidential authority. But in giving the President functions to exercise in his discretion, and by creating a special council to assist him, Rau had also narrowed the usual scope of cabinet authority. He made his intention to do this even clearer when he parenthetically noted that the President, with his Council of State, should have discretionary authority in regard to the protection of minorities and in the superintendence of elections (including the delimitation of constituencies) because such action should be taken 'free from party bias'.[45] Yet despite the possession of these extraordinary powers, the President should have, in the main, the very limited authority of a constitutional head of state. The relations between the President and his ministers, according to a clause in Rau's Memorandum, should 'as far as possible, be the same as between the King and his ministers in England'.[46]

The members of the Union Constitution Committee refused to split the Executive in this fashion and rejected Rau's provisions. Nor did it adopt the clause binding the President to observe the conventions of parliamentary government. The questions of limiting ministerial and presidential power were not closed, however; they would reappear on the Assembly floor. But the Union Constitution Committee did reject once and for all the idea of discretionary powers for the President; they were too reminiscent of arbitrary, imperial authority.[47] When Rau drafted his second Memorandum embodying the decisions of the Union Constitution Committee, he omitted these provisions.

It was with the methods Rau used to control the Executive and the head of state that the Union Constitution Committee, and later the Assembly, quarrelled, not with his aims; these the Assembly achieved in other ways. In the appointment of Supreme and High

---

[44] 1935 *Act*, Section 12
[45] Rau, *India's Constitution*, pp. 71–73.
[46] Ibid., p. 71.
[47] The UCC took all these decisions at its meeting of 8 June 1947; see minutes, *Prasad papers*, File 3-C/47.

Court justices, for example, the Assembly provided that the President should act neither in his discretion nor on the advice of his council of ministers but in consultation with the Chief Justice and other justices. Although the welfare of minorities in the nation would be a responsibility of the Union and provincial governments, and not of the President as Rau had envisaged, the Draft Constitution did provide for a special officer, appointed by the President, to oversee minority welfare. The President could also create special commissions to investigate the condition of minorities in relation to their constitutional safeguards. The Executive's authority to appoint the Public Service Commission was not to be circumscribed, however, and appointments were to be made by the President on the advice of the cabinet.[48] In practice the Public Service Commission has been a non-party body and its membership has not been tampered with for political reasons.

The members of the Assembly also agreed with Rau—though the idea cannot be credited entirely to him—that the control and supervision of elections should be in the hands of an independent body. The Draft Constitution provided for an Election Commission to assume the task. This commission, although appointed by the President, is a non-party, quasi-judicial body and, like the Public Service Commission, it has not suffered from political interference in the performance of its duties. Finally, the Assembly took from the President the discretionary responsibility given him by Rau for the maintenance of the financial stability and public security of the country—powers so sweeping that it is hard to conceive how anyone could have thought them compatible with the responsible, parliamentary constitution envisaged for India. Not only did the Assembly limit presidential authority in this regard, however; it went further and limited the power of the Executive branch as a whole. Although the Executive can initiate action to preserve public order and financial stability during an emergency, it must present its programme to Parliament for approval.[49]

[48] See Article 316 of the Constitution (Draft Article 283). At one time the UCC contemplated Presidential appointment of members of the Public Service Commission in his discretion. Governors appoint the members of State Public Service Commissions with ministerial advice (Article 316) although Governors at one time were to exercise this power in their discretion also; see Draft Article 285.

[49] See the Emergency Provisions of the *Constitution* and Chapter 8 below.

With the rejection of the letter, although not the spirit, of all of Rau's provisions controlling the Executive, it appeared that the device of a supervisory council was dead. Rau omitted it from his Draft Constitution of September 1947 and the Drafting Committee left it out of the Draft Constitution. Yet sometime between April and October 1948, three members of the Drafting Committee, Mohammed Saadulla, N. Madhava Rau, and Dr. Ambedkar, submitted an amendment to the Draft that would have re-created Rau's Council of State in another form. By Ambedkar's amendment (one presumes that he was its main advocate), the President was instructed to choose his ministers and to exercise his other functions in accordance with a new Instrument of Instructions.[50]

The Instrument further enjoined the head of state to form an Advisory Board composed of not less than fifteen members of both Houses of Parliament (who were to be elected to the board by proportional representation) to advise him when making the following appointments: the Chief Justice and other Supreme and High Court justices, ambassadors to foreign states, the Auditor General of India, the chairman and members of the Public Service Commission, and the members of the Election Commission. In the event of any dispute between the President and his Advisory Board regarding appointments, the two sides were to submit their views to Parliament.

Although the written conventions of Ambedkar's amendment were concerned primarily with the President, the Advisory Board was apparently intended to curb the power of the cabinet. The functions of the board cut directly across the normal channels of decision-making in parliamentary government and would have been an endless source of conflict within the Executive. The cabinet in any Executive, as far as any observer could reasonably predict in 1948, would for a long time be a Congress cabinet. In this presumption and in the political backgrounds of the sponsors, would seem to lie the motives

---

[50] Amendment 3404, *Amendment Book II*, p. 366. The new Instrument was also numbered Schedule IIIa. Ambedkar also moved an amendment (Number 3406, p. 368, ibid.) that laid down in a new Fourth Schedule nearly identical provisions applying to state Governors. It would be repetitious to discuss the provisions of, and the argument pertaining to, the Governor's Instrument of Instructions, and therefore this discussion will be confined to the President's Instrument of Instructions. The new Schedule IV was an amplification of the easting Fourth Schedule, which already embodied an Instrument of Instructions to Governors.

behind the amendment. None of the three were on cordial terms with the Congress. N. M. Rau had for many years served governments in the Princely States and although not strongly anti-Congress was hardly a supporter of the party. Saadulla had most recently been a member of the Muslim League and had only joined the Assembly after Partition. Ambedkar 'never took kindly' to the Congress, in B. Shiva Rao's delightfully mild phrase,[51] having had a running fight with it, largely over Untouchable causes, since the twenties.

And Ambedkar's pamphlet on States and Minorities and how to secure their rights in a free India plainly expresses the thoughts that gave rise to the Advisory Board. The application of the British parliamentary system to India, he wrote, will mean that the cabinet will be formed by the majority party, but although in England this would mean a political majority, in India 'the majority is a communal majority. No matter what social and political programmes it may have, the majority will retain its character of being a communal majority'.[52] The majority under the British system, Ambedkar continued, was under no obligation to bring representatives of the minority communities into the cabinet. This was 'full of menace to the life, liberty, and pursuit of happiness of minorities in general and the Untouchables in particular . . . It would make the majority community a governing class and the minority community a subject race.' His scheme (of having in essence an irremovable ministry with ministers from the various communities elected by single transferrable vote, as noted above) would prevent the exclusive control of the administration by the majority party, Ambedkar wrote, and would prevent the exclusion of minorities from the cabinet. Furthermore, it would prevent the inclusion in the Executive by the majority party of minority representatives who lacked the confidence of the minorities[53]—certainly a reference to Congress Untouchable leaders if not to certain 'tame' Congress Muslims.

Ambedkar's plan had not been adopted by the Assembly (there is no evidence that this aspect of it was even considered), and he

---

[51] In an interview with the author.

[52] Ambedkar's definitions here were ones he had long held: The majority community to him meant, as it had at the time of the Poona Pact in 1932, the caste Hindus. The Untouchables were a separate community in fact outside the Hindu fold as were other groups like the Muslims or Parsis.

[53] Ambedkar, *States and Minorities*, pp. 36–38.

evidently hoped to achieve some of his ends with the Advisory Board, which, elected by proportional representation, would presumably contain suitable minority representatives and would not be a creature of the caste Hindus. The Advisory Board failed to gain the approval of the first meeting of the Drafting Committee, to consider it. For three days until 20 October 1948 the members of the Drafting Committee met to sift the many amendments to the Draft Constitution, in preparation for the forthcoming seventh session. As a result, the Advisory Board and Ambedkar's Schedule IIIa were rejected. Remaining was the Drafting Committee's Instrument of Instructions regarding minority representation and the conventions of cabinet government along with the new Clause 62(5)a referring to the Schedule.[54] These, as we shall see, the Assembly would eliminate later.

2. Written Provisions Versus Tacit Conventions

Running parallel to these schemes for limiting Executive power by the use of supervisory councils was a second issue: should the well-known conventions of cabinet government, as practised in England, be included in the Constitution in the form of written provisions, or could India rely on the honesty of her leaders and their grounding in the traditional behaviour demanded by the parliamentary system to protect the democratic working of her political institutions?

All those many members of the Assembly who supported the British system against rival claims believed that its forms and conventions should be adopted along with the general framework. But opinion was divided as to whether the conventional forms should be written or unwritten. K. M. Munshi, in his Draft Constitution, provided for a head of state with powers like those of the British

---

[54] See Consolidated Minutes of the meetings, 18–10 October 1948; B. Shiva Rao, *Select Documents*, III.

   The relevant documents cause some confusion here. In late October 1948 the Assembly published the *Draft Constitution* (Second Edition), *Reprint indicating recommendations for amendment by the Drafting Committee*. In this edition, the amendments recommended by the committee were printed in italics facing the text of the original draft of the previous February. The text of Clause 62(5)a appears in italics, but so does the entire Schedule IIIA as moved by Ambedkar including the Advisory Board. One can only assume that the inclusion of Ambedkar's Schedule was a clerical error, it having been rejected by the Drafting Committee. See ibid., Clause 62(5)a and new Schedule IIIA.

monarch. Munshi explicitly laid down that he was to act, barring certain exceptions, only on the advice of his ministers.[55] S. P. Mookerjee also made it clear that he believed that the head of state should act only on ministerial advice, and he would have expressly provided that the council of ministers be jointly responsible to Parliament.[56] Ayyar and Ayyangar, in their joint memorandum, advocated the British form of cabinet government; they did not suggest the writing-in of the rules usually left to convention. The Union Constitution Committee omitted all reference to the authority of the President, to his relations with the council of ministers (excepting that their function was to aid and advise the President), and to the relations of the cabinet with Parliament.

In his Draft Constitution of September 1947, Rau added flesh to the bare bones of the Union Constitution Committee's Executive provisions. Among other things, he laid down that the cabinet was collectively responsible to the House of the People, and this major convention of parliamentary government became part of the Constitution. The members of the Drafting Committee were uncertain about including this provision, however—first including it, then taking it out, and then putting it back again. Rau also gave the President the power to return a Bill to Parliament for reconsideration, along with his recommendations, without at the same time establishing a procedure by which Parliament could again pass the Bill.[57] Rau had, in fact, given the Executive the power to block legislation, using almost the words employed for the same purpose in Section 32 of the 1935 Act. Surprisingly, the Drafting Committee repeated the provision in the Draft Constitution and the Assembly adopted it with only one dissenting voice in December 1948. It was only in May 1949 that the Assembly removed this excessive Executive power and made provision for the repassage of legislation over a presidential veto.[58] Nowhere in the Assembly Debates is there an explanation of this extraordinary affair.

During its preparation of the Draft Constitution, the Drafting Committee clarified the relationship between the council of ministers and the President; the Prime Minister was to keep the President

[55] Munshi, *Draft Constitution*, op cit., Article XX.
[56] Mookerjee's reply to B. N. Rau's questionnaire, op. cit.
[57] Rau, *Draft Constitution*, Clause 76.
[58] *CAD* VIII, 5, 191–6.

informed about ministerial decisions and proposed legislation and to provide the President with such information concerning administrative affairs as he should desire. On Ambedkar's suggestion, the Drafting Committee laid down that the President should address each new session of Parliament in the manner 'prevalent in the Parliament of the United Kingdom regarding the King's speech . . . and the debate thereon'.[59]

The Drafting Committee also adopted a provision designed to limit presidential power by preventing the head of state from serving more than two terms in office. The article was taken word for word by Rau from the Irish Constitution for his memorandum of 30 May 1947; it was approved by the Union Constitution Committee, and Rau repeated it in his Draft Constitution. The members of the Drafting Committee approved this limitation and the Assembly adopted the provision in December 1948 without substantial debate.[60] Yet in a version of the Draft Constitution printed on 28 October 1949, the restriction of presidential terms to two had been omitted from the Constitution. The article now said simply that a person who had held the office of President was 'eligible for re-election to that office'.[61] The number of terms a President could serve was presumably a matter that could be left to convention.

This unpublicized change in the Constitution which was apparently not debated by the Assembly, would have been easily forgotten had it not been that fears subsequently arose that convention, or conscience, might not be enough to cause an incumbent President to relinquish his office. What, in fact, was the convention? No-one had made it clear; it appears that the subject had not been discussed. And the major precedent for limiting a President to two terms—if that was the intention—was uncertain since Franklin Roosevelt had ignored convention in 1940 and had run for and won his third and fourth terms as President of the United States.[62]

---

[59] Minutes of meetings, 5 and 6 December 1947; *Prasad papers*, File I-D/47.

[60] See Article 12(3) of the Irish Constitution; also Rau, *India's Constitution*, p. 67, Rau, *Draft Constitution*, Clause 45, and *Draft Constitution*, Article 46. The provision read: 'A person who holds, or has held, office as President shall be eligible for re-election to that office once, but only once.'

[61] *Draft Constitution, Articles agreed to by the Constituent Assembly at the consideration stage*, edition of 28 October 1949, Article 46.

[62] It was evident, however, that the United States might make it a constitutional provision that no President could serve more than two terms. The Congress had

The length of a President's tenure became an important constitutional concern in 1960, although it had been a political and personal issue in 1957. In each case the incumbent President had been Rajendra Prasad. Prasad had been first elected President of India by the Constituent Assembly on 24 January 1950, and was elected President under the normal working of the Constitution in 1952. When the time came in 1957 for a new presidential election, Nehru hoped and expected that Prasad would step down in favour of the Vice-President, Radhakrishnan. Prasad declined to do this and there was a minor crisis within the Congress Party.[63] By the summer of 1960 the question was being asked publicly whether Prasad would run for a third term, and in early 1961 it appeared that there was some popular resistance to his again taking office. The issue had come so much to the fore by April 1961 that a member of the Rajya Sabha moved an amendment to the Constitution restricting a President to two terms, an effort that came to naught.[64] Prasad himself cleared the air in the autumn of the year by announcing that he would not run. In the following spring, Dr. Radhakrishnan was elected as India's second President.

What in retrospect seems to have been a storm in a teacup was not considered such at the time. The issue was one greater than the incompatible views of Nehru and Prasad or than right- versus left-wing in the Government and the Congress; it was one of propriety and of constitutional convention. That this was so, that individuals both within and without the Government evidently feared that Prasad might violate an incipient convention, may well have been due to the several previous attempts that he had made to stretch presidential powers beyond their conventional limits.

In April 1948, less than two months after the Draft Constitution had been published, Prasad wrote to B. N. Rau that he did not find a provision 'laying it down in so many terms' that the President of the Union was bound to accept and act upon the advice of his

---

passed the 22nd Amendment to the Constitution, which effected this change, in March 1947. By November 1949 more than twenty states had ratified it—and in February 1951 it received the necessary thirty-six ratifications.

[63] See Brecher, *Nehru*, p. 507.

[64] *The Times*, 24 April 1961. The amendment was moved by Bhupesh Gupta, a Communist MP.

ministers.[65] Prasad was writing in connection with Article 285(1) of the Draft, which he interpreted to mean that the President, in his discretion, appointed the chairman of the Public Service Commission, and he asked Rau whether the President was not bound 'at all in any case or that he is bound . . . in all cases' to accept ministerial advice.[66] That Prasad interpreted Article 285(1) in this way showed that he had, wilfully or otherwise, misread it and that he had not paid sufficient attention to the debate on the subject in the Assembly.[67] Not only had he apparently forgotten that it had been made clear many times in speeches, notes, and memoranda that the President of India was to be, like the British monarch, a constitutional head of state; he had forgotten that A. K. Ayyar had reiterated this point specifically in connection with the appointment of the chairman of the Union Public Service Commission.[68] Rau's reply to this letter is not available, but we may assume that he pointed out Prasad's error to him.

On 8 August, Prasad again wrote to Rau. He asked whether a Governor could in his discretion withhold assent from a Bill passed by the legislature; and if the Governor referred the Bill to the President, could the President then assent or withhold assent in his discretion. Prasad's argument was that if the ministry in New Delhi was the same as that in the province (presumably meaning that both could easily be Congress ministries), the provision would be meaningless.[69] The answers to Prasad's questions lie in the Draft Constitution

---

[65] In a letter dated 9 April 1948; *Prasad papers*, Random Letters File.

[66] Ibid.

[67] The article was not easy to read clearly, and it embodied one of the several discrepancies that existed at that time between the powers of the President and Governors. Clause (1) of the article read: 'The Chairman and other members of a Public Service Commission shall be appointed, in the case of the Union Commission, by the President, and in the case of a State Commission, by the Governor of the State in his discretion.' It is understandable that it might take several readings to realize that the power was not discretionary in the case of the President.

[68] The UCC report, Clause 21, had stipulated that the President appoint the members and chairman of the Public Service Commission on the advice of his ministers; *Reports, First Series*, p. 58. Replying to a suggestion that it was necessary to leave this part of the provision intact, Ayyar said that it need not be included because 'whenever the word President is used what is understood is the President in consultation with the Cabinet'. *CAD* IV, 12, 909.

[69] Letter of 8 August 1948; *Prasad papers*, Random Letters File.

itself[70]—the relevant Articles are 175, 176, and 143(1). The Governor had as discretionary powers only those explicitly given him by the provisions of the Draft Constitution (Article 143). And this power was not given in the case of assenting to or withholding assent from Bills or of referring them to the President, except that in certain situations the Governor could in his discretion refer a Bill back to the legislature with his recommendations; if the legislature repassed the Bill in any form, however, the Governor must assent to it (Article 175). When presented with a Bill referred to him by a Governor, the President could assent to it, withhold assent, or refer it back to the provincial legislature. No mention of discretionary power was made (Article 176). It was clear, therefore, that the President was in this case, also, bound to act on the advice of his ministers. Prasad's point that the value of the relevant provisions would be undermined if the central and state ministries were of the same party was a doubtful one. The Indian experience had been, at least since 1946, that in disputes between the central-government and a provincial ministry each side had taken its own particular interests more to heart than common membership in the Congress Party.

Prasad's interest in the extent of presidential power was almost certainly more than academic. It would have been unusual if there had not been speculation about who the first President of India would be. Assembly members had once believed that the first President would be elected in the autumn of 1947 when, it was hoped, the Constitution would be completed.[71] The Union Constitution Committee report, submitted to the Assembly in early July 1947, provided in its Transitional Provisions for a provisional President to be elected by the Constituent Assembly. From this time onward, the question of who this man should be must have been pondered by the Assembly members, Prasad included. If, by virtue of his seniority and general popularity, Prasad was not already a likely choice, he was made so by a memorandum that A. K. Ayyar submitted to the Drafting Committee in January 1948. Ayyar pointed out that

---

[70] Unfortunately, Rau's reply to this letter is also not available.

[71] During the July 1947 session of the Constituent Assembly both Prasad and Munshi expressed the hope that the Constitution would be finished in October, and the Assembly schedule was at first planned around this completion date. See *CAD* IV, 1, 541 and 546.

there must be a transitional government and that ways to constitute it must be considered. He recommended that the President of the Constituent Assembly and the then functioning ministers should, be the provisional government until one could be created under the provisions of the Constitution.[72] Less than three months later Prasad wrote his first letter to Rau inquiring about the scope of Presidential power. It may well be that Ayyar's memorandum was one of the factors that prompted his pen. But Prasad's interest in the scope of presidential authority must not be understood as personal aggrandizement. He may have believed that he would be President and that the President must have greater authority, but later evidence, as we shall see, indicates that he was more concerned for the welfare of the nation than for his own personal power.

Despite the honesty of his motives, it may have been Prasad's inquiries to Rau that led the Drafting Committee during the summer of 1948 to recommend including in the Constitution an Instrument of Instructions definitively limiting the President's power. The Instrument among other things enjoined the President to choose as Prime Minister the person most likely to command a stable majority in Parliament (a provision earlier considered and rejected by the Union Constitution Committee), and, in all matters within the scope of the Executive power of the Union, to be guided by the advice of his ministers. This fear that the head of state might exceed his constitutional authority was shared by many Assembly members, although in their case perhaps the fear sprang more from the colonial experience than it did from any knowledge of Prasad's possible intentions. Members of the Assembly again and again had wanted to be reassured that the President could act only on the advice of his ministers, and Ambedkar's Instrument of Instructions gave them some confidence that this would in fact be true. One member, for example, said he was pleased that according to the Instrument the President had to choose the leader of the majority party in Parliament as Prime Minister, because Indians could remember when Governors under the 1935 Act had chosen provincial prime ministers to suit their own ends.[73]

---

[72] Ayyar, *Memorandum on Transitional Provisions*, 23 January 1948; *Ayyar papers*.

[73] *CAD* VII, 30, 1181; R. K. Sidhwa. Governors, said Sidhwa, had 'created hell and mischief' by choosing prime ministers who lacked majority support. The irony of this was that the provision Sidhwa was praising was an almost exact

It seemed that the Drafting Committee, the leaders, and the rank and file of the Assembly were as one. The Assembly, as we have seen, adopted Ambedkar's Clause 62(5)a, thus giving implicit approval to the Instrument of Instructions to which it referred. Yet ten months later the Assembly reversed itself. The Instruments of Instructions directed at the President and the Governors were removed from the Constitution. There were to be no written conventions excepting those few, like the collective responsibility of the cabinets to legislatures, that had been included in the main body of the Constitution. Why? The Assembly was never in so many words given the reasons. Ambedkar was in the unenviable position of having to support the withdrawal of the Instruments from the Constitution after his own committee had put them there. It is through his speeches that we must attempt to understand the Assembly's change of mind.

The essence of Ambedkar's argument in December 1948, when he moved the inclusion of the President's Instrument of Instructions, was that the Instrument had moral force. It established a code of behaviour, of procedure. A provincial legislature or the Union Parliament, said Ambedkar, could, by citing the Instrument, force a Governor or the President to heed the advice of his ministers or face impeachment proceedings for violation of the Constitution.[74] Ambedkar admitted that

---

copy of that directed at Governors under the 1935 Act. The great difference lay in the discretionary powers of British Governors, which would be denied their Indian successors.

[74] It was here, of course, that the situation differed from that under the 1935 Act. Although Instruments of Instructions to the Governor-General and Governors of Imperial India were not justiciable, they were enforceable. Superior in authority to the Governor and able to see that he followed his Instructions, or lost his post, was the Governor-General, and superior to both of them was the authority of the Secretary of Sate and of Parliament in London. See Sections 13, 14, 53, and 54 of the 1935 Act. Had the Constituent Assembly so desired, it could have kept the Instrument of Instructions for Governors on this precedent, for once Governors came to be appointed by the President (and the power to place in office implied the power to remove from office) there was an authority superior to them to see that they acted in consonance, with their Instructions. The Assembly decided, however, that the Governor's status was to be a replica of the President's and that he should not be the object of a special Instrument of Instructions. Speaking in support of the withdrawal of the Governor's Instructions, T. T. Krishnamachari merely said that what had once been thought 'necessary' could now 'be left entirely to convention'. (CAD X, 4, 114;.on 11 October 1949). Ambedkar told the Assembly that the Instrument was useless because 'there is no

the provisions of the Instrument were not, strictly speaking, enforceable or justiciable. And he rejected Naziruddin Ahmad's suggestion that they be made justiciable—by allowing the President to be questioned as to whether he had followed the advice of his ministers—because this would permit the courts to interfere in the affairs of Parliament and the Executive.[75] The system of checks and balances would be upset.

Moving the deletion of Clause 62(5)a and Schedule IIIA in October 1949, Ambedkar told the Assembly that the members of the Executive, Legislative, and Judicial branches of the government 'know their functions, their limitations, and their duties . . . The Executive is bound to obey the legislature without any kind of compulsory obligation laid down in the Constitution'.[76] Thereupon this exchange ensued:

> *Skri H. V. Kamath:* If in any particular case the President does not act upon the advice of his ministers, will that be tantamount to a violation of the Constitution and will he be liable to impeachment? *The Honourable Dr. S. R. Ambedkar:* There is not the slightest doubt about it.[77]

From this, one is forced to deduce that Ambedkar and the members of the Drafting Committee, perhaps under pressure from Nehru or Patel, had come to the conclusion that the written provisions of a non-justiciable Instrument of Instructions and the tacit conventions of cabinet government had equal value: both were legally unenforceable, but both provided a mechanism by which the legislature could control the Executive; and of the two, conventions were the tidiest and the simplest way of limiting Executive authority.

Not all the members of the Assembly were happy about the removal of the written conventions, although Ambedkar's categorical statement to Kamath had quieted most fears. Ayyar attempted to soothe the suspicions that remained. He warned the Assembly that including a partial list of conventions in the Constitution might cause the Executive to suppose that all powers not specifically denied them were theirs, and the result, he said, could be conflict between the Executive and the

---

functionary . . . who can see that this Instrument of Instructions is carried out by the Governor' (*CAD* X, 7, 260), a statement that may not have been entirely correct.

[75] *CAD* VII, 30, 1189.

[76] *CAD* X, 7, 269—14 October 1949.

[77] Ibid.

Legislature. Ayyar concurred with Ambedkar that a President who did not heed the advice of his ministers would in fact be thwarting the will of Parliament, for which he could be impeached.[78] With the Instruments of Instructions gone, the protection of parliamentary government in India was left to convention, to the vigilance of Parliament, and ultimately, 'to the will of that power which . . . is the true political sovereign of the State—the majority of the electors or . . . the nation'.[79]

Executives Since 1950

India has now gone through more than a decade with parliamentary Executives both at the centre and in the states. As far as one can tell, the Executive has functioned in very much the manner envisaged by the members of the Constituent Assembly. Both the written and the tacit provisions of the Constitution have been followed. That cabinet government has provided India with stable and strong government is obvious, and if one attributes this to the almost unchallenged ascendency of the Congress, then one must also admit that Congress ministries have not aggrandized their authority at the expense of constitutional government either in the states or in New Delhi. This is not to paint a picture of flawless governing or of human perfection, but it is to say that cabinet government has worked because it has been understood and because the will to make it work has generally been present.

Legislative vigilance may have been needed to preserve democratic government in the states; certainly it has been necessary to maintain the constitutional form of parliamentary government at the centre. This, however, has been the proof of the pudding. The fears, with which some Indian observers greeted the Executive provisions of the Constitution— that the seeds of responsible government would not grow in Indian soil, as they had in British—have not so far been borne out.[80] Nor have the doubts of a distinguished foreign authority, Professor Alan Gledhill, who expressed concern

---

[78] Ibid., p. 170.

[79] Dicey, *Law of the Constitution*, on the aim of conventions; p. 429.

[80] For some of these fears, see, for example, articles published in the *Indian Journal of Political Science*, during 1950–52, Vols. XI, 4, XII, 1 and 3; and XIII, 3 and 4.

that the President might use the powers apparently granted him by the Constitution to make himself a dictator. Professor Gledhill conjured up the following situation: A President who has been aggrandizing his powers learns that Parliament intends to impeach him. During the stipulated lapse of two weeks between the notice of, and the movement of, the impeachment motion, the President dissolves Parliament. If a new Parliament is elected, writes Professor Gledhill, the President need not summon it for six months. In the meantime the President may dismiss his ministers and appoint others of his choice, himself governing the country by Ordinance during this period. This situation could easily justify a proclamation of emergency, and in this manner the President could step by step take over control of the nation.[81]

Professor Gledhill projected a 'constitutional' take-over of power. But according to the constitutional practices existing in India, this would be impossible. The President could not dissolve Parliament without the advice of his Prime Minister, in the first place. Nor could his other hypothetical actions be described as constitutional. That a President or a Prime Minister, perhaps with the backing of the armed forces, could assume power in India is possible, but that would be revolution. And, as Sir Ivor Jennings has written, constitutions do not contemplate revolutions.[82] If the Federal Executive in India becomes autocratic it will be because Parliament and the body politic have defaulted in their responsibility and have acquiesced in their own downfall, not because the intent of the Constitution has been 'constitutionally' circumvented.

Even so, President Rajendra Prasad on several occasions attributed to his office enormously greater powers than those given by the Constitution. Had his first attempt to ignore conventional restrictions and to act the part of his own Prime Minister not been foiled, parliamentary government in India would have disappeared before it was two years old. On 18 September 1951 Prasad sent a note to Nehru in which he expressed the desire to act solely on his own judgement, independently of the council of ministers, when giving assent to Bills, when sending messages to Parliament, and when

---

[81] Gledhill, *The Republic of India*, p. 108.
[82] Jennings, *Cabinet Government*, p. 297.

returning Bills to Parliament for reconsideration.[83] This was a fla-
grant attack on the conventions of cabinet government, and there
can be little doubt that it was inspired by the Hindu Code Bill, which
had just been introduced in the Provisional Parliament. This would
have largely invalidated Hindu personal law and was to Prasad, a
conservative Hindu, extremely distasteful. But Prasad's motives were
not entirely personal. He maintained that the Provisional Parliament
did not have the authority to enact such major legislation, because it
was in-directly elected and its members lacked the public 'mandate'
of a general election.[84] (The Provisional Parliament was a carry-over
from the Constituent Assembly; the first general elections to the Lok
Sabha took place in 1952.)

Prasad's argument had some moral force, but the point at issue
was that he desired to use the power of his office either to force the
Provisional Parliament to shelve the measure or, failing that, to veto
it even against the advice of his cabinet.[85] He was willing to endanger the Constitution in pursuit of his own point of view. But more
surprising was the way he mis-read the Constitution, misinterpreting
the very evident intent of the Constituent Assembly, in an attempt to
prove that he possessed the powers he desired. He cited, for example,
the absence from the Constitution of any mention of conventional
limitations. The British precedent for the scope of the functions of a
head of state was not pertinent, he wrote, because if these limitations
were to have applied in India the Assembly would have included
an equivalent to Article 105, in which the British precedent had
been named as the basis of the powers, privileges, and immunities
of members of Parliament. Prasad also relied on a technical Article
to support his desire for freedom of action—Article 254, which laid

---

[83] The actual text of Prasad's note to Nehru is nor available, but it can be reconstructed from the replies to it by Ayyar and others.

[84] Prasad had made this view clear on an earlier occasion when the Hindu Code
Bill had been before the Constituent Assembly (Legislative); see *The Hindu*, 1
May 1949.

[85] Prasad's intention (or desire) to use the power of his office to thwart the Hindu
Code Bill had leaked out. On 16 September a newspaper story had indicated
that Prasad might attempt to withhold his assent from the Bill if Parliament
passed it and that he might address the House on the subject; *The Hindu*, 18
September 1950. Questions on this news item, when asked on 17 September in
the Lok Sabha, were turned aside unanswered; ibid.

down that a law could prevail in a state if it pertained to an item on the Concurrent List and had received Presidential assent even though it was repugnant to a law made by the Union Parliament.[86]

Prime Minister Nehru immediately transmitted the President's views to A. K. Ayyar in Madras and to the Attorney-General, M. C. Setalvad, for their opinions. A secret correspondence followed. The Attorney-General wrote to Nehru that 'by Article 74(1) the President is required to act in all matters with the aid and advice of his Council of Ministers', and he cited innumerable constitutional authorities to prove his point.[87] He also used the argument which Ayyar had put forward in the Assembly, that because sovereignty lies with 'the people' and because 'the People' elect the Parliament, from which comes the council of ministers, power lies with the council of ministers, not with the President.

Ayyar replied to Nehru's queries in two letters. The first was brief, apparently written hastily to apprise Nehru of his views; the second, written some three weeks later, goes into greater detail. In his earlier letter Ayyar wrote that it was 'perfectly clear' that the President's position was analagous to that of 'a constitutional monarch in England . . . and there is no sphere of his functions in respect of which he can act without reference to the advice of his ministers'.[88]

Ayyar began his second letter by saying that 'the President's note raises points of such constitutional importance that, if conceded (they) will upset the whole constitutional structure envisaged at the time when the Constitution was passed (and will) make the President a kind of dictator . . . .' Prasad, Ayyar wrote, 'seems to read every Article of the Constitution in which the expression "President" occurs as conferring powers upon the President in his personal capacity without reference to the Cabinet'. Article 74, wrote Ayyar, was 'all pervasive' in its character; it would be 'constitutionally improper for the President not to seek or not to be guided by the advice of his ministers'.[89] Ayyar attacked Prasad's citation of Article 105, in

---

[86] This account of Prasad's note is reconstructed per footnote 83.

[87] Note by the Attorney-General to Nehru, dated 14 September 1951; *Ayyar papers*. Among his authorities were Anson and Dicey.

[88] Ayyar letter to Nehru, dated 20 September 1951; *Ayyar papers*.

[89] Ayyar letter to Nehru, dated 8 October 1951; *Ayyar papers*. Ayyar also feared that if Prasad's contentions were conceded, Governors could also break loose from conventional limitations, for on paper their powers were much the same.

support of his contention that British precedent did not apply to conventional limitations of Presidential power, by recalling that the article had been adopted simply because it was easier to do so than to enumerate the privileges one by one.

As to Prasad's other argument, Ayyar replied that Article 254 conferred no special power on the President, who must abide by ministerial advice and not set himself up as an 'umpire' between the states and the Union Government. And the President could not give or withhold assent from Bills because he had no 'revisional or appellate authority over the Cabinet'.[90]

Prasad retreated before the firmness of these arguments (the Hindu Code Bill had meanwhile been shelved due to conservative resistance), and it was not until 1960 that he again made a public issue of the scope of Presidential authority. In a speech to the India Law Institute given in November 1960, he asked to what extent Indians were entitled to invoke and incorporate into our written Constitution by interpretation the conventions of the British Constitution, which is an unwritten constitution'. Resurrecting his oft-used argument, he noted that 'there is no provision in the Constitution which in so many words lays down that the President shall be bound to act in accordance with the advice of his ministers'. To support his doubt that the President had the same constitutional status as the King, Prasad pointed out that the President was both elected and liable to impeachment (arguments that had been answered many times in the past) and 'the fact that our conditions and problems are not on a par with the British'.[91]

Prasad's motive in raising these shop-worn arguments seems to have been to enable the Presidency to assume authority and continuity should the nation, or more particularly the Union Government, ever undergo political upheaval. He evidently believed that the President should have the power to act in a crisis of authority at

---

[90] Ibid.

[91] From the text of the speech, delivered 28 November 1960, in New Delhi, as issued by the President's Public Relations Officer. Ironically enough, both Nehru and Setalvad, who was still the Attorney-General, were present. The New Delhi Press reported the President's speech thoroughly: *The Times of India* (on 30 November 1960) reported that Parliamentary circles were 'non-plussed' by the speech and that the President had raised an issue of grave constitutional importance.

the centre as the Union Executive could in a like crisis in a state government.[92] Yet he never said this publicly and weakened his case by using arguments fallacious in view of the clear intention of the founding fathers. Prasad may have seen himself in the role of the rock in the flood; one cannot divorce personal pride entirely from his behaviour. But more likely his intentions were unselfish, for during his stay in office he was personally self-effacing and, barring the lapse over the Hindu Code Bill, never attempted to exceed his meagre powers.[93]

For ill or creditable motives, however, Prasad attempted to read into, the Constitution what was never intended to be there. Fortunately he failed. In fact, his efforts may have strengthened the Constitution by establishing the firm precedent that within the Executive the cabinet is all powerful. There is no reason to believe that President Radhakrishnan shares his predecessor's views. And Indians may with some confidence hope that the state Executive and the Union Executive will continue to function as Professor Alexandrowicz has described them. Governors, he wrote, 'have under the present Constitution, apart from a few exceptions, a nominal position only and depend entirely on the Ministry'[94]. And as for the Federal Executive, despite Rajendra Prasad's attempts to the contrary, 'the examination of constitutional practice in the post-independence years show(s) beyond doubt that . . . the President is by convention reduced to a mere figurehead while the Ministry is the real Executive'.[95]

[92] This is the view of a variety of observers in India.
[93] The opinion of numerous political figures of the period, including B. Shiva Rao and Vishwanath Verma, former private secretary to President Prasad.
[94] Alexandrowicz, op. cit., p. 143.
[95] Ibid., p.127; see also ibid., Chapter 7.

6

The Legislature—
Unity Through Popular Government

The root of the trouble lay in the decision to introduce parliamentary democracy into a society which was far from homogenous and riven with a deep Hindu-Muslim cleavage.

Penderel Moon

A satisfactory solution of questions pertaining to minorities will ensure the health, vitality, and strength of the free State of India.

Govind Ballabh Pant

THE members of the Constituent Assembly had one predominant aim when framing the Legislative provisions of the Constitution: to create a basis for the social and political unity of the country. They chose to do this by uniting Indians into one mass electorate having universal, adult suffrage, and by providing for the direct representation of the voters in genuinely popular assemblies. Unexceptional as this programme for a newly independent state may now seem, it meant in 1947 that the Constituent Assembly had to overturn the constitutional pattern left by British rule. The Executive and Judicial provisions of the 1935 Act were adapted to India's needs by the Assembly with some major changes of substance, but with few of form; not so with the Legislative provisions. These had to be entirely remade.

Under the terms of the 1935 Government of India Act not only did the provinces lack even a semblance of popular government (the situation in the Princely States was worse), but the small electorate that existed was itself thoroughly fragmented. The franchise was restricted by property, educational, and other qualifications to approximately 15 percent of the country's population, and the resulting electorate was split into no less than thirteen communal and functional compartments for whose representatives seats were reserved in the various parliamentary bodies. Seats in the federal lower house—traditionally a popular assembly—were filled entirely by indirect election, largely from the lower houses of provincial assemblies, and in all cases on the basis of communal or functional electorates. Quite evidently, the members of the Constituent Assembly could not pursue the goals of national unity and stability by perpetuating a system of government that accentuated existing cleavages in Indian society and tended to create new ones.

For this reason the Assembly decided to attempt a drastic cure—knowing that half-way measures would be almost sure to fail. The Constitution provided for universal, adult franchise; joint electorates, in which all groups could contest for seats, replaced separate, communal electorates. There were to be neither weightage of representation for minorities nor reservation of seats (except for Scheduled Castes and Tribes).[1] The lower houses both in the states and at the centre were to be directly elected by adult suffrage. Only the relatively powerless upper houses were to be, even in part, indirectly elected. At the centre, members of the upper, federal house, or the Council of States, were to be chosen by the members of the lower houses in state assemblies. In the upper houses of provincial assemblies, called Legislative Councils, one-third of the membership was to be elected by the members of the Legislative Assemblies and the remainder was to be directly elected from territorial constituencies by special electorates consisting of the members of municipal, district, and other forms of local government, of university graduates, and of teachers in higher schools.[2]

---

[1] Seats were to be reserved for Scheduled Castes and Tribes for ten years from the commencement of the Constitution in the lower houses of state assemblies and in the Lok Sabha, the lower house of Parliament. The President was empowered (likewise state Governors) to appoint up to two Anglo-Indians to the lower house if he believed that community to be insufficiently represented. *Constitution*, Part XVI. This provision was extended for a further ten years (until 1970) by the Eighth Amendment Act of 1959.

[2] In upper houses there were also to be members nominated by the President (12) and the Governor (one-sixth of the membership of the upper house) with special qualifications in the fields of literature, science, art, and social service. The representatives elected to the upper houses by the Legislative Assembly were to

The powers of legislatures under the 1935 Act and the new Constitution, as one would suspect, differed as greatly as their composition and manner of election. Their authority had been circumscribed and limited in various ways. The British-appointed Governors and the Governor-General had the power both to block legislation and to create it by the process of 'certification', or by enacting a Governor-General's (or Governor's) Act, which had 'the same force and effect' as a provision enacted by the legislature. These officials had also extensive discretionary powers that put their actions beyond the reach of legislatures. But the Union Parliament and the state legislatures under the new Constitution had the full powers commonly possessed by parliamentary bodies in representative, federal democracies.

Although the Assembly's main task of achieving strength through unity overshadowed everything else during the framing of the Legislative provisions, there were other issues that had to be resolved. Should Indian legislatures, for example, have second chambers, either in the provinces or at New Delhi? This was a question which, at the national level, involved the place of second chambers in federal unions. Then, once it was decided to have upper houses, there arose the subsidiary question of their composition. The Assembly did not consider in detail the authority and powers of the legislatures when framing the legislative provisions. Their wide powers would be made apparent elsewhere in the Constitution, as in the clause giving legislatures almost unlimited authority to expropriate property.

The subject of political parties received little attention in the Assembly. Members made obeisance to the ideal of a 'loyal opposition' and to the desirability of having two strong parties to ensure the traditional working of parliamentary democracy and cabinet government, but they wasted no time on what in India, at least, was a largely theoretical question. India, Assembly members knew, would have dominant-party, Congress government for a long time to come; they were aware of the beneficial results this unifying force could have during the early years of independence. They believed that, even lacking a two-party system, Indians could make parliamentary democracy work—and time has so far proved them right.

---

come from outside the Assembly's membership. See *Constitution*, Arts. 80 and 171. Not all states were to have bicameral legislatures.

The Fight Against Schism

If the British made a mistake in introducing the parliamentary system into India, as Penderel Moon has said,[3] their even more damaging error was not to have let Indians work the system unhindered by outside influence.

> The inherent dangers (Moon wrote) of this British-sponsored experiment would have been lessened if the British, having once launched it, had hastened to transfer all political power to Indian hands before the constant appeals to the gallery inseparable from democratic processes had time to inflame feelings and accentuate the Hindu-Muslim division.[4]

But the British did not go after the introduction of quasi-parliamentary democracy in 1919. They remained for nearly thirty more years—during which they not only became the unloved third party in a bitter political triangle, but they so encrusted the parliamentary systen with aberrations called minority safeguards that Indian political life became more fragmented than before. Without going into the divide-and-rule controversy, we may agree with Moon that the Raj 'certainly took advantage of the divisions that existed (in Indian society) in order to justify the prolongation of their rule, and they failed, until quite near the end, actively to promote unity'.[5]

The leaders of the Independence Movement understood clearly that the different devices for communal and functional representation embodied in the 1919 and 1935 Government of India Acts prevented the achievement of either social or political unity, and they attacked them with varying degrees of thoroughness in the Nehru and Sapru Reports. The former went much farther—nearly, in fact, as far as the Constitution—than the Sapru Committee, probably because communal feeling was not running so high in 1928 as in 1945. The unicameral provincial legislatures and the lower house at the centre, according to the Nehru Report, were to be directly elected

---

[3] Penderel Moon, *Divide and Quit*, p. 284; see quotation at the head of this chapter.

[4] Ibid.

[5] Ibid., p. 285. Moon believed that the opportune time for the British to have left India to the Indians was in 1929 when the Montagu-Chelmsford reforms came up for review; ibid.

by universal, adult suffrage. Electorates were to be mixed and joint, not separate and communal. Seats were to be reserved for Muslims at the centre and in provinces where they were a minority. There was to be reservation for the Hindu minority in the North-West Frontier Province, but there was to be no reservation for any minority in the legislatures of the Punjab and Bengal. The members of the federal upper house were to be elected by members of the provincial legislatures according to the Hare system of proportional representation, but there was to be no representation of special interests in the upper house.[6] As the Nehru Report phrased it, there was no justification for a chamber comprised of obscurantists and people belonging to special classes whose chief aim is to protect their own interests and obstruct all liberal measures'.[7]

The four members of the Sapru Committee, who, as it has already been pointed out, styled themselves a conciliation committee, took a more cautious approach to the minorities issue. To begin with, however, the committee came down in favour of adult suffrage on grounds that would be difficult to fault. After citing the educative effect on the 'average man' of the 1937 elections, the committee's report pointed out that although the voter's 'judgement may be faulty, his reasoning inaccurate, and his support of a candidate not infrequently determined by considerations removed from a high sense of democracy, he is yet no better or worse than the average voter in many parts of Europe where adult franchise has been in force for some time.'[8] The report added that if power was to be transferred by the British, the risk of enfranchising the adult population should be taken to prevent its concentration 'in the hands of a powerful few'.[9]

The Sapru Committee recommended that the lower house of the Union assembly should be directly elected except for ten per cent of the seats, which were to be filled from special constituencies representing landlords, labour, women, commerce and industry, etc The members chosen by direct election were to fill reserved seats, however—i.e., seats from Muslims, Hindus, Scheduled Castes,

6   *Nehru Report*, op. cit. Recommendations: Paragraphs 8, 9, 31 and that entitled 'Communal Representation'.
7   Ibid., p. 94.
8   *Sapru Report*, para. 209, p, 170.
9   Ibid.

Sikhs, Anglo-Indians, and Indian Christians. The committee hoped that Hindus would agree to letting Muslims have an equal number of seats to theirs, in return for which Muslims should agree to joint electorates.[10] From the standpoint of the Nehru Report, these provisions went several steps backward. The members of the Sapru Committee justified their position by expressing the hope that the demand for special representation in the legislature would gradually disappear, and the belief that it would be unwise 'to start a constitution in a spirit of conflict with any section'.[11]

The members of the Constituent Assembly did not have to attempt to solve a problem of such dimensions. Partition and independence reduced it to a manageable size. The drafting of provisions for the Legislature, so long inseparable from the Hindu-Muslim conflict, was made possible by the departure of the British from India and the absorbtion of more than 60 per cent of India's Muslims into Pakistan.[12] Yet even then there remained in India forty million Muslims, nearly as many Untouchables, and numerous other minority groups. To protect their interests, thus freeing them from fear of oppression, was no small task. During its early days the Constituent Assembly was forced to mark time on these and other major issues. Representatives of the Muslim League were absent and impending events created an atmosphere of indecision. But on 3 June 1947 the British announced the formation of Pakistan and set the date of independence ten weeks away. Work on the main principles of the Constitution could at last begin.

The Provincial and Union Constitution Committees, as we have seen, took their first major decisions during the first week of June. On 9 June the members of the Union Constitution Committee decided that elections to the lower house of the federal legislature should be direct, on the basis of territorial constituencies, and by adult suffrage. The committee also recommended that there should be an upper house whose composition would be determined later—but it was

[10] Ibid., para. 201, p. 165. The committee placed great emphasis on this point.
[11] Ibid., para. 203, p. 167. The Sapru Committee made no recommendations concerning either provincial legislatures or a central upper house.
[12] Perhaps the formation of Pakistan was not needed. Perhaps even so late as 1947 the absence of the British would have been enough: Indians, free at last to face the Hindu-Muslim problem without the presence of a divisive third party, might have settled it. But that was not the way it happened.

not to be along the lines of functional representation.[13] At about the same time the Provincial Constitution Committee voted to recommend to the Assembly that the lower houses of provincial legislatures be elected in the same way. The provinces were to be given a choice in the matter of upper houses, but where second chambers were to exist, half their members were to be elected according to the Irish system of functional representation.[14] The two committees left the question of communal representation to the Advisory Committee, but unity had suffered an initial setback with the inclusion of special interest representation in the provincial upper houses.

The Advisory Committee and its Minority Rights Sub-Committee had begun work earlier in the spring, but, as we have seen in Chapter 3, they were concerned primarily with the negative rights of minority groups. The sub-committee turned its attention to the state's positive obligations towards minorities in mid-July. From 21 to 27 July, the sub-committee members, under H. C. Mookerjee's chairmanship, considered the question of protected minority representation in legislatures, executives, and in the public services. Several days later the entire Advisory Committee made its recommendations on the basis of the sub-committee's report. Sentiment in the Assembly at this time seems to have been in favour of reserving seats for minorities in legislatures, but strongly against separate electorates.[15] Certainly most minority groups and their representatives in the Assembly sought reservation for themselves. These included Congressmen and non-Congressmen. The Sikhs wanted reservation, including the Akali Sikh leader and Union Defence Minister, Baldev Singh. The Parsi leader, Homi Modi, supported reservation for his community until Sardar Patel dissuaded him. The leader of the Congress Untouchables, Jagjivan Ram, plus H. J. Khandekar, as well as Ambedkar, desired reservation for the Scheduled

---

[13] Minutes of the meeting; 9 June 1947; *INA*.

[14] Clause 19, PCC Reports; *Reports, First Series*, op. cit., p. 41. Article 18(7) of the Irish Constitution provided for election to the Seanad Eireann of members representing national language, art, literature, or other professional interests, agriculture, and allied interests, labour, industry and commerce, and public administration and public services.

[15] Of the ten answers to Rau's Questionnaire from UCC and PCC members, only three plainly disapproved of reservation, although eight flatly opposed separate electorates. K. M. Panikkar and S. P. Mookerjee, both caste Hindus, among others, supported reservation.

Castes. Although H. C. Mookerjee, leader of the Indian Christians, himself wanted to forego reservation, he feared that his community would not agree.[16] Yet under pressure from Patel, exercised by K. M. Munshi, he ultimately decided to disavow reservation,[17] and become a leader of the movement against it. The Anglo-Indians under Frank Anthony demanded special treatment. And among the Muslims, including the 'nationalist', Congress Muslims, as well as League representatives, there was strong support for reservation. Several voices were even raised in favour of separate electorates.

After considering these views and holding prolonged discussions among themselves, the members of the Minorities Sub-Committee rejected separate electorates by twenty-six votes to three, and by the same margin accepted the principle of reserved seats for certain minorities for a ten-year period, after which the question would be reconsidered.[18] The Advisory Committee took up the sub-committee's decision at a meeting held on 28 July. Voting on the sub-committee's recommendation that separate electorates be ended, only three of the fifty-eight members present opposed abolition.[19] The committee's report noted that separate electorates had been rejected by 'an overwhelming majority' because 'this system has in the past sharpened communal differences to a dangerous extent and has proved one of the main stumbling blocks to the development of a healthy national life'. It seemed especially necessary to avoid the dangers of schism, the report continued, in view of the 'new political conditions that have developed in the country'[20]—certainly a reference to India's opportunity to make

[16] See letter from Mookerjee to Prasad, 22 March 1947; *Law Ministry Archives*, File CA/24/Com/47-I.

[17] K. M. Munshi in an interview with the author.

[18] Report of the Minorities Sub-Committee, dated 28 August 1947; ibid., File CA/24/ Com/47-II. The votes were given incorrectly in the Report, but a correction was subsequently issued.

[19] Minutes of the meeting, 28 July 1947; *Prasad papers*, File 4-C/47. These three may have been Chaudhri Khaliquzzaman, Mohammed Saadulla, and Ismail Chundrigar, the three Muslim League representatives appointed to the Advisory Committee and the Minorities Sub-Committee by Prasad in late June. Khaliquzzaman and Saadulla later supported separate electorates for Muslims on the floor of the Assembly.

[20] *Report of the Advisory Committee on the Subject of Minority Rights*, dated 8 August 1947, para. 3; *Reports, Second Series*, p. 30.

a fresh start now the main stream of separatist fervour had been channelled towards Pakistan.

But to prevent communal minorities feeling 'apprehensive', the report continued, seats were to be reserved for them on the basis of their percentage in the general population.[21] The representatives of the Parsis and the Indian Christians on the Advisory Committee had turned down reservation for their communities, and decision on Sikh representation was postponed because it was impossible until the details of Partition had been settled. The Anglo-Indians on the committee, led by the doyen of the community, Frank Anthony, at first called for a form of special representation in legislatures that amounted to weightage, but ultimately gave up this demand in favour of a provision allowing the President and provincial Governors to nominate Anglo-Indians to legislatures if they were inadequately represented as a result of a general election.[22]

The Advisory Committee's report, signed by Patel, claimed that the committee's decisions 'where they were not unanimous, were taken by very large majorities composed substantially of members belonging to minority communities themselves'.[23] This may have been true. Partition had intervened since Ambedkar had demanded separate electorates for the Scheduled Castes' in his States and Minorities pamphlet. And Partition also altered the view of many Muslims, who now thought that they must drop this highly controversial point in order to ingratiate themselves with the Congress. So far as reservation or special representation was concerned, the Sikhs were still free to press their demands and otherwise reservation had been conceded. Whether the Christians and Parsis, in general, supported the stands of Mookerjee and Modi, it is difficult to say. There can be little doubt that Patel, despite his belief that the minorities must make their own decisions on such issues and not be simply outvoted by caste Hindus, quietly and privately put a great deal of pressure on the minorities to relinquish special privileges. On the other hand, it is quite possible that the minorities themselves realized

---

[21] Ibid., para. 4, pp. 30–31.

[22] Ibid., para. 6, pp. 31–32. Weightage was representation in excess of the number that would have resulted had a community been represented according to its percentage of the general population of the country. The Advisory Committee had flatly rejected weighted representation for any community.

[23] Ibid., para. 2, p. 30.

that the nation's best interests would be served by their self-denial and the creation of an at least politically homogeneous society. The Indian Muslims' position on this issue was especially delicate. Partition had made them a smaller— and hence less powerful—and a highly suspect group. Should they, therefore, give up all special protection and throw themselves on the mercy of the Congress? Or did they need the protection of separate electorates and reservation even more than previously? The community was deeply split by the issue.[24] Ultimately it would decide, along with the other minorities—excepting the Anglo-Indians and the Untouchables— to forego even reservation in the Legislature, hoping by its sacrifice to ensure fair treatment from the Hindu majority.

During its sessions of July and August the Assembly again considered functional representation, the divisive nature of which had not yet been fully understood. The Provincial Constitution Committee's provisions regarding functional representation in provincial upper houses were accepted. And the Assembly modified the Union Constitution Committee report so that instead of ten members nominated by the President, the Union upper house, by this time named the Council of States, was to have twenty-five members elected according to functional representation along the lines of the Irish Constitution, as well as the members elected by provincial legislatures.[25] All these provisions appeared virtually unchanged in Rau's Draft Constitution.

When the Draft Constitution appeared, however, functional representation in the Council of States had been done away with and the President was again empowered (as he had been in the original Union Constitution Committee report) to nominate a small group of members to represent the professions. The Drafting Committee had removed special representation for commerce and industry and labour as no longer necessary 'in view of adult suffrage', and because it had learned that 'the panel system of election hitherto in force under the

[24] See speeches by Muslim members in *CAD* VIII, 8 and 9, especially that of Tajamul Husain, *CAD* VIII, 9, 336ff. It is alleged that some Congress Muslims, as well as Muslim League members, favoured separate electorates as well as reservation of seats.

[25] Reports of the UCC as adopted by the Assembly, para. 14; *Reports, Second Series*, p. 16.

Irish Constitution had proved very unsatisfactory in practice'.[26] This intelligence had come to the Drafting Committee by way of B. N. Rau, who, during his visit to Ireland in November 1947, had been told by both the Irish Attorney General and De Valera that functional representation had been working badly. De Valera had told Rau that it was one of the three things in the Constitution that he would change if he could.[27] The Drafting Committee, however, left untouched the provisions for functional representation in the provincial constitutions.

Debate on the Legislative provisions of the Draft Constitution began on 3 January 1949, when the Assembly, in its clause-by-clause consideration of the Draft, reached Article 67, relating to the composition of Parliament. Several days earlier, the Advisory Committee had met to reconsider minority representation in legislatures. It may be illuminating to examine the debate in the Assembly in the light of what happened at this meeting.

Several members had suggested that due to the vast changes since August 1947 reservation of seats for minorities should be abolished. Three members of the committee had actually given notice of resolution to this effect,[28] and it was apparent that sentiment had begun slowly to flow in this direction. Patel, however, was too considerate of minority fears—and too much the strategist—to force the issue, preferring to wait until time and other persons had achieved his ends for him. The giving up of reservation should not be forced on any minority, he said. 'For example, if the Muslims by general agreement among themselves felt that they did not want any reservation, their view should be accepted, but the proposal should come from them and not from a

---

[26] *Draft Constitution*, footnote to Article 67, p. 28. During the period the Congress Constitution Committee had also been considering the possibility of incorporating functional representation in the party constitution. In a note dated 22 January 1948, the AICC recorded that it 'warmly endorsed the idea of functional representation' but believed the idea would be difficult to implement; *Prasad papers*, File 3-A/48.

[27] From Rau's account of his trip to U.S.A., Canada, Ireland, and England; *India's Constitution*, pp. 309 and 311.

[28] The members were H. C. Mookerjee, a Christian; Tajamul Husain, a Shia Muslim; and L K. Maitra, a Hindu. Husain's membership in the Shia community was of some importance. The Shia in India had not been strong advocates of reservation during the British period, as had Sunni Muslims, nor had they been strong supporters of Jinnah or the Muslim League. See minutes of the Advisory Committee meeting, 30 December 1948; *Prasad papers*, File 4-C/47.

member of any other community.'[29] Although a final decision had not been made, reservation had been threatened, and it must have been clear to Assembly members that it might soon be done away with.

Four days later, in apparent response to the mood of the Advisory Committee meeting, four Muslims and an important Sikh figure demanded in the Assembly that both the Council of States and the House of the People should be elected by proportional representation. They apparently believed that the presence of their minority groups in Parliament would be endangered by the end of reservation, and sought to secure the representation of their community in another way. Hukum Singh, once leader of the Akali Sikhs and since 1962 Speaker of the Lok Sabha, said that he believed proportional representation would protect minority interests and at the same time avoid the communalism implicit in separate electorates and reservation of seats.[30] K. S. Karimuddin, speaking for the Muslims, advocated proportional representation because the single vote system and single member constituencies produced the 'tyranny of the majority'.[31]

As regards the House of the People, the movement for proportional representation found almost no support. The Assembly rejected it because it was too complicated to administer and too difficult for the illiterate voter to understand. But the main reason was its incompatability with the parliamentary system. Dr. Ambedkar pointed out to the Assembly that proportional representation produced an effect of fragmentation, and that the successful working of cabinet government demanded a majority party. India needed unity and strength. India, he said, must have 'a stable government to maintain law and order. (Hear, Hear)'.[32]

---

[29] Ibid. See also Advisory Committee report of 11 May 1949; *Reports, Third Series*, p. 241.

[30] *CAD* VII, 32, 1249–50. At a meeting held on 25 October 1948, the Akalis decided to demand separate electorates for Sikhs, plus 50 per cent weightage in the East Punjab Legislative Assembly and 5 per cent weightage in the House of the People because of what the 'Sikhs have stood for and suffered'. These demands came as a result of the 'aggressive communal mentality brought into play during the past ten months by the majority community'. *Views of the Akali Dal on the Draft Constitution*; *Prasad papers, Special File*.

[31] Ibid., p. 1233.

[32] Ibid., p. 1262. The members of the Assembly were aware, through B. N. Rau's account of his trip to Ireland, that both the Irish Attorney General and De Valera were against proportional representation as much as functional representation.

In the case of the Council of States, however, the reverse was true: the Assembly voted in favour of proportional representation after a brief and inconsequential debate—indicating that, as usual, the issue, had already been decided in the party meeting before it came to the floor of the House. There were perhaps several reasons for this. The precedent had already been established in the provincial constitution, where one-third of the upper house was to be elected by the lower house according to proportional representation, and there were also the precedents provided by the constitutions of other countries. It may also have been in part a concession to minority fears, although it is difficult to understand how either communal or political groups could gain any especial advantage from this provision, particularly considering the relative powerlessness of the Council of States.[33]

The Assembly took the final decisions on the reservation of seats in legislatures for communal minorities during May 1949. On 11 May the Advisory Committee met to take up H. C. Mookerjee's resolution—for which support had been solicited during the previous months—that reservation be abolished. All that religious groups needed for their protection, said Mookerjee, moving the resolution, were the negative rights already in the Constitution and not safeguards in the legislatures. There should be no more thinking in terms of sub-national, minority groups. 'I have all along held', he said, 'that India is one nation.'[34] Nearly everyone present agreed or said he did. R. K. Sidhwa said that he had opposed reservation for Parsis, but that Homi Modi had wanted it. The Sikhs agreed, after a lengthy discussion, to drop their claims for reservation and weightage if certain conditions were met in relation to the Sikh Scheduled Castes—a matter that had been considered at an earlier meeting between the Sikhs in

---

Rau reported that De Valera 'would do away with proportional representation in any shape or form'. *India's Constitution*, op.cit., p. 310. For some interesting comments on elections in India in the light of the Assembly's rejection of proportional representation, see Alexandrowicz, op. cit., Chapter 9.

[33] This provision in the second general elections resulted, for example, in the Muslims gaining 10.7 per cent of the membership of the Rajya Sabha (Council of States), a percentage slightly greater, than the Muslim proportion of the national population.

[34] Proceedings of the Advisory Committee meeting, 11 May 1949; *Law Ministry Archives*, File CA/19(11)/Cons/49. All references here to this meeting have been taken from this source.

the Constituent Assembly and those of the East Punjab Legislative Assembly. Naziruddin Ahmad, a Muslim League representative in the Assembly, was reported to have written President Prasad that the Muslims of West Bengal did not want reservation. Begum Aizaz Rasul, a League representative from the United Provinces, found herself thrust forward as spokesman for the Muslim community. The Muslims, she said, now realized that it was in their own best interests no less than in the country's that reservation be abolished.

Nehru thought that, with separate electorates ended, most of the 'poison' had gone; had the minorities demanded it, he would have accepted some scheme of reservation, he said. Nevertheless, he believed that it was 'manifestly absurd to carry on with this reservation business'. The dissenters were the Scheduled Caste members. Speaking for them, Muniswami Pillai said that he was surprised that Mookerjee's resolution had not provided for reservation for the Scheduled Castes and tribes, particularly since at the time of the committee's report of August 1947 Gandhi had personally 'set his seal on it'. The meeting accepted Pillai's amendment to Mookerjee's resolution and adopted the resolution 'That the system of reservation for minorities other than Scheduled Castes in Legislatures be abolished'.[35]

Two weeks later the Assembly took up the Advisory Committee's report. During the two-day debate, members expressed almost complete support for the committee's decision. Two Muslim members, Mohammed Ismail and Mohammed Saadulla, supported reservation but were opposed by other Muslims. As it had in the Advisory Committee, schism lost and unity won the day. 'Let God give us the wisdom and the courage to do the right thing to all manner of people', said Patel. And with this benediction, the Assembly abolished the statutory basis of communalism.[36]

---

[35] Ibid. According to Patel, of the approximately forty members present at the meeting, only one voted against the resolution; see *CAD* VIII, 8, 271. For the committee's report, see *Report of the Advisory Committee*, 11 May 1949; *Reports, Third Series*, pp. 240–5.

[36] *CAD* VIII, 9, 354. So far as the Muslims are concerned, they have not fared badly in the legislatures without reservation, but they have not been represented according to their proportion in the population—in part this has been their own fault for not running enough candidates. The Muslims, according to their population, were entitled to 49 seats in the Lok Sabha in the 1952 and 1957 general elections; they secured only 28 and 26 seats. And in the state legislatures,

There remained only one more provision in the Draft Constitution that smacked of the special-interest representation of the British period—Article 150, establishing functional representation in the upper houses of provincial legislatures. Dissatisfaction began to be voiced in the Assembly Party in May 1949 and on the first day of the Ninth Assembly Session, 30 July 1949, the Assembly showed publicly that it was unhappy with functional representation but was unable to decide on an alternative form of composition for the Legislative Councils. Dr. Ambedkar pointed out that it would be inconsistent to have functional representation in the province when it had been discarded at the centre. T. T. Krishnamachari recalled the advice given to Rau in Ireland that functional representation there had not worked well. Mrs. Banerji said that no one should find a place in Legislative Councils simply because he possessed 'large properties'.[37] Yet with all the criticism of Article 150, no substitute provision was forthcoming, and Ambedkar moved a new article that laid down the size of the upper houses but left their composition to be determined by Parliament.[38] This provision, too, received a great deal of criticism. Members asked why the Constituent Assembly should leave such problems to Parliament, and why Parliament would be in a better position than the Assembly to make the decision. Outside the House, spokesmen for commerce and industry in speeches and letters to the Assembly, protested at the abolition of their special privileges. After several hours debate the article was held over.

Nearly three weeks later, on 19 August, Ambedkar produced a new provision, one that ultimately appeared as Article 171 of the Constitution. One-half of the seats in Legislative Councils should be filled by direct election from special electorates in territorial constituencies, electorates consisting of municipal, district, and other local governing bodies and of university graduates and higher-school teachers. One-third of the members were to be elected according

---

Muslim representation also fell, generally speaking, below their proportion of the population. For an excellent article on this subject, see Sisir K. Gupta, Moslems in Indian Politics, 1947–60, in *India Quarterly*, Vol. XVIII, No. 4, 1962.

[37] *CAD* IX, 1, 33. For the entirety of this debate, see ibid., pp. 1–37.

[38] This had been the decision reached by the meeting of the provincial premiers with the Drafting Committee on 22 July 1949; see minutes of the meeting, *Law Ministry Archives*. Nehru was strongly of this opinion.

to proportional representation by the members of the lower houses from outside their own number, and the final one-sixth of the membership was to be nominated by the Governor. There remained a tentative air about these arrangements, however, for the new article provided that Parliament could alter the composition of the upper houses if it desired.[39] This has not so far come about.

The members of the Constituent Assembly could only set the stage for the development of India's political life. They could not themselves knit up the ravelled sleeve of national unity. But they had removed the constitutional barriers to political (and therefore social) union and amity that had existed since the introduction of separate electorates in 1909 and, in fact, since the introduction of functional representation in municipal councils in 1885. Whether Indians could prove that their country possessed the fundamental unity they claimed for it was a question for the future.

The Problem of Second Chambers

One of the most vexing questions of political science, wrote B. N. Rau in his Constitutional Precedents, is the problem of second chambers. Because the Assembly was in effect drafting two constitutions, the federal and the provincial, it was forced to answer the question twice, although many of the classic arguments for and against second chambers applied in both cases.

The first bicameral legislature as the national assembly for India was established by the 1919 Government of India Act, but the upper house in New Delhi was never to have a 'federal' role in the sense of providing for equal representation of the various provinces and states in the country. In 1919, of course, the federal issue did not arise,

---

[39] *CAD* IX, 13, 473–4. It seems likely that the special electorates of graduates, teachers, and local officials was derived from an amendment to Article 150 of the Draft moved by S. L. Saksena on 30 July when the article first came up for debate; see *CAD* IX, 1, 24. That Ambedkar moved the new article was due in part to Prasad's intervention. Prasad had written to Ambedkar on 29 July that leaving the composition of upper houses to Parliament would hold up elections and cause other difficulties. Prasad suggested that some scheme be devised to establish Legislative Councils, but that Parliament could be allowed to make changes in their composition. Prasad letter to Ambedkar, 29 July 1949; *Prasad papers*, Random Letters File.

because India was not then to have a government constructed on federal principles, but rather, on the basis of devolution of authority from the centre. In the federal structure envisaged by the Nehru Report, the upper house would have existed primarily to provide an opportunity for the reconsideration of legislation in a 'somewhat cooler atmosphere' than that provided in the lower house—a precaution especially necessary in India, the authors of the report believed, owing to the existence of communal feelings.[40] The report rejected the example of the U.S. Senate 'in view of the great difference in size and population of our provinces'. Yet it did recommend that in the upper house the number of members from the smaller provinces could be increased so that their relationship to the great provinces 'should not be wholly disproportionate'. That the members of the upper house were to be elected by the provincial legislatures would, however, give the provinces a feeling of being represented at the centre, according to the report.[41]

The same reasons for not having equal representation of the constituent units in the upper house were cited by the Federal Structure Sub-Committee at the Round Table Conference. The sub-committee added that it doubted if equal representation 'would commend itself to general public opinion'.[42] The 1935 Act gave expression to this viewpoint. The Sapru Committee made no recommendations on the subject, and thus the issue came to the Constituent Assembly.

In his Precedents, Rau dealt rather extensively with second chambers, pointing out that although they were 'regarded as an essential element of federal constitutions', they were the exception rather than the rule in the constituent units of federations—other than those of the United States of America and Australia. He cited four commonly used arguments in favour of second chambers: tradition; the desire of propertied and other interests to protect themselves from the majority; the desire, even held by 'sincere democrats', to have a body to impose checks on hasty legislation; and the desire to provide representation for interests difficult to include in lower houses. The argument generally used against upper houses, according to Rau, was that they were undemocratic and needlessly slowed down the

[40] *Nehru Report*, p. 94. .
[41] Ibid., pp. 94–95.
[42] *Report of the Federal Structure Sub-Committee* to the RTC; Cmd. 3778, p. 218.

democratic process.[43] These points and the anecdotes that Rau used to illustrate them became the source-book for Assembly members during the debates on the issue.

The Union and Provincial Constitution Committees considered this question at their meetings held early in June 1947. The former was in favour of an upper house elected by the members of the lower houses of provincial legislatures. Provincial representation was to be one member for each million of population up to five millions and one for each two millions of population thereafter. The maximum provincial delegation was to be twenty.[44] The Union Constitution Committee report offered no explanation for its rejection of equal representation, but we may surmise that the committee members agreed with the views expressed in the Nehru Report and at the Round Table Conference. They may also have feared, as B. N. Rau did, that if they allowed equal representation for all the constituent units of the federation, the provinces 'would be swamped' by the Princely States.[45]

In the Provincial Constitution Committee, second chambers soon proved to be a controversial issue. Five of the six answers submitted to Rau's questionnaire on provincial constitutions had recommended single chamber legislatures. Only K. N. Katju had supported bicameralism, while among its opponents was B. G. Kher, the powerful Prime Minister of Bombay, which already had two houses under the 1935 Act. B. N. Rau had foreseen the difficulty. In his 'A Model Provincial Constitution', written in late May for the consideration of the Provincial Constitution Committee, he noted that the existence and composition of second chambers would 'probably have to be left to the decision of the representatives of that province in the

[43] Rau, *Precedents*, Third Series, pp. 146–8.

[44] UCC report, para. 14; *Reports, First Series*, p. 54. This ratio mechanism was set up by a UCC sub-committee consisting of Ambedkar, N. G. Ayyangar, Munshi, and Panikkar. Minutes of the UCC meeting of 9 June 1947; *INA*. Applied to the provinces, this system gave twenty representatives to Madras, the U.P., and Bihar, twelve members to Bombay and West Bengal, etc.

[45] Rau, in a note in his *Memorandum on the Union Constitution* of 30 May 1947; Rau, *India's Constitution*, p. 75. Of the UCC members answering Rau's questionnaire, only Panikkar favoured equal representation for the units on the American model. All four members favoured an upper house in the federal legislature and believed its members should be elected by the lower houses.

Constituent Assembly'.[46] The Provincial Constitution Committee did indeed leave the decision on upper houses to the provincial delegations in the Assembly, but it laid down what the composition of the second chamber would be if a province chose to have one. It was to be one-fourth the size of the lower house and, as we have seen, was to be one-half elected by a system of functional representation, one-third elected by the lower houses according to proportional representation, and one-sixth nominated by the Governor. Neither the Union nor the Provincial Constitution Committee made extensive recommendations concerning the powers of the upper houses. The latter followed Rau's example of suggesting that the 1935 Act should be used as a model. The Union Constitution Committee went somewhat farther and laid down that the lower house was to have almost exclusive power over Money Bills, the power of the Council of States being limited to suggesting amendments to them, which the lower house was under no obligation to accept.[47] In other respects, the powers of the two houses were much the same.

The Assembly considered the reports of these two committees during July and August 1947. In both cases the debate centred on the role of second chambers in modern democracies; the place of an upper house in federal legislatures was discussed only once, and then cursorily. N. G. Ayyangar told the Assembly that 'the need for a second chamber has been felt practically all over the world wherever there are federations of any importance', yet he did not attempt to justify the existence of the Council of States on any of the commonly accepted 'federal' grounds, such as giving equal representation to the federating units. 'The most that we expect the Second Chamber to do', said Ayyangar, 'is perhaps to hold dignified debates on important issues and to delay legislation which might be the outcome of passions of the moment.'[48] The idea of a second chamber at the centre received less criticism, however, than in the provinces. H. V. Kamath, for example, admitted that an upper house in New Delhi was acceptable, but in the provinces, he said, such houses were 'pernicious and vicious'.[49]

---

[46] Rau, *India's Constitution*, p. 147 (note).
[47] UCC report, para. 15; *Reports, First Series*, p. 17.
[48] *CAD* IV, 11, 876.
[49] *CAD* IV, 5, 679.

Not all Assembly members, however, agreed with Kamath. The argument bounced back and forth between those who believed that upper houses were a 'good check upon democratic outbursts', and members who thought that second chambers 'safeguard(ed) the interests of the propertied-classes and vested interests', the classes that 'buttressed and bolstered up British rule'. There was argument between those who believed that upper houses introduced 'an element of sobriety and second thought', and those who thought that they acted as 'clogs in the wheels of progress'.[50]

K. Santhanam believed that second chambers were not necessary to avoid the hasty enactment of legislation because the modem legislative process was suffciently slow to accomplish this end itself. But he did suggest that a minor check, or brake, be put on the legislative process in the provinces. The Governor, according to Santhanam's plan, was to have the authority in his discretion to return a Bill to the legislature with suggestions for amendment. If the legislature repassed the Bill, with or without amending it, the Governor was bound to assent to it. This 'veto power', said Santhanam, would prevent hasty action by a legislature or a ministry.[51] The provision found a good deal of support and the Assembly adopted it, yet without at the same time laying down that provincial legislatures should be unicameral.

The Draft Constitution closely followed the terms of the Union and Provincial Constitution Committee reports, including the minor additions made during the July and August debates. The major exception, as we have seen, was that functional representation in the upper house of the Union Parliament was removed. The decision on second chambers in the provinces still awaited action by provincial delegations. This was to come in November 1948. The powers of the second chambers, as laid down in the Draft Constitution, were nearly identical. The Council of States and the Legislative Councils could delay for six months the passage of a Bill sent to them by a lower house, but then the issue had to be resolved by a joint sitting of the two houses; to be enacted, all Bills, excepting Money Bills, had to be passed by both houses. An upper house could delay a Money Bill only for thirty days, however. If it failed to act within that span of time, the Bill was to be deemed passed by both

[50] Ibid., pp. 675 and 679, and *CAD* IV, 11, 926–7.
[51] *CAD* IV, 6, 704.

houses. If the upper house returned the Bill to the lower house with amendments or suggestions, the lower house could accept or reject them and the Bill was deemed to have been adopted by both houses. Bills, other than Money Bills, could be introduced in either house, both in Parliament and in the provincial legislatures.[52]

During the summer and autumn of 1948, members of the Assembly submitted no substantive amendments to the Legislative provisions and they were not debated again until January 1949. In November 1948, however, the provincial delegations in the Assembly voted on the question of second chambers in their provinces. Despite the occasional opposition of prominent figures within the delegations, most of the provinces chose to have bicameral legislatures. Bombay had set the example in July 1947, when despite the objections of its Prime Minister, B. G. Kher, it had decided in favour of two houses.[53] The Madras delegation adopted a second chamber by a majority, with M. A. Ayyangar, T. T. Krishnamachari, and K. Santhanam in opposition. The Bihar delegation voted sixteen to seven in favour; the East Punjab did likewise by a vote of ten to one; the United Provinces made the decision by a 'majority'; Orissa did so by a vote of six to one. The West Bengal delegation found itself evenly divided at the first meeting on 24 November, but the next day voted twelve to three for a second chamber. Assam, with three members voting, and the Central Provinces, with nine members voting, decided unanimously against having a second chamber.[54]

The January 1949 debate on the upper houses and their powers was, generally speaking, inconsequential. The stock arguments were repeated. When announcing the results of the voting on upper houses in the provinces, Ambedkar spoke against them, thus indicating that, if he had voted at the Bombay delegation's meeting, the decision was taken against his will as well as against Kher's.[55] Only one member revived the issue of a 'federal' house in Parliament by suggesting that each of the provinces have three representatives in the Council of

[52] *Draft Constitution*, Articles 88, 89, 172, and 174.
[53] The vote was taken on 20 July 1947. *Prasad papers*, File 7-R/48.
[54] This information has all been derived from File 7-R/48 of the Prasad papers. Unfortunately, no other details of these meetings have been included.
[55] *CAD* VII, 34, 1317–8. We may recall here that Ambedkar, originally elected to the CA from Bengal, lost his seat with Partition. The Congress secured his re-election from Bombay.

States. It was at this time that the Assembly removed the provision giving the Princely States the right to 40 per cent representation in the Council of States—a weighted representation that dated to the 1935 Act and the Round Table Conference.[56] The provision in any event was obsolescent since the absorption of the smaller Princely States into provinces and the formation of unions of other Princely States. A new Schedule was added to the Draft giving the number of representatives of each Princely State, which had been calculated in the same way as provincial representation.

In May 1949 the Assembly moved to curtail the already small powers of the Council of States. It reduced from thirty to fourteen days the time that the upper house could retard the passage of a Money Bill.[57] And later in the month, the dislike of second chambers in the provinces again came to the surface. Assembly members from Madras, Bombay, and the United Provinces, whose delegates had six months previously decided in favour of upper houses, demanded in the Assembly Party meetings that the issue be reopened. Opinion, however, was sharply divided.[58] This resistance to upper houses, supported as it was by several major provincial leaders, was the likely reason for Ambedkar's move during July and August to lessen still' further the powers of the Legislative Councils. First, he moved an amendment allowing Parliament to abolish the Legislative Council of a province if the lower house of the provincial legislature passed a resolution to this effect by a majority of the whole house with two-thirds of the members present and voting.[59] This amendment sparked a further debate on the merits and demerits of second chambers, but it was soon adopted.

The second diminution of the authority of provincial upper houses came in the form of an amendment removing the mechanism of the joint sitting of both houses and allowing for the passage of any Bill by the lower house, or Legislative Assembly, over the objection of the Legislative Council. Pant had strongly supported such a move during the July meetings of the provincial premiers and the Drafting

[56] *Draft Constitution*, Article 67.

[57] *CAD* VIII, 5, 184–5; see also *Constitution*, Article 109.

[58] *The Hindustan Times*, 2 June 1949.

[59] *CAD* IX, 1, 13; this was Draft Article 148A. See the *Constitution*, Article 169. K. T. Shah had moved a similar amendment, which had at the time been voted down, during the debate on the Legislative provisions in January 1949; see *CAD* VII, 34, 1305–6.

Committee. According to the amendment, if a Bill were passed by the Assembly and rejected by the Council, not acted upon by the Council for two months (later raised to three), or amended by the Council in a manner objectionable to the Assembly, the Assembly could repass the Bill in any form it liked. The Bill thereupon became law as enacted by the Assembly even if the Legislative Council rejected it, again made amendments not to the liking of the lower house, or simply did not act on it for one month. Presenting this provision to the Constituent Assembly, Ambedkar explained that the joint sitting had been kept at the centre because of the Federal character of the Central Legislature'. But in the case of the provinces, he believed that 'the decision of the more popular House representing the people as a whole ought to prevail in case of a difference of opinion which the two Houses have not been able to reconcile by mutual agreement'. This new provision also reduced from six to three months the period that the second chamber could retard the passage of a Bill.[60] As Professor Morris-Jones has written, 'Whatever uncertainty there may have been on the purposes of an Upper House, there was at no stage any doubt that the House of the People would be the more powerful', and this statement applied equally to the Legislative Councils in the provinces.[61]

A majority in the Assembly wanted bicameral legislatures in their provinces, yet despite this members had reduced the powers of the second chamber until they had, one might say, only a nuisance value. Why, then, have second chambers at all? Presumably because, in the view of Assembly members, the upper house 'could perform the very good and useful function of being a revising body' whose 'views may count but not its votes'.[62] A body that could, in effect, do little more than express its views could not seriously fragment the politics of a province. With a bicameral legislature of this

---

[60] See *CAD* IX, 2, 43–44, and the *Constitution*, Article 197. Although this would seem to have been part of a movement to reduce the powers of the upper houses, and the author believes it was such, Ambedkar later said it was not a matter of principle, but of 'expediency and practicality'; ibid., p. 52.

[61] Morris-Jones, *Parliament*, p. 90. The Council of State has been called 'one of the weakest second chambers in the world, weaker than even the House of Lords'. See Palmer, *The Indian Political System*, p. 118. Alaxandrowicz, op. cit, disagrees with the comparison with the House of Lords, see p. 165 (footnote).

[62] *CAD* IX, 1, 33. Mrs. P. Banerji.

sort, the political life of a province would largely find its expression in the lower house of the legislature and in the majority party of that house. We may reasonably assume from this that the Assembly drastically curtailed the powers of the provincial upper houses in the interests of greater unity.

It is here that the questions of the powers and of the composition of second chambers meet. We have discussed the issue of functional representation in a separate section because, in the eyes of Assembly members, it was very much a part of the legacy of schism from the British period. To reject functional representation in second chambers was to minimize their divisive effect on Indian politics (and thus on society), and to reduce their legislative authority was a further application of the same principle. In the case of the Council of States, this aim was taken to the limits thought advisable in a federal parliament in May 1949, when the Assembly cut down to fourteen days the period that the upper house could delay a Money Bill. Relative to the provincial upper houses, as we have seen, the principle was taken much further. It was not accidental that during the same three-week period in July and August 1949 the Assembly moved finally to abolish functional representation in Legislative Councils and to reduce their authority to the vanishing point. Both actions were intended to remove obstacles from the path of political unity.

The goals of the Constituent Assembly when drafting the Legislative provisions of the Constitution were to bring popular opinion into the halls of government and, by the method of bringing it there, to show Indians that although they were many peoples, they were but one nation.

7

The Judiciary and the
Social Revolution

The seat of Justice is the Seat of God.

Mahavir Tyagi

THE members of the Constituent Assembly brought to the framing of the Judicial provisions of the Constitution an idealism equalled only by that shown towards the Fundamental Rights. Indeed, the Judiciary was seen as an extension of the Rights, for it was the courts that would give the Rights force. The Judiciary was to be an arm of the social revolution, upholding the equality that Indians had longed for during colonial days, but had not gained—not simply because the regime was colonial, and perforce repressive, but largely because the British had feared that social change would endanger their rule.

The courts were also idealized because, as guardians of the Constitution, they would be the expression of the new law created by Indians for Indians. During the British period, despite the presence of Indians in government, Indians had not been responsible for the laws that governed them. Indians had neither law nor courts of their own, and both the courts and the law had been designed to meet the needs of the colonial power. Under the Constitution, all this would be changed. The courts were, therefore, widely considered one of the most tangible evidences of independence. And to the lawyers with which the Congress—and the Assembly—abounded, the opportunity to draft the judicial system under which they would function must have seemed the chance to write their own scriptures. Nor must it be forgotten that the Judicial provisions were framed during a period of the most appalling lawlessness that India had ever seen. The orderly processes of the courts must have seemed doubly a haven in days when tens of thousands were dying by the rifle, the kirpan, and the club.

The subjects that loomed largest in the minds of Assembly members when framing the Judicial provisions were the independence of the courts and two closely related issues, the powers of the Supreme Court and judicial review. The Assembly went to great lengths to ensure that the courts would be independent, devoting more hours of debate to this subject than to almost any other aspect of the provisions. If the beacon of the judiciary was to remain bright, the courts must be above reproach, free from coercion and from political influence:

Judicial review, Assembly members believed, was an essential power for the courts of a free India, and an India with a federal constitution. The Assembly's aim, when framing the Judicial provisions, was to establish clearly the foundations of the Judiciary's review power and its duty to uphold the Constitution. The members' interest centred, quite reasonably, on the Supreme Court, for it would be the final authority on the interpretation of the Constitution even if points of constitutional law were raised—and the Assembly provided that they might be—in lower courts. Much less attention was paid in the Assembly to the High Courts and the subordinate Judiciary. The Supreme Court also captured the imagination of Assembly members because of its special responsibility for safeguarding the Fundamental Rights. The question of review was taken up not only during the drafting of the Judicial provisions, but, as will be recalled, during the framing of the Fundamental Rights as well. In the Judicial provisions the Assembly was concerned with establishing the basic power of review; in the Rights, the members placed certain restrictions on the courts' review power—principally in cases concerning property and personal liberty. The role of the courts in the conflict between the individual's rights and society's needs has been considered in Chapters 3 and 4. The present chapter is concerned with the origins of judicial review and with how the Supreme Court, in particular, despite the apparent paradox of its restricted power, became the citadel of Indian justice.[1]

---

[1] As the present work is concerned with the political background of the Constitution, and not with the legal aspects of its functioning, the author has avoided discussion of the courts' methods of interpretation and the effect of their

Review and the independence of the Judiciary were the main issues that spawned a variety of subsidiary questions. Should the jurisdiction of the Supreme Court, for example, be confined to 'federal' issues, as had been the case under the 1935 Act? Or should it have original and appellate jurisdiction in a wide variety of civil and criminal matters? Should India have a dual system of courts, state and federal, as in the United States? Or should the Constitution retain the unified structure of High Courts surmounted by a Federal Court embodied in the 1935 Act? And how centralized should the Judiciary be? Although national unity was constantly a goal, the independence of the High Courts must not be endangered.

To answer these questions the Assembly did not have to begin afresh. From the British, India had inherited a well-constructed and smoothly functioning judicial system, many of whose forms and details could readily be adapted by the members. Yet the drafting of the Judicial provisions was not a matter of copying, for under the 1935 Act the power of the courts was limited, on constitutional issues strictly so. Assembly members had to ask themselves which of the provisions should be retained, and, if retained, how they should be modified and how the jurisdiction and powers of the courts should be widened to meet the needs of an independent state.

The Assembly embodied its decisions on these issues in two sections of the Constitution: the Union Judiciary—i.e., the Supreme Court—and the High Courts in the States. The Constitution provides that the justices of both the Supreme Court and the High Courts be appointed by the President, the former in consultation with justices of the Supreme Court and of the High Courts, and the latter in consultation with the Chief Justice of the Supreme Court, the High Court, and the Governor of the state. Judges hold office during good behaviour until reaching the retirement age laid down in the Constitution, but can be removed by Parliament. The qualifications, salaries, and certain allowances of High and Supreme Court judges are laid down in the Constitution.

---

decisions on the working of the Constitution. For comment on the application of judicial review to laws made under the Constitution, the reader should consult Alexandrowicz, op. cit.; McWhinney, *Judicial Review in the English-Speaking World*, pp. 13ff, 129–40; Durgadas Basu, *Commentary on the Indian Constitution;* and Gledhill, *Fundamental Rights in India.*

The Supreme Court has, according to the Constitution, original jurisdiction in all 'federal' disputes between the units, and between the units and the Union government. It has also broad appellate jurisdiction. Any civil or criminal case may be appealed to it if an interpretation of the Constitution is involved and if certain other qualifications are met, for instance if the High Court certifies that the case is a fit one for appeal, or if the Supreme Court grants special leave to appeal. Parliament can extend the Court's jurisdiction in several directions, including to matters enumerated on the Union List. The President may submit a matter to the Supreme Court for an advisory opinion. Generally speaking, the Court may make its own rules of procedure, and appoint its own officers. The administrative expenses of the Supreme Court, including salaries, allowances and pensions, are charged to the revenues of the Union Government and are not dependent upon appropriation by Parliament.

The Constitution lays down that there shall be a High Court for each state. Since States Reorganization in 1956, therefore, India has had fourteen High Courts as well as three Judicial Commissioners Courts in centrally administered territories. The jurisdiction of each High Court, excepting where altered by the terms of the Constitution or legislative act, is to be that of the court existing prior to the Constitution. Every High Court has the power to issue prerogative writs for the enforcement of the Fundamental Rights or for any other purpose. (The Supreme Court, unless otherwise empowered by Parliament, can only issue them to enforce the Rights.)[2] As in the case of the Supreme Court, the expenses of the High Courts are chargeable to revenue and are not dependent upon appropriations. The High Courts are responsible for the superintendence of all inferior courts within their jurisdiction.

The centralization of the Indian judicial system is made clear not only by the single hierarchy of courts—there are no autonomous state courts in the American sense—but by the uniformity of law provided for by the Legislative Lists. Criminal Law and procedure, laws dealing with marriage, divorce, succession, and the transfer of property (other than agricultural land), contracts, 'actionable wrongs', civil procedure, and many other such categories, are on the Concurrent Legislative List and therefore subject to legislation by

---

[2] *The Constitution*, Articles 32 and 139.

either Parliament or a state legislature. Although the 'administration of justice', the constitution of subordinate courts, and, within limits, the jurisdiction of High Courts are on the State List, the constitution and organization of the High Courts, in addition to the Supreme Court, lie within the province of Parliament—as do the qualifications of persons entitled to practice before High Courts. The extension of a High Court's jurisdiction beyond the state in which it has its seat is also a Union subject. In the intricate process of framing these provisions, it was the Supreme Court that first occupied the Constituent Assembly's attention.

The Supreme Court

The first important reference to a Supreme Court for India appears in the Nehru Report, which, as it envisaged a federal constitution for an independent nation, proposed several important additions to the existing judicial system. This system, established by the British, consisted of inferior courts and High Courts, of which the High Courts in Calcutta, Madras, and Bombay were the most important. Appeals could lie from these three courts to the Judicial Committee of the Privy Council in England. The Nehru Report recommended that this hierarchy of courts be kept, but that at the apex of the Judiciary there should be a Supreme Court with original jurisdiction in all 'federal' matters and where interpretation of the constitution was concerned—in fact, the power of judicial review. The appellate jurisdiction of the Court was to extend to cases that at the time could be appealed from a High Court to the Privy Council. The Court was to be the highest in the land, but in certain circumstances appeals could still go to the Privy Council. Parliament (meaning the Parliament of the Commonwealth of India) could legislate on the jurisdiction of the Court, and its justices could be removed by the Governor-General on an address from both Houses.[3]

During the investigations of possible constitutional reforms in India conducted by various bodies from the Simon Commission to the Joint Parliamentary Committee, the question of a Federal Court and of a Supreme Court was again studied in some detail. The White

---

[3] *Nehru Report*, Clauses 46–52. There are direct precedents for these provisions in Clauses 55–65 of Mrs. Besant's *Commonwealth of India Bill*.

Paper of 1933 proposed that there should be in India a Supreme Court, in addition to the Federal Court, to hear appeals from the provincial High Courts in civil cases and certain criminal cases, provided an appeal did not already lie to the Federal Court. The Supreme Court would have, in general, replaced the Privy Council, excepting that certain appeals would still be allowed to the Judicial Committee. The Joint Committee rejected this suggestion and proposed the establishment of only a Federal Court, stating that such a court was 'an essential element in a Federal Constitution, . . . at once the interpreter and guardian of the Constitution and a tribunal for the determination of disputes between the constituent units of the Federation.'[4]

The Joint Committee recommended that the original jurisdiction of the Federal Court should extend to disputes involving the interpretation of the constitution, disputes among the units and between them and the federal government, and disputes concerning the interpretation of laws enacted by the federal legislature. The appellate jurisdiction of the Court was to include cases involving the interpretation of the constitution and federal laws. But despite the noble phrases about the need for a Federal Court, appeals on constitutional questions were to lie to the Privy Council without the Court's permission.[5] The Federal Court, in reality, was to be a body with very limited powers of constitutional interpretation, for cases would almost certainly go to the Judicial Committee on appeal, especially if the appellant happened to be the Government of India.

The Federal Court was actually established by Section 200 of the 1935 Government of India Act, and its original jurisdiction, which in essence was that suggested by the Joint Committee, was laid down in Section 204. The actual authority of the Court was again to be restricted. It was not to 'pronounce any judgement other than a declaratory judgement',[6] which meant that it could declare what the law was but did not have the authority to exact compliance with its decision. And, as the Joint Committee's report had suggested, appeals could lie to the Privy Council without the Court's leave from decisions involving the interpretation of the 1935 Act itself. The Federal Court's power of judicial review was, therefore, largely

---

[4] *Report of the Joint Committee*, H.C. 5, para. 322.
[5] Ibid., para. 326.
[6] 1935 *Government of India Act*, Section 204(2).

a paper power, hardly surprising, perhaps, in a colonial situation, but contrasting ironically with the pronouncements in favour of a Federal Court by the Joint Committee.[7]

Reviewing the history of the functioning of the Federal Court, the Sapru Committee in 1945 noted that it had exercised its appellate jurisdiction in a number of cases, but that it had considered only one case within its original jurisdiction.[8] Under a new constitution, said the report, the position of the Federal Court 'will have to be greatly strengthened'. It would need to have wider jurisdiction, and must be the 'interpreter and guardian' of the constitution. This expanded jurisdiction should include a special responsibility for difficult cases concerning 'the civil rights and liberties of people' who might otherwise have to spend years in litigation in inferior courts before their cases reached the Federal Court.[9] The courts should have appellate jurisdiction for civil and criminal cases throughout India, the committee asserted. And the scope of the Court should also extend to enforcing the guarantees given to minorities.[10]

The Supreme Court first appeared in the proceedings of the Assembly in its role as guardian of the social revolution: even before a committee was established to enquire into its functions, it was called upon to safeguard civil and minority rights. The Advisory Committee's report on Fundamental Rights showed the powerful appeal of a Supreme Court to a people attempting to establish their own just society. In the Introduction to its draft clauses, the committee explained that it attached 'great importance to the constitution making these rights justiciable', and noted that the right of the citizen to such protection was a 'special feature' of the American Constitution.

---

[7] For two expositions of the legal basis for judicial review in Indian courts, see Dicey, *Law of the Constitution*, pp. 99–102 and 163–5, and also McWhinney, op. cit., pp. 13–15.

[8] *Sapru Report*, para. 245, pp. 187–8. The Court's original jurisdiction had been 'practically in abeyance', said the report. This case was The United Provinces *v.* The Governor-General in Council; Federal Court Reports 1939, Vol. I—(1939) FRC—pp. 124–58. It concerned whether the provincial or Federal Government was competent to levy certain taxes in certain areas.

[9] Ibid., para. 247, p. 189.

[10] Ibid., para. 249, p. 190, and para. 253, p. 192. The Sapru Committee found itself unable to decide whether the existing Federal Court of the 1935 Act should be immediately expanded into a Supreme Court, but believed that in a free India a court with such powers should exist.

'Suitable and adequate provision will have to be made to define the scope of the remedies for the enforcement of these Fundamental Rights', said the report.[11] And in the Rights provisions themselves, as we have seen in Chapter 3, the committee recommended that the Supreme Court should have the power to issue the prerogative writs to enforce 'the rights guaranteed in this part of the Constitution'.

Yet the unborn Supreme Court, and the principles of liberty that it was to protect, had already been caught in the contest that was developing in the Assembly between conflicting concepts of the individual's rights and society's needs. The Advisory Committee report itself qualified the exercise of the basic freedoms of speech, assembly, etc., with provisos, and had removed from the right to property the protection of due process—and presumably, therefore, of judicial review. As time went on, the Assembly would further curb the Court's power.

The task of framing draft provisions establishing the Supreme Court was actually begun while the Advisory Committee's report on rights was being debated. An *ad hoc* Committee of five members—B. N. Rau, Munshi, Ayyar, B. L. Mitter, and S. Varadachariar—undertook the work. Munshi, Ayyar, and Mitter were Assembly members; Rau and Varadachariar were not. Mitter was the Dewan of Baroda and had entered the Assembly as the representative of that Princely State. He had been an advocate in Calcutta, was the Law Member of the Viceroy's Executive Council from 1928 to 1934 and Advocate General of India in the early forties, and had been a member of Lincoln's Inn. Later in the year, Mitter was for a brief period a member of the Drafting Committee. Varadachariar, the committee's chairman, had similar qualifications. He had for many years been an advocate in Madras and editor of the Madras Law Review. He had been a judge on the Madras High Court and was a judge of the Federal Court from 1939 to 1946. Rau, Munshi, and Ayyar, as we have seen, were advocates of distinction.

At meetings held during the first three weeks of May 1947, the members of the *ad hoc* Committee found themselves in substantial agreement concerning the powers of the Supreme Court. The first recommendation of their report bestowed the power of judicial review upon the Court. 'A Supreme Court', the report read, 'with

---

[11] Advisory Committee's *Interim Report on Fundamental Rights*, para. 3; *Reports, First Series*, p. 21.

jurisdiction to decide upon the constitutional validity of acts and laws can be regarded as a necessary implication of any federal scheme.'[12] Such power need not belong exclusively to the Supreme Court, however, and constitutional issues could be raised in any court, as had been possible under the 1935 Act. Having established why a Supreme Court was a necessity, the report went on to recommend what the remainder of the Court's jurisdiction should be. The Court was to have exclusive jurisdiction in disputes between the Union and a unit and between units. The central legislature should be able to legislate concerning the jurisdiction of the Court. As to protecting individual liberties, the Court should have revisory and appellate jurisdiction in rights cases and its jurisdiction should cover areas where that of other courts did not reach. But it would be a mistake the report said, to give the Supreme Court exclusive jurisdiction over rights issues. As the Court could not possibly handle all the cases, this would in effect deny many persons the right, of redress. Other courts should have full powers in rights cases. The Supreme Court was, in general, to have the appellate jurisdiction held previously by the Privy Council. Although the members of the committee recognized that the idea had many opponents, they also 'considered it expedient' to confer upon the Court advisory jurisdiction like that given the Federal Court under Section 213 of the 1935 Act.[13]

The importance of giving the Supreme Court the power of judicial review was pointed out by Ayyar and Munshi in separate memoranda. Munshi believed that this power was especially necessary for the safeguarding of fundamental rights and for ensuring the observance of due process. He hoped, however, that judicial review would have a more direct basis in the Constitution than simply due process,[14] and in his Draft Constitution he had already provided that the Supreme Court should have the authority to examine the constitutionality of legislation. Munshi had further suggested that

[12] *Report of the* Ad Hoc *Committee of the Supreme Court*, para. 3; *Reports, First Series*, p. 63. The report was dated 21 May 1947 and was attached as an Appendix to the UCC report of 4 July. See also minutes of the meeting, 28 April 1947; *Law Ministry Archives*, File CA/4/Cons/49-II.

[13] Report, para 11; ibid., pp. 64–5. The committee did not state who opposed giving the Court advisory jurisdiction, nor their reasons for opposing it.

[14] Munshi, *Note to the* Ad Hoc *Committee on the Union Judiciary*, dated 26 April 1947; *Munshi papers*.

the appellate jurisdiction of the Court should extend to civil cases involving sums of more than Rs.10,000 where a point of law was concerned and to any civil or criminal case where there had been a miscarriage of justice.[15]

Ayyar pointed out that judicial review in the United States, although favoured by Hamilton and others, had been inferred from the Constitution. Despite Justice Marshall's decision, it should not be assumed, wrote Ayyar, that judicial review 'is a necessary incident of a written constitution or even a federal constitution', and he cited the Swiss Constitution in support of his view. Therefore, it was all the more necessary, he believed, that judicial review ought to be explicitly named as one of the Court's powers.[16] For his belief that in India 'the final word on the interpretation of the Constitution rests with the Supreme Court', Ayyar turned for support, interestingly enough, to British legal tradition. By passing the well-known fact that the Judiciary in England could not declare an Act of Parliament void, Ayyar cited the power of English courts to review actions taken by bodies on authority granted by Parliament. British law, said Ayyar, had always recognized that legislative acts of limited jurisdiction could be brought before any court. He believed that India must apply this aspect of the 'rule of law' to the jurisdiction of the Supreme Court.[17]

The members of the Union Constitution Committee considered the report of the *ad hoc* Committee and made its recommendations their own, with the exception of changing the manner of choosing the justices of the Court—an issue that will be taken up subsequently. During the debate on the Union Constitution Committee report in the Assembly, in August 1947, the jurisdiction and powers of the Supreme Court were hardly touched upon. It was not until the publication of the Draft Constitution that Assembly members had the details of the Union Judiciary before them.

---

[15] Munshi, *Draft Constitution*, Clause XXXVIII; *Munshi papers*.

[16] Ayyar, in a memorandum entitled *Courts Under the New Constitution*, undated (possibly summer 1948); *Ayyar papers*. See also Dr. Wheare on this point; *Federal Government*, pp. 60–61.

[17] Ibid. Ayyar thought that the Supreme Court should have the final word on constitutional matters because of the experience that other Dominions, particularly Canada, had had with judgements of the Privy Council going against the wishes of the framers.

Following the general recommendations of the *ad hoc* Committee, the Draft Constitution laid down the Supreme Court's jurisdiction in detail. The Court's original jurisdiction extended to 'federal' matters involving the central government and the units—a proposition so commonly accepted that the Assembly never really debated it. The Court's appellate jurisdiction extended to all High Court judgements whether civil or criminal if the interpretation of the Constitution was in question, to civil cases where more than Rs.20,000 was concerned, and to cases where the Supreme Court had granted special leave to appeal.[18] The jurisdiction of the Court could be extended by Act of Parliament to any item on the Union List and additional jurisdiction could be conferred on the Court by either the Union or a state government with Parliament's consent. The Court also had advisory jurisdiction in the case of a presidential request for an advisory opinion.

By Draft Article 25 of the Fundamental Rights, the right to move the Supreme Court for the enforcement of the Rights was guaranteed and the Court was empowered to issue the prerogative writs. Parliament could empower the Court to issue these writs for other purposes. Article 25 also provided that Parliament could extend the power to issue these writs for rights protection to other courts in India, and, as we have seen, the Assembly, on Ayyar's suggestion, later empowered High Courts to issue the writs. The 'rights to freedom' of the Draft were, as will be recalled, still encumbered by provisos and the due process clause had been removed entirely. Although due process would never reappear, the Courts would regain some measure of their power of judicial review with the adoption of Bhargava's amendment inserting the word 'reasonable' in the provisos to the 'freedoms' article.[19]

The Judicial provisions of the Draft Constitution were debated for the first of several times in December 1948. During the ensuing year Assembly members were almost entirely concerned with enlarging the Supreme Court's jurisdiction relative to criminal

---

[18] The Court's appellate jurisdiction where the Princely States were concerned was somewhat restricted; see Articles 112 and 113.

[19] As K. Santhanam wryly remarked, in the United States the courts were to restrict the misuse of liberty, whereas in India the courts would have 'to restrict the scope of the limitations' on the Rights; *CAD* VII, 3, 262.

appeals[20]—in marked contrast to their efforts, in the continuing Rights debate, to limit the Court's power in matters concerned with property and personal liberty insofar as it related to preventive detention. The members frequently expressed the sentiment that appeals should lie to the Supreme Court on questions of law even if they did not involve interpretation of the Constitution, that all cases where the sentence was transportation or death should be appealable to the Court, and that the limit for civil appeals should be lowered to Rs.10,000.[21] Ambedkar and T. T. Krishnamachari countered these demands by explaining that most of them were already met by the terms of appeal in Articles 110 and 111. In this they were correct, but the attitudes of Assembly members revealed the prevailing belief that the Court should be the citadel of justice—an attitude Ayyar supported when he claimed the Court had the widest jurisdiction of any superior court in the world.

The movement to ensure that appeals in certain criminal cases could be taken to the Supreme Court continued, however, and culminated in an amendment submitted by Thakur Das Bhargava. This amendment incorporated many of the ideas that had been expressed on the floor of the House and provided principally for appeal where the sentence was transportation or death. Forced by this amendment and by the general atmosphere in the Assembly to make concessions, Ambedkar moved a new Article IIIA, which provided that the Supreme Court could entertain appeals in criminal cases from High Courts where the High Court had reversed the judgement of a lower court and sentenced a prisoner to death, where it had withdrawn a case from an inferior court, tried it, and sentenced the accused to death, and where the High Court thought the case one fit for appeal. 'Parliament was empowered to confer on the Supreme Court the right to hear other criminal appeals.[22] After a debate on the

---

[20] There were, however, other suggestions made for widening the Court's responsibilities. It was suggested, for example, that the Chief Justice should preside at impeachment proceedings fat the President or Vice-President; *CAD* VII, 27, 1066. The Court was by that time the final authority in disputes over the election, of the President and Vice-President; *Draft Constitution*, Article 58.

[21] This lengthy debate took place during June 1949; see *CAD* VIII, 15, 59off, and 16, 621–43.

[22] For the text of Ambekar's amendment, see *CAD* VIII, 21, 840 and the *Constitution, Article* 134, which is, in all essentials, the same.

two amendments lasting the better part of two days, the Assembly adopted Ambedkar's amendment. Barring drafting changes, the provisions establishing the Supreme Court were completed.

The members of the Assembly had established the Supreme Court. They had given it wide original jurisdiction in 'federal' matters. They had given it original jurisdiction in fundamental rights cases, thereby making it the supreme guarantor of the Rights. They had given the Court extraordinarily wide appellate jurisdiction in fundamental rights and in civil and criminal cases. Assembly members would go to great lengths, as we shall see, to keep the Court and the judicial system pure and independent. The Assembly had come close to deifying the Supreme Court and the entire judicial system. Yet it had also greatly circumscribed the Judiciary's power of review where rights to property and personal liberty were concerned. And the Judiciary's review power in rights matters, in general, had been almost obliterated in the Emergency Provisions, by which the Executive had authority to deny for uncertain periods the right to the prerogative writs. The Supreme Court's involvement in federal issues—compared with that of the Supreme Court in the United States—was of course diminished, although not limited, by the provision in the Constitution for a strong central government. The Constitution itself expressed the centralizing tendency apparent in modern federations, said A. K. Ayyar, 'instead of leaving it to the Supreme Court to strengthen the centre by a process of judicial interpretation'.[23]

The Assembly had created an idol and then fettered at least one of its arms. But although the curbs on the Judiciary's power were greater than some persons wished, they are not so extensive as others have claimed, and in the Assembly the curbs had the support of the large majority of members. The limitations on the courts' review power, both during the framing of the Fundamental Rights and the Judicial provisions, were drafted in the name of the social revolution. As Ayyar put it:

> While there can be no two opinions on the need for the maintenance of judicial independence, both for the safeguarding of individual liberty and the proper working of the Constitution, it is also necessary to keep in view one important principle. The doctrine of independence is not to be raised to the level of a dogma so as to enable the Judiciary

[23] *CAD* VII, 4, 335.

to function as a kind of super-Legislature or super-Executive. The Judiciary is there to interpret the Constitution or adjudicate upon the rights between the parties concerned. As has been pointed out recently in a leading decision of the Supreme Court (of the United States), the Judiciary as much as the Congress and the Executive, is depending for its proper functioning upon the cooperation of the other two.[24]

As far as the Rights were concerned, B. N. Rau had another explanation for the limitation of the Judiciary's power. 'It may be asked', he wrote in an article on the Draft Constitution, 'why we cannot trust our courts to impose any necessary limitations (on the Fundamental Rights) instead of specifying them in the Constitution itself'.[25] His answer was that the Draft, unlike the American Constitution, laid down that any provision inconsistent with the Rights should be void (Article 8). Hence, wrote Rau, unless the 'Constitution itself lays down precisely the qualifications subject to which the rights are conferred, the Courts may be powerless in the matter'. There would seem to be an echo of Rau's legalistic argument in Chief Justice Kania's opinion in the Gopalan Case when he said, 'The Courts are not at liberty to declare an act void because in their opinion it is opposed to a spirit supposed to pervade the Constitution, but (which is) not expressed in words.[26]

The desire to restrict the purview of the courts in certain matters was not restricted to 'liberals' like Ayyar and Rau. Patel led the way in giving the Executive authority, largely unsupervised by the courts, to impose preventive detention. He had also opposed the inclusion in the Constitution of rights to secrecy of correspondence and to inviolability of an individual's person and home. And when Ayyar and Rajgopalachari explained, during the discussion of the property provision in the Advisory Committee, that 'due process' might endanger tenancy and zamindari-abolition legislation, Patel had shown a wariness of conservative judges. 'There is a danger', he said, 'that a certain old type of judges may misinterpret this new process of law.'[27]

---

[24] CAD XI, 9, 837.

[25] An article published in The Hindu of 15 August 1948; cited in Rau, India's Constitution, p. 364.

[26] Gopalan's Case, 1950, SCR 88; the quotation is cited in P. N. Sapru, The Relation of the Individual to the State under the Indian Constitution, p. 29.

[27] Proceedings of the Advisory Committee meeting, 21 April 1964; Shiva Rao, Select Documents, II.

Despite the restrictions placed upon it, the Judiciary in India has wide powers. If Constitutional amendments since 1950 have further limited the authority of the courts in property questions, legislation has extended their power to scrutinize Executive action in preventive detention cases. In fact, laws made under most provisions of the Constitution are subject to judicial review. The members of the Constituent Assembly believed that in some areas of the social revolution, the Legislative branch of the government should be supreme; in these areas, they could not bring themselves to trust the judges, whose function was to be limited to interpreting the law as written. Assembly members would have agreed, however, that but for these exceptions it was the duty of the Judiciary itself to 'keep the charter of government current with the times and not allow it to become archaic or out of tune with the needs of the day'.[28]

An Independent Judiciary

The members of the Constituent Assembly envisaged the Judiciary as a bastion of rights and of justice. The question was how to render the fortress impregnable to sapping by private interests. The Assembly had been careful to keep the Judiciary out of politics. How was politics to be kept out of the courts?[29] The Assembly's answer was to strengthen the walls of the fortress with constitutional provisions. At first glance, the Assembly's debates on the Judicial provisions seem to have been disproportionately concerned with the administrative aspects of the judicial system, with the tenure, salaries, allowances, and retirement age of judges, with the question of how detailed the

---

[28]   William O. Douglas, *From Marshall to Mukherjea, Studies in American and Indian Constitutional Law*, p. 332.

[29]   The firm belief in, one might even say the impassioned advocacy of, an independent Judiciary at the level of the High Courts and the Supreme Court was in large part a product of common experience at a much lower level. The District Officer of the British period (whether the official concerned was an Englishman or an Indian) was both the administrative officer and the magistrate, the Executive and the Judiciary, in his area. He made the regulations and then sat as the magistrate to interpret and to enforce them. The vast dislike of this system (which has not been entirely rooted out to this day) first found expression in the Directive Principles, where it was stated that 'the state shall take steps to separate the Judiciary from the Executive in the public services of the State'; *Constitution*, Article 50.

Judicial provisions of the Constitution should be, and more pertinently, with the mechanism for choosing judges. A closer look, however, shows that the members' interest in these apparently routine matters—which did at times become tedious—was prompted by the desire to insulate the courts from attempted coercion by forces within or outside the government. In this respect, the attitude of the Sapru Committee must have greatly influenced Assembly members.

The Sapru Committee report recommended that the justices of the Supreme Court and the High Courts should be appointed by the head of state in consultation with the Chief Justice of the Supreme Court and, in the case of High Court judges, in consultation additionally with the High Court Chief Justice and the head of the unit concerned. The justices of all courts could be removed on grounds of misbehaviour or infirmity of mind by the head of state, with the concurrence of the Supreme Court in the case of High Court justices, and with the concurrence of a special tribunal in the case of Supreme Court justices.[30]

The salaries of all judges (and the strength of the courts) should be 'fixed in the Constitution Act', said the Sapru Report, and should be neither varied to a justice's advantage or disadvantage during his term of office, nor in any way modified without the sanction of the head of state and the recommendation of the High Court, the Supreme Court, and the government concerned. Such provisions must be included, the members of the committee believed, in order 'to secure the absolute independence of the High Courts (and presumably the Supreme Court as well) and to put them, above party politics or influences'.[31] Although these conditions might seem to infringe provincial autonomy, the independence of the courts was of greater importance, the report argued. Nothing could undermine public confidence more than 'the possibility of executive interference with the strength and independence of the highest tribunal of the provinces'.[32] The Sapru Committee also suggested special provisions for the removal of judges because it was not satisfied with the

---

[30] *Sapru Report*, Clause 13, pp. xi–xii. In its recommendations of general constitutional provisions, the Sapru Committee used the words Supreme Court instead of Federal Court despite its refusal in the body of the report to commit itself fully on the issue of a Supreme Court Ibid., para. 253, p. 192.

[31] Ibid, para. 261, p. 196.

[32] Ibid.

mechanism in the 1935 Act,[33] yet it rejected the idea of an address by
Parliament—which was used in England and would later be adopted
by the Constituent Assembly—because it did 'not consider it right
and proper that the judge's conduct should form the subject of discussion in the heated atmosphere of a political Assembly'.[34]

The members of the Constituent Assembly's *ad hoc* Committee
on the Supreme Court took a somewhat different view of these matters, but the Assembly would ultimately frame provisions closer to
those of the Sapru Committee. The members believed that the salaries and pensions of justices should be laid down in statutory rules
and that only their main recommendations need be embodied in
the Constitution. Detailed provisions, including those establishing
the procedure for the issuance of writs in civil rights cases, could be
laid down in a 'Judiciary Act', said the *ad hoc* Committee.[35] In the
matter of choosing justices, however, the committee sought greater
safeguards. Its report declared that it would not 'be expedient' to
leave the appointment of Supreme Court judges 'to the unfettered
discretion of the President of the Union', and it offered alternative
suggestions. According to the first of these, the President should
nominate puisne judges with the concurrence of the Chief Justice,
and this nomination would then be subject to confirmation by a
panel composed of High Court Chief Justices, 'some members' of
both houses of the central legislature, and the law officers of the
Union. The second scheme was that the panel should submit three
names to the President who would choose one of them with the concurrence of the Chief Justice.[36]

The Union Constitution Committee, considering these recommendations at its 11 June meeting, decided that the salaries,
allowances, etc. of Supreme Court justices need not be included in

[33] 1935 Act, Sections 200 and 220; judges could be removed by the monarch with
the concurrence of the Judicial Committee of the Privy Council.

[34] *Sapru Report*, para. 266, p. 198. We may recall here that two of the four members
of the Sapru Committee, Sapru himself and M. R. Jayakar, had been judges' of
the Federal Court and members of the Privy Council.

[35] Ad Hoc *Committee Report*, para. 15–16; *Reports, First Series*, p. 66. The committee
confined itself to the subject of the Supreme Court, and made no recommendations about other aspects of the Judiciary. See also minutes of the meeting, 28
April 1947; *Law Ministry Archives*, File CA/4/Cons/49-II.

[36] Ibid., para. 14, p. 65.

the Constitution, but disagreed with the *ad hoc* Committee's suggestions for the selection of judges. Instead, returning to the method
of the Sapru Report, the Union Constitution Committee recommended to the Assembly that justices be appointed by the President
in consultation with the Chief Justice of the Supreme Court and such
other Supreme or High Court Justices as might be necessary.[37] This
provision ultimately became part of the Constitution. The Provincial
Constitution Committee had no expert report for its guidance. In a
joint meeting with the Union Constitution Committee to consider
the *ad hoc* Committee's report, the members decided, however, to
adopt the same system for appointing judges: High Court justices
were to be appointed by the President in consultation with the Chief
Justices of the Supreme Court and the High Court concerned and the
Governor of the State.[38] Otherwise the provisions of the 1935 Act,
with the necessary adaptations, were to be used. Along with the Union
Constitution Committee, the members of the Provincial Constitution
Committee believed that the salaries and allowances of justices could
be provided for in a Judicature Act, but they also believed that the
bench needed greater security in the interim. Pending the passage of
such an act, therefore, the salaries and allowances of judges were to be
enumerated in a constitutional schedule.[39]

Introducing the Provincial Constitution Committee report to the
Assembly, Patel explained that the committee had paid special attention to the manner of appointing judges, for 'the judiciary should be
above suspicion and should be above party influences'.[40] The debate
on this report was brief and marked by only one major change.
Adopting an amendment moved by A. K. Ayyar, the Assembly gave
to High Courts the power to issue prerogative writs in fundamental
rights cases, entrusted them with the superintendence of subordinate
courts within their jurisdiction, and empowered them to consider
cases concerning revenue matters.

Turning to the Union Constitution Committee report a week later,
the Assembly accepted with little debate the committee's provisions

---

[37] Minutes of the meeting, 11 June 1947; *INA*. See also UCC report Clause 18;
Reports, First Series, p. 57.
[38] Minutes of the third joint UCC–PCC meeting, to June 1947; *INA*. See also
PCC report, Part II, *Reports, First Series*, p. 43.
[39] Ibid.
[40] *CAD* VI, 2, 579.

that judges should be appointed by the President, but considered at somewhat greater length several methods of removing justices from the bench. Two main amendments were moved. That of A. K. Ayyar provided that justices could be removed by the President for incapacity or proved misbehaviour, on receipt of an address by both houses of Parliament.[41] K. Santhanam moved a similar amendment. Both were opposed by M. A. Ayyangar, according to whose amendment judges could be removed on like grounds but by a special tribunal of acting and former Supreme and High Court judges.[42] Ayyar argued that the weighty procedure of a Parliamentary address enhanced the dignity of the Supreme Court and that his method was preferable to a simple tribunal. The Assembly adopted Ayyar's amendment. Ayyar also defended the exclusion from the Constitution of provisions laying down the salaries of judges. He believed that 'from the very nature of things' all such provisions could not be included in the Constitution, which should embody only the 'main heads'. It should be left, he said, 'for a Judicature Act to be passed by the Assembly to implement the powers that are conferred under the Constitution'.[43] On this the Drafting Committee would not agree with him.

The Drafting Committee held regular meetings from early November onwards. During the week between 10 and 17 December, the members framed nearly all the Judicial provisions, including many of the details omitted the previous summer. The committee set the number of justices on the Supreme Court at seven, subject to change by Parliament, and confirmed the retirement age at sixty-five years.[44] The committee also laid down the qualifications necessary for justices. The procedure for the removal of judges was stiffened by requiring the address by Parliament to be passed by a two-thirds majority. Former judges were not to be allowed to return to the Bar, a provision that had the strong support of both Sir Tej Bahadur Sapru and B. N. Rau. On the question of writing the salaries, allowances, leave, and pensions of justices into the Constitution, the Drafting

---

[41] *CAD* IV, 12, 889.

[42] Ibid., p. 895. The removal of judges by a tribunal may also have had B. N. Rau's support. See Rau, *India's Constitution*, pp. 305ff.

[43] Ibid., p. 890.

[44] The retirement age of judges in India had been a subject of minor controversy since the Round Table Conference. The age of 65 years was laid down in the 1935 Act and recommended by the *ad hoc* Committee.

Committee compromised. Parliament was empowered to legislate on these subjects; until it did so, however, salaries and so on were to be as laid down in a Schedule to the Draft. But none of these rights could be varied to a justice's disadvantage during his tenure of office. The Draft Constitution provided that the salaries etc. of the administrative personnel and officers of the Supreme Court were to be fixed by the President in consultation with the Chief Justice and that all the expenses of the Court were to be chargeable to the revenues of the country. The method of appointing judges remained unchanged.

The provisions for the High Courts were largely the same. Judges were to be appointed by the President, as previously agreed upon, and removed by him on receipt of a parliamentary address. The salaries and other emoluments of judges were laid down in a schedule, but could be legislated upon by the provincial legislature provided that the minimum salary of a Chief Justice was kept at Rs.4,000 monthly and that of puisne judges at Rs.3,500. These salaries were laid down in the Second Schedule of the Draft, along with figures of Rs. 5,000 monthly for the Chief Justice of the Supreme Court and Rs.4,500 for other Supreme Court judges. It is likely that the Drafting Committee adopted these amounts on the recommendation of the Home Ministry, which suggested them in a note to the committee.[45]

The first reaction to the Judicial provisions of the Draft Constitution came from the judges themselves. In late December 1947, the Chief Justice of the Federal Court, H. J. Kania (to whom the provisions had presumably been shown as soon as they had been drafted), wrote a letter to Nehru about them.[46] Kania made no comment on the jurisdiction and powers of the courts, confining his letter entirely to the independence of the Judiciary. He suggested that the Draft Constitution should cover the relationship of the Executive with the Judiciary so that the courts would be free from suspicion of Executive control. Kania particularly stressed that, when recommending to the President a person for a judgeship on a High

---

[45] See note, undated (but possibly drafted in November 1947); *Ayyar papers*.

[46] The Chief Justice's letter to Nehru was circulated to the Drafting Committee on 30 December 1947; the copy of the letter examined by the author lacked a date; *Prasad papers*, File 1(2)-D/47. Kania had been a justice of the Federal Court since 1946 and Chief Justice since August 1947.

Court, the Governor and the High Court Chief Justice should be in direct contact so that the provincial Home Ministry would not be an intermediary in the proceedings. Otherwise, Kania said, local politics might affect the selection of judges.

These points and many others were elaborated at a meeting held by the justices of the Federal Court and the Chief Justices of all the High Courts a month after the publication of the Draft Constitution. The sense of the meeting was that under the Raj the Judiciary had, in the main, been independent, but that certain tendencies to encroach upon its independence were becoming apparent. India must preserve, in the justices' opinion, 'the fearless functioning of an independent, incorruptible, and efficient Judiciary'. Taking up the point of Kania's earlier letter, the meeting deplored 'the growing tendency to treat the High Court as a part of the Home Department of the Province', and recommended that the Chief Justice of the High Court, after consulting with the Governor, should send his suggestions for appointment directly to the President, thus excluding all provincial ministers from the selection process.[47] This recommendation was to eliminate the procedure, claimed by the justices to be followed in some provinces, by which the High Court Chief Justice made his suggestion on appointments to the provincial prime minister, who passed it to his home minister, who in turn sent his views to the Union Home Minister in New Delhi for communication to the Union Prime Minister and the Governor-General. By this procedure, it was claimed, the High Court Chief Justice's original written recommendation never reached New Delhi at all. Reading the substitute provision put forward by the meeting of justices, however, one finds it difficult to defect any difference from that already in the Draft Constitution.

Further to ensure the independence of the Judiciary, the justices' meeting recommended that the salaries, leave, and allowances of High Court judges should be a Union subject, and if not, that all

---

[47] The meeting was held 26–27 March 1948 in New Delhi. All the High Court Chief Justices were present excepting those from Calcutta and Patna; these courts were represented by senior puisne judges. Their opinions were, for the most part, unanimously expressed. See the Memorandum expressing these views in the *Comments* volume, op. cit., pp. 10–28; *INA*. The tone of the Memorandum and the style in which it was written indicate that Kania was the author. See also *Law Ministry Archives*, File CA/21/Cons/48, for the original documents of this meeting as well as other background material.

provincial legislation on these matters should be reserved for the President's consideration.[48] The responsibility for district judges and all subordinate courts should, in the justices' view, be taken from the provincial government and placed within the power of the High Courts. It was also suggested that either former judges be allowed to return to the Bar—outside the jurisdiction of the High Court on which they had sat—or that pensions be increased. (Although the Assembly rejected this suggestion at the time, the Seventh Amendment Act of 1956 provided that retired justices could return to the Bar.) Salaries, too, should be raised, the justices said. The sum of Rs.4,000 had been established seventy years earlier and the standard of living of judges must be kept up, for to 'lower their dignity and status' *vis-a-vis* the other members of the community would be detrimental to the larger interests of everyone concerned. To maintain the independence of the Judiciary by preventing the use of politics as a stepping-stone to the bench, the justices finally recommended that no former minister could become a judge.[49]

Ayyar, replying to the justices' memorandum, took a firm line.[50] The provisions in the Draft Constitution concerning subordinate courts must be made to work, he said, and these courts could not be put in the charge of the High Courts. An independent Judiciary was an admirable principle, but the High Courts could not be vested with administrative responsibility and then placed above criticism.[51] As to the justices' other comments, the Judiciary was remarkably independent, Ayyar said. There was no authority that could interfere with it in the exercise of its functions. Judges had security of tenure and could only be removed by the most rigorous procedure;

---

[48] Ibid. In the Draft Constitution, the provincial legislatures had much wider authority to legislate on High Courts than in the Constitution; see items 2 and 3 of the State List, Seventh Schedule.

[49] Ibid.

[50] This note (in the *Ayyar papers*) is undated, but the contents mark it as a reply to the memorandum issued by the Justices' meeting. Ayyar referred to his note as a reply to the 'Chief Justice's Memo', which is further evidence that Kania prepared it. Ayyar's note was probably written in April 1948.

[51] Ibid. Much of the administration of the subordinate courts was placed in the hands of the High Courts by Article 203 of the Draft, but all actions on these matters by High Courts were subject to existing law and needed the Governor's previous approval.

no judge's salary could be altered to his disadvantage during his term of office; the salaries and allowanaces of all justices were not subject to the vagaries of legislative appropriations, but were charged to the revenues of the Union or provincial government; and the administrative establishment of courts was fixed by Chief Justices.[52] The Drafting Committee did, however, accept an amendment suggested by several High Court Chief Justices to the effect that any Bill passed by a provincial legislature derogating the authority of a High Court should be reserved for the President's consideration.[53]

The Assembly did not undertake detailed consideration of the Judicial provisions of the Draft until a year after these recommendations were presented. When on 24 May 1949 the Assembly took up Article 103 on the appointment of Supreme Court Judges, it became evident that keeping politics out of the courts continued to be a matter of great concern. One member, for example, suggested that the appointment of judges should be confirmed by two-thirds of both houses of Parliament so that their independence would not be 'compromised'.[54] Ambedkar defended the draft provision, saying that it was a middle way between the English system of appointment by the Lord Chancellor and the American system of confirmation of judicial appointments by the Senate. The English method was too unsupervised, said Ambedkar, and, in India, the American way too open to politics.[55] The majority of the Assembly agreed with Ambedkar and the provision was adopted.[56]

---

[52] Ibid.

[53] For the amendment, see *Prasad papers*, File 1-M/48. The amendment was submitted for consideration at the Special Committee meeting of 10 April 1948 and drew its inspiration from a like provision in the Instrument of Instructions for Governors issued under the 1935 Act. See also *Constitution*, Article 200. The Special Committee was composed of the members of the Drafting, Union Powers, and Union Constitution Committees plus other Assembly leaders.

[54] *CAD* VIII, 7, 231; S. L. Saksena.

[55] Ibid., p. 258. Ambedkar had earlier attempted through his Advisory Board to make the appointment of judges subject to special procedures.

[56] There is disagreement as to how satisfactory the appointment of judges has been. The International Commission of Jurists has said that although the appointment of justices in India is potentially political, 'in fact no case has yet occurred where any appointment has been made without the concurrence of the Chief Justice of India'. Political patronage in High Court appointments, reported the jurists, has been 'very rare'. See International Commission of Jurists, *Rule of Law-in a Free Society*, p.

It proved much more difficult to resolve the matter of judges salaries, however, and the status of the provisions naming them. The
quality as well as the independence of the Judiciary were considered
to be at stake, and the decision, which the Assembly was left to ratify,
was taken by the Cabinet. Article 104 of the Draft Constitution, it will
be recalled, laid down that the salaries, allowances, leave, pensions,
etc. of judges could be legislated upon by Parliament, but that until
such time they should be provided for in the Second Schedule. There
was a like provision for the High Courts. This article was apparently
already under discussion at the highest level when it came up for
consideration in the Assembly on 27 May, and Ambedkar requested
that debate on it be postponed. Four days later a secret note written
by Patel was circulated in the Cabinet. It recalled discussions on the
issue six months earlier and said that in the light of these and of the
views of the Chief Justice, the Prime Minister and he had agreed that
to have 'a first-rate Judiciary in India' the salaries of judges should be
fixed in the Constitution in order to attract 'first-rate men to accept
these appointments'. The note also listed the salaries and allowances
considered to be necessary to achieve this.[57]

The following day, Ambedkar submitted a note in which he said the
salaries named by Patel were in some cases too high. He did not seem to
question the idea of fixing the salaries in the Constitution.[58] Discussion

285. The Indian Law Commission, however, has noted that appointments to the
Supreme Court have been criticized, and added, 'It is undoubtedly true that the
best talent . . . has not always found its way to the Supreme Court'. Government of
India, *Law Commission of India, Fourteenth Report*, p. 34. In regard to High Court
judges, the Commission reported that the large volume of responsible criticism that
selection had been inferior, that there had been undue Executive influence, and
that expediency and communal considerations had influenced the appointment of
justices appeared 'well-founded'; ibid., pp. 69–70.

[57] *Note for Cabinet*, 31 May 1949, signed by Patel as Home Minister; *Law Ministry
Archives*.

[58] *Note for Cabinet*, 1 June 1949, by Ambedkar as Law Minister; ibid. Patel and
Nehru had suggested these figures: Chief Justice of the Supreme Court, Rs.5,000
monthly; puisne judges, Rs.4,500 monthly; Chief Justice, High Courts, Rs.4,200
monthly; puisne judges Rs.4,000 monthly; in all cases emoluments and allowances were to be in addition to these figures. These salaries were the same as those
in the Draft Constitution in the case of the Supreme Court; they were higher
than those the Draft laid down for High Court judges. Ambedkar's figures, in
the above order, were: Rs.5,000; Rs.4,000; Rs.3,500 and Rs.3,000.

continued but no decision had been reached when the Assembly rose on 16 June. On the first day of the following session, however, 30 July 1949, Ambedkar moved on the Assembly floor a new Article 104 that provided that judges should be paid the salaries specified in the Second Schedule, but that the privileges and allowances of justices should be determined by Parliament. Until Parliament decided on them, however, they should be as specified in the Schedule. The Assembly adopted the new provision after an inconsequential debate.[59] The schedule itself was adopted in mid-October. The salaries for justices specified in it showed that Nehru and Patel had been forced by their cabinet colleagues to lower their sights in every case save that of the Chief Justice. In the main, the salaries embodied in the Constitution were those laid down in the Draft nearly two years before.[60]

Believing that they had established a Judiciary both independent and powerful, Assembly members then wished to give their work some permanence. There would, of course, be in the Constitution a mechanism for amending it. How, then, could the sanctity of the courts be protected? The Assembly solved the problem by including among the entrenched provisions of the Constitution all the articles dealing with the Union Judiciary, the High Courts in the states, and the Legislative Lists—on which appeared the authority for the several legislatures to act on matters concerning the Judiciary.[61]

---

[59] *CAD* IX, 1, 10–13.

[60] *CAD* X, 5,119–53. A later difficulty was also settled by Patel's intervention. Although there was agreement in the Cabinet on the salaries of judges appointed under the new Constitution (in fact, judges appointed after 31 October 1948), disagreement arose about those appointed before that date. An understanding had been reached between justices in this category and the Government with the result that their salaries were somewhat higher than those of judges appointed under the new Constitution. The Cabinet evidently moved on 7 June 1949 to reconsider this agreement, however, and reaffirmed its decision on 26 July. On 19 August Patel prepared a note for the Cabinet in which he said that such action would constitute 'a serious breach of faith' because it would be departing from the 'pledged word' given judges during earlier negotiations. He 'earnestly exhort(ed)' the Cabinet not to do this. The salaries were not reduced. See *Note for Cabinet*, 19 August 1949, signed by Patel as Home Minister; in the author's possession. The salaries of Supreme and High Court justices in 1964 continued to be those laid down in the Second Schedule. There have been, however, Acts passed in regard to justices' conditions of service.

[61] *Constitution*, Article 368.

Although much of the Constitution can be changed by Parliament itself, the entrenched provisions require additionally the approval of not less than one-half of the legislatures of the states. Only certain provisions pertaining to the Executive and to the federal structure were also included in this special category.

The Union Constitution Committee had recommended, in a supplementary report of mid-July 1947, that the articles pertaining to the Supreme Court should require the consent of the provinces before being amended. This was included in the Draft Constitution, but no mention was made of the High Courts. By the time the Draft was presented to the Assembly in November 1948, Ambedkar, Saadulla, N. M. Rau, and several others had submitted amendments giving the same status to the provisions regarding the High Courts.[62] The Drafting Committee agreed to this principle and recommended to the Assembly that it be accepted,[63] and the members adopted the provision in September 1949 during the debate on the amending process. Thus the Assembly finally provided all the measures it believed necessary to preserve the independence of the Judiciary.

The Recurrent Theme of Unity

When B. N. Rau circulated his questionnaire on the Union and provincial constitutions, the only question concerning the Judiciary was: 'Should there be a separate chain of courts to administer Union laws?'[64] Of the eight members of the Union and Provincial Constitution Committees who answered the question, one believed that the answer should be left to Parliament and the remaining seven said 'No'.

In his note to the *ad hoc* Committee, Munshi stressed the unifying effect of a uniform interpretation of the laws by a Supreme Court. With the units autonomous and with the growing enthusiasm for linguistic provinces, wrote Munshi, there will naturally be a tendency towards the growth of 'petty nation states'. Although the Union government could oppose such a trend, Munshi believed the courts

---

[62] Ambedkar, Saadulla, and Rau's amendment was No. 3253, *Amendment Book*, II, p. 348. The very next amendment was identical, and bore the names of Santhanam, M. A. Ayyangar, Mrs. Durgabai, and T. T. Krishnamachari; ibid.

[63] See *Draft Constitution, Revised Edition* of October 1948, under Article 304.

[64] Rau, *India's Constitution*, p. 37.

could have an even greater effect, because 'the unconscious process of consolidation which a uniformity of laws and interpretation involves makes the unifying unconscious and therefore more stable'.[65]

There can be no doubt that this proposition found universal favour in the Assembly. Of the many basic principles of government that Assembly members adopted in large measure because they were used to them, the unitary judicial system seems to have been accepted with the least questioning. The Assembly first approached the issue from the standpoint of the enforcement of the Fundamental Rights; the Supreme Court was to have a special, country-wide responsibility for the protection of individual rights—a responsibility that remained even when the High Courts were empowered to issue prerogative writs. Later, other aspects of uniformity received approval, such as uniform qualifications for High Court justices and like provisions for the appointment and removal of judges. The meeting of the justices advocated making the salaries and allowances of High Court Judges a Union subject because it 'yielded a desirable uniformity'.[66] This principle was extended ultimately to advocates. The Assembly adopted Ambedkar's amendment that 'persons entitled to practice before the Supreme Court or any High Court' be made a subject on the Union List.[67] Ayyar and Ambedkar defended this move—against a few claims that it infringed provincial 'autonomy'—on the grounds that uniform qualifications set by Parliament were needed to permit advocates to follow their cases from court to court, which at that time was not always possible, and because it would keep newly-formed High Courts from setting standards that departed radically from the norm.

Ambedkar was perhaps the greatest apostle in the Assembly of what he described as 'one single integrated Judiciary having jurisdiction and providing remedies in all cases arising under the constitutional law, the civil law, or the criminal law'. For him, such a judicial systems, plus uniformity of law, were 'essential to maintain the unity of the country'.[68]

---

[65] Munshi *Note to the* Ad Hoc *Committee on the Union Judiciary*. In his *Draft Constitution*, Munshi had advocated a dual system of courts in which High Courts could act as Union Courts in specified circumstances and with the Supreme Court empowered to create inferior courts to administer Union laws.

[66] Memorandum reporting the sense of the Justices' meeting; *Comments* volume, op. cit.

[67] *CAD* IX, 21, 787.

[68] *CAD* VII, 1, 37.

8

Federalism—I
The Amicable Union

Personally, I do not attach any importance to the label which may be attached to it—whether you call it a Federal Constitution or a Unitary Constitution or by any other name. It makes no difference so long as the Constitution serves our purpose.

Rajendra Prasad

THE political structure of the Indian Constitution is so unusual that it is impossible to describe it briefly. Characterizations such as 'quasi-federal' and 'statutory decentralization' are interesting, but not particularly illuminating. The members of the Assembly themselves refused to adhere to any theory or dogma about federalism. India had unique problems, they believed, problems that had not 'confronted other federations in history'.[1] These could not be solved by recourse to theory because federalism was 'not a definite concept' and lacked a 'stable meaning'.[2] Therefore, Assembly members, drawing on the experience of the great federations like the United States, Canada, Switzerland, and Australia, pursued 'the policy of pick and choose to see (what) would suit (them) best, (what) would suit the genius of the nation best. . . .'[3] This process produced new modifications of established ideas about the construction of federal governments and their relations with the governments of their constituent units. The Assembly, in fact, produced a new kind of federalism to meet India's peculiar needs.

---

[1] *CAD* V, 1, 38; N. G. Ayyangar.
[2] *CAD* XI, 11, 950; T. T. Krishnamachari.
[3] *CAD* XI, 5, 654; L. K. Maitra.

The most singular aspect of the drafting of the federal provisions was the relative absence of conflict between the 'centralizers' and the 'provincialists'. The proceedings of the Assembly revealed none of the deep-seated conflicts of interest evident in Philadelphia in 1787 or like that between Ontario and Quebec. There was no dearth of argument in the Assembly over the distribution of powers, over the effect of the Emergency Provisions on the federal structure, or over the distribution of revenue, but, in general, these disagreements concerned techniques as much as federal principles. As we shall see in the debate on the financial provisions, Assembly members loudly demanded increased revenue for provincial governments, yet they agreed that the Union Government should collect the money and then distribute it among the units. This could hardly be called a traditional defence of provincial autonomy.

The Assembly was perhaps the first constituent body to embrace from the start what A. H. Birch and others have called 'cooperative federalism'.[4] This 'new phase' that has emerged largely since World War II, although its roots extend back to the thirties and early forties, has been characterized by the increasing interdependence of federal and regional governments—a development, it is usually argued, that has not destroyed the federal principle. This concept is clearly different from that prevailing when the federal systems of the United States or Australia were set up, and which gave rise to Dr. Wheare's definition of federalism: 'The general and regional governments of a country shall be independent each of the other within its sphere.'[5] Cooperative federalism produces a strong central, or general, government, yet it does not necessarily result in weak provincial governments that are largely administrative agencies for central policies. Indian federalism has demonstrated this.

Cooperative federalism, according to Birch, is distinguished by

. . . the practice of administrative cooperation between general and regional governments, the partial dependence of the regional governments upon payments from the general governments, and the fact that the general governments, by the use of conditional

---

4   A.H. Birch, *Federalism, Finance, and Social Legislation in Canada, Australia, and the United States*, p. 305.

5   K. C. Wheare, *Federal Government*, p. 97.

grants, frequently promote developments in matters which are constitutionally assigned to the regions.[6]

This definition applies to India with the exception of conditional grants, a device rarely used under the Constitution. Federal disbursements within the framework of national planning, however, have had the same centralizing effect to some extent, but this has been over and above the normal operation of federal finance. Although the federal structure of the Constitution in its day-to-day working is certainly centralized, the larger powers of the Union Government to intrude into provincial affairs have been infrequently used. And none of them, except in some cases for a brief initial period, lies solely in the hands of the Union Executive. Proclamations of Emergency, for example, and the use of 'President's rule', in which the Union Government may take over the operation of a unit government, must be laid before Parliament—in which, of course, the provinces are represented. Parliament can, in certain circumstances, legislate on matters included in the State List, but only with the approval of a two-thirds majority in the Council of States or during a proclaimed emergency. In Dr. Ambedkar's well known description, the Constitution 'is a Federal Constitution inasmuch as it establishes what may be called a Dual Polity (which) . . . will consist of the Union at the Centre and the States at the periphery each endowed with sovereign powers to be exercised in the field assigned to them respectively by the Constitution'. Yet the Constitution, said Ambedkar, avoided the 'tight mold of federalism' in which the American Constitution was caught, and could be 'both unitary as well as federal according to the requirements of time and circumstances'.[7]

The development of this remarkable federal system will in this chapter be treated in six parts devoted to the following subjects: the distribution of powers, the Union's emergency powers, the distribution of revenues, national planning, the linguistic provinces issue, and the integration into the federal structure of the former Princely States. The amending process, because of its vital importance to the working of the Constitution as a whole, will be treated separately in Chapter 11. The role of Parliament, and particularly that of the

---

[6] Birch, op. cit., p. 306.

[7] *CAD* VII, 1, 33–34; Ambedkar was introducing the Draft Constitution in the Assembly.

Council of States, in the federal system, it will be recalled, has been treated in Chapter 6.

Before examining, the way in which the Assembly framed these provisions, however, it may be helpful to consider briefly the forces bearing on its decisions. These impelled the Assembly almost exclusively in one direction, toward a centralized, cooperative federation. They had earlier caused the Assembly to adopt a direct, parliamentary constitution as distinct from one based on 'Gandhian' decentralization. The antecedents of both decisions lay in the history of the previous thirty years, in the great pressure exerted by conditions existing during the framing period, and in the belief of Assembly members that the renascence of India demanded strong central government.

It would seem that a country so large in size and diverse in population as India was fated to have a governmental system in which local initiative and strong control were blended. India's size and diversity equally prevented the efficient working of a too unified administration and demanded a central authority powerful enough to prevent its administrative structure from disintegrating. Mogul and British rule had been based on these two principles. During British times, the great increase in the rapidity of communication had made the central government more powerful and had correspondingly diminished the authority and independence of local governing bodies. This was an imperial, as well as an administrative, necessity. To hold India, the British had to control it, and as a result of their tightening control the balance of power tipped heavily towards the central government. No matter how substantial the devolution of authority to the provinces under the 1919 Government of India Act or how apparently federal the provisions of the 1935 Act, or to what extent Indians held office in either the federal or provincial governments, power was centralized and always in British hands. As the Report of the Joint Parliamentary Committee phrased it, the government in New Delhi under the 1935 Act would, in the main, cease to have authority over matters within the provincial sphere, but 'in virtue of his power of supervising the Governors (the Governor-General), will have authority to secure compliance in certain respects with directions which he may find it necessary to give'.[8] This reliance on central power by the British profoundly affected India's future. Because of it, Indians had

---

[8]   *Joint Parliamentary Committee Report*, P. 29.

neither experienced nor participated in the working of a more traditional federal system like that of the United States or Australia. Their immediate experience with government, therefore, almost inevitably led them towards centralization. As Nehru said in 1936, 'It is likely that free India may be a Federal India, though in any event there must be a great deal of unitary control.'[9]

An equally forceful influence towards centralization was the national preoccupation with communalism in the years from the late twenties until Partition, For Indians, the emotionally charged, the politically significant, issue, other than independence, was community rights and status. 'States rights' issues were secondary and never assumed the importance they had in America and Australia. During the drafting of the 1919 and 1935 Acts, for example, far more emphasis was placed on ensuring community rights than on the distribution of powers. That this was true in part because the geographical dispersion of the minorities prevented them from couching their demands for communal security in federal form does not alter the situation. And when communal demands did take federal form, as in the case of the Muslims, the explosiveness of the mixture made Congress leaders more wary of the concept of provincial autonomy as well as of communalism itself. In such an atmosphere, unity gained further significance. Responsible Indian leaders, already confronted with a fragmented society, believed no new, divisive forces should be introduced. In the Constituent Assembly, therefore, allegiance to provincial governments was muted. As Ambedkar said, introducing the Draft Constitution: 'The proposed Indian Constitution is a dual polity with a single citizenship. There is only one citizenship for the whole of India . . . There is no State citizenship.'[10] Local allegiances, as they existed, for example, in the United States, were to be avoided not encouraged.

The effect of communal tensions on plans for a federal structure is evident in the reports of the Nehru and Sapru Committees. After devoting two chapters to what it called 'The Communal Aspect', the Nehru report said, 'We are called upon to determine the principles of the Constitution after considering these divergent views.'[11] It then went on to recommend, however, a

---

[9] IAR 1936, II, p. 226.
[10] CAD VII, 1, 34.
[11] Nehru Report, p. 24.

centralized federal structure based on the devolution of powers of the 1919 Act. The members of the Sapru Committee were even more torn between what they believed necessary for India and what they considered politically feasible. They believed that 'it would be unfortunate if the residuary powers were placed in the hands of the Provinces and that a strong Centre was most necessary in India'. Yet 'for the sake of peace and amity', the members agreed to recommend the establishment of a loose federal system in which residuary powers, 'in accordance with the Muslim view', would be vested in the provinces.[12]

The Cabinet Mission Plan took this line of reasoning even further, proposing a political system closer to confederation than federalism. But as a result of Partition the Assembly was able to bring the nation back to a more normal course of development. 'The severe limitation on the scope of central authority in the Cabinet Mission's Plan was a compromise accepted by the Assembly much, we think, against its judgement of the administrative needs of the country in order to accommodate the Muslim League', said the second report of the Union Powers Committee. The members of the committee, the report continued, were unanimously of the view that 'it would be injurious to the interests of the country to provide for a weak central authority which would be incapable of ensuring peace, of coordinating vital matters of common concern, and of speaking effectively for the whole country in the international sphere. . . . The soundest framework for our constitution is a federation with a strong Centre.'[13]

The exigencies of the present as well as the pattern of the past impelled the Constituent Assembly to create a strong central government. Lessons pointing to this conclusion were to be had in the streets outside the Assembly. Only a strong government could survive the communal frenzy preceding and accompanying Partition, accomplish the administrative tasks created by Partition and the transfer of power, and resettle the refugees. Only with centralized coordination and control could the food crisis be met and the economy of the country saved from disaster. 'We have to deal', said Nehru, 'with a situation in which, if I may say so, if we do not try our utmost

---

[12] *Sapru Report*, para. 226, p. 177.
[13] The second *Report of the Union Powers Committee*, para. 2, dated 5 July 1947; *Reports, First Series*, pp. 70–71. This summary of the committee's views bears Nehru's signature.

the whole of India will be a cauldron within six months. . . . And I don't know whether it will not be a cauldron in the next six months due to the economic situation.'[14] Only a strong central government could deal with the problem of the Princely States, few of which had any semblance of modern government or effective administration or seemed inclined to cooperate with the new government. There was some danger, too, that provincial governments might not be able to bear the strains of their new responsibilities, particularly in regard to public security and the food crisis.

In such a situation, talk of union versus provincial powers was 'a dead issue', K. M. Panikkar believed. 'Federation is a fair weather constitution', he said, and to have one would be 'definitely dangerous to the strength, prosperity, and welfare of India'. The provincial governments should by devolution have large powers, Panikkar believed, and the basic principle of the constitution 'should be a unitary one'. 'In a federation, the All-India Centre will not have authority over the provinces', he warned, 'and the structure of administrative unity built up in Hindustan will fall to pieces unless the Centre is given an overriding power.'[15] It is likely that Panikkar was neither rejecting a tightly-knit federation, nor suggesting a unitary constitution in the strict sense of the term, but that he was advocating a constitution in which the central government would have extensive powers—and in this he was speaking for many Assembly members.[16]

The immediate goals of the social revolution—improving the standard of living and increasing industrial and agricultural productivity— provided yet another reason for a strong central authority. Although some Assembly members argued that the welfare

[14] Nehru in a speech to a meeting of the Negotiating Committee of the Chamber of Princes and the Assembly's States Committee, held on 8 February 1947; *Prasad papers*, File 11-C/46-7-8.

[15] Panikkar, *A Note on Some General Principles of the Union Constitution*, printed in May 1947, PP. 1–8; *Prasad papers*, File 3-C/47.

[16] Among them was P. S. Deshmukh, who became so alarmed by the world situation, by the unstable conditions in India, and by the need for greater cooperation between the Union and provincial governments that in 1949 he recommended scrapping the Draft Constitution in favour of unitary government, The two problems that concerned Deshmukh most were the agitation for the formation of linguistic provinces and the need for uniformity in economic and taxation policies. See P. S. Deshmukh motion submitted to the Steering Committee for debate on 19 May 1949; *Prasad papers*. File 2-S/48. For a further discussion of these matters, see below.

of the people was the responsibility of the provincial governments,[17] most believed that the burden rested primarily with the Union Government, and that only a national effort could effect the necessary gains. 'Only on the basis of the total wealth of the country', said D. P. Khaitan, soon afterwards to become a member of the Drafting Committee, could India 'build up the edifice of education, health, culture, and so on.'[18] 'The attributes of a strong Centre', said Balkrishna Sharma, 'are that it should be in a position to think and plan for the well-being of the country as a whole, which means . . . having the authority . . . to coordinate (and) . . . the power of initiative. . . . It should be in a position to supply the wherewithal to the provinces for their better administration whenever the need arises. . . . It should have the right in times of stress and strain to issue directives to the provinces regulating their economic and industrial life in the interests of the nation as a whole.'[19] Yet as we have seen, the members of the Assembly did not consider it their task to lay down precisely how the aims of the social revolution should be pursued. They believed that their function was to prepare the way for this revolution by giving the Union Government the powers to meet its economic and social responsibilities.

Logical, perhaps even necessary, as the creation of a cooperative federation was in view of the country's constitutional experience and the exigencies of prevailing conditions, one other fact made a cooperative approach to constitution-making imperative: the provinces of India were already members of a federal union during the framing period, and, in terms of political reality, this union was indissoluble. 'The Federation was not the result of an agreement by the States to join in a Federation', Ambedkar told the Assembly, and 'the Federation not being the result of an agreement, no State has the right to secede from it.'[20] The members of the Constituent Assembly were not the representatives of separate states come together, as in the United States, to frame a constitution making them one nation. They were the members of a family who, for the first time in possession of

[17] One of the few expressing this view was K. Santhanam, *CAD* V, 3, 55–79

[18] *CAD* V, 4, 99; during the debate on the second Union Powers Committee report.

[19] *CAD* V, 4, 77.

[20] *CAD* VII, 1, 43.

their own house, must find a way to live together in it. If their life was not to grind to an acrimonious halt, the members' relationship must by compromise be made mutually satisfactory.

This task was made much easier, of course, by the existence of a powerful political party with nationwide authority and by the absence of strong regional or provincially-based political parties. Had these existed, they would have complicated the achievement of a harmoniously working federal system. Nor did the Provincial Congress Committees assume the role of protectors of provincial 'rights'. Files of communications exchanged between the Provincial Congress Committees and the Congress high command contain no mention of the work of the Constituent Assembly. The local Congress Committees were not only too busy mending political fences, in preparation for forthcoming elections, but the centres of power had shifted from them to the provincial governments. It was the leaders of these governments, as we shall see, who would negotiate with the Union leaders—both groups being in the Assembly—concerning the shape of the federal structure. Finally, Partition had its effect. By providing an example of the dangers inherent in separatism, it served to unite Indians. And by removing the greatest body of separatist fervour from India it left no real barrier to the creation of a cooperative federation.

It should not be thought, however, that the concept of tight federation went unchallenged. There was a good deal of sentiment in favour of administrative decentralization. Moreover, as Professor Morris-Jones has pointed out, the 1935 Act 'introduced on to the stage the provincial politician' and had given him a taste of power. 'It was unlikely that these men, when they came to form a significant proportion of the members of the Constituent Assembly . . . would allow much talk of a purely unitary constitution.'[21]

Although they were well aware of the many forces necessitating a tight federal structure, Assembly members were able to take their first step in this direction only after the announcement of Partition. Before June 1947, little time had been devoted to considering the federal system. The Assembly had created a Union Powers Committee under Nehru's chairmanship in January 1947, but the committee had been limited by the terms of the Cabinet Mission Plan. Its first

[21] Morris-Jones, *Parliament in India*, p. 17.

report, therefore, provided in general terms for a very weak central government. By mid-April 1947, however, when the Union Powers Committee submitted its report to the Assembly, Partition was being discussed between Congress and Muslim League leaders and Lord Mountbatten, and the Assembly postponed debate on the report.[22] With the decision to divide India into two States, the Union Powers Committee report became outdated and was consigned to the dust of library shelves. The prologue had ended.

Mountbatten announced Partition on 3 June 1947. Within four days the Assembly had embarked on a centralized federal union. On 5 June the Union and Provincial Constitution Committees, having spent much of the first month of their lives marking time, met in joint session and concluded that in the light of the June Third Statement the Cabinet Mission Plan no longer applied to the Assembly.[23] The following day the Union Constitution Committee met alone. Present were Nehru, the chairman, Prasad, Azad, Pant, Jagjivan Ram, Ambedkar, Ayyar, Munshi, Shah, S. P. Mookerjee, V. T. Krishnamachari, Panikkar, N, G. Ayyangar, and P. Govinda Menon. These men took the following tentative decisions:

> That the Constitution would be federal with a strong centre;
> That there should be three 'exhaustive' legislative lists, and that residuary powers should vest in the Union Government;
> That the Princely States should be on a par with the provinces regarding the Federal List, subject to special matters; and
> That generally speaking the Executive authority of the Union should be co-extensive with its legislative authority.[24]

The next day, 7 June, the two committees again held a joint session to consider the decisions that the Union Constitution Committee had taken the day before and to decide whether India should be 'a Unitary State with Provinces functioning as agents and delegates of Central authority, or whether India should be a Federation of

---

[22] *CAD* III, 1, 360ff. N. G. Ayyangar introduced the UPC report into the Assembly and then suggested that it should not be debated because 'the present political conversations' might result in 'the division of India into two or more independent states'. For the text of the first UPC report, dated 17 April 1947, see *Reports, First Series*, pp. 1–5.

[23] Minutes of the meeting, 5 June 1947; *INA*.

[24] Minutes of the meeting, 6 June 1947; ibid.

autonomous Units ceding certain specified powers to the Centre'. The assembled members voted to accept the recommendations of the Union Constitution Committee.[25]

During the following five weeks, the Union Constitution and Union Powers Committees prepared reports giving preliminary form to these decisions. The second Union Powers Committee report included detailed legislative lists as well as recommendations concerning the absorption of the Princely States. The two reports drafted by the Union Constitution Committee treated such federal matters as the distribution of powers, the extent of Union Executive authority, the distribution of revenue, and amendment. In each case the committees began the slow building of central power.

The Distribution of Powers

The basic provisions laying down the distribution of powers between the Union and the provincial governments are found in Part XI of the Constitution, entitled Relations Between the Union and the States. Part XI is divided into two Chapters, Legislative Relations, which establishes the list system, and Administrative Relations. Yet throughout the Constitution there are articles profoundly affecting the power relationship of the various governments. Two articles of the Temporary and Transitional Provisions give the Union the power to control trade in certain vital commodities within a province and to control, if it so desires, the governments of the former Princely States.[26] The Emergency Provisions in their entirety bear directly on the distribution of powers; likewise the provisions for the distribution of revenue. Perhaps not usually considered a part of the division of powers, although they are important to it, are such provisions as those establishing the limited authority of the upper, 'federal' house of Parliament, the single judicial system, the one Election Commission with nationwide authority, and the amending process—all of which weigh the scales of power in favour of the Union.

Nor is the distribution of powers under the Constitution static. Although the provisions of Part XI are entrenched so far as amendment goes, the power relationship may be greatly changed, but not

---

[25] Minutes of the meeting, 7 June 1947; ibid.
[26] *Constitution*, Part XXI, Articles 369 and 371.

permanently upset, in three ways. Under the provisions for meeting emergencies, the Union Executive and the Parliament can direct a provincial government in the use of its powers or assume all of its powers, the Union Executive acting for the provincial Executive and Parliament enacting legislation as if it were the provincial legislature. Thus, in Ambedkar's words, India may in certain circumstances become a unitary state. The power relationship may also be changed in a second way: by the use of Union Executive power. Union Executive authority normally extends only to subjects on the Union list, yet according to Article 73 Parliament may extend its authority to the Concurrent List. Articles 256 and 257 provide that the Executive power of a province must be exercised so as to comply with Union laws and so as not to impede or prejudice the exercise of Union Executive authority. To ensure that both these stipulations are obeyed, the Union Executive may give directions to a provincial government as to the manner in which it should act, and if a provincial government does not comply with these directions, the Union, under the Emergency Provisions, may take over the running of the government (Article 365). The Union Executive may also devolve upon a provincial government, with that government's consent, the exercise of any of its powers. Finally, Article 249 provides that the Council of States may empower Parliament to legislate on any matter included in the State Legislative List, thus allowing government to become nearly as unitary as under the Emergency Provisions.

1. The Division of Powers in the Legislative Lists

The first two articles of Part XI deal with the most central aspect of the distribution of powers, the competence of the Union and provincial legislatures as elaborated in the legislative lists. A third provision vests residuary powers in the Union, and another lays down that in cases where a provincial law is repugnant to a Union law, the provincial law shall be void. The remaining articles concern the potential modification of the basic distribution by action of the Council of States and by the Union Executive.

The list system of the distribution of legislative powers originated in India with the 1919 Government of India Act. Under the Devolution Rules made in accordance with the Act, authority to legislate on various matters was granted to the provinces, and the list of these subjects became the model for the Provincial Legislative List developed at the Round Table Conferences and by the Joint Parliamentary Committee. The corollary to the Provincial List, of course, was a list of subjects reserved for the federal legislature, which found its precedent in the Canadian and Australian Constitutions. At the Round Table Conferences there was also conceived the idea of a third, or Concurrent, List to embody those subjects that 'cannot be allocated exclusively either to a Central or to a Provincial Legislature', but where the federal legislature should have jurisdiction 'to enable it in some cases to secure uniformity in the main principles of law throughout the country . . . to guide and encourage provincial effort, and . . . to provide remedies for mischiefs arising in the provincial sphere'.[27]

The members of the Joint Parliamentary Committee believed that the lists would provide a sound basis for a federal system, and found in the exhaustive description of the jurisdiction of the federal and provincial legislatures an escape from the vexing issue of residuary powers—which was a serious bone of communal contention, with Hindus claiming that residuary powers should vest in the centre and Muslims strongly holding the opposite view. (Residuary powers would remain a subject of hot controversy until Partition, despite the unreality of the issue resulting from the completeness of the lists.) If, however, a matter should arise that had not been foreseen when drawing up the lists, the Governor-General under the 1935 Act was to make an *ad hoc* decision, assigning this residuary subject to the federation or the provinces as he believed fit.[28] The provision establishing the superiority of federal over provincial law also dates from this period; it was designed to decide conflicts that might arise in connection with the Concurrent List.

The 1935 Act embodied the list system as it had been envisaged by the Joint Committee, and the reports of the Union Constitution and Union Powers Committees reproduced these provisions of the 1935 Act little changed into the Assembly. The second Union Powers Committee report—transmitted under Nehru's letter to President Prasad in which he said that 'the soundest framework for our

---

[27] *Report of the Joint Parliamentary Committee*, para. 51, pp. 30–31.

[28] Ibid., paras. 56 and 230, pp. 33 and 143.

constitution is a federation with a strong centre'[29]—dealt almost entirely with the legislative lists. These were given in detail and, except for drafting changes, the items were taken directly from the Seventh Schedule of the 1935 Act. The important point here is less that this was done, than that the provinces readily agreed to it: the decision was taken by the Provincial and Union Constitution Committees in joint session. The prime ministers of Bombay, Assam, the United Provinces and a former prime minister of Madras were members of these committees.[30] The report also recommended that residuary powers should be vested in the Union.

The report of the Union Constitution Committee presented only brief, preliminary suggestions concerning the federal structure and the distribution of powers. Recapitulating the decisions taken during the first week of June, the committee recommended that the Constitution should be federal with a strong centre, that there should be exhaustive legislative lists, and that the Princely States should be on a par with the provinces in regard to the Union Legislative List.[31] The absence from the Committee's report of more specific provisions concerning the federal structure can be attributed to the atmosphere of uncertainty during the previous months. It seemed fruitless to draft federal provisions when unity and Partition were in the balance. Rau, for example, in his memorandum on the Union Constitution, devoted little attention to the distribution of powers, noting that if the Cabinet Mission Plan was abandoned, 'the whole matter may have to be considered afresh'.[32] Work on the federal system could only begin in earnest after the question of Pakistan had been decided.

The Assembly did not extensively debate the federal provisions in the reports of the Union Constitution and Union Powers Committees during the sessions of July and August 1947. There was some general debate on the extent of Union power during the consideration of the Union Constitution Committee report, but the sole suggestion of substance concerning the distribution of powers was that the devolution of

---

[29] Second UPC report; *Reports, First Series*, pp. 70–80; the quotation is from p. 71.

[30] See minutes of meeting, 2 July 1947; *INA*.

[31] UCC report, ibid., p. 58.

[32] Rau, *India's Constitution*, p. 92,

Union authority upon a provincial government should be only with the province's consent. To this, N, G. Ayyangar, the committee's spokesman in the debate, objected that as a general proposition having to seek provincial approval for Union action would 'be going against the root principles of the exercise of (Union) Executive authority in relation to federal subjects'.[33] Nevertheless the Draft Constitution, and the Constitution both provided that the Union Executive must have such consent before devolving its authority.

Introducing the Union Powers Committee's report, N. G. Ayyangar, again the spokesman, instead of Nehru who was the committee's chairman, explained the members' position. 'The committee came to the conclusion', he said, 'that we should make the Centre in this country as strong as possible consistent with leaving a fairly wide range of subjects to the Provinces in which they would have the utmost freedom to order things as they liked.'[34] Another general debate about a Strong versus a weak Union Government followed. Several members claimed that the centre was being strengthened at the cost of the provinces; others disagreed. Turning to the question of residuary powers, the Assembly decided to vest them in the Union. Although it had long been Congress policy that they should vest in the units, with Partition a fact this 'kind of bargaining for communal considerations' could be ended.[35]

Turning to the legislative lists in the UPC report, the Assembly commenced a brief debate on Union subjects—only the first thirty-seven items of the Union List and neither of the other two lists were discussed because of lack of time. Three things marked this and future debates on the lists: the suspicion by a minority of back-benchers that provincial rights might be encroached upon, the greater-than-average sensitivity of some Muslim and Princely States representatives to this issue, and the lack of change that would be wrought in the lists as a result of their consideration on the floor of the House. Setting the precedent for future debates, the Assembly at this time made no material alterations, the majority believing in the need to maintain Union power unimpaired.

The legislative lists prepared by the Drafting Committee and included as the Seventh Schedule of the Draft Constitution differed

---

[33] *CAD* IV, 13, 982–3.
[34] *CAD* V, 3, 39.
[35] *CAD* V, 4, 80; G.L.. Mehta

little from those of the Union Powers Committee report. Commenting on the three lists, Ayyar said that they merely distinguished between what was of common and of provincial concern, and that the items of the Concurrent List did not dangerously enlarge the scope of Union authority, for they were no greater than the powers exercised concurrently in the United States and Canada. When drafting the lists, Ayyar said, the committee had 'profited by the historical and constitutional development of these various countries'.[36] Ayyar would presumably have agreed with Jennings that legislative lists might be a source of litigation, but that a general description of the distribution of legislative powers—as in the United States—presented even more dangerous opportunities for court action that could cripple or delay a government's programme.[37]

The Assembly had two main purposes when bestowing such broad powers on the Union Government in the Union and Concurrent Lists. One was constitutional flexibility. Federalism, as Ambedkar put it, traditionally suffered from rigidity, and the countries adopting federal government throughout the years had sought to reduce this disadvantage. Australia had attempted to do so 'by conferring upon the Parliament of the Commonwealth large powers of concurrent legislation'. Profiting by the Australian example, said Ambedkar, the Draft Constitution had taken the process one step further. While both constitutions gave their central governments a large number of concurrent powers, he said, 'the exclusive authority of the Australian Parliament to legislate extends only to about three matters; the authority of the Indian Parliament as proposed in the Draft Constitution will extend to ninety-one matters. In this way the Draft Constitution has secured the greatest possible elasticity in its federalism, which is supposed to be rigid by nature'.[38]

The second purpose of these extensive powers was to enable the Union to meet the needs and to withstand the pressures of the times. The problems facing the Government, which confronted the Assembly through the dual role of the leadership, directly shaped the content of the Constitution. A memorandum assessing the

---

[36] Ayyar in a lecture to the Ranade Association, given during the early spring of 1948; *Ayyar papers*.

[37] Jennings, *Some Characteristics*, p. 60.

[38] *CAD* VII, 1, 35–36.

problems facing the Interim Government (September 1946 to 14 August 1947)[39] noted, as needing immediate attention, agricultural production policy, price control for agricultural products, the establishment of central higher technical institutions, and food distribution. Also demanding, urgent consideration were controls on coal and textiles. A second memorandum, containing less pressing matters, listed the need to formulate a sound and firm economic policy, to increase production of consumer goods, to hold back inflation, and to bring down prices. This memorandum also said that the state must create administrative machinery in the fields of agricultural and general economic development.[40] These documents were prepared for the Government, not for the Assembly; yet it was evident that if the Government was to fulfil its responsibilities in these matters, it must have the constitutional powers to do so.

More explicit were two other memoranda. Jagjivan Ram, Labour Minister in the Interim Government, prepared a note for the Cabinet and the Union Powers Committee stating his strong belief that labour policy and administration, including social Welfare and labour planning, should be a Union responsibility.[41] The Union Minister of Agriculture, Jairamdas Daulatram, wrote to Dr. Ambedkar, whilst the Drafting Committee was preparing the legislative lists, explaining that the difficulties of feeding an ever-growing population meant added responsibility for the Union Government. To facilitate the Government's work the Draft Constitution must, as a minimal provision, give the Union authority to coordinate agricultural production on a national scale.[42]

An official policy resolution issued in April 1948 made the Government's position even clearer. The Draft Constitution, to a great extent incorporating the principles of cooperative federalism, had by that time been published, but the views in the resolution had been formed over a period of time and were certainly reflected in the Drafting Committee's decisions. The resolution indicated, moreover, the argument that Government leaders in the Assembly would use

---

[39] The memorandum was entitled 'Important Tasks facing the Interim Government' and was dated 19 August 1946, author not given; *Prasad paperst*. File I-I/46-7.

[40] Memorandum entitled 'Major Tasks Before the Interim Government', dated 3 April 1947, no author given; ibid.

[41] Note dated 29 May 1947; *Munshi papers*.

[42] Memorandum dated 16 January 1948, *Comments* volume; *INA*.

during the subsequent debates. The Government's resolution envisaged an increasingly active role for the state in the development of industry and agriculture, particularly in promoting such industries as coal, iron and steel, aircraft manufacture, and shipbuilding. Although the resolution included unit governments and other public authorities, like municipal corporations, in its definition of 'state', most of the initiative would have to come from the Union as the only government able to undertake such projects. Furthermore, the resolution specifically stated that the management of state enterprises would, as a rule, be under public corporations statutorily controlled by the Union. Basic industries ranging from salt to automobiles, from rubber to cotton, from cement to machine tools, should be under Union control. Not only should the overseeing of these industries be a Union responsibility, according to the resolution, but also the location of the factories, so that the needs of the national economy would be served.[43]

The drafting of the legislative lists entered its last phase in July 1949. On 14 July the secretaries of the Union ministries met under the chairmanship of B. N. Rau to discuss the lists. The suggestions for changes were largely technical and legal in nature, but questions concerning the distribution of powers were raised. The secretary of the Ministry of Works, Mines and Power, for example, said that in the view of his ministry, oil, including oilfields and petroleum products from well to distribution, should be a Union subject, although in the Draft they were divided between the Union and the states. Rau replied that this was a matter for the forthcoming meeting between the Drafting Committee and the provincial prime ministers, because Assam would certainly oppose such a change.[44] The secretaries of the ministries of agriculture and education would also have broadened Union power, and a frequently heard response to suggestions was, 'Will the provinces agree?'

Just a week later the Drafting Committee met to discuss the federal provisions of the Draft Constitution. The prime ministers of the provinces and of certain Princely States, several Union ministers, and the members of the Union Powers Committee were invited. The meeting had for its consideration recommendations from several provincial governments and Union ministries, as well

[43] *Government of India Resolution on Industrial Policy*, 8 April 1948.
[44] Proceedings of the meeting, 14 July 1949; *Law Ministry Archives*, File CA/59/Cons/ 49. All references here are from these proceedings.

as the proposals made by the previous week's meeting of ministerial secretaries—many of which were adopted. The discussions led
to few changes of substance in the legislative lists, but they illustrate the conflicts that could arise between the 'centralizers' and the
provincial politician. For example, the Union Minister for Health,
Rajkumari Amrit Kaur, had long advocated making public health a
concurrent and not merely a state subject. Munshi and Nehru supported her. Pandit Pant, premier of the United Provinces, opposed
this. He argued that too much central power would impair the
sense of responsibility of provincial governments. To this Nehru
responded that 'according to Pandit Pant there need not be a
Concurrent List at all'.[45] On the matter of forests—in the State
List in the Draft Constitution—a like argument took place. Pandit
Pant opposed a move to make 'forests' a concurrent subject. He was
reported as saying that India had worked decentralization 'not only
as a matter of theory but also in actual practice', and that India was
too large for such a degree of centralization. B.C. Kher, premier
of Bombay, interjected here that if the centrists' attitude prevailed
there might as well be only two lists, the Union and the Concurrent.
Then Nehru asked what if the Union adopted legislation relating to
forests under its authority to undertake national planning. Pant's
reply went to the core of Indian federalism, expressing the mutual
dependence of the Union and the units upon which the system
rests. 'If it is hoped', said Pant, 'that the provinces can be made to
cooperate against their own will by means of central legislation,
that hope is not likely to materialize.'

The meeting also discussed making education a concurrent
or a Union subject instead of leaving it almost entirely with the
province, as under the 1935 Act. Maulana Azad, the Minister
of Education, strongly opposed leaving it with the provinces; he
believed it should be under 'Central guidance if not Central control', so that 'the intelligentsia of the country will be thinking
on similar lines'.[46] Azad also believed that educational planning
and the standards of higher educational institutions should be a

---

[45] Proceedings of the meeting, 21 July 1947; *Law Ministry Archives*. All subsequent
references are from these proceedings.

[46] Azad in a letter to the Drafting Committee, 28 April 1948. See *Comments*
volume; *INA*. Under cover of a letter dated 18 November 1948, Azad submitted
provisions embodying these Ideas; see *Ayyar papers*.

Union subject. Nehru and others supported him, but sentiment in general favoured the continuance of provincial authority in this sphere. The meeting agreed, however, that coordination and standards of higher education, scientific and technical institutions, and several other categories might be placed in the Union List—a decision arrived at earlier by the Cabinet, to which the issue had been referred because of its very controversial nature. Vocational and technical training for labour was to be a concurrent subject: otherwise education would remain with the states.[47] With agreement on the lists reached by the heads of the Union and provincial governments, the debate in the Assembly was of little consequence. The lists were adopted in September 1949.

The wide range of authority given the Union Government by the list system was enhanced by three provisions for the temporary assumption of provincial legislative power by the Union Parliament. Under one article, this could occur during times of emergency, and it will be considered later. Another, adapted from the Australian Constitution and the 1935 Act, enabled two units to request Parliamentary regulation of a matter normally reserved for provincial action.[48] The third provision, Article 226 of the Draft, laid down that Parliament could, with the previous approval of a two-thirds majority in the Council of States, legislate on any matter on the State List.

Dr. Ambedkar described Article 226 as an Indian innovation in the process of making federal government less rigid and legalistic. It empowered Parliament, he said, to legislate 'on exclusively provincial subjects in normal times' if they became 'a matter of national concern'.[49] This was certainly true; yet it appears that the origins of the provision lay more in a desire to effect social change and economic gains than solely in the wish to make the federal structure more flexible. While on his trip to America and Europe during the autumn of 1947, B. N. Rau had considered deeply the moral aspects of fundamental rights issues and had come to the general conclusion

---

[47] Proceedings of the meeting, op. cit.

[48] *Draft Constitution*, Article 229, *Constitution*, Article 252. For the precedents from which this provision was derived, see *Australian Constitution*, Article 51 (xxxvii) and, more closely, the 1935 *Act*, Section 103.

[49] *CAD* VII, I, 36

that 'the general welfare should prevail over the individual right'.[50] Federalism with its independent spheres of legislative power could, however, be a hindrance in this respect. It might prove necessary, Rau said, 'in order to raise the standard of living of the Indian people as a whole', to introduce 'a system of cooperative farming and of price control of agricultural products on a national scale'. Yet with agriculture, cooperative societies, and the production, supply, and distribution of goods provincial subjects, the Union Government could not achieve its aim. Because the goal was in fact national welfare, 'the Centre should not be precluded from legislating in respect of the above subjects', Rau believed. He continued:

> The essence of the matter is that where legislation is called for on a national basis, the Central legislature should have power to enact it without amending the Constitution. Such legislation may be needed not only in such spheres as education, cooperative farming, or public health, but also in a matter which is coming to be regarded as one of national and indeed almost international importance, namely, the safeguarding of the civil rights of ail citizens, e.g., removing the social disabilities of Harijans.[51]

Therefore, Rau believed his Draft Constitution should be amended to allow Parliament to legislate upon any matter on the Provincial List, provided that the Council of States by a two-thirds majority had declared that such action was 'necessary and expedient in the national interest'. A like majority could revoke the resolution.[52] The members of the Drafting Committee agreed, supporting their belief with a reference to the opinion, handed down in a Canadian case, that matters affecting peace, order, and good government were the responsibility of Parliament even if they touched upon matters reserved for provincial legislatures.[53] The committee included Rau's recommended version of the article word for word in the Draft

[50] Rau, *India's Constitution*, p. 313. This portion of his report to Prasad and the Assembly, Rau forwarded by airmail from the United States.

[51] Ibid., p. 315. Rau had been very much influenced by the Report of the President's (of the United States) Committee on Civil Rights and its recommendation that the national government must take the lead, in safeguarding civil rights, with Congress enacting the necessary legislation; ibid.

[52] Rau, op. cit., p. 314.

[53] See *List of Amendments to the Draft Constitution*, November 1948, including comments by the Drafting Committee; *Law Ministry Archives*. The opinion

Constitution, omitting, however, provision for the revocation of such a resolution if passed by the Council of States. This would be changed, and other alterations would be made, at a later date.

Ayyar attempted to limit the anti-federal character of Article 226 by eliminating part of Article 228 which permitted a provincial legislature to act on a matter while Parliament was empowered to do so by virtue of a resolution passed under Article 226. He reasoned that treating such a subject as if it were on the Concurrent List, instead of as a provincial matter temporarily under Union control, 'would offer a premium for the Union gradually encroaching on the State field and striking at the federal structure of the Constitution'.[54] *The Hindu* supported Ayyar, but the Drafting Committee took a contrary view. It refused to accept Ayyar's suggestion because 'to go quite so far' would encroach on provincial rights.[55]

Article 226 had vociferous critics both inside and outside the Assembly, although the debate in the House was remarkably short. *The Hindustan Times* claimed in an editorial that it dealt a death blow to provincial autonomy. Several law professors expressed the belief—later voiced by members of the Assembly—that it perverted the amending process and ought, therefore, to be removed from the Draft. Jayaprakash Narayan recommended this.[56] The legislatures of both Bombay and the East Punjab, when debating the merits of the Draft in the autumn of 1948, favoured its omission, regarding it as a grave infringement of provincial rights.[57] Many Assembly members held this view, and twenty proposed an amendment deleting the article. Among the supporters of the amendment were K. Santhanam, M. A. Ayyangar, Mrs. Durgabai, T. T. and V. T. Krishnamachari, Acharya Jugal Kishore, and five Muslims.

Opening the debate on the article in the Assembly, Ambedkar moved an amendment limiting the life of a resolution passed by the Council of States under the article to one year, and laying down that a

---

cited was that of the Privy Council in Attorney-General of Ontario *v.* Canada Temperance Federation', 1946.

[54] *Draft Constitution,* second footnote, p. 104. See also Ayyar's note on the subject submitted to the Drafting Committee and appended to the *Draft Constitution,* pp. 213–14.

[55] List of Amendments, op. cit.; *Law Ministry Archives.*

[56] Suggestions for Amendments file; *Prasad papers.*

[57] See *Bombay Legislative Assembly Debates,* 20 October 1948 and *East Punjab Legislative Assembly Debates,* extracts, 21–28 October 1948; *INA.*

law passed under the terms of Article 226, if Parliament would otherwise not have been competent to pass it, would lapse in six months.[58] There can be little doubt that Ambedkar's amendment was a compromise measure intended to mollify the opposition in the Congress Assembly Party. None of the ranking members of the Assembly spoke on the issue except T. T. Krishnamachari, who, by this time a member of the Drafting Committee, reversed his earlier position and now supported the provision. The Assembly adopted Ambedkar's amendments and Article 226 passed into the Constitution.

2. Union Executive Authority and the Division of Powers

The distribution of legislative powers filled Chapter I of Part IX of the Draft. Chapter II of the Relations Between the Union and the States, on Administrative Relations, contained three articles that modified the basic distribution of powers established by the lists. Two of these articles empowered the Union Executive to give directions to a unit government to ensure that the Executive of a unit complied with, and did not impede or prejudice, the laws of the Union and the Union Executive in the exercise of its authority. The third provision empowered the President, with the consent of the unit government, to devolve upon it any function of the Union Executive. These three articles, based on nearly identical sections of the 1935 Act, were considered unobjectionable, and the Assembly adopted them with little consequential debate.[59]

On 15 November 1949, however, just eleven days before the completion of the Constitution, Ambedkar introduced a new article, 365, in the Assembly. This put teeth in the existing provisions by laying down that if a unit failed to give effect to, or to comply with, the directions given by the Union Executive, the President

---

[58] *CAD* VIII, 20, 799–800.

[59] For the debate, see *CAD* VIII, 20, 816–17. The sections of the 1935 Act used as models were 122, 124, and 126. The only change of any note made by the Assembly to the draft provisions was to extend the Executive authority of the Union to the giving of directions to a unit government with regard to the protection of the railways. Such powers had been included in the 1935 Act, but not in the Draft Constitution, and finally were inserted at the insistence of the Ministry of Railways, which cited the failure of provincial governments in 1946 to protect railways and trains from looting, arson, and murder. See ministry's letter of 22 July 1949 (*Munshi papers*) and a note of 9 August 1949 (*Prasad papers*).

could declare that the government of the unit was not being carried on in accordance with the Constitution. The President could then, under the Emergency Provisions, assume any of the functions of the unit government.[60]

Angry voices denounced the new provision. Thakur Das Bhargava and Pandit Kunzru opposed it, as did several others. They were dismayed by the 'drastic power' of the article and argued that the Drafting Committee had exceeded its authority by introducing the provision when the drafting was so nearly completed. Other opponents of the article said it resembled the hated Section 93 of the 1935 Act 'in all its nakedness and power'.[61] They damned the Union for its lack of faith in the provinces, and the argument raged for several hours. Ambedkar defended the provision, arguing that it introduced no new principle, but that it followed from the articles giving the Executive the power to issue directions, and that it merely completed the President's powers—the authority to give directions was useless without the power to enforce them. He compared Article 365 with Section 126 of the 1935 Act, according to which the Governor-General in his discretion could order a provincial Governor to comply with a federal directive.[62] Despite the vehemence of the opposition, the Assembly passed the article.

Two articles of the Temporary and Transitional Provisions also affected the distribution of powers. In both, the basic distribution established by the list system was subjected to temporary modifications to resolve immediate problems. The terms of Article 306 of the Draft Constitution (Article 369 of the Constitution) were a direct product of the Government's assessment of the nation's administrative needs. They provided that for five years the. Union could legislate, as if the subjects were part of the Concurrent List, on trade and commerce in, and the production of, textiles, paper, foodstuffs, petroleum, coal, iron, steel, and motor vehicle spare parts they also made the Union

[60] *CAD* XI, 2, 503. This Article first appeared as Article 365 in the *Draft Constitution as Revised by the Drafting Committee*, dated 3 November 1949. This Draft renumbered all articles in a manner largely coinciding with the final Constitution.

[61] *CAD* XI, 2, 516. Section 93 gave the Governor of a province the authority in his discretion to assume any of the functions of the government—thus the Governor-General, through the Governor, could take over the government of a province.

[62] Ibid., pp. 507–9.

responsible for the relief and rehabilitation of displaced persons. The Drafting Committee noted that such unusual power was necessary 'in view of the present conditions'.[63] The memoranda setting out the problems facing the Interim Government and the resolution stating the Government's industrial policy make clear what existing conditions were. And Prasad, when he was Minister of Agriculture, wrote to Lord Mountbatten, then the Governor-General, about the shortage of wheat supplies due to 'the colossal failure which had overtaken our wheat crop'. Already a twelve-ounce ration had been imposed in Madras. Prasad predicted that 'half-starvation or starvation' would occur unless India acquired food, and he feared that restrictions on consumption might lead to great popular pressure against food controls.[64] There was only desultory discussion of the measure when it reached the floor in October 1949. Although four members had at least a year earlier submitted an amendment to delete the article, they did not move it during the debate. Good sense, if not the Whip, prevailed, and the Assembly adopted the article.[65]

The second article of the Temporary and Transitional Provisions that so greatly weighed the distribution of power towards the Union Government was introduced in the Assembly as Article 306B and ultimately became Article 371 of the Constitution. It provided that for ten years, or a longer or shorter period, if Parliament so decided, the 'Part B' states—the former Princely States—should be under the

[63] *Draft Constitution*, footnote, p. 151. The committee also noted that a precedent for the measure lay in the India (Central Government and Legislature) Act of 1946, which granted similar powers to the Federal Government; ibid. This provision has been given additional force by Item 33 of the Concurrent list of the Constitution. This item, included at the request of the Finance Ministry, laid down that Parliament could legislate on the production and distribution of certain commodities after declaring that such legislation was in the national interest. John Matthai, the Finance Minister, had noted that the Union could not be at the mercy of any unit on such matters and must be able to control commodities such as cotton that were "of equal importance to the well-being of the country'. Matthai letter to Drafting Committee, 1 November 1949; *Law Ministry Archives.*

Added to Item 33 by the Third Amendment Act, 1954, were many of the products and foodstuffs that had been named in Article 369, thus keeping them subject to Union legislation even though the effect of Article 369 had expired

[64] Prasad letter to Mountbatten, 11 June 1947; *Prasad papers*, File 19-C/47.

[65] For this debate, see *CAD* X, 2, 3–7.

control of, and comply with, any directions given by the President. Failure to comply with such directions could result, under Article 365, in a take-over of the government by the Union Executive.

The provision was one of several that marked the final integration of the Princely States—a subject that will be considered in detail in Chapter 10. In the Assembly, a number of provincial representatives supported the article, while the States' representatives were almost equally divided in criticism and praise. Some critics were perhaps silenced by the Whip, and others may have been reassured by Patel's statement that 'the provision involve(d) no censure of any government', that it was a 'safety-valve', and that the Government did 'not wish to interfere with the day-to-day administration of any State'.[66] The opponents of the measure claimed that it unfairly discriminated between the former Princely States and the provinces and that it would inhibit the growth of democratic government in the States.[67] Two States, Mysore and Travancore-Cochin, objected to the provision and exacted a promise from Patel that they would receive preferential treatment.[68] And in 1951 Mysore successfully resisted a Presidential order under Article 371, showing that New Delhi's power under the provision was not so great as might have been presumed.[69] As a result of the reorganization of the states and the Seventh Amendment to the Constitution, the provision disappeared.

Finally, two other Articles claim brief attention. These demonstrate clearly enough the danger of classifying the Indian Constitution on the basis of its text rather than of how it has been worked. Article 175 of the Draft laid down, among other things, that a Governor could reserve a Bill passed by the provincial legislature for the consideration of the President. Article 176 provided, in general, that the President could assent to, or withhold assent from, such a Bill. Thus, on paper, the Union Government possessed a veto power on all provincial legislation. These provisions, which

[66] *CAD* X, 5, 164.

[67] *CAD* X, 6, 185–201. The Report of the States Reorganization Commission called Article 371 'unfedetal in character', but said that it did not alter the basic relation-ship between the Union and the States, established by the clear division of power. *Report*, p. 6.

[68] V. P. Menon, *The Integration*, p. 468; see also Patel in the Assembly, *CAD* X, 5,164.

[69] Alexandrowicz, op. cit., pp. 160–1.

had their origins in the 1935 Act, came up for debate in June 1949; they were held over. On 1 August they were again presented to the Assembly and passed, Article 176 without debate, and Article 175 with an amendment, proposed by Ambedkar, that a Money Bill could not be reserved by the Governor. They became Articles 200 and 201 of the Constitution. In theory they invalidate the division of powers, for 'there is no means of overriding the President's veto in the case of State legislation'.[70] Yet, in practice, there is little danger of the federal structure being upset. As one of the leading authorities on the working of the Constitution has written, since a Governor may reserve a Bill only on the advice of his ministers, 'the scope for the exercise of these powers in the case of Government Bills, which are sponsored by Ministers, is not much evident'.[71]

The Union's Long Arm; the Emergency Provisions

The effect that India's peculiar situation had on the shape of her federal system is nowhere more apparent than in the Emergency Provisions of the Constitution, by which the distribution of powers can be so drastically altered that the Constitution becomes unitary rather than federal. The Emergency Provisions comprise the nine articles of Part XVIII of the Constitution. According to the first of these, Article 352, the President may proclaim that a state of emergency exists if he is satisfied that national security is threatened by external aggression or internal disturbance. Such a proclamation must be laid before each house of Parliament and expires automatically after a two-month period, unless extended by Parliament. If the President is satisfied that the financial credit or stability of India or any part of it is threatened, he may issue, under the authority of Article 360, a similar proclamation. While this is valid, the Union Executive may give directions to unit Executives to observe 'such canons of financial propriety as may be specified in such directions'.[72]

---

[70] Basu, *Commentary*, p. 37.

[71] Ibid.

[72] *Constitution*, Article 360. It is perhaps helpful to reiterate here that the words 'the President' in the Emergency. Provisions, as elsewhere in the Constitution, mean the President as advised by his ministers.

During an emergency, Union Executive power extends to giving directions to states concerning the exercise of their Executive power, and Parliament may legislate on any matter whether or not it is normally on the Union Legislative List. Under a proclamation of emergency, the President may also temporarily modify the provisions laying down the distribution of revenues between the Union and the states, and Parliament need not be restricted by the 'freedoms' article of the Fundamental Rights from making laws that would otherwise be unconstitutional. Moreover, the right to move the courts for the enforcement of any of the Fundamental Rights may be suspended by the President.

Article 355 of the Emergency Provisions lays down that it is the duty of the Union to protect the units from external aggression and internal disturbance and to ensure that 'the government of every State is carried on in accordance with the provisions of this Constitution'. Therefore, if the President believes, because he has been so advised by a Governor or has himself decided, that a unit cannot be governed according to the Constitution, he may by proclamation assume the functions of the unit Executive and declare that 'the powers of the Legislature of the State shall be exercisable by or under the authority of Parliament'.[73] Such proclamations expire after two months unless approved by both houses of Parliament, but if approved may be renewed at six-monthly intervals for a period not to exceed three years. If Parliament has assumed the powers of the state legislature, it may confer this power on the President with the authority to delegate it as he thinks fit.

Governors, it must be noted, have no 'emergency powers' of the kind given to the President. But Governors, as well as the President, have legislative powers with which to meet certain emergency situations. These are laid down separately in two articles that give the President and Governors the power to promulgate Ordinances when the Union Parliament or state legislatures are not in session. Generally speaking, the power at both levels is the same: Governors and the President, facing the need for 'immediate action', may promulgate Ordinances having the force of legislative Acts, but they must lay Ordinances before the legislature when it reassembles. Unless approved by both houses, the Ordinance expires six weeks after reassembly. Governors may not use their legislative power to circumvent the restrictions on

[73] Ibid., Article 356(1) (b).

their authority imposed elsewhere in the Constitution. They may not, without instructions from the President, promulgate an Ordinance if a Bill containing the same provisions would have needed presidential sanction before introduction into the state legislature or if the Bill, once enacted, would have had to be reserved for the consideration of the President.[74]

The legislative powers of the Governors and the President, and the power vested in the President and the Union Government to meet emergencies have in part descended from similar provisions in the 1935 Government of India Act. This is particularly true of the Ordinance power. The all-important difference between the Union's emergency powers and those vested in the Governor-General and Governors under the 1935 Act is that under the Constitution all such actions are subject to legislative ratification. The President may shift the balance of federal power entirely to the Union Government, but his actions are subject to approval by a popular assembly in which the unit governments are represented. He has no powers that he can exercise in his discretion, or in his individual judgement', as had the Governor-General and his Governors; he must always act on the advice of ministers drawn from a popular assembly.

The Assembly drafted the provisions giving the President and Governors legislative powers with a minimum of debate and difficulty. It quickly adopted the provisions as embodied in the Union Constitution Committee and Provincial Constitution Committee reports, and when the Assembly considered the legislative powers in the Draft Constitution their reception was similar. Pandit Kunzru would have reduced the life-span of a presidential Ordinance from six weeks to thirty days and he believed that within that time Parliament should be summoned to consider the Ordinance. Equally, he would have shortened Governors' Ordinances to two weeks. Kunzru feared that in a province or at the Union level, Ordinance rule might last for six months, the period of time that could elapse between sessions of Parliament or provincial legislatures.[75] To this Ambedkar replied that since both Parliament and provincial assemblies were obliged by the Constitution to meet twice a year and their sessions would be of some duration, there was little possibility of an Ordinance

---

[74] Ibid., Article 213.
[75] *CAD* VIII, 6, 201ff and VIII, 21, 869–72.

existing six months before it was scrutinized by the legislature.[76] The Ordinance provisions, little changed from Rau's drafts of May 1947, were adopted in May and June 1949.

The long and involved progress of the Emergency Provisions through the Constituent Assembly began with the deliberations, under Nehru's chairmanship, of the Union Powers Committee in February 1947. The committee believed that for the effective discharge of its defence responsibilities, the Union should have powers similar to those of Sections 126A and 102 of the 1935 Act, and the power 'to deal with grave economic emergencies in any part of the Union' if they would affect the Union.[77] Although the Assembly postponed consideration of the first Union Powers Committee report in late April, as we have seen, and later shelved it as outdated, the suggestions for emergency provisions and several other recommendations were saved.

With the Union Powers Committee's recommendation in mind, Rau drafted his Memorandum on the Union Constitution and his Model Provincial Constitution, in which he considered emergency situations. At the Union level, according to Rau, the President had a special responsibility, which he was to fulfil in his discretion, to prevent grave menace to the peace and tranquillity of the Union and to safeguard its financial stability and credit. And the Governors were to have discretionary power to prevent grave menace to the peace and tranquillity of their provinces. But Rau presented no detailed picture of how the President and the Governors were to fulfil these special responsibilities.[78]

The Union and Provincial Constitution Committees both jointly and separately considered Rau's suggestions. The former did

[76] *CAD* VIII, 6, 212.

[77] UPC report, Paras. 2A and 3(14); *Reports, First Series*, pp. 1 and 4. Section 102 of the 1935 Act provided that if the security of India was threatened by war or internal disturbance, the Governor-General in his discretion could proclaim an emergency, whereupon the Federal Legislature could with the Governor-General's sanction, given also in his discretion, legislate upon matters on the Provincial Legislative list. Section 126A was added to the 1935 Act by the Government of India Act (Amendment) Act, September 1939. It empowered the Central Government to take over the administration of subjects on the Provincial and Concurrent Lists.

[78] Rau, *India's Constitution*, p. 71 (President), and pp. 145–6 (Governor).

not elaborate on the recommendations of the first Union Powers Committee and confined itself to providing that the President could extend a session of Parliament during an emergency for a year beyond its normal four-year term. Nor did the Union Powers Committee, when preparing its second report, enlarge upon its earlier suggestions. Turning to the provinces, a joint session of the Union and Provincial Constitution Committees, on Patel's suggestion, decided that a Governor should be limited to reporting a grave menace to the peace of the province to the President, who would take action under his own powers.[79] *The Hindustan Times* interpreted this as tacitly recognizing 'the right of the Union to directly administer the affairs of a province on emergent occasions'.[80] The following day, the committees approved the Governor's taking such action in his discretion without consulting his ministers.[81] When the Provincial Constitution Committee's report was presented to the Assembly; however, the reach of Union authority had been lessened and the authority of Governors increased. Fulfilling his special responsibility to prevent grave menace to the peace of the province, the Governor was to act in his discretion, and he need only report the situation to the President if he could not secure essential legislation in the local legislature. On receiving such a report the President would take appropriate action under his own emergency powers.[82]

The Assembly debate on the Provincial Constitution Committee report revealed sharp differences of opinion about the Governor's relations with his own ministers and the relationship of the provincial Executive to the Union Government. Reduced to personalities, it was Pandit Pant against the leaders of the Assembly. It was Pant's belief that, contrary to the terms of the Provincial Constitution Committee report, the Governor should act on the advice of his ministers when issuing and acting under a proclamation of emergency, but that he could report or refrain from reporting the state of emergency to the President in his discretion—thus making the Union's entry into provincial affairs dependent on the discretionary power of the Governor (who at this time was to be elected,

---

[79] Minutes of the meeting, 10 June 1947; *INA.*

[80] *The Hindustan Times*, 11 June 1947.

[81] Minutes of the meeting, 11 June 1947; *INA.*

[82] PCC report, Clause 15; *Reports, First Series*, p. 40.

not nominated).[83] The Assembly leadership held that the Governor could in emergencies act in his discretion so far as his own ministers were concerned, but that he was bound to communicate the proclamation of emergency to the President, who could then take what action he deemed necessary.[84] Munshi moved an agreed amendment to this effect. Pant, in obedience to the Whip, did not oppose the official position. But although he was 'bound by the decision of the party', he nevertheless told the Assembly that he believed his amendment sound because Governors did not become all-wise simply because they were elected.[85] Kunzru, however, who shared Pant's views, ignored the Whip—to which he was not so subservient, not being a true Congressman. He attacked the Governor's power to issue proclamations in his discretion, pointing out that even under the 1935 Act [Section 93(5)], Governors must have the Governor-General's 'concurrence' before issuing a proclamation.[86] Munshi's amendment was carried and, in essence, appeared later as Article 188 of the Draft Constitution.

The Emergency Provisions of the Draft Constitution were far more comprehensive in their scope than the committee reports of mid-1947 had presaged, and they greatly resembled those finally embodied in the Constitution. Two changes by the Assembly, however, increased Union power at the expense of provincial authority. In one change, Article 188 of the Draft was removed. This provision gave the Governor the authority in his discretion to proclaim an emergency and to assume all functions of the government excepting those of the High Court. The Governor had to communicate the proclamation of emergency to the President, who could revoke it or take action under his own emergency powers. The second change was the inclusion of a new provision giving the President power in regard to financial emergencies in the provinces.

The Assembly debate on the draft Emergency Provisions and its modifications of them took place principally in August 1949. The question was first reopened, however, in late May when, while

---

[83] See Supplementary List of Amendments, *Orders of the Day*, 16 July 1947; *INA*.

[84] *CAD* IV, 8, 818. For the text of this provision as adopted, see *Reports, Second Series*, pp. 3–4.

[85] Ibid., p. 809.

[86] Ibid., pp. 798–801.

considering the provincial constitution, Article 188 came up for debate. Opposition to Governors proclaiming emergencies in their discretion had been steadily growing. Pant and Kunzru continued their resistance, begun in August 1947s and were joined by many who believed that a Governor should not be permitted to take action in emergencies without the President's consent or the advice of his ministers. The Cabinet had by this time come to dislike Article 188 for a very different reason: it considered it inadequate. Under the article, the President, in effect the Union Government, could not act in a provincial emergency unless the Governor had first proclaimed that an emergency existed. The Cabinet believed that the President should be able himself to suspend the Constitution in a province and assume the functions of its government in case of a breakdown in the constitutional machinery. It therefore approved a new provision, Article 277A, drafted by Patel's Home and Ambedkar's Law Ministries, and sent it to the Assembly Secretariat.[87] In the Assembly, Article 188 was held over for further consideration.

Article 277A laid down that it was the duty of the Union to protect every province from external aggression and internal disturbance, and to ensure that government in the provinces was carried on according to the Constitution. Thus the Union was given a constitutional responsibility for the good government of the provinces. Article 188 remained un-changed. It came up for scrutiny again, along with Article 277A, during the July meetings between the Drafting Committee and the provincial prime ministers. Pant then reiterated his objections to the discretionary power of the Governor to proclaim emergencies, and Ambedkar reiterated his belief that the Union must have a clear constitutional responsibility to intervene in a province. Union action must not be 'a pure invasion' of provincial autonomy, said Ambedkar.[88] The meeting also discussed the role of Parliament in emergencies. Ayyar claimed that it would be administratively impossible for Parliament to assume the functions of a state legislature. N. G. Ayyangar, however, believed that this was a logical corollary of the Union's emergency, powers.

---

[87] See a memorandum to the CA Secretariat from the Ministries of Home and Law, 5 June 1949; *Munshi papers*. The text of Article 277A is, in essence, that of the *Constitution*, Article 355.

[88] Proceedings of the meeting, 13 July 1949; *Law Ministry Archives*.

T. T. Krishnamachari agreed. Ultimately, the group approved Article 277A and decided to omit Article 188 from the Constitution. It then redrafted Article 278 so that the President, on the receipt of a report from a Governor 'or otherwise', could assume the functions of the provincial Executive, and Parliament those of the legislature, if the government of the province could not be carried on in accordance with the Constitution.[89]

A week later on 2 August, the Assembly took up these and the remaining articles of the Emergency Provisions. First Ambedkar's amendment to Article 275 was adopted, reducing the life-span of an emergency proclamation from six months to two, unless approved by Parliament. The Assembly then empowered the Union Executive to give directions to state Executives concerning the exercise of their functions. *The Hindustan Times* chose this moment to support the Emergency Provisions editorially. Critics of the provisions must remember, the paper said, that 'in the face of unconstitutional challenge to any authority within the Union, the only power in a position to safeguard the States, the Union, and the Constitution is the Central Executive and there is no escape from it.'[90]

The third article, entitling the President during emergencies to suspend any or all of the provisions concerning the distribution of revenue, sustained several strong attacks. Pandit Kunzru believed that Article 277 was 'practically subversive of the financial rights of the states', reducing them, by removing their fiscal autonomy, to the status of municipal and district boards.[91] B. Das said that the Drafting Committee had made the President into a 'new Frankenstein'.[92] A. K. Ayyar replied, somewhat speciously, that the provinces lost little by the provision because the collection and distribution of revenue was in any case controlled by Parliament. (In fact, the financial provisions of the Draft did vest some such powers in Parliament,

---

[89] Minutes of the meeting, 28 July 1949; *Munshi papers*. See also *Constitution*, Article 356. K. Santhanam had suggested in July 1947 that the President need not wait for notification by a Governor before taking action under his emergency powers, but could himself decide that constitutional government in a province was impossible and assume the functions of the government; *CAD* IV, 13, 948–9.

[90] *The Hindustan Times*, 4 August 1949.

[91] *CAD* IX, 13, 505.

[92] *CAD* IX, 14, 517.

but they also laid down what sources of revenue were to be divided between the Union and the provinces. It was Union interference with these provisions during emergencies that Kunzru and others most feared.) Moreover, Ayyar told the Assembly, it should not be feared that the President would abrogate all the financial provisions at once. The Union Finance Ministry supported the provision because the Union would bear the brunt of the cost of an emergency and must therefore have the necessary funds.[93] The article was carried.

Introducing Article 277A, Ambedkar repeated the argument he had used in the Drafting Committee meeting with the provincial prime ministers. India had a federal system, he said, which meant that the provinces were in certain ways sovereign and had 'plenary authority to make any law for the peace, order, and good government of the province'. For the Union to intervene in a province's government would, therefore, be a 'wanton invasion' of provincial affairs. Hence Article 277A was needed to impose on the Union an 'obligation' to protect the units and to maintain the Constitution.[94]

Article 277A evoked little reaction in the Assembly. Not so the consequent modifications of the existing draft provisions, which created new powers for the Union in times of emergency. There were three of these. By the first two, Article 278 was made into two articles, 278 and 278A, and, as we have seen, to Article 278 the word 'otherwise' was added, empowering the President to assume the functions of a provincial government whether or not he had received a request to intervene from the Governor. Article 278A, which consisted largely of Clause (4) of Article 278, itself embodied two major changes. It empowered Parliament, upon the proclamation by the President that he had assumed the functions of the provincial government, to confer on the President 'the power of the Legislature of the State to make laws' and gave him the authority to delegate this power. It also authorized the President to spend money from the state's revenues if Parliament happened not to be in session.

These two articles, now commonly referred to as 'President's rule', were not opposed on the floor of the Assembly by any of its ranking members. Other members, however, condemned the

---

[93] Letter from the Joint Secretary, Finance Ministry, to Joint Secretary, Constituent Assembly, 9 August 1949; *Munshi papers*.

[94] *CAD* IX, 4, 113.

provisions as 'far too sweeping', thus 'reducing provincial autonomy to a farce'.[95] Perhaps the most colourful objections came from H. V. Kamath, who informed the Assembly that he foresaw the possible end of democracy in India in the form of a Hitler-like takeover by the Union Government. 'Other-wise' . . . is a diabolical word in this context', he said, 'and I pray to God that it will be deleted from this article.'[96] P. S. Deshmukh believed that bestowing such powers on the President was both impractical and unfederal because it placed too great a burden upon Parliament and gave the President authority to override 'at his own sweet will the provisions of the Constitution itself'[97]. Kunzru's attack went much deeper into the problems of government and the responsibilities, in a free society, of the governed. He argued that Articles 275 and 276 gave the Union the necessary power to intervene in a province when its government was menaced by external aggression or internal disturbance. Therefore it was 'obvious' that the leaders of the Assembly were not thinking of peace and tranquillity but of good government when they drafted Articles 277A, 278, and 278A. 'The Central Government', Kunzru said, 'will have the power to intervene to protect the electors against themselves.' He deplored this because it would rob the people of their initiative. The power to redress bad government, Kunzru believed, should rest with the electors and they should be made to feel their responsibilities.[98]

The major speakers in support of the complex of provisions and particularly of Articles 278 and 278A were Ayyar, Santhanam, and Ambedkar. Ayyar's principle argument was that Union power under the Emergency Provisions was not so horrific as it might at first appear, for the power of 'the President' in fact meant the cabinet, which in turn represented a parliament comprised of members representing the provinces. 'Parliament', he said, 'can exercise its control and supervision over the Cabinet which has undertaken the responsibility of the Executive function of the state.' He concluded by invoking as the *raison d'etre* of the provisions the 'grave and

---

[95] *CAD* IX, 4, 141–4; S. L.Saksena.

[96] Ibid., p. 140.

[97] Ibid., p. 146.

[98] Ibid., p. 156. Kunzru held this view firmly enough to submit an amendment to delete Article 278, and Pant joined him in this. See amendment 3012, *Amendment Book* II, P.319.

difficult times' facing the nation[99]—by which he must have meant the lawlessness and terrorism in Bengal, the continuing activities of the Communists in Telengana, as well as the uncertain agricultural and financial situation.

In their defence of the Emergency Provisions, Santhanam and Ambedkar showed themselves very much alive to Kunzru's arguments. Santhanam, for example, expressed the hope that in cases where government in a province could not be carried on, the Union would see to it that the legislature was dissolved and new elections held, thus giving the province a second chance to manage its own affairs before the Union intervened. Ambedkar agreed. He said that he approved the deletion of Article 188 because the Governor's emergency powers amounted to naught if the President was sure to step in, but that the President should give the provincial government warning before assuming its functions, and then order an election, thus 'allowing the people of the province to settle matters by themselves'.[100]

Two months later, Ambedkar introduced the last of the Emergency Provisions into the Assembly, new Article 280A, which laid down that if the financial stability or credit of the nation or of any province was in danger, the President could issue a proclamation to that effect and then take action in the same manner as under a proclamation of emergency, which would include directing provincial governments to observe unnamed 'canons of financial propriety'.[101] Pandit Kunzru disliked this provision even more than its predecessors. He rejected Ambedkar's contention that it resembled the American National Recovery Act because, he said, that Act was a temporary measure designed to meet a particular situation, the Great Depression. How did this new provision, Kunzru asked, square with Nehru's statement, made just three days previously, to the U.S. Congress, in Washington, that the Indian Constitution was

---

[99] *CAD* IX, 4, 151. Ayyar also advanced the very specious argument that the Union could not interfere with the working of the provincial constitution because its provisions were part of the Constitution—a point true only in the strictest, most legalistic sense, for what Assembly members feared was not the use, but the misuse of Union power.

[100] *CAD* IX, 5, 177.

[101] This new article was introduced in mid-October, and became Article 360 of the Constitution. See *CAD* X, 9, 361.

federal and based on the American Constitution?[102] Kunzru also wondered aloud just how far the Union could go under the article. Many provinces were enforcing prohibition to their financial detriment, he said, and the Union Government was advising them against this action. Could such a difference of opinion be used as an excuse to invoke Article 280A?

Ambedkar had presented the provision to the Assembly with the explanation that it was necessary in view of the 'present economic and financial situation in this country'.[103] 'He cited the National Recovery Act as a type of measure that might be needed to meet economic problems in India, and pointed out that in the United States this had been declared unconstitutional. Rather than risk such an eventuality in India, he said, Article 280A should be included in the Constitution. Munshi supported Ambedkar when replying to Kunzru's speech. 'The country is on the brink of a precipice', he said, as dangerous as that faced by the United States in 1933 and France in 1937, and extraordinary powers might be needed by the Union. Munshi was no doubt referring to the grave financial situation involving the devaluation of the rupee—which the Constituent Assembly (Legislative) had debated several days previously. The provision was not for normal times, he continued, and showed that the economic life of the nation was indivisible. 'There is no provincial autonomy, there is no federation by and for itself, Munshi said, 'these are not sacrosanct words.'[104] The Assembly adopted the provision.

Between 1950 and 1960 there were no proclamations of national emergency made under the President's powers; the first proclamation of national emergency came in October 1962 after the attack on the Northeast Frontier by China. Through 1964 there were, however, seven instances of President's rule.[105] In each case the

---

[102] *CAD* X, 9, 370. Nehru made this speech to a joint session of Congress in Washington on 13 October 1949. The text appears in the *The Hindustan Times* of 14 October. The text also is given in *Jawaharlal Nehru's Speeches*, 1949–53, P. 122. But the date of the speech is wrongly given as 19 October and the place as New York City.

[103] Ibid., p. 361.

[104] Ibid., pp. 371–2.

[105] The seven instances: the Punjab, 1951; PEPSU (Patiala and East Punjab States Union), 1952; Andhra, 1954; Travancore-Cochin, 1956; Kerala, 1960; Orissa, 1961; Kerala, 1964.

Union entered the affair at the last moment, usually at the invitation of the Governor, after other solutions had failed. In each case the intervention was made when parliamentary government temporarily failed, when fresh elections could not produce a majority for one party, or a coalition, and therefore no government could be formed. The Union Government was quite evidently loathe to enter Kerala in 1960. It intervened in Orissa in 1961 at the request of the coalition government there, which found that it could not function effectively. In 1953 the Union actually refused to assume the functions of the Travancore-Cochin Government and a solution to the impasse was found without recourse to President's rule. The Union in each of these cases relinquished power in the state at the earliest possible moment, preserving what Professor Alexandrowicz has called the 'two-way convertability' of the Constitution and maintaining the Constitution's essentially federal.[106]

---

[106] See Alexandrowicz, op.cit., p. 162.

9

Federalism—II
The Distribution of Revenues

OTHER parts of the Constitution may demonstrate the unique aspects of Indian federalism and the degree to which the Union and state governments are coordinate in their activities, but none fly so directly in the face of the classical federal tradition as the provisions for the distribution of revenues. Under classically federal constitutions, 'both general and regional governments must each have under its own independent control financial resources sufficient to perform its exclusive functions', wrote Dr. Wheare.[1] In the Constituent Assembly, however, there was apparently little importance attached to the adage that 'he who pays the piper calls the tune', and when provincial representatives called for increased provincial revenues they did so out of pride and the desire that their province might meet its social responsibilities rather than from any dream of 'provincial autonomy'. The Assembly's approach to the framing of these portions of the Constitution, as well as the financial provisions themselves, exemplify Birch's description of cooperative federalism.

Alladi Krishnaswami Ayyar, for example, told the Assembly that although 'an independent source or sources of revenue are certainly necessary for the proper functioning of a federal government, there is a distinct tendency in the several federations for the central government to act as the taxing agency', taking care at the same time that the units shared in the proceeds of the taxes and received other subsidies.[2] Mohammed Saadulla, a Muslim League member

---

[1] Wheare, *Federal Government*, p. 97.
[2] *CAD* VII, 4, 336–7.

representing Assam, who was critical of the 'over-centralization' of the Constitution and who charged that the Emergency Provisions constituted the 'utmost interference' in provincial affairs, nevertheless called on the Union Government to give liberal aid to Assam and deplored 'the absence (from the Constitution) of any provision for financial help to the poorer and needy provinces'.[3] In twenty memoranda from provincial governments to the Assembly about sales tax and on the distribution of revenues, each placing the strongest possible claim for increased funds, no provincial government couched its demands in terms of protecting its autonomy or of 'states rights'.[4] Nor, with one or two exceptions, did members of the Assembly stand up in the House and claim that for the proper working of the federal system the provinces should control sufficient sources of revenue to be able to meet their budgetary needs. And the members certainly knew that under the scheme contemplated for the Constitution—which was very similar to that of the 1935 Act—provincial tax heads would not produce enough income to meet expenditures. The statistics presented by the first Finance Commission showed, in fact, that the revenues of most states fell approximately 15 per cent short of meeting the expenses of normal administration, and the states were, therefore, dependent upon the Union for at least this revenue—apart from any other grants for capital development purposes.[5]

The provincial governments, however, did want as much money as they could get, and believed that they should not have to place themselves completely at the mercy of the Union Government to get it. These governments, and their representatives in the Assembly, put forward strong claims to an increased share of the proceeds from income tax and Union excise duties, as well as for a portion of corporation tax revenues—under the 1935 Act an exclusively Union revenue source. Yet the provincial governments were willing to let the Union levy, collect, and distribute these taxes and did not

---

[3] *CAD* XI, 7, 734. For the entirety of this most informative speech, see ibid., pp. 732–6.

[4] For the ten memoranda on the distribution of revenues, see *Memoranda by the Government of India and the Provincial Governments to the Expert Committee on the Financial Provisions of the Constitution*, as compiled by the CA. For the ten memoranda on sales tax, see *Munshi papers*.

[5] *Report of the Finance Commission* (1952); the calculations are the author's.

suggest that they be placed within the legislative competence of the provinces. The Expert Committee on the Financial Provisions of the Constitution recommended that the provincial governments have 'adequate resources of their own, without having to depend on the variable munificence or affluence of the Centre', yet the committee did not believe it practicable to increase the areas in which the provinces could levy taxes. There must continue to be, said the Expert Committee's report, 'divided heads' of taxation with the 'shares of the Centre and the provinces in these heads . . . adjusted automatically (and) without friction or mutual interference'.[6] The members of the Assembly left this task to Finance Commissions. This willingness to leave adjustments in the distribution of revenues to post-constitutional commissions rather than demanding that the distribution be laid down in detail in the Constitution contrasts strongly with the case of Nigeria, where mutual distrust produced several fiscal commissions, which were to establish the division of revenues between the federal government and the units, and which lead ultimately to the entrenchment of the units' shares of tax receipts.[7]

The provisions embodying this cooperative system of revenue distribution are found in the first two chapters of Part XII of the Constitution, and can be roughly divided into four categories: the allocation of taxing power and the distribution of tax receipts; the power of the Union, particularly, to make grants-in-aid; the articles regulating borrowing; and the provisions providing for Finance Commissions.

In the division of the taxing power, generally speaking, 'taxes that have an inter-state base are under the legislative jurisdiction of the Union, while those that have a local base fall under the legislative jurisdiction of the states'.[8] Union taxes are of several types. There are taxes levied and collected by the Union and of which the Union retains the proceeds—corporation taxes, customs duties, taxes levied on companies, surcharges levied on Union or state tax

[6] *Report of the Expert Committee on the Financial Provisions of the Constitution*, para. 28; *Reports, Third Series*, p. 129. This report was dated 5 December 1947.

[7] See John P. Mackintosh, 'Federalism in Nigeria', *Political Studies*, October 1962, p. 227.

[8] R. N. Bhargava, '*The Theory and Working of Union Finance in India*, p. 79. This summary of the taxation scheme in the Constitution has been drawn, in part, from Bhargava.

heads, and a variety of other taxes.[9] Second, there are taxes levied and collected by the Union, but the proceeds of which are to be shared with the states—primarily income tax and excise duties, excepting that agricultural income tax and certain excise duties are reserved for the states. Third, there are taxes levied and collected by the Union, but the proceeds of which are assigned wholly to the states—succession and estate duties, terminal taxes on goods and passengers, etc. And fourth, there are taxes levied by the Union, but collected by the states—such as stamp duties and excise on medicinal preparations.

Within the jurisdiction of the state governments are most taxes concerned with land, such as land revenue, agricultural income and land succession taxes, estate duties in respect of agricultural land, and also the excise duties on alcoholic liquors and narcotics. Also among state tax heads are sales taxes, taxes on professions and callings, and taxes on vehicles, on passengers travelling by roads or inland waterways, and on luxuries and amusements.[10]

According to the Constitution, both the Union and the states are empowered to make grants. By virtue of the sums at its disposal, the Union's power is, of course, the most significant. The Union may make grants for a public purpose even though the purpose is one concerning which Parliament cannot normally legislate, and it is under this provision that many of the large capital grants for national development schemes are made. The Union may make grants-in-aid of the revenues of any state to defray budgetary deficits, etc. Also, the Union may make specific purpose grants to Assam, Bihar, Orissa, and West Bengal in lieu of their share of the jute export duty, and to Assam and other states to pay for improvements undertaken in tribal areas.

The Union may borrow on the security of the national revenues within such limits as are established by Parliament. The state governments may also borrow within limits set by their legislatures, but only under restrictions imposed by the Constitution. State governments may borrow only within the territory of India, and then only with the Union's consent if there is outstanding any part of a

[9] These taxes are enumerated primarily in the Union List, Seventh Schedule, Items 82–92, as modified by the articles of Part XII, particularly articles 270, 271, and 272.

[10] See Constitution, Seventh Schedule, State List, Items 45–63.

previous loan from the Union, or from the Government of British India. Making such loans, the Union may impose conditions as it thinks fit. As nearly all the state governments have long had Union loans outstanding, their borrowing activities, since the inception of the Constitution, have been carried on with the cooperation and consent of the Union.

Guardians of the equitable and fiscally sound distribution of the revenue from the shared tax heads and of the effective use of grants-in-aid are the Finance Commissions—quasi-judicial bodies of five members appointed by the President. The first commission was to be appointed two years after the inauguration of the Constitution, and there were to be successors created every five years thereafter unless needed sooner. The commissions, according to the Constitution, are to make recommendations concerning the distribution of tax revenues between the Union and the states, concerning the principles that should govern grants-in-aid, and on any other matters referred to them by the President. The President must lay the commission's recommendations, together with an explanation of the action taken on them, before Parliament.

Although the Finance Commissions may not recommend changes in the content or form of the finance provisions themselves, the power of the commissions is very great because, as we have seen, the Constitution lays down only how certain revenues are to be levied and collected, and not how the proceeds from them are to be distributed. For example: income tax is to be levied and collected by the Union. Yet 'such percentage as may be prescribed' of this revenue shall be paid to the states.[11] Or another example: the Union is to levy and collect duties on the succession of property and terminal and certain other taxes. This revenue is all assigned to the states, but the manner in which it is to be distributed among them may be legislated upon by Parliament. In both of these cases a Finance Commission may make recommendations; in the first it suggests what proportion of the total sum should be allotted to the states, and in both cases it may suggest how the revenue cake is to be cut and which states are to receive the biggest pieces. As it has become a convention that Finance Commission

---

[11] The *Constitution*; Article 270. 'Prescribed' is defined as meaning prescribed by the President after considering—and by convention, accepting—the recommendations of the Finance Commission.

reports are accepted without question by all parties, the power of the commission to make adjustments in the distribution of revenues and thus affect the balance of the federal system is very great indeed.

I. The Background to Indian Federal Finance

Why did the members of the Constituent Assembly frame provisions making the Union Government the banker and collecting agent for the state governments? How could it do so and still avoid the corrosive argument that had eaten away at the spirit of unity in many other countries? Certainly the long experience first with unitary and then with tightly federal colonial government had a great effect, for the financial provisions of the Constitution resemble very closely their predecessors in the 1935 Act. And perhaps of equal influence was the existence of a strong federal structure during the framing period. When drafting the financial provisions, as well as the other aspects of the federal system, the provinces could not bargain from a position of sovereign power; no provincial delegation could quit the Assembly, so a workable compromise had to be reached.

Two new factors, however, greatly reinforced the pressure toward centralization exerted by these inherited constitutional patterns. One was the unstable financial situation prevailing during the framing period. The other was the Assembly members' belief that the 'need' of the provinces should determine how revenues were distributed. And the need of the provinces for increased funds, with few exceptions, was stated in terms of the social revolution. P. C. Ghosh, the prime minister of West Bengal, for example, in a memorandum expressing his province's claim for an increased share of Union tax heads, wrote that the additional sums were needed to support the 'constantly growing social services and nation-building activities' of the province.[12] The investigations of the Expert Committee on the Financial Provisions of the Constitution confirmed that this was a view common to all the provinces. 'Every province has drawn pointed attention to the urgency of its programme of social service and economic development and to the limited nature of its own resources, both existing and potential', the Expert Committee's report stated, and it noted that all the provinces had asked 'for a substantial

---

[12] In a memorandum to the Assembly, dated 30 September 1947; *Munshi papers.*

transfer of revenue from the Central sources'.[13] The provinces' needs 'in relation to welfare services and general development' were 'almost unlimited', the report continued. And the provinces, it said, must have adequate financial resources 'if these services, on which the improvement of human well-being and the increase of the country's productive capacity so much depend, are to be properly planned and executed'.[14]

But where were the provinces to get these funds? The answer was that either the Union had to provide them or the provinces must find the revenue themselves. Yet this posed two more questions. Where could the Union, even with its almost unlimited borrowing power, raise the necessary sums? And if the provinces were left to their own devices, what would happen to those provinces that must draw their tax revenue from poor, agricultural populations? They would never he able to meet their responsibilities and obligations.

The Assembly had its answer to these questions: certain basic taxes and the revenue from them should be left within the legislative jurisdiction of the provincial governments, but the most lucrative tax heads should be levied and collected by the Union and distributed among the provinces according to their need. The Union was to have its own revenues and from these could distribute some of the proceeds, or make grants, to the provincial governments, again on the basis of need. 'If federation means anything,' said Pandit Kunzru, 'it means that there should be a transfer of wealth from the richer to the poorer provinces.'[15] Sri Krishna Sinha, the prime minister of Bihar, informed the Assembly that it was the 'duty of the Centre to give greater assistance to the poorer provinces' and to raise them to the level of the richer.[16] The members of the Experts Committee had 'no doubt that the Centre, when distributing specific purpose grants . . . will bear in mind the varying circumstances of the different provinces'.[17]

The logical result of these views was increased Union authority. With the provinces—or at least seven out of the nine of them, not

---

[13] Expert Committee's report, para. 23; *Reports, Third Series*, p. 218.

[14] Ibid., para. 28, p. 129.

[15] *CAD* IX, 6, 117.

[16] In a memorandum to the Assembly, dated 31 October 1947; *Munshi papers*. Bihar was the fourth richest province on the basis of revenue earnings according to the Expert Committee report; *Reports, Third Series*, p. 149.

[17] Expert Committee report, para. 48; *Reports, Third Series*, p. 133.

counting the former Princely States—in favour of sharing revenues on the basis of need, there had to be an agency to fulfil this coordinating role, to collect the revenues of the richer provinces and to distribute them among the poorer. Certainly revenues could not be effectively divided by province-to-province negotiations. The inevitable third party between the wealthy and the poorer provinces was the Union Government—whose pact as dispenser of bounty would be watched over by the Finance Commissions.

The focus of the problem was the three richest provinces—Bombay, West Bengal, and Madras. On their willingness to share depended much of the effectiveness of a cooperative system of revenue distribution. And, as might be expected, these governments entered the negotiations proclaiming their right to the largest percentage of tax revenue collected within their province. Because the personal income tax provided the largest sum of divisible revenue, it evoked the most interest. The Government of Bombay expressed to the Expert Committee the belief that it should receive one third of the total divisible revenue from income and corporation taxes, as it was the largest contributor under these heads.[18] The Government of West Bengal believed that the distribution of income tax proceeds should be on the basis of 'collection' or derivation.[19] Madras apparently put forth no demands of this sort. According to these demands, Bombay would have received 33 per cent of income tax revenues, after having contributed 45.8 per cent of the total revenue, and West Bengal would have received her contribution of 28.6 per cent of income tax revenue. Together the two provinces would have received between them approximately 62 per cent of the divisible amount, although they had but 17 per cent of the nation's population.[20] Fortunately, neither Bombay nor West Bengal held fast to these demands which were morally untenable, anyway, because their large tax revenues were mainly due to the fortuitous location in Bombay and Calcutta of the head offices of many large business concerns. And in the end they agreed to leave the distribution to Parliament,

[18] See Expert Committee report; ibid., p. 151.

[19] From the *Debate and Resolution of the West Bengal Legislative Assembly* on the Draft Constitution, held September 1948; *INA*.

[20] These revenue figures for Bengal and Bombay are taken from a minute by R. K. Rao to the *Report of the Finance Commission* (1952), p. 112.

subject to later adjustments by the Finance Commissions. This demonstration of a cooperative spirit again contrasts with the Nigerian experience, where the richer Western province was most reluctant to support the poorer Northern and Eastern provinces.

The other provincial governments joined Bombay, Bengal, and Madras in demanding an increased share of revenues from the Union, but for the provinces as a group, not merely for themselves. They were content, however, to cite 'need' as the principle upon which revenue distribution should be based and to leave the details of distribution to subsequent negotiations—in fact, to the Finance Commissions. Although the role the Union Government was to play in disbursing funds may not have been wholly satisfactory to the provincial governments, as there was no alternative it had the attraction of the inevitable. One provincial government, the Central Provinces and Berar, went so far as to suggest that the Union's role be increased. It stated its view that estate and succession taxes on agricultural land, for long provincial tax fields, should, for the sake of uniformity, be collected by the Union and distributed among the provinces.[21] The Finance Minister, John Matthai, also believed that the Union should have the maximum power of taxation, and he thought it unnecessary to have rigidly defined tax heads for the provinces,[22] The prevailing view of Union Government leaders, however, was probably that expressed by N. G. Ayyangar to Matthai: that even with the strong central government contemplated for India, the provinces could not be expected to depend entirely on the Union for their money.[23]

The attitude in the Assembly towards the financial provisions—the necessary reliance of the provinces on the Union, which they feared might be niggardly when distributing revenues, the provinces' suspicions of each other, and the belief in the principle of 'need'—were quaintly, although inadvertantly, summed up by President Prasad. Addressing the House, and particularly Matthai, who was sitting immediately in front of him, Prasad said that there was 'a considerable feeling

[21] *Report of the Committee of the Whole*—of the C.P. and Berar Legislative Assembly, forwarded to the Constituent Assembly by the Speaker of the lower house, G. S. Gupta, on October 1948; *INA.*
[22] See notes on a *Discussion Held in the Finance Minister's Office*, held on 4 September 1947; *Prasad papers.* File 12-A/47. Present on this occasion were Matthai, Prasad, N. G. Ayyangar, and Finance Ministry officials.
[23] Ibid.

in the provinces that their sources of revenue have been curtailed . . . (and) that the distribution of the income tax is not such as to give them satisfaction. I desire to ask the Finance Minister to bear this in mind . . . so that it may not be said that the policy of the Government of India is such as to give more to those who have much and to take away the little from those who have little.'[24]

The Finance Commissions of 1952 and 1957 have indeed made this their policy, increasing the provinces' share of divisible revenues and basing the distribution of revenue among the provinces on the basis of need. The report of the first Finance Commission declared that the scheme of revenue distribution 'should attempt to lessen the inequalities between states',[25] and the second commission demonstrated its faith in the principle by recommending that 10 per cent of divisible revenues should be distributed on the basis of collection, and the remaining 90 per cent according to population.[26]

The second factor that gave new meaning to the constitutional pattern inherited from the British period was the uncertain financial condition of the country. For example, the members of the Drafting Committee cited the 'unstable conditions' prevailing during the framing period as grounds for their rejection of the Expert Committee's recommendation that a more generous allocation of revenues than presently existed should be made to the provinces.[27] The Drafting Committee suggested that the system of distribution laid down by the 1935 Act should be retained for at least five years, when a Finance Commission might review the situation. Pandit Kunzru, who frequently defended provincial interests from what he considered to be Union encroachments, supported the Drafting Committee. He opposed an amendment that would have given the provinces a 60 per cent share of income and corporation taxes, both because he believed a statutory division of revenue too rigid and because of the 'parlous . . . position of the Central

[24] *CAD* X, 9, 340.

[25] *Report of the Finance Commission* (1952), p. 7.

[26] *Report of the Finance Commission* (1957), p. 40.

[27] Although the Drafting Committee did not specify which of the Expert Committee's recommendations it disliked, we may safely assume that it was recommendations 7 and 13, which laid down that the Union should share corporation as well as income tax with the provisions and that not less than 60 per cent of these revenues should go to the provinces. Expert Committee report para. 100; *Reports, Third Series*, pp. 144–5.

finances'.[28] And the Expert Committee itself suggested that the Constitution should grant the President special power to suspend or vary the financial provisions in time of emergency.

The Union Finance Ministry also opposed disbursements to the provinces. It believed that in the near future there would be a decrease in Union revenue from customs duties, from income and corporation taxes (due to the removal of the excess profits tax), and because of the abolition of the domestic salt tax. Moreover, the ministry estimated that Union outlays would increase in the future because of the large-scale importation of food grains, the cost of defence, of refugee resettlement, and of civil administration.[29]

Although their arguments did not spring from federal considerations, various commercial interests expressed to the Assembly an equal belief in the need for a strong central government and for increased Union participation in tax matters. Union control of certain types of tax was advocated because the multiplicity of provincial taxes had been harmful to trade; it was easier to operate under a coherent system of regulations emanating from a single source. Furthermore, commerce and industry could only prosper in a stable political situation. The Magora Chemical Company Limited of Poona, for example, circulated a letter among Assembly members advocating the assumption of excise taxes by the Union because the provincial excise on alcohol made it difficult to ship tinctures from one province to another.[30] This letter apparently had some effect, for in the Draft Constitution medicinal preparations containing alcohol were to be subject to a Union excise tax although the tax was to be collected by the states, whereas under the 1935 Act the levy as well as the collection of excise duties on such products were reserved for the provinces.[31]

Among the several memoranda submitted to the Assembly and to the Government recommending active Union participation

---

[28] *CAD* IX, 6, 215.

[29] Finance Ministry memorandum, circulated with the agenda for the meeting of the Drafting Committee with the provincial prime ministers to be held on 21 July 1949; *Munshi papers*.

[30] In a letter dated 26 July 1947; *Prasad papers*.

[31] 1935 *Act*, Seventh Schedule, Federal List, item 45. *Draft Constitution*, Seventh Schedule, Union List, item 86. A footnote to this entry states that it was included because 'uniform rates of excise duty' were needed 'for the sake of the development of the pharmaceutical industry'. ibid., p. 195.

in the economic life of the country, was that from the All-India Manufacturers Association of Bombay. This group communicated to Prasad, in his capacity as Food Minister, a resolution in favour of a strong central government to enforce laws and to remedy shortages of food and clothing.[32] These sentiments are reminiscent of those expressed by many of the thirteen colonies at Philadelphia in 1787; provincialism in any age, it seems, is bad for trade. With occasional exceptions, such as that of the Magora Chemical Company's letter, it is almost impossible to assess the influence of these views on the leadership in the Congress or the Assembly. They represented, at least, one more weight in the scales on the side of cooperative federalism.

2. Drafting the Financial Provisions

The financial provisions of the Constitution were from the first based closely on the 1935 Act. This was foreshadowed even by the loose federalism of the first Union Powers Committee report. In the second Union Powers report, which reproduced almost intact the Legislative Lists of the 1935 Act, including the division of tax heads, and in the very general recommendations of the first Union Constitution Committee report, which cited as precedents various sections of the 1935 Act, the reliance on the example of the Government of India Act became even more apparent. The more detailed clauses and articles of Rau's Draft Constitution and that framed by the Drafting Committee were in many cases copies of the provisions of the 1935 Act, although by this time certain important changes had crept in.

When preparing the Draft Constitution, the members of the Drafting Committee had for their consideration the recommendations of the Expert Committee and detailed memoranda from nearly all the provincial governments. The memoranda were the result of a request made on 30 August 1947 by the Drafting Committee for the views of the provinces on the distribution of revenues under the 1935 Act. That there should be an expert committee to advise during the framing of the financial provisions was decided by Prasad, N. G. Ayyangar, and Matthai at a meeting held in the Finance Minister's office to discuss the general principles involved in the division of taxing powers. The intention of this small group was that the special

[32] Letters dated 20 July 1947; *Prasad papers.*

committee should include members representing the provincial point of view, and the Constituent Assembly Secretariat submitted a list of possible candidates to Prasad for his consideration. They were: Pant, Kher, R. S. Shukla, N. R. Sarkar, Sitaramayya, and Biswanath Das.[33] With the exception of Sarkar, all were powerful figures in the politics of their provinces, Shukla, Pant, and Kher being prime ministers. It appears, however, that the Congress leadership preferred to 'keep the issue out of politics' or to keep provincial leaders away from the committee. When Prasad made his appointments to the new Expert Committee on the Financial Provisions, the members proved to be V. S. Sundaram and M. V. Rangachari, two civil servants, and N. R. Sarkar, who, although he had been Member for Commerce in the Viceroy's Executive Council in 1942, and would be Finance Minister and acting Prime Minister of Bengal in 1949, was best known as a businessman. The Expert Committee submitted its report to the Assembly in December 1947.

The Drafting Committee, in conjunction with the Union Powers and Constitution Committees and the Provincial Constitution Committee, met during 1948 to consider proposed changes in the Draft. The provincial finance ministers also met in New Delhi several times during 1948 and 1949 to consider the distribution of revenues. A large number of Assembly members submitted amendments to the Draft and the ministries of the Union Government as well as the provincial governments drew up barrages of memoranda expressing their views on all aspects of the issue. In July 1949, the Drafting Committee met with the provincial finance and prime ministers to thrash out the thornier subjects of contention. Then, during the first week of August, the Assembly began full debate on the financial provisions. By this time letters, speeches both within the Assembly and outside, memoranda, and ceaseless lobbying had aired nearly all the major arguments and the viewpoints of most persons concerned. Yet the most controversial issues defied solution through weeks of attempts at compromise, and the Assembly did not adopt the last of the financial provisions until mid-October.

The most difficult problem to solve, one that provoked a 'battle royal' in the Assembly and the one that best demonstrates the basic

[33] Minutes of the meeting, 4 September 1947, and appended information and documents; *Prasad papers*, File 12-A/47. See also footnote 22 above.

differences between the Union and provincial governments is the sales tax issue. The provinces wanted their right under the 1935 Act to levy a sales tax left untouched, and the Union aimed at restricting the tax in order to promote smoother and more effective commercial intercourse within the country and to prevent high prices as a result of multiple taxation. During the first year of the Assembly, the Union Government had shown little interest in the sales tax. The Drafting Committee troubled itself only to insert an item in the Provincial List, making minor changes in the wording of the equivalent entry in the 1935 Act. In the autumn of 1948, however, the Union Finance Ministry initiated action on the issue, but in the form of negotiations with the provincial governments not as a constitutional provision. At a meeting with provincial finance ministers during October, the Union ministry recommended, for example, that there should be no sales tax on the export from one province to another of essential food items such as grain, pulse (lentils), flour, and several other articles, and that sales taxes on raw materials should be held to a minimum.[34]

This effort evidently failed, for the Finance Ministry next sought to control the use of the sales tax by means of a provision in the Constitution. It prepared several amendments to the Draft Constitution, which were discussed at a number of meetings, but the final approval of the Finance Ministry's ultimate draft was given by the Cabinet. The provision in the form of new Article 264A was then sent to the Drafting Committee.[35] This amendment resembled the present Article 286 of the Constitution. Among other things, it prohibited the taxing of the sale or purchase of goods by a province when the sale took place outside the boundaries of the province or in the course of export from or import into India, and it also prohibited the taxing of purchases or sales in the course of interstate trade and the taxing of essential goods—as defined by Parliament— without Presidential consent. 'Taxes on the sale or purchase of goods' was still to be, however, a provincial subject.

On 24 July 1949, several days after it received the Finance Ministry's new Article 264A, the Drafting Committee met with

[34] The records of this meeting are not available. Many of the views expressed at it were recapitulated, however, in a letter from the Government of Bombay to the Assembly, dated 12 August 1949; *Munshi papers.*

[35] See letter from the Ministry of Finance to the Constituent Assembly Secretariat, 8 July 1949; *Law Ministry Archives.*

Prasad, Nehru, and Matthai and the provincial finance and prime ministers to consider the question. The presence of Prasad and Nehru indicates the importance the issue had assumed. All three of the Union leaders explained that it was agreed to leave the sales tax as an exclusively provincial subject, but they emphasized that the use of the tax should be restricted to safeguard the Union's programme of industrial development and to ensure a uniform application of the tax. Ambedkar added that the terms of Article 264A would reinforce the right to freedom of trade laid down in Article 16.[36]

The Government had some support for its position. Organizations such as the Federation of Indian Chambers of Commerce and Industry thought that the Union should either take over the sales tax or ensure its uniform application to prevent double taxation, sales taxes on raw materials, and rising trade barriers between the provinces.[37] And several provincial governments later rallied to the Union's position.[38] Generally speaking, however, the provincial representatives at the meeting held that the sales tax constituted the one major source of income left to the provinces—it averaged 15 per cent of provincial revenues in 1951[39]— and the Union's restrictions on its use were too severe. But although the provincial governments were eager to increase their revenues from sales tax, their unity ended there. Policies that earned profits for one province hurt the purse of another. This doubtless strengthened the Union's bargaining position, yet the chaotic diversity of the demands nearly defied solution. Faced with these conflicting claims, the Union Government became adamant. Government and Congress leaders informed the provincial ministers that their governments might submit exact amendments to Article 264A, but that suggestions for the deletion of the article and for the removal of Union controls of sales tax would not

[36] Proceedings of the meeting, 24 July 1949; *Law Ministry Archives*.

[37] Letter from the Federation to the Ministry of Finance, dated 8 June 1949; *Munshi papers*.

[38] For the views of these governments, see: Letter to the Assembly from the East Punjab, dated 14 August 1949; letter from the Government of Orissa to the Joint Secretary of the Assembly dated 30 July 1949; and A Summary of Views of Assam Government on Subjects Scheduled for Discussion at Provincial Finance Ministers Conference, undated, but presumably written in early July 1949. All of these documents are in the *Munshi papers*.

[39] *Finance Commission Report* (1952), p. 49.

be considered.[40] During the following two months, the provincial governments restated their positions, making the conflict of interests clearer than ever.

The Prime Minister of Bihar, S. K. Sinha, for example, expressed to Ambedkar the opinion that there should be no ban on taxing materials for use in manufacturing (products destined for Bihar's steel mills), and that goods for sale outside a province should not be taxed within the province.[41] On the other hand R. S. Shukla, the prime minister of Central Provinces and Berar, favoured a sales tax on raw materials. Berar products were sold in Calcutta, which reaped all the Central Provinces' tax profits, he said. But he, along with the Assam Government, disapproved of a tax on food grains.[42]

The Government of Madras, on the other hand, found the proposed prohibition on taxation of essential food items such as wheat, rice, pulse, salt, and condiments 'unacceptable' because the government would lose so much revenue. The Madras Government also approved multi-stage taxation, and would have exempted from sales tax only the last transaction before export from the province.[43]

As in the case of other knotty problems, the sales tax question was settled in private negotiations and in the Assembly Party. The Union leaders held to their position of July and the provinces eventually capitulated. The disunity and avarice of the provinces proved their undoing. When Article 264A was introduced in the Assembly on 16 October 1949, it occasioned few speeches and was passed after barely an hour's debate.

Since 1950, Union control over sales tax has been increased beyond the point envisaged in Article 264A. The Union and state governments have agreed that a Union excise tax should replace the sales tax on millmade textiles, sugar, and tobacco and the resulting revenue should be distributed so that each province would receive amounts

---

[40] Proceedings of the meeting, 24 July 1949; *Law Ministry Archives.*

[41] In a letter to Ambedkar, dated 2 September 1949; *Munshi papers.*

[42] In a letter to Ambedkar, with a copy to Munshi, dated 5 September 1949, and in an official letter as C.P. and Berar Prime Minister to Ambedkar of 29 July 1949; *Munshi papers.*

[43] Letter to the Assembly, dated 2 August 1949; *Munshi papers.* In the year 1950–51, Madras income from sales tax reached 28.8 per cent of her total revenue; *Finance Commission report* (1952), p. 49.

at least equal to that formerly derived from the sales tax.[44] The sales tax problem still plagues Indian commerce and industry, however, and it is generally conceded that the provision in the Constitution has proved inadequate to the situation, and that Article 286 was one of the Assembly's few conspicuous failures.

The problem of the distribution of revenues from divided tax heads did not prove so knotty as the sales tax issue. Nevertheless there was a definite conflict between the interests of the provinces and between the provinces and the Union. The problems posed by divided tax heads were not new ones, however; they dated from the drafting in the early 1930's of the 1935 Act and had for years been a subject of controversy. The basic issue in each case was how to decide which of the two parties concerned, the federal government or the units, had the more legitimate demands for available funds and how to divide the nation's taxable capacity between them. Within this issue were two others. These were, in the words of the Joint Parliamentary Committee, that the provinces had 'rarely had means adequate for a full development of their social needs, and that the existing division of heads of revenue between Centre and Province leaves the Centre with an undue share of those heads which respond most readily to an improvement in economic conditions'.[45] To help remedy this situation, the 1935 Act provided that income-tax revenues were to be divided between the federation and the provinces.

The situation in 1947 was essentially the same as that obtaining earlier; the provinces were short of money because their expenditures had risen sharply—due partly to a broadened concept of the government's social responsibilities—while the taxable capacity of their exclusive revenue sources had increased relatively little. As a result, the provinces demanded in the Constituent Assembly an increased portion of income tax revenue and that from the other divisible heads instituted by the 1935 Act—such as certain excise and export duties. The provinces also demanded in 1947 that additional heads, particularly the corporation tax, be made divisible. During the autumn of 1947, each of the provincial governments expressed the belief to the Expert Committee that the provinces share of income tax revenue should be raised above the figure of 50 per cent established in

---

[44] See *Finance Commission report* (1957), p. 2.
[45] *Report of the Joint Parliamentary Committee*, para .245, 246, pp. 161–2.

the 1935 Act. Demands went as high as 75 per cent.[46] There began also at this time a strong movement on the part of the provinces to have the proceeds of the corporation tax, which had been a central government tax head under the 1935 Act, added to the funds accruing from the income tax for distribution among the provinces. Seven provinces expressed this demand to the Assembly in some form.[47]

Although the provincial, governments were agreed that they should receive a greater share of this revenue, they could not decide how it should be distributed among them. The rich manufacturing and entrepot province of Bombay, as we have seen, claimed one third of the total income and corporation tax pool for itself. Bihar, on the other hand, advocated distribution on the basis of population, with special attention to the place where the income was actually earned—meaning, as Prime Minister Sinha's memorandum clearly stated, in Bihar where the steel mills were, not in West Bengal and Bombay because the head offices of firms like Tata's happened to be in these provinces.[48] The United Provinces, with more people than any other province, also favoured distribution on a population basis, and the prime minister of the East Punjab believed in distribution on the basis of need.

During 1948 and 1949, there was a weakly supported movement to have the provincial share of divisible tax heads entrenched in the Constitution. This view was expressed with regard to both the income tax and the divisible excise taxes, but the former had greater support. These suggestions for entrenchment appeared first in the form of eight amendments to the Draft Constitution, which were submitted by nearly twenty Assembly members representing six provinces.[49] And of these twenty persons, six were ranking members of the Assembly.

---

[46] See a memorandum from V. K. R. V. Rao, for the Government of Assam, to B. N. Rau, dated 17 October 1947; *Munshi papers.*

[47] Two provinces called for the allocation of 50 per cent of the joint pool of income and corporation tax to the provincial governments, and Bombay and the Central Provinces and Berar thought that the provincial share should be 75 per cent. The remaining four provinces believed 60 per cent to be a reasonable figure. See memoranda and letters from the provincial governments; *Munshi papers.* See also debates in East Punjab Legislative Assembly; op. cit., *INA.*

[48] Memorandum to the Assembly, dated 31 October 1947; *Munshi papers.*

[49] For these amendments, see *Amendment Book* II, pp. 298–9.

This movement for entrenching the provincial share of these revenues appears to have had little force behind it. Entrenchment was not advocated in any of the many memoranda and letters sent to the Assembly by the provincial governments, despite the universal claims for an increased share of income tax proceeds and for the inclusion of the corporation tax among divisible revenues. Nor did the question receive serious attention on the floor of the House. Had the provinces been advocating that their share of divisible revenues should be fixed in the Constitution in order to protect themselves against the interference of the Union Government, the issue might well have assumed greater importance. But one gains the impression that even those who favoured entrenchment did so to ensure that the provinces were not cheated of their due by a Union more eager to spend money on its own projects than on those dear to a provincial government. This view is borne out by the quiet demise of the issue at the meeting between the provincial prime and finance ministers and the Drafting Committee on 22 July 1949 and by the willingness to leave the matter to the Finance Commissions. When the question of entrenchment was raised by a representative from Bihar, presumably the Finance Minister, A. Sinha, the meeting considered it only briefly, and it was sharply opposed by K. C. Neogy and Pandit Pant on the grounds that such a rigid means of allocation would make future adjustments in revenue distribution too difficult. The matter should be left to the Finance Commissions, said Pant, and no-one at the meeting pressed the issue further.[50] It was not seriously raised again.

The Assembly adopted draft Article 251 on the income tax very much as it had been originally framed—the tax was to be levied and collected by the Union and the revenue divided between the Union and the provinces in a manner to be determined by Parliament. The Union retained the corporation tax as an exclusive subject. Acting on the advice of two Finance Commissions, Parliament has now raised the provincial share of income tax revenue to 60 per cent.[51] The chairman of the second commission, which brought the provinces' share to this level, was K. Santhanam, who a decade before had believed that the provinces should receive at least 50 per cent of this revenue.

[50] Minutes of the meeting, 22 July 1947; *Munshi papers*.
[51] *Finance Commission Report* (1957), p. 39.

The pattern of demands in the Assembly for the distribution of excise revenue was similar to that for income tax revenue. Article 253 of the Draft Constitution, which became Article 272 of the Constitution, provided that, in general, the Union should levy and collect excise duties named on the Union List (Entry 86: duties of excise on tobacco and other goods manufactured or produced in India), but could, if Parliament so legislated, pay out the equivalent sums to the provinces in which the excise was collected. The consensus of the suggestions on this provision was that from 50 to 60 per cent of the profits from excise duties should be assigned to the provinces. A number of Assembly members as well as two provincial governments suggested that all such excise revenue should be made over to the provinces. An early note from the United Provinces Government advocated pooling the revenue from income and corporation taxes with excise and export duties for division among the provinces on a population basis.[52] There were also cases of what may be described as special pleading. Madras, for example, with its important tobacco industry, wanted the excise duty on tobacco transferred from the Union to the State Legislative List. The Assam Government claimed as its due 75 per cent of the excise duty on kerosene and petrol and a like amount of the export duty on tea.[53] The Assembly rejected all these recommendations, but the two Finance Commissions have assigned increasing amounts of Union excise revenue to the states.[54]

The Assembly adopted the provisions in the Draft Constitution concerning 'Borrowing' with little difficulty. It will be recalled that the provincial governments with outstanding loans from the Union or its predecessor government were not to borrow without the Union's consent. When this article was under consideration seven of the nine provinces had outstanding loans.[55] Yet the provincial governments evidently did not believe that this put them unduly in the grip of

[52] Memorandum from the United Provinces to the Assembly, undated, but probably drafted in August 1947; ibid.

[53] For Madras's views, see minutes of the Drafting Committee meeting, 22 July 1949. Also memorandum from the Government of Assam, dated 17 March 1948; both in *Munshi papers*.

[54] See especially *Report of the Finance Commission* (1957), pp. 40ff.

[55] See a note prepared by the Union Finance Ministry on borrowing, circulated to the Drafting Committee for use at its meeting of 21 July 1949; *Munshi papers*.

the Union and did not oppose either the article or the proviso. Nor, it seems, has the working of this article during the past decade been detrimental to the interests of the states.[56]

The Union Government may come to the financial assistance of a province not only through the devolution of revenues and with loans, but with grants-in-aid of provincial revenues and other grants. This power, as we have seen, is, practically speaking, unlimited, for the Union can make grants for purposes outside its legislative jurisdiction. It has been the practice under the Constitution to make grants-in-aid on the basis of budgetary need, to aid provinces whose revenues, even after devolution, fall short of their expenditures. And it has been the aim to keep these grants-in-aid to a minimum by making devolution adequate.[57]

The question of grants is somewhat different. Grants may be broadly characterized as conditional or unconditional. The Union's practice since independence has been to make grants unconditionally,[58] with the obvious exception of grants to provinces such as Assam for the development of backward areas and tribes. There can be little doubt that the Assembly expected that the use of grants and grants-in-aid would follow the lines eventually recommended by the Finance Commissions, for neither of the articles of the Draft caused much discussion at the July 1949 meeting of the Drafting Committee and provincial ministers, and the Assembly adopted the provisions with equally little debate. In fact, the opposite was true: instead of evincing suspicion of the grants procedure, at least five provinces made specific pleas for special subventions for social and economic development. There is no evidence that the provincial governments or their representatives in the Assembly feared that the Union Government would try to reduce their independence by means of the mechanism for making grants.

The huge sums involved in capital expenditures under the Five Year Plans is a subject in itself and far beyond the scope of this work.

---

[56] The opinion of C. D. Deshmukh, India's first Union Finance Minister tinder the Constitution, expressed in an interview with the author in 1960.

[57] Grants-in-aid are usually if not always unconditional. See *Finance Commission Reports* of 1952 and 1957; pp. 91 and 25.

[58] Bhargava, *The Theory and Working of Union Finance*, p. 110.

It was hardly touched upon by the Assembly, although brief mention was made of national planning (see below). Apparently the dimensions that the issue would assume were not envisaged and only the more common uses of grants were considered. Despite the successful working of the financial provisions of the Constitution, which has in large part been due to the application by the Finance Commissions of the principle of need, the relationship between the Union and the states continues to be a subject of controversy. Ambedkar described the distribution of revenues as 'better than any financial system that I know of' but with the defect that 'the provinces are very largely dependent for their resources upon grants made to them by the Centre'.[59] Compared with the 1935 Act, however, the states under the Constitution have greater autonomy in both their financial and administrative relations with the Union. But the coordinate nature of state and Union activities under the Constitution gives the Union, at least potentially, great power to interfere in state affairs. Yet neither the working of the financial provisions, nor of the Indian brand of cooperative federalism as a whole, would seem to justify the description of India 'as a Federation in which paramountcy powers which the British Government had over the Indian States have been taken over by the Union Government and applied to all its units'.[60] This is to miss an essential point: that India is not New Delhi alone, but the state capitals as well. The states need Union funds, but the Union without the cooperation of the states could not long exist. The state governments may often be instruments of Union (national) policy, but without their help the Union could not give effect to its programme. The two, therefore, are mutually dependent. This relationship has been summed up by the authority on public administration, Paul Appleby, who wrote:

> No other large and important national government, I believe, is so dependent as India on theoretically subordinate, but actually rather distinct units responsible to a different political control, for so much of the administration of what are recognized as national programmes of great importance to the nation.[61]

---

[59] *CAD* X, 9,339.
[60] K. Santhanam, *Union-State Relations in India*, p. 13.
[61] P. Appleby, *Public Administration in India, Report of a Survey*, p. 22.

10

Federalism—III
National Planning

THE importance that national or economic development planning has assumed in India since the formation of the Planning Commission in March 1950 was not foreshadowed in the proceedings of the Constituent Assembly. The Assembly's only direct contact with the subject was to inscribe 'Economic and Social Planning' on the Concurrent Legislative List. The need, widely recognized both in the Assembly and outside it, for a nationally planned effort to raise the economic and social Standard of the country certainly supported the arguments for a Strong central government. But as there were other, more compelling, reasons for creating a tight federal Structure, one may doubt the importance of even the indirect effect of the necessity for planning on the decisions of Assembly members.

Nevertheless, Congress Party leaders had long emphasized the importance of planning as well as their belief that it should be among the Union's powers. Nehru and others had preached the virtues of planning since the later 1920's, and the Congress established a National Planning Committee, with Nehru as chairman, in 1937.[1] Three times during the negotiations with the Cabinet Mission, the Congress leadership made it clear that the central government under any constitutional scheme must bear the responsibility for national planning.[2] The members of the Mission would not agree to

---

[1] For a synopsis of the very extensive work of this committee, see K. T. Shah, *National Planning, Principles and Administration.*

[2] Maulana Azad in a letter to Pethick-Lawrence, 9 May 1946; in the Congress scheme of 12 May 1946; and Azad in a letter to Wavell, 13 June 1946. See *IAR*

this, however, and the first report of the Union Powers Committee merely expressed the hope that planning would by 'agreement' be included within the scope of Union powers. But the Second Union Powers Committee report, drafted after the announcement of Partition, included 'Economic and Social Planning' as an item on the Concurrent List. There it remained in the Draft Constitution, to be adopted by the Assembly after several minutes of inconsequential debate on 3 September 1949.

The advocacy of planning was by no means restricted to the Congress. Contrary to the United States and Europe, where planning was considered either dangerously Marxist or conducive to an excessive concentration of power in the hands of the government, planning in India had the support of eminently respectable capitalists. There was a Member for Planning and Development in the Viceroy's Executive Council, and in 1945 eight prominent industrialists and bankers (among them John Matthai) published a booklet entitled *A Plan of Economic Development for India.*[3] The 'Bombay Plan', as it was nicknamed, as well as making a number of remarkably forward-looking suggestions, recommended the creation of very comprehensive plans by a national planning committee and their execution by 'a supreme economic council working alongside the national planning committee under the authority of the central government'.[4] Such support among the business community, where one might have expected it to be lacking, was confirmed by the report of the Fiscal Commission in 1949. The answers to a questionnaire circulated by the commission showed a 'preponderance of opinion among all sections of witnesses in favour of an organization for the *overall* planning of the economic activities of the country'.[5]

Even so, there was no clear idea during the framing period of how planning would affect the federal Structure. It was certainly not forseen that the Planning Commission would in effect supersede the Finance Commissions—whose purview would revert to the non-Plan aspects of federal finance established by the

1946,1, pp. 140, 142–4, and 167.

[3] P. Thakurdas and others, *A Plan of Economic Development for India.*

[4] Ibid., p. 8.

[5] Government of India, *Report of the Fiscal Commission*, p. 254.

Constitution. Nor is there any evidence that Assembly members foresaw that planning would mould the federal Structure as much as, or more than, any of the more explicit federal provisions. Yet time has shown that, along with the dominant-party political situation, planning has been a Strong unifying force within Indian federalism.[6]

The Linguistic Provinces Issue and the Constitution

'One of the most difficult problems in the framing of India's new Constitution', wrote B. N. Rau, 'will be to satisfy the demand for linguistic provinces and other demands of a like nature.'[7] In the sense that this issue would both agitate and plague the Assembly throughout its three-year lifetime, Rau was quite right. The Assembly did not, however, attempt to resolve the question, despite Strong pressures to do so, and the demand for the reorganization of the provinces on a linguistic-cum-cultural basis directly affected the content of the Constitution in only one way: it assured the inclusion of Article 3.

Article 3 provides that Parliament may form a new State by combining two States or by the separation of territory from a State, may increase or diminish the area of any State, and may alter its boundaries or name. No Bill for these purposes may be introduced in Parliament except on the recommendation of the President after he has 'ascertained' the views of the legislature(s) of the State(s) concerned. Thus the face of India can be changed by Parliament without recourse to the more cumbersome mechanism of constitutional amendment.[8]

[6] G. L. Nanda, now Union Home Minister and member of the Planning Commission, early expressed the view that planning would be effective in India only if the Congress provided the impetus and acted as a unifying force in support of the plans. Nanda in a note entitled: 'The Role of Planning in a Federal System', written in January 1950; *Prasad papers*, File 1-A/50.

[7] Rau, *Constitutional Precedents, First Series*, p. 17.

[8] The companion to Article 3 is Article 2, which provides that Parliament may admit to the Union, or establish, new States 'on such terms and conditions as it thinks fit'. There can be little doubt that when framing Articles 2 and 3, Assembly members also had in mind the absorption of the Princely States into the Union. For a discussion of this subject, see the following section of this chapter. The Fifth Amendment Act, 1955, slightly changed the proviso to Article 3, Stipulating that the President must refer the proposed Bill to the State legislature for its views.

The precedent for Article 3 was Section 290 of the 1935 Act, by which Parliament at Westminster had the power to alter provincial boundaries. Section 290, in turn, closely followed the terms of Chapter VI of the Australian Constitution, and the parent of all such provisions has been Article IV, Section 3 of the United States Constitution.

B. N. Rau had included a provision similar to Section 290 in his Memorandum on the Union Constitution of May 1947. The Union Constitution Committee accepted his recommendation, having the support of a joint sub-committee of the Union and Provincial Constitution Committees, called the Linguistic Provinces Sub-Committee, and included such a provision in its report, citing as its precedents the 1935 Act and the Australian Constitution. In this early form, however, Parliament was obliged to obtain the 'consent' of the legislatures of all the provinces concerned before creating a new province or changing the boundaries of an existing one.[9] The wording of this clause was to cause the Drafting Committee some difficulty.

Taking up the clause on the second day of its consideration of Rau's Draft Constitution, the Drafting Committee decided that Parliament need not obtain the consent of the provinces concerned, but must simply ascertain the 'views' of the legislatures of provinces that would be affected by the proposed changes. Several members apparently believed that in this form the provision did not give sufficient protection to minority groups, for the next day the Drafting Committee added a proviso to the article. This Stated that such Bills could be introduced in Parliament only by the Government, and only if a majority of the representatives in the provincial legislature of the areas immediately concerned in the boundary changes had in writing requested the Government to introduce a Bill. The views of the provincial governments were still to be sought. The following day yet another safeguard was added: the legislatures of all the provinces involved must also request Governmental action before a Bill changing the existing delimitation of the provinces could be introduced in Parliament.[10]

Six weeks later, on 19 January 1948, the committee adopted the form in which the provision would appear as Article 3 of the Draft

[9]   Report of the UCC, para, 2 and 3; *Reports, First Series*, pp. 46–47.
[10] Minutes of the meeting, 29 and 30 October 1947; *INA*.

Constitution. Bills affecting provincial boundaries were to be introduced in Parliament only by the Government and must either have the approval of the representatives of the area concerned (written approval was not stipulated) or the sanction of a resolution passed by the provincial legislature.[11] Yet slightly more than a month after the publication of the Draft, the Drafting Committee, on Rau's recommendation, decided to revert to an earlier version of the article. Rau suggested that Bills realigning boundaries should be introduced on the recommendation of the President and that Parliament need only ascertain the views of the provincial legislatures. The members of the Drafting Committee adopted this rewording of the article and commended it to the Assembly.[12]

From all this it would seem that the members of the Drafting Committee and the Congress leadership had been trying to find a way to solve the linguistic States issue within the framework of a federal system, while at the same time protecting minority interests. Yet one suspects that the Oligarchy, being opposed to linguistic redistribution (see p. 243), would not have been displeased had the intricacy of the mechanism for a time postponed the formation of provinces on this basis. Realizing that the outcome was almost inevitable, however, the party leadership finally chose the simplest method of implementing a redistribution of provinces in order to provide a safety-valve for the ever increasing pressure for the creation of linguistic provinces. And as to the interests of minorities, if one accepts Dr. Ambedkar's explanation, the Drafting Committee chose Rau's version in order to prevent the voice of a minority group from being totally silenced by an adverse vote in the provincial legislature.[13]

Not everyone in the Assembly was satisfied with the draft provision. Ayyar believed that giving Parliament the 'drastic power' of draft Article 3 was 'not consistent with the Federal principle of the Constitution itself', because the majority in Parliament might not reflect the views of the provinces. But as there was 'consensus' on the need for linguistic

[11] Minutes of the meeting, 19 January 1948; ibid.

[12] For Rau's suggestion, see *Prasad papers*, File 1-M/48. For the Drafting Committee's decision, see minutes of the meeting, 28 March 1948; *Prasad papers*, File I-D/48. At this time the consent of the governments of the former Princely States was still needed.

[13] *CAD* VII, 7, 439ff.

provinces, said Ayyar, the requirement of the consent of provincial governments could be dispensed with for a three-year period.[14] Many Assembly members agreed with both of these views—except that few supported the three-year limitation—and adopted Article 3 after a wordy debate devoted more to the linguistic provinces issue in general than to the merits of the provision before them.

The indirect influence of the linguistic provinces question on the shape of the Constitution is nearly impossible to assess. One may assume that the fear of separatist forces tended to work in favour of a Stronger central government, although there are few examples of such thinking. A motion submitted by P. S. Deshmukh to the Steering Committee did, however, express this view. Deshmukh recommended that for a variety of reasons, including the 'bitter passions' aroused by the linguistic provinces controversy, the Draft Constitution should be forgotten and instead the Assembly should draw up a constitution providing India with a unitary govern-ment.[15] A note by Azad is another example. He thought that 'the demand for linguistic provinces and (other) particularistic ten-dencies' were gathering Strength in the country. Faced with this situation, 'the only way of maintaining Indian solidarity', Azad believed, was 'to give a commanding position to the Centre in the new constitutional set up'.[16] Nehru and Patel Strongly opposed the formation of linguistic provinces, particularly at this time. But there is no evidence that they supported a Strong centre for this reason. The supporters of linguistic provinces, and there were many in the Assembly, did not consider themselves separatists, however, or as representing 'fissiparous tendencies'. They aimed at the 'con-structive consolidation of the country', and supreme in their minds was the good of all India.[17] Why should Assembly members wish to frame a Constitution to protect the nation against themselves?

[14] Ayyar in a note on Article 3, undated, but written presumably during the late spring or summer of 1948; *Ayyar papers*.

[15] Motion submitted to the Steering Committee for debate at its meeting of 19 May 1949. Minutes of the meeting; *Prasad papers*, File 2-S/48.

[16] Azad in a note on 'Education in the Union and Concurrent Lists', dated 18 November 1948; *Munshi papers*.

[17] From a Statement in *The Hindustan Times* of 29 November 1947, signed by six Assembly members: Diwakar, Pataskar, Nijalingappa, Munawalli, Jedhe, and S. V. Krishnamurthy.

Could the Constitution, in fact, protect Indian unity from any ill-effects resulting from the formation of linguistic provinces? It was doubtful. Making the Union Government powerful and the federal Structure tight, and keeping the provinces tied to the Union by financial necessity might to some degree prevent separatist sentiment from gaining momentum. But the Assembly had already framed a tight federal system in response to recent events, the uncertainty of public security, and the provinces' demand for revenue distribution on the principle of need. It had not done so in the belief that constitutional provisions could end the widespread agitation for linguistic provinces, which the Assembly treated as a separate question from that of the Structure of the Constitution. Referring to several demands that the Union and Provincial Constitution Committees should take up the question of linguistic provinces, President Prasad told the Assembly, 'the model constitution(s) (to be prepared by these committees) need not necessarily require linguistic provinces for that purpose'.[18] In short, the relations of the provinces to the Union were to be the same no matter on what basis the provinces were constituted.

Nor has the formation of linguistic provinces and the growth of linguistic sub-nationalism in the years since independence affected the constitutional relationship between the States and the Union— although the growth of linguism may yet prove a threat to Indian unity. Tamil-speaking Madras and Telegu-speaking Andhra have the same constitutional relationship to New Delhi as had undivided Madras before 1953. It might have been supposed that this sub-national feeling would have 'operated against the encroachments of the centre', K. M. Panikkar has written; yet this has not proved true. 'It cannot be emphasized too much that regional feeling in India has not been in relation to the Centre, except perhaps to a small degree in the State of Madras, but in a sense of rivalry, *to other regions.* All are claimants for the patronage and bounty of the Centre.'[19]

Although the linguistic provinces issue had only a nebulous effect on the drafting of the Constitution, excepting for the terms of Article

---

[18] *CAD* III, 3, 473; 30 April 1947.

[19] Panikkar, *The Foundations of New India*, p. 242. For a most able and detailed, although perhaps too pessimistic, account of the danger linguism poses to Indian unity, see Seliq Harrison, *India, The Most Dangerous Decades.*

3, it nevertheless made frequent appearances in the Constituent Assembly. We may, therefore, briefly examine some of them. That the issue entered the Assembly in the first place was a result of the policy of Congress during the previous three decades. The party had organized its administrative Structure on the basis of linguistic units at the Nagpur Congress of 1920 and from then on attacked as arbitrary and irrational the provincial boundaries drawn by the British. The Nehru Report had recommended provincial redistribution in which the 'main considerations must necessarily be the wishes of the people and the linguistic unity of the area concerned'.[20] Each linguistic group believed that independence should bring the fulfilment of its particular wishes, and after the War focussed its hopes on the Constituent Assembly. The resistance of the Oligarchy, however, as well as their own conflicting claims, frustrated the desires of the various groups—and continued to do so until the formation of Andhra in 1953 and States Reorganization in 1956.

The crescendo of demands began in August 1946, little more than a month after the elections to the Constituent Assembly. Pattabhi Sitaramayya, a member of the Congress Working Committee and Congress president in 1948, called for the formation of linguistic provinces and said that 'the whole problem must be taken up as the first and foremost problem to be solved by the Constituent Assembly'.[21] Sitaramayya continued to lead the pack during the ensuing months. The supporters of linguistic provinces held a conference in New Delhi on 8 December 1946, the day before the inaugural meeting of the Assembly. In his presidential address, Sitaramayya repeated his demand of August, and a resolution of the conference called upon the Assembly to accept the principle of the formation of linguistic provinces and to set up the machinery for redistribution. During the first three weeks of the first Assembly session four similar resolutions were submitted. Supporters included a minister of State, the deputy speaker of the Constituent Assembly (Legislative), a future member of the Drafting Committee, three Provincial Congress Committee presidents, and other Congress officials.[22] At its first meeting, the

---

[20] *Nehru Report*, op. cit, p. 61.

[21] *The Hindustan Times*, 31 August 1946.

[22] See *Prasad papers*, File 2-S/48 for the texts of these resolutions. Among those supporting them were: R. R. Diwakar, K. V. Rao, B. M. Gupte, Nalavade, S.

Steering Committee under Prasad's chairmanship, and with Patel and Azad present, decided that the Assembly was not competent to take up the issue at that time[23]—a stand the committee would continue to take throughout the lifetime of the Assembly. The Objectives Resolution, however, indicated the possibility of redistribution by declaring that India would be made up of the Princely States and the provinces, 'whether with their present boundaries or with such others as may be determined by the Constituent Assembly'.[24]

During the early months of 1947, despite the frowns of the Assembly leadership, the pressure for linguistic provinces continued. Finally, the leaders agreed that the Provincial and Union Constitution Committees could appoint a joint sub-committee to consider the matter. It met under Sitaramayya's chairmanship on 12 June 1947 and unanimously recommended that immediately after independence the Government should appoint a commission to consider creating the new provinces of Andhra, Karnataka, Kerala, Maharashtra, and possibly others. The commission should report in time for the Assembly to list any newly-formed provinces in the Constitution.[25]

After Independence Day, the agitation increased and the Drafting Committee recommended a commission to 'inquire into all relevant matters not only as regards Andhra, but as regards other linguistic regions'.[26] Yet the Government made no move to establish, a commission. Prasad, perturbed by this inactivity, asked B. N. Rau on 9 April 1948 to try to get Nehru and Patel to take action.[27] Presumably a decision was made within a month, for in mid-May Prasad wrote

---

K. Patil, Jedlie, Pataskar, Mane, Nijalingappa, M. A. Ayyangar, Sanjeeva Reddy, Mrs. Durbagai, V. C. K. Rao, Narasimha Raju, D. P. Khaitan, H. Sitarama Reddy, B. Shiva Rao, and P. Subbarayan.

[23] Minutes of the meeting, 23 January 1947; ibid. Among the members of the Steering Committee at this time were three supporters of the resolutions in favour of linguistic provinces; M. A. Ayyangar, Mrs. Durgabai, and S. N. Mane.

[24] CAD I, 5, 57.

[25] Minutes of the meeting, 12 June 1947; INA. It was planned to enumerate the constituent units of the Union in a schedule to the Constitution in much the manner of Section 46 of the 1935 Act. As no linguistic provinces were created before 1950, however, there were no new provinces to include in Schedule I of the Constitution.

[26] Draft Constitution, footnote, p. 159.

[27] Prasad in a letter to Rau, 9 April 1947; Prasad papers, Random letters file.

to various provincial prime ministers asking them to name a representative to a Linguistic Provinces Commission.[28] But this might have produced a body composed of supporters of provincial redistribution, the last thing the Government—or at least Nehru and Patel—wanted, and Prasad's idea was dropped. When the Linguistic Provinces Commission came into being on 17 June 1948, its three members were an undistinguished Congress Assembly member from Bihar, J. N. Lal; a Gray's Inn lawyer, Cambridge graduate, and retired senior Indian Civil Service official, Panna Lall; and the chairman, a retired judge of the Allahabad High Court, S. K. Dar—whence the commonly used name of the Dar Commission.

After an exhaustive enquiry, the Dar Commission concluded that 'the formation of provinces on exclusively or even mainly linguistic considerations is not in the larger interests of the Indian nation and should not be taken in hand'.[29] The report, dated 10 December 1948, could hardly have been pleasing to the many supporters of linguistic redistribution, including their unofficial leader, Pattabhi Sitaramayya, who had been elected president of the Congress the previous October. As a result, eight days after the publication of the Dar report the annual Congress session at Jaipur approved a resolution forming the 'JVP' committee—so called from the initials of the first names of its members, Nehru, Patel, and Sitaramayya—to take a second look at the question.[30]

The JVP Report, submitted on 1 April 1949, contained a perceptive analysis of the situation, and two of its sentences reflect its own difficulties as well as the dilemma racking India: 'We feel that the present is not an opportune moment for the formation of new provinces.' Yet the members also believed that 'If public sentiment is insistent and overwhelming, we, as democrats, have to submit to it, but subject to certain limitations in regard to the good of India as a whole. . . .'[31] The supporters of linguistic provinces knew a half-open

---

[28] Letters of 16 May 1948; *Prasad papers*, File 1-P/48.

[29] *Report of the Linguistic Provinces Commission*, para. 152(1); *Reports, Third Series*, p. 217.

[30] For an account of these events, see Ralph Retzlaff, 'The Indian Constituent Assembly and the Problem of Indian Unity', p. 471; an unpublished PhD. thesis, Cornell University, 1959.

[31] Indian National Congress, *Report of the Linguistic Provinces Committee*, pp. 9 and 15.

door when they saw one, publicly welcomed the JVP Report, and continued to press their claims.

But the months of confused lobbying that followed—largely outside the Assembly—did not produce the hoped-for result. This was primarily because the Oligarchy, Nehru, Patel, Prasad, and Azad, opposed the redistribution of provinces on a linguistic basis.[32] Nehru believed that 'some kind of re-organization' was 'inevitable', but that cultural, geographic, and economic factors as well as language must be taken into account. Nor should the Assembly attempt to solve the problem 'when passions are roused', said Nehru, 'but at a suitable moment when the time is ripe for it'.[33] Azad, as we know, deplored the increasing demand for 'linguistic provinces and (other) particularistic tendencies'. Patel forthrightly denounced the idea of redistribution. History had taught the hard lesson, he told an audience in Nagpur in 1948, that linguistic separatism imperilled national solidarity and unity.[34] Prasad apparently opposed redistribution less strongly than the other three, but he still believed that '. . . there is an urgent need amongst all of us of thinking and acting as Indians rather than as belonging to any particular province, or group or community'.[35] With the inauguration of the Constitution in January 1950, the Assembly was quit of its burden, having refused to include the formation of linguistic provinces in its task of constitution-making.

Extending the Constitution to the Princely States

The total absorption of the Princely States into the Indian constitutional Structure, which occupied the decade between the announcement of the Cabinet Mission Plan on 16 May 1946 and States Reorganization in 1956, was very largely accomplished during the life-span of the Constituent Assembly. At the beginning

---

[32] The Congress Working Committee, however, did agree in November 1949 to, the formation of Andhra, although this did not actually take place until 1953. See minutes of the W.C. meeting, 16–17 November 1949; *Prasad papers*, File 4-A/49.

[33] *CAD* VII, 4, 320–1.

[34] *The Hindustan Times*, 5 November 1948.

[35] Prasad in a letter to B. P. Podder, of the Marwari Association of Calcutta, dated 8 April 1948; *Prasad papers*, File 1-P/48.

of this period, the Princely States were in no way part of the Union. Somewhat later most of them became loosely attached to the Union Government in a relationship more closely resembling confederation than federalism—although several threatened to remain completely independent. Yet by the time the Constitution was inaugurated, few distinctions remained between the former Princely States and the other States of the Union, previously the provinces of British India.

Article 1 and the First Schedule of the Constitution enumerate the component units of the Union. Before 1956 there were the Part A States, the former provinces, the Part B States, the former Princely States, and the Part C States, which were centrally administered areas and included the former Chief Commissioners provinces. Among the ten Part C States were seven former Princely States, which, for the time being, were to be centrally administered.[36] The provisions of the provincial constitution applied equally to both Part A and Part B States, and the relationship of the latter with the Union was, with few exceptions, the same as that enjoyed by the Part A States.

Article 371 expressed the only major difference between the two, laying down that for a period of at least ten years the governments of Part B States were to be subject to the general control of the President.[37] Part B States also had to forego to the Union their properties and assets if the purposes for which these assets were held pertained to matters on the Union List. At the same time, the Union assumed the liabilities of Part B States if they concerned items on the Union List. The other differences between the former provinces and Princely States worked in favour of the latter. Although their armed forces must form part of the armed forces of the Union, Part B States might continue to maintain them until Parliament provided otherwise. The Union could make special grants to Part B States in lieu of revenues lost by the Union assumption of tax heads. And the Part B States were allowed in most cases to keep their

---

[36] There were also Part D States, limited to the Andaman and Nicobar Islands. All these categories of States were wiped out by the Seventh Amendment Act, which reorganized the States largely on the basis of the recommendations of the States Reorganization Commission. Most of the Part C States were absorbed in surrounding States, with the exception of the following, which became centrally administered Union Territories: Delhi, Himachal Pradesh (including Bilaspur), Manipur, Tripura, and the Andaman, Nicobar, and Lakshwadeep Islands.

[37] For a discussion of the drafting of this article, see above, p. 206.

former rulers as Rajpramukhs, or governors—an arrangement satisfying to the Princes and not too distasteful to their former subjects, protected as they now were by the Constitution from the rulers' previously arbitrary and sometimes tyrannical authority.[38] The State of Kashmir had, and continues to have, a privileged position under the Constitution.[39]

At the beginning of the States' metamorphosis in 1946–47, the Assembly conducted the negotiations with the rulers, for these were beyond the competence of the Interim Government. But after its establishment in July 1947, the States Ministry under Sardar Patel assumed the primary responsibility for bringing the Princes into the Union. The Assembly, however, continued to be closely involved with what Patel called the 'unionization' of the States, although largely as a ratifying body, drafting the provisions to implement the agreements reached between the States Ministry and the Princes. It is only the Assembly's role that concerns us here; the work of the States Ministry has been recounted by V. P. Menon in his book, *The Integration of the Indian States.*

The problem of bringing the Princely States into an Indian federation, bequeathed to the Assembly and the Union Government by the departing British, was one the British themselves had never been able to solve. For over a hundred years before independence these States had had a special relationship with the Paramount power. Their treaties with the British had left them a good deal of internal autonomy—glorified by the ruling Princes into 'sovereignty'—although the Viceroy's power to bring them to heel was ever present in the person of the Resident. During the Round Table Conference, fearful of the possibility of an Indian federation, the Princes sought to protect their special Status. They refused to agree to Paramountcy being within the purview of the federal government, and they clung leech-like to the manifestations of their 'sovereignty'.[40] As a result,

---

[38] This was the case, for example, in the Rajasthan Union, in Madhya Bharat, Travancore, etc. These arrangements were not specifically provided for in the Constitution, but were arrived at in negotiations between the Union Government and the Princes. For the relevant provisions of the Constitution, see Clause (21) of Article 366.

[39] *The Constitution*, Article 370.

[40] For an excellent summary of the Princes' attitudes, see N. D. Varadachariar, *Indian States in the Federation*, pp. 94–99.

the 1935 Act provided only that the States could accede to the federation if they so desired. The negotiations concerning the terms of accession were to be undertaken with each State separately by the Viceroy, in his capacity as Crown Representative. Initiated in 1937, on the coming into force of the 1935 Act, these negotiations dragged on until the War, with the result that none of the Princely States became members of the federation.

The Congress's policy towards the States began to emerge in the 1920's. Resolutions urged the Princes 'to introduce responsible government based on representative institutions' in their States and to guarantee elementary fundamental rights.[41] Another resolution asserted that the Congress stood for 'the same political, social, and economic freedom in the States as in the rest of India', and that the party considered the States 'as integral parts of India'.[42] The only federation acceptable to the Congress, stated a third resolution, referring to the 1935 Act, was 'one in which the States participate as free units enjoying the same measure of democratic freedom as the rest of India'.[43] The annual Congress Session of 1946, held at Meerut the month before the opening of the Assembly, reiterated most of these sentiments and damned the rulers as reactionaries who were trying to crush the political aspirations of their subjects.

With the end of the War and the approach of independence, it became evident that there would be a confrontation of these two forces, the one favouring arbitrary rule and seeking to preserve its privilege and its freedom from central government influence, and the other dedicated to spreading popular government and the social revolution throughout the country. Certain features of the situation were plain to every discerning eye. Federalism in the new India would not work if there existed among the units both monarchical and democratic governments—the two were incompatible. This contrast in political institutions had been one reason why the

[41] Resolution of the Calcutta Session 1928; see Chakrabarty and Bhattacharya, op. cit., pp. 27–28. See also *Nehru Report*, p. 83.

[42] This resolution was passed at the Haripura Session 1938; see *IAR* 1938, 1, pp. 299–300. Some months later, in his inaugural speech to the All-India States Peoples Conference of February 1939, Nehru described most States as 'sinks of reaction and incompetence'; see Nehru, *Unity of India*, p. 30.

[43] Ibid.

federation envisaged in the 1935 Act had never come to fruition. And in the new India, said Nehru, 'no State can have an administration which goes against our fundamental principles or gives less freedom than obtains in other parts of India'.[44] Moreover, unless, the Princely States were brought into a close relationship with the Union, it would be difficult or impossible to extend to their peoples the benefits of social reform, to bring them up to the level of the provinces in such matters as labour welfare and agricultural and industrial development.

The acuteness of the problem lay in its threat to Indian unity. The Princely States occupied one third of the country's land area and contained one fourth of its people. Although many States were insignificant, many were powerful. The larger States were financially self-sufficient, and at the time of independence forty-four had their own military forces.[45] Had the havoc of Hyderabad been repeated in even two or three other States, the result could have been chaos and anarchy and the Assembly might never have finished its work.

The Constituent Assembly's authority to negotiate with the Princely States originated with the Cabinet Mission. The Mission projected a 'Union of India, embracing both British India and the States' in which the Union would be responsible for the subjects of Defence, Foreign Affairs, and Communications, while the States would retain jurisdiction over all subjects not ceded to the Union.[46] It also recommended that the States should send representatives to the Assembly and that, until they were chosen, the States should be represented in the negotiations by a Negotiating Committee. One of the first bargains that had to be struck was the manner of choosing the States' members. Were they to be appointed by the rulers or elected by bodies within the State, or a combination of the two? Negotiations produced an agreement according to which not less than 50 per cent of each State's representatives were to be elected, and the remaining number could be nominated by the rulers.

---

[44] *CAD* I, 5, 56.

[45] Government of India, *White Paper on the Indian States*, p. 77.

[46] Cabinet Mission Plan, para.15(1) and (4); cited in Gwyer and Appadorai,op. cit.,p. 580.

The Cabinet Mission Plan stated flatly that 'Paramountcy can neither be retained by the British Crown, nor transferred to the new Government'. This meant, the Mission explained, that with the transfer of power, 'all rights surrendered by the States to the Paramount Power will return to the States'.[47] The Mission also informed the Princes that, with Paramountcy ended, they should either enter into 'a federal relationship with the successor Government', or enter into 'particular political arrangements with it'.[48] Precisely what this entailed, the rulers, and apparently the Mission itself, were not certain. Some Princes believed that they must accede to the Union on the basis of the three subjects, others thought in terms of looser ties, while yet others thought they could remain completely independent.

Thus the integration of the States apparently presented the Assembly with the federal problem in its most familiar form. Contrary to the provinces, the States were, once Paramountcy had lapsed, sovereign governments that had never been parts of the nation's constitutional Structure; possessing, as many of them did, their own financial resources and military power, they were in a strong bargaining position. In reality, however, this greater independence and power availed them little, for the 'facts of geography', the relatively greater power of the Union, the dissension among the Princes themselves, and, ultimately, the national consciousness of the great majority of the Princes made the States' entry into the Union nearly inescapable.

In response to the Cabinet Mission Plan, the Princes agreed in June 1946 to form a Negotiating Committee, and the committee met sporadically during the next six months defining and redefining the States' position and aims.[49] On 21 December, the

---

[47] *Memorandum on States' Treaties*, etc. presented by the Mission to the Chancellor, Chamber of Princes, 12 May 1946; ibid., p. 767.

[48] Ibid.

[49] The Negotiating Committee, formally speaking, represented the Chamber of Princes, whose Chancellor was the Nawab of Bhopal. Founded by the British in 1921, the Chamber was a consultative body comprised of the rulers and their representatives; it was not a governmental body. Neither Mysore nor Hyderabad were members. The members of the Chamber of Princes Negotiating Committee in mid-November 1946 were: the Nawab of Bhopal, leader, the Maharajdhiraja of Patiala, the Maharaja of Nawangar, C.P. Ramaswami Aiyar, Sir Sultan Ahmed, Sir Mirza Ismail, Sardar D. K. Sen, Sir A. Ramaswami Mudaliar, Sardar

Assembly established its own States Committee to negotiate with the Princes' Negotiating Committee.[50] A month later, the adoption of the Objectives Resolution and Nehru's speech on it made the lines of the Assembly's States policy clear: the Indian Union would include the States, which must accede on at least the three subjects suggested by the Cabinet Mission, and the Princes must take Steps to introduce representative government in their States. On 8–9 February 1947, the committees representing the Princes and the Assembly met for the first time, and the process of integration began in earnest.

At this meeting, Nehru and Patel elaborated the Assembly's position. The States would not be compelled to join the Union and, should they join, they would retain all but ceded subjects. Fundamental Rights were likely to be a Union subject, however, and, to safeguard the rights, the jurisdiction of the Federal Court would presumably extend to the States. Nehru and Ayyangar also pointed out that Assembly committees would soon be meeting to consider important aspects of the Constitution, and it behoved the States to join the Assembly in order that their representatives might participate in these discussions.[51]

The Princes held that their participation in the Assembly would not imply a commitment to join the Union—a matter that must be negotiated separately. Should they join, they would retain their 'sovereignty and all rights and powers' except where expressly ceded. The Assembly had no authority to interfere with the internal administration of the States, the institutions of which must remain inviolate. The Princes also claimed that the Assembly's negotiations with the States should be carried on only through the Negotiating Committee. Nehru, however, asserted that the Assembly did have the right to deal with individual States concerning their joining the Assembly. He had already opened negotiations with the Dewan of Baroda, B. L. Miner, for Baroda's entry into the Assembly, and Mitter's decision

---

K. M. Panikkar, and Maharaj Virbhadra Singhji. The eleventh place was vacant due to the death of Sir Manubhai Mehta; secretary to the committee was Mir Maqbul Mahmood.

[50] The members of the States Committee were: Nehru, chairman, Azad, Patel, N. G. Ayyangar, Deo, and Sitaramayya.

[51] Proceedings of the meetings, 8–9 February 1947; *Prasad papers*, File 11-C/46-7-8. All citations here are from this source.

to send three representatives (including himself) was announced the following day, 9 February.

This first meeting achieved little, although it seems that an impassioned reminder by Nehru of the dangers facing India, of the revolutionary spirit of the masses, and of the near chaos of the country, impressed the members of the Negotiating Committee as well as silenced the Nawab of Bhopal, its chairman, who displayed a most uncompromising and condescending attitude throughout the talks. Bhopal continued to oppose joining the Assembly even after the meeting between the two committees on 1 March, at which Nehru had pressed the Princes—in the light of the urgency imparted to the situation by Prime Minister Attlees's 20 February speech—to send representatives to the Assembly.[52] The split in the rulers' ranks, begun by Baroda's entry into the Assembly, widened, however; the Maharajas of Patiala and Bikaner decided to join the Assembly, and at the beginning of the third Assembly session on 28 April sixteen representatives from seven States signed the register as Assembly members. But as yet no ruler had signed an Instrument of Accession—indeed, none had been drafted—nor established even a loose federal relationship with the Interim Government and the federation.

The Viceroy's June Third Statement, announcing that Independence Day was barely ten weeks away, galvanized the Assembly and the Interim Government into action. The reason for this furious activity was clear: dealing with the States would be far easier before independence, while there remained some political attachment to New Delhi, even if only to the Crown Representative, the Viceroy, than it would be when the States had dropped into a limbo, attached to no one.[53] On 5 June, at a meeting of a sub-committee of the Assembly's States Committee and the Negotiating Committee, members of the States Committee urged the Princes speedily to select representatives who could be present at the July session of the Assembly. The Secretary of the Assembly, H. V. R. Iengar, wrote to the Dewans of all the States informing them that there could 'no longer by any

---

[52] Proceedings of the meeting, 1 March 1947; ibid. See also States Committee report, para. 5; *Reports, First Series*, p. 8.

[53] Evident as the motivation was, it was not stated openly. Lord Mountbatten almost certainly held this view, for he refused the request of several rulers that Paramountcy lapse before independence.

justification for letting this indeterminate position continue', and the States must choose their Assembly representatives.[54] And Nehru wrote to the Viceroy's chief of Staff that the States must inevitably join the Union, for 'the facts of geography cannot be ignored'.[55]

Four days later, Nehru told the Viceroy that the time had come for the Interim Government—as the *de facto* Government of India—to take a hand in the States issue. Nehru recommended that the Political Department be merged with a Government bureau and thus be brought under Indian control. If this was not possible, Nehru said, a new agency to deal with the States had to be formed immediately.[56] Within three weeks, the States Ministry had been established, and several days after that, Sardar Patel, with V. P. Menon as the ministry secretary, entered the arena. From this point onward, the role of the Assembly in the absorption of the States became secondary to that of the Government.

The month of July saw a steady increase in the pressure brought to bear on the States. The States Ministry and the Viceroy, in conjunction with the Princes, drafted an Instrument of Accession and a Standstill Agreement—which provided that the relations existing between the Union Government and the States would remain in force until altered by mutual agreement. The All-India Congress Committee met and passed a resolution condemning the threatened 'balkanization' of the country. Nehru announced to the Assembly that some of the States that had joined the Assembly were willing to cede to the centre wider powers than had been contemplated in the Cabinet Mission Plan. But the Assembly's policy, he said, continued to be 'that the application to the States in general of the federal list of subjects, insofar as it goes beyond the 16th May Statement, should be with their consent'.[57] In

[54] Sub-Committee of the States Committee and the Negotiating Committee, minutes of the meeting, 5 June 1949; *Prasad papers*, File II-C/46-7-8.

[55] Nehru in a letter to Lord Ismay, dated 19 June 1947—concerning an early draft of the Standstill Agreement; *Prasad papers*, File 19-C/47.

[56] Nehru in a letter to Mountbatten, dated 9 June 1947; ibid. On the same day, Nehru wrote a secret letter to the Viceroy protesting against the 'highly improper' behaviour of the Political Department, which was, among other things, Nehru charged, handing over Central Government property to the States; ibid.

[57] Second report of the Union Powers Committee, para. 3; *Reports, First Series*, p. 71.

another move, the Assembly, over the opposition of several States' representatives, adopted the provision in the Union Constitution Committee's report extending Union Executive authority, when it related to Union subjects, to the States. N. G. Ayyangar explained that

> . . . the general principle should be that it is the Federation that is responsible for the executive administration of federal subjects, but . . . it will not, unless it considers it necessary, interfere with the States' administration of federal subjects where it is in existence today and where it is efficient according to proper Standards.[58]

The Viceroy himself brought perhaps the most effective pressure on the States to accede to the Union. He did this not only privately during the lengthy negotiations, but also in a forceful and persuasive speech to the Chamber of Princes. 'You cannot', he told the Princes, 'run away from the Dominion Government that is your neighbour'.[59] By Independence Day, all the States, excepting Hyderabad, Kashmir, Junagadh, and two insignificant ones, had joined the Union, ceding as a minimum their authority over Defence, Communications, and Foreign Affairs. And nearly three dozen States and Groups of States—comprised of many small States—had representatives in the Assembly.

During the following two-and-a-half years, the States Ministry, using a variety of devices, brought the States more and more deeply into the Union. Some were absorbed into adjacent provinces. Others were taken over and administered in the manner of Chief Commissioners Provinces. Many were formed into Unions of States. Only the largest maintained their territorial and governmental identity. In each case, the Government several times renegotiated the Covenants laying down the relationship of the individual States and the Unions of States to the Union so that their powers came closer and closer to those possessed by the provinces. These changes in the constitutional status of the States were in general brought about by the States ceding further powers to the Union Government or by ceding authority over a subject already included on the Union List.

---

[58] *CAD* IV,10, 851.
[59] Mountbatten delivered this speech on 25 July 1947; see Gwyer and Appadorai. op. cit., p. 775.

Hence alterations in the Draft Constitution to reflect these changes were seldom necessary. So far as it concerned the position of the States, the Draft would be altered little between its publication in February 1948 and October 1949, when it was greatly amended to bring the States fully into the Union.

The provisions of the Draft Constitution on its appearance in early 1948 showed that the integration of the States had made progress since the preceding August, but that their position was still much different from that of the provinces. In order 'to mark this difference' the Draft divided the units of the Union into three classes that exactly corresponded to the Part A, B, and C States of the Constitution: the former provinces, the former Princely States, and the centrally administered areas, called Chief Commissioners Provinces.[60] This division of the units into categories having a different status in the federation dated from Section 5 of the 1935 Act, which had listed the provinces and the States as the two components of the federation. B. N. Rau had used the device in his Draft Constitution, but had increased the categories to three, adding the Chief Commissioners Provinces. The provisions of the Draft granting the States this extraordinary status numbered nearly two dozen. The articles of the Draft concerning the Public Services, for example, did not apply to the States; nor would civil appeals lie to the Supreme Court from a High Court in a State, as they would from High Courts in the provinces; more importantly, neither the provisions of the provincial constitution, nor those laying down the distribution of powers applied to the former Princely States, although the latter could be extended to the States with their consent.

That the units of a federation should have different relationships to the federal government was not thought of as an innovation by Assembly members; it was merely a recognition of the existing situation. But, in general, they found the exceptional autonomy of the States galling, and they believed it dangerous to the viability of the Union. It was 'unfortunate and . . . indefensible', Ambedkar said, that the States were on a different footing from the provinces. 'This disparity', he continued, 'may even prove dangerous to the efficiency of the State. So long as this disparity exists, the Centre's

---

[60] Draft Constitution, p. iv.

authority over all-India matters may lose its efficacy. For power is no power if it cannot be exercised in all cases and in all places.'[61]

The Assembly then found itself confronted by the problem of constitutions for the States. The Covenants establishing the relationship between the Union and the various States and Unions of States, laid down that the States and Unions could convene their own constituent assemblies and frame their own constitutions. By the autumn of 1948, however, few constituent assemblies had been formed, and those functioning lacked direction. On 25 October 1948, P. Govinda Menon of Cochin State moved in the Steering Committee that the Assembly set up a committee to prepare a model constitution for the State constituent assemblies to follow. Although several Assembly members opposed this on the ground that there should be no such constituent assemblies and the States should use the constitution drafted for the provinces, the Assembly, including States representatives, and the States Ministry favoured the idea. In November B. N. Rau was chosen to head the committee, which was to work in cooperation with the States Ministry, and by mid-March 1949 the committee's report was ready. The committee reported that its model constitution varied little, from that already framed for the provinces. The only major difference, in fact, was that the State legislatures were empowered to amend their constitution, whereas the provincial legislatures were denied constituent powers in relation to any of the provisions of the Indian Constitution.[62]

With the rapid pace of events, this plan, too, became outmoded. A conference of the prime ministers of the States and Unions of States with officials of the States Ministry decided on 19 May 1949 that constituent assemblies in the various States and Unions should not frame their own constitutions on the basis of the model prepared by Rau, but that a constitution for all the States and Unions should be included in a special chapter of the Constitution. Rau's model was

---

[61] *CAD* VII, 1, 42.

[62] The original members of this committee were: B. N. Rau, Munshi, P. Govinda Menon, and Dr. R. U. Singh. Under pressure from the convention of States Representatives in the Constituent Assembly, the following were added to the membership: Hanumanthaiya, R. Shankar, and C. C. Shah. See *Report of the Committee on a Model Constitution for Indian States and Unions*, dated about 21 March 1949; *Munshi papers*. See also letter from Y. S. Parmar to Munshi dated 8 December' 1948; ibid.

presumably to be used for this purpose. The legislatures of the States were to continue to have constituent powers under the arrangement, however, and even after that promulgation of the Constitution they were to be allowed to make recommendations for changes in the Constitution as it pertained to the States.

By October, this scheme had in turn become outdated. The Assembly adopted a new article (Article 238 of the Constitution), which applied, with certain minor exceptions, the constitution of the provinces to the States. This meant not only that both would have the same political institutions, but that the States would never get the exceptional constituent power once contemplated for them. Patel summed up the reasons behind this change. 'As . . . the States came closer to the Centre,' he said, 'it was realized that the idea of separate constitutions being framed for the different constituent units of the Indian Union was a legacy of the Rulers' polity and that in a people's polity there was no scope for variegated constitutional patterns.'[63]

During July and August 1949, the Assembly began taking the final steps towards extending the provisions of the Constitution as a whole to the States. In July, for example, the Secretariat of the Assembly, in co-operation with the States Ministry, circulated long lists of amendments to the Draft Constitution that had as their aim 'assimilating so far as possible the position of the Indian States to that of the Provinces'.[64] Most of the governments in the States and the majority of Assembly members by now supported this, but there remained one strong barrier: the States' fears of the economic consequences of integration. Accession to the Union had not cost the States their revenues, nor had the larger States and Unions lost their financial autonomy during the whittling away of their political authority. Faced with complete absorption into the Union, however, 'all were afraid that if they were to part with "federal" assets and sources of revenue without adequate "compensation", their progress would be arrested and they would continue for a long time as backward members of the Indian Union'.[65] To calm these fears by prescribing a just financial settlement, the Government established the Indian States Finances Enquiry Committee, with

---

[63] See *CAD* X, 5, 162–3.

[64] See two lists of amendments sent to members of the Drafting Committee on 19 July 1949; *Munshi papers*.

[65] Menon, *Integration*, pp. 456–7.

the doyen of the States representatives in the Assembly, V. T. Krishnamachari, as its chairman; one Congressman, S. K. Patil, and one member of the Indian Civil Service (I.C.S.), N. Dandekar, were its other members.

The committee's report was circulated on 14 August 1949. It argued that for the units to have different relations with the federation would be 'a source of weakness and . . . produce a sense of unfairness among the less favoured units . . . fatal to friendly relations and orderly progress'.[66] They suggested that the Union Government 'guarantee the whole amount of the loss' to the States resulting from their relinquishing to the Union customs duties and other revenue heads. And the committee recommended that:

> Union authority should be the same in the States and the provinces;
> the Union Government 'should exercise its functions in the States through its own administrative agencies as in the provinces', and
> the States 'should contribute to the finances of the Union on exactly the same basis as the provinces and receive grants and other forms of financial assistance on the same basis'.[67]

The Committee's report cleared the way for the final Stages of integration, and two months of furious activity ensued. Meeting on 31 August, the Steering Committee decided that a series of amendments to the Draft Constitution designed to bring the States wholly into the Union should be circulated among the State Governments by the States Ministry. If this could be done immediately, the Steering Committee hoped that the States' replies would reach the Assembly by 1 October, when all points of view would be considered and the issue finally settled.[68] It was late in September before the lists of amendments were prepared, but they were then flown to the various State capitals. Several governments accepted them immediately, others sent delegations to New Delhi to discuss them. Meanwhile, from 26 September to 9 October, officials of the States Ministry and States members in the Assembly discussed the recommendations of the States Finances Enquiry Committee. All these discussions proved successful. On 12 October, Dr. Ambedkar placed the amendments 'unionizing' the former Princely States before the Assembly. With

---

[66] *Report of the Indian States Finances Enquiry Committee*, Part I, para. 11, p. 8.
[67] Ibid., para. 14, p. 9.
[68] Minutes of the meeting, 31 August 1949; *Prasad papers*, File 2-S/48.

the exception of Article 371 giving the President general control over the governments of Part B States for ten years, the many amendments were passed with hardly a voice raised in dissent.

So far as the Assembly was concerned, the States issue came to its triumphant ending on 26 November 1949, the day the members signed the completed Constitution. On that day, Patel announced that the Constitution had been accepted by 'all nine States specified in Part B of the First Schedule of the Constitution, including the State of Hyderabad'.[69] Just over six years later, the States Reorganization Act came into effect. All references to Part B States were removed from the Constitution and the Princely States issue breathed its last. On that occasion, Indians might well have remembered Patel's words to the Constitutent Assembly: 'Unlike the scheme of 1935', he had said, 'our new Constitution is not an alliance between democracies and dynasties, but a real Union of the Indian people based on the basic concept of the sovereignty of the people.'[70] Indians had finally united India.

[69] *CAD* XI, 12, 983.
[70] *CAD* X, 5, 164.

11

Amendment—
The Flexible Federation

*One can therefore safely say that the Indian Federation will not Suffer
from the faults of rigidity or legalism. Its distinguishing feature is that it
is a flexible federation.*

B. R. Ambedkar

THE ease or difficulty with which a constitution may be amended has
come to be used by constitutional theorists as the primary measure of
its 'flexibility' or 'rigidity'. By this yardstick the Indian Constitution
during the decade and a half of its existence has proved very
flexible—in fact too flexible for the critics who charge that the
'sanctity' of the Constitution has been destroyed by the seventeen
amendments to it.[1] The consideration of flexibility should also take
into account the changes that can be wrought in a constitution by
custom and usage, without resorting to amendment. By this yardstick too, the Indian Constitution has proved flexible—as the effects
of national planning on the federal structure show.

The amending process, in fact, has proved itself one of the most
ably conceived aspects of the Constitution. Although it appears
complicated, it is merely diverse, providing three ways of ascend-
ing difficulty for altering the Constitution. Certain provisions of the
Constitution may be amended by a simple majority in Parliament and
others by a two thirds majority; amendments to a third category of
provisions must be ratified by one half the states. These mechanisms

---

[1] For two early views that the Indian Constitution was or would prove difficult to
amend, see Jennings, *Some Characteristics*, p. 10 and Max Beloff, *The American
Federal Government*, p. 16.

have worked smoothly—as demonstrated by the ease of amendment. The 'wise variety' of the amending process has been praised by Dr. Wheare, who has commented that it 'strikes a good balance' by protecting the rights of the states while leaving the remainder of the Constitution easy to amend.[2]

The Assembly's success is the more noteworthy in view of the members' lack of immediate experience—a Government of India Act could be changed only by Britons and only in Westminster—and in view of the small amount of time devoted to the issue. Whereas most provisions of the Constitution were born in committees, debated several times on the floor of the House, returned to committees for redrafting, and debated once again before being adopted, the amending article was almost entirely framed in committees. It was discussed in the Assembly—and then briefly—only several hours before being adopted. This was certainly the result of circumstance and not of design. Nor should it be concluded that the members or the leadership of the Assembly showed a cavalier attitude towards the matter. A more likely explanation of this ready agreement is that the blend of amending techniques commended itself as reasonably satisfactory both to those supporting easy amendment and to those members eager to protect the federal nature of the Constitution.

Of the three ways of amending the Constitution, two are laid down in the amending article itself and the third is provided for in at least twenty-two other articles.[3] The amending article (Article 368) provides that an amendment Bill can be introduced in either House of Parliament. If it is passed by a majority in each house with two thirds of the members present and voting, and has the assent of the President, it becomes an amendment. The stated exceptions to this procedure are the amending article itself and the articles dealing with the election of the President, the extent of the Executive power of the Union and the state governments, the Judiciary, the distribution of powers (including the Legislative Lists), and the representation of the states in Parliament. Amendments to these provisions must not only be passed by Parliament, in the manner just described, but

---

[2]   Wheare, *Modern Constitutions*, p. 143.
[3]   For a list of these articles, to which the author believes several more can be added, see Alexandrowicz, op. cit, p. 323.

need also to be ratified by the legislatures of one half of the states. Of the seventeen Amendment Acts to the Constitution adopted since 1950 nine have needed only Parliamentary approval, and eight have been ratified by the states.[4]

According to the third method of amendment, the Constitution can be changed by a simple majority vote in Parliament, followed by Presidential assent. Nearly two dozen articles of the Constitution thus provide for their own alteration, and the pattern is a standard one. Whatever the article establishes—e.g. the qualifications for citizenship, the salaries of Supreme or High Court Justices, the states that are to have bicameral legislatures—is to remain in force 'until Parliament otherwise provides'. Articles 1, 2, and 3 provide perhaps the most striking example of this aspect of the amending process. Article 1 lays down that India shall be a Union of States, and these states are named in the First Schedule. Yet by Articles 2 and 3, Parliament is empowered to establish new states, increase or decrease the area of any state, change the name of any state, alter its boundaries, or cause it to disappear entirely (as happened to Hyderabad) by merging it with other states. The efficacy of this form of amendment has been amply demonstrated by the reorganization of the states in 1956 and, in general, by the adjustability of the Constitution to the demand for the formation of linguistic provinces.

The three mechanisms of the amending process were a compromise worked out by the Drafting Committee, and were designed, as Dr. Ambedkar said when introducing the Draft Constitution, to achieve a flexible federation. The compromise was between a small group of Assembly members, who recommended the adoption of an amending process like that of the United States, and a somewhat larger group that advocated amendment of the entire Constitution, at least during an initial period, by a simple majority of Parliament. This group counted Nehru among its adherents.

The drafting of the amending process began in June 1947. The documents before the Union Constitution Committee when it began its meetings early in the month, advocated, in general, the more conservative approach to amendment. The draft

---

[4] Needing state ratification: Amendment Acts, Third, Sixth, Seventh, Eighth, Thirteenth, Fourteenth, Fifteenth, and Sixteenth.

constitutions of Munshi and K. T. Shah, Panikkar's and S. P. Mookerjee's answers to Rau's questionnaire, and Ayyar's and Ayyangar's joint memorandum on the Union Constitution, recommended that amendments should first be passed by a two-thirds majority in each house of Parliament and then be ratified by a like majority of provincial legislatures. Munshi would have reduced the number of ratifications needed to one half of the provinces, and Shah would have required, in addition to ratification, approval by a majority of the population in a referendum.[5] These recommendations largely ignored the amending process suggested in the Nehru and Sapru Reports. The Nehru Report had recommended amendment by Parliament. It was suggested that a Bill that passed through two readings and was passed at the Third Reading by two thirds of both Houses in a joint sitting could amend the constitution.[6] The Sapru Committee, in pursuit of communal harmony, had gone to the other extreme: only formal amendments could be enacted by the central legislature. For consequential amendments, six months notice had to be given. At the end of that period, the amendment Bill could be introduced in the legislature, and, if passed by a two-thirds majority and ratified by the same majority of provincial legislatures, it became an amendment. Certain vital provisions, which were to be listed in a schedule, were to be excluded from amendment for five years.[7]

In his memorandum on the Union Construction, B. N. Rau provided for amendment in two ways. He recommended the procedure favoured by Ayyar, Ayyangar, and the others—passage by a two-thirds majority in Parliament and ratification by a like majority of provincial legislatures. But in the Transitional Provisions of his memorandum he provided that Parliament, notwithstanding anything in the amending clause, could make 'adaptations and modifications' in the Constitution and could make temporary provisions for the removal of any difficulties that might arise when implementing it. He explained that such a 'removal-of-difficulties

---

[5]   See Munshi, *Draft Constitution*, op. cit, Article L, *Munshi papers*; Shah, *Draft Constitution*, *INA*; Panikkar and Mookerjee replies, op. cit., *Prasad papers*, File 3-C/47; and Ayyar and Ayyangar, memorandum, op. cit., *INA*.

[6]   *Nehru Report*, Clause 87, p. 123.

[7]   *Sapru Report*, Clause 20, p. xv.

clause is now quite usual' and that it was like Section 310 of the 1935 Act. He had made the clause effective for three years after the example of the Irish Constitution.[8] Although one cannot be sure, it appears that Rau was stretching the customary meaning of a removal-of-difficulties clause into a device for the easy amendment of the Constitution—the need for which he strongly believed. The grounds for thinking this are that the like provision in the Union Constitution Committee's report is nearly identical to that in Rau's memorandum with the additional sentence in the explanatory note that 'This clause will make the process of amendment comparatively easy during the first three years'.[9] Speaking about the UCC report, Munshi reinforced this point by pointing out that easy amendment for three years would allow Parliament 'to remedy short-comings in the Constitution resulting from the members working under pressure'.[10] In the Transitional Provisions of his Draft Constitution, Rau made this provision into two. The first gave the President the power to make adaptations in the Constitution in order to remove difficulties, but only until the first Parliament was convened. The second clause laid down that for three years from the commencement of the Constitution, Parliament could 'by Act amend this Constitution whether by way of variation, addition, or repeal'. Rau again noted that the provision was derived from Article 51 of the Irish Constitution.[11]

To return to the drafting of the amending clause, the Union Constitution Committee at first adopted the clause as Rau had recommended it. Several days later the committee decided that ratification of amendments need be by one half, and not two-thirds, of the provinces. Such was the amending process, along, with the clause in the Transitional Provisions, embodied by the UCC in its first report, dated 3 July 1947. There was dissatisfaction with this method of amendment, however, and a sub-committee was appointed to

---

[8] Rau, *India's Constitution*, p. 96. The reference was to Article 51 of the Irish Constitution. See also Rau's second 'Memorandum on The Union Constitution', dated 21 June 1947; *Prasad papers*, File 3-C/47. This embodied the UCC decisions to that date.

[9] UCC report. Part XI, para. 6; *Reports, First Series*, p. 62.

[10] *CAD* IV, 1, 546.

[11] Rau, *Draft Constitution*, of September 1947, Clause 238.

consider the matter further.[12] It met twice, on 11 and 12 July. At
the first meeting the members upheld the provision demanding
that amendments should be ratified by provincial legislatures, but
changed the provision concerning the majority needed: The sub-
committee recommended that amendments should be ratified by
legislatures representing one half the total population of the units,
including one third of the population of the Princely States.[13]

At the second meeting the amending clause was further modified,
and amendment made much easier. Foreshadowing the provision
that would ultimately appear in the Constitution, the sub-committee
decided that only changes in the Union Legislative list, the representation of the units in Parliament, and the powers of the Supreme
Court need be ratified by provincial legislatures; other provisions
could be amended simply by a two-thirds majority in Parliament.[14]
This decision was embodied in a supplementary report drafted by the
Union Constitution Committee the following day.[15] This overnight
change may have been due to Nehru's influence. He was not present
at the first meeting, but did attend the second. And Nehru, as we
shall see, favoured amendment by a simple majority in Parliament.
Moreover, it is likely that he was the only person present who was
strong enough to reverse the opinions of others in that fashion. At
neither meeting was the subject of the removal-of-difficulties clause
raised. It was allowed to stand, and the supplementary report of the
Union Constitution Committee did not refer to it.

The provisions for amendment as drafted by the Union Constitution
Committee were never debated by the Assembly. When they came
up for debate, they were held over. N. G. Ayyangar requested that
there be no debate on the clauses because the possibility of giving

[12] The members of the sub-committee were: Nehru, Prasad, N. G. Ayyangar,
Ambedkar, Munshi, V. T. Krishnamachari, Panikkar, Zaidi, Ayyar, and Pant.
B. N. Rau also attended the meetings.

[13] Minutes of the meeting, 11 July 1947; *INA*. This system of amendment could
have meant, for example, that, speaking only of provinces not of the States, a
constitutional amendment could be ratified by the legislatures of the United
Provinces, Bihar, and Bombay, over the opposition of the other six provinces,
for in these three provinces resided over half the population of provincial India.

[14] Minutes of the meeting, 12 July 1947; ibid.

[15] *Supplementary Report of the Union Constitution Committee*, dated 13 July
1947; *Reports, First Series*, pp. 68–9. Both UCC reports were presented in the
Constituent Assembly on 21 July.

provincial legislatures constituent powers over provincial constitutions was being considered.[16] This idea was soon dropped, however, presumably in view of the indescribable confusion that would have resulted had each province been allowed to modify the Constitution in its own way.

These were the happenings of July and August 1947. In late September, Rau completed his Draft Constitution. In the amending article of his draft he had followed the Union Constitution Committee's sub-committee. But he had added a proviso prohibiting for ten years, amendment to the clauses establishing reserved seats in the provincial legislatures and Parliament for Muslim, Sikhs, and other minorities—an addition apparently inspired by the Sapru Report.[17] There was also the method of easy amendment in the Transitional Provisions. In October Rau began his trip to Europe and the United States where he found support for his views on amendment. He reported to Prasad, who passed the information to the Drafting Committee and to the Assembly, that in his talks with justices and statesmen throughout his trip, 'the provision in Clause 238 was regarded as a wise precaution'.[18] President De Valera of Ireland told Rau that the three year period for parliamentary amendment 'was also far too short . . . he would suggest a period of not less than five years'.[19]

Yet the members of the Drafting Committee rejected such a provision in spite of Rau. The Transitional Provisions of the Draft Constitution did not provide for easy amendment, although the removal-of-difficulties clause was retained. The principle of amendment by a simple majority in Parliament had not been entirely cast aside, however; instead, it had been incorporated in a variety of articles that provided for their own amendment. Among these were Articles 1-3 concerning the creation of new states and the provisions laying down the salaries and other conditions of Supreme and High Court Justices. The Drafting Committee also somewhat changed the amending clause of Rau's Draft, reverting to the earlier version of the

16 CAD IV, 14, 979. The debate on the UCC report was closed in favour of a debate on the Advisory Committee's report. Due to this shortening of the debate, the Transitional Provision and the removal-of-difficulties clause were not taken up.
17 Rau, Draft Constitution, Clause 232, Part XIII.
18 Rau, India's Constitution, p. 303. This portion of Rau's report to Prasad was dated 24 November 1947; see original of report in Prasad papers, File 3-C/47.
19 Ibid., p.311.

Union Constitution Committee. Amendments requiring provincial ratification were to have the support of the legislatures of one half the provinces and one third of the former Princely States, and not the support of legislatures representing a majority of the population. The Drafting Committee further provided that changes in any of the Legislative Lists (instead of only the Union List) must be ratified by the provinces.[20]

The Drafting Committee kept Rau's provision prohibiting amendment of the articles reserving seats in the legislatures for minorities. This would remain in the Draft until it became inoperative in May 1949, when the minorities relinquished their claims for reservation. The amending article also envisaged granting provincial assemblies the power to legislate on the number of houses in their legislatures. This authority as we have seen, was removed from this article and embodied in what later became Article 169 of the Constitution.

Although the Drafting Committee had rejected amendment by a simple majority of Parliament, the principle continued to have supporters. Among them was Nehru, who submitted an amendment to the Draft by which for five years any provision of the Constitution, excepting the entrenched provisions, could be amended by Parliament.[21] Four other amendments had a similar intent, though several opposed this view. One would have raised the percentage of provinces needed to ratify an amendment to the Constitution from two-thirds to three-fourths. Another, submitted by V. T. Krishnamachari, the senior States representative in the Assembly, would have increased from one-third to one half the number of Princely States needed to ratify an amendment.[22]

B. N. Rau took the opportunity on two occasions during the summer of 1948 to reiterate his support for the cause that had apparently become largely his and Nehru's. In a letter to Prasad, written in June, he said that the remedy for difficult questions, like minority demands and the pressure for linguistic provinces, lay 'in making the Constitution flexible'. Therefore, he wrote, easy amendment during the early years should be made possible, and he

---

[20] *Draft Constitution*, Article 304.

[21] Amendment No. 3267, *Amendment Book II*, op. cit., p. 350.

[22] Amendment No. 3258, ibid., p. 349.

again cited De Valera's advice on the subject. We must avoid the anomaly, he continued, that a Constituent Assembly, not elected by adult suffrage, can draft a Constitution by simple majority, 'but a Parliament elected by adult suffrage cannot amend it except by special majorities followed, in some cases, by special ratification'. Rau concluded, associating himself with Nehru's amendment, that for five years the Constitution should be amended 'by the ordinary process of law-making'.[23] He repeated these arguments in an article published in *The Hindu* of 15 August 1948, the anniversary of independence. He called the amending process 'illogical' and said that the justification for easy amendment lay in the 'rapidly changing conditions' in India and the nation's economic and political 'state of flux'.[24]

Introducing the Draft Constitution to the Assembly in November 1948, Ambedkar explained in some detail the form and meaning of its federal system. He pointed to what he called the rigidity and legalism of the American and Australian federations and cited two methods that Australians had adopted to render their constitution more flexible. One of these was 'making some of the articles of the Constitution of a temporary duration to remain in force only 'until Parliament otherwise provides'. Following the Australian example, Ambedkar continued, there were 'as many as six articles in the Draft Constitution (actually there were more) where the provisions are of a temporary duration and which could be replaced by Parliament at any time by provisions suitable for the occasion'.[25]

Ambedkar, at the time, evidently considered such a mechanism a substitute for, rather than part of, the amending process, which he described as a second way of keeping the Constitution flexible. 'The second means adopted to avoid rigidity and legalism', he said, 'is the provision for facility with which the Constitution (can) be amended.'[26] He then went on to outline the dual mechanism of the amending process in Article 304—the amending article—and concluded with the statement, quoted at the head of this chapter, that India was to be a flexible federation.

---

[23] Letters of 17 June 1948; *Prasad papers.*
[24] Cited in Rau, *India's Constitution,* pp. 365–6.
[25] *CAD* VII, 1, 35.
[26] Ibid., p. 36.

Prime Minister Nehru was the only member to reply to Ambedkar during these initial speeches on the Draft. He told the Assembly that solid and permanent as the Constitution must be, it must also permit national growth. He argued that because the new Parliament would represent every adult in India, 'it is right that the House elected so . . . should have an easy opportunity to make such changes as it wants to'.[27] As the individual articles of the Draft were not being debated, Nehru did not move the amendment he had submitted. The amending process then disappeared from view for a second time, not to reappear until mid-September 1949. In drafting other provisions, however, the Assembly would increasingly use the device of the 'temporary' provision susceptible to change by Parliament.

The debate on the amending article took place on 17 September 1949 in the relative calm following the stormy controversies on the questions of compensation, preventive detention, and language that had occupied the previous weeks. Opening the debate, Ambedkar moved two amendments to Article 304, bringing them into the form that finally appeared in the Constitution. The amendments produced no substantial change other than increasing the categories of entrenched subjects somewhat beyond those named in the Draft as it had been first published.[28] Ambedkar reserved his right to speak, saying that he would answer later what he expected would be the 'considerable debate' on the issue. His estimation of the interest that would be shown was exaggerated, however; there were only eight speakers besides himself, and none of them were important members of the Assembly.

Six of the eight speakers believed that the Constitution should be much easier to amend, and proposed that for at least an initial period of three to five years amendment should be by simple

[27] CAD VII, 4,323.

[28] It is one of the many surprising aspects of constitution-making in India that entrenching the Fundamental Rights provision was apparently never seriously considered. During the debates on the Rights, the issue was not mentioned. During the passing of the amending process, only five members submitted amendments calling for the entrenchment of the Rights, and none of them bothered to defend their amendments on the floor of the Assembly. See Amendments 3256, 3257, and 3259, Amendment Book II, pp. 348–9. Three of those supporting these amendments were ranking members of the Assembly: R. R. Diwakar, Shankarrao Deo and Acharya Jugal Kishore.

majority. The grounds for demanding simple amendment were nearly always the same. 'We are conscious', said P. S. Deshmukh, ' . . . that there are many provisions which are likely to create difficulties when the Constitution actually starts functioning. . . . This Constitution is bound to be and will prove to be defective in many respects.' It would be better to change the Constitution, this member continued, than to risk 'the whole Constitution being rejected . . . by further Parliaments and their resorting to something much more drastic and radical.'[29]

H. V. Kamath, deploring—as did others—that Nehru had never moved his amendment, doubted the basic premise of the amending process. 'I understand', he said, 'that amendment is not to be taken lightly because the Constituent Assembly of any country is superior in constitutional status to any future Parliament of that country.' 'But', he added, 'the Constituent Assembly has been created by indirect election from communal electorates and from a very restricted franchise; hence, this Assembly cannot be deemed to be superior in constitutional status to a future Parliament.'[30] This argument was supported by Mahavir Tyagi, who called the Assembly's work a 'Congress Constitution',[31] and by others who said that the trying conditions of the framing period had doubtless produced provisions that in the days ahead would prove to have been ill-conceived. Naziruddin Ahmad and Jugal Kishore accepted Ambedkar's amendments and supported the adoption of the amending process as put forward by the Drafting Committee, but Kishore thought that there might be sufficient errors in the Constitution to warrant easy amendment for a few years. The one member who supported the amending process outright, R. K. Sidhwa, told the Assembly that the members were representative of the country and that therefore he preferred to abide by their decisions.

Replying, Ambedkar attacked each of the opposition views, and he laid great stress on the importance of the amending process in federal constitutions. He 'utterly repudiated' the argument that the Assembly, because of its indirect election, was unfit to frame a Constitution. 'The Constitution is a fundamental document', he

---

[29] *CAD* IX, 37, 1644–5.
[30] Ibid.
[31] Ibid., p. 1656.

said and 'utter chaos' would result if it could be amended by a simple parliamentary majority.[32] He again explained how the Drafting Committee had provided for amendment in this fashion in selected articles and that other provisions could be amended by a two-thirds majority in Parliament. As to the parts of the Constitution that demanded provincial ratification for amendment, Ambedkar told the Assembly, 'We cannot forget the fact that while we have in a large number of cases invaded provincial autonomy, we still intend, and have as a matter of fact seen to it, that the federal structure of the Constitution remains fundamentally unaltered.' To amend the provisions laying down the distribution of powers and of revenue 'without permitting the provinces or the States to have any voice', he said, 'is in my judgement altogether nullifying the fundamentals of the Constitution'.[33]

Nehru's silence during the debate, as well as that of other Assembly leaders, has never been explained. Perhaps he had changed his mind and had come to believe that the amending process was sufficiently easy in such cases as the language provisions and the creation of new states, and that the other mechanisms were necessary to inspire confidence in the permanence of the federal structure. If his silence indicates dissent, it is perhaps also a measure of the opposition facing him. Even if Nehru held to his earlier view, it is extremely doubtful if the members of provincial governments in the Assembly would have agreed to an amending process that would have put them at the mercy of the Union Parliament. At the conclusion of Ambedkar's rebuttal, the Assembly adopted the Drafting Committee's version of the article.

The provisions for amendment were quite evidently a compromise between the view that Parliament should be empowered to amend any part of the Constitution and the more traditional concept of amendment in federations. Yet why was the compromise between such disparate view-points reached with apparently so little difficulty? Primarily, it seems, because the members of the Constituent Assembly realized that their efforts were subject to error and that therefore, except where it was necessary to safeguard certain institutions (such as the Judiciary and the federal system), the

---

[32] Ibid., pp. 1662–3.
[33] Ibid., p. 1661.

Constitution should be easily amended. Moreover the members, in general, acknowledged the force behind the arguments for entrenchment and thought that as both views were reasonable, and because each was strongly supported, they should be accommodated. There was no necessary contradiction between easy and difficult amendment; the two techniques could be applied to separate parts of the Constitution. It must not be assumed, however, that by making parts of the Constitution relatively easy to amend, the Assembly favoured parliamentary sovereignty. The members believed that the Assembly had superior status and that its product should be the supreme law of the land.

The very successful functioning of each of the three mechanisms for amendment—due in part, to the existence of a virtual one-party system— may have surprised, as well as gratified, even the Founding Fathers. Yet the 'extraordinary diversity' of the amending process was designed to meet a variety of circumstances. By permitting efficient change in the Constitution, it has borne out Ambedkar's prediction that Indian-federalism would be flexible. And the amendments to the Constitution, if they do nothing more, according to Professor Alexandrowicz, 'testify . . . to the existence of a proper machinery of constitutional development'.[34]

---

[34] Alexandrowicz, op. cit., pp. 232–3.

12

Language and the Constitution—
The Half-Hearted Compromise

How shall we promote the unity of India and yet preserve the rich diversity of our inheritance?

Jawaharlal Nehru

WHAT India needed most was unity. What would most effectively unite her was a common language. But in India there were a dozen major regional languages—each written in a different script—and none of them was spoken by a majority of the population. Even Hindustani, defined in the broadest terms as a bazaar language comprised of Hindi, Urdu, Punjabi, and words from other Indian languages as well as English, was spoken by only approximately 45 per cent of the population.[1] The common tongue of India in 1946 was the language of the conqueror, English.

Yet the strong emotional appeal of a national language, of an Indian language for Indians, could not be denied. It was politically and psychologically necessary that the Assembly should find a solution to the problem despite the apparent impossibility of the task. Not only did the emotional void have to be filled, but, it was self-evident, Indians must be able to communicate with one another.

---

[1] The 1951 Census of India reported that nearly 150 million, or about 42 per cent of India claimed to have as their native tongue Eastern and Western Hindi, Urdu, Hindustani, and Punjabi, collectively known as Hindustani. India has also over 700 minor languages and dialects. See *Census of India*, 1951, Paper No. 1, pp. 2ff. Of the fourteen languages recognized by the Eighth Schedule of the Constitution, one, Kashmiri, is spoken by less than 100,000 people, and another, Sanskrit, is a dead language.

And the speakers of each of the regional languages were clamouring for recognition and status for their languages.

Faced with this situation, what were the members of the Constituent Assembly to do? What language should the Assembly designate as the means of communication between Indians generally, between provincial governments, between the provinces and the Union, and within the countrywide structure of the Union Government? Could any of the Indian languages be given precedence over the others? If so, which? And then, what would be the status of the other languages? If an Indian language was given special status, what would be the position of English?

The members of the Constituent Assembly did not attempt the impossible; they did not lay down in the language provisions of the Constitution that one language should be spoken over all India. Yet they could not avoid giving one of the regional languages special status, so they provided, not that there be a 'national' language, but, using a tactful euphemism, that Hindi should be the "official language of the Union'.[2] Hindi would also be used for inter-provincial communication. For an initial period of fifteen years, however, English was to continue to serve as the official language. After this time, Hindi would supplant English unless Parliament legislated otherwise; but English would be retained for use in the courts and for official texts after the expiration of the fifteen-year period and until Parliament otherwise legislated. The provincial governments were permitted to choose one of the regional languages, or English, for the conduct of their own affairs and the major regional languages were listed in a schedule to the Constitution. Finally, the members also attempted a definition of Hindi, and provided for language commissions to report on the language situation and on how to further the spread of the 'official language'.

The language provisions are thus a compromise. Although from the first Assembly members favoured adopting Hindi, or Hindustani, and finally decided this in near unanimity, they split into bitterly contending factions over the other issues. The central points of the controversy were the length of time English should continue to be used as the language of government and the status to be accorded

---

[2] The language provisions are to be found in the *Constitution*, Part XVII, and comprise Articles 343–51.

the other regional languages. A third major issue proved to be the definition of Hindi. A group of Hindi-speaking Assembly members from the provinces of North-central India, led by a hard-core of linguistic extremists, whom we shall call the Hindi-wallahs, constituted one faction.[3] This group believed that Hindi should be not only the 'national' language by virtue of an inherent superiority over other Indian languages, but that it should replace English for official Union purposes immediately or in a very short time. It also held that Hindi should soon replace English as the second language of the provinces. In opposition were the moderates, who believed that Hindi—which they defined much more broadly—might be declared the 'official' language of the Union because the largest number of Indians spoke it, but that it should be simply the first among equals, the other regional languages having national status. And the moderates demanded that English, as the *de facto* national language, should be replaced very, very slowly and cautiously. Nehru, joined by several other Assembly leaders, led this group. The other moderates came largely from South India, Bombay, and Bengal, areas where Hindi was not spoken and where English had been the only link between the speakers of the regional languages. But as the controversy grew hotter, a number of Hindi-speakers joined the ranks of the moderates.

The Assembly was not separated into such distinct factions in its early days. At first, the general sentiment in favour of an Indian national language blinded all concerned to the problems involved. But as the members framed the language provisions, they became aware of the difficulties and of their disagreements. Then the split began to grow slowly and steadily. The Hindi-wallahs, unremittingly militant, pressed their demands. The moderates retreated in an attempt to preserve national unity and peace within the Assembly. Doing so gained them nothing. And by August 1949 their resistance was hardening. They had realized that acceptance of the Hindi-wallahs' demands would lead to the destruction, not the creation, of unity. In August and September they rallied to a last-ditch defence against the final attacks of the extremists. As a result, the moderates preserved much of their position, but largely

---

[3] The *Concise Oxford Dictionary* defines 'wallah' as meaning a 'person or thing employed about or concerned with something, (a) man'. 'Wallah' is a common word in India: a 'Delhi-wallah' is a man from Delhi; a 'carpet-wallah' sells carpets;' a 'khabadi-wallah' is the old-clothes man.

in the negative form of exceptions to the overall intent of the language provisions, which bore the stamp of the Hindi-wallahs. Parliament, for example, could extend the use of English by an Act, but if it failed to do so Hindi was automatically to replace English in 1965. During the interim period the Union was to promote the spread of Hindi and the President could authorize its use by the Union in addition to English. The presence of Nehru as Prime Minister from 1950 to 1964 kept the hard core of Hindi speakers from using these provisions to force their language on the rest of the country. Nehru, supported by moderate opinion, also used the loopholes in the provision—e.g., that Parliament may provide for the use of English after fifteen years, etc.—to prevent the use of English from lapsing and to preserve national unify.

The Hindi-wallahs were ready to risk splitting the Assembly and the country in their unreasoning pursuit of uniformity. They thus denied the Assembly's belief in the concept of accommodation and in decision-making by consensus. Assembly members preferred to take decisions by consensus or by as near to unanimity as possible. Not only was this method deeply embedded in the Indian tradition, it was manifestly the most practical way to frame the Constitution. A system of government would not work effectively, Assembly members knew, if large segments of the population were opposed to it. Every attempt had to be made, therefore, to achieve the broadest possible agreement. The Hindi-wallahs, however, announced that they would impose Hindi on the country if they had a one-vote majority. To prevent this, the moderates went to great lengths to find a compromise. They ultimately acquiesced in the language provisions, although they were not happy with them, in the hope that they would provide a framework within which an amicable settlement could be reached. The moderates' fears that the extremists had not accepted the provisions in the spirit of consensus have, unfortunately, been borne out. Since 1950 the extremists have continued to scorn this spirit and have pursued their original aims on the basis of the letter of the Constitution, ignoring the intention of the compromise, which was to resolve the language issue without unduly harming the interests of any linguistic group.

According to the concept of accommodation, apparently incompatible principles can co-exist because they operate in different spheres, on different levels, and thus do not conflict.[4] The Hindi-wallahs, held that

---

[4] For a further discussion of consensus and accommodation, see Chapter 13.

the use of English was incompatible with India's independence and therefore Hindi must become the national language. They preached that multi-lingualism was incompatible with Indian unity and that for this reason, also, the nation should adopt Hindi. The moderates, however, did not consider the question as one of *either* English *or* Hindi. They believed that English and all the regional languages could be effectively utilized in their proper spheres, like liquids seeking their own levels. Hindi—broadly defined—might be given a special place because it was spoken by a relatively larger number of persons, but the use of English, they believed, was not incompatible with Indian nationalism. The extremists, although finally forced into a compromise by the resistance of the moderates, spurned accommodation as they had consensus. Theirs was a half-hearted compromise, and the issue of language thus remained a source of great danger to Indian unity.

Language assumed such surpassing importance in the Assembly because, like Fundamental Rights, it touched everyone. The power of the Executive or the Judiciary would rarely affect most individuals. Federalism was a question for politicians. But in a nation composed of linguistic minorities, where even provinces were not linguistically homogenous and there were, for example, Tamil enclaves existing in Oriya-speaking areas,[5] problems of language were an everyday affair. Language meant the issue of mother-tongue instruction in primary schools—an issue well known in every country where there are substantial minority groups —as well as the question of the medium of instruction in universities. The language of the Union and provincial civil services meant money and social status to the middle and upper classes, for the services were their primary source of prestigious employment. Politicians and administrators would be no less affected by the language provisions. The language issue was also made real because it involved the cultural and historical pride of the linguistic groups, and, in the case of Muslims and Sikhs particularly, religious sentiments. Finally, there was one aspect that proved to be especially important, affecting even Hindi-speakers themselves, namely, the definition of Hindi.

If Hindi became too narrowly defined by 'purifying' it of words derived from other Indian languages, particularly Urdu and English,

---

[5] Such enclaves were to a large extent removed and most states made more nearly unilingual by the States Reorganization of 1956.

and by coining modern technical and scientific terms on the basis of archaic Sanskrit roots, it would become the language of a learned coterie. Not only would everyday communication be impeded, but progress towards the social revolution would be greatly retarded, perhaps stopped. Nevertheless, the Hindi-wallahs made insistent attempts in this direction in the Assembly. This, as much as their efforts to eliminate English, brought the Assembly to the verge of a public split. It revealed the lengths to which the extremists' zealotry was leading them. In the end, the extremists succeeded in getting a partial expression of their view placed in the language provisions of the Constitution, which lay down that Hindi, for its vocabulary, must draw 'primarily on Sanskrit and secondarily on other languages'.[6] For their part, the moderates exacted a *quid pro quo* to the effect that Hindi must serve as an expression of the 'composite culture of India' and should assimilate 'the forms, style, and expressions used in Hindustani' and in the other major languages of India.[7] Neither faction believed in this compromise definition, either then or today. The Hindi-wallahs show no tendency towards broadening their views on Hindi, and the majority of Indians realize that to Sanskritize Hindi would make it the language of the few. This issue declined in importance, however, as the time came closer for Parliament to decide on the future status of English as the second official language of India.

The language issue in other major federations, such as Pakistan, Canada, and Switzerland, and in South Africa, despite its importance to the framing and working of their constitutions, cannot be compared in intricacy or dimensions with that faced by India. Although its language problem is an especially difficult one, Pakistan has, basically, only Bengali, Punjabi, and Urdu (little different in its spoken form from Punjabi) to contend with—Pushtu being spoken by only a very small minority and Sindhi, which is dying out, being much like Urdu. Because Urdu and Bengali speakers rarely learn each other's language, however, Pakistan uses English as the common language at the federal government level. Canada and South Africa also have only two languages, and compared with India, linguism is a small issue. Six million more persons speak Tamil, for example, than there are people in all Canada. Switzerland has three major languages, but they are spoken by a population of only six million in an area only

---

[6] *Constitution*, Article 351.
[7] Ibid.

slightly larger than Kerala, India's smallest state. In each of these countries it is possible for government officials and many citizens to speak each of the major languages. It was found possible, therefore, to give all the major languages the status of official languages either in the Constitution or in practice.[8] As such a solution obviously was out of the question in India, the Constituent Assembly had to find its own solution to the nation's most delicate problem.

The Assembly actually framed the language compromise during the six weeks from 1 August to 14 September 1949. The negotiations will be treated in the latter half of this chapter. The language issue appeared in the Assembly, however, within several days of its convening, and its roots reach back many years. It is to this background and to the development of the various aspects of the problem that the first portion of the chapter will be devoted.

From the Coming of Gandhi to the Constituent Assembly

Gandhi placed the language issue at the heart of the Independence Movement. 'It is my humble but firm opinion', he said in 1918, 'that unless we give Hindi its national status and the provincial languages their due place in the life of the people, all talk of Swaraj is useless.'[9] India must assert its real self if it was to regain its soul and thus truly become independent. It had lived too long 'under the spell of English' and as a result its people 'were steeped in ignorance'.[10]

---

[8] For comment on the language provisions of these constitutions, one may consult Callard, *Pakistan*; R. M. Dawson, *The Government of Canada*; E. H. Walton, *The Inner History of the National Convention of South Africa*; C. Hughes, *The Federal Constitution of Switzerland*; and texts of the various constitutions. It should be noted how far the Swiss were willing to go on the language issue for the sake of national unity. The language of the majority of the inhabitants of Switzerland is Swiss-German. Yet because the speakers of French, Italian, and Romanche would learn high-German in school, it has become a convention that high German and *not* Swiss-German must be spoken in the Federal Parliament. See Hughes, op. cit., p, 128.

[9] In a speech to the Hindi Sahitya Sammelan at Indore. Reproduced in Gandhi, *Thoughts on National Language*, p. 14. Gandhi, as we shall see, used the words Hindi and Hindustani at different times for several reasons, but he was always speaking of the same tongue, that is, broad Hindustani written in both the Urdu and Devanagri scripts.

[10] Ibid., p. 9.

Therefore English must no longer be used in legislatures and on public platforms. Two years later Gandhi asserted that 'as political knowledge and education grows, it will become more and more necessary to use a national language'.[11] Under Gandhi's urging the Congress changed to a mass movement in 1920, and the party went to the people in their own languages. The new constitution, adopted at Nagpur that year, formed the party into Provincial Congress Committees based on linguistic areas instead of—as had previously been the case—on the administrative boundaries of existing provinces. The new Provincial Congress Committees were encouraged to use the local language in their affairs. The Cocanada Congress of 1923 amended the party constitution, laying down that the proceedings of the annual sessions should be conducted as far as possible in Hindustani. Yet it proved impossible to avoid using English, and the party constitution provided that English and the provincial languages could also be used.[12]

The Nehru Report continued to support this policy. Its authors were 'strongly of the opinion that every effort should be made to make Hindustani the common language of the whole of India as it is today of half of it'.[13] As to the provincial languages, they were to be the instruments for achieving national democracy. Culture depends on language, said the report. 'It becomes essential therefore to conduct the business and politics of the country in a language which' is understood by the masses. So far as the provinces are concerned, this must be in the provincial language. . . . Provincial languages will have to be encouraged.'[14] But again English proved inescapable: the members of the Nehru Committee discussed their report, and wrote it, in English.

This pattern continued during the thirties and early forties. Purushottam Das Tandon wrote that 'India's real self must assert itself through her own languages.'[15] For Nehru, it was 'axiomatic

---

[11] From an article in *Young India*, 1920; ibid., p. 17.

[12] Chakrabarty and Bhattacharya, op. cit., p. 220. Azad later seemed to take the credit for the introduction of Hindustani into the Congress Constitution; see *CAD* IX, 34, 1454. Cocanada was in Madras at that time and is now in Andhra.

[13] *Nehru Report*, p. 62.

[14] Ibid.

[15] In an article contributed to Z. Ahmad, *National Language for India*, p. 93.

that the masses can only grow educationally and culturally through the medium of their own languages'. But he approached the question of the status of English more realistically and cautiously than some others. He wrote in 1937 that 'English will inevitably remain an important language for us because of our past associations and because of its present importance in the world.' But it was 'manifestly impossible' for English to serve as a common tongue in India 'if we think in terms of the masses'.[16] The general view of this formative period was well summed up by Z. Ahmad in 1941 in a book entitled *National Language for India*. 'All sensible persons', Ahmad wrote, 'are agreed that we have to forge a medium of thought and expression which can cement our common efforts and urges for the rehabilitation and development of our national life.'[17] Throughout these years, English remained the language of the Independence Movement, at least in its upper echelons. Little attention was paid to the details of the language question, and the exact position of English in independent India seems not to have been discussed, nor the status of the regional languages, nor other details that would confront the Constituent Assembly, such as the language of the courts, of Parliament, and of the Constitution itself. Even the difficulties that the choice of Hindustani as the national language would pose to North-South relations could be glossed over because the issue could not be put to the vital test of action. It was enough at this time to proclaim that Indians must speak an Indian language.

The Congress had made Hindustani, at least on paper, its official language.[18] Gandhi had hundreds of times said that Hindustani should be the national language, and Nehru said it was 'bound to become the all-India medium of communication'.[19] Why did the Congress choose Hindustani? What qualifications had it for a national role? What effect did the choice have on the non-Hindustani-speaking areas, and particularly on the South? What, indeed, did Hindustani mean?

---

[16] In 'The Question of Language', written in 1937. Included in Nehru, *The Unity of India*, pp. 243–4.

[17] Ahmad, op. cit., p. 7—Ahmad's Introduction to the compilation of articles.

[18] The Congress Constitution of 1934, 'for the first time in Congress and Indian history', prescribed Hindustani as the language of all Congress proceedings. See N. V. Rajkumar. *Development of the Congress Constitution*, p. 70.

[19] Nehru, *Unity of India*, pp. 20–21.

Hindustani meant what Gandhi said it meant and for him it was the language of the masses of North India.[20] Only four months before his death, Gandhi summed up his life-long views about Hindustani:

> This Hindustani (Gandhi wrote) should be neither Sanskritized Hindi nor Persianised Urdu but a happy combination of both. It should also freely admit words wherever necessary from the different regional languages and also assimilate words from foreign languages, provided that they can mix well and easily with our national language. Thus our national language must develop into a rich and powerful instrument capable of expressing the whole gamut of human thoughts and feelings. To confine oneself exclusively to Hindi or Urdu would be a crime against intelligence and the spirit of patriotism.[21]

Congress leaders, especially the Oligarchy, had long accepted this definition. And Rajgopalachari suggested broadening Hindustani even furthering by writing it in the regional scripts as well as in the Devanagri script of Hindi and the Persian-like Urdu script of Urdu.[22]

This choice of a simple bazaar language posed certain problems, however. Hindustani might be the language of the masses, but was it sufficiently developed to meet the needs of science, technology, and politics? Bengali and Tamil were much more developed and better met the needs of a modern state; yet even they were not wholly adequate to the task, and were far less widely spoken than Hindustani. Hence the problem. What language should be chosen: one less well developed, but more widely spoken, or *vice versa*? In pre-independence days this issue received little attention. For the Assembly, however, it was of major importance, particularly in the light of the Hindi-wallahs' campaign to purge Hindustani of Urdu and English—the major source of technical terms as well as many other words and phrases—and to substitute unknown, Sanskrit-derived words in their place.

The widespread use of Hindustani was what first attracted the Congress leadership to it. Gandhi claimed in 1928 that one hundred and twenty million persons spoke Hindustani and that eighty millions more understood it.[23] Nehru used the same figures in

---

[20] See, for example, his speech to the Hindi Sammelan at Indore in 1918; ibid, p. 10.

[21] From *Harijansevak* of 12 October 1947; see *Gandhi Thoughts*, p. 174;

[22] In an article included in Ahmad, op. cit, p. 201.

[23] Gandhi in *Young India*, 23 August 1928; cited in Gandhi, *Thoughts*, p. 30.

1937. These estimates, in the light of the 1931 Census, appear to be somewhat high, but nevertheless Hindustani-speakers outnumbered Tamil-speakers (twenty millions) six to one and Bengali-speakers (fifty-three millions, halved by Partition) by more than two to one.

The Congress leadership also chose Hindustani as the language of the Independence Movement because it bridged the widening gulf between Hindus and Muslims. Hindustani, as the leadership understood it, drew its vocabulary from both Sanskrit and Arabic-Persian roots. It could be written in either the Devanagri (Nagari) or Urdu scripts. Muslims, on one side, might be expected to use a more Persianized vocabulary and the Urdu script—which had religious overtones for them because of its relationship to Arabic, the holy language of the Koran. Hindus, would, in general, use the Nagari script and a more Sanskritized vocabulary both of which had links with Hindu scripture. This was commonly called the Hindi language. But except for the extremists on each side, North Indians shared the vernacular speech, and many intellectuals wrote in both scripts. Many Hindus, Nehru among them, considered Urdu their mother tongue. Hindustani provided a happy example of cultural synthesis sorely needed in an atmosphere of increasing communal tension.

Gandhi and Nehru emphasized time after time that only Hindustani could link the two communities. In 1945, for example, Gandhi wrote Purushottam Das Tandon that he intended to resign from the Hindi Sahitya Sammelan because it preached that only Hindi in the Nagari script could be the national language.[24] Tandon replied that he could not agree that all Indians should learn Urdu and Hindi and he believed instead that it was more important to oust English from its position and to convert the speakers of regional languages to Hindi.[25] Several days later Gandhi resigned, from the Sammelan saying, 'my definition of Rashtra Bhasha (national language) includes a knowledge of both Hindi and Urdu and both the Nagari and Urdu scripts. Only thus can a happy fusion of Hindi and Urdu take place.'[26] For his part, Nehru summed up the situation

---

[24] Gandhi to Tandon, 28 May 1945. See Gandhi, *Thoughts*, p. 133.
[25] Tandon to Gandhi, letters of 8 June and 11 July 1945; ibid., p. 134 and pp. 136–7.
[26] Gandhi to Tandon, 15 July 1945; ibid., p. 141.

thus: 'Scratch a separatist in language and you will invariably find that he is a communalist and very often a political reactionary.'[27]

The choice of Hindustani as the official language of the Congress and as the prospective national language affected North-South relations very little before independence—largely because the issue was not forced. But on one occasion in 1937 when Rajgopalachari, as premier of Madras, and P. Subbarayan, his education minister, introduced Hindustani as a compulsory subject in the first three forms of high schools, there was a violent reaction. For weeks afterwards, according to Subbarayan, he left his house to cries of 'Let Hindi die and let Tamil live. Let Subbarayan die and Rajgopalachari die.'[28] It was one of the unfortunate coincidences of Indian history that Hindustani was a northern language and that it was given special status by North Indians, like Nehru, Prasad, and Azad and by north-oriented Gujaratis like Gandhi and Patel, who held the balance of power in the Congress. These men were above choosing Hindustani because they were born to it or had adopted it, but nevertheless Hindustani became forever tarred with the brush of northern power in the party. And after independence politicians from the North would have little more success in spreading Hindi in the South than had party leaders in previous years.

Early Skirmishes in the Assembly

I. Through the Framing of the Draft Constitution

The language issue entered the Assembly through the door of the Rules Committee. The committee, under Prasad's chairmanship, decided on 14 December 1946 that in the Assembly business should be 'transacted in Hindustani (Hindi or Urdu) or English' and that, with the President's permission, a member could address the house in his mother-tongue. Records of the Assembly were to be kept in Hindustani (Hindi or Urdu) and English.[29] This rule remained

---

[27] Nehru, *Unity of India*, p. 248.

[28] *CAD* IX, 33,1401.

[29] Minutes of the meeting, 14 December 1946, in *Orders of the Day* for that date; *INA*. The rule in question was numbered 18 during the debate. It was number 30 in the first edition of the Rules, and was renumbered 29 in subsequent editions. For the membership of the Rules Committee, see Appendix II.

unchanged throughout the life of the Assembly. The Assembly debate on the draft rules, held 'in camera' on 22 December, demonstrated clearly how controversial was the continuance of English and the antagonism the subject could arouse between Hindi extremists and South Indians. The two principle amendments proposed to the rule on language bore the names of Seth Govind Das, a Hindi extremist from Mahakoshal in the Central Provinces, and K. Santhanam, a prominent Madrassi. Govind Das had moved that the language of the Assembly should be Hindustani and that anyone not able to speak it could use his mother-tongue or English. Speaking on his amendment, Govind Das said it was 'painful' that the Constituent Assembly of free India 'should try to make English its national language'. (Govind Das had expressed a common equation: whatever was designated the language of the Assembly or, later, of Parliament, equalled the national language.) He continued: 'I want to tell my brethren from Madras that if after twenty-five years of efforts on the part of Mahatma Gandhi they have not been able to understand Hindustani, the blame lies at their door. It is beyond our patience that because some of our brethren from Madras do not understand Hindustani, English should reign supreme in a Constituent Assembly . . . assembled to frame a Constitution for a free India.'[30]

Santhanam's amendment to the rules provided that all motions and amendments in the Assembly be tabled in English and that English should be spoken on the floor of the House whether or not the member knew Hindustani. Supporting his provision and replying to Govind Das's speech, Santhanam remarked that in time all India would learn Hindustani, but he doubted the ability of many persons to use it in technical discussions.[31] As if to emphasize Santhanam's point, A. K. Ayyar had requested that Govind Das's speech, which had been made in Hindustani, be translated into English for him. Prasad had agreed that the substance of the speech be translated because Ayyar was too old to learn Hindustani. Speaking after the closure motion, K. M. Munshi said that no one

[30] *CAD* I, 11, 233. This number of the CAD was kept confidential at the time—for other reasons than the rules debate, it seems, most likely because the budget of the Assembly was under discussion. It is now available in the Indian National Archives. For the texts of both Santhanam's and Govind Das's amendments, see *Orders of the Day*, 22 December 1946; *INA*.

[31] Ibid., p. 235.

doubted that Hindustani was the national language and that in the Assembly it would have precedence, but, said Munshi, English could not be omitted altogether.[32] The Assembly passed the rule relating to language unamended by a large majority.

Three months later, the language issue was again under discussion, this time in the Fundamental Rights Sub-Committee. At two meetings in late March 1947 the members debated the necessity of including a clause on language in the Rights. They decided in favour of a language clause 'in view of the peculiar conditions of this country'—meaning, primarily, the Hindu-Muslim conflict.

The clause read:

> Hindustani, written at the option of the citizen either in the Devnagari (sic) or the Persian script, shall, as the national language, be the first official language of the Union. English shall be the second official language for such period as the Union may by law determine.[33]

In their report to the Advisory Committee of 16 April, the Rights Sub-Committee members recommended this provision and, additionally, that the records of the Union be kept in Hindustani, in both scripts, and in English.[34]

The sub-committee's recommendation was not moderate enough for Masani and Mrs. Mehta. They submitted a minute of dissent reiterating their earlier suggestions that Roman be an optional script for the writing of Hindustani, along with Urdu and Nagari, in view of 'the lakhs of Indians . . . particularly in the South' who were not familiar with the two Northern scripts.[35]

The Advisory Committee considered the Rights Sub-Committee's report during the latter half of April. At the meeting of 22 April it postponed consideration of the language provision, and subsequently the clause was dropped from the Rights. This had been done, Patel informed the Assembly, because responsibility for the

---

[32] Ibid., p. 327.

[33] Minutes of the meetings, 24 and 25 March 1947; *Prasad papers*, File 1-F/47. Present when the decision was made were: Kripalani, Ayyar, Harnam Singh, Shah, Munshi, Kaur, Masani and Mrs. Mehta. Absent were Azad, Panikkar, Daulatram, and Ambedkar.

[34] See report of the Fundamental Rights Sub-Committee to the Advisory Committee, dated 16 April 1947; ibid.

[35] See their joint minute, dated 14 April 1947; *Prasad papers*. File 1-F/47.

matter had been assumed by the Union Constitution Committee.[36] Although this was in fact the case, it may have been equally true that the party leaders wished to preserve harmony and to avoid muddying the waters of the rights debate with so controversial a subject as language.

There is no evidence that the UCC devoted much time or thought to the language question beyond recommending in its report that the language of the Union Parliament should be Hindustani (Hindi or Urdu) and English, with the members permitted to use their mother-tongue if necessary. This provision descended directly from the Assembly Rules by way of Rau's memorandum on the Union Constitution. The Provincial Constitution Committee took up the question of language during the same period as the Union Constitution Committee. Its report recommended that in provincial legislatures business should be conducted in the provincial language, or languages, or in Hindustani or in English. Unexceptional as this provision appears, it was much more moderate than that suggested by Rau, who granted the provincial languages no status even in their own legislatures. According to his model Provincial Constitution, the languages were to be Hindustani or English.[37]

The opening of the fourth Assembly session on 14 July 1947 began a new phase in the language controversy. Meeting under the shadow of Partition, the Assembly witnessed a concerted attack, led by the Hindi-wallahs, on Hindustani, English, and the provincial languages. On the first day of the session, Patel introduced the report of the Provincial Constitution Committee. The next day the order paper carried five amendments that would have substituted 'Hindi' for Hindustani as an alternative language in provincial legislatures.[38]

[36] *CAD* V, 11, 361–2. See also Supplementary Report of the Advisory Committee on Fundamental Rights; *Reports, Second Series*, p. 47.

[37] See Rau, *India's Constitution*, pp. 147–8. There is reason to believe that Munshi shared this view, for he made a handwritten note to this effect in the margin of his suggested minority rights. See a draft of rights provisions dated 15 April 1947; *Munshi papers*.

[38] Amendments 92–95 and 98, *Orders of the Day*, 19 July 1947; *INA*. Moving these amendments were Balkrishna Sharma, Purushottam Das Tandon, H. V. Pataskar, D. P. Khaitan, who would later become a member of the Drafting Committee, and H. J. Khandekar. Others submitting strongly pro-Hindi amendments at this time were Guptanath Singh, R. V. Dhulekar, and S. L. Saksena.

That day and the next the order paper also carried amendments that would have prevented English from being spoken in the provincial legislatures; only the provincial language and Hindi could be used, according to these amendments. The evening of the third day the Congress Assembly Party took up the issue and there occurred 'the rare phenomenon of the Congress leaders and the rank and file being ranged in opposite camps and the leaders being heavily outvoted'. The meeting voted sixty-three to thirty-two that Hindi, not Hindustani 'should be the national language of India'. In a second vote, the meeting designated Nagari the national script by a majority of sixty-three to eighteen. English was favoured as a second language.[39] In the Assembly the following morning, Patel asked that the question of the language in provincial legislatures be held over.

Less than a week later this pattern recurred in regard to the UCC report. Several amendments by Hindi-wallahs would have changed the name of the language of Parliament from Hindustani to Hindi. Other amendments went much further, however, providing that Hindi should be the national language and Nagari the national script and that only Hindi might be used in Parliament,[40] that Hindi be the official language of the state but that English might be used for five or ten years, and that Hindi should be the national language but that English might be used in Parliament if Parliament so decided. There is no evidence that these amendments were discussed in the Assembly Party meeting, and the Assembly did not debate the provision in the UCC report naming Hindustani as the language of Parliament. Contrary to the National Convention of South Africa, which considered the language issue one that 'must be dealt with and settled satisfactorily before any real progress (in constitution-making) could be hoped for',[41] the Constituent Assembly was apparently postponing coming to grips with the problem in the belief that the enmities roused by debating it might endanger other aspects of the Assembly's work.

In the two months between the third and fourth sessions, the Assembly had passed a watershed in the language controversy.

---

[39] *The Hindustan Times*, 17 July 1947.

[40] Amendment 305, submitted by Seth Govind Das, List 2, *Orders of the Day*, 12 July 1947; *INA*.

[41] Walton, *Inner History*, p. 97.

This watershed was Partition. Partition killed Hindustani and endangered the position of English and the provincial languages in the Constitution. 'If there had been no Partition, Hindustani would without doubt have been the national language,' K. Santhanam believed, 'but the anger against the Muslims turned against Urdu.'[42] Assembly members 'felt that the Muslims having caused the division of the country, the whole issue of national language must be reviewed afresh', said an article in *The Hindustan Times*.[43] Having seen the dream of unity shattered by Partition, by the 'treachery' of the Urdu (Hindustani) speakers, the Hindi extremists became even more firmly committed to Hindi and to achieving national unity through it. Speakers of the provincial languages must learn Hindi and the regional languages must take second place, the Hindi-wallahs believed. And as to English, it should go as Urdu had gone. Were not both un-Indian?

Hindustani might have been eliminated as a term, but its spirit still lived. Gandhi, Nehru, and other members of the Assembly who had believed in Hindustani would in the future support 'broad' Hindi. Many would remember the words Gandhi had written just two weeks after the Assembly Party meeting had rejected Hindustani:

> The Congress has always kept a broad vision . . . The omens of today seem to point to the contrary. During the crisis the Congress must stand firm like a rock. It dare not give way on the question of the *lingua franca* for India. It cannot be Persianized Urdu or Sanskritized Hindi. It must be a beautiful blend of the two simple forms written in either script.[44]

When the Draft Constitution appeared in February 1948, it had no separate language provision, but it established that the language of Parliament was English or Hindi and that these languages could be used in the provincial legislatures as alternatives to the provincial languages. It is not clear why the members of the Drafting Committee changed Hindustani to Hindi without the official sanction of the Assembly. According to the committee's own version, it did so by a majority vote after being informed

---

[42] K. Santhanam in an interview with the author.

[43] *The Hindustan Times*, 17 July 1947.

[44] Gandhi in *Harijan*, 10 August 1947, but written on 31 July; Gandhi, *Thoughts*, p. 170.

by Munshi of 'the Congress Party's resolution for the changing of the words "Hindustani (Hindi or Urdu)" to "Hindi" '.[45] The resolution alluded to must have been that of the previous July. One presumes that the Oligarchy had agreed to the change, and that it again did so to postpone conflict. 'Hindustani became a bad word after Partition,' as one observer put it, 'and the party leaders were reluctant to divide the party over it.'[46]

2. Events of 1948

Nineteen forty-eight was a busy year for the Hindi-wallahs. They seemed at the beginning to hold views that a large number of Assembly members could support—sixty-three members had voted to replace Hindustani by Hindi. But by the end of the year many members had come to distrust their 'linguistic fanaticism'. Alienating their erstwhile followers was their attack on the provincial languages and on English, and their attempts to Sanskritize Hindi. The Hindi-wallahs made their views clear not only in amendments to the Draft Constitution but during the framing of the new Congress constitution and in their attempts to have the nation's Constitution adopted in Hindi as well as in English.

The Hindi extremists submitted twenty-nine amendments to the Draft Constitution between February and November 1948.[47] Some of these would have revised the articles concerning the language of Parliament and the legislatures; others would have added new language provisions to the Draft. Compressed into one provision, the amendments would have read somewhat like this:

---

[45] See comments by the Drafting Committee on amendments suggested to Article 99 of the Draft—written in March 1948, preparatory to the meeting of the Special Committee, in April; *Prasad papers,* File 1-M/48. The committee took the original decision on 10 December 1947; see minutes of the meeting, *Prasad papers*, File 1-D/47.

[46] K. Santhanam in an interview with the author.

[47] Sponsoring these provisions were several new figures on the language scene—G. S. Gupta, Dr. Raghuvira, Algurai Shastri, and B. A. Mandloi—as well as Govind Das, Tandon, S. L. Saksena, V. D. Tripathi, and Balkrishnu Sharma. Oddly absent was the name of Ravi Shankar Shukla, who, by the following summer, was to emerge as one of the most militant leaders of the group.

National Language

> Hindi (Bharati) shall be the national (official) language of India.
> Devangari shall be the national script of India.
> In provinces where Hindi is not spoken or Nagari used, the language to be used may be decided by the local legislature.
> Provinces may use English as a second official language so long as the legislatures so desire (or, in several amendments, for seven or five years only).
> English may be used as a second official language of the Indian Union for as long as Parliament may determine. (In a variety of amendments the use of English was to be limited to five or seven years.)
> In Parliament, business shall be transacted in Hindi in Nagari. But for as long as Parliament may prescribe, English may be used. (Or, in several versions English might be used for only five or seven years.)[48]

The members of the group who believed that English should not be used after a five- or seven-year period were Gupta, Govind Das, Saksena, and Tripathi.

To these amendments, there were counter-amendments. With the exceptions of two submitted by K. T. Shah and the venerable Sachchidananda Sinha (both supporting Hindustani), they came from Muslims and South Indians. The Muslims all supported Hindustani in both scripts as a national language, but ignored the problem of English. The South Indians were willing to use the term Hindi, but believed that the official language should be English for fifteen years, after which Hindi should be recognized as the official language and Hindi and English would be the language of Parliament.

The Congress's decision to redraft its constitution gave the Hindi-wallahs an opportunity to attack both Hindustani (and the spirit of broad Hindi) and the regional languages. In November 1947, the All-India Congress Committee appointed a new drafting committee, the drafts of several previous committees having proved unacceptable.[49] On 7 April 1948, the convenor of the committee sent a draft constitution prepared by the committee and an accompanying circular to all AICC members. The language provision of the draft, much as

---

[48] *See Amendment Book* I, pp. 19–25. See especially pp. 19–21: and 30.

[49] The members of the new committer were Sitaramayya, Tandon, Narenda Dev, Diwakar, S. K Paul, S. M. Ghose, and Jugal Kishore, convenor.

in the past, laid down that Hindustani in the Nagari script was the language of Congress proceedings, but that provincial languages or English could be used. In Provincial Congress Committee proceedings, the provincial language, Hindustani, or English could be used.[50] The draft also listed, in accordance with long practice, the names, headquarters-cities, and the languages of the various Provincial Congress Committees. For such PCC's as those of the United Provinces, Bihar, and Mahakoshal (Central Provinces) the language listed in the 1948 draft was Hindustani.

Tandon, however, objected to Hindustani being the language of Congress proceedings, Kishore explained in the circular letter; he wanted Hindi to be used. The tone of the letter indicated that the committee supported Hindustani. Discussing the draft later in April, the AICC meeting in Bombay passed over the language provision as too controversial. When the draft came before the Jaipur Congress in December—and was approved—all mention of language had been removed—even the list of regional languages used by the PCC's had been deleted. Evidently the high command had again temporized in the interests of party unity. Tandon's success in forcing Hindustani from its place of political birth (it had been named the language of Congress proceedings and placed in the 1920 constitution as a result of Gandhi's advocacy) was a blow to moderation. More than anything else, it was a reminder that a few months previously the greatest champion of linguistic moderation had been killed by a member of a Hindu communalist organization that detested Hindustani.[51]

The Congress presidential election of 1948 also played a part in the development of the language controversy, although the question of language was not directly involved, by embittering North-South relations. The election was to take place in October 1948, less than a month before the beginning of the seventh Assembly session, when Rajendra Prasad's year of office expired. Who should replace him? Pattabhi Sitaramayya, a Telegu-speaker from Madras province, very much wanted to do so, and he believed that he had the support of the South. The other major candidate was Purushottam

[50] Article XXVI of the Draft Congress Constitution. Sent under cover of Congress Circular Letter of 7 April 1948; *Prasad papers*, File 3-A/48.

[51] The RSS. See, for example, articles printed in *Organizer* in 1947–8, which was the publication of the Rashtriya Swayamsevak Sangh (the RSS).

Das Tandon. It is doubtful if Tandon decided to stand for the presidency because of the language issue; ideological conflicts and the desire for greater power in the party were more important. But Tandon may have decided to remain a candidate—instead of withdrawing his name as Prasad requested—in part to uphold his views on language. Certainly, many opposed him on language grounds. In any case a contest between a northerner and a southerner at this time was bound to have linguistic overtones. Prasad, for example, did not like the prospect of an election in which Sitaramayya would be opposed by a candidate from the North. 'I have a feeling', he wrote, 'that the sentiments of South Indians that they do not get full recognition in the Congress deserves consideration . . . I think that a contest against Dr. Pattabhi, who is the only candidate from the South, will assume the form of a contest between the North and the West on the one hand and the South on the other, and I think it would be a most unfortunate thing to have that kind of contest.'[52] Despite all efforts to get him to do so, Tandon refused to withdraw so that Sitaramayya might be elected unanimously. In the election Sitaramayya won by a small majority. And although it was not a central issue, the question of language, according to *Harijan's* post-mortem on the election, affected the vote.[53]

The efforts of the Hindi-extremists to have the Constitution adopted in a Hindi version produced resentment among both southerners, who could not speak Hindi, and among Hindi-speakers who found that the Hindi versions had been so Sankritized as to make them unintelligible. Vernacular versions of the Constitution were not only feasible but necessary if the general public was to understand its government. A Sankritized translation, however, would not only be unintelligible except to a tiny group of the initiate, but it was doubtful if a Sankritized Constitution could be superimposed on the base of Parliamentary government and the British common-law tradition to which the nation was accustomed and which Assembly members wanted to retain. Having become aware of these obstacles, the Assembly framed and adopted

---

[52] Prasad to P. C. Ghosh, 1 October 1948; *Prasad papers.* File 1-A/48.
[53] *Harijan*, 7 November 1948.

the Constitution in English. There is today no version of the Constitution with legal standing in any Indian language.[54]

The possibility of framing it in the national language had been considered as early as January 1947. The matter first achieved prominence, however, in early May that year when Prasad asked in the Assembly (of no one in particular) if India 'forever in future' should have a constitution in English and have to rely on English-speaking judges to interpret it. Perhaps, he suggested, 'we could have a translation made of this Constitution as it is drafted as soon as possible, and ultimately adopt that as our original Constitution. (Cheers.)'[55] Prasad pursued the idea through the summer, apparently thinking in terms of only a Hindi translation. On 1 November 1947, the Hindi translation committee met for the first time with Prasad present. Later Hindustani and Urdu committees would be created.

The two chief members of the Hindi committee were G. S. Gupta and Dr. Raghuvira. Gupta was the Speaker of the Legislative Assembly in the Central Provinces and a Hindi purist who opposed the incorporation of international political and legal terms into Hindi. New words should be coined from a Sanskrit base, he believed.[56] Raghuvira, a Punjabi from Lahore residing in Nagpur, was the author of *The Great English-Indian Dictionary.* He opposed taking 'Hindustani people' on to the Hindi translation committee.[57] In the autumn of 1947, neither Gupta nor Raghuvira were Assembly members. They believed that they should be, apparently the better to pursue their aim of a Hindi constitution, and succeeded in getting themselves seats with the

[54] In an only slightly similar situation, South Africa had chosen an English original version for its Constitution, instead of versions in Dutch and English, which would have conflicted. See Walton, op. cit., pp. 108ff. The Burmese, however, have made both English and Burmese language versions of the Constitution 'authentic' versions, and in cases where the meaning is in doubt, both versions are consulted. See Maung Maung, *Burma's Constitution,* pp. 206–7.

[55] *CAD* III, 5, 533–4.

[56] Gupta expressed these views many times. See, for example, Government of India, *Verbatim Record of the Educational Conference,* 16–18 January 1948, pp. 62–65.

[57] Raghuvira to C. Sharan, private secretary to Prasad, in a letter dated 7 October 1947. Raghuvira was almost demanding that he be made a member of the Hindi committee. *Prasad papers,* File I-H/47-8-9.

aid of Ravi Shankar Shukla, the prime minister of the Central Provinces, who also was a Hindi extremist.

By the summer of 1948, the Hindi translation, as well as the Urdu and Hindustani translations, had been completed. Nehru saw a copy and wrote to Prasad 'that he did not understand a word of it'.[58] Sanskritization, as even Hindi speakers later charged, had made the translation incomprehensible. Continuing his campaign, Gupta sent a resolution to the Steering Committee saying that because English 'cannot and must not' long remain the language of India, the Constitution should be framed in Hindi 'side by side' with English. For five years English would be recognized as the authoritative version and then it would yield to the Hindi.[59] S. L. Saksena took this a step further, recommending that the English and Hindi versions be framed jointly and that the Hindi version passed by the Assembly should be considered the original version of the Constitution.[60] The Steering Committee decided that the resolutions should be held over until the Assembly had considered the provision on the language of Parliament.

The views of the Hindi-wallahs, or at least one section of them, were also made brutally plain in three recommendations by a committee of the C.P. and Berar Legislative Assembly. Headed by Ravi Shankar Shukla, the premier, and with G. S. Gupta as one of its members, the committee recommended that the official language of the Union should be Hindi and Nagari with English optional during a transitional period, that a knowledge of Hindi should be mandatory for entrants into the Union Public Service (and Hindi-speaking entrants should know a provincial language), and that the Constitution should be framed in Hindi. Elucidating these basic tenets, the committee said that the grace period for English should be five years and that Hindi's source of 'learned terms . . . can only be Sanskrit'. The committee did not recognize Urdu as an Indian script and said of Hindustani: 'Hindustani by itself is no language . . . As a vehicle of learned thought it is non-existent . . . The highest dictates

---

[58] Related by Prasad to G. S, Gupta in a letter, 29 June 1948; ibid.

[59] Agenda for Steering Committee meeting of 25 October 1948; *Munshi papers*. When Hindi became the authorized version, the English version would remain 'valid', said Gupta.

[60] See agenda for Steering Committee meeting of 10 November 1948; *Munshi papers*.

of nationalism require that our terms of any technical value must be based on Sanskrit. This way lies the linguistic unity of India.'[61] These recommendations were printed on 22 October 1948 and copies were forwarded by Gupta to all members of the Constituent Assembly. When the Assembly reconvened on 4 November, the effect of the Hindi-wallahs' activities became evident. Speakers referred to the intolerance, thoughtlessness, and fanaticism of the Hindi campaign. It was 'no use repeating *ad nauseam*', one member said, 'the new dictum that independence will be meaningless if we all do not start talking in Hindi or conducting official business in Hindi from tomorrow'.[62] G. G. S. Musafir, who favoured framing the Constitution in Hindi, accused the Hindi-wallahs of Sanskritizing the language and called for the use of simple words that everyone could understand. Two speeches sum up the adverse reaction to the extremists. T. T. Krishnamachari of Madras told the Assembly:

> I would, Sir, convey a warning on behalf of the people of the South for the reason that there are already elements in South India who want separation and it is up to us to tax the maximum strength we have to keeping those elements down, and my honourable friends in U.P. do not help us in any way by flogging their idea 'Hindi-Imperialism' to the maximum extent possible.[63]

L. K. Maitra of Bengal warned the Hindi-wallahs 'not in their over-zealousness (to) mar their own case'. He continued:

> This is a sort of fanaticism, this is linguistic fanaticism, which if allowed to grow and develop will ultimately defeat the very object they have in view. I therefore plead to them for a little patience and forbearance towards those who, for the time being, cannot speak the language of the North.[64]

The battle over language was not to be joined at this time, however. Assembly leaders, desirous of a just and lasting solution to the controversy, refused to permit debate. Neither consensus nor accommodation could be achieved in the heat of the moment. Prasad told the Assembly that, for the very reasons the extremists wanted immediate

---

[61] *Report of the Committee of the Whole*, dated 18 October 1948, op. cit., *INA*.
[62] *CAD* VII, 2, 249; L. K. Maitra.
[63] Ibid., p. 235.
[64] Ibid., p. 249.

discussion of the language issue, he intended to delay it and to turn to other aspects of the Draft. 'I suggest', he said, 'that it is much better to discuss at any rate the fundamentals of the Constitution in a calm atmosphere before our tempers get frayed.'[65] Nehru agreed that debate on language at that time might delay completion of the Constitution. 'Urgency may ill serve our purposes', he counselled. And he warned the Assembly to seek consensus. 'If we proceed in an urgent matter to impose something, maybe by a majority, on an unwilling minority in parts of the country, or even in this House, we do not really succeed in what we have started to achieve.'[66]

At least half the Assembly were against the Hindi-wallahs, who nevertheless were prepared to ignore the major concepts of consensus and accommodation in order to force their will upon the Assembly and the nation. Their intolerance and cohesiveness never faltered. What were the bonds or similarities of background, if any, that impelled these extremists to pursue this course in concert? They all were, of course, Hindi speakers. Although three of the group (Tandon among them) had attended Christian mission schools, which might have increased their dislike of English and its alien culture, the majority had received a university education at the famous Hindu institutions of Allahabad and Benares. None had been educated outside India or outside Hindi areas. Few of these men, if any, could be called orthodox Hindus: they would dine with Muslims, for example. But several were revivalists—Balkrishna Sharma, Tandon, Govind Das—and envisaged the new India in terms of the glories of ancient Hindu kingdoms. Tandon also led the opposition to the Hindu Code Bill. G. S. Gupta had for many years been a member of the fundamentalist Arya Samaj. And Dr. Raghuvira ran for Parliament in 1962 on the ticket of the communalist Jan Sangh Party. Others among the extremists, however, like Algurai Shastri, V. D. Tripathi, and S. L. Saxena were quite secular in outlook and had socialist political views. Although each of these men would have claimed that he was not anti-Muslim, there can be little doubt that their attitudes were at least tinged with communalism. There would be little other reason to attempt to purge Hindustani of words of Arabic and Persian origin. Only on the language question did these men act as a group, so presumably religious conservatism

[65] *CAD* VII, 1, 21.
[66] *CAD* VII, 4, 321.

was not the unifying force—although such sentiments must not be entirely discounted. The extremists' attitude towards English and the regional languages supported this view. The principal motive, then, was apparently a narrow nationalism generating its own fervour and tolerating no deviation from its own vision of what was truly Indian.

3. Events of 1949, January to August

The language controversy continued to develop along these lines in 1949. Outside the Assembly groups like the Socialists called for the gradual introduction of a national language, and this was to be 'simple Hindustani using one script only'.[67] The Hindi extremists conducted themselves in such a way that Nehru condemned the 'narrow-minded', near-communal tone of the controversy. 'Everybody knows', he said, 'that obviously Hindi is the most powerful language of India . . . But it is the misfortune of Hindi that it has collected round it some advocates who continually do tremendous injury to its cause by advocating it in a wrong way.'[68] The question of a Hindi Constitution continued to agitate the Assembly during the first half of the year. Most important as background to the events of August and September was the steadily increasing assertiveness of regional language speakers, not only towards the Hindi extremists, but often towards each other. This spirit was manifest particularly in multilingual areas and in the field of education.

The 'original version' question was re-opened in January and, as spring arrived, it developed into a contest between Prasad and Nehru. Nehru agreed that the Constitution should be translated, but he favoured having this done by experts and not Assembly members,[69] and he continued to oppose adopting the Constitution in a Hindi version. On 5 January 1949, apparently inflicting a defeat on the Hindi-wallahs, the Steering Committee empowered Prasad to appoint an expert committee to prepare a translation that would 'as far as possible be precise and easily understood by the common

---

[67] Socialist Party, *Resolutions of the 7th Annual Socialist Party Conference*, March 1949, p. 25.

[68] At a ceremony at the Central Institute of Education, New Delhi, 18 April 1949; *Charka*, May 1949.

[69] Munshi in a letter to Satyanarayan Sinha, the Chief Whip, 2 January 1949; *Munshi papers*.

man'.[70] Prasad, however, still argued in support of a Hindi original version, although he was willing to have the Constitution passed also in English and the English version would be the authoritative one for an initial period.

Prasad pressed his view in a series of letters and memoranda. He wrote to the secretary of the Assembly on 4 June that the Assembly should appoint a committee to examine the expert committee's translation so that the Assembly might pass it. The Hindi version could then, after fifteen years, 'become the authoritative version of the Constitution'.[71] On the same day, he wrote to Nehru that when the Assembly's committee had examined the translation, he proposed to ask the House to set aside a day a week to pass it article by article. After ten to fifteen years, wrote Prasad, the Hindi version would become 'crystallized', the language of the Union would 'become more and more Hindi or Hindustani, and people from the South will get an opportunity of adjusting themselves'. To support his arguments, Prasad cited the precedent of the Irish Constitution.[72]

Nehru's reply to Prasad's manoeuvres throughout the spring had been that the Constitution might be translated, then an Assembly committee could examine the translation, and even that it could be accepted as 'an original text'.[73] He rejected Prasad's other views. Consideration of the Hindi version in the Assembly, he believed, would 'give rise to fierce argument at every step and on almost every word. It will thus tend to raise passions which will be reflected in the consideration of the English version and delay matters there.'[74] The English version of the Constitution must inevitably be authoritative, Nehru told Prasad—although 'many years after' a Hindi version might have equal or greater authority. As to the Irish experience, he had discussed it with De Valera and had been informed that the Irish had found Gaelic 'hard going' and were reverting more and more to

---

[70] Minutes of the meeting, 5 January 1949; *Munshi papers*. Present at this meeting were: Patel, Satyanarayan Sinha, M. A. Ayyangar, Durgabai, P. G. Menon, Nalavade, J. N. Lal, and S. M. Ghose. There by special invitation were: Nehru, Pant, Ambedkar, Kher, and B. G. Reddi.

[71] Prasad to H. V. R. Iengar, 4 June 1949; *Law Ministry Archives*.

[72] Prasad to Nehru, 4 June 1949; *Prasad papers*, File RP-5/49.

[73] Nehru to Prasad, 24 May 1949; ibid.

[74] Nehru to Prasad, 5 June 1949; ibid.

English.[75] Despite Nehru's opposition, Prasad placed his ideas before the Steering Committee meeting of 10 June 1949. The committee, no doubt wisely, decided that 'no decision should be taken at this stage'.[76] The issue never again assumed serious proportions in the Assembly.

Prasad's adamant stand on translation presents an odd contrast to his moderation on other aspects of the language issue. Sensitive to the feelings of both Muslims and other Hindustani speakers, he had advocated first Hindustani and then broad, inclusive Hindi. He had, it is true, said that technical terms could be drawn from Sanskrit, but he had not objected to the incorporation of English words. Aware of the belief among South Indians that they occupied an inferior position in the Congress, he helped Pattabhi Sitaramayya gain the presidency of the party. He had supported the use of English as the language of the Constituent Assembly. Yet his efforts to have the Constitution adopted in either an authoritative or an original Hindi version directly opposed the interests of non-Hindi speakers. The reason he pursued this course so strongly was apparently that he believed, like Gandhi, whose thought he understood so well, that Indians would not be truly independent so long as they relied upon English.

The agitation over the national language quite obviously involved the status of the regional languages in relation to Hindi. Long before this became a burning question in the Constituent Assembly, however, language in multilingual areas and in education—issues that themselves overlapped—had been a source of conflict involving the pride of the various linguistic groups. In the closing months of the Assembly the resurgence of these sub-issues fueled the fires of the central controversy.

India, as has been pointed out, was a land of linguistic minorities where no one language was spoken by a majority of the population and where there were not only true linguistic minorities but also relative minorities—groups of speakers of one of the more important languages living in enclaves controlled by the speakers of other major languages. This was one of the basic facts of Indian political life, and, recognizing it as such, the Congress laid down in the 'Karachi Rights' of 1931 that 'the culture, language, and scripts of the minorities and

[75] Ibid.
[76] Minutes of the meeting, 10 June 1949; *Munshi papers*.

of the different linguistic areas should be protected'.[77] In 1938 a committee of the Central Advisory Board of Education supported one of the perpetual demands of linguistic minorities by espousing the principle of mother-tongue instruction in primary schools, and official support for this, and for the use of mother-tongue instruction at higher educational levels, increased during the years 1940–45.[78]

The Congress Experts Committee in the summer of 1946 suggested that the Constitution should protect linguistic minorities by providing that the members of a group not speaking the language of their area should not be restricted in developing their language and culture and that, in areas where a considerable proportion of the population used a language other than the provincial language, public authority must provide facilities for mother-tongue education.[79] Munshi recommended a similar provision to the Minorities Sub-Committee of the Advisory Committee in mid-April 1947. Neither suggestion was accepted. Instead, the Advisory Committee drafted a set of provisions that, generally speaking, provided that minorities should have the right to conserve their language, script, and culture; that no minority could be discriminated against on language grounds in regard to entrance into state educational institutions; that minorities could establish and maintain their own educational institutions; and that, when providing aid for schools, the state could not discriminate against schools maintained by language minorities.[80] To ensure that all types of minorities were protected by these rights, including speakers of major languages residing in an area where another major language was spoken, special phraseology was used.[81]

---

[77] See Chakrabarty and Bhattacharya, op. cit., p. 28. Nehru wrote in 1937 that state education should be given in the language of the student and that minority groups of sufficient size could demand education in their own language. See 'Question of Language', in Nehru, *Unity of India*, p. 256.

[78] See for the period, Government of India, *Reports and Proceedings of the Central Advisory Board of Education.*

[79] See draft fundamental rights prepared by the Experts Committee; *Prasad papers,* File 16-P/4 5-6-7.

[80] See Advisory Committee report, *Reports, First Series,* p. 33; also *CAD* V, 11, 365–71; also the *Constitution,* Arts. 29–30.

[81] Instead of using an earlier form 'Minorities in every Unit shall be protected' relative to language, etc., Ambedkar chose 'Any section of citizens residing in the territory of India or any part thereof having a distinct language . . .' shall, etc. The purpose of the change, Ambedkar explained, was to include

These were negative rights: neither the state nor society should prevent a minority from using its own language. But had linguistic minorities any positive rights in the educational field? Munshi and Ambedkar held that they did not. Explaining the minority provisions, Munshi said:

> This minority right is intended to prevent majority controlled legislatures from favouring their own community to the exclusion of other communities. ... Is it suggested that the State should be at liberty to endow schools for minorities? Then it will come to this, that the minority will be a favoured section of the public. This destroys the very basis of a fundamental right.[82]

Ambedkar agreed that the provisions cast 'no burden upon the State'. But he believed that the state had a moral, if not a political, obligation to linguistic minorities. He held that because the state was not prohibited from legislating on such matters, provided the legislation was not oppressive, and because mother-tongue education was 'such a universal principle', no provincial government could justifiably abrogate the principle 'without damage to a considerable part of the population in the matter of its educational rights'.[83] By the time Ambedkar made this speech in the Assembly (8 December 1948), these views had already been expressed in a policy statement by the Union Government. Mother-tongue instruction for children, said a Government resolution, was an accepted principle. And to achieve this, as well as administrative efficiency, the resolution continued, most provinces must be, to some degree multilingual. Provincial governments must not force linguistic conformity on minorities.[84]

These principles were severely tested by a variety of conflicts during the autumn of 1948 and in 1949, conflicts that had a direct bearing on the language issue in the Assembly. In Oriya-speaking Orissa, for example, the large Telegu-speaking minority in Ganjam and Koraput districts charged that although both Oriya and Telegu

---

groups which 'although not minorities in the technical sense, (were) cultural minorities'—meaning Tamil-speaking Madrassis living in Bombay, for example. *CAD* VII, 22, 922.

[82] *CAD* V, 11, 367.

[83] *CAD* VII, 22, 923.

[84] Government of India, Ministry of Education, *Resolution Number* D.3791/48—D.I., dated 3 August 1948.

were recognized languages, Oriya-speaking court officers were refusing to accept documents written in Telegu. In the Manbhum district of Bihar, the large Bengali-speaking minority claimed that Hindi was being used to the detriment of Bengali in schools.[85] In the Central Provinces, Nagpur University announced its intention to make Hindi the compulsory medium of instruction, starting in the autumn of 1949,[86] even though it was in a largely bilingual province and in a division of the province where Marathi speakers outnumbered Hindi speakers two to one.

To try to meet these and like situations, the Congress Working Committee drafted the well-known Resolution on Bilingual Areas, which was published on 5 August 1949. The resolution, although as the name suggests devoted primarily to problems in multilingual areas, also tried to weave together into a coherent—and conciliatory—policy statement the party's ideas on the issue of language generally. A further reason for publishing the resolution was to dampen the linguistic provinces agitation. The leaders of the major language groups were demanding that the problems of multilingual areas should be solved by territorial readjustment. But the Working Committee had no intention, at this time at least, of approaching the problem in this way. Pressed on the issue, it had, therefore, to suggest a positive alternative.

The resolution, largely drafted by Prasad,[87] laid down that certain 'principles' might be applied to the various aspects of the language controversy. For example, each province should choose its own language, which should be used in the courts and for administrative purposes and as the medium of instruction at all educational levels.

---

[85] See note by the Working Committee, approximate date 20 May 1949, and memorandum prepared for the W.C. by P. Mishra and P. C. Ghosh, 7 June 1949; Prasad papers, File4-A/49.

[86] Government of India, Ministry of Education, *Report of the Committee on the Medium of Instruction at the University Stage*, p. 3. Report published November 1948.

[87] Minutes of the Working Committee meeting, 31 July 1949; *Prasad papers*, File 4-A/49. Present during the drafting of the resolution were: Sitaramayya, Prasad, Patel, Azad, Nehru, Pant, P. C. Ghosh, Kamaraj Nadar, Deo, Ram Sahai, Patil, Pratap Singh, Debeshwar Sharma, Sucheta Kripalani, K. V. Rao, and Nijalingappa. Eight of the group were Hindi speakers. The native tongue of the other members were: Patel, Gujarati; Ghosh, Bengali; Patil and Deo, Marathi; Rao and Sitaramayya, Telegu; Nijalingappa, Kannada; Kamaraj, Tamil.

Bi-lingual areas were the only exceptions to this. In these 'fringe' areas, if the minority was 'of a considerable size, i.e. 20 per cent of the population', public documents should be in both languages.[88] This was followed by other recommendations regarding education at various levels.

On the subject of the national language, the resolution laid down that there should be 'a State language in which the business of the Union will be conducted'. And, the resolution continued, the State language will be the language of correspondence with the Provincial and State Governments. All records of the Centre will be kept and maintained in that language. It will also serve as the language for inter-Provincial and inter-State commerce and correspondence. During a period of transition, which shall not exceed fifteen years, English may be used at the Centre and for inter-Provincial affairs provided that the State language will be progressively utilized until it replaces English.[89]

Several aspects of the resolution deserve comment. First, its generality. Compared with the language provisions of the Constitution, the terms of the 5 August Resolution were very broad. Perhaps it could not have been otherwise, but the detail of the Constitution demonstrates the great lengths to which the extremists and the moderates thought it necessary to go in order to give fullest expression to their own views and to protect their interests from the insidious intentions of their opponents. The Working Committee's resolution suggested, for example, that the provincial language should be used in the courts. If by this the members meant the subordinate, district courts, etc. they were on relatively safe ground. Yet the courts in a province included the High Court, and in the Constitution the uses of English in the High Courts and the Supreme Court would be set out in some detail. The resolution also indicates that Congress leaders had decided that it would be impolitic to single out any tongue for the honour of being the 'national' language, and that the Hindi-Hindustani

---

[88] For the text of the resolution, see Indian National Congress, *Resolutions on Language* Policy (1949–57), pp. 1–3. The Working Committee went to special pains to point out that Urdu was one of the languages recognized for all purposes mentioned in the resolution.

[89] Ibid.

dispute remained so sensitive that they avoided specifying what the state language should be.

The Working Committee also recommended that during a fifteen-year grace period, when English might be used by government, Hindi could progressively be employed. In the Assembly the Hindi-wallahs would make this their position, while South Indians, particularly, would fight fiercely against it. That the Working Committee found it necessary to publish the language resolution shows the temperature to which the controversy had risen under the pressure of the Hindi-wallahs and how unaccustomed the party leadership was to facing opposition of such militancy. The resolution also testifies to a strong belief in the necessity for a national language. As one observer later wrote, many Indians of the time believed that 'India lacked that linguistic unity which was thought to be so vital for a free people'.[90] Most of all the resolution, particularly the fifteen-year grace period for English, reflected the hopeful belief that within a few years most difficulties could be ironed out and that the 'next generation' could settle the language issue once and for all.[91] This hope has been rudely shattered.

The Battle is Joined

The reaction to the 5 August Resolution began immediately. Although the Assembly did not sit on 6 or 7 August, the Congress Party's office was reported to be flooded with 'thousands' of letters about language policy, especially as it applied to bilingual areas. And on these two days the Hindi Sahitya Sammelan, under President Seth Govind Das, held a National Language Convention in New Delhi, to 'obtain a considered decision about the national language'.[92] Although the sponsors of the convention claimed that prominent litterateurs representing all Indian languages would be present to produce this decision, few of the writers who attended

---

[90] S. K. Chatterji in his Minority Report to the *Report of the Official Language Commission*, p. 282.

[91] B. Shiva Rao and K. M. Munshi in interviews with the author have testified to the commonness of this belief.

[92] Seth Govind Das, *Self Examination (An Autobiography)*, p. 124. This book is written in Hindi and was translated for the author.

were well-known.[93] The convention was intended, in fact, to be a claque for Hindi and for Govind Das. At the end of its discussions, it demanded that 'Sanskritized Hindi' and the Nagari script be made the national language of India and said that Hindi should progressively replace English for Union and inter-governmental correspondence during a period not to exceed ten years. 'This arrangement was quite in accordance with the nation's will', proclaimed Govind Das subsequently.[94] But the convention, in fact, must have hurt rather than helped the cause of unity.

In a public speech in Delhi on 7 August, Purushottam Das Tandon made the Hindi-wallah's position even clearer. 'Those who oppose acceptance of Hindi as the national language and Nagari as the single national script', he said, 'are still following a policy of anti-national appeasement and are catering to communal aspirations.'[95] When the Assembly met on 8 August, the order paper bristled with language amendments to the Draft Constitution. Postponement was over, the battle had begun. Many of the amendments embodied the commonly-known views of the extremists, including a provision that during a ten-year transition period, Parliament could provide for the use of *either or both* Hindi and English for Union purposes. The moderates opposed this wording, recognizing it as a loophole that would permit the immediate exclusion of English. One such amendment bore the names of eighty-two members, forty-five of whom were from Bihar, the Central Provinces, and the United Provinces, and of whom at least fifty-eight were Hindi speakers. The name of Acharya Jugal Kishore, a general secretary of the Congress in 1948 headed this list, and several southerners, surprisingly enough, were also among the sponsors.[96] This amendment clearly demonstrated the support that the extremists had at this time from many Hindi-speaking back-benchers, and to some extent among non-Hindi speakers. Other amendments would have reduced the grace-period, for English to five years, and yet others would have lengthened it or have given Parliament the authority to provide for the continued

---

[93] For a list of those attending, see ibid., Appendix.

[94] Ibid., p. 126. The convention was also reported in the press; see *The Hindu* and *The Hindustan Times* of these days. The convention dismissed Urdu as 'the language of military camps'; *The Hindustan Times*, 8 August 1949.

[95] *The Hindustan Times*, 8 August 1949.

[96] Amendment number 4, *Orders of the Day*, 8 August 1949; *INA*.

use of English at its expiration—a provision that would appear in the Constitution.

The next day the non-Hindi bloc, led by the Southerners, protested against these amendments and launched a counter-attack. At the Assembly Party meeting in the afternoon, they insisted that English should be used as the official language for at least fifteen years and they flatly refused to agree to the progressive substitution of Hindi during this time. They did concede, however, that by a two-thirds majority Parliament could authorize the use of Hindi *in addition to* English in the transitional period. The Hindi-wallahs objected, saying that the complete replacement of English by Hindi at the end of fifteen years would only be possible by progressive substitution.[97]

The meeting was able to agree unanimously, however, that 'Hindi should be the official language of the Indian Union and that Devnagari should be the script'.[98] That Hindi should have this special status was never again in doubt. But there was, predictably, a 'divergence of opinion' over the meaning of Hindi. Nehru explained that Hindi should be defined as having the style and form of Hindustani—a phrase that would appear in the Constitution— and he and Prasad criticized the Hindi extremists for trying to purge Urdu from the language.[99] With an easy and peaceful solution of the controversy out of the question, the members at the meeting decided to appoint a committee to draft a compromise provision. It consisted of the members of the Drafting Committee (N. G. Ayyangar, T. T. Krishnamachari, Ayyar, Munshi, Ambedkar, Saadulla, and N. M. Rau), plus Azad, Pant, Tandon, Balkrishna Sharma, S. P. Mookerjee, and Santhanam.[100]

That evening, after the party meeting, the non-Hindi speakers gathered together to draft an amendment to answer those proposed the day before by the Hindi supporters. The result was an amendment signed by forty-four members, twenty-eight of whom came

---

[97] *The Hindu*, 12 August 1949.

[98] Ibid. According to *The Hindustan Times*, 12 August 1949, the meeting agreed that 'Hindi, as understood by the common man, should be chosen the national language.'

[99] *The Hindustan Times*, 12 August 1949.

[100] Ibid. According to *The Hindustan Times*, 12 August 1949, G. S. Gupta, Moti Satyanarayana and Amrit Kaur were also members. In most cases, references to *The Hindu* have been cross-checked with *The Hindustan Times*.

from Madras; the remainder were also from the South with the exception of two Assamese and three Biharis. K. Santhanam's name headed the list of supporters, which included T. T. Krishnamachari, Mrs. Durgabai, A. K. Ayyar, and M. A. Ayyangar. The amendment itself closely resembled a recommendation made by Santhanam a month earlier. It accepted Hindi with Nagari as the official language and proposed that English continue in use for fifteen years and for a further period if so determined by both Houses of Parliament. During the transition period, Hindi could be used in addition to English, and the Union Government should make funds available for teaching Hindi. Up to this point, both factions had talked in generalities. But the forty-four members now inserted a vital detail, probably at Santhanam's behest. They provided that 'For all official purposes of the Union or any State, numbers shall be indicated by Arabic numerals.'[101] The question of numerals was to become the sorest point in the language controversy.

The week from 10 to 17 August saw the language issue debated in 'stormy meetings' of the Assembly Party, according to the press; Prasad was reported to have said that the official language must be 'the language that is generally understood in Northern India', and that although there should be a fifteen-year grace period for English, Hindi should be progressively introduced for use 'in all-India matters'.[102] An editorial in *The Hindu* expressed the contrary view, saying that South Indian, Assamese, and Bengali members of the Assembly had 'good reason' to oppose the progressive substitution of Hindi because Hindi must be developed before it could attain the stature of a national language. Cultural changes take centuries not

---

[101] Amendment 52, *Orders of the Day*, 10 August 1949; *INA*. While the southerners were at work, Dr. Raghuvira was drafting an amendment that was nearly the ultimate in extremist sentiment. It appeared on the same order paper. It laid down that Hindi with Nagari constituted the national and the official language and listed recruitment to the Union Public Services as one of the areas in which Hindi should be used. Within three to five years, English should be replaced 'totally, entirely, and absolutely', wrote Raghuvira. After five years, English could no longer be used either in Parliament or in the legislatures or in the administration of the provinces, where the regional language or Hindi must be used. And the English version of the Constitution would be valid for only five years. Amendment 36; ibid.

[102] A Press Trust of India (PTI) dispatch in *The Hindu*, 17 August 1949.

years, said the editorial.[103] In Delhi a female Sanyasi promised to fast to the death unless Hindi was adopted as the national language and India renamed Bharat. Nehru, among others, visited her. She broke her fast on 12 August, claiming that Nehru and other Congress leaders had assured her that Hindi would be adopted. And Pandit Pant was reported to have made a suggestion that, had it been accepted, would have avoided years of bitterness. Pant suggested that 'it should be left to the non-Hindi speaking regions to suggest the time limit' for the replacement of English by Hindi in Union affairs.[104]

The special committee presented its report to the party meeting on 16 August. It pleased no one and was particularly offensive to the moderates. According to the most important of its provisions, English would be the sole official language for ten years and for five more if Parliament agreed by a two-thirds majority. If Hindi replaced English at the end of ten years, Parliament could, by a simple majority, provide for the continued use of the 'International numerals'. This tactful change from 'Arabic numerals' unfortunately did not mollify the Hindi extremists, who demanded the adoption of Nagari numerals. An 'influential section' of the committee, it was also reported, desired that Hindustani and Urdu as well as Sanskrit be named as sources of Hindi vocabulary.[105] Azad had resigned from the committee over this issue, claiming that the members would neither accept the word Hindustani nor 'accept any such interpretation which can widen the scope of Hindi'.[106] S. P. Mookerjee accurately labelled the committee a failure. The swing of moderates among the Hindi speakers away from the extremists appears to date from this time.

The special committee's efforts having been of no avail, the party meeting left it to the 'Drafting Committee to produce a compromise article. On 22 August, Ambedkar presented this newest in the series of attempted compromises. It provided that English would be used for fifteen years for official Union purposes and that Parliament could extend the period. The question of numerals, however, was

---

[103] *The Hindu*, 13 August 1949. The editorial also said that the term Hindi must mean broad and inclusive, not Sanskritized, Hindi.

[104] *The Hindu*, 11 August 1949; reported in *The Hindustan Times* of the same date.

[105] *The Hindu*, 17 August 1949.

[106] *CAD* IX, 34, 1476. See also ibid., p. 1452.

left unresolved. In the interim, the President could provide for the use of Hindi in addition to English; English was to be the language of the courts, and the regional languages were to be protected and listed in a schedule to the Constitution. After the inauguration of the Constitution, a language commission would be established to study such matters as the progressive use of Hindi, the choice of numerals, etc.[107]

Numerals and the fifteen-year transition period dominated the debate in Assembly Party meetings during the succeeding ten days. During this time, the language provisions were hammered out in greater and greater detail until they became what was called the 'Munshi-Ayyangar formula', which was the basis of the language provisions of the Constitution. On 26 August, the debate over numerals lasted a tense and acrimonious three hours. Sitaramayya was in the chair. Ultimately the question came to a vote. The result, by a show of hands, was sixty-three in favour of International numerals and fifty-four in favour of Nagari numerals. The Hindi-wallahs called for a division. The count in the lobbies yielded a seventy-four/seventy-four tie. At this the Hindi side claimed that it had had seventy-five votes when the voting first commenced, but that one of its members had left the House after the show of hands.[108] The meeting decided, however, evidently on Sitarammayya's and Nehru's urging, that Nagari numerals could not be forced on the country by such a narrow margin. In two other moves, the meeting agreed that Hindi-speaking provinces might use Hindi rather than English as the inter-provincial language during the transition period and removed English from the list of fourteen languages that would be named in the schedule to the Constitution.

For the next few days, the Hindi-wallahs under Tandon's leadership continued to refuse to accept the International numerals and maintained that English must not be used beyond fifteen years. Other members of the Hindi-bloc pressed for a reduction in the transition period and for the progressive substitution of Hindi as well as for the use of Hindi in the civil services, etc. The pressure

---

[107] *The Hindu*, 23 August 1949.

[108] For reports of this meeting see *The Hindu*, and *The Hindustan Times* of 27 August 1949. The reports are substantially the same.

of the extremists, particularly on the numerals issue, drove many Gujarati, Marathi, Bengali, and even Bihari Assembly members from the Hindi group into the ranks of the moderates. The South Indians among the moderates, as might be expected, took the strongest stand. Their views were expressed by *The Hindu,* which editorially condemned the stupidity and uselessness of the fight over numerals and cited the frequently used arguments that the International numerals were of Indian origin (which was true) and that they must be retained for the sake of efficiency in such matters as the census, federal statistics, commerce, and so on.[109]

Nehru and Azad now led the moderates quite openly. Patel, although not deeply interested in the language issue, brought his influence for compromise to bear from his sick-bed in Bombay. He wrote to Nehru, who read the letter at the party meeting, that fifteen years was sufficient for the change-over to Hindi, but that in the interim period, when Hindi might be authorized as an additional language to English, care should be taken not to upset administrative procedures.[110] Patel, conservative by nature, seems to have been in general sympathetic to Tandon's position and somewhat annoyed by the southern resistance to Hindi.[111] Yet he was sufficiently Gandhian for us to assume that he opposed Sanskritized Hindi, and, as the practical man, he must simply have wanted above all a settlement of the dispute. For this reason he probably supported the Munshi-Ayyangar formula.

On 2 September, this was ready, and its authors (who included Ambedkar) presented it to the party meeting held, as usual, in the afternoon at Constitution House on Curzon Road. This compromise, generally speaking, suited everyone but the Hindi extremists, who opposed it two weeks later in one of the bitterest debates in the Assembly's history. Barring a few changes, the formula closely

---

[109]   *The Hindu,* 30 August 1949.

[110]   *The Hindu,* 24 August 1949. The Home Ministry, presumably on Patel's direction, had earlier recommended that the official language of the Union (whether it be Hindi or English) should be the language of the High Courts, not the regional language. Home Ministry letter 11–a/48, dated 16 May 1948; R. S. *Shukla papers.*

[111]   An article published in *Harijan,* 21 November 1948 (Vol. XII, No. 38), indicated that Patel was displeased because Congress proceedings still had to be in English 'because of the South Indian bloc'.

resembled Part XVII of the Constitution, and it is worthwhile here to review its major provisions.

The formula provided that the official language of the Union was to be Hindi with the Nagari script but that International numerals would be used.[112] Notwithstanding this, English was to be used for Union affairs for fifteen years and Parliament could extend the period. The President could, during this period, order the use of Hindi and the Nagari numerals in addition to English and the International numerals. The language of the Supreme Court and the High Courts, the authoritative texts of Bills, Acts, Ordinances, etc., should be in English, and for fifteen years no Bill to alter this provision could be introduced in Parliament without the sanction of the President. It was the duty of the Union to promote the spread and development of Hindi so that it could serve as a medium of expression for the 'composite culture of India' and to secure Hindi's enrichment by seeing that it assimilated the 'forms, style, and expressions used in Hindustani and in the other languages of India'. For its vocabulary, Hindi should draw 'primarily on Sanskrit and secondarily on other languages'. An attached schedule listed thirteen living Indian languages, but not English or Sanskrit.

States could adopt any language used in the state, or Hindi, as their official language, the formula laid down, but English was to be used until the state legislature otherwise provided. The language in use by the Union was to be the language of Union-state and inter-state communications but Hindi-speaking states could use Hindi. The formula called for the formation of language commissions in 1955 and 1960 to survey the progress of Hindi. When drawing up its recommendations, the commission was to have due regard, among other things, for 'the just claims and the interests of the non-Hindi speaking areas in regard to the public services'.[113]

The roots of the Munshi-Ayyangar formula are apparent in the debates of the previous weeks and years. Two aspects of the

---

[112] The Munshi-Ayyangar formula was, officially, Amendment 65 'Relating to Language' on the Fourth List of Amendments, *Orders of the Day*, 5 September 1949; *INA*. For the text, see also *CAD* IX, 32, 1321–23. Listed as its sponsors were N. G. Ayyangar, Munshi, and Ambedkar:

[113] Ibid.

compromise, however, included for the benefit of regional language speakers, deserve special comment. They are: the listing of regional languages in the Constitution and the reference to the interests of non-Hindi speakers in regard to the public services. The services provided one of the largest sources of prestige employment for the middle and upper classes in India. They exerted 'a disproportionate pull on the educated youth of the country'.[114] Any move that would detrimentally affect the chances of Bengali or Tamil speakers, for example, entering the services would therefore be furiously resisted. Making Hindi the language of the services by the rapid replacement of English, as the Hindi-wallahs frequently advocated, was such a move.[115] For even if Hindi-speakers were obliged to learn a regional language, as some Hindi supporters were willing to agree, having the entrance examinations for the services in Hindi would place non-Hindi speakers at a great disadvantage. And so long as English remained the medium of instruction in universities (as it must for 'some time', in the view of the Universities Education Commission[116]), it would be unrealistic to demand that non-Hindi speaking university graduates should have a command of Hindi equalling that of native Hindi speakers—hence the

---

[114] *Report of the Official Language Commission*, p. 186.

The other aspect of the provisions regarding the public services that interested the Assembly was the matter of minority representation. The Minorities Sub-Committee, at its July 1947 meetings, voted that places should be reserved in the services for certain minorities. The Advisory Committee rejected this decision several weeks later, however, and no such provision was included in the Constitution. But by the Fundamental Rights the state is permitted to reserve places for 'backward classes' of citizens.

[115] Some examples of this: G. S. Gupta submitted a resolution to the Steering Committee on 25 October 1948 that all candidates to the Union Services pass tests in Hindi and one other Indian language; *Munshi papers*. Mahavir Tyagi moved an amendment in the Assembly that provided that 'all tests, examinations, and competitions' held to select candidates for the Union Services should be in the official language. *CAD* IX, 28; 1106.

[116] Government of India, *Report of the Universities Education Commission*, p. 325. The report, although dated January 1950, was completed and presented to Nehru and Azad— as Minister of Education—on 24 August 1949. Radhakrishnan, the chairman, was quoted as saying at a press conference held the next day that 'We have also recommended that there must be no attempt at hasty replacement of English as a medium of instruction.' See *The Hindu*, 26 August 1949.

provision of the Constitution protecting the interests of the non-Hindi speakers.

The plan to list thirteen living Indian languages in the Constitution was unique, yet what was its significance? The Munsghi Ayyangar formula provided that each language should be represented on the language commission; later it was agreed that these languages should be the sources from which Hindi should broaden itself.[117] But these were the only tangible advantages accruing to the regional languages from being listed in the Constitution. As the first Language Commission observed, 'there is no particular distinction bestowed on a language' because it is named in Schedule VIII.[118] The languages were not made either national or official languages on the pattern of the Swiss, Pakistan, and South African Constitutions, the only constitutions in which the languages of the country are given by name.[119] Why, then, was such a list included in the formula, and why did its inclusion assume such importance in the eyes of regional language speakers?

The answer was: 'for psychological reasons and to give these languages status', according to Mrs. Durgabai Deshmukh. 'We had these languages listed in the Constitution to protect them from being ignored or wiped out by the Hindi-wallahs.'[120] According to Nehru the regional languages should be enumerated so that they would be assured 'their due place' in the new India.[121] And he once suggested that they be called 'Officially Recognized Languages' instead of regional languages.[122] That the fears of the regional-language speakers were far from baseless was borne out by the attitude of Ravi Shankar Shukla, who opposed the listing of the languages in

---

[117] *See Constitution*, Article 351.

[118] *Report*, op. cit., p. 51.

[119] The Canadian Constitution lists no languages, although it does accord special status to French as well as English. The Soviet Constitution (1936) does even less, providing in Article 40 only that laws passed by the Supreme Soviet must be published in the languages of the Republics of the Union.

[120] Mrs. Durgabai (now Mrs. Durgabai Deshmukh), in an interview with the author. This explanation has been corroborated by T. T. Krishnamachari, also in an interview with the author.

[121] *The Hindustan Times*, 24 August 1949.

[122] Nehru letter to Ambedkar, Munshi, and N. G. Ayyangar regarding their new language formula, dated 23 August 1949; *Law Ministry Archives*, File CA/19(II)/Cons/49.

the Constitution as 'wholly unnecessary in view of the precarious conditions in the country'. Listing the languages, he believed, was a 'reactionary provision' because a commission representing these languages would 'delay the introduction of Hindi as the Official Language of the Union'.[123]

With such opinions current among the Hindi-wallahs, no wonder the speakers of other languages feared for the status of their tongues. As Mrs. Durgabai from Madras said:

> ... The people of the non-Hindi speaking areas have been made to feel that this fight or this attitude on behalf of the Hindi-speaking areas is a fight for effectively preventing the natural influence of other powerful languages of India on the composite culture of the nation.[124]

S. P. Mookerjee, a former president of the communal Hindu Mahasabha, but a Bengali, welcomed the listing of the regional languages. Why, he asked, have 'many people belonging to non-Hindi speaking provinces. .. become a bit nervous about Hindi?' Because 'people speaking other languages, not inferior to Hindi by any means, have not been allowed the same facilities which even the much-detested foreign regime did not dare deprive them of'.[125]

Pattabhi Sitaramayya occupied the chair on the afternoon of 2 September when the Munshi-Ayyangar formula was debated. He requested the meeting to treat the formula as a whole and as a compromise designed to satisfy the major points of view. The heated discussion revolved about two points: the content of the formula and how the formula was to be sponsored on the Assembly floor. The debate on the compromise itself covered familiar ground. The debate on the sponsorship of the formula—which, it will be recalled, took the form of an amendment to the Draft

---

[123]   Shukla letter to the chairman of the Drafting Committee, 1 September 1949; *Shukla papers*.

[124]   *CAD* IX, 34, 1426.

[125]   *CAD* IX, 33, 1391. The speakers of the regional languages had reason for pride. Nearly all these languages were older, more developed tongues than Hindi—particularly Bengali and Tamil. Hindi was a relative newcomer, dating from the later half of the eighteenth century. (Chatterji, *Languages and the Linguistic Problem*, p. 18). Even the Official Language Commission noted that Hindi lacked 'such natural ascendancy over the other provincial languages as to incline inhabitants of these provinces to accept a secondary position for the language in their own regions'. (Report, op. cit., p. 320.)

Constitution—involved an important matter of policy. If the party meeting voted to endorse the formula and it was then moved in the Assembly, it would be an official amendment, recognized as expressing Congress policy, and thus be binding on Congress members. If moved on the floor by its sponsors without the Assembly Party's sanction, it would have only the status of a member's private amendment. The moderates fought for passage by the party meeting; the Hindi-wallahs opposed it.[126] Finally the issue came to a division. On the side of the moderates, it was reported, voted members from Bombay (primarily Gujaratis), Bengal, Assam, Madras, and the South, plus Nehru, many ministers of the Union Government, and members of the Drafting Committee. Opposing the party's adoption of the amendment were Assembly members from the United Provinces, the Central Provinces, the East Punjab, Bihar, and Rajasthan. The result was a tie vote, seventy-seven to seventy-seven. Sitaramayya declined to use his casting vote, and the deadlock remained unresolved.

The question that continued to defy solution was numerals. The Hindi-wallahs had opposed adoption of the formula because it recognized the International numerals. The moderates, in the face of extremist insistence on Nagari numerals, had threatened to break off negotiations entirely.[127] The language dispute thus went to the Assembly unresolved. There was to be no Whip, and the vote in the Assembly would be free.

We may pause here to bury a minor controversy. The closeness of the votes on language in the party meetings has given rise to the legend that Hindi became the official language of India by a majority of only one vote.[128] This seems very doubtful. Issues of *The Hindu* on 12 and 28 August 1949 reported that two meetings of the Congress Assembly Party 'unanimously' named Hindi as the official language. *The Hindustan Times* throws no doubt on this and in its report of 12 August on the previous day's party meeting said that it had been agreed to make Hindi as spoken by the common man the

---

[126] The following account is based on reports in *The Hindu* and *The Hindustan Times* of 3 September 1949.

[127] Ibid. Also Mrs. Durgabai Deshmukh in an interview with the author.

[128] See for example, Harrison, *Dangerous Decades*, p. 9—in which Harrison cites an article published in 1958 in *The Hindu*.

national language. Had this been decided by one vote, it presumably would have been reported in the same manner as the one-vote margins on numerals and the sponsorship of the Munshi-Ayyangar formula. Moreover, there seems never to have been any doubt that either Hindi or Hindustani would be given all-India status, and the choice of the word Hindi instead of Hindustani was apparently made in July 1947 by a large majority.[129]

One is left with the conclusion that the 'one-vote' legend is based on the events at the party meeting of 26 August 1949, when there may have existed briefly a one-vote majority in favour of Nagari over International numerals. Accounts of the language controversy by Ambedkar and Seth Govind Das in fact support this view, although they apparently uphold the legend. In his *Thoughts on Linguistic States,* Ambedkar wrote:

> . . . There was no Article which proved more controversial than Article 115, which deals with the (Hindi) question. No Article produced more opposition. No Article more heat. After a prolonged discussion, when the question was put, the vote was 78 against 78. The tie could not be resolved. After a long time when the question was put to the meeting once more, the result was 77 against 78 for Hindi. Hindi won its place as the national language by one vote.[130]

Govind Das, in his autobiography, has written:

> . . . When the votes were taken, 78 were in favour of Hindi and 77 in favour of Hindustani . . . This was not liked by the supporters of Hindustani and they descended to rowdyism . . . Kaka Bhagwant Rai (Roy) of Patiala, having cast his vote in favour of Hindi and knowing the result to have been in favour of Hindi left the Assembly due to some urgent work. When votes were again taken, on the matter being pressed by the supporters of Hindustani, the Hindi side had one less vote and therefore both sides were equal at 77. A wave of enthusiasm ran through the opposition group.[131]

Neither of the authors gives a date for the events recounted. But they bear sufficient resemblance to the 26 August party meeting

---

[129] See above, p. 177.

[130] Ambedkar, *Thoughts*, p. 14. In none of the many draft versions of the Constitution does an Article 115 deal even remotely with the language question.

[131] Govind Das, *Self Examination*, pp. 118–9.

for it to be assumed that that is what they describe. *The Hindustan Times* also reported that the departure of a Patiala representative reduced the one-vote majority to a tie. The most reasonable conclusion one can draw is that Ambedkar and Govind Das have confused the facts or have interpreted the one-vote majority for Nagari numerals, if such there was, as a victory for Hindi, but this would in no way justify the claim that Hindi became the official language of India by one vote. And in the context of the Assembly Party's belief in consensus, the one-vote, legend loses all meaning. For the close voting in the party meeting produced not decisions, but only further attempts at compromise in order that the controversy might be settled with maximum agreement or, if possible, unanimously.

During the week following the 2 September party meeting, the Assembly continued, as it had during the past month, to devote its time to problems of federalism, special minority provisions, tax matters, and so on. Off the floor of the House, the Hindi-wallahs persisted in their attacks on the Munshi-Ayyangar formula while the moderates stood firm on it. The debate on language in the Assembly was scheduled to open on 12 September. On 10 September, the dammed waters of extremist fury burst upon the compromise formula. The order paper bulged with forty-five pages of language amendments, most of them submitted by Hindi-wallahs. They would have wiped out, or made unrecognizable, the provisions by which the formula intended to save Indian unity.

The amendments by Govind Das conveyed the tone of extremist sentiment. One of them, which would have replaced the formula with a wholly new language section, provided that states adopting Hindi as their language could print the texts of Bills, Acts, and the judgements of courts in Hindi and could use it instead of English in High Court proceedings.[132] This amendment omitted mention of International numerals, provided that Hindi should replace English as the official language after ten years (or after fifteen if Hindi had been used additionally to English for all purposes during the interim). It made no provision for Parliament to extend this period, nor for Hindi to have a composite, all-India character. Another amendment by Govind Das (like provisions were submitted by Shukla, Mandloi,

---

[132] Fourth List of Amendments, *Orders of the Day*, 10 September 1949; *INA*.

Gupta, and others) would have deleted from the formula the schedule naming the regional languages. Amendments by other extremists called for the complete replacement of English in five years and for the progressive substitution of Hindi.

The disgust and dismay with which many Assembly members by this time looked on the controversy was shown by the amendments that would have made Sanskrit the official language. Heading the list of twenty-eight members who submitted such amendments were the names of Ambedkar and T. T. Krishnamachari.[133] Neither could have believed that their amendment would be accepted, but they would have agreed with L. K. Maitra, who told the Assembly that choosing Sanskrit would put all the regional languages on an equal footing and put an end to the 'jealousies' aroused by the choice of Hindi.[134] *The Hindustan Times* called the suggestion 'a council of despair'.[135]

The final confrontation on language began late in the afternoon of 12 September, the morning session having been devoted to the finale of the compensation issue, and in a short time the pattern of the debate became established. President Prasad opened the proceedings by enjoining a calm approach and temperate language. Speakers, he said, 'should not let fall a single word or expression which might hurt or cause offence'. And he further called for the decision on the language provisions of the Constitution to be taken by consensus. 'The decision of the House should be acceptable to the country as a whole,' he said. '. . . Therefore, members will remember that it will not do to carry a point by debate in this House.'[136]

N. G. Ayyangar then introduced the Munshi-Ayyangar formula, saying that it embodied not his or his co-sponsors' ideas, but that it was 'a compromise between opinions which were not easily reconcilable'. There were two basic principles behind the formula, Ayyangar explained. One was that 'we should select one of the

---

[133] Amendment 71, *Orders of the Day*, 10 September 1949; *INA*. Ambedkar had at one time expressed a strong belief in linguistic homogeneity for India. He had suggested that the language chosen as the national language by the Assembly should be 'the language of the State, i.e. of the Union as well as the Units.' Ambedkar, minute of dissent to the Fundamental Rights Sub-Committee, 19 April 1947; *Prasad papers*. File 1-F/47.

[134] *CAD* IX, 33, 1352–60.

[135] *The Hindustan Times*, 19 September 1949.

[136] *CAD* IX, 32, 1312.

languages in India as the common language of the whole of India'. Yet this could not be achieved immediately and English must continue to be used because Hindi 'is not today sufficiently developed and must be given time to establish itself'. The second principle was 'that the numerals to be used for all official Union purposes should be what have been described as the all-India forms of Indian numerals'. For the sake of compromise, Ayyangar said, the drafters of the formula had made two concessions on the latter principle. The first was that the President could order the use of Nagari numerals in addition to International numerals; the second, that the language commission might make recommendations on the subject of numerals. Otherwise, said Ayyangar, the basic principles of the compromise must stand.[137]

Seth Govind Das, speaking in Hindi, replied to Ayyangar. The distance between his views and those of Prasad and Ayyangar was great. He rejected Prasad's appeal for consensus, although he called for reaching decisions 'in an amicable spirit'.

> We have accepted democracy (Govind Das said) and democracy can only function when majority opinion is honoured. If we differ on any issue, that can only be decided by votes. Whatever decision is arrived at by the majority must be accepted by the minority respectfully and without any bitterness.[138]

Govind Das also rejected International numerals and the idea that English might not be completely replaced by Hindi in fifteen years. To the charge that the extremists were narrowing the scope of Hindi and behaving in a communal and revivalist fashion, he replied, 'It is a great injustice to accuce us of communalism.' He then charged that 'Urdu has mostly drawn inspiration from outside the country' and used *Bulbul* instead of *Koyal* to mean cuckoo. India, he said, had had one cultural tradition for thousands of years. 'It is in order to maintain this tradition that we want one language and one script for the whole country. We do not want it to be said that there are two cultures here.'[139]

That evening, the leaders of the Hindi-wallahs met and drew up an amendment that may be regarded as their 'official' position.

[137] Ibid., pp. 1317–19.
[138] Ibid., p. 1325.
[139] Ibid, p. 1328.

Signed by Tandon, Shukla, Balkrishna Sharma, Govind Das, Govind Malaviya, and six others, it appeared on the next day's order paper. The amendment provided that the official Union language would be Hindi with the Nagari script and with both Nagari and International numerals. It laid down, however, that during a fifteen-year interim period in which English would be used, the President could authorize the use of *either or both* forms of numerals for official purposes and could also authorize the use of Hindi in addition to English in all fields 'other than auditing, accounting, and banking'. Parliament was empowered to extend the use of English.[140] Here the amendment ended. It made no mention of language in the states or in the courts, and it contained no schedule of regional languages and no directive that Hindi should absorb the style and forms of Hindustani and the other Indian languages.

The debate of the following day was marked by speeches from S. P. Mookerjee and Nehru. Mookerjee repeated the call for a decision based on consensus.

> If it is claimed by anyone (he said) that bypassing an article in the Constitution of India one language is going to be accepted by all by a process of coercion, I say, Sir, that that will not be possible to achieve. (Hear, Hear.) Unity in diversity is India's keynote and must be achieved by a process of understanding and consent and for that a proper atmosphere has to be created.[141]

Nehru, speaking thoughtfully, rambled typically to the heart of the matter. The Munshi-Ayyangar formula was the best solution under the circumstances, therefore he supported it, he said. Although English must continue to be a most important language in India no nation could become great on the basis of a foreign language. The language India chose for itself must be 'a language of the people, not a language of a learned coterie', he continued. Gandhi had used the word Hindustani to represent the people's language, to represent 'the composite culture of India', and it was the references to Hindustani that had allowed him to support the Munshi-Ayyangar formula. Had those references not been made, he said, 'then it would have been very difficult for me to accept this

---

[140] Amendment 333 of the Eighth list of Amendments, *Orders of the Day*, 13 September 1949; *INA*.

[141] *CAD* IX, 33, 1389.

Resolution'.[142] Nehru criticized the 'tone of authoritarianism' in the speeches of the Hindi-wallahs, and told them they could not force a language on the people. In conclusion he attacked the attempts to narrow and to Sanskritize Hindi, the attempts to cut India off from the English-language aspects of its heritage.

> We stand on the threshold of a new age (Nehru said) . . . What sort of India do we want? Do we want a modern India—with its roots steeped in the past . . . in so far as it inspires us—do we want a modern India with modern science and all the rest of it, or do we want to live in some ancient age, in some other age which has no relation to the present? You have to choose between the two. It is a question of approach. You have to choose whether you look forward or backward.[143]

The third day of debate Dr. Raghuvira attacked Urdu, and Jaipal Singh deprecated 'the puritanical fanaticism that has gripped so many people'.[144] Tandon, Maulana Azad, and Shankarrao Deo made long contributions. Although Deo, a general secretary of the Congress, supported the Munshi-Ayyangar formula, International numerals, and broad Hindi, he said that the very aims of the formula conflicted: 'I cannot understand how these things can go together', he said. 'We cannot hope to have one language for the whole country and at the same time work for the enrichment of the regional languages.' Deo hoped that India could retain its cultural diversity. He was an Indian, he said, but his language was Marathi. If having Hindi as the official language meant 'one language for the whole country, then I am against it', he said.[145]

Tandon, not surprisingly objected to the formula at nearly every point. He had hoped that the substitution of Hindi for English would begin immediately, and spoke, therefore, of the 'hard provision in regard to Hindi not being used at all except in addition to English for five years and more until a commission makes a recommendation and that recommendation is accepted by the President'. He called the continued use of English in the provinces 'palpably retrograde'. He described the Nagari numerals as 'an ancient heritage', and said

[142] Ibid., pp. 1410–11.
[143] Ibid., p. 1416.
[144] *CAD* IX, 34, 1440.
[145] Ibid., pp.1430–1.

that 'Hindi, with the backing of Sanskrit can face all the difficulties of vocabulary with ease.'[146]

Azad replied to Tandon in a speech noteworthy for its reasonableness and perceptiveness. He explained how he had come to realize the need for a gradual approach to the replacement of English. 'The Union of North and South', he said, 'has been made possibly only through the medium of English. If today we give up English, then this linguistic relationship will cease to exist.' Azad closed by expressing the hope that 'the present atmosphere of narrow mindedness' would give way to an atmosphere 'in which people freeing themselves from all sorts of sentiments would see the problem of language in its real and true perspective'.[147]

This was 14 September. The sitting adjourned at 1 p.m. for lunch. Most members must have eaten a sober meal. Decision was due that afternoon, but the debate had brought agreement no closer. The members in general looked forward with distaste to a division. The Assembly Party met at 3 p.m. to try to break the deadlock. Sitaramayya presided over two hours of 'strenuous and stormy discussion' that brought no result. Just at five o'clock, when the Assembly was scheduled to reconvene, the members reached an agreement. They trooped into the Assembly room and requested the Chair for a further hour to work out details. At six o'clock the work was done. The members breathed 'a genuine sigh of relief that the matter had been settled.[148]

The compromise consisted of five amendments to the Munshi-Ayyangar formula, each of which was a concession to the extremist bloc. These provided that after fifteen years, Parliament could legislate on the use of Nagari numerals as well as on the continued use of English, that Hindi might be used in the proceedings of a High Court with the sanction of the President, that Bills, Acts, Ordinances, etc., could be issued in the official language of a state if an official English translation was published, and that Sanskrit be added to the list of languages in the Schedule.[149]

---

[146] Ibid, pp. 1443–9.

[147] Ibid., pp. 1453 and 1459.

[148] This account of the meeting was taken from *The Hindu* of 15 September 1949. It has been largely corroborated by interviews.

[149] For the texts of the amendments as finally moved, and for the formula as amended, see *CAD* IX, 34, 1486–9. The Drafting Committee on its own ini-

With the final compromise on paper, the party meeting agreed that the members should withdraw the nearly 400 language amendments they had submitted and support the final version of the formula. A Whip was issued to this effect. Back in the Assembly chamber, the members heard Munshi read the agreed amendments, and all but five members withdrew their own amendments. Three of them were Congressmen, Brajeshwar Prasad, S. L. Saksena, and Tandon. The two others were League Muslims, Naziruddin Ahmad and Z. H. Lari.[150] The Assembly rejected their amendments by overwhelming majorities. The new Munshi-Ayyangar formula was then put to the vote, to be carried 'amidst deafening cheers'.

Epilogue

'We have done the wisest possible thing', Prasad told the Assembly immediately after the adoption of the language provisions, 'and I am glad, I am happy, and I hope posterity will bless us for this.' He predicted that a common language would 'forge another link that will bind us all together from one end (of the country) to the other'.[151]

Yet India, even North India, despite the increasing efforts of the extremists, has not rushed to embrace Hindi. An editorial written in *The Hindu* at the time foresaw the future more closely than Prasad had, when it said that fifteen years was more like a minimum than a maximum for the replacement of English. In the fifteen years since the inauguration of the Constitution the Union Government has put Hindi to only minor uses in the conduct of

---

tiative later changed the last article of the formula so that the sources of Hindi were to be the 'other languages of India specified in the Eighth Schedule', and not simply the 'other languages of India', as had been the earlier wording; see *Constitution*, Article 351.

[150] Tandon resigned from the Assembly Party 'as a protest against the mandate' (*The Hindu*, 16 and 17 September 1949), apparently in the meeting of 14 September, so that he would be free to press his amendments on the floor of the House. The Congress two days later requested that he withdraw his resignation, and he did so; ibid. Z. H. Lari resigned from the Assembly because Hindustani and the Urdu script were not mentioned in the language provisions; *The Hindu*, 17 September 1949.

[151] *CAD* IX, 34, 1490–1.

its affairs. Only the Hindi-speaking states have been using Hindi, and then not always widely. The regional languages in other states, generally speaking, have replaced English as the language of subordinate courts and of legislative proceedings, but otherwise English has continued to be the principal language of state as well as of Union affairs.[152]

The principal reason for this is that India has produced very little feeling of linguistic nationalism. It was not, and is not, generally speaking, un-Indian to speak English. The Congress (as apart from Gandhi himself) proclaimed the virtues of speaking Hindustani, yet continued to use English at all but the local level. In the Constituent Assembly speeches were made calling for a national language and emphasizing its importance to national unity as a 'cement' to hold the various parts of India together. Yet more than half the members of the Assembly, one may reasonably estimate, voted for the Munshi-Ayyangar formula because it did not make inevitable the *de facto* adoption of an Indian tongue as the national language. The element of linguistic nationalism—or, better, linguistic chauvinism—was injected by the Hindi extremists. Since the coming into force of the Constitution, the Official Language of the Union has not replaced English, and the use of English after 1965 has been provided for by the Official Languages Act of 1963.[153]

India's problem has been and is, rather, one of sub-national sentiment and sub-national competition, which often take the form of linguistic rivalries.[154] In the Assembly, these rivalries had not assumed their present proportions or many of their present guises; they were expressed as resistance to the linguistic chauvinism of another sub-national group, the Hindi speakers—who came, unfortunately, to be represented by a group of extremists. The language provisions of the Constitution were designed, in a typically Indian fashion, to meet such a situation: Assembly members believed that

[152] For a description of the language situation after the first five years of the language provisions, see Government of India, *Report of the Official Language Commission*, 1956, esp. pp. 442–62.

[153] *The Official Languages Act*, 1963, Government of India, Act No. 19 of 1963.

[154] For a comprehensive treatment of the forms inter-provincial competition has taken—over allocation of funds for development plans, etc.—and how this often expresses itself in language rivalries, see Harrison, *Dangerous Decades*.

India should, ideally, have an indigenous national language; Hindi (or Hindustani) was the most suitable, so it was named for the role. Yet for Hindi to be in practice the national language was impossible, for the only language in national use was English. Moreover, the other sub-nations feared the introduction of Hindi and had pride in their own languages. Hence the Constitution makes clear what the national ideal is, and then, realistically, compromises, laying down how the nation is to function, linguistically speaking, until the ideal is achieved. More than this, as the furious controversy among the members testifies, the Assembly was unable to do. Yet the language provisions are not just an unhappy compromise; they have a more positive side. They show that the large majority of the Assembly believed that the use of many Indian languages and of English was compatible with national unity and with the evolution of a national spirit.

13

Conclusion—
Comments on a Successful Constitution

By independence we have lost the excuse of blaming the British for anything going wrong. If hereafter things go wrong, we will have nobody to blame except ourselves.

B. R. Ambedkar

WITH the adoption of the Constitution by the members of the Constituent Assembly on 26 November 1949, India became the largest democracy in the world. By this act of strength and will, Assembly members began what was perhaps the greatest political venture since that originated in Philadelphia in 1787. A huge land with the second largest population in the world, socially and economically retarded, culturally diverse, and, for the first time in 150 years responsible for its own future, was to attempt to achieve administrative and political unity and an economic and social revolution under a democratic constitution. The nation was to do this, moreover, under a constitution whose provisions and principles, although compatible with Indian thought and recent history, were nevertheless almost entirely of non-Indian origin, coming as they had largely from the former colonial power.

The Assembly rejected the example of China and Russia, in which, no matter what the constitutional euphemisms, national unity and social renovation were being sought by arbitrary means. And Indians, during the decade and a half since independence, have stood by their choice when smaller nations, with problems certainly no greater than India's have not dared to risk the gamble of democracy, settling for 'guided democracy' or some other arrangement denying the citizens a direct voice in their government.

In the years since its inauguration, the Indian Constitution has worked well; the Assembly's faith in its creation and in the nation has been warranted. Although the safety of democracy is never assured, the gamble never finally won, and although the social revolution is only slowly being achieved, the evidence in India bears out Percival Spear's judgement that the Constitution 'must on the whole be pronounced a signal success'.[1]

When considering the effectiveness of a constitution, it must first be understood that it has real existence only in the way it is used. A constitution can be judged only by its adequacy to situations it was designed to meet—and by the extent to which the situations it might reasonably be expected to meet were foreseen—and by the extent to which it commands the allegiance of those who are to govern themselves by it. Presumably, the closer the sense of a constitution is to the inclinations of a people, the greater will be their allegiance to it. Applying these criteria to the Indian Constitution, the primary example of its effectiveness has been the smoothness with which a successor government to that of Prime Minister Nehru was chosen. The succession of a more ordinary mortal to the place occupied by a charismatic, all-powerful leader is difficult in any political system, but hardest of all in a young democracy. But within hours of Nehru's death in May 1964 an interim government had been formed and in less than two weeks the Congress Parliamentary Party, with the assistance of the organizational wing of the Congress, had chosen a new leader and he had been asked by the President to form a government.

The very teething troubles that democratic government has had in India emphasise the soundness of the Constitution. On the occasions when there has been a failure of government in the states, 'President's rule' has been invoked under the Emergency Provisions and the Union has governed the state until by fresh elections or other means normal government could be restored; central power has then been withdrawn. Thus has the Constitution successfully met anticipated situations. In Uttar Pradash in 1964 there was a confrontation of the High Court and the state legislature over the release by the court on a writ of habeas corpus of an individual committed to jail for contempt of the legislature. This test of power between the Legislature and the

---

[1]   Spear, *India*, p. 427.

Judiciary generated a great deal of heat and aroused wide interest. The matter was referred by the President under the Constitution to the Supreme Court for an advisory opinion—and it upheld the action of the High Court. The issue has not yet run its course, but so far the course has been fixed by the Constitution.

The Constitution has been accepted as the charter of Indian unity. Within its limits are held the negotiations over the working of the federal system. The realignment of state boundaries on linguistic lines was done within its definition of Indian nationalism. The question of the Official Language has been debated in Parliament within the framework of a compromise designed to preserve national unity. The Constitution has established the accepted norms of 'national' behaviour.

The Constitution's greatest success, however, lies below the surface of government. It has provided a framework for social and political development, a rational, institutional basis for political behaviour. It not only establishes the national ideals, more importantly it lays down the rational, institutional manner by which they are to be pursued—a gigantic step for a people previously committed largely to irrational means of achieving other-worldly goals. There are not only the Fundamental Rights and the Directive Principles and the structure of national planning, there is the direct electoral system. This has been widely accepted as a means for bringing pressure to bear on government—as certain key bye-elections even more than the three mammoth general elections show—and has charged India's traditional, hierarchical society with new energy. The Constitution has thus created another norm, one of democratic political behaviour based on the belief that man can shape his own destiny. This is not to claim that there is no more apathy in India or that Indian life, political and social, is completely democratic or that constitutional democracy has no enemies in India. But it is to say that a strong, positive counterforce to political and social authoritarianism has been established. The Constitution has so far been a success because both the ends it has proclaimed and the means it has laid down for achieving them have been popularly accepted and have already worked beneficial changes in Indian society.

Finally, it must be said that the success of a constitution is neither so easy to document nor so spectacular as its failure. So, in one sense, the absence of comment about the constitutional situation in India is a mark of the Constitution's effective working. It has been accepted as the basis for democracy in India in the matter of fact way that a family presumes the soundness of the foundations of the house in which it lives.

The credit for the success of the Constitution has been ascribed to various causes. Some observers have said that it has been due to its close derivation from Euro-American—particularly from British—constitutional precedent. (There have also been doubts that a constitution so indebted to foreign precedent would be suitable for a country with great and ancient traditions of its own.) Credit has also been given to the pre-independence experience with parliamentary government and to the presence of varying extraneous factors during the framing period and the first years of the Constitution's working—such as the presence of unusually able leaders and a dominant-party system.

Although the importance of these factors must be granted, the explanation of the Constitution's success lies principally in its having been framed by Indians, and in the excellence of the framing process itself. The members of the Assembly drafted a Constitution that expressed the aspirations of the nation. They skilfully selected and modified the provisions that they borrowed, helped by the 'experts' among their number and the advice given by ministries of the Union and provincial governments. The Assembly members also applied to their task with great effectiveness two wholly Indian concepts, consensus and accommodation. Accommodation was applied to the principles to be embodied in the Constitution. Consensus was the aim of the decision-making process, the single, most important source of the Constituent Assembly's effectiveness.

India's Original Contribution

I. Decision-making by Consensus

Consensus, as has been briefly noted earlier, is a manner of making decisions by unanimity or near-unanimity, of elevating the means by which a decision is made to an importance perhaps even higher than that of the decision itself. It is a recognition that majority rule may not be a successful way to decide political conflicts in which human emotions are very deeply involved, that, in some situations, it may be politically unwise, if not morally unjust, for fifty-two persons to impose their will on forty-eight. It is a realization, to continue the arithmetic, that a decision would have more moral and political force if, say, ninety of the one hundred persons agreed to it.[2] Assembly leaders understood this well and bent their energies towards this goal in the hope and expectation that the Constitution, framed by consensus, would work effectively and thus prove durable. Their efforts were rewarded. During the Third Reading one of the more independent-minded Assembly members, Thakur Das Bhargava, was able to say, 'I am really very glad that we have been able to prepare such a splendid constitution with unanimity'[3]—an exaggeration to be sure, but evidence of the very large extent of agreement with which the Assembly completed its work.

Consensus has deep roots in India. Village panchayats traditionally reached decisions in this way, and even if the process was in practice often manipulated by the more powerful members the ideal was still there—as it continues to be today. Caste panchayats have steadily maintained the policy of reaching decisions by consensus. Certainly Indians prefer lengthy discussion of problems to moving quickly to arbitrary decisions. Consensus thus had a general appeal in the Assembly: to the leadership as an ethical and effective way of reaching lasting agreement and to the rank and file as an indigenous institution that suited the framing of an 'Indian' constitution.

Early in the proceedings, Nehru informed the Assembly that the Constitution should be framed 'in the proper time and with as great a respect for unanimity as possible'.[4] And the members set about doing this in a variety of ways. Most important among them were the Congress Assembly Party meetings where each provision of the Constitution was subjected to frank and searching debate, and whose approval was in fact as important as that of the Assembly itself. Everyone elected to the Assembly on the Congress ticket, as

---

[2]   K. G. Mashruwala—in his *Some Particular Suggestions for the Constitution*—tried to put consensus into concrete form. He said that a fifty over forty-nine majority was bad in a country which was not 'well-knit' and that decisions should be made by the consent of the majority of the members present with no greater dissent than 35 per cent of the members of the House. This might avoid 'majority tyranny'.

[3]   *CAD* XI, 5, 685.

[4]   *CAD* II, 3, 299.

we have seen, could attend these meetings, from party stalwarts to non-Congressmen, like Ayyar, Ambedkar, and N. G. Ayyangar, who were brought into the Assembly because the leadership believed that their talents should not be wasted. Also a part of this process were the Assembly's committee system, the dialogue between provincial and Union government leaders in the Assembly, the many inter-governmental communications, and the off-the-record discussions between Assembly leaders and dissidents among the members. All constituted a reasoned and reasonable approach to unity.

The primary examples of decision-making by consensus were perhaps the federal and the language provisions. The Assembly worked out the details of the Indian federal structure in nego-tiations that lasted from the first meeting of the Union Powers Committee in the spring of 1947 until November 1949. The provi-sions had to be framed to satisfy the representatives of the Union and the provincial governments in the Assembly because the prov-inces could not opt out of India nor could federalism be worked by coercion. Hence provincial political figures of stature were included on important committees and in the making of major decisions. On the Union Powers Committee, for example, were Pant, premier of the U.P., and three prominent States representa-tives, Miner, V. T. Krishnamachari, and Ramaswami Mudaliar. On the Provincial Constitution Committee were two provincial prime ministers, Mahtab of Orissa and Kher of Bombay, as well as power-ful figures from provincial Congresses such as Biyani, Ujjal Singh, Deo, Diwakar, and Nagappa. More important in the framing of the federal provisions, however, was the series of meetings held at various times between the Drafting Committee, the Union Powers Committee, the members of the Union Cabinet (and their ministe-rial secretaries), and the provincial prime ministers and ministers of education and finance. The meetings of late July 1949, as we have seen, were the culmination of this effort.

In the pursuit of agreement on the federal provisions, several issues went to the Cabinet. Azad's campaign to expand Union power in the field of education by establishing uniform national standards was considered in the Cabinet before being settled in the July con-ferences between the provincial prime ministers and Union leaders. Security for the railways also became a Cabinet matter. Although 'railways' was a subject in the proposed Union List, railway police was to be a state subject. The Union Ministry of Railways, however, wanted constitutional authority to deploy police to protect the railways—largely as a result of depradations that had taken place during Partition. The Home Ministry objected to this, believing that in case of unrest it would be better to keep the police available for general duties. Also, the issue directly concerned the power of provincial governments. Apprised of the dispute, the Cabinet decided to place the matter before the July meetings with the provincial premiers and then to take action.[5] The issue was quietly settled in mid-November, the provinces retaining their power over railway police and the Union Executive gaining the right to give directions to the states in this regard. The Cabinet played a major role in the framing of the Emergency Provisions, approving, for example, the revision of Article 188 of the Draft Constitution so that the President could suspend the Constitution in case of a breakdown of provincial government without waiting for an emergency to be proclaimed by the Governor. The Cabinet itself could not effect this change, however, and desired that the Drafting Committee prepare the necessary amendments to give effect to the proposal.[6] The question was then, as we have seen, taken up and settled in the July 1949 conferences with the provincial premiers. The Cabinet, in collaboration with other select Assembly members, also considered in the early summer of 1949 the Finance Ministry's recommendations for the article on sales tax. The resulting draft provision was to be placed before the Drafting Committee and the premier's conference.[7] Commenting on these and other efforts to reach decisions by consensus, and in particular on the federal financial provisions, B. G. Kher said, 'I am very glad that good sense has prevailed and we have now evolved formulae which have met with a very generous measure of approval both in the provinces and at the Centre.'[8]

[5] See secret correspondence on this affair, including an extract from Cabinet minutes, in a letter from S. S. Ramasubban in the Ministry of Railways to S. N. Mukerjee of the Assembly Secretariat (undated, but Cabinet minutes dated 13 August 1949); *Law Ministry Archives*, File CA/65/Cons/49.

[6] See Ministry of Home Affairs letter to S. N. Mukerjee, 5 June, 1949, ibid., File CA/19/Cons/49.

[7] Letter from Finance Ministry to Assembly Secretariat, 8 July 1949; *Law Ministry Archives*.

[8] *CAD* XI, 5, 667.

The language question strained the Assembly's decision-making machinery to the utmost. For nearly three years the members searched for a generally acceptable solution. The Munshi-Ayyangar formula was drafted almost in desperation. Opening the final Assembly debate on language, Prasad announced that he would not put the issue to a vote. If an agreement was not acceptable to the whole country it would be most difficult to implement. Therefore, he said, 'it will not do to carry a point by debate in this House'.[9] The lack of enthusiasm for the final compromise, particularly on the part of the Hindi extremists, in one way represented a major failure of the decision-making process in the Assembly. Yet it was also a triumph, because it showed the lengths to which the Assembly was willing to go in search of agreement by consensus.

Consensus, and the decision-making process in general, was made possible largely by the atmosphere of unity, of idealism, and of national purpose that pervaded the Assembly. The members had come through the valley of the shadow, as Nehru put it, into the sunlight of independence. Many of them were not long out of jail. And suddenly they were given the opportunity to frame a constitution embodying the ideals and dreams of an independence movement. The Congress had led a national freedom struggle; now the party, expressing in its own ranks the talent and the diversity of the country, had an opportunity to make India whole for the first time in its history. For this reason the president of the Congress, not the Prime Minister of the Union Government, presided over Assembly Party meetings. Agreement on particular issues in the Assembly might result largely from pressure by the leadership, but it was a spontaneous sense of national purpose that motivated the members in their three-year task of laying the foundations for the new India. Symbolic of the times, a film drawing large audiences in New Delhi was entitled *Shaheed—a national drama of Independence*.

It must not be thought, however, that Assembly members on all occasions proceeded smoothly to inevitable conclusions on a cloud of goodwill. Consensus, and even agreement on a narrower basis, involved a great deal of work and the use of an assortment of political techniques. The rank and file of the Assembly although men of

[9]   *CAD* IX, 32, 1312.

unusual calibre, needed to be led.[10] The philosophy of leadership was expressed, with perhaps unusual paternalism, by N. G. Ayyangar. 'I believe', he wrote to B. N. Rau, ' . . . in preliminary decisions on these issues (of the basic principles of the Constitution) being taken by small numbers of selected people including party chiefs after those issues have been investigated from all points of view with the help of informed persons like you . . . Public opinion in such matters requires both a firm lead and skilled guidance.'[11] The Oligarchy and the 'experts' provided this leadership, the one through its political power and experience in government and the other through their knowledge of law.[12] On occasion the Oligarchy simply made its will known and was obeyed. The debate on the national anthem—certainly a hare that the Assembly at the time could refrain from chasing—was put off for nearly a year because Nehru informed the Steering Committee that it should be. But in general the Oligarchy used persuasion to gain support for its views. Nehru and Patel frequently called in dissidents and converted them with reasoned explanations of their policies—Patel often holding court during his sunrise walks among the fifteenth century tombs of Lodi Gardens. And when Nehru or Patel was called to the Assembly to quell a rebellious House, he did so with argument.

Nehru and Patel were the focus of power in the Assembly. When they were divided on an issue, as in the case of the property clause, factions could line up behind them and the debate would be lengthy. But when they settled their differences, the factions among the rank and file could do little else but shake hands and make the decision unanimous. Nehru and Patel appear to have had a much more amicable relationship than is generally believed. Each depended upon the other to complement his own abilities—Nehru on Patel perhaps more than Patel on Nehru. Each had his especial interests—Patel in

[10] In the opinion of several former Assembly members who are now Members of Parliament and of several observers of both bodies, the level of capability was higher in the Assembly than in Parliament today.

[11] N. G. Ayyangar letter to B. N. Rau, 20 March 1947; *Law Ministry Archives*, File CA/18/Cons/47.

[12] Ambedkar's manner towards the Assembly was often quite haughty, although his explanations when he chose to give them were brilliantly lucid. He was described as explaining a minor point 'with the air of a Sherlock Holmes making things clear for his Watson'. *The Hindustan Times*, 4 June 1949.

the Princely States, the public services, and the working of the Home Ministry (as it existed and would be under the new Constitution), and Nehru in Fundamental Rights, protection of minority rights, and the social reform aspects of the Constitution—and each let the other have almost free rein in these areas. The two men spent an hour together in private conversation on most evenings and often settled matters on which they had differed during the day, confronting their supporters with their agreement the following morning in the Assembly.[13] The blend in the Constitution of idealistic provisions and articles of a practical, administrative, and technical nature is perhaps the best evidence of the joint influence of these two men.

Nehru and Patel were not, however, the only powerful figures in the Assembly. Their colleagues in the Oligarchy, Azad and particularly Prasad, exercised much influence. Prasad could not do this openly; his position as the presiding officer of the Assembly prevented that. But his suggestions made behind the scenes carried considerable weight. As a basically conservative individual, his sympathies often lay with Patel and key provincial figures like Purushottam Das Tandon—who often used Prasad as a channel to communicate his ideas to the inner circle of Assembly leaders. Prasad's stand on many issues is difficult to determine, but on others, such as the Munshi-Ayyangar language formula, his councils of moderation must have been enhanced by his reputation for conservatism. Close to the fringes of the Oligarchy was Pandit Pant, who seems to have been the unofficial spokesman of the provincial premiers in the Assembly. Pant's contribution to the framing of the federal provisions and to a lesser extent in the language and due process controversies was substantial.

The Assembly leadership exercised its authority informally through political power and personal popularity and formally by the Assembly Party Whip. The use of the Whip began during the first session of the Assembly in December 1946 and Whips were issued continuously thereafter. They did not take the form of one-, two-, and three-line Whips, but were simply mimeographed lists of provisions and amendments that were to be accepted or rejected when they were introduced on the Assembly floor. They were signed by

[13] According to several persons interviewed by the author, including K. M. Munshi and Mrs. Durgabai Deshmukh, both members of the Constituent Assembly.

Satyanarayan Sinha, the Chief Whip. The Whip had the weight of Assembly Party discipline behind it, and although it frequently did not prevent debate on an issue in the Assembly, generally speaking it controlled the vote. All members elected to the Assembly on the Congress ticket, whether Congress Party members or not, were subject to this discipline. On occasion it silenced even such important figures as Pandit Pant, and Tandon believed it incumbent upon him to resign from the Assembly Party because he refused to obey the Whip at the time of the vote on the Munshi-Ayyangar formula. The Whip was certainly a mechanism by which the leadership controlled the behaviour of the Assembly, particularly the back-benchers, but it must not be equated with a three-line Whip in the British Parliament or in the Lok Sabha of today. In the first place it could be violated with impunity. Pandit Kunzru frequently disobeyed the Whip, as did H. V. Kamath, S. L. Saksena, Thakur Das Bhargava, and others, who were members of the Congress Party. Disciplinary action against Kamath and Saksena, contemplated at one time, was never taken.[14] One suspects that Pant obeyed the Whip more from self-discipline than because he feared ensure. The Whip also served as a guide for Assembly members through the welter of decisions taken in the party meetings. The Assembly might be scheduled to consider a dozen or more provisions of the Draft Constitution in a sitting. To each provision there might be dozens of amendments, and on each of them the party meeting had taken action. Assembly members could not be expected to keep these clear in their minds and the Whip provided a routine ready-reference to their previous decisions.

In the context of the Assembly's desire to make decisions by consensus, the Whip lost much of its importance, for even at its firmest, the Whip recorded decisions taken after lengthy discussion in the Assembly Party meetings. In these discussions everyone could have his say—experts like Ambedkar, cabinet ministers like Matthai, influential persons outside the leadership circle, and back-benchers as well as the leaders themselves. In these discussions the rank and file of the Assembly, although largely unacquainted with the intricacies of constitution-making, played an important part. On many issues, particularly technical ones, they were willing to be quietly led. But on matters that touched their interests they participated actively in the

---

[14] See a news report on this subject in *The Hindustan Times*, 23 August 1949.

discussions and several times imposed their will on the leadership. The language and linguistic provinces issues, the Fundamental Rights and Directive Principles, the minorities issue as it affected the Legislative and Executive provisions, aspects of the federal provisions, and several other issues were cases in point.

Nearly two-hundred and fifty members spoke in the Assembly, over two-hundred of them frequently. Groups of like-minded members formed on various occasions behind figures like Nehru and Patel, and behind spokesmen outside the leadership like Kunzru, Tandon, Santhanam, and Thakur Das Bhargava to press their views on the federal provisions, the language issue, or the provisos to the Fundamental Rights. One group made more or less constant contributions to the debate during the three years and submitted many amendments to the Draft Constitution. The members called themselves the 'Canning Lane Group' because they lived while attending Assembly sessions in Canning Lane, which joins Curzon Road not far from Constitution House where the Assembly Party held its meetings. Among the members were Mrs. Durgabai, M. A. Ayyangar, Pattabhi Sitaramayya, and Thakur Das Bhargava. Despite general participation in the debates, however, there can be no doubt that the bulk of the work in the Assembly was done by a group of about fifty individuals, and that a strong lead was given and initial decisions taken by an even smaller circle of less than twelve. Often the Assembly had little real choice but to go where its nose had been pointed. On the other hand, the rank and file of the Assembly were far from a rubber-stamp for the decisions of the leadership. The beneficial effects of consensus could only be gained from active agreement on issues. Procedural consensus was not enough; the Constitution, if it were to last, had to be based on consensus on the substantial issues. It has been largely because the Assembly pursued this ideal so diligently that its product has worked so well.

One more matter should be considered in regard to consensus. If decision-making by consensus had so commended itself to the Assembly, why was it not provided for in the Constitution? Probably because, as Pandit Kunzru put it, 'You can't run a modern government by consensus.'[15] Moreover, it would have been extremely difficult to draft such a provision. Consensus would have to be defined (would it

---

[15] In an interview with the author.

be 85, 95, or 100 per cent, agreement by voters?) and, more difficult, the subjects to which it would apply, for every Bill before Parliament could not be passed with consensus. The major categories to which consensus should apply might be easily chosen, but not the less important subjects.[16] Taken all in all, it was best to wait upon the individual occasion to decide whether consensus should be sought, and then to rely, as had been done in the Assembly, on good will and good sense.

2. The Principle of Accommodation

The second of India's original contributions to constitution-making, accommodation, is, as has been suggested in Chapter I, the ability to reconcile, to harmonize, and to make work without changing their content, apparently incompatible concepts—at least concepts that appear conflicting to the non-Indian, and especially to the European or American observer. Indians can accommodate such apparently conflicting principles by seeing them at different levels of value, or, if you will, in compartments not watertight, but sufficiently separate so that a concept can operate freely within its own sphere and not conflict with another operating in a separate sphere. Accommodation is not compromise. Accommodation is a belief or an attitude; compromise is a technique. To compromise is to settle an issue by mutual concession, each party giving up the portion of its desired end that conflicts with the interests of the other parties. It is the search for a mutually agreeable middle way. The provisions of the language chapter of the Constitution are a compromise.

With accommodation, concepts and viewpoints, although seemingly incompatible, stand intact. They are not whittled away by compromise, but are worked simultaneously. This attitude has been described thus:

> . . . The most notable characteristic in every field of Indian activity
> . . . . is the constant attempt to reconcile conflicting views or actions,
> to discover a workable compromise, to avoid seeing the human
> situation in terms of all black or all white . . . As India's philosopher

---

[16] K. G. Mashruwala, in his *Suggestions for the Constitution*, had proposed a 'scale' of subjects to which his system of 'consensus' would apply. But the actual agreement to institute this system would have been, as suggested above, most difficult to achieve.

Vice President (now President) Sarvapalli Radhakrishnan has put it: Why look at things in terms of this or that? Why not try to have both this *and* that?[17]

The writer is perceptive and has simply confused compromise with accommodation. Another observer agrees that accommodation may 'reflect an Indian style of thought, and that it might conceivably be accepted as an Indian tradition of political behaviour'.[18]

The Constituent Assembly's attitude towards consensus was accommodation applied to procedural techniques. Majority rule—i.e., decision-making by vote—and decision-making by consensus are conflicting concepts. The Assembly wished to proceed by consensus, but clearly the wording of every provision of the Constitution could not be arrived at this way. Moreover, the Assembly was a parliamentary body, drafting a constitution for a parliamentary democracy, or government 'by counting heads'. In such a situation, how could consensus be achieved? The Assembly resolved the issue by treating it on two levels: on less important questions consensus might be sought, but, if necessary, decision would be taken by vote. On important issues, however, decisions would be taken by consensus.

India's constitutional structure is a good example of the principle of accommodation on matters of substance. Federal and unitary systems of government are apparently incompatible. A constitution, an American or an English constitutional lawyer would say, must be one or the other. Yet the Indian Constitution is either, depending on the circumstances. The question of India's membership in the Commonwealth is another such example. The Assembly had decided in 1946 that India was to be a republic. Yet in 1949 the Assembly decided that India was to be a member of an organization with a monarch at its head. India was thus the first nation to reconcile the incompatibles of republicanism and monarchy. This it did at the time when Ireland was breaking away from the Commonwealth and was proclaiming itself a republic in reaction, primarily, to the unpleasant symbol of the monarchy.[19] India, however, reconciled

---

[17] Vera M. Dean, *New Patterns of Democracy*, p. 2.

[18] Francis Camell, 'Political Ideas and Ideologies in South and South-East Asia.' Ch, XIV of S. Rose (Ed.), *Politics in Southern Asia*, p. 182.

[19] For the definitive presentation of this point, see K. C. Wheare, *The Constitutional Structure of the Commonwealth*, pp. 153 and 155.

the two by viewing her own sovereignty on a level untouched by her recognition of the British Monarch as a 'symbol of association and as such the Head of the Commonwealth'.[20]

The solution of the panchayat question was also based on accommodation. The leaders of the Assembly had successfully separated the demand for panchayats in the Constitution from support for a completely Gandhian system of indirect government, thus avoiding a major conflict between panchayat supporters and the proponents of a direct, parliamentary Constitution. But there still remained a strong demand for panchayat development in terms of administrative decentralization versus centralization. Nehru, and in fact most Assembly members, recognized the need for a strong central government and, at the same time, for as much decentralization as possible. Could these incompatibles be accommodated? The question had long dogged the Congress in pre-independence days, and it had been a matter of particular importance to Nehru and Gandhi. Now the Assembly had to provide the answer.

The Assembly resolved the dilemma by placing both principles in the Constitution, and by applying them to different levels of government. Centralization was made a constitutional principle and would primarily affect the relationship of the provincial governments to the Union. Decentralization was to take place below the level of provincial government, and legislation to this end would be left largely to the provincial legislatures. The inclusion of Article 40 was a conscious device to accommodate apparent incompatibles—and the development of panchayats since 1950 suggests that the device can be successful.

The Constituent Assembly's adoption of the present Constitution is perhaps the most remarkable example of accommodation. The first concern of newly independent peoples is to establish, in their own eyes, and in those of the world, their national identity and *raison d'etre*. As a person desires to be distinguishable from his fellows by his singular personality, so newly created nations are concerned with their nationality. India was no exception to this. 'It is surely desirable', Nehru told Assembly members during the first session,

> that we should give some indication to ourselves, to those who look to this Assembly, to those millions in this country who are looking up

---

[20] Ibid., p. 154.

to us, and to the world at large as to what we may do, what we seek to achieve, whither we are going.[21]

The need to re-establish nationality may have been even greater in India because the country was apparently so anglicized: some Assembly members believed that the country and its institutions were so bereft of their Indianness that a special effort was needed to reassert it.

Feeling deeply the importance of being Indian, how could the members of the Constituent Assembly be satisfied with a Constitution whose political principles, and very provisions, were almost entirely European or American in origin? The majority of members could do so for the astoundingly simple reason that they saw no incompatability between the two. 'No Constitution can have an isolated existence', said K. C. Sharma. 'It is but right that we should gain from the experience of others and from the British Constitution and the American Constitution.'[22] A large number of Assembly members also believed that the apparent inconsistency between Indianness and a basically non-Indian constitution would be reconciled by working the Constitution in an Indian way. The very fact that a provision of, say, the Irish Constitution had been included to meet an Indian situation, made the provision effectively Indian. The techniques of the modern constitution would help preserve the true India; Seth Govind Das, certainly a conservative Hindu in outlook, believed this.

> I do not think that any one of us can transform the India of today into the India of Rigvedic times (said Govind Das, speaking in Hindi), but while I hold this view, I would like to make it clear at the same time that the civilization and culture which is the heritage of our early history . . . should not be rejected by us. We should adopt all that the modern world has to give us to fulfil our needs . . . . Modern India should be so built up that we may be able to retain our culture and civilization.[23]

India's long and glorious history was a fact not to be tarnished even by the adoption of a non-Indian constitution: as the two occupied different periods of time, so they occupied different levels of reality.

---

[21] *CAD* I, 5, 59 Professor Berlin refers to the 'wish to assert the "personality" of my class, or group or nation', as one of the sources of nationalist sentiment in modern times. See Berlin, *Two Concepts*, p. 45.

[22] *CAD* XI, 5, 677.

[23] *CAD* XI, 4, 611.

The roots of accommodation rest in the soil of Indian thoughts—thought that is characterized by its lack of dogmatism. What Spear has called the 'absorbtive and syncretistic features of Hinduism',[24] attributes that could flourish only in an undogmatic atmosphere, have become the basis of the Indian (Indian Muslim as well as Hindu) approach to life. 'Religion in India is not dogmatic', wrote Radhakrisnnan. 'It is a rational synthesis which goes on gathering into itself new conceptions as philosophy progresses. It is experimental and provisional in its nature . . .'[25] Such an attitude of open examination of all thought makes accommodation possible, for new ideas are not held at arms-length.

The ability to think at different levels, without dogmatism, refusing to confine speculation within narrow systems, pervaded Indian society. 'The whole history of India for thousands of years past shows her essential unity and the vitality and adaptability of her culture', wrote Nehru.[26] Indians generally, and Constituent Assembly members no less, believed that these attributes were both an historical truth and a continuing source of the nation's strength, and they naturally applied them to constitution-making.

The Art of Selection and Modification

For the Assembly to have discovered new constitutional principles in 1947 would have been difficult or impossible.[27] Thus the Indian Constitution is, on the surface, largely derivative. To consider that

---

[24] Spear, op. cit, p. 39.

[25] Radhakrishnan, *Indian Philosophy* I, pp. 25–26.

[26] Nehru, *Unity of India*, p. 17. It may be objected that India's inability to absorb the Muslims and, finally, Partition, invalidate the whole concept of accommodation. Of two possible answers to this, the first is the simpler: the separateness of Muslims in India, resulting in the final cultural and political divorce of Partition was the major failure of largely Hindu India to accommodate disparate forces. Such an answer would not be entirely true, however, which leads us to a tentative second answer. This is that the initial defensive reaction of Hinduism to the arrival of a new political and religious force in India was softening during the heyday of the Mogul Empire—under the benevolence of Akbar, etc.—and that accommodation might have taken place had it not been prevented from doing so first by Aurangzeb and then during the years 1830 to 1947 largely by the presence of the British in India.

[27] Dr. Ambedkar believed that 'the only new things, if there can be any, in a constitution framed so late in the day are the variations made to remove the faults (of

the Assembly was merely imitative, however, would be to forget that borrowing did not relieve the Assembly of choice, and that the borrowed provisions had to be adapted to suit Indian conditions. An appraisal of the Assembly's work must consider both the skilfullness with which it selected the provisions it borrowed and the quality of its modifications, for in each lay the possibility of creativeness and originality, success and failure. And, it has turned out, the Assembly successfully played the alchemist, turning foreign metals into Indian coin.

One example of selection and modification is constitutional amendment. The three mechanisms of the system devised by the Assembly, contrary to predictions, have made the Constitution flexible while at the same time protecting the rights of the states. They have worked better than has the amending process in any other country where federalism and the British parliamentary system jointly form the bases of the constitution. Particularly noteworthy was the Assembly's foresight in leaving in the hands of Parliament the language issue and the creation and admission into the Union of new states and territories, which anticipated the early reorganization and renaming of several provinces, the integration of the former Princely States, and the nationwide reorganization of 1956. The Assembly had a clear precedent for this in the 1935 Act and in the formation by the British of Sind and Orissa provinces. But the Assembly's foresight in leaving a safety-valve for such pressures was exceeded by the wisdom of making the creation of new states (and therefore the changing of existing ones) a procedure demanding only a parliamentary majority instead of a constitutional amendment. This contrasts favourably with the examples of Australia and of Nigeria, where constitutional difficulties have impeded the creation of new states.

Impugning the Assembly's creativeness misses the point most widely when it centres on the debt that the federal provisions of the Constitution owe to those of the 1935 Act.[28] Although the resemblance between the two federal systems is great, the legislative

---

its antecedents) and to accommodate it to the needs of the country'. *CAD* VII, I, 37.

[28] One might interject here that the federal provisions of the 1935 Act were derived largely from the constitutions of the Dominions, and that the Congress had called for a federal constitution for India in the nineteen-twenties.

list system and many of the provisions relating to revenue collection and distribution having been kept, the Assembly made vital changes. It brought the former Princely States into the federal system with the same status as the provinces; it provided for national planning to grow within the federal structure; and it created Finance Commissions to protect the States' interests and to make the revenue provisions flexible. The essential point, however, is neither the copying nor the changes, but that the provincial leaders of a newly independent country adopted voluntarily the tight federalism that had been originally designed to support a strong, centralized, colonial administration. The British imposed such a system on India, but independent Indians, aware of the national need, and despite the tendency in some newly independent nations to distrust even tight federalism as fostering schism, adopted cooperative federalism for themselves.

The Constituent Assembly could be creative in its rejection of precedent as well as in its borrowing. The Assembly rejected much of the 1935 Act in order to draft a constitution making Indians for the first time politically 'one people'. In so far as the Constituent Assembly was able, it united India's communal and other minorities. To do so it turned away from the detailed minority provisions that characterized post-World War I constitutions in Europe—with which the members were familiar through the *Constitutional Precedents* of B. N. Rau—and from the maiming precedent of the 1935 Act.

The 1935 Act, with a mixture of shrewd calculation and of genuine solicitude for the welfare of the minorities, encouraged factions by giving them political being.[29] The 1935 Act as has been seen earlier, employed such constitutional devices as functional representation, separate electorates, reserved seats, and weightage. In the lower and theoretically 'popular' House of the federal legislature, there were eleven categories of reserved seats for communal and functional representation. Members were to be elected to these seats, in general, indirectly and separately by the respective electoral groups in the

---

[29] Britain's negative attitude towards Indian unity was to be expected. Because the road to Indian unity was the road to declining British power, it was a wiser policy for Britain to encourage factions and then to hold the balance between them. The British did not create factions or communalism in India, but their policies and, indeed, their very presence abetted it. Sadly enough, Indians themselves, generally speaking, contributed greatly to their own downfall in this regard.

lower houses of provincial assemblies. With this support of faction, the British enacted the paradox of colonial regimes: in the guise of protecting the rights of indigenous minorities from the depredations of indigenous majorities, they denied liberty to both.

Desiring above all to promote national unity, members of the Constituent Assembly rejected these devices by substituting direct elections for indirect in lower houses, by rejecting separate electorates in favour of joint electorates and by abolishing weightage and, except for Scheduled Castes and Tribes, reserved seats. The Assembly believed, in Jennings's words, that 'to recognize communal claims . . . is to strengthen communalism',[30] and so it had decided to ignore them. The great reduction in the size of the Indian Muslim community because of Partition doubtless made the Assembly's task easier, and the horrors, attending Partition certainly underlined the necessity for communal peace, but the Assembly's positive approach to communal unity resulted primarily from Indians being free to grapple with their own affairs.

The Assembly selected and modified the provisions from other constitutions with a great deal of professional help. This began even before the Assembly was convened, with the Constitutional Precedents prepared by the Assembly Secretariat under the supervision of B. N. Rau. And the Assembly drew freely on Rau's advice throughout the framing of the Draft Constitution, before his departure to New York to represent India at the United Nations. The members depended equally on the talents of the non-Congressmen that the Congress had brought into the Assembly, such as N. Gopalaswami Ayyangar, Alladi Krishnaswami Ayyar, and Dr. Ambedkar. The assistance rendered by the Ministry of Law, under Ambedkar, and the Ministry of Finance, under John Matthai, both of whom, of course, participated in the Assembly Party meetings, was of especial importance. Other Union Government ministries also submitted large numbers of memoranda to the Assembly. There were, additionally, hundreds of communications from provincial governments on subjects varying from revenue and taxes through fundamental rights to suggestions about which groups should be listed in the Constitution as Scheduled Castes and Tribes. Then there were the reports of the 'expert' committees on the financial provisions of the Constitution, the linguistic provinces

---

[30] Jennings, *Some Characteristics*, p.65.

issue, the powers of the Supreme Court, the citizenship article, and so on. Adding perspective to the creation and interpretation of these views was the actual experience of governing the country, a responsibility that fell, in varying degrees, on nearly all Assembly members. The practical knowledge resulting from this dual role, as has been seen, materially affected the content of the Constitution.

Public bodies and private individuals in substantial numbers also made their views known to the Assembly. Among the organizations were chambers of commerce and industry and private companies, bar associations, linguistic associations, and minority groups. Individuals who wrote to the Assembly were primarily interested in legal technicalities, the language issue, and in fundamental and minority rights— communications on the latter two subjects ran into thousands. There were several letters from 'God Kalki' signed by one 'S. R. Chari—God Incarnate'.[31] The Assembly Secretariat acknowledged nearly all these communications and frequently summarized them for the Drafting Committee or Assembly leaders. Their affect on the Assembly is difficult to judge. Some suggestions were rejected outright, such as that from chambers of commerce and industry that there be functional representation in the legislatures. The pressure from lawyers, justices, and others to liberalize certain of the Rights provisions, however, bore fruit. It is doubtful whether many of the views expressed by outsiders were not already held by some Assembly members. It also seems that members accurately sensed the strength of public opinion on various issues. Thus it would probably be correct to assume that these communications to the Assembly served primarily to warn the members that their efforts were being watched and that they must use particular care in framing certain provisions. And because very few letters criticized the Assembly's choice of federalism and parliamentary democracy, members could see that there was little opposition to the borrowing of constitutional provisions and a good deal of interest that the work should be done well.

If the nobility of a constitution's goals is a measure of a constituent body's intent, then the efficacy of the provisions for attaining these ideals should be the measure of its skill. The Constituent Assembly intended that the Constitution would bring to Indians liberty,

---

[31] Although communications from the public are to be found in several collections of papers, the bulk of them are to be found in the Law Ministry Archives.

equality, fraternity, and justice. It intended that the Constitution should foster India's rebirth. The events of the past fourteen years indicate that the Constitution has helped towards the achievement of these aims. What is important, therefore, is not the foreign origin of the means, but that, properly adapted, they have subserved the national goals.

Criticisms of the Constitution

Not all Assembly members believed that foreign precedent could be adapted to India's needs. Some held that a constitution so 'un-Indian', so alien in its forms if not its principles, could not be a success. Yet other authorities, particularly the British constitutionalist Sir Ivor Jennings, have approved of the reliance on British precedent, but have argued that the provisions borrowed were not always well selected and that the Constitution, generally speaking, was too long and complicated. Let us consider these views.

The most frequently expressed fear, and the most easily understandable, was that the largely foreign origin of the Constitution would make it unworkable in India. 'The ideals on which this Draft Constitution is framed have no manifest relation to the fundamental spirit of India', charged one member of the Assembly. 'I can assure you', he went on, that this Constitution will 'not prove suitable' and will 'break down soon after being brought into operation.'[32] 'We wanted the music of Veena or Sitar', lamented another Assembly member, 'but here we have the music of an English band.'[33] A third Assembly member characterized the Constitution as 'a slavish imitation of—nay, much more—a slavish surrender to the West'.[34]

---

[32] *CAD* XI, 4; 613; L. Sahu.

[33] Ibid., p. 616; K. Hanumanhaiya.

[34] *CAD* VII, 2, 242; Lokanath Misra. The Speaker of the C.A. (Legislative), later to gain eminence as the Speaker of Lok Sabha, G. V. Mavlankar, also doubted that the constitution suited the 'genius' of the country. Mavlankar believed that the level of political consciousness was so low in India that a democratic constitution could not work. See *The Hindustan Times*, 15 September 1949. Mavlankar obviously was not willing to gamble—as were Nehru and Patel—that the introduction of democratic government would over 10 years produce the political consciousness needed for the Constitution's survival.

These critics believed that the Constitution was un-Indian or anti-Indian because it neither incorporated nor represented the 'genius' or the 'ancient polity' of India. By it India was robbed of her patrimony, if not of her identity. India must be governed under Indian institutions, they said, and the Assembly had gone wrong by ignoring indigenous institutions and Gandhi's teaching.

Yet the Assembly members who complained that the Constitution did not reflect the 'genius' of the nation did not favour a 'Gandhian' constitution, and they never explained what that 'genius' was—the reason being that they were not sure. No one has ever successfully defined 'Indian' in this context either in the Assembly or since. Even such extreme Hindu organizations as the Rashtriya Swayamsevak Sangh (RSS) and the Hindu Mahasabha have not challenged parliamentary government on the grounds that it is contrary to the mystical 'Hindu polity', and the constitution proposed by the Hindu Mahasabha was parliamentary in form. To declare that the Constitution is un-Indian or anti-Indian is to use the undefined—if not the undefinable—as a measuring stick.

Most of the Constitution is plainly non-Indian, but this is different from being un-Indian, or being inconsistent with Indian ways of thought and action. If any real inconsistency between the assumptions of the Constitution and the values of a 'Hindu tradition' or an 'Indian tradition' existed, if the Constitution was un-Indian and therefore not suited to be the basis for government, its inadequacy, its repugnancy to the community, would surely by now have become apparent in an adverse reaction to it by the conservative—some would say reactionary—masses. There has been no such adverse reaction. On the contrary, the Indian masses, whether factory workers or behind the plough, have adopted with alacrity the aims of the Constitution as their own guarantee of a better life—perhaps without being aware of precisely where they come from. And they have with equal eagerness used the mechanisms of the Constitution—adult suffrage, the Judiciary, the Fundamental Rights and Directive Principles —as their means to attain these goals.

The heart of the issue is that most Indians—no matter how strong the attachment to traditional life—have shown little fondness for traditional politics, understood as rule of the many by the privileged few; they do not see any necessary connection between the two. The evidence increasingly shows that Indians in general are eager to use democratic politics to overthrow all but the most personal aspects of tradition in favour of increased political and social freedom. Moreover, criticisms that the Constitution is anti-Indian ignore the fact that it has been secular democracy in India that has permitted the existence of such 'Indian' forms of politics as satyagraha, the fast, and the Bhoodan movement of Vinobha Bhave.[35] This, and not criticism of the Constitution as un-Indian, represents the syncretism and the spirit of accommodation of which Indians are so proud.

The Constitution has been criticized, particularly by Sir Ivor Jennings, as too long and detailed and too rigid.[36] Long and detailed the Constitution certainly is. Rigid it has not proved to be. There were sound grounds in the eyes of most Assembly members for the inclusion of so many details in the Constitution. Certain of them were put into the Constitution because they were thought to be of fundamental importance and should, therefore, not be on the level of ordinary legislation. For example, the provisions relating to the public services and to the Judiciary were included so as to put the independence of the services and of the Judiciary beyond the reach of Parliament, thereby giving them a special sanctity. The Judicial provisions were included in the Constitution as the result of an express decision in the Assembly not to relegate them to a Judicature Act. As Dr. Ambedkar put it, such details must be found in the Constitution because 'it is perfectly possible to pervert the Constitution without changing its form by merely changing the form of administration'.[37] To lessen the chances of their intentions being subverted, the members of the Assembly took care to state them clearly in the Constitution. We shall never know if Dr. Ambedkar's scepticism was justified, but as the Constitution's detail has not prevented its efficient working, his caution has done no harm.

A further reason for including a variety of detail in the Constitution, Assembly members believed, was to effect a smooth transfer of authority from the British Indian Government to the governments of India, thus preserving administrative efficiency. At independence, India inherited a well-established system of constitutional law. To have recreated this

---

[35] For further discussion of this point, see Morris-Jones, *Parliament in India*, pp. 37–38.

[36] Jennings, *Some Characteristics*, pp. 9–16.

[37] *CAD* VII, 1, 38. For more on Dr. Ambedkar's views on this subject, see Chapter 1.

body of law in the form of legislation to be passed after drafting a constitution of broad principles seemed to Assembly members a difficult
if not a dangerous proposition. Why should they desert the firm shore
of precedent for the seas of political uncertainty? Assembly members
also believed that the detail of the Constitution might diminish rather
than increase the amount of litigation testing its meaning and their
intentions. This would be particularly true if the provisions of the
Constitution embodying administrative detail were drawn from the
1935 Act, already well known both to politicians and members of
the legal profession. Moreover, the inclusion of such detail from the
1935 Act and from other constitutions would mean that the existing
case law concerning the interpretation of these provisions would be
available to aid in interpreting the Constitution. Time has supported
all these assumptions. There have not been an undue number of cases
involving interpretation of the Constitution, but when these have
arisen case law from America and other countries as well as Indian
precedent have frequently been drawn on by the Supreme Court. And
Indian administration has been remarkably effective largely because it
did not have to be created afresh after independence.[38]

Time, therefore, has happily proved most criticisms of the
Constitution ill-founded. That the Indian Constitution was an ably
conceived and drafted document, showing a creative, if not an original, approach to the nation's constitutional needs, we cannot justly
doubt. This is borne out, if in no other way, by the success of democratic, parliamentary government in India, for if it is quite possible
to govern badly with a good constitution, it is nearly impossible to
govern well with an inadequate one.

The Credit Goes to the Indians

The successful working of the Constitution has been attributed by
some observers largely or entirely to the favourable conditions that

---

[38] In this regard, it is well known that many Indians in 1947 envied Pakistan's
opportunity to create a nation and an administration relatively unencumbered
by existing traditions and machinery. Yet Pakistan, and many other countries,
have found this a most difficult task. India's task has not been made simple; the
legacies of the past hinder, as well as help, and may eventually have to be cast
away. But in the early years of independence, a working administration is an
enormous asset.

have existed from 1950 to the present, to the inculcation of Indian society with democratic principles during the colonial period, and to the inclusion in the Constitution of the tried and true institutions of parliamentary democracy. The value and importance of American and British constitutional precedent to the framers of the Constitution is everywhere present in the proceedings and documents of the Assembly and in the text of the Constitution itself. The debt to the 1935 Act in particular is very great. But it is often forgotten that the 1935 Act was as seriously flawed as parts of it were skilfully drafted, and that the members of the Assembly did not use many of its chief provisions. Certainly the Indian experience of, and direct participation in, the institutions of democratic, parliamentary government during the British period immeasurably enhanced the Constitution's chances of success. The beneficial effect of this aspect of colonial rule can hardly be questioned, but neither should it blind critics to the achievement of the Assembly in drafting a constitution that Indians have been able to work so well.

Those who argue that certain circumstances conspired to allow the Constitution to work well are referring to India's possession at independence of the three factors necessary for the stability of a new state: a charismatic leadership, a mass party, and a well-trained bureaucracy.[39] Nehru and other leading figures, with their popularity and gifts of statesmanship, have given India direction, and have in themselves been a point of focus for the nation. The Constitution has worked partly because the leaders knew where they were going and the mass of people were reasonably content to follow them. The mass party, with its generally accepted set of goals, its spirit of cooperative endeavour, and its discipline—which in great part flowed from loyalty to the leaders—not only made more widespread the national sense of purpose, but held the nation together. The power and magnetism of the Congress high command, and, the discipline it enforced, have, to date, assured the effective working of the federal system. The bureaucracy, both during the framing period and under the Constitution, has kept the machinery of government going; taxes were collected, railways ran.

---

[39] For the concise statement of these factors the author is indebted to the late Francis Carnell.

Because day to day administration has continued, because of the nation's faith in its leadership, and because of the cohesive effect of the party, there has never been in India a crisis of popular confidence; hence there has been no anarchy. These factors helped India survive the chaos of Partition. Ordered life continuing, there was time for the niceties of parliamentary democracy, for the thoughtful consideration and solution of problems including, of course, the framing of the Constitution. The Constitution has been a success, one might say, summing up this line of argument, because there have been no direct attacks on it or on the institutions it created, and because the colonial experience, the leadership, the mass party, and the bureaucracy have provided a favourable constitutional environment.

No one can say what would have happened to the Constitution or, indeed, if there would have been one, had the colonial experience not been successful. But what if there had not been present in India a great leader, a mass party, and civil servants? Would the best of constitutions have survived Nehru's early disappearance from the scene and the possibly consequent disappearance of Congress ascendancy?

This is to ask if newly independent states in the mid-twentieth century should adopt democratic constitutions at all. The question implies that, had Congress ascendancy disappeared, there would have been various parties contending ineffectively for power and that there would have been anarchy. No democratic constitution can protect itself against such a situation any more than it can, without losing its own democratic character, protect itself, against the ineptness of, or subversion by, governments originally based upon it. For its continued existence, a democratic, constitution demands a belief in democracy especially by the governed and by the members of the government it establishes—who are, it is hoped, also effective governors. And democratic federations also presuppose a will towards union.

Lacking these, a democratic constitution is likely to be mortally threatened, as it was in the United States in 1861, or overturned, as in Weimar Germany. A democratic constitution can be smothered, as in Ghana, by the very factors that have protected it in India, a charismatic leader and a mass party, because there each gives only lip-service to democracy. We may ask, therefore, should the Indian Constitution have been framed to project itself against the presence, as well as the absence, of such a leader and such a powerful party? The answer is that constitutions can achieve only so much; democracy in new states is simply a calculated risk. The events of 1964 indicate that in India the risk has paid off, that parliamentary democracy can survive the death of Nehru, the last of the great leaders.

In India the risk was smaller, the chances of success greater, than in most new states because the Indian tradition and Indian society were congenial to democratic government. It was less the invaluable colonial experience that assured the working of the Constitution than that the ideas and spirit of English liberal democracy fell on fertile ground. This, and the fact that the charismatic leader and the mass party have protected democracy and not made a mockery of it, both stem, as do all reasons for the success of the Constitution, from one cause: the Indian receptivity to democratic ways.

The ideal of consensus is the most democratic of standards. The ideal of non-violent, non-coercive self-rule, also strongly established in India, is equally so. The Indian cultural tradition, rich, deep, and undogmatic, has been able to absorb the most advanced intellectual concepts. Indian intellectuals were able to meet the early representatives of European culture on equal terms. They easily mastered both the philosophy and practice of modern government. The Indian's natural receptiveness to democratic processes, and his ability to employ them, are illustrated by the history of the Indian National Congress. Unlike most nationalist movements, the Congress was democratic in its internal organization. In its conduct of the Independence Movement, terrorism was the exception rather than the rule, and bargaining, the rule rather than the exception. In the sixty years before independence, the Congress had practised democracy as well as demanding democratic government for India.

The Indians' sense of their rich cultural heritage, their record of professional achievement in the arts and sciences of the modern world, and their faith in their ability to govern themselves, combined to give them a national maturity that allowed a reasoned approach to the creation and working of government. Equipped with the basic qualifications, attitudes, and experience for creating and working a democratic constitution, Indians did not default their tryst with destiny.

Appendix I

Statement by the Cabinet Mission to India and His Excellency the Viceroy, 16 May 1946 (Called the Cabinet Mission Plan.)
Paragraph 18 and a portion of 19.

18. In forming any assembly to decide a new constitutional structure the first problem is to obtain as broad-based and accurate a representation of the whole population as is possible. The most satisfactory method obviously would be by election based on adult franchise, but any attempt to introduce such a step would lead to a wholly unacceptable delay in the formulation of the new Constitution. The only practicable course is to utilize the recently elected Provincial Legislative Assemblies as electing bodies. There are, however, two factors in their composition which make this difficult. First, the numerical strengths of Provincial Legislative Assemblies do not bear the same proportion to the total population in each province. Thus, Assam, with a population of 10 million, has a Legislative Assembly of 108 members, while Bengal, with a population six times as large has an Assembly of only 250. Secondly, owing to the weightage given to Minorities by the Communal Award, the strengths of the several communities in each Provincial Legislative Assembly are not in proportion to their numbers in the Province. Thus the number of seats reserved for Moslems in the Bengal Legislative Assembly is only 48 per cent of the total, although they form 55 per cent of the provincial population. After a most careful consideration of the various methods by which these points might be corrected, we have come to the conclusions that the fairest and most practical plan would be:

    (a)   to allot each Province a total number of seats proportional to its population, roughly in the ratio of one to one million, as the nearest substitute for representation by adult suffrage;

(b) to divide this provincial allocation of seats between the main communities in each Province in proportion to their population;

(c) to provide that the representatives allocated to each community in a Province shall be elected by the members of that community in its Legislative Assembly.

We think that for these purposes it is sufficient to recognize only the three main communities in India, General, Moslem and Sikh, the 'General' community including all persons who are not Moslems or Sikhs. As smaller minorities would upon a population basis have little or no representation, since they would lose the weightage which assures them seats in the Provincial Legislatures, we have made the arrangements set out in paragraph 20 below to give them a full representation upon all matters of special interest to Minorities.

19. (i) We therefore propose that there shall be elected by each Provincial Legislative Assembly the following numbers of representatives, each part of the Legislative Assembly (General, Moslem or Sikh) electing its own representatives by the method of proportional representation with a single transferable vote:

Table of Representation

Section A			
Province:	*General*	*Moslem*	*Total*
Madras	45	4	49
Bombay	19	2	21
United Provinces	47	8	55
Bihar	31	5	36
Central Provinces	16	1	17
Orissa	9	0	9
	167	20	187

Section B				
Province:	*General*	*Moslem*	*Sikh*	*Total*
Punjab	8	16	4	28
North-West Frontier Province	0	3	0	3
Sind	1	3	0	4
	9	22	4	35

(*Continued*)

(*Continued*)

Section C			
Province:	*General*	*Moslem*	*Total*
Bengal	27	33	60
Assam	7	3	10
	34	36	70
Total for British India		292	
Maximum for Indian States		93	
Total		385	

Note: In order to represent the Chief Commissioners' Provinces there will be added to Section A the member representing Delhi in the Central Legislative Assembly, the member representing Ajmer-Merwara in the Central Legislative Assembly and representatives to be elected by the Coorg Legislative Council...

Appendix II

Listed below are the members of the most important Assembly Committees

Rules Committee

Rajendra Prasad, Chairman
Jagjivan Ram
Sarat Chandra Bose
(who later lost his seat in the
Assembly)
Frank Anthony
A.K. Ayyar
Baksi Tek Chand
Rafi Ahmed Kidwai

Joseph Alban D'souza
N. G. Ayyangar
Purushottam Das Tandon
Gopinath Bardoli
Pattabhi Sitaramayya
K. M. Munshi
Mehr Chand Khanna
Harnam Singh
Mrs. G. Durgabai

Steering Committee

Rajendra Prasad, Chairman
Maulana Abul Kalam Azad
Vallabhbhai Patel
Ujjal Singh
Mrs. G. Durgabai
S. H. Prater

Kiran Shankar Roy
Satyanarayan Sinha
M. A. Ayyangar
S. N, Mane
Diwan Chaman Lall
K. M. Munshi

States Committee (Committee appointed to negotiate with the States
Negotiating Committee)

Jawaharlal Nehru, Chairman
Maulana Abul Kalam Azad
Vallabhbhai Patel

Pattabhi Sitaramayya
Shankarrao Deo
N. G. Ayyangar

Drafting Committee

B.R. Ambedkar, Chairman

Mohammed Saadulla

B. L. Mitter (who soon after
his appointment ceased to
be a member of the Assembly)
N. G. Ayyangar
A. K. Ayyar
K. M. Munshi

N. Madhava Rau
D. P. Khaitan (who died
in 1948, and who was
replaced on the committee
in January 1949 by)
T. T. Krishnamachari

Advisory Committee (membership as of May 1949)

Vallabhbhai Patel, Chairman
Surendra Mohan Ghose
Prithvi Singh Azad
H. J. Khandekar
P.R.Thakur
S. H. Prater
Mehr Chand Khanna
Shyama Prasad Mookerjee
Dharam Prakash
Jagjivan Ram
B. R. Ambedkar
Jogendra Singh
Partap Singh
Gyani Kartar Singh
Joseph Alban D'souza
J. L. P. Roche-Victoria
Frank Anthony
Homi Mody
Rup Nath Brahma
Abdul Samad Khan
Phool Bhan Shah
Jaipal Singh
Maulana Abdul Kalam Azad
Rajkumari Amrit Kaur
Govind Ballabh Pant
Purushottam Das Tandon
K.T. Shah
A.V. Thakur
Raj Krushna Bose
Abdul Qayum Ansari
Hussainbhay A. Lallejee

V. I. Muniswami Pillai
Baldev Singh
Ujjal Singh
H. C. Mookerjee
P. K. Salve
N. Madhava Rau
Darbar Gopaldas Desai
Chengalroya Reddy
Lakshmi Kant Maitra
Sarangdhar Das
Tajamul Husain
R. K. Sidhwa
Khan Abdul Ghaffar Khan
J. J. M. Nichols-Roy
Devendra Nath Samanta
J. B. Kripalani
Jairamdas Daulatram
Mrs. Hansa Mehta
Gopinath Bardoli
A. K. Ayyar
K. M. Munshi
M. Ruthnaswamy
Hafizur Rehman
Mohammed Saadulla
Saiyid Jafar Imam
Kameshwara Singh
Mohan Singh Mehta
Gokulbhai Bhatt
Seth Govind Das
Thakur Das Bhargava
Giani Gurumukh Singh

Kasturbhai Lalbhai   Begum Aizaz Rasul

Fundamental Rights Sub-Committee (of the Advisory Committee)

J. B. Kripalani, Chairman	K. M. Munshi
M. R. Masani	Harnam Singh
K. T. Shah	Maulana Abdul Kalam Azad
Rajkumari Amrit Kaur	B. R. Ambedkar
Mrs. Hansa Mehta	Jairamdas Daulatram
A.K. Ayyar	K. M. Panikkar

Minorities Sub-Committee (of the Advisory Committee)

Because of the particular relevance of the individual's community to his membership on the sub-committee, the community of the members has been given. It will be noted that several members were not members of the Constituent Assembly; they were co-opted by the other committee members.

H. C. Mookerjee, Chairman	Christian
Jagjivan Ram	Scheduled Castes
Maulana Abul Kalam Azad	Muslim
B. R. Ambedkar	Scheduled Castes
Jogendra Singh	Sikh
S. P. Mookerjee	Hindu
Ujjal Singh	Sikh
Harnam Singh	Sikh
Bakshi Tek Chand	Hindu
Gopichand Bhargava	Hindu
H. J. Khandekar	Scheduled Castes
P. R. Thakur	Scheduled Castes
Homi Mody	Parsi
P. K. Salve	Christian—Notan Assembly member
S. H. Prater	Anglo-Indian
Frank Anthony	Anglo-Indian
C. Rajgopalachari	Hindu
Rajkumari Amrit Kaur	Christian
Jairamdas Daulatram	Hindu
R. K. Sidhwa	Parsi
Rup Nath Brahma	Scheduled Tribes, Assam—Not a member of the Assembly

M. Ruthnaswamy	Hindu—Not an Assembly member
M. V. H. Collins	Anglo-Indian—Not an Assembly member
Joseph Alban D'souza	Christian
K. M. Munshi	Hindu
Govind Ballabh Pant	Hindu

Appointed to the Sub-Committee by President Prasad in June 1947:

Ismail Chundrigar	Muslim
Mohammed Saadulla	Muslim
Chaudhri Khaliquzzaman	Muslim

Union Powers Committee (as of 28 July 1947)

Jawaharlal Nehru, Chairman	Col. Himmatsinghji
B. L. Miner	A. Ramaswami Mudaliar
N. G. Ayvangar	A. K. Ayyar
V. T. Krishnamachari	Govind Ballabh Pant
Biswanath Das	Jairamdas Daulatram
Sarat Chandra Bose	K.M. Munshi
Pattabhi Sitaramayya	Bakshi Tek Chand
D. P. Khaitan	M. R. Masani

Union Constitution Committee

Jawaharlal Nehru, Chairman	S. P. Mookerjee
Maulana Abul Kalam Azad	V. T. Krishnamachari
Govind Ballabh Pant	K. M. Panikkar
Jagjivan Ram	N. G. Ayyangar
B. R. Ambedkar	P. Govinda Menon
A. K. Ayyar	M. A. Srinivasan
K. M. Munshi	B. H. Zaidi
K. T. Shah	

Ad Hoc *Committee on the Supreme Court*

S. Varadachariar, Chairman	B. L.Mitter
(Not an Assembly member)	K. M. Munshi
A. K. Ayyar	B. N. Rau, Constitutional Adviser

Provincial Constitution Committee

Vallabhbhai Patel, Chairman	Radhanath Das
P. Subbarayan	Satyanarayan Sinha
Pattabhi Sitaramayya	Rafi Ahmed Kidwai

B. G. Kher

Brijlal Biyani

K. N. Katju

Phulan Prasad Verma

Harekrushna Mahtab

Kiran Shankar Roy

Jairamdas Daulatram

Ujjal Singh

P. K. Sen

Mrs. Hansa Mehta

Rajkumari Amrit Kaur

H.C. Mookerjee

J. B. Kripalani

Shankarrao Deo

R. R. Diwakar

S. Nagappa

Diwan Chaman Lall

C. M. Poonacha

Appendix III

Part A

The first part of this Appendix is devoted to brief biographical sketches of the twenty-one most important figures in the Assembly. The second part lists the names of all Assembly members mentioned in this work and gives the party and the province that they represented and their community and probable caste affiliation.

There is room for an entire work on the personal backgrounds of the members of the Constituent Assembly somewhat along the lines followed by Charles Beard in his work on the American Constitution. This would, however, be a work of great difficulty, for biographical information is extremely hard to come by in India. Efforts have been made in this direction in regard to the Provisional Parliament of 1950–52 and for the Parliament of India after 1952 by Professor Morris-Jones. (See his *Parliament in India,* pp. 114ff and 156ff.) Yet it would, without deeper research, be unwise to apply these facts to the members of the Constituent Assembly. The information in the following sketches has been gleaned from a variety of sources, among them the Who's Who section of the *Times of India Directory and Yearbook,* the *India and Pakistan Yearbook,* also published by the *Times of India,* the Rajya Sabha and Lok Sabha *Who's Who* published by the Government, of India, and two other books, T. Peters, *Who's Who in India* and W. P. Kabadi, *The Indian Who's Who.* The author has also drawn personally on the knowledge of qualified observers.

Immediately under the names of the Assembly members in Part A are given the community they were elected to represent in the Assembly (General, Muslim, or Sikh), their caste, if the member happens to be a Hindu, and the party on whose ticket they were elected. Thus Dr. Ambedkar represented the General community, was a Hindu and a member of the Scheduled Castes, and was elected to the Assembly first by the Scheduled Castes Federation and then by the Congress Party. Bengal and Bombay were provinces from which he was elected.

AMBEDKAR, Dr. Bhimrao
General (Hindu, Scheduled Castes—Mahar)

Scheduled Castes Federation—
Bengal; Congress—Bombay
Born: 1893   Died: 1956
Mother tongue (M.T.): Marathi
Educated at Satara and Bombay; Columbia University, New York City, M.A., and Ph.D. (Attended on a scholarship of Gaekwar of Baroda.) University of London, D.Sc.; Grays Inn. Bar 1923.
Taught in college in Bombay. Delegate to Round Table Conference 1930–32 and member Joint Parliamentary Committee on Constitutional Reform. Member for Labour, Governor-General's Executive Council 1942–46. A leader of the Untouchables and an opponent of Gandhi and the Congress. Author of works on economics, finance, politics, and the Untouchables. Minister of Law, Government of India 1947–51. In the Constituent Assembly:
    Chairman Drafting Committee
    Member   Advisory Committee
        „   C.A. Committee on Functions
        „   Union Constitution Committee
After Assembly:
    Retirement from public life, convert to Buddhism, Member Parliament.

AYYANGAR, M. A. (Ananthasayanam)
General (Hindu, Brahmin)   Congress—Madras
Born: 1889
M.T.:Telegu
Educated almost entirely in Madras, including taking a law degree at Madras Law College.
Teacher, advocate. Interested in uplift of Untouchables and Indian culture—tended to believe in its superiority over Euro-American culture. Jail sentence of eight months in 1940 after offering

individual satyagraha, and jail term from 1942 to December 1944.
Chittor District Congress Committee Secretary 1931, President
1937. Deputy Whip, Congress Party in Central Assembly 1937;
AICC 1938.
Deputy Speaker of the C.A. (Legislative).
In the Constituent Assembly:
    Member of the Steering Committee.
After Assembly:
Deputy Speaker and later Speaker of Lok Sabha. Member Provincial
Congress Committee and All-India Congress Committee. State
Governor.

AYYANGAR, Dewan Bahadur (Sir) N. Gopalaswami
General (Hindu, Brahmin)   Congress—Madras
Born: 1886   Died: 1953
M.T.: Tamil
Educated in Madras at Wesley, Presidency, and Law Colleges.
A lifetime in public service. Joined Madras Civil Service 1905 and
    worked upwards to Collector and Deputy Magistrate. Member
    Indian Legislative Assembly. Inspector Municipal Councils
    and Local Boards. Secretary to Government in Public Works
    Department. Prime Minister of Kashmir 1937–43 (during which
    time he received his knighthood from the British Government).
    Member of the Sapru Committee 1945. Minister without
    Portfolio in the Government of India 1947–48; Leader Indian
    Delegation to U.N. Security Council 1948; Minister of Transport
    and Railways in the Government of India 1948–50.
In the Constituent Assembly:
    Member Rules Committee
        „   Business Committee
        „   Union Subjects Committee
        „   States Committee
        „   Committee on Chief Commissioners Provinces
        „   Drafting Committee
        „   C.A. Functions Committee
        „   Union Constitution Committee
After Assembly:
    Minister for States 1950–52. Minister of Defence 1953; as well as
    other portfolios.

AYYAR, Dewan Bahadur (Sir) Alladi Krishnaswami
General (Hindu, Brahmin)   Congress—Madras
Born: 1883   Died: 1952
M.T.: Tamil, but brought up in a Telegu-speaking area.
Educated entirely in Madras at Christian College and Law College.
Advocate before Madras High Court of Judicature; Standing
    Counsel for Zamindars of Madras Presidency. Advocate-General,
    Madras 1929–44. Knighted 1931. Fellow of Madras University.
    Government of India Committee to amend law of Partnership
    and of Sale of Goods 1929.
In the Constituent Assembly:
    Member Rules Committee
        „   Drafting Committee
        „   Advisory Committee
        „   C.A. Functions Committee
        „   Union Powers Committee
        „   Union Constitution Committee
        „   ad hoc Committee on the Supreme Court
After Assembly:
    Retired from public life.

AZAD, Maulana Abul Kalam
Muslim   Congress—N.W.F.P. and U.P.
Born: 1888 in Mecca   Died: 1958
M.T.: Urdu.
Educated privately in both Arabia and India, to which he returned
    in 1898. Educational tour of Arab countries and Europe prior
    to 1912.
Publisher of Al-Hilal, pre-World War I. Urdu nationalist journal invit-
    ing Muslims to join the Congress. A full time Congress man after
    his release from internment in 1920. Negotiated with Cripps in
    1942, with Wavell at Simla in 1945, and with the Cabinet Mission
    as Congress President. Author and Muslim theologian. Minister of
    Education in the Government of India 1947 until his death.
In the Constituent Assembly:
    Member Steering Committee
        „   Advisory Committee
        „   States Committee
        „   Union Constitution Committee

After Assembly:

Until his death, Minister of Education; from May 1952 until his death also Minister of Natural Resources and Scientific Research. After Gandhi, perhaps Nehru's closest associate and friend.

DAULATRAM, Jairamdas
General (Hindu, Amil—near-Brahmin)   Congress—Sind and
                                      E. Punjab
Born: 1890
M.T.:Sindhi
Educated at Sindh College, Karachi, and at Elphinstone College and Law College, Bombay—B.A., LL.B.
Advocate, journalist (Editor *The Hindustan Times* 1925–6). Member Bombay Legislative Council 1926–9. Most of lifetime in Congress and Independence Movement since 1919. General Secretary of Congress 1930–35, and Member of Working Committee 1925–41; AICC from 1922 onwards. Governor of Bihar 1947. Minister of Food and Agriculture 1947–50.
In the Constituent Assembly:
  Member Advisory Committee
    „   Union Subjects Committee
    „   Provincial Constitution Committee
After Assembly:
  Governor of Assam.

DEO, Shankarrao (Dattatraya)
General (Hindu, Brahmin)   Congress—Bombay
Born: 1895
M.T.: Marathi
Educated at Bhave School, Poona; Baroda College, Baroda; St. Xaviers College, Bombay; and at Bombay University—B.A., 1918.
Bombay Home Rule League; at Champaran Satyagraha. Maharashtra PCC President 1931–8. Since 1936 full-time Congressman, and a member of the AICC and Working Committee. A devoted Gandhian. General Secretary of the Congress. Never a member of the Government. Espoused Marathi causes.
In the Constituent Assembly:
  Member Advisory Committee

„   Provincial Constitution Committee
„   Minorities Sub-Committee
„   Fundamental Rights Sub-Committee
„   Union Powers Committee
After Assembly:
  Remained a figure of some importance in the Bombay Congress
  and movements for a Marathi-speaking state. Did not hold public
  office.

DURGABAI, Mrs. G.
General (Hindu, Brahmin)   Congress—Madras
Born: 1909
M.T.: Telegu
  Educated in Madras, then at Benares Hindu University, and at
  Waltair and Law College, Madras.
Advocate Madras High Court. Longtime Congresswoman and par-
  ticipant in charitable and public causes in South India. Aided
  Gandhi in the propagation of Hindustani in the South.
In the Constituent Assembly:
  Member Steering Committee
     „   Rules Committee
After Assembly:
  Public activities. Wife of C. D. Deshmukh. Advocate, Supreme
  Court.

KRIPALANI, Acharya J. B.
General (Hindu, Amil—near-Brahmin) Congress—United Provinces
Born: 1888 in Hyderabad, Sind.
M.T.: Hindustani—Sindhi.
  Educated at Sind College, Karachi; Wilson College, Bombay, and
  Ferguson College, Poona.
Kripalani has been primarily an educator and a Congressman, also
  a follower of Gandhi. Has been a professor at Benares Hindu
  University and principal of Gandhi's Gujarat University in
  Ahmedabad, 1923–8. A member of the Working Committee
  1934–46, also a General Secretary of the Congress and Congress
  President. Author.
In the Constituent Assembly:
  Member Advisory Committee
     „   Steering Committee

    „   Provincial Constitution Committee

    „   and Chairman, Fundamental Rights Sub-Committee

After Assembly:

A leading member of opposition to Congress in Kisan Mazdoor Praja Party and later the Praja Socialist Party. Member Parliament.

KRISHNAMACHARI, T. T.

General (Hindu, Brahmin)   Congress—Madras

Born:1899

M.T.: Tamil

Educated at Christian College, Madras and Madras University.

Businessman primarily. Elected to Madras Assembly in 1937–42 from Indian Commerce constituency. Also a member of the Central Assembly 1942–5. Member Financial Delegation to London 1948.

In the Constituent Assembly;

Member of the Drafting Committee from January 1949.

After Assembly:

It was largely after the period of the Constituent Assembly that T. T. Krishnamachari achieved prominence. Minister for Commerce and Industry 1952–6; Minister of Iron and Steel 1955–7; Finance Minister 1956–8 and 1963–

MOOKERJEE, H. C

General (Christian)   Congress—Bengal

Born: 1877   Died: 1956

M.T.: Bengali.

Educated in Calcutta at Ripon College and Presidency College.

Mookerjee was first and foremost an educator. Professor of English at City College, Calcutta, from 1898–1914, then at Calcutta University from 1918–37, and then head of the English Department until 1942. President of various teachers' associations. Also President of All-India Council of Indian Christians. Member Bengal Legislative Assembly 1937–42. Author.

In the Constituent Assembly:

Vice-President of the Assembly (with V. T. Krishnamachari)

Member Advisory Committee

    „   and Chairman, Minority Rights Sub-Committee

    „   Provincial Constitution Committee

After Assembly:

Governor of Bengal.

MUNSHI, K.M.
General (Hindu, Brahmin)   Congress—Bombay
Born: 1887
M.T.: Gujarati
    Educated at Dalai High School, Broach, and at Baroda College,
    Baroda—B.A. and LL.B.
Advocate 1913. Fellow of Bombay University 1926 until the present.
Member Bombay Legislative Council and Assembly 1926–42.
Home Minister Government of Bombay, 1937–9. Author in several
languages, historian of Gujarati language. Early associate of Gandhi.
President Hindi Sahitya Sammelan 1944. President of Bharatiya
Vidya Bhavan since 1938—a publishing house which fosters studies
of Hindu culture. Member Congress Working Committee 1930,
and AICC 1931–7; six months in prison during 1930 satyagraha;
two-year sentence 1932—during Civil Disobedience Movement;
four months detention 1940–1. Resigned from Congress July 1941.
Present All-India Penal Reform Committee 1940. Government of
India's Agent in Hyderabad 1947–8.
In the Constituent Assembly:
    Member Rules Committee
        „   Steering Committee
        „   Advisory Committee
    Member Union Subjects Committee
        „   and Chairman, Order of Business Committee
        „   Union Constitution Committee
        „   ad hoc Committee on the Supreme Court
        „   Drafting Committee
After Assembly:
    Minister of Food and Agriculture 1950–52. Governor of U.P.
    1952–6. A founder of the Swatantra Party.

NEHRU, Pandit Jawaharlal
General (Hindu, Brahmin)   Congress—United Provinces
Born: 1889   Died: 1964
M.T.: Urdu—Hindustani
    Educated privately until his departure for England, Harrow, and
    Trinity College, Cambridge, and the Inner Temple.
Advocate, Allahabad High Court. Associate of Gandhi from World
    War I until Gandhi's death. Lifetime in Congress work. Member

AICC since 1918 and member Working Committee and party president. The party's foreign affairs expert. Author. Chairman Allahabad Municipal Government 1923–26. Vice-President Viceroy's Interim Government and then, after independence, Prime Minister and Minister of External Affairs.

In the Constituent Assembly:
Chairman States Committee
    „   Union Subjects Committee
    „   Union Constitution Committee

After Assembly:
Prime Minister and Foreign Minister of India and holder of various other portfolios as the occasion has demanded.

PANT, Pandit Govind Ballabh
General (Hindu, Brahmin)   Congress—United Provinces
Born: 1887   Died: 1961
M.T.: Hindi—Hindustani.
Educated at Muir Central College and Law College, Allahabad.
Advocate, Allahabad High Court and at Naini Tal. Pant had been a Congressman since 1921, first on the provincial level in U.P. (President UPPCC 1927), and, then on the national level in the late thirties. He was a member of the Working Committee after 1946. His great political power came from his pre-eminent position in the U.P., which has been the seat of Congress power. Pant remained largely on the provincial scene politically until after the period of the Assembly. He was in the U.P. Assembly and Legislative Council from 1923–30. Was Deputy Leader Congress Party in Central Assembly in 1934. Prime Minister of U.P. 1937–9, a position he resumed in 1946 and held throughout the framing period.

In the Constituent Assembly:
Member Advisory Committee
    „   Union Subjects Committee
    „   Union Constitution Committee

After Assembly:
Prime Minister of U.P. (holding other portfolios as well) until 1955. Home Minister in the Government of India 1955 until his death.

PATEL, Sardar Vallabhbhai J.

General (Hindu, Vaishya)　　　　　Congress—Bombay
Born: 1875　　　　　　　　　　　Died: 1950
M.T.: Gujarati.

Educated Nadiad High School and the Middle Temple.

Advocate in Ahmedabad on return from England in 1913. Became associated with Gandhi in 1916 and began full-time existence of worker in Independence Movement. Was ranking Congressman of central group in the twenties and was Congress president in 1931. He was on, or near, the Working Committee from that time until his death. President Ahmedabad Municipal Government 1924–8. Became Home plus Information and Broadcasting Minister in Interim Government in 1946. Minister for States after July 1947 and Minister of Home and States after 1948. The man who shared power in Congress with Nehru.

In the Constituent Assembly:

Chairman Provincial Constitution Committee
　　　　,,　　Advisory Committee
Member Steering Committee
　　　　,,　　States Committee

PRASAD, Rajendra

General (Hindu, Kayasth)　　　　　Congress—Bihar
Born: 1884　　　　　　　　　　　Died: 1963
M.T.: Bihari (Hindi—Hindustani).

Educated at Presidency College, Calcutta and then became a teacher of English there; academic career considered brilliant.

Advocate, Calcutta and Patna High Courts. Joined Gandhi and the Independence Movement in 1920 and thereafter devoted his life to it, being a general secretary of the Congress and Congress president three times, 1934, 1939, and 1948; on, or near, Working Committee since early thirties. Minister of Food and Agriculture in Interim Government and until January 1948.

In the Constituent Assembly:

Assembly President 1946–50
Chairman Rules Committee
　　　　,,　　Steering Committee

After Assembly:

President of India 1950–62.

RAU, (Sir) Benegal Narsing
Hindu, Brahmin   Not a member of the
                                        Constituent Assembly
Born: 1887   Died: 1953
M.T.: Konkani.
Educated at Presidency College, Madras, and at Trinity College, Cambridge.
Rau joined the I.C.S. in 1910 and soon began what was to be a career in legal work. He was a District or Sessions Judge 1919–23, and a judge of the Calcutta High Court from 1935–9. At other times he did legal work for the Government of India on committees, commissions, and as acting Reforms Commissioner in 1928. Presented Assam's case to Joint Select Committee of Parliament in 1933. He was prime minister of Kashmir in 1944–5. He returned from Kashmir to the Reforms office of the Goverment of India, where he remained until his appointment as Constitutional Adviser in July 1946. Rau several times represented India, or acted as adviser to the Indian Delegation, at the United Nations. He served as a member of the International Court at The Hague for a year during 1952–3.

RAU, N. Madhava
General (Hindu, Brahmin)   Congress—Orissa States
Born: 1887
M.T.: Kannada.
Educated at Noble College, Masulipatam, Pachaiyappa's and Government Law College, Madras.
Rau spent his adult life, prior to his work in the Assembly, in administrative capacities in Princely States, primarily in Mysore. He joined the Mysore Civil Service in 1907 and rose through a variety of positions to that of Dewan of Mysore from 1941–6. This included accompanying Sir Mirza Ismail to the Round Table Conference. He was a member of the Viceroy's Executive Council in 1935. In the early days of the Assembly, he was Constitutional Adviser to the Eastern (Orissa) States, and himself joined the Assembly in July 1947.
In the Constituent Assembly:
Member Drafting Committee
After Assembly:
Member of Provincial Parliament 1950–1. Retired, in South India, from public life.

SAADULLA, Saiyid Mohammed
Muslim   Muslim League—Assam
Born: 1886   Died: 1961
M.T.; Assamese and Urdu.
Educated at Cotton College, Gauhati, Assam, and at Presidency and
    Ripon Colleges, Calcutta. From Presidency College he received
    an M.A. in Chemistry and from Ripon College the following year
    a Bachelor of Law Degree.
Lawyer in Gauhati 1909–19; advocate before Calcutta High Court
    1920–24. Member Assam Legislative Council 1912–20, and from
    1923 onwards. Minister of Education and Agriculture, Assam
    Government 1924–9 and Minister of Finance and Law 1930–34.
    At one time a Nationalist Muslim and later a leader of the Muslim
    League in Assam. Prime Minister of Assam April 1937 to September
    1938 and from November 1939 to June 1942 and from August
    1942 until March 1945. Knighted 1928, made K.C.I.E. 1946.
In the Constituent Assembly:
    Member Steering Committee
        „   Drafting Committee
After Assembly:
Retired to private life.

SINHA, Satyanarayan
General (Hindu, Rajput)   Congress—Bihar
Born: 1899
M.T.: Bihari (Hindi—Hindustani).
Educated at Muzafarpur Zilla School and Patna University.
Has spent life as a Congressman and a legislator, although maintaining his
    agricultural and zamindari interests; he came from a family of minor
    zamindars. Joined Independence Movement in 1920. Member AICC
    since 1924. President, Darbhanga District Congress Committee
    1930–47. General Secretary Bihar PCC 1942–7. Member Bihar
    Legislative Council in 1926; Central Legislative Assembly 1934–9.
    Minister of Parliamentary Affairs 1948 onwards.
In the Constituent Assembly:
    Chief Whip
    Member Steering Committee
        „   Provincial Constitution Committee
After Assembly:
    Chief Whip and Minister of Parliamentary Affairs.

SITARAMAYYA, Dr. B. Pattabhi
General (Hindu, Brahmin)   Congress—Madras
Born: 1880   Died: 1959
M.T.: Telegu
Educated in Madras. Took a medical degree.
Practised as a doctor 1906–16 and then became a full-time
    Congressman, maintaining, however, some business interests.
    A member of the Working Committee fourteen times between
    1929–48, when he became president of the Congress. President
    Andhra PCC 1937–8. President of the All-India States Peoples'
    Conference 1936, 1938, and 1946–8. Author.
In the Constituent Assembly:
    Member Rules Committee
        „   States Committee
        „   Union Subjects Committee
        „   Provincial Constitution Committee
    Chairman Committee on Chief Commissioners Provinces
After Assembly:
    Governor of Madhya Pradesh.

Part B

Below are listed the names of all members of the Constituent Assembly who have been named in the text. Other persons appearing in the text have been identified when mentioned. Information on caste included here is tentative. Also, the meaning of this information must be carefully weighed because there is no immediate correlation between the member's caste and his behaviour in the Assembly.

Name	Community (under the terms of the cabinet Mission Plan)	Community	Caste† (probable)	Party	Province
Ahmad, Naziruddin	Muslim	Muslim		Muslim League	West Bengal
Alagesan, O. V.	General	Hindu	non-Brahmin	Congress	Madras
Ali, Asaf	Muslim	Muslim		Congress	Delhi
Ambedkar, B. R.*	General	Hindu	S.C.†	Schd. Castes Fed.	West Bengal
				Congress	Bombay
				Congress	Madras
Anthony, Frank	General	Anglo-Indian		Congress	Madras
Ayyangar, M. A.*	General	Hindu	Brahmin	Congress	Madras
Ayyangar, N. G.*	General	Hindu	Brahmin	Congress	Madras
Ayyar, A. K.*	General	Hindu	Brahmin	Congress	Madras
Azad, Maulana A. K.*	Muslim	Muslim		Congress	NWFP and United Provinces

(Continued)

Name	Community (under the terms of the cabinet Mission Plan)	Community	Caste† (probable)	Party	Province
Bahadur, Raj	Princely States	Hindu	Kayastha	Congress	Matsya Union
Baig, Mahboob Ali	Muslim	Muslim		Muslim League	Madras
Banerjee, S. C.	General	Hindu	Brahmin	Congress	West Bengal
Banerji, Mrs. Purnima	General	Hindu	Brahmin	Congress	United Provinces
Bhargava, M. Bihari Lal	General	Hindu	Brahmin	Congress	Ajmer-Merwara
Bhargava, Thakur Das	General	Hindu	Brahmin	Congress	East Punjab
Bhatt, Gokulbhai	Princely States	Hindu	Brahmin	Congress	East Rajputana
Biyani, Brijlal	General	Hindu	Marwari	Congress	C.P. and Berar
Chand, Bakhshi Tek	General	Hindu	Khatri	Congress	East Punjab
Chattopadhyaya, M. L.	General	Hindu	Brahmin	Congress	West Bengal
Chaudhury, R. K.	General	Hindu	Kayastha	Congress	Assam
Chettiyar, T. A. R.	General	Hindu	non-Brahmin	Congress	Madras
Chundrigar, Ismail	Muslim	Muslim		Muslim League	Bombay
Das, B.	General	Hindu	non-Brahmin	Congress	Orissa

Das, Biswanath	General	Hindu	non-Brahmin	Congress	Orissa
Das, Saranghdar	Princely States	Hindu	Kayastha	Congress	Eastern States
Das, Seth Govind	General	Hindu	Marwari	Congress	C.P. and Berar
Datta, D. N.	General	Hindu	Brahmin	Congress	West Bengal
Daulatram, Jairamdas*	General	Hindu	Amil	Congress	Sindh and East Punjab
Deo, Shankarrao*	General	Hindu	Brahmin	Congress	Bombay
Deshmukh, P. S.	General	Hindu	Maharatta	Congress	C.P. and Berar
Dhulekar, R. V.	General	Hindu	Brahmin	Congress	United Provinces
Diwaker, R. R,	General	Hindu	Brahmin	Congress	Bombay
Durgabai, Mrs. G.*	General	Hindu	Brahmin	Congress	Madras
Gadgil, N. V.	General	Hindu	Brahmin	Congress	Bombay
Ghose, Surendra Mohan	General	Hindu	Kayastha	Congress	West Bengal
Ghosh, Profulla Chandra	General	Hindu	Kayastha	Congress	West Bengal

(Continued)

Name	Community (under the terms of the cabinet Mission Plan)	Community	Caste[†] (probable)	Party	Province
Goenka, Ramnath	General	Hindu	Marwari	Congress	Madras
Gupta, G. S.	General	Hindu	Vaishya	Congress	C.P. and Berar
Gupte, B. M.	General	Hindu	Brahmin	Congress	Bombay
Hanumanthaiya, K.	Princely States	Hindu	non-Brahmin		Mysore
Himatsingka, P. D.	General	Hindu	Marwari	Congress	West Bengal
Husain, Tajamul	Muslim	Muslim		Muslim League	Bihar
Ibrahim, K. T. M. A.	Muslim	Muslim		Muslim League	Madras
Ismail, Mohammed	Muslim	Muslim		Muslim League	Madras
Jain, Ajit Prasad	General	Jain		Congress	United Provinces
Jayakar, M. R.	General	Hindu	non-Brahmin	Congress	Bombay
Jedhe, K. M.	General	Hindu	Maharatta	Congress	Bombay
Kamath, H. V.	General	Hindu	Brahmin	Congress	C.P. and Berar
Karimuddin, K. S.	Muslim	Muslim		Muslim League	C.P. and Berar
Katju, K. N.	General	Hindu	Brahmin	Congress	United Provinces
Kaur, Rajkumari Amrit	General	Christian		Congress	C.P. and Berar

Name	Category	Religion	Caste	Party	Province
Keskar, B. V.	General	Hindu	Brahmin	Congress	United Provinces
Khaitan, D. P.	General	Hindu	Marwari	Congress	West Bengal
Khaliquzzaman, Chaudhri	Muslim	Muslim		Muslim League	United Provinces
Khan, Azis Ahmad	Muslim	Muslim		Muslim League	United Provinces
Khan, Khan Abdul Ghaffar	Muslim	Muslim		Congress	NWFP
Khan, Mohammed Ismail	Muslim	Muslim		Muslim League	United Provinces
Khare, N. B.	Princely States	Hindu	Brahmin		Alwar
Kher, B. G.	General	Hindu	Brahmin	Congress	Bombay
Kishore, Jugal	General	Hindu	Vaishya	Congress	United Provinces
Kripalani, J. B.*	General	Hindu	Amil	Congress	United Provinces
Krishnamachari, T. T.*	General	Hindu	Brahmin	Congress	Madras
Krishnamachari, V. T.	Princely States	Hindu	Brahmin		Jaipur
Kunzru, H. N.	General	Hindu	Brahmin	Congress	United Provinces
Lahiri, Somnath	General	Hindu	Brahmin	Communist	West Bengal
Lal, J. N.	General	Hindu	Kayastha	Congress	Bihar
Lari, Z. H.	Muslim	Muslim		Muslim League	United Provinces

(Continued)

Name	Community (under the terms of the cabinet Mission Plan)	Community	Caste† (probable)	Party	Province
Maitra, L. K.	General	Hindu	Brahmin	Congress	West Bengal
Majumdar, Suresh Chandra	General	Hindu	Kayastha	Congress	West Bengal
Malaviya, Govind	General	Hindu	Brahmin	Congress	United Provinces
Mandloi, B. A.	General	Hindu	non-Brahmin	Congress	C.P. and Berar
Mane, S. N.	General	Hindu	S.C.	Congress	Bombay
Masani, Minoo R.	General	Parsi		Congress	Bombay
Matthai, John	General	Christian		Congress	United Provinces
Mehta, G. L.	Princely States	Hindu	Brahmin		Guarat States
Mehta, Mrs. Hansa	General	Hindu	Brahmin	Congress	Bombay
Menon, K. Madhava	General –	Hindu	non-Brahmin	Congress	Madras
Menon, P. Govinda	Princely States	Hindu	non-Brahmin		Cochin
Misra, Lokanath	General	Hindu	Brahmin	Congress	Orissa
Mitter, B. L.	Princely States	Hindu	Brahmo Samaj		Baroda
Mookerjee, H. C.*	General	Christian		Congress	West Bengal
Mookerjee, S. P.	General	Hindu	Brahmin	Congress	West Bengal

	Princely States	Hindu	non-Brahmin		Deccan States
Munavalli, B.	General	Hindu	Brahmin	Congress	Bombay
Munshi, K. M.*	Sikh	Sikh		Congress	East Punjab
Musafir, G. G. S.	General	Hindu	non-Brahmin	Congress	Madras
Nadar, Kamaraj	General	Hindu	S.C.	Congress	Madras
Nagappa, S.	General	Hindu	Brahmin	Congress	Bihar
Naidu, Mrs. Sarojini	General	Hindu	S.C.	Congress	Bombay
Nalavade, R. M.	General	Hindu	Brahmin	Congress	United Provinces
Nehru, Jawaharlal*	General	Hindu	Kayastha	Congress	West Bengal
Neogy, K. C.	General	Hindu	Lingayat	Congress	Bombay
Nijalingappa, S.	General	Hindu	Brahmin	Congress	United Provinces
Pandit, Mrs. V.	Princely States	Hindu	non-Brahmin		Bikaner
Panikkar, K. M.	General	Hindu	Brahmin	Congress	United Provinces
Pant, Govind Ballabh*	General	Hindu	Kshatriya	Congress	Orissa
Parlakimedi, Maharaja of	General	Hindu	Rajput	Congress	Himachal Pradesh
Parmar, Y. S.	General	Hindu	Brahmin	Congress	Bombay
Pataskar, H. V.	General	Hindu	Vaishya	Congress	Bombay
Patel, Vallabhbhai*	General	Hindu	Maharatta	Congress	Bombay
Patil, S. K.					

(Continued)

Name	Community (under the terms of the cabinet Mission Plan)	Community	Caste† (probable)	Party	Province
Pillai, V. I. Muniswami	General	Hindu	S.C.	Congress	Madras
Pillai, P. S. N.	Princely States	Hindu	non-Brahmin		Travancore
Pocker, B.	Muslim	Muslim		Muslim League	Madras
Prasad, Brajeshwar	General	Hindu	Kayastha	Congress	Bihar
Prasad, Rajendra*	General	Hindu	Kayastha	Congress	Bihar
Radhakrishnan, S.	General	Hindu	Brahmin	Congress	United Provinces
Raghuvira, Dr.	General	Hindu	Brahmin	Congress	C.P. and Berar
Rajgopalachari, C.	General	Hindu	Brahmin	Congress	Madras
Raju, P. L. Narasimha	General	Hindu	non-Brahmin	Congress	Madras
Ram, Jagjivan	General	Hindu	S.C.	Congress	Bihar
Ranga, N. G.	General	Hindu	non-Brahmin	Congress	Madras
Rao, B. Shiva	General	Hindu	Brahmin	Congress	Madras
Rao, Kala Venkata	General	Hindu	Brahmin	Congress	Madras
Rao, V. C. Kesava	General	Hindu	S.C.	Congress	Madras
Rau, N. Madhava*	Princely States	Hindu	Brahmin		Orissa States

Rasul, Begum Aizaz	Muslim	Muslim		Muslim League	United Provinces
Reddi, B. Gopala	General	Hindu	non-Brahmin	Congress	Madras
Reddi, H. Sitarama	General	Hindu	non-Brahmin	Congress	Madras
Reddi, Sanjeeva	General	Hindu	non-Brahmin	Congress	Madras
Roy, Kiran Shankar	General	Hindu	Kayastha	Congress	West Bengal
Saadulla, Mohammed*	Muslim	Muslim		Muslim League	Assam
Sahai, Ram	Princely States	Hindu	Kayastha	Congress	Gwalior
Sahaya, Syamandan	General	Hindu	Kayastha	Independent	Bihar
Sahu, L.	General	Adibasi		Independent	Orissa
Saksena, Mohan Lal	General!	Hindu	Kayastha	Congress	United Provinces
Saksena, Shibban Lal	General	Hindu	Kayastha	Congress	United Provinces
Santhanam, K.	General	Hindu	Brahmin	Congress	Madras
Satyanarayana, Moturi	General]	Hindu	Brahmin	Congress	Madras
Seth, Damodar Swarup	General	Hindu	Vaishya	Congress	United Provinces
Shah, C. C.	Princely States	Hindu	Vaishya		Saurashtra
Shah, K. T.	General	Hindu	Vaishya	Congress	Bihar
Sharma, Balkrishna	General	Hindu	Brahmin	Congress	United Provinces
Sharma, K. C.	General	Hindu	Brahmin	Congress	United Provinces

(Continued)

Name	Community (under the terms of the cabinet Mission Plan)	Community	Caste† (probable)	Party	Province
Shastri, Algurai	General	Hindu	Brahmin	Congress	United Provinces
Shukla, Ravi Shankar	General	Hindu	Brahmin	Congress	C.P. and Berar
Sidhwa, R. K.	General	Parsi		Congress	C.P. and Berar
Singh, Baldev	Sikh	Sikh		Akali	East Punjab
Singh, Guptanath	General	Hindu	Bhumihar	Congress	Bihar
Singh, Harnam	Sikh	Sikh		Akali	East Punjab
Singh, Hukam	Sikh	Sikh		Akali	East Punjab
Singh, Jaganath Bakhsh	General	Hindu	Thakur	Independent	United Provinces
Singh, Jaidev	Princely States	Sikh		Independent	Patiala
Singh, Jaipal	General	Adibasi		Independent	Bihar
Singh, Pratap (Kairon)	Sikh	Sikh		Congress	East Punjab
Singh, Ramnarayan	General	Hindu	Rajput	Congress	Bihar
Singh, Ujjal	Sikh	Sikh		Akali	East Punjab
Singhji, Raja Sardar of Khetri	Princely States	Hindu	Kshatriya		Jaipur

Name	Category	Religion	Caste	Party	Province
Sinha, Anugrah Narayan	General	Hindu	Rajput	Congress	Bihar
Sinha, Sachchidananda	General	Hindu	Kayastha	Congress	Bihar
Sinha, Satyanarayan*	General	Hindu	Rajput	Congress	Bihar
Sinha, Sri Krishna	General	Hindu	Brahmin	Congress	Bihar
Sitaramayya, Pattabhi*	General	Hindu	Brahmin	Congress	Madras
Subbarayan, P.	General	Hindu	non-Brahmin	Congress	Madras
Tahir, Mohammed	Muslim	Muslim		Muslim League	Bihar
Tandon, Purushottam Das	General	Hindu	Kshatriya	Congress	United Provinces
Tripathi, K. M.	Princely States	Hindu	Brahmin		Eastern States
Tripathi; V. D.	General	Hindu	Brahmin	Congress	United Provinces
Tyagi, Mahavir	General	Hindu	Taga Brahmin	Congress	United Provinces
Vijayavargiya, G	Princely States	Hindu	non-Brahmin	Congress	Gwalior
Vyas, Jainarayan	Princely States	Hindu	Brahmin		Jodhpur
Zaidi, B. H.	Princely States	Muslim			Rampur and Benares

* See Part.   † In some cases the Varna and not the caste in given   ‡ Scheduled Castes

Bibliography

A. Primary Sources

The most important original sources of information for a work on the framing of the Indian Constitution are the published and unpublished documents of the Constituent Assembly and the private correspondence of leading Assembly members. Seeking these documents out and patching together the story of the drafting of the Constitution, however, is complicated by the dispersion of the material and its lack of organization. When the Constituent Assembly wound up its business early in 1950, the Ministry of Law, and not the newly created Lok Sabha Secretariat, became the inheritor of most of the Assembly's records. Hence the Law Ministry possesses the most complete collection of official Assembly material. The Indian National Archives became the custodians of only odds and ends of unpublished documents. The researcher, therefore, must seek in every nook and cranny for his material, and depend for Assembly documents largely on private collections of papers.

Further sources of information denied to the student of Indian affairs are the personal memoirs and the written records of political parties and other organizations that are major sources for the study of European and American politics. It is simply that there has not been in India the same tradition of preserving political minutae, or even vital records, that exists in Europe and America. It is, for instance, almost certainly true that no formal records were kept of the meetings of the Congress Assembly Party during the framing period, despite the great importance of these meetings. Indeed, it is a moot point whether or not even notes of the proceedings exist. The author, who has been informed by reliable persons that such notes do and do not exist, never succeeded in finding any.

Of the published primary sources on the creation of the Constitution, the Constituent Assembly Debates and the reports of Assembly committees are the most important to the researcher. The Assembly Debates are the record of the public proceedings of the Assembly, and they contain a wealth of information about the views of the members. But to obtain the full value of the Debates, they must be used in conjunction with the unpublished documents. The Assembly also printed a variety of material that supplements the usefulness of the Debates and of the committee reports. All these documents were published by the Manager of Publications, Delhi, and were printed by the Government of India Press. They are listed below.

Constituent Assembly Debates—12 Volumes, 9 December 1946 to 26 January 1950; including two records of confidential debates (held in camera) and not yet officially made public, although readily available in the Indian National Archives.

Reports of Committees of the Constituent Assembly of India—First, Second, and Third Series (published by the Parliament Secretariat); dated 1947, 1948, and 1950.

Constituent Assembly Excluded and Partially-Excluded Areas (other than Assam) Sub-Committee, Vol. II. Evidence.

Ditto for Assam. Both undated. The Advisory Committee's report to the Constituent Assembly based on the sub-committee reports and their volumes of evidence appear as an Advisory Committee report on the subjects of North East Frontier tribes; see report 7 in *Reports of Committees, Third Series.*

Constitutional Precedents, First Series, Second Series, Third Series. Prepared by B. N. Rau, the first volume was circulated to Assembly members by the Assembly Secretariat on 25 September 1946. The series of three volumes was sent bound to members on 6 December 1946.

First Draft of the Constitution of India and Schedules, prepared by the Constitu tional Adviser. The first draft was dated 22 September 1947 and was printed with corrections on 7 October 1947 in a horizontal, folio format. The Schedules were published 18 October in the same format. Both were reprinted in book format by the Lok Sabha Secretariat in 1960.

Draft Constitution of India, as prepared by the Drafting Committee. Published on 26 February 1948; contains a letter of transmittal (Ambedkar to Prasad) dated 21 February.

Draft Constitution of India, as prepared by the Drafting Committee, Reprint indicating recommendations for amendment by the Drafting Committee. Published in October 1948; letter of transmittal (Ambedkar to Prasad) dated 26 October 1948. Printed originally in large, horizontal, folio size with February text and suggested amendments (in italics) in two columns on one page with blank facing page for members' notes. Reprinted in folio, book format by the Lok Sabha Secretariat in 1960.

Draft Constitution of India: Articles agreed to by the Constituent Assembly at the consideration stage. Issued approximately seven times from 8 January 1949 through 28 October 1949.

Draft Constitution of India, as revised by the Drafting Committee. Dated 3 November 1949. This final draft incorporated the changes made by the Assembly preparatory to the Third Reading.

List of Amendments to the Draft Constitution of India, List I, II, and III, sometimes bound together, sometimes separately. List I apparently consists of amendments submitted before the meeting of the Special Committee on 10–11 April 1948. Lists II and III date from the summer and early autumn of 1948.

Notes on Amendments to the Draft Constitution, notes written in large measure by B. N. Rau, but embodying comments made by others, especially the Special Committee, on amendments to the Draft Constitution. Printed during the summer (August) 1948.

Notice of Amendments to the Draft Constitution of India (referred to in the footnotes as Amendment Books). In two volumes, these books list by articles the Assembly members' amendments to the Draft of February 1948. The books were published in November 1948 and contain amendments submitted to 11 November.

Printed List of Amendments, dated 5 May 1949.

Ditto, dated 10 July 1949. These two lists were supplemental to the lists in the Amendment Books.

Statistical Handbook, numbers 1 and 2. The former concerned the *Population of India According to Communities;* the latter was concerned with the *Population of India According to Languages.* Both were based on the Census of 1931.

Memoranda, etc. Submitted by the Government of India and the Provincial Governments to the Expert Committee on Financial Provisions of the Union Constitution. Fifteen items, some of them lengthy. Printed 12 July 1949, but most, if not all, of the material therein was circulated in mimeographed form during the previous year.

Rules of Procedure and Standing Orders. Four editions 1946–9.

Comments on the Provisions of the Draft Constitution. Printed in late 1948, this volume (referred to in the footnotes as Comments Volume) contains thirty-three items submitted to the Assembly during 1948, with one or two from late 1947, including letters, memoranda and notes from Government of India ministries, provincial governments, provincial legislatures and legislative councils, Federal and High Court justices, etc., etc. Bound, separately, but evidently part of this series of 'comments' are copies of the debates in several provincial legislatures on the Draft Constitution.

Although copies of these publications are scattered throughout India, all of them are in the library of the Indian School of International Studies (Sapru House) or in the Indian National Archives, or in the Law Ministry Library, New Delhi. The Archives have the most complete collection.

The unpublished documents of the Constituent Assembly are innumerable. Those that the author has used number in the thousands. To list them here would be impractical, particularly as their general character is made evident in the footnotes. A description of these documents according to the more important categories into which they fall may, however, be useful.

The largest single body of material, and a most important one, is called the *Orders of the Day* (bound by the National Archives in seven volumes). These Orders contain the agenda of each day's business and a list of the amendments to be moved on that day. In some cases these amendments are the same as those in the Amendment Books, but more frequently they are short notice amendments to amendments (usually to those listed in the Amendment Books or on the smaller *Printed Lists of Amendments*) and appear only in the *Orders of the Day*. Only successful amendments appear in the actual Debates. The Orders also sometimes contain committee reports and less essential information. The great value to the researcher of this collection of documents can be imagined. A complete set of the Orders is in the National Archives.

Other categories of unpublished Assembly documents are:

Committee reports—These are those of the Fundamental Rights and Minority Sub-Committees of the Advisory Committee to the parent Advisory Committee and several lesser committees.

Committee minutes and proceedings—These documents include agenda of meetings as well as minutes and verbatim proceedings of meetings, and minutes of dissent to committee reports or to provisions recommended by majority vote in committee meetings. The value of the researcher of the content of these documents varies greatly. The minutes of the meetings of the Fundamental Rights Sub-Committee, the Minorities Sub-Committee, and of the Union Constitution Committee, for example, often give important details of what was said in the meeting, who said it, and, if there was a vote on an issue, who was on which side. The minutes of Drafting Committee meetings, however, give only the decisions taken at the meeting. The names of members only appear in a list of those attending a particular meeting. The appendixes to these minutes list the changes to articles that have been agreed to, and thus the researcher can trace the progressive development of a particular provision, but it is very difficult to discover why a certain change was made and who were its supporters and opponents. The proceedings of the Drafting Committee meetings with the provincial premiers and the proceedings of several Advisory Committee meetings are very valuable. They are to be found in the Law Ministry Archives. Rarely are the sets of committee documents complete, nor are they gathered together in one place. The most comprehensive collections for the Union and Provincial Constitution Committees are in the Law Ministry Archives, with the National Archives next. The Law Ministry has few records of the Drafting Committee, however. The researcher must compile his own set of committee proceedings from fragments—large and small—scattered among collections of private papers and in official archives. To the author's knowledge, the committee documents extant (and hence used by him) are those of the States, Drafting, Provincial Constitution, Union Constitution, Union Powers, and Steering Committees; also the Advisory Committee and its sub-committees, and the Rules Committee.

Documents submitted to the Assembly to support a particular point of view make up the fourth category of unpublished Assembly documents. There are hundreds of these documents, varying from official notes and memoranda to personal and official letters. They were sent to the Assembly Secretariat, to committees, and to influential Assembly members by pressure groups (such as the Federation of Indian Chambers of Commerce in Bombay), private individuals, by ministers and legislators in provincial governments and legislatures, by Union Government ministers, by other Assembly members, and so on. Frequently they were attached to the agenda for committee meetings and were circulated to committee members. Ministries also prepared informational briefs for the use of Assembly committees, which likewise were attached to agenda. There are also the working papers of various committees. It is from this body of material that the author has drawn a good deal of his evidence for the creation of certain of the Constitutions' provisions. These documents are available to the researcher somewhat more in private collections than in official archives.

A fifth and last category of unpublished Assembly documents is the major notes on policy and programme prepared either by B. N.

Rau, or by N. G. Ayyangar, Ayyar, Munshi, Prasad, and others on such matters as rules, minority rights, the form of federalism, legal ramifications of the wording of a provision, etc., etc. There are some dozens of these notes and most of them can be found in collections of private papers.

Leaving the documents of the Constituent Assembly, we turn to a second major source of unpublished material bearing on the framing of the Constitution: the unpublished documents of the Indian National Congress. Here the researcher again meets the frustrating tendency of Indian political figures and organizations not to write things down. If any unpublished Congress documents of the period are kept at Congress headquarters on Jantar Mantar Road in New Delhi, the author failed to prise them loose from the officials of the Congress and he had, again, to rely on material in private collections of papers. Among such collections one finds agenda for Working Committee meetings (rarely minutes), letters from the high command to PCC's, letters between ranking Congress officials (often productive of material bearing on the Assembly), and informational background material on party economic and social ideas and programmes. It is impossible to estimate how much of this material exists, but that seen by the author in private papers has been most valuable to understanding both Assembly affairs and the milieu in which the Assembly did its work.

A third group of original, unpublished material is the private correspondence among ranking Constituent Assembly, Congress, and Government members available in private papers. In this field the correspondence of President Prasad has been especially valuable.

The repositories of the sources so far mentioned in this note are:

The Indian National Archives, New Delhi.

The Archives of the Ministry of Law, New Delhi—These archives are, with the Prasad papers (see below), the best repository of Constituent Assembly documents. They are less useful in the way of private correspondence, but are equally productive of official documents. The collection is extensive, including the originals of many of the letters and petitions sent to the Assembly by members of the general public. The material on the Princely States and the Assembly is especially good. Prior to June 1964, the archives had not been organized, and were carelessly kept. This situation has since been remedied by an able secretary in the Ministry.

The Library of the Lok Sabha Secretariat, New Delhi.

The Library of the Indian School of International Studies (Sapru House), New Delhi.

Collections of private papers:

The Prasad papers; most valuable. Forty-seven files, of which ten are primarily concerned with Congress Party affairs. These were in the possession of President Prasad in New Delhi.

The Munshi papers; of great value. A dozen files almost entirely concerned with Assembly affairs. In Mr. Munshi's possession, New Delhi.

The Sapru papers; interesting but of less value. Excellently catalogued by, and in the possession of, the National Library, Calcutta.

The Ayyar papers; valuable, but far from complete. In the possession—those that the author has seen—of Mr. Munshi.

The Ravi Shankar Shukla papers; very fragmentary. Copies in the author's possession.

The Ambedkar papers; extremely fragmentary—at least those that the author has seen. These seen by the author were in the library of Siddharth College, Bombay. The exact whereabouts of Dr. Ambedkar's papers is uncertain.

The V. T. Krishnamachari papers; helpful, but incomplete. In the possession of the Indian Institute of Public Administration, New Delhi.

Nehru papers; the author did not attempt to consult these papers.

The Azad and Patel papers are still not available to research scholars.

The author was also permitted by the Indian National Archives to consult certain of the Reforms Office Papers on the Constituent Assembly—primarily its formation—and in regard to the elections of 1945–6 to provincial legislatures and the Central Legislative Assembly and of the 1937 elections to the provincial legislatures.

Interviews were a further source of original material for the author. Of the several dozen interviews granted him, only the most important are listed below. The brief identification given after the name of the person interviewed indicates his position during the period of the Constituent Assembly, or his importance to this work.

N. Rajgopala Aiyangar—Justice, Supreme Court, 1960–.

Mrs. B. R. Ambedkar—wife of Dr. Ambedkar.

Thakur Das Bhargava—member of the Constituent Assembly (MCA).

N. C. Chatterjee—Calcutta advocate; ranking member of the Hindu Mahasabha.

Seth Govind Das—MCA.

C. D. Deshmukh—First Finance Minister under the new Constitution.

Mrs. Durgabai Deshmukh—MCA. .

Durga Das—Joint Editor, *The Hindustan Times*.

N. V. Gadgil—MCA.

A. C. Guha—M.CA

Tajamul Husatn—MCA.

P. C. Joshi—Ranking Communist party organizer; Right wing faction of party.

H. V. Kamath—MCA.

Humayan Kabir—Member of Congress Experts Committee on the Assembly.

M. N. Kaul—Secretary of the C.A. (Legislative) and of the Lok Sabha.

J. B. Kripalani—MCA.

K. R. Kripalani—Convenor of the Congress Experts Committee.

T. T. Krishnamachari—MCA.

H. N. Kunzru—MCA.

Somnath Lahiri Communist MCA.

A. K. Majumdar—Historian.

M. R. Masani—MCA.

V. K. Krishna Menon—Attended Congress Experts Committee meetings; was Indian High Commissioner in London during Commonwealth negotiations.

S. N. Mukerjee—Drafting Officer of the Assembly.

K. M. Munshi—MCA.

K. C Neogy—MCA; associated with early committees on planning.

Sri Prakasa—MCA.

Rajendra Prasad—President of the Assembly.

S. Radhitkrishnan—MCA (now President of India).

B. Shiva Rao—MCA; brother of B. N. Rau.

K. Santhanam—MCA; editor of *The Hindustan Times.*

Vishwanath Verma—Secretary to President Rajendra Prasad, 1957–62.

B. Secondary Sources

The number of books that have been written on the Constitution is very large. With one or two exceptions, however, these books do not treat the framing period nor do they find their sources in original documents. Many books, on the other hand, do deal with the history, political or intellectual, of India leading to the Assembly period. Because a people's experience, its vision of the past as well as the future finds expression in its constitution, very little of its history does not have some bearing on what is included in that document. Hence a list of works treating subjects that are in some way relevant to the Indian Constituent Assembly's work would be of great length. Yet the number of works having a direct bearing on the subject of constitution-making in India is not long. A list of such published (and largely secondary) sources is given below. In the main, this list consists of works cited in the text.

Adarkar, B. P. *Principles and Problems of Federal Finance,* P. S. King and Son Ltd., London, 1933.

Agarwal, Shriman Narayan. *Gandhian Constitution for Free India,* Kitabistan, Allahabad, 1946.

The Gandhian Plan of Economic Development for India, Padma Publications Ltd., Bombay, 1944.

Ahmad, Z. A. *National Language for India, A Symposium,* Kitabistan, Allahabad, 1941.

The Indian Federation—Congress Economic and Political Studies pamphlets No. 10, Indian National Congress, Allahabad, 1938.

Aiyangar, N. Rajgopala. *The Government of India Act of* 1935, *with a ommentary critical and exploratory,* Madras Law Journal Office, Madras. 1937.

Aiyar, Alladi Krishnaswami. *The Constitution and Fundamental Rights,* The Srinivasa Sastri Institute of Politics, Madras, 1955.

Alexandrowicz, Charles H. *Constitutional Developments in India,* Oxford University Press, Bombay, 1957.

All Parties Conference. *Report of the Committee appointed by the Conference to determine the principles of the Constitution for India (The Nehru Report),* Indian National Congress, Allahabad, 1928.

Altekar, A. S. *State and Government in Ancient India,* Motilal Banarsidass, Publisher, Delhi, 1958. Third Edition.

Ambedkar, B. R. *States and Minorities—What are their rights and how to secure them in the Constitution of Free India,* Thacker and Co., Bombay, 1947.

Thoughts on Linguistic States, Published by Ambedkar, Delhi, 1955.

Appleby, Paul. *Public Administration in India, Report of a Survey,* Government of India (Cabinet Secretariat), New Delhi, 1953.

Aundh, Government Press of. *Aundh State Constitution Act No. 1 of* 1939.

Azad, Maulana Abul Kalam. *India Wins Freedom,* Orient Longmans Co., Calcutta, 1959.

Azad's Speeches, 1947–1955, Government of India, Delhi, 1957.

Banerjee, A. C. *The Constituent Assembly of India,* A. Mukherjee and Co., Calcutta, 1947.

Indian Constitutional Documents, Three Volumes, A. Mukherjee and Co., Calcutta, Second Edition, 1948.

Banerjee, D. N. *Our Fundamental Rights, Their Nature and Extent,* World Press Private Ltd., Calcutta, 1960.

Basu, Durga Das. *Commentary on the Constitution of India,* Third Edition, Two Volumes, S. C. Sarkar and Sons, Calcutta, 1955.

Bayley, David H. *Preventive Detention in India,* Firma K. L. Mukhopadhyay, Calcutta, 1962.

Beard, Charles. *An Economic Interpretation of the American Constitution,* Macmillan Co., New York, Sixteenth Printing, 1959.

Beer, Max. *A History of British Socialism,* George Allen and Unwin, London, Reprinting of 1948.

Beloff, Max (Ed.). *The Federalist,* Basil Blackwell, Oxford, 1948.

The American Federal Government, Oxford University Press, London, 1959.

Berlin, Isaiah. *Two Concepts of Liberty,* Clarendon Press, Oxford, 1961.

Bhargava, R. N. *The Theory and Working of Union Finance in India,* George Allen and Unwin, London, 1956.

Birch, A. H. *Federalism, Finance, and Social Legislation in Canada, Australia, and the United States,* Oxford University Press, London, 1955.

Brecher, Michael. *Nehru—A Political Biography,* Oxford University Press, London, 1959.

Callard, Keith. *Pakistan, A Political Study,* George Allen and Unwin, London, 1957.

Chakrabarty, D. and Bhattacharya, C. *Congress in Evolution,* The Book Co. Ltd., Calcutta, 1940.

Chanakya—See Panikkar, K. M., for *Indian Revolution.*

Chanakya (pseudonym for Raghavan). *Indian Constituent Assembly,* Bombay Book Depot, Bombay, 1947.

Chanda, Ashoke. *Indian Administration,* George Allen and Unwin, London, 1958.

Chatterji, S. K. *Languages and the Linguistic Problem* (Oxford pamphlets on Indian Affairs, No. 11), Oxford University Press, Bombay, 1943.

Clark, Jane. *The Rise of a New Federalism,* Columbia University Press, New York, 1938.

Constitutions—The texts of the following Constitutions have been used: *United States; USSR,* 1936; *Eire,* 1922 and 1937; *Weimar Germany; Canada; Japan,* 1946; *Australia; South Africa; Switzerland; Pakistan,* 1956 and 1962; *Burma,* 1947; *Nigeria,* 1954; and 1961; *Ghana,* 1960.

Coupland, Reginald. *The Indian Problem,* Three Volumes, Oxford University Press, London, 1944.

India: A Re-Statement, Oxford University Press, London, 1945.

Dawson, R. M. *The Government of Canada,* University of Toronto Press, Toronto, 1958.

Dean, Vera M. *New Patterns of Democracy in In£a,* Harvard University Press, Cambridge, Mass., 1959.

Desai, A. R. *Social Background of Indian Nationalism,* Oxford University Press, Bombay, 1948.

Deshmukh, C. D. *Economic Developments in India*, 1946–1956, Asia Publishing House, Bombay, 1958.

Dev, Acharya Narenda. *Socialism and the National Revolution*, Padma Publications, Bombay, 1946.

Dey, S. K. *Panchayat-i-Raj*, Asia Publishing House, London, 1961.

Dicey, A. V. *Law of the Constitution*, Edited by E. C. S. Wade, Macmillan and Co., London ('Papermac' Edition), 1961.

Douglas, William O. *From Marshall to Mukherjea, Studies in American and Indian Constitutional Law*, Eastern Law House Private Ltd., Calcutta, 1956.

Farrand, Max. *The Framing of the Constitution of the United States*, Yale University Press, New Haven, 16th Printing, 1958.

Fite, E. D. *Government by Co-operation*, The Macmillan Co., New York, 1932.

Frankfurter, Felix. *Felix Frankfurter Reminisces* (Edited by H. B. Philips), Seeker and Warburg, London, 1960.

Gadgil, D. R. *Some Observations on the Draft Constitution*, Gokhale Institute, Poona, 1948.

The Federal Problem in India, Gokhale Institute, Poona, 1947.

Gandhi, M. K. *Hind Swaraj*, Navajivan Press, Ahmedabad, Reprinting of 1958.

Thoughts on National Language, Navajivan Press, Ahmedabad, 1956.

Delhi Diary, Navajivan Press, Ahmedabad, 1948.

Ghoshal U. N. *A History of Indian Political Ideas*, Oxford, University Press, Bombay, 1959.

Gledhill, Alan. *Fundamental Rights in India*, Stevens and Sons, London, 1955.

India (British Commonwealth Series), Stevens and Sons, London, 1951.

Green, T. H. *Literal Legislation and Freedom of Contract* (Edited by R. L. Nettleship, in *T. H. Green*, Three Volumes), Longmans, Green and Co., London, 1885.

Government of Great Britain publications:

1918. *Report on Indian Constitutional Reforms* (Montague-Chelmsford Reforms), Cmd. 9109.

1919. *Government of India Act*, 1919, 9 and 10 Geo. 5 Ch. 101.

1925. *A Bill to Constitute within the British Empire a Commonwealth of India* (Annie Besant Bill), 16 Geo. 5.

1929. *Indian States Committee Report* (Butler Committee), Cmd. 3302.

1930. *Report of the Indian Statutory Commission* (Simon Commission), Cmd. 3568–9.

Report of the Federal Structure Sub-Committee, Cmd. 3778. (To the First Round Table Conference.)

1931. *White Paper on Indian Constitutional Reform,* Cmd. 3972.
   Indian-Round Table Conference (Second Session), Cmd. 3997.
1932. *Report of the Federal Finance Committee* (Percy Committee), Cmd. 4069.
   Indian Round Table Conference (Third Session), Cmd. 4238.
1933. *Proposals for Indian Constitutional Reform* (White paper), Cmd. 4268.
1934. *Report of the Joint Committee on Indian Constitutional Reform,* H.C. 5.
1935. *Government of India Act,* 1935, 25 and 26 Geo. 5 Ch. 42.
   Instrument of Instructions to the Governor-General and Governors (Under the 1935 Act), Cmd. 4805.
1936. *Indian Financial Enquiry Report* (Niemeyer Report), Cmd. 5163.
1942. *Lord Privy Seal's Mission, Statement and Draft Declaration* (Cripps Mission), Cmd. 6350.
1945. *Statement of the Policy of His Majesty's Government,* Cmd. 6652.
1946. *Statement by the Cabinet Mission and His Excellency the Viceroy* (May 16 Statement or Cabinet Mission Plan), Cmd. 6821.
   Correspondence and Documents connected with the Conference between the Cabinet Mission and His Excellency the Viceroy and Representatives of the Congress and the Muslim League, May 1946, Cmd. 6821.
   Statement by the Mission dated 25 May, Cmd. 6835.
1947. *Indian Independence Act,* 10 and 11 Geo. 6.
Government of India publications:
   Proceedings of the Central Advisory Board of Education, 1938–49, Delhi.
   Federal Court Reports, Vols. I-X, Delhi, 1937–48.
   Census of India, 1931 and 1951, Delhi.
   Report of the Fiscal Commission, 1949–50, Delhi, 1950.
   Return Showing the Results of Elections to the Central Legislative Assembly and the Provincial Legislatures in 1945–46, Delhi, 1948.
   Report on the Medium of Instruction at the University Stage, Delhi, 1948.
   Verbatim Record of the Education Conference, Delhi, 1948.
   Resolution on Educational Policy, No. D.3791/48 D.I., Delhi, 1948.
   Resolution on Industrial Policy, No. 1(3)-44(13)/48, Delhi, 1948.
   Report of the Indian States Finances Enquiry Committee, Delhi, 1949.
   White Paper on the Indian States, Delhi, 1950.
   Report of the Universities Education Commission, Delhi, 1950.
   Supreme Court Reports, Delhi, 1950 to the present.
   Parliamentary Debates, Delhi, 1950 to the present.
   The Constitution (Amendment) Acts, I–VII, Delhi, 1951–56.
   First Five Year Plan—A Draft Outline, Delhi, 1951.

First Five Year Plan, Delhi, 1953.

Second Five Year Plan, Delhi, 1956.

Third Five Year Plan, Delhi, 1961.

Report of the Finance Commission, Delhi, 1952 and 1957, First and Second Commissions.

Report of the States Reorganisation Commission, Delhi, 1955.

Report of the Official Language Commission, Delhi, 1956.

Report of the Committee of Parliament on Official Language, Delhi, 1958.

Report of the First General Elections, 1951–52, Delhi, 1955.

The Constitution of India, editions of 1950, 1958, and 1963.

Law Commission of India, Fourteenth Report, Delhi, 1958.

The Official Language Act, 1963, No. 19 of 1963, Delhi.

Government of Bombay Province. Bombay Act No. XXII of 1938, *Bombay Code.* Vol. II, 1921–1949.

Government of Uttar Pradesh. U.P. Zamindari Abolition and Land Reforms Act, 1950 (U.P. Act No. 1 of 1951). *U.P. Code,* Seventh Edition, Vol. IV of 1955.

Govind Das, Sethi, *Self Examination* (An Autobiography), in Hindi, Three Volumes, Bharatiya Vishva Prakashan, Delhi, 1958.

Gwyer, Maurice and Appadorai, A. *Speeches and Documents on the Indian Constitution,* Oxford University Press, London, 1957.

Hand, Learned. *The Spirit of Liberty* (Edited by Irving Dillard), Alfred A. Knopf, New York, 1954.

Harrison, Selig. *India—The Most Dangerous Decades,* Princeton University Press, Princeton, 1960.

Headlam-Morley, Agnes. *The New Democratic Constitutions of Europe,* Oxford University Press, London, 1928.

Hicks, U. K., Carnell, F., and others. *Federalism and Economic Growth in Underdeveloped Countries,* George Allen and Unwin, London, 1961.

Hindu Mahasabha. *Constitution of Hindus than Free State,* Poona, 1944.

Hughes, C. *The Federal Constitution of Switzerland,* Clarendon Press, Oxford, 1954.

Ilbert, C. P. *Government of India,* Oxford University Press, London, Third Edition, 1915.

Indian National Congress:

Bulletins, published in Allahabad and New Delhi, 1946–1950.

Reports of the General Secretaries, 1940–1950, three volumes, Allahabad and New Delhi.

Election Manifesto, 1945.

Constitution of the Indian National Congress, New Delhi, 1948.

Our Immediate Programme, New Delhi, 1950.

Report of the 45th Indian National Congress, Allahabad, 1931.

Congress and the Problem of Minorities, Resolutions since 1885, New Delhi, 1947.

Resolutions on States Reorganisation, 1920–1956, New Delhi, 1957.

Resolutions on Economic Policy and Programme, 1924–1954, New Delhi, 1954.

Resolutions on Language Policy, 1949–1957, New Delhi, 1958.

Report of the Linguistic Provinces Committee (the 'JVP Report'), New Delhi, 1949.

The First Year of Freedom, The Second Year, etc., New Delhi, 1948 to the present.

Constituent Assembly and its Work, by K. P. Mallikerjunudu, Congress Publication Board, Bombay, 1946.

Various other publications.

International Commission of Jurists. *Rule of Law in a Free Society,* A Report from a Congress in New Delhi, Geneva, 1959.

Iqbal, Mohammed. *The Law of Preventive Detention in England, India, and Pakistan,* Punjab Religious Book Society, Lahore, 1955.

Jayaswal, K. P. *Hindu Polity,* Bangalore Printing and Publishing Co., Bangalore, 1955.

Jennings, Ivor. *Cabinet Government,* Cambridge University Press, Cambridge, Reprinting of 1947.

Some Characteristics of the Indian Constitution, Oxford University Press, Madras, 1953.

Karunakaran, K. P. *Modern Indian Political Tradition,* Allied Publishers, New Delhi, 1962.

Kogekar, S. V. and Park, Richard. *Reports on the Indian General Elections,* 1951–52, Popular Book Depot, Bombay, 1956.

Laski, Harold. *A Grammar of Politics,* George Allen and Unwin, London, 1960.

Majumdar, Biman Bihari (Ed.). *Gandhian Concept of State,* Bihar University by M. C. Sarkar, Calcutta, 1957.

Majumdar, R. C. and others. *An Advanced History of India,* Macmillan and Co., London, Second Edition, 1960.

Malaviya, H. D. *Land Reforms in India,* Indian National Congress, New Delhi, Second Edition, 1955.

Masani, R. P. *Dadabhai Naorji: The Grand Old Man of India,* George Allen and Unwin, London, 1939.

Mashruwala, K. G. *Some Particular Suggestions for the Constitutin of Free India,* Hamara Hindustan Publications, Bombay, 1946.

Maung, Maung. *Burma's Constitution,* Martinus Nijhoff, The Hague, 1959.

McWhinney, Edward. *Judical Review in the English-Speaking World,* University of Toronto Press, Toronto, 1956.

Mehta, Ashoke. *The Opposition in New States,* Paper read to a Seminar held under the auspices of the Congress for Cultural Freedom at Rhodes, Greece, 1958.

The Political Mind of India, Socialist Party, Bombay, 1952.

Mitra, N. N. (Ed.). *Indian Annual Register,* Annual Register Office, Calcutta, 1919–47.

Menon, V. P. *The Transfer of Power in India,* Orient Longmans, Calcutta, 1957.

The Story of the Integration of the Indian States, Orient Longmans, Calcutta, 1956.

Moon, Penderel. *Divide and Quit,* Chatto and Windus, London, 1961.

Morris-Jones, W. H. *Parliament in India,* Longmans Green, London, 1957.

Narayan, Jayaprakash. *A Plea for the Reconstruction of Indian Polity,* A. B. Sarva Seva Sangh Prakashan, Wardha, 1959 (For Private Circulation).

Nehru, B. K. and Adarkar, B. P. *Report on the Australian System of Federal Finance and its Applicability to Indian Conditions,* Delhi, 1947.

Nehru, Jawaharlal. *The Unity of India,* Lindsay Drummond, London, Third Impression, 1948.

A Bunch of Old Letters, Asia Publishing House, London, 1960.

An Autobiography, Bodley Head, London, Reprinting of 1958.

Discovery of India, Meridian Books Ltd., London, 1956.

Independence and After (Speeches 1946–1949), Government of India, Delhi, 1949.

Speeches 1949–53, Government of India, Delhi, Second Edition, 1957.

Palmer, Norman D. *The Indian Political System,* George Allen and Unwin, London, 1961.

Panikkar, K. M. *Hindu Society at the Crossraods,* Asia Publishing House, Bombay, 1955.

The Foundations of New India, George Allen and Unwin, London, 1963.

Geographical Factors in Indian History, Bharatiya Vidya Bhavan, Bombay, 1959.

Indian Revolution (Written under pseudonym of 'Chanakya'), National Information and Publications Ltd., Bombay, 1951.

Panjabi, K. L. *The Indomitable Sardar,* Bharatiya Vidya Bhavan, Bombay, 1962.

Parikh, N. D. *Sardar Vallabhbhai Patel,* Two Volumes, Navajivan Press, Ahmedabad, 1953–56.

Patel, G. D. *The Indian Land Problem and Legislation,* N. M. Tripathi Ltd., Bombay, 1954.

Patel, Vallabhbhai, *Speeches on Indian Problems* 1947—48, Government of India, Delhi, 1949.

Phillipson, S. and Hicks, J. R. *Report of the Commission on Revenue Allocation,* Government of Nigeria Press, Lagos, 1951.

Prakash, Indra. *A Review of the History and Work of the Hindu Mahasabka and the Hindu Sanghatan Movement,* Akhil Bharatiya Hindu Mahasabha, New Delhi, 1938.

Prasad, Rafendra. *An Autobiography,* Asia Publishing House, Bombay, 1947.

Speech at Cornerstone Laying Indian Law Institute, issued by Public Relations Officer Rashtrapati Bhavan, New Delhi, 1960.

Pyarelal, U. N. *Mahatma Gandhi, The Last Phase,* Two Volumes, Navajivan Press,. Ahmedabad, 1956.

Radhakrishnan, S. *Indian Philosophy,* Two Volumes, George Allen and Unwin Ltd., London, 1929, Revised Edition.

The Hindu View of Life, Unwin Books (First paperback edition), London, 1960.

Rajgopalachari, C. *Rajaji's Speeches,* Government of India, Delhi, 1948.

Rajkumar, N. V. *Development of the Congress Constitution,* Indian National Congress, New Delhi, 1948.

Ramaswamy, M. *The Law of the Indian Constitution,* Longmans Green, London, 1938.

Rao, B. Shiva. *The Framing of India's Constitution: Select Documents,* Volumes I–III of a five-volume series, Indian Institute of Public Administration, Delhi, 1965–66.

Select Constitutions of the World, Madras, 1934.

Rao, K.V. *Parliamentary Democracy in India, A Critical Commentary,* World Press Private Ltd., Calcutta, 1961.

Rau, Benegal Narsing. *India's Constitution in the Making* (Edited by B. Shiva Rao), Orient Longmans, Calcutta, 1960.

Retzlaff, Ralph. *The Indian Constituent Assembly and the Problem of Indian Unity,* unpublished PhD. thesis, Cornell University, 1959.

Rose, Saul. *Socialism in Southern Asia,* Royal Institute of International Affairs at the Oxford University Press, London, 1959.

(Ed.) *Politics in Southern Asia,* Macmillan Co., London, 1963.

Roy, M. N. *Draft Constitution for Free India,* Radical Democratic Party, Delhi, Second Impression, 1945.

Sampurnanand. *Indian Socialism,* Asia Publishing House, London, 1961.

Santhanam, K. *Union-State Relations in India,* Asia Publishing House, London, 1960.

The Constitution of India, Hindustan Times Press, New Delhi, 1951.

Sapru, P. N. *The Relation of the Individual to the State under the Indian Constitution,* University of Calcutta, Calcutta, 1959.

Sapru, Tej Bahadur and others. *Constitutional Proposals of the Sapru Committee,* Padma Publications Ltd., Second Edition, 1946.

Shah, K. T. *National Planning, Principles and Administration,* Vora and Co. Publishers, Bombay, 1948.

Sharma, Ram. *The Supreme Court in the Indian Constitution,* Rajpal and Sons, Delhi, 1959.

Sitaramayya, Pattabhi. *History of the Indian National Congress,* Two Volumes, Padma Publications, Bombay, Reprinting of 1946.

Current History in Questions and Answers, Automatic Publishers Ltd., Calcutta, 1948.

Socialist Party:

Programme, Socialist Party, Bombay, 1947.

Draft Constitution of the Indian Republic, Bombay, 1948.

Resolutions of the Seventh Annual Socialist Party Conference, at Patna, 1949, Bombay, 1949.

Seventh Annual Socialist Party Conference—Presidential Address of Acharya Narenda Dev, Bombay, 1949.

Resolutions of the National Executive at Belgaum, 1948, Bombay, 1948.

Report of the Sixth Annual Conference, at Nasik, 1948, Bombay, 1948.

Resolutions of the Fifth Annual Party Conference at Kanpur, March 1947 *and General Council Meeting at Nagpur, August* 1947 *and National Executive Meetings of* 1947, Bombay, 1947.

Spear, Percival. *India,* University of Michigan Press, Ann Arbor, 1961.

Tendulkar, D. G. *Mahatma, Life of Mohandas Karamchand Gandhi,* Volume VII, Jhaveri and Tendulkar, Bombay, 1953.

Thakurdas, P. and others. *A Plan of Economic Development for India* (The Bombay Plan), Penguin Books, 1945.

Thompson, E. J. and Garratt, .G. T. *Rise and Fulfilment of British Rule in India,* Central Book Depot, Allahabad, 1958.

Varadachariar, N. D. *Indian States in the Federation,* Oxford University Press, London, 1936.

Visvesvaraya, M. *Reconstructing India,* London, 1920.

Planned Economy for India, Bangalore Press, Bangalore, 1936, Second Edition.

Van Doren, Carl. *The Great Rehearsal,* Viking Press, New York, 1948.

Walton, E. H. *The Inner History of the National Convention of South Africa,* Longmans and Green (T. M. Miller, Capetown), London, 1912.

Watson, V. C. *The Indian Constitution and the Hindu Tradition: The Conflict of Basic Political Values,* unpublished PhD. thesis, North-Western University, Chicago, 1957.

Weiner, Myron. *Party Politics in India,* Princeton University Press, Princeton, 1957.

Wheare, K. C. *Modern Constitutions,* Oxford University Press, London, Reprinting of 1958.

Federal Government, Oxford University Press, London, Third Edition, 1956.

The Constitutional Structure of the Commonwealth, Clarendon Press, Oxford, 1960.

Who's Who:

The India and Pakistan Yearbook and Who's Who, Times of India, Bombay, 1945–53

The Times of India Directory and Yearbook, Times of India, Bombay, 1951 and after.

Parliament of India Who's Who, Government of India, New Delhi, 1950 and after.

Parliament of India—Rajya Sabha—Who's Who, Government of India, New Delhi, 1957 and after.

The Indian Who's Who, by W. P. Kabadi, published by Kabadi, Bombay, 1935.

Who's Who in India, by T. Peters, Modern Press and Publicity, Bombay, 1954.

Indian Elections and Legislators, by S. P. Singh Sud, All-India Publications, Ludhiana, 1953.

Eminent Indians, by D. B. Dhananpala, Nalanda Publications Co., Bombay, 1947.

Great Men of India, by L. F. Rushbrook Williams, Home Library Club, Times of India and Statesman, 1939.

The Muslim Year Book of India and Who's Who, by S. M. Jamil, Bombay Newspaper Co. Ltd., Bombay, 1948–49.

Articles:

Aiyer, S. P. 'India's Emerging Co-operative Federalism', *Indian Journal of Political Science,* October-December 1960.

Banerjee, D. N. 'The Position of the President in India', *Modern Review,* June and December 1950 and June 1951.

Mackintosh, John P. 'Federalism in Nigeria', *Political Studies,* October 1962.

Maddick, Henry, 'Panchayat-i-Raj', *Journal of Local Administration Overseas,* October 1962.

Morris-Jones, W. H. 'The Exploration of Indian Political Life', *Pacific Affairs,* December 1959.

'Mahatma Gandhi—Political Philosopher', *Political Affairs,* February 1960.

Tinker, Hugh. 'Authority and Community in Village India', *Pacific Affairs,* December 1959.

'A Symposium on Co-operative Federalism', *Iowa Law Review,* Volume 23, 1938.

Index